COMPARATIVE LAW AND SOCIETY

RESEARCH HANDBOOKS IN COMPARATIVE LAW

Series Editors: Francesco Parisi, *Oppenheimer Wolff and Donnelly Professor of Law, University of Minnesota, USA and Professor of Economics, University of Bologna, Italy* and Tom Ginsburg, *Professor of Law, University of Chicago, USA*

The volumes in this series offer high-level discussion and analysis on particular aspects of legal systems and the law. Well-known scholars edit each handbook and bring together accessible yet sophisticated contributions from an international cast of top researchers. The first series of its kind to cover a wide range of comparative issues so comprehensively, this is an indispensable resource for students and scholars alike.

Comparative Law and Society

Edited by

David S. Clark

Willamette University, USA

RESEARCH HANDBOOKS IN COMPARATIVE LAW

Edward Elgar
Cheltenham, UK • Northampton, MA, USA

Published by
Edward Elgar Publishing Limited
The Lypiatts
15 Lansdown Road
Cheltenham
Glos GL50 2JA
UK

Edward Elgar Publishing, Inc.
William Pratt House
9 Dewey Court
Northampton
Massachusetts 01060
USA

A catalogue record for this book
is available from the British Library

Library of Congress Control Number: 2012938057

ISBN 978 1 84980 361 8 (cased)

Typeset by Servis Filmsetting Ltd, Stockport, Cheshire
Printed and bound by MPG Books Group, UK

Contents

Figures

Tables

Contributors

Michael Adler is Emeritus Professor of Socio-Legal Studies at Edinburgh University, School of Social and Political Science, and a part-time Member of the Scottish Committee of the Administrative Justice and Tribunals Council. He is the author or editor of numerous books and, in recent years, his research and publications have been concerned with problems that arise at the interface between social policy and public law, in particular with administrative grievances and the means by which they can be redressed. He edited *Administrative Justice in Context* (Oxford: Hart, 2010) and is currently writing *Do Parties in Tribunal Proceedings Still Need Representation?* (New York: Palgrave Macmillan, forthcoming).

Neil Brewer is Dean of the School of Psychology at Flinders University (Adelaide, South Australia). He has authored numerous journal articles, books and chapters on eyewitness memory and identification, including edited books such as *Psychology and Law: An Empirical Perspective* (New York: Guilford Press, 2005, with Kipling D. Williams) and *Psychology and Policing* (Hillsdale, NJ: Lawrence Erlbaum, 1995, with Carlene Wilson). He is invited regularly to present to conferences of judges and magistrates around Australia.

David S. Clark is Maynard and Bertha Wilson Professor of Law and Director, Certificate Program in International and Comparative Law, Willamette University (Salem, Oregon). He was editor in chief of the three volume *Encyclopedia of Law and Society: American and Global Perspectives* (Thousand Oaks, CA: Sage, 2007) and co-author of *Comparative Law: Historical Development of the Civil Law Tradition in Europe, Latin America, and East Asia* (New Providence, NJ: Matthew Bender & Co., 2010, with John Henry Merryman and John Owen Haley). He is a titular member of the International Academy of Comparative Law and past president of the American Society of Comparative Law (2002–06).

Roger Cotterrell is Anniversary Professor of Legal Theory at Queen Mary University (London) and a Fellow of the British Academy. His books include *Living Law: Studies in Legal and Social Theory* (Aldershot, UK: Dartmouth, 2008), *Law, Culture and Society: Legal Ideas in the Mirror of Social Theory* (Aldershot, UK: Ashgate, 2006), *The Politics of Jurisprudence: A Critical Introduction to Legal Philosophy* (London: LexisNexis, 2nd edn, 2003) and *Émile Durkheim: Law in a Moral Domain* (Edinburgh: Edinburgh University Press, 1999). His edited works include *Émile Durkheim: Justice, Morality and Politics* (Aldershot, UK: Ashgate, 2010) and the two volume *Sociological Perspectives on Law* and *Law in Social Theory* (Aldershot, UK: Ashgate, 2001, 2006).

Brian L. Cutler is Professor in the Faculty of Social Science and Humanities at the University of Ontario Institute of Technology in Oshawa, Ontario. In his 25 years of academic experience in the US and Canada, Professor Cutler has published numerous books, book chapters, and journal articles about forensic psychology in general and eyewitness memory in particular. He also has served as an expert witness in US courts and testified about the psychology of eyewitness identification.

Tom Ginsburg is Leo Spitz Professor of Law at the University of Chicago. He is co-director of the Comparative Constitutions Project (http://www.comparativeconstitutionsproject. org), an effort to document the contents of the world's constitutions. His books include *The Endurance of National Constitutions* (Cambridge: Cambridge University Press, 2009, with Zachary Elkins and James Melton), *Judicial Review in New Democracies: Constitutional Courts in Asian Cases* (Cambridge: Cambridge University Press, 2003) and *Rule by Law: The Politics of Courts in Authoritarian Regimes* (Cambridge: Cambridge University Press, 2008, editor with Tamir Moustafa).

Mark Goodale is Associate Professor of Conflict Analysis and Anthropology at George Mason University (Fairfax, Virginia) and Series Editor of Stanford Studies in Human Rights. He is the author of *Surrendering to Utopia: An Anthropology of Human Rights* (Stanford: Stanford University Press, 2009) and *Dilemmas of Modernity: Bolivian Encounters with Law and Liberalism* (Stanford: Stanford University Press, 2009) and co-editor of *Mirrors of Justice: Law and Power in the Post-Cold War Era* (Cambridge: Cambridge University Press, 2010, with Kamari Maxine Clarke). He is currently at work on two new books: the first, a study of revolution and the meanings of radical social change based on research in Bolivia since 2005; the second, a set of essays on the relationship between human rights and moral creativity.

Carlo Guarnieri is Professor of Political Science at the University of Bologna. His comparative interest in courts and judges is illustrated by his English book, *The Power of Judges* (Oxford: Oxford University Press, 2002, with Patrizia Pederzoli) and, more recently 'Judicial Independence in Authoritarian Regimes: Lessons from Continental Europe', in Randall Peerenboom (ed.), *Judicial Independence in China: Lessons for Global Rule of Law Promotion* 234 (Cambridge: Cambridge University Press, 2009) and 'Judicial Independence and the Rule of Law: Exploring the European Experience', in Shimon Shetreet and Christopher Forsyth (eds), *The Culture of Judicial Independence: Conceptual Foundations and Practical Challenges* ch. 6 (Leiden, Netherlands: Martinus Nijhoff 2011, with Daniela Piana).

Ruth Horry is a postdoctoral Research Fellow in the School of Psychology at Flinders University (Adelaide, South Australia). She completed her PhD in 2009 at Sussex University, England. She has authored several journal articles on face recognition and eyewitness identification.

Barbara Luppi is a Research Scholar in the Department of Political Economy, University of Modena and Reggio Emilia. She has published journal articles on issues of law and economics and contributed a chapter to *Methodology of Comparative Law* (Cheltenham, UK and Northampton, MA, USA: Edward Elgar, 2011, edited by Pier Giuseppe Monateri).

Stephen C. McCaffrey is Distinguished Professor and Scholar at the University of the Pacific, McGeorge School of Law (Sacramento, California). A worldwide authority on international water law, he served as special *rapporteur* for the commission's draft articles on the law of non-navigational uses of international watercourses, which formed the basis of the 1997 UN Convention on that subject. His books include *Global Issues in Environmental Law* (St. Paul, MN: West Group, 2009, with Rachael E. Salcido), *Transnational Litigation in Comparative Perspective: Theory and Application* (New York: Oxford University Press, 2010, with Thomas O. Main), and *Public International Law* (New Providence, NJ: LexisNexis, 2010).

Elizabeth Mertz is John and Rylla Bosshard Professor of Law at the University of Wisconsin (Madison), Senior Research Professor at the American Bar Foundation and a Fellow of the American Anthropological Association. In 2010–11, she was a Visiting Fellow at the Program in Law and Public Affairs at Princeton University, where she also taught graduate and undergraduate courses in anthropology. She has served as editor of *PoLAR: Political and Legal Anthropology Review* and *Law & Social Inquiry*, as guest editor of the *Law & Society Review* and as co-editor of the Ashgate book series, Transforming Legal Education. She was co-winner of the Herbert Jacob Prize of the Law & Society Association for her book, *The Language of Law School: Learning to 'Think Like a Lawyer'* (Oxford: Oxford University Press, 2007).

David Nelken is Distinguished Professor of Legal Institutions and Social Change at the University of Macerata (Italy), Distinguished Research Professor of Law at Cardiff Law School, and Visiting Professor of Criminology at the London School of Economics and Political Science as well as at Oxford University. He is an Academician of the Academy of Social Sciences (UK) and received a Distinguished Scholar award from the American Sociological Association (1985) and the Sellin-Glueck prize of the American Society of Criminology (2009). Two recent books include *Beyond Law in Context* (Aldershot, UK: Ashgate, 2009) and *Comparative Criminal Justice: Making Sense of Difference* (London: Sage, 2010). His preferred email address is sen4144@gmail.com.

Francis Pakes is Reader in Comparative Criminology at the University of Portsmouth (UK), where he teaches assorted topics in comparative and international criminology. His research involves issues in comparative criminology, in particular with reference to the Netherlands and lately with a focus on the impact of globalisation on criminal justice arrangements. He has revised his book *Comparative Criminal Justice* (Cullompton, UK: Willan, 2nd edn, 2010) and is finishing a new work, *Globalisation: The Challenge for Criminology*, expected in 2012.

Matthew A. Palmer is a Lecturer in the School of Psychology, University of Tasmania. He conducts research in several areas of forensic psychology, including eyewitness memory and juror decisions. He has published research in leading international journals, such as *Acta Psychologica* and *Journal of Experimental Psychology: Applied*.

Francesco Parisi is Oppenheimer Wolff and Donnelly Professor of Law at the University of Minnesota (Minneapolis) and a Distinguished Professor of Economics (*Professore Ordinario per Chiara Fama*) at the University of Bologna. He is the author of ten books and over two hundred articles in the field of law and economics. These include *The Economics of Lawmaking* (Oxford: Oxford University Press, 2009, with Vincy Fon) and *The Language of Law and Economics* (Cambridge: Cambridge University Press, 2011). Parisi is currently the editor-in-chief of the *Review of Law and Economics* and served as editor of the *Supreme Court Economic Review* from 2002 to 2008. He is a member of the board of editors of the *International Review of Law and Economics*, the *Journal of Public Choice* and the *American Journal of Comparative Law*, and serves on the board of advisors of the Social Sciences Research Network.

Jonathan T. Polk is a PhD candidate in the Department of International Affairs at the University of Georgia (UGA, in Athens), focusing on comparative politics, particularly parties and other political institutions. He completed his MA in Political Science at UGA and received his BA from St. John's College (Annapolis, Maryland). Since 2006, he has worked as a research associate at UGA's Center for the Study of Global Issues (Globis) and he joined (in 2009) the research team of the Chapel Hill Expert Survey on party positioning in Europe. He has taught courses on European and Latin American politics in UGA's study abroad programs in Costa Rica and Italy.

John C. Reitz is Edward L. Carmody Professor of Law at the University of Iowa (Iowa City), where he teaches comparative and administrative law and directs the LL.M. program in international and comparative law and the visiting scholar program. He was the Pao Yu-Kong Distinguished Visiting Professor of Law at Zhejiang University (2008–10) in Hangzhou, China, where he continues to hold the post of visiting professor. He is an editor of *Constitutional Dialogues in Comparative Perspective* (New York: St. Martin's Press, 1999, with Sally J. Kenney and William M. Reisinger) and lectures widely to law school audiences on various aspects of US law in Germany, Russia, the Ukraine, Romania, Hungary, Nigeria, China and Vietnam. He has served as a consultant to the UN Development Projects in Vietnam on civil procedure and administrative court reform and is a titular member of the International Academy of Comparative Law and currently the President of the American Society of Comparative Law.

Rachael E. Salcido is Professor of Law and Director of the Sustainable Development Institute at the University of the Pacific, McGeorge School of Law (Sacramento, California). She is the Pacific McGeorge trustee to the Rocky Mountain Mineral Law Foundation and serves on the Foundation's scholarship committee. Professor Salcido teaches property, natural resources, environmental law, and ocean and coastal law. She is an expert in environmental restoration and offshore development and is co-author of *Global Issues in Environmental Law* (St. Paul, MN: West Group, 2009, with Stephen C. McCaffrey).

Sara Stendahl is Associate Professor of Public Law at Göteborg University (Sweden), School of Business, Economics and Law. Using a framework of theories on legitimacy and justice, she has written in Swedish and English on issues concerning social security law (health, disability, occupational injury and unemployment). Within this area, she has also taken a special interest in the legal practices of courts and administrative bodies. Her recent publications include two co-edited books: *The European Work-First Welfare State* (Göteborg: Centre for European Research-Cergu, 2008, with Thomas Erhag and Stamatia Devetzi) and *Too Sick to Work? Social Security Reforms in Europe for Persons with Reduced Earnings Capacity* (Alphen aan den Rijn, Netherlands: Kluwer Law International 2011, with Stamatia Devetzi).

Julie C. Suk is Professor of Law at Yeshiva University, Benjamin N. Cardozo School of Law (New York). Her research focuses on the intersection of comparative law and public policy, especially employment law, antidiscrimination law and the relationship between litigation and regulation and between law and the social welfare state. She teaches comparative law, employment law and civil procedure and is fluent in French and Korean and proficient in German, Italian and Latin. Before joining the Cardozo faculty, she was a fellow at Princeton University's Program in Law and Public Affairs. She has been a Jean Monnet Fellow at the European University Institute and a visiting professor at the University of Chicago and UCLA.

G. Alan Tarr is Director of the Center for State Constitutional Studies and Distinguished Professor of Political Science at Rutgers University-Camden. He is the author or editor of several books on federalism, including *Understanding State Constitutions* (Princeton: Princeton University Press, 1998), *Constitutional Origins, Structure, and Change in Federal Countries* (Montreal: McGill-Queen's University Press, 2005) and *Federalism, Subnational Constitutions, and Minority Rights* (Westport, CT: Praeger, 2004). Three times the recipient of fellowships from the National Endowment for the Humanities and more recently of a Fulbright Fellowship, he has lectured on federalism and constitutionalism throughout the United States and in Africa, Asia, Europe and South America.

Stephen C. Thaman is Professor of Law at Saint Louis University, where he teaches criminal law and procedure, international criminal law and comparative law. His primary research interest is in the area of comparative criminal procedure. He has written extensively on jury systems, evidence exclusionary rules, plea bargaining and other criminal procedure topics. His recent books include *Comparative Criminal Procedure: A Casebook Approach* (2nd edn, 2008) and *World Plea Bargaining: Consensual Procedures and Avoidance of the Full Criminal Trial* (2010), both published by Carolina Academic Press in Durham, NC.

Koen van Aeken is Assistant Professor (Docent) at Tilbug Law School (Netherlands), Department for Public Law, Jurisprudence and Legal History. He has a PhD in legal sociology from the University of Antwerp. His main teaching and research focus involves the empirical study of law, with such topics as the effects of regulation, legislative evaluation, access to justice and the legal profession.

Howard J. Wiarda is the Dean Rusk Professor of International Relations at the University of Georgia (Athens). In Washington, DC, he is a Senior Associate at the Center for Strategic and International Studies (CSIS) and Senior Fellow at the Woodrow Wilson International Center for Scholars. He is the author of many books, including *The Soul of Latin America* (New Haven: Yale University Press, 2001), *Dilemmas of Democracy in Latin America* (Lanham, MD: Rowman & Littlefield, 2005) and the best-selling textbook *Latin American Politics and Development* (Boulder, CO: Westview, 7th edn, 2011). In the field of comparative politics, he has authored *New Directions in Comparative Politics* (Boulder, CO: Westview, 3rd edn, 2002) and edited *Introduction to Comparative Politics* (Fort Worth, TX: Harcourt College, 2nd edn, 2000).

Preface*

The field of comparative law and society embraces the common or overlapping area of two constituent disciplines: comparative law, and law and society. That means that some comparative law aims, typically among many professional objectives and methods, such as most statutory interpretation and case analysis, would be of little interest to socio-legal scholars. Conversely, sociological or cultural aims and some professional objectives in comparative law, such as institution building, normally would be of interest. On the other side, socio-legal research that focuses on a single legal jurisdiction in which the comparatist resides—by itself—would not be useful to comparative law. Only when the researcher combines that work with other similar research on a foreign jurisdiction does the comparatist's curiosity arise.

Approaches to comparing legal systems or parts of legal systems often involve a broad view for the discipline of comparative law, something other than the narrow focus on legal rules for a professional or practical purpose. Since there have been many philosophies and definitions of law, ideas about legal systems have been similarly diverse. A legal system may refer to the rules of a tribe, city, nation, the international order or the natural rules for humankind itself. If the purpose of investigation is to accumulate knowledge or to test general explanatory propositions, it may be relevant for socio-legal scholars.

In general, a system involves regular interactions among elements that together make up an entity with boundaries. Thus, lawyers, judges, legislators, administrators, the police and legal scholars all work with rules in regularized ways that involve cultural expectations about their roles and the legal institutions with which they interact. This view of a legal system is greater than the rules themselves. Since comparison contemplates more than one legal system in the search for similarities and differences among them, one way to explore the field of comparative law and society is to consider the different approaches to and classifications of law and legal systems that various philosophers, jurists and researchers use. This volume provides 19 chapters that illustrate the diversity existing in this field.

Historically, Europe is the origin of most comparative law and socio-legal activity. Of the two subject matters, comparative law is the older field due in part to the traditional importance of law as a faculty (in reality two faculties—Roman law and canon law) at European universities. In addition, most law graduates took jobs working in local and regional secular government that had its own customary systems of law. By the second half of the nineteenth century, there were a few national organizations (some sponsoring scholarly journals) of comparative law, which increased in number during the early twentieth century along with international meetings of scholars. During this same period, there emerged national organizations with international congresses in most of the social science disciplines discussed in Part I. Some of these scholars, as illustrated, had an interest in law.

Comparative law is the science or practice of identifying, explaining or using the

---

*   An earlier version of some material in this preface appeared in David S. Clark, 'Comparative Law Methods in the United States', 16 *Roger Williams University Law Review* 134–8 (2011).

similarities and differences between two or more legal systems or their constituent parts. The objectives or aims of comparative law include those that are practical or professional, scientific and cultural. Its scientific aspirations can be looser, in the sense of accumulating or applying systematic knowledge (*Wissenschaft*), tighter, such as empirically testing general explanatory propositions, or some intermediate endeavor. These activities involve many distinct methods. Legal systems can be international, national or subnational. They contain a complex mixture of distinctive legal norms, institutions, processes, actors and culture.

Comparatists confront many challenges in carrying out their objectives. First, they must select a legal element for study, such as a contract rule, the standard of proof in criminal procedure, the expected or actual role for prosecutors, civil discovery, legal education, the relationship among government structures, or people's attitudes toward mediation as a form of dispute resolution. As suggested earlier, this volume will primarily provide examples that are not rule focused. Second, comparatists should identify the aim of their inquiry—whether it is professional, scientific or cultural. Third, they must choose at least two legal systems, which typically are their home system and that of a foreign nation. This one often does implicitly. The investigator may state that she is only interested in a foreign example, such as the presence of rule of law in Indonesia, but she has to begin somewhere in her conceptual organization. That somewhere is usually the relevant element in the researcher's own home legal system. The two systems need not be contemporary; one may be historical or idealized. It is here that one can see overlap with legal history or legal philosophy. Fourth, comparatists must select a method or methods to use in making their comparison. These methods may have developed within other disciplines, which can make the activity interdisciplinary as is typical in law and society research.

There is further discretion in determining the nature and extent of the similarities or differences the investigator will emphasize. Some comparatists prefer identifying similarities in what they find, while others accentuate differences. This will often vary depending on the use or objective that the comparatist has.

Some comparative law utilizes a level of generality above the nation state. The classification of the world's national and subnational legal systems into families or traditions is an effort to simplify the universe by focusing on the similarities of selected components within a legal tradition and then often pointing out the differences between that tradition and others. For instance, legal scholars commonly speak of the civil law tradition or the Islamic law tradition. Further analysis may lead to the recognition of mixed jurisdictions that reflect legal pluralism within a single legal system, such as in Louisiana or Scotland.

From this portrayal, one can see that comparative law is not a discipline with fixed boundaries, either by subject or by method, and, certainly, it is not doctrinal in the narrow sense. Over the course of world history, many legal scholars and lawyers who worked on issues related to law that involved a foreign element did not think of themselves as comparatists. Chapter 1 traces much of this history.

Part I of the volume, Methods and Disciplines, then discusses a variety of comparative law methods with illustrative examples in six chapters, organized by discipline. These are the principal academic areas that include law as one of their interests: sociology, criminology, anthropology, economics, political science and psychology. All of these disciplines view law and its elements as integral parts of society, but analyze law's impact from a variety of perspectives.

Part II, Core Issues, covers major legal institutions, processes, professionals and cultures associated with certain legal subjects. Each chapter takes a comparative perspective that involves at least two legal systems, expertly presented by authors from England, Wales and Scotland in the United Kingdom, from Italy, the Netherlands and Sweden in continental Europe, and from Australia, Canada and the United States. These issues include the separation of government powers, federalism, judges and judicial independence, civil courts and alternative dispute resolution, criminal courts, administrative agencies, constitutional courts, legal cultures, legal education, legal professions and law firms, legal protection of the environment and the treatment of preventive health at work.

I am grateful to the authors for their prompt and cheerful participation in this project and to Jane Bayliss, Tara Gorvine, Alexandra Mandzak and Virginia Williams at Edward Elgar Publishing for their guidance in the production process. I am also indebted to Galin Brown, Willamette University Law Library Access Services Manager, for helpful interlibrary loan assistance and to the College of Law for a summer research grant that facilitated completion of Chapter 1.

David S. Clark
Salem, Oregon
January 2012

For Marilee and
Lee, Susanna, Eliina, Liisa, and David

1 History of comparative law and society

*David S. Clark**

1 INTRODUCTION

1.1 Comparative Law

Comparative law is as old as the existence of law. It arose with the first complaint of injustice directed against human action justified by a legal rule. The complainer, not having that law on her side, had to rely on a rule existing outside the actor's legal system, perhaps on a higher law. Ancient illustrations of law and justice may be of significance to theologians, philosophers or shamans. However, other than a legal anthropologist's interest in preliterate human societies, most comparatists today would not consider historical examples older than three millennia and much of that consideration is about classical European legal systems. Nevertheless, modern legal comparatists are continuing to push the boundaries of their discipline outward, intruding on sister fields in the social sciences and humanities—from economics to rhetoric—and expanding their consideration to ancient use of legal comparison in China and other parts of Asia.

The modern view is that comparison is inherent to humans and probably to other species. This insight comes from diverse disciplines ranging from social psychology to human evolutionary genetics.[1] Social comparison is how we make sense of the world in which we live and even understand ourselves. Legal comparison concerns that part of social reality involving laws and legal institutions. From this perspective, comparison does not need to be justified any more than rationality requires justification. Consciously rational comparison will involve aims and methods, but intuitive comparison may be subconscious. In thinking about legal norms, values and institutions, scholars for centuries have argued, sometimes violently, between concepts that are rooted in essentialism and nominalism. Comparison is integral to both these philosophical approaches and it applies to law as much as to other matters. Dialectical reasoning is another example involving comparison, since one must identify the antithesis to the thesis. One finds that dyadic conceptualism has dominated legal doctrine, principles and values across human cultures.

Sustained scholarly comparative law activity in the United States began in the early twentieth century. It developed together with organized networks of communication, often extending abroad, and the successful effort to establish scientific teaching and

* Maynard and Bertha Wilson Professor of Law and Director, Certificate Program in International and Comparative Law, Willamette University. I thank the College of Law for a summer research grant that facilitated completion of research for this chapter and participants from the 2012 American Society for Comparative Law Works-in-Progress Workshop at Princeton University for valuable comments.

[1] See, e.g., Jerry Suls and Ladd Wheeler (eds), *Handbook of Social Comparison: Theory and Research* (New York: Kluwer Academic 2000).

research at private and public American law schools, which were mostly university-based.[2] In Europe—particularly in France and Germany—organized comparative law began in the second half of the nineteenth century with societies and journals of comparative legislation.[3]

The earliest example of an attempt to mix comparative law themes with history and the social sciences at an international meeting was the initial 1862 congress of the Association Internationale pour le Progrès des Sciences Sociales. Held at its seat in Brussels, it dedicated one of the five sections (and membership categories) to comparative legislation. The First Section defined its aims as the 'study of civil, political, and penal laws in various countries, their effects on the people's social condition, their imperfections and resulting evils, and their susceptibility to improvement and reform'.[4] Delegates at the first congress discussed and delivered reports on topics such as: (1) What are the bases and means for a good codification of laws? (2) What legislation controls the press in European countries? (3) The introduction of improvements in legislation concerning aliens, and (4) International recognition of foreign corporations. The Association's officers lived in several countries other than Belgium: France, Germany, Great Britain, Italy, The Netherlands, Poland, Portugal, Russia, Spain, Switzerland and the United States.[5]

The first major international meeting of scholars that exclusively treated comparative law, including its broader social dimension, was the Congrès International de Droit Comparé held in Paris in 1900. The French Société de Législation Comparée organized the event in conjunction with the 1900 Paris World Exposition. Foreign delegates (from outside France) attended from 15 countries, including Japan, Mexico, Russia, the United States and Turkey.[6] The next world congress of comparative law was held in St. Louis in 1904, also in conjunction with a world fair in addition to the third modern Olympics. Unlike the 1900 international comparative law congress in Paris, lawyers and judges from the American Bar Association (ABA) organized and ran the American Congress, with a smaller representation from academia. This yielded a more pragmatic legal focus with less concern for the social context in which law operates. Delegates attended from 17 countries.[7] In 1907, the ABA authorized the organization of the Comparative Law Bureau, which published its first *Annual Bulletin* surveying foreign legislation and legal literature in 1908.[8]

---

[2]   See David S. Clark, 'The Modern Development of American Comparative Law: 1904–1945', 55 *American Journal of Comparative Law* 587–8, 591–600 (2007).

[3]   David S. Clark, 'Nothing New in 2000? Comparative Law in 1900 and Today', 75 *Tulane Law Review* 871, 873–4 (2001).

[4]   1 *Annales de l'Association internationale pour le progrès des sciences sociales* 131 (Brussels: A. Lacrois, Verboeckhoven & Co. 1863); see ibid. 10–11. For the social context of this organization within the transnational reform movement in Europe, see Christian Müller, 'Designing the Model European-Liberal and Republican Concepts of Citizenship in Europe in the 1860s: The *Association Internationale pour le Progrès des Sciences Sociales*', 37 *History of European Ideas* 223–31 (2011).

[5]   1 *Annales* (note 4) 4–5, 53–66, 133–226.

[6]   Clark (note 3) 875, 878.

[7]   Ibid. 888–90; Clark (note 2) 593–6; see V. Mott Porter (ed.), *Official Report of the Universal Congress of Lawyers and Jurists* (St. Louis: Congress Executive Committee 1905).

[8]   Clark (note 2) 596. The Bureau held annual meetings and had an active book publishing agenda. Ibid. 596–600.

1.2   Law and Society

Law and society, sometimes referred to as socio-legal studies, also has its classical examples—typically shared with comparative law—such as Aristotle (384–22 BCE) and Plato (428–347 BCE). More commonly, law and society scholars point to the discipline's origins from the period of the European Enlightenment. Scholars first created a national association emphasizing law and sociology in Japan in 1947.[9] Italy had a similar organization, founded in 1948.[10] Sociology of law appeared in Europe at an international level in 1962, but without a strong organizational basis in the early years and without a journal.[11] As an influential field, however, with an organization, journal and meetings, law and society first developed in the United States in the 1960s. It continued to expand in several European countries and Japan, and later spread to other parts of the world. Scholars active in the law and society community have utilized a wide range of methods from the social sciences and humanities, frequently in an interdisciplinary manner. They also sometimes worked with lawyers and legal scholars who might have special insight into ways that people and legal professionals understand and use legal rules and institutions.

The Law and Society Association, founded in 1964 by a group of young scholars attending the American Sociological Association's annual meeting, began the *Law & Society Review* in 1966 and held its first independent society meeting in 1975. Although most of its annual meetings have been in the United States, some have been held abroad—including Amsterdam (1991), Toronto (1995), Glasgow (1996), Budapest (2001), Vancouver (2002), Berlin (2007) and Montreal (2008).[12]

The *Review*'s first editor, Richard Schwartz, nicely summarized the journal's (and the Society's) aims in its first issue in 1966.

> [There is] a growing need on the part of social scientists and lawyers for a forum in which to carry on an interdisciplinary dialogue. During the past decade, each of the social sciences has found it necessary to face legal policy issues of highest relevance to the disciplines themselves and to the society as a whole. In political science, the decision process in the courts and administrative agencies have been explored to an extent which parallels earlier and continuing work on the legislatures. Political scientists have also turned their attention to the implementation of legal decisions, especially where the institutions of government have been seen as an important determinant of the impact of law. Sociologists, too, are showing increasing interest in the legal process. Their studies have been concerned with the manner in which the population is affected by law in such areas as civil rights, poverty, and crime. Both professions have joined with the anthropologists in studying the relationship between society and culture on the one hand and the nature and operation of legal institutions on the other. In addition, other professional groups—notably

---

[9]   Setsuo Miyazawa, 'Japan', in David S. Clark (ed.), *Encyclopedia of Law and Society: American and Global Perspectives* 2, 835–6 (Thousand Oaks, CA: Sage 2007). The Japanese Association of Sociology of Law began its journal in 1951. Ibid. 836.

[10]   Vincenzo Ferrari, 'Centro Nazionale di Prevenzione e Difesa Sociale (National Center of Crime Prevention and Social Defense)', in Clark (ed.) (note 9) 1, 166–7.

[11]   The International Sociological Association created the Research Committee on Sociology of Law in 1962. Johannes Feest, 'ISA Research Committee on Sociology of Law', in Clark (ed.) (note 9) 2, 825–6.

[12]   Lawrence M. Friedman, 'Law and Society Association, The', in Clark (ed.) (note 9) 2, 922–3; Law and Society Association, Meeting Sites of the Law and Society Association, http://www.lawandsociety.org/ann_mtg/meeting_lst.htm.

economists, social workers, clinical and social psychologists, and psychiatrists—are increasingly called upon for information thought to be of value in the formulation of legal policy. Above all, the legal profession has moved from a position of reluctant consumer of such information to an active participant in the research process.

With so many diverse disciplines attending to legal issues, it becomes increasingly important and valuable that there be created a forum for the interchange of ideas on law and the social sciences. Even if there were need only to coordinate the kind of information utilized in legal policy making, some locus for the exchange of ideas would be needed. Since legal policy characteristically affects the whole of society, policies formulated with reference to only one of its facets would surely be inadequate. But in addition, an analysis of origins and effects of legal policy constitutes a crucial task for the theoretical understanding of the nature of the social order. Whatever the case for individual disciplines developing independently, few would deny the value of social sciences ultimately combining insights to understand the larger picture. If law is correctly viewed as a conduit through which all of the diverse institutional elements of the society simultaneously flow, it must constitute a critical point for effective interdisciplinary collaboration.[13]

Schwartz's emphasis was on both the significant number of disciplines interested in law, legal institutions and legal policy and the usefulness of interdisciplinary cooperation in developing a better understanding of the nature of law and social order. He had already recognized the importance of comparison among legal jurisdictions—both historical and modern—to build a solid corpus of knowledge about law. His 1964 study (with James Miller) of 51 societies analyzed the relationship between emergence of forms of legal organization—such as counsel, mediation and police—and societal complexity.[14] Foreign and comparative research appeared in the *Review* from its beginning[15] and in the first published teaching materials for the field in 1969: *Law and the Behavior Sciences*.[16]

2   NATURE OF COMPARATIVE LAW AND SOCIETY

The easiest way to conceptualize the topic of comparative law and society is to think of its two constituent parts—comparative law, and law and society—as two circles with an overlapping area. It is that joint area that comprises our subject. That means that some comparative law aims, typically among professional objectives and methods, such as most statutory interpretation and case analysis, would be of no interest to socio-legal scholars. Conversely, sociological or cultural aims and some professional objectives in comparative

---

[13]   Richard D. Schwartz, 'From the Editor', 1 *Law & Society Review* 6–7 (1966: 1).

[14]   Richard D. Schwartz and James C. Miller, 'Legal Evolution and Societal Complexity', 70 *American Journal of Sociology* 159 (1964).

[15]   E.g., Aaron V. Cicourel, 'Kinship, Marriage, and Divorce in Comparative Family Law', 1 *Law & Society Review* 103 (1966–7); Gregory J. Massell, 'Law as an Instrument of Revolutionary Change in a Traditional Milieu: The Case of Soviet Central Asia', 2 ibid. 179 (1967–8); Masaji Chiba, 'Relations between the School District System and the Feudalistic Village Community in Nineteenth-Century Japan: A Study of the Effect of Law upon Society', 2 ibid. 229 (1967–8); Howard J. Wiarda, 'Contemporary Constitutions and Constitutionalism in the Dominican Republic: The Basic Law within the Political Process', 2 ibid. 385 (1967–8). Richard Abel also mentions many comparative studies in his survey of the *Review*. 'Law and Society: Project and Practice', 6 *Annual Review of Law and Social Science* 1–23 (2010).

[16]   Lawrence M. Friedman and Stewart Macaulay, *Law and the Behavior Sciences* ch. 6 (Indianapolis: Bobbs-Merrill 1969) (on Law, Culture and History).

law, such as institution building, normally would be of interest. On the other side, socio-legal research that focuses on a single legal jurisdiction in which the comparatist resides—by itself—would not be useful to comparative law. It is only when such research is combined with other similar research on a foreign jurisdiction that the comparatist's curiosity arises.

Approaches to comparing legal systems or parts of legal systems often involve a broad view for the discipline of comparative law, something other than the narrow focus on legal rules for a professional or practical purpose. Since there have been many philosophies and definitions of law, ideas about legal systems have been similarly diverse. A legal system may refer to the rules of a tribe, city, nation, the international order or the natural rules for humankind itself. If the purpose of investigation is to accumulate knowledge or to test general explanatory propositions, it may be relevant for socio-legal scholars.

In general, a system involves regular interactions among elements that together make up an entity with boundaries. Thus, lawyers, judges, legislators, administrators, the police and legal scholars all work with rules in regularized ways that involve cultural expectations about their roles and the legal institutions with which they interact. This view of a legal system is greater than the rules themselves. Since comparison contemplates more than one legal system in the search for similarities and differences among them, one way to explore the history of comparative law and society is to consider the different approaches to and classifications of law and legal systems that various philosophers, jurists and researchers have used. Sections 3 and 4 emphasize the classifications of legal systems that jurists have used from an historical perspective. Such classification is necessary, since meaningful comparison without categories is not possible. Section 5 then turns to the various approaches that distinct modern academic disciplines take toward the law and society inquiry.

3   COMPARISON IN CLASSICAL LEGAL TRADITIONS

3.1   Athens

Ancient Greeks made the earliest recorded efforts explicitly to classify legal systems based on their interest in political structure, philosophical speculation, and the comparative study of law. For instance, Plato in the *Laws* discussed the rules of several Greek and other *poleis* (city-states) in formulating his ideal code and legal institutions for Magnesia. He showed how differing constitutional forms yielded either a good state or a bad state. In the *Republic*, he sought to ground law and politics in a model state with a transcendental metaphysics to be implemented by elite Guardians with an educated vision of the Form of the Good. This approach to achieving justice resonated with subsequent natural law jurists who would have the basis to compare an actual system of legal rules with a utopian system. Karl Marx (1818–83) used Plato's class-based society in his own theory of law, where each ruling class he analyzed applied law—the product of economic forces—to control society's lower classes.[17]

---

[17]   Edgar Bodenheimer, *Jurisprudence: The Philosophy and Method of the Law* 6–10, 13–14, 79–80 (Cambridge, MA: Harvard University Press, rev. edn, 1974); Gerhard Dannemann,

Aristotle examined many legal structures in his *Politics* before settling on the three preferred categories of kingship, aristocracy and constitutional government (*politeia*) with their deviant siblings, tyranny, oligarchy and democracy. He rejected Platonic transcendentalism as well as the Sophists' relativism and skepticism. Aristotle's approach was empirical, rooted in how humans actually govern themselves. He found virtue in the moderation (golden middle) of a legislator, judge or legal rule.[18] Aristotle's successor, Theophrastus (372–287 BCE), examined comparative commercial law.[19]

3.2   Rome

In Rome, jurists' interest in foreign law was more practical, particularly with the creation of the office of *praetor peregrinus* in 242 BCE. This praetor supervised jurisdiction over disputes involving non-Romans. It was here that the mixture of a less formalistic Roman *ius civile*, Greek law and other foreign legal norms led to an internationalized *ius gentium*. Roman political authorities allowed distinct ethnic groups in the provinces to rule themselves in most matters, but Roman jurists did not have a philosophical interest in studying and classifying foreign legal systems since they believed in the superiority of their own law. Cicero (106–43 BCE) illustrated this view. An exception that makes the point was the fourth century *Collatio legum Mosaicarum et Romanarum*, in which excerpts from Roman jurists were paired with the laws of Moses, either to improve the stature of Christianity or to demonstrate that Rome had implemented Mosaic law.[20]

3.3   China[21]

The experience with law in Chinese history is completely different. For most of the past two and a half millennia, Chinese philosophers and political leaders have de-emphasized the use of law in society and therefore found no need to make comparisons with legal rules and institutions in foreign places. Like the Romans, the Chinese believed in the superiority of their own approach to ordering society and maintaining peace. This separation from foreign legal

---

'Comparative Law: Study of Similarities or Differences?' in Mathias Reimann and Reinhard Zimmerman (eds), *The Oxford Handbook of Comparative Law* 383, 396–7 (Oxford: Oxford University Press 2006); William B. Ewald, 'Plato', in Clark (ed.) (note 9) 3, 1109–10; see Plato, *The Laws* (London: Penguin, Trevor J. Saunders trans. and notes, 1970); Plato, *Republic* (Oxford: Oxford University Press, Robin Waterfield trans. and notes, 1993).

[18]   Bodenheimer (note 17) 6–10, 13–14; Charles Donahue, 'Comparative Law before the Code Napoléon', in Reimann and Zimmerman (eds) (note 17) 3–5; William B. Ewald, 'Aristotle', in Clark (ed.) (note 9) 1, 92–3; see Aristotle, *Politics* (Oxford: Oxford University Press, Ernest Barker trans., 1995); David S. Clark, 'Comparative Legal Systems', in Clark (ed.) (note 9) 1, 225.

[19]   Konrad Zweigert and Hein Kötz, *Introduction to Comparative Law* 49 (Oxford: Oxford University Press, Tony Weir trans., 3rd edn, 1998).

[20]   Clark (note 18) 225–6; Donahue (note 18) 5–8.

[21]   See Geoffrey MacCormack, *The Spirit of Traditional Chinese Law* (Athens: University of Georgia Press 1996); Werner Menski, *Comparative Law in a Global Context: The Legal Systems of Asia and Africa* 493–569 (Cambridge: Cambridge University Press, 2nd edn, 2006); John Henry Merryman, David S. Clark and John Owen Haley, *Comparative Law: Historical Development of the Civil Law Tradition in Europe, Latin America, and East Asia* 553–73 (New Providence, NJ: Matthew Bender & Co. 2010); Zweigert and Kötz (note 19) 286–94.

sources ended in the mid-nineteenth century when European governments (and the United States) forced Chinese emperors during the Qing Dynasty into unequal treaties granting Western powers and their citizens special rights, including in Chinese territory.

In place of law, the Chinese in East Asia during the Zhou Dynasty developed the idea that human nature is inherently good, social relations are part of the natural order, and virtuous conduct can be achieved through education and deference to the example of community rulers. Confucius (K'ung fu-tze, 551–479 BCE) refined these ethical tenets to serve also as the basis for government and politics. Subsequent philosophers, such as Dong Zhongshu (179–104 BCE), further elaborated a form of Confucianism emphasizing cosmic harmony. This underlay Chinese ideology until the twentieth century and informs national legal cultures up to the present in those legal systems that China has influenced.

Confucianism directs humans to keep their thoughts, feelings and actions in conformity with cosmic harmony—silently guiding all things in the universe—so that they in their conduct will not upset the natural balance of existing social and other relations. *Li*—rites or norms of proper behavior—depend on a person's social status: within the family, village, economy or political structure. Each person has many relations relevant to maintaining harmony that are based on one's characteristics, such as age, gender, family rank, type of employment or social prestige. *Li* provides guidance for each situation, depending on whether it involves dealings between family members, friends, strangers, political or social superior and inferior, older and younger, and so on. Within each category, appropriate behavior may be further defined, such as between older brother and younger brother, or husband and wife within a family.

The ideal person within this ideology is one learned in *li* who follows the rules modestly and instinctively, thereby repressing his own self-interest for the greater good of maintaining harmony. It is obvious that such a community would not need a large legal apparatus with its own set of rules to control human conduct, maintain social order and facilitate justice. Order and justice are subsumed within harmony. Nevertheless, Werner Menski emphasizes that one should not underestimate the importance of pluralistic customary law in imperial China.[22]

Before Confucianism prevailed as the spiritual and philosophical basis of the Chinese state during the Han Dynasty (206 BCE–220 CE), the political reality of the 'Warring States' Period (481–221 BCE) involved continued armed conflict among rival territorial princes. This reality—so unlike Confucian society—supported the emergence of the Legalist School, with philosophers such as Han Fei Zi (280–233 BCE). Legalists held that humans, in essence, were selfish, looking out for their own interests. When education could not induce proper behavior, the state must punish individuals—both to control them and to set an example for others—with legal rules (*fa*) and processes.

Although Confucianism triumphed, from the Han Dynasty until the beginning of the Republic of China (1912), emperors issued a series of codes that dealt almost completely with administrative and criminal matters.[23] The Tang Code (624) is the earliest that has

---

[22] Menski (note 21) 518–21.
[23] Karen Turner argues that legal scholars have underestimated the importance of law in China and that a reassessment is necessary. Karen Turner, 'Rule of Law Ideas in Early China?' 6 *Journal of Chinese Law* 1–44 (1992).

survived intact. Even when the issue appears to be family or succession law, the rules treat those subjects in an administrative (such as taxation) or penal context. The codes recognize the Confucian notion that legislation is a necessary evil, required only when the social order is seriously disrupted or the state threatened. The Confucian influence on penal law appears in the gradation of penalties based on the social status of the criminal and victim as much as the actor's intent or surrounding circumstances. Beyond China, Confucianism has been a major influence on the legal systems of Japan, Korea, Taiwan and Vietnam.

As far as private law was concerned, the teachings of Confucianism emphasized modes of dispute resolution outside courts. Emperors sent imperial magistrates—men educated in the Confucian literature—to the provinces to carry out administrative and judicial duties and to encourage obedience to Confucian virtue.[24] Disputes should be settled within the smallest unit with authority, whether the family, kin-group, village or commercial guild. Conciliators—with prestige due to age or rank—used the standards of *li* to seek compromise. Community pressure supported that solution. Reconciliation was justice. Only when the conciliators failed would a disputant take the matter to a provincial magistrate, suffering censure for that decision and experiencing the delay, expense and corruption of the state courts.

3.4   India and Hindu Law[25]

As in China with Confucianism, Hinduism in India is an ancient system of thought, with religious, philosophical and social underpinnings, that has served as a guiding force in society to control human conduct. The aim of Hinduism is to provide the individual with a moral compass to guide virtue and piety. Karma from good deeds in this life will permit the transmigration of the soul to a better existence in the next life, perhaps to a higher caste, or ultimately the soul's release as a higher spiritual being. There is no record of efforts among classical Hindu legal scholars to compare legal systems, but distinct schools of law in India developed in the eleventh and twelfth centuries that might have stimulated such interest.

Hindu law has passed through several periods of reconfiguration from Vedic times (1500 BCE), the classical phase (500 BCE to 1100 CE), the postclassical era, to English influence in India through the East India Company in the seventeenth century. Unlike Islam, scholars do not largely derive Hindu law from ancient religious scripture. Hindus do not need to hold specific religious beliefs. Rather, Hindu law is a kind of common law, continuously developed through customary practices and the historical records of Brahmin scholars until British officials took a greater interest in Hindu law after 1772.

---

[24]   Randall Peerenboom, 'Chinese Legalist School', in Clark (ed.) (note 9) 1, 179–80. In the *Analects* (2:3), Confucius stated, 'Lead the people with government regulations and organize them with penal law (*xing*), and they will avoid punishments but will be without shame. Lead them with virtue and organize them through the *li*, and the people will have a sense of shame and moreover will become humane people of good character'. Quoted in ibid. 179.
[25]   See Marc Galanter, *Law and Society in Modern India* (New York: Oxford University Press, Rajeev Dhavan ed., 1989); Menski (note 21) 193–278; Zweigert and Kötz (note 19) 313–19; Shubhankar Dam, 'Hindu Law', in Clark (ed.) (note 9) 2, 701–04.

After that time, an Anglo-Hindu case law developed together with British statutory intervention in India, which today legal scholars distinguish from pre-modern Hindu law.

Two points are relevant here. First, Hindu law was less connected to central government activities than the situation with Confucianism in China. India did not have a similar series of imperial codes or imperial magistrates such as those in China. Second, Hindu law was more diverse than Chinese law, with a large number of local variations. It also had a richer private law. It emphasized the practice of plurality and relative justice, with little interest in uniformity of law. What the two systems shared was a de-emphasis of law in society compared to Western traditions. Like the Romans, Indian authorities permitted Christians, Jews, Parsis and Muslims to use their own family and succession law. Hindu law today applies beyond India to Nepal and parts of Africa and southeast Asia.

The ancient Hindu texts (in Sanskrit) related to law were *smritis* (remembered knowledge of priests and scholars). They include *dharmasūtras* and *dharmaśāstras*, or rites, duties and rules of conduct, a moral guidance for righteousness. The key concept is *dharma*, the obligation of every person to do the right thing at all times, to take the virtuous path. The pluralism of Hindu law lies in the diverse implementation of this principle in the infinite socio-cultural circumstances of Indian life, by historical period, region, caste status, gender, age, and so on.[26]

The tension with modern Western law is obvious. Hindu law teaches that fixed rules might cause injustice. The endless distinctions treat individuals as separate units, linked all the same by a common conceptual bond in a macrocosmic order (*rita*) or secular truth (*satya*). Dharma, the appropriate action, must consider all the circumstances with a view to promote the common good. In one sense, the individual is the ultimate agent to determine the 'law' in any particular situation, consequently reducing the role for the state as lawmaker.

3.5   Islamic Law[27]

Islam, including its law, developed in the Arabian Peninsula in the seventh century CE. It considered Muhammad (570–632) the last in a series of prophets for the monotheistic faith of Abraham, Moses and Jesus. Islamic law (shari'a) encompasses the system of duties incumbent upon a Muslim by virtue of his religious belief. It is the expression of Allah's command for the Muslim community, the revealed word of God (Qur'an). Spread by conquest and trade, Islam has had a proselytizing appeal, since it recognized no barriers of race or class.

Shari'a is, as is canon law for Roman Catholics or Jewish law for Jews, the law of a religious community. Canon law prior to 1500 had almost universal applicability in Europe, since the Christian church had all the attributes of government (categories of jurisdiction) it shared with secular European rulers. Jurists consider canon law as an early example of 'modern' in the Western sense since it borrowed some of the sophisticated legal norms

---

[26]   Donald R. Davis, Jr., 'A Realist View of Hindu Law', 19 *Ratio Juris* 287, 291–310 (2006).

[27]   See Menski (note 21) 279–379; Lawrence Rosen, *The Justice of Islam: Comparative Perspectives on Islamic Law and Society* (New York: Oxford University Press 1999); Bernard G. Weiss, *The Spirit of Islamic Law* (Athens: University of Georgia Press 1998); Mahmood Monshipouri, 'Islamic Law', in Clark (ed.) (note 9) 2, 827–30.

and lawmaking and interpreting techniques from Roman law. However, its aspiration of universality with a single descending hierarchy from the pope down impeded interest in comparative law. Together with rediscovered and elaborated Roman law, canon law constituted the *jus commune* of Europe. Canon law declined in importance with the rise of statism and nationalism in Europe.

Shari'a today dominates the Middle East, most of the north half of Africa, southwest Asia, Malaysia and Indonesia. It is also influential in other parts of the world with more than one billion believers. Islamic law is a total belief system, since it regulates a person's relationship not only with others and with the state, but also with God. Shari'a is a comprehensive normative system that embraces both private and public conduct. It thus includes ritualistic practices as well as a system of legal rights and duties.

Fundamental to Islamic law is the belief, largely abandoned in Western secular law, that law is an expression of divine will. With the death of Muhammad in 632, communication of the divine will to man ceased. Unlike Western law, which jurists expect to evolve in response to major changes in society, the dominant Muslim jurisprudence states that it should not be society that frames the law, but rather the divine law that molds and controls society. The 'unchanging character of Islamic law' created interesting problems of interpretation for the scholars and operators of Islamic law, and differing views concerning the appropriate solution to such problems account for some of the differences between 'schools' of Islamic law. The major Sunni schools, established by the eleventh century, are Hanafi (Egypt, west Africa, Pakistan, Bangladesh and India), Maliki (north, central and west Africa), Shafi'i (east Africa, Malaysia and Indonesia), and Hanbali (the Arabian Peninsula). About 10 percent of believers are Shi'a, most of whom live in Iran, Iraq, Pakistan, India, Turkmenistan, Kazakhstan and Uzbekistan.

These Sunni schools, and their difference with the Shi'a jurists, provided the opportunity to develop comparative law, but there is little evidence that this occurred.[28] As with the split of western Christendom into Roman Catholics and Protestants, the divergence in religious law most often led to hostility and the attempt to exclude or conquer the nonconforming believers. Nevertheless, there were many examples in classical Islam of tolerance for Jews and Christians to live with their own laws.

Islamic jurists, besides the Qur'an, rely on *sunna*, the collection of stories (*hadith*) about the action and statements of Muhammad. These two sources provide guidance about living the good life to ensure the obedient Muslim life in paradise. The most comprehensive 'legal' aspect of jurist work, with principles, comes from the *fuqaha* of each of the various schools. This applies the two central sources to interpret particular circumstances (*ijtihad*) by analogy (*qiyas*) and consensus (*ijma*). In addition, a jurist (*faqih*) or religious figure (*mufti*) may issue a *fatwa* or opinion about an obligation for Muslims. The sophistication of this system was supplemented by Islamic law courts staffed by judges called *qadis*, learned in the law, serving as quasi-governmental agents, and issuing judicial decisions that serve as jurisprudence (*fiqh*).

---

[28]   Contra Hossein Modarressi Tabataba'i, *An Introduction to Shi'i Law: A Bibliographical Study* 43, 46 (London: Ithaca Press 1984), cited in H. Patrick Glenn, *Legal Traditions of the World: Sustainable Diversity in Law* 211 (New York: Oxford University Press, 4th edn, 2010).

With the expansion of Western colonization in the nineteenth century, Islamic law declined in importance. In the twenty-first century, however, there is renewed debate in Muslim countries about the place for classical Islam in modern society. Its importance is obvious and comparatists are not ignoring its relevance for understanding the legal systems of much of Africa and Asia. The utility of humanistic and social science methods is apparent.

3.6 Influence of the Classical Legal Traditions

From this survey of the classical modes of thinking about law and its classification, the only one to leave a lasting legacy for modern comparative law was Roman law. Of all the great ancient civilizations, the thousand-year history of Rome as it developed in western Europe first accommodated foreign law within the republic through the institutional framework of the *praetor peregrinus*.[29] This praetor's annual edict, regulating jurisdiction in disputes between foreigners, and later between citizens and foreigners, together with its juristic interpretation, was a pragmatic response to the reality of conquest and trade. During the empire, jurists interpreted the legal norms that developed within this institution as *ius gentium*, the law of peoples. Romans thought of this as one version of a universal law in comparison to the other universal, less practical, natural law, or the *ius civile* peculiar to Roman citizens. The Romans borrowed and absorbed some Greek thinking about law, which saw, in addition, a second life during the Renaissance as university law masters rediscovered Aristotle and Plato.

An importance difference between Roman law and the other classical laws considered here was that Roman law did not have a strong ideological or religious basis for its existence and authority. Jurists had differentiated it from religion, morality or philosophy. The important elements of Roman law were pragmatic, with private jurists developing most legal norms in a highly decentralized fashion that they incorporated into classical Roman law, eventually embodied in Emperor Justinian's *Corpus juris civilis* (529–34). This compilation served as the basis for university law study and influence on canon law in Europe after the twelfth century. Law faculties in the large number of European universities, teaching and studying Roman and canon law, served as the natural place to develop interest in comparative law after the Enlightenment forces of statism and nationalism began to support national law as their alternative in the eighteenth century.[30]

Moreover, while the Chinese, Hindu-Indian, and Islamic legal systems continue in force up to the present, and therefore governments supporting those systems have a strong interest in maintaining their mythic authority, such is not the case for Roman law. In the eighteenth and nineteenth centuries, Roman law often served as the alternative to national law in utilizing comparative law methods. This was as true for Sir William Blackstone (1723–80) at Oxford, in his thesis that English law was as rational as Roman law, as it was for John Adams (1735–1826) in arguing against English law as applied in the American

---

[29] See T. Corey Brennan, 1–2 *The Praetorship in the Roman Republic* (Oxford: Oxford University Press 2000).

[30] See David S. Clark, 'The Medieval Origins of Modern Legal Education: Between Church and State', 35 *American Journal of Comparative Law* 653 (1987).

colonies.[31] The major exception to this was the new German Empire, which embraced Roman law as part of the *usus modernus pandectarum*.

As for the origin of law and society research, beyond that of Plato and Aristotle, one needs to look at the early modern classifications of law that we turn to in section 4. It would be incongruous in classical Hindu or Islamic law (or Chinese law) to use the conjunction 'and', since one could only really describe law as substantially undifferentiated within the social and cultural settings of those legal traditions. These are traditions where the term 'socio-legal studies' would be superior to the use of 'law and society'.

4   COMPARISON BY MODERN EUROPEAN JURISTS

4.1   Early Modern Classifications

In the early modern era, some natural law jurists such as Hugo Grotius (Hugo de Groot, 1583–1645),[32] Samuel Pufendorf (1632–94) and Baron Charles-Louis de Montesquieu (1689–1755) used comparative law methods to provide empirical backing for natural law principles.[33] Others such as Blackstone had the additional objective of providing prestige for their national law: his four-volume *Commentaries on the Laws of England* (1765–9) emphasized similarities in English common law, Roman law and natural law.

Montesquieu's extensive speculation about the relation of law to natural and social forces and explicit classification of legal systems emphasized the distinct manners (*moeurs*) of a particular people in a particular era. His *Lettres Persanes* (1721), published anonymously, used the device of two Persians traveling in Europe who satirized the customs of French and European society. They pointed to the abuses and cruelties of criminal justice systems and argued for a rational theory of punishment adjusted to the settled sensibilities of the people.

Montesquieu's relativist view of humans' ability to achieve justice was further developed in *De l'esprit des lois* (1748), which drew upon causative factors such as climate, soil, population size, a people's morals and customs, religion and commerce. He classified governments along with the appropriate principle for their constitutive societies. Therefore, democracy required civic virtue; aristocracy, moderation against the people; monarchy, honor for the law and intermediate institutions; and despotism, fear to maintain order. He found different mechanisms for lawmaking and adjudication in the first three types of legal systems, but pointed out that law was not necessary for despotism.[34]

Besides Montesquieu's contribution to comparative law, socio-legal scholars also often see him as the father of their discipline.[35] Montesquieu had an important impact

---

[31]   See David S. Clark, 'Comparative Law in Colonial British America', 59 *American Journal of Comparative Law* 637 (2011).

[32]   Edward Keene, 'Grotius, Hugo', in Clark (ed.) (note 9) 2, 677–8.

[33]   Donahue (note 18) 23–31; Paul O. Carrese, 'Montesquieu, Charles-Louis de', in Clark (ed.) (note 9) 2, 1035–7.

[34]   Clark (note 18) 226.

[35]   See, e.g., Henry W. Ehrmann, *Comparative Legal Cultures* 5 (Englewood Cliffs, NJ: Prentice-Hall 1976); Klaus F. Röhl, *Rechtssoziologie: Ein Lehrbuch* 5–7 (Cologne: Carl Heymanns Verlag 1987).

on others, including Cesare Beccaria (1738–94), and in the nineteenth century, Alexis de Tocqueville and Émile Durkheim. Beccaria shared Montesquieu's concern with injustice and cruelty in criminal law and procedure in Europe. Beccaria's *Dei delitti e delle pene* (1764), soon translated into English, French and German, led to restrictions on the use of torture, judge-interpreted crime and punishment, and punishment that exceeded a proportionality standard measured by social harm.[36]

4.2   Nineteenth and Early Twentieth Century Classifications

By the nineteenth century, many European jurists and other scholars were developing comparative socio-legal studies. A few of the best known were Léon Duguit (1859–1928), Eugen Ehrlich (1862–1922), Otto von Gierke (1841–1921), Eugenio María de Hostos (1839–1903), Cesare Lombroso (1835–1909), Lewis Henry Morgan (1818–81), Gustav von Schmoller (1838–1917), William Graham Sumner (1840–1910), Gabriel de Tarde (1843–1904) and Alexis de Tocqueville (1805–59).[37] Of these, only Morgan was an American, and one could consider him the first law and society scholar with an international reputation in the young republic.[38]

Further sophistication in comparative law and society came with attempts to classify law and legal systems within two or more categories. Nineteenth century evolutionary theorists developed elaborate classifications of local and national legal systems. Law in these schemes was part of the larger social system that changed over time. For instance, Sir Henry Maine (1822–88), interested in the striking parallels between the development of English common law and classical Roman law, posited in *Ancient Law* (1861) stages of social development common to different peoples that could be correlated with particular instruments of legal growth. Jurists could characterize legal systems by whether social change occurred primarily by legal fictions, equity or natural law, or conscious creative legislation.[39]

Karl Marx, schooled in Roman law as well as history and philosophy, accepted the reigning concepts of his time about the nature of man and society. After he added the study of economics, he developed (along with Friedrich Engels, 1820–95) a conception of law that was materialist. Law, in *Zur Kritik der politischen Ökonomie* (1859), assumed a pivotal role in his base-superstructure model of social evolution. In essence, Marx's works supported a theory of law as an instrument of social power, which itself was a reflection of economic relations. In turn, it was people's gradual conquest of nature, a matter of technology, which determined economic relations.[40] Marxist historical materialism

---

[36]   Mario A. Cattaneo, 'Beccaria, Cesare', in Clark (ed.) (note 9) 1, 117–18.

[37]   There is an entry describing each of these persons in Clark (ed.) (note 9) 1–3.

[38]   Russell A. Judkins, 'Morgan, Lewis Henry', in Clark (ed.) (note 9), 2, 1044–5. Morgan had a classical education, including in Greek and Latin, then read law and became a lawyer in 1842. A few years later, he began to collect kinship data from a variety of indigenous tribes to support his theory that the peoples of the New World originally came from Asia. See note 49 below.

[39]   Clark (note 18) 226; Dante J. Scala, 'Maine, Henry Sumner', in Clark (ed.) (note 9) 2, 980–81.

[40]   Heath D. Pearson, 'Marx, Karl', in Clark (ed.) (note 9) 2, 996–8; see *Zur Kritik der politischen Ökonomie* (1859), translated as *A Contribution to the Critique of Political Economy* (New York: International Library Publishing, N.I. Stone trans., 1904). Marx reworked this as part of *Das Kapital* (1867). In *Kritik* (1859: 263) he wrote: 'In the social production of their life, men enter

comprehends society as structured by the material conditions at any given time. It identified five successive stages in the evolution of these material conditions in Europe, each with a different role for law. These stages were primitive communism, slavery, feudalism, capitalism, socialism and perhaps, one day, communism without the state or law.

Émile Durkheim (1858–1917), the first university sociologist recognized as such in France, had wide-ranging interests that included law. In his first book, *De la Division du Travail Social* (1893), Durkheim described the evolution of societies from mechanical solidarity to organic solidarity. He argued that forms of law provide an index of the type of social solidarity that exists. Repressive law, concerned with punishing offenses, represents mechanical solidarity or the type of social cohesion based on people's shared beliefs and personal ties. A limited degree of religious or cultural diversity could exist in such a society. By comparison, restitutive law, which restores the status quo if social relations are disturbed, represents organic solidarity or cohesion based on functional interdependence. Here, there is substantial division of labor and comprehensive contract, tort and commercial law mediates among diverse individual and social interests. In Durkheim's later writing, he emphasized the sacredness of abstract individuals, a religion of humanity to replace traditional religion found in repressive law regimes. This was not an egoistic individualism, but a moral individualism that would enhance human dignity and autonomy.[41]

In the twentieth century, Max Weber (1864–1920) used many of the same historical sources as legal evolutionists, but in *Wirtschaft und Gesellschaft* (1922) constructed ideal types to facilitate the comparison of actual social and legal systems in trying to explain the rise of industrial capitalism. His four-cell typology for lawmaking and law application considered the rationality or irrationality of legal thought as well as whether legal norms and decision making were highly differentiated from religion, ideology or emotion. He argued that the category of formal (autonomous) rationality, with a consistent body of general legal norms, provided the predictability facilitating modern capitalism.[42]

In an effort to make American lawyers and political scientists less parochial, John Wigmore (1863–1943) in 1928 published the three-volume *A Panorama of the World's Legal Systems*. He covered 16 historic and contemporary legal systems by the pictorial method, using between 20 and 50 pictures accompanied by text for each legal system to enliven its justice buildings, principal legal actors and characteristic legal materials. Organized historically, these systems included the Egyptian, Mesopotamian, Chinese, Hindu, Hebrew, Greek, maritime, Roman, Celtic, Germanic, canon, Japanese, Mohammedan (Islam), Slavic, Romanesque (civil law) and Anglican.[43]

---

into definite relations that are indispensable and independent of their will . . .. The sum total of these relations of production constitutes the economic structure of society, the real foundation, on which rises a legal and political superstructure and to which correspond definite forms of social consciousness . . .. At a certain stage of their development, the material productive forces of society come in conflict with the existing relations of production, or—what is but a legal expression for the same thing—with the property relations within which they have been at work hitherto . . .. Then begins an epoch of social revolution.' Quoted from Pearson: 997.

[41]   Roger Cotterrell, 'Durkheim, Émile', in Clark (ed.) (note 9) 1, 443–5; see Roger Cotterrell, 'Durkheim School', in Clark (ed.) (note 9) 1, 442–3.

[42]   Ronen Shamir, 'Weber, Max', in Clark (ed.) (note 9) 3, 1573–5.

[43]   Clark (note 2) 607–10; Clark (note 18) 226–7.

5 COMPARISON BY DISCIPLINES RELATED TO LAW

Drawing on these earlier scholars and their classifications of law, and with a common concern for the connection between law and society, anthropologists, criminologists, economists, political scientists, psychologists and sociologists generally believe that they should de-emphasize formal legal rules when comparing legal systems. A few examples will have to suffice.

5.1 Anthropology of Law

Anthropologists frequently observe that some societies operate without government but have social order and law-like institutions. In modern nations, there may be many levels or discrete groups in societies (with their own 'legal' systems) so that it becomes appropriate to speak of legal pluralism. Comparing legal systems then depends on the characteristics of different societies or their subgroups. Leopold Pospíšil, for example, described this situation as a patterned mosaic of subgroups that belong to certain identifiable types with different memberships.[44] Each subgroup owes its existence to a legal system that regulates the behavior of its members. These legal systems then form a hierarchy reflecting the degree of inclusiveness of the corresponding subgroups that one categorizes by legal level, such as the family, lineage, community, state or nation. People are simultaneously members of several subgroups of different inclusiveness, which may lead to contradictory legal loyalties.[45]

Mark Goodale and Elizabeth Mertz place the beginning of legal anthropology in the nineteenth century, with its emphasis on comparative and evolutionary studies.[46] European scholars were fascinated by ancient and 'primitive' societies, which by their nature they would have to compare with contemporary European legal systems to provide meaning for the reader. Henry Maine is an obvious illustration, but so too were the studies of Johann Bachofen (1815–87),[47] John McLennan (1827–81)[48] and the American, Lewis Morgan.[49] Although modern anthropologists find most of this research inadequate due to

---

[44] See Leopold Pospíšil, *Anthropology of Law: A Comparative Theory* 106–26 (New York: Harper & Row 1971).

[45] Clark (note 18) 227.

[46] Mark Goodale and Elizabeth Mertz, 'Anthropology of Law', in Clark (ed.) (note 9) 1, 68–70; see Elizabeth Mertz and Mark Goodale, 'Comparative Anthropology of Law', in this volume, ch. 4, sec. 2.1.

[47] J.J. Bachofen, *Das Mutterrecht. Eine Untersuchung über die Gynaikokratie der alten Welt nach ihrer religiösen und rechtlichen Natur* (Stuttgart: Krais & Hoffman 1861.) Selected work of Bachofen was translated into English in 1967, including excerpts from *Mother Right*. It argued that people originally conceptualized law and morality within matriarchies.

[48] John F. McLennan, *Primitive Marriage: An Inquiry into the Origin of the Form of Capture in Marriage Ceremonies* (Edinburgh: Adam & Charles Black 1865). McLennan, a Scot, argued that early conditions of economic scarcity led to female-centered social rules and structured family relationships and kinship systems. Its evolutionary premise was common for the time. 'In the sciences of law and society, old means not old in chronology, but in structure: that is most archaic which lies nearest to the beginning of human progress.' Ibid. 8–9.

[49] Lewis H. Morgan, *Ancient Society: Researches in the Lines of Human Progress from Savagery through Barbarism to Civilization* (New York: Henry Holt & Co. 1877). As illustrated in the book's

its armchair methods, the emphasis on cultural and historical context remains important. The shift in methodology in the twentieth century to intensive ethnographic research in the subjects' culture and language led to less comparative work, although there have been a few exceptions.[50]

5.2   Criminology

Criminology was the first social science closely connected to law to develop in Europe. It encompasses all aspects of crime and punishment, including the nature and causes of crime, characteristics of criminals and victims, and the efforts of police, prosecutors, defense lawyers, judges and correctional officials to control crime and punish offenders.[51] Besides Beccaria,[52] early philosophical approaches to crime in the nineteenth century, often with a comparative perspective, included those of Jeremy Bentham (1748–1832),[53] Lombroso[54] and Marx.[55] By the late nineteenth century, sociologists, statisticians, psychologists and psychiatrists more widely used their methodologies to examine crime, criminal justice and punishment.[56]

Franz von Liszt (1851–1919) is good example of the interdisciplinary interest in crime. He studied law in Vienna and became a professor. He was a co-founder of the German criminal law journal, *Zeitschrift für die gesamte Strafrechtwissenschaft* in 1871 and one year later moved to Marburg. There he taught a seminar in criminology and established the sociological school in criminal policy (Marburg School). He fought the metaphysical theory of reprisal punishment with a positivist approach that looked to a deviant's motives in acting and the role of prevention in punishment. In 1889, he co-founded the International Criminalist Union, which influenced legislators in many countries to implement probation instead of short prison sentences, rehabilitation and special rules

---

title, Morgan used three stages of history to explore comparatively changes in kinship and property relations as they affected social structure and governance systems. Technological innovation was an important factor in this evolution. See Daniel Noah Moses, *The Promise of Progress: The Life and Work of Lewis Henry Morgan* (Columbia: University of Missouri Press 2009); notes 37–8 and accompanying text.

[50]   See, e.g., Michael Freeman and David Napier (eds), *Law and Anthropology* (Oxford: Oxford University Press 2009); Laura Nader (ed.), *Law in Culture and Society* (Chicago: Aldine Publishing 1969, reprinted 1997).

[51]   See Peter Becker and Richard F. Wetzell (eds), *Criminals and their Scientists: The History of Criminology in International Perspective* (Cambridge: Cambridge University Press 2006); Robert Agnew, 'Criminology', in Clark (ed.) (note 9) 1, 340–45.

[52]   See note 36 and accompanying text.

[53]   Bentham, the founder of classical utilitarianism, devised the panopticon prison (1787), a circular structure that facilitated inmate surveillance from a central watchtower to guarantee their good behavior. It inspired the Eastern State Penitentiary in Philadelphia, which opened in 1829. Philip Schofield, 'Bentham, Jeremy', in Clark (ed.) (note 9) 1, 121–2.

[54]   See text accompanying note 37.

[55]   See note 40 and accompanying text.

[56]   Lombroso's use of psychiatry was an early example of law and medicine and the idea of the born *homo criminalis*. Scholars today discredit most of this early psychiatric interest in crime and criminal law, with its phrenology, sterilization and eugenics.

for juveniles. He taught in Berlin from 1898 to 1916, which provided him with a visible platform for his ideas.[57]

Another example is Raffaele Garofalo (1851–1934), a student of Lombroso, who published a popular, comprehensive and comparative treatise on criminology using examples from Europe, Asia and North and South America. Garofalo took a thoroughgoing socio-logical approach to crime, criminal law, procedure and punishment, adding elements of anthropological and psychological theory. He was president of the International Institute of Sociology (Paris), procurator-general of the Venice Court of Appeal, and professor of criminal law and procedure in Naples.[58] He not only prepared his most important work, *Criminologia*, in Italian, he worked on an updated French translation,[59] which later served (with his participation) in the English translation published in the US. This later volume was part of the Modern Criminal Science Series published under the auspices of the American Institute of Criminal Law and Criminology. It supported translations of European work to 'inculcate the study of modern criminal science, as a pressing duty for the legal profession and for the thoughtful community at large'.[60] In general, comparative criminology has had an important place in criminology's history, which has increased recently along with the incidence of transnational crime.[61]

5.3   Law and Economics

Francesco Parisi traces the origins of law and economics to Adam Smith's (1723–90) discussion of the economic effects of legislation regulating economic activities, and Bentham's theory of legislation and utilitarianism. Both of these classical economists were explicitly comparative in their analysis. Much of this comparative writing about economics and government or law, such as that of Marx, continued in the nineteenth century. Nevertheless, the modern worldwide success of law and economics began in the United States with scholars such as Henry Simon, Aaron Director (1902–2004), Henry Manne, George Stigler (1911–92), Armen Alchian and Gordon Tullock.[62]

---

[57]   Florian Herrmann, 'Liszt, Franz von', in Clark (ed.) (note 9) 2, 958–9.

[58]   Raffaele Garofalo, *Criminology* xi–xii (Boston: Little, Brown & Co., Robert Wyness Millar trans., 1914).

[59]   The first Italian edition appeared in 1885—*Criminologia: Studio sul Delitto, sulle sue Cause e sui Mezzi di Repressione* (Turin: Bocca)—with subsequent editions. Garofalo personally worked on the French translation, which he updated for the fifth French edition in 1905. There were also Spanish and Portuguese translations. Garofalo (note 58) xiii.

[60]   Garofalo (note 58) viii. John Wigmore, a leading comparatist, was the chair of the translation committee. Ibid. ix; see Clark (note 2) 599–600, 607–10; text accompanying note 43.

[61]   See, e.g., Piers Beirne and David Nelken (eds), *Issues in Comparative Criminology* (Aldershot, UK: Dartmouth 1997); Gregory J. Howard and Graeme Newman (eds), *Varieties of Comparative Criminology* (Leiden: Brill 2001); James Sheptycki and Ali Wardak (eds), *Transnational and Comparative Criminology* (London: Glass House 2005); John Winterdyk, Philip Reichel and Harry Dammer (eds), *A Guided Reader to Research in Comparative Criminology/Criminal Justice* (Bochum: Universitätsverlag Brockmeyer 2009); Francis Pakes, 'Comparative Criminal Justice', in Clark (ed.) (note 9) 1, 218–20; Francis Pakes, 'Comparative Criminology' in this volume, ch. 3; Robert Winslow, 'A Comparative Criminology Tour of the World', http://www-rohan.sdsu.edu/faculty/rwinslow/index.html (by country).

[62]   Francesco Parisi, 'Economics, Law and', in Clark (ed.) (note 9) 1, 451–8; Warren J. Samuels,

Although the first twentieth-century applications of economics to law tended to focus on areas related to labor law, corporate law, tax law and competition law, in the 1960s, the pioneering work of Ronald Coase and Guido Calabresi brought to light the pervasive bearing of economics on all areas of the law. The methodological breakthrough occasioned by Coase and Calabresi allowed immediate expansion to the areas of tort, property and contract. The analytical power of their work did not confine itself to these fields, however, and subsequent law and economics contributions demonstrate the explanatory and analytical reach of its methodology in several other areas of the law.

By the 1970s, several important applications of economics to law gradually exposed the economic structure of every aspect of a legal system: from its origin and evolution, to its substantive, procedural and constitutional rules. An important ingredient in the success of law and economics research, illustrating its international and comparative reach, has been the establishment of specialized journals. The first such journal, the *Journal of Law and Economics*, appeared in 1958 at the University of Chicago. Others that followed include the *Journal of Legal Studies* (1972), *Research in Law and Economics* (1979), *International Review of Law and Economics* (1981), *Supreme Court Economic Review* (1982), *Journal of Law, Economics and Organization* (1985), *European Journal of Law and Economics* (1994), *American Law and Economics Review* (1999), *Journal of Empirical Legal Studies* (2004), and *Review of Law and Economics* (2005).[63] In recent years, some economists and comparatists have found each other's disciplines attractive.[64]

5.4   Law and Political Science

Comparative law and political science has its origins in the earliest classifications of legal institutions discussed in sections 3.1 and 4.1. Aristotle, Montesquieu and Tocqueville are obvious examples with their emphasis on constitutional structures and legal culture.[65] By the eighteenth century, European theorists (some of whom had university teaching positions) secured the field of political economy as one that examined the usefulness of political and legal institutions and policies at the level of the state to develop economic production, exchange, distribution and wealth. Those working in this tradition could claim some of the same scholars important in law and economics, such as Smith and Marx. Much of the work was comparative and explicitly dealt with legal institutions and processes.[66]

'Smith, Adam', in 3 ibid. 1378–9; Peter R. Senn, 'Stigler, George J.', in 3 ibid. 1435–6. Other historical examples described in the *Encyclopedia* (ibid.) are John R. Commons (1862–1945), Carl Menger (1840–1921), Gustav von Schmoller (1838–1917) and Werner Sombart (1863–1941).

[63]   Steven G. Medema, 'Chicago School of Law and Economics', in Clark (ed.) (note 9) 1, 167–70; Parisi (note 62) 452.

[64]   See, e.g., Ugo Mattei, *Comparative Law and Economics* (Ann Arbor, University of Michigan Press 1997); Florian Faust, 'Comparative Law and Economic Analysis of Law', in Reimann and Zimmerman (note 17) 837–65.

[65]   Alison Dundes Renteln, 'Political Science, Law and', in Clark (ed.) (note 9) 3, 1137; see Mark Hulliung, *Montesquieu and the Old Regime* 1–14, 25–53, 212–30 (Berkeley: University of California Press 1976).

[66]   An example of this type of research is John C. Reitz, 'Comparative Law and Political Economy', in this volume, ch. 6. A detailed treatment of important political economists, many

The comparative politics revolution in the United States during the 1950s shifted law and political science from a field that tended to emphasize public law and to describe the legal institutions of foreign governments to the explanation of political behavior in structural and functional terms. Gabriel Almond and Bingham Powell, for instance, used the developmental variable of cultural secularization and structural differentiation together with the low or high level of political subsystem autonomy associated with interest groups and political parties to classify political systems. Modern systems could be pre-mobilized, mobilizing, or penetrative, and within each of these categories either authoritarian or democratic.[67]

By the 1980s and 1990s, an emphasis on empirical and comparative methods to analyze government institutions and processes and the ways in which people relate to them had spread beyond the United States to Europe and elsewhere. Alison Renteln describes some of this research in studies on judicial behavior, juries, courts and their processes, criminal justice systems (overlapping criminology), administrative law, dispute transformation and resolution, constitutional courts and civil and human rights. She identifies globalization as one of the forces sparking the increased interest in comparative research.[68]

5.5   Psychology and Law

Andreas Kapardis dates the beginning of modern experimental psychology and its interest in legal psychology from the end of the nineteenth century. Much of the research was transnational or comparative.[69] Prior to that time, psychology was a branch of philosophy. Early work began at German universities and spread to the United States and shortly thereafter to other parts of Europe. Hugo Münsterberg (1863–1916) was a pioneer in this field. He studied psychology and medicine at Leipzig and accepted his first teaching position at Freiburg. At the initial International Congress of Psychology in 1891, he met the American William James, who invited him to chair the psychology laboratory at Harvard. Harvard's president, Charles Eliot, who had initiated or supported laboratory methods at most of Harvard's faculties, including the case method at the Law School, offered Münsterberg a professorship (in experimental psychology) at Harvard, which he held until his death.[70] In 1908, he published *On the Witness Stand*, a series of essays that explored psychological factors that can affect a trial's outcome, including witness memory and the use of hypnotism. In a book chapter, entitled 'The Mind of the

---

educated in law, by country, is in John Kells Ingram, *A History of Political Economy* 55–195 (New York: Macmillan & Co. 1894).

[67]   Gabriel A. Almond and G. Bingham Powell, Jr., *Comparative Politics: System, Process, and Policy* (Boston: Little, Brown, 2nd edn, 1978); Clark (note 18) 227.

[68]   Renteln (note 65) 1138–43.

[69]   Andreas Kapardis, 'Psychology and Law', in Clark (ed.) (note 9) 3, 1227–8.

[70]   See Matthew Hale, Jr., *Human Science and Social Order: Hugo Münsterberg and the Origins of Applied Psychology* (Philadelphia: Temple University Press 1980). Münsterberg was an exchange professor from Harvard during the academic year 1910–11 to the University of Berlin, during which time he founded the Amerika Institut in Berlin. Ibid. 166–8. On Eliot and the Law School, see David S. Clark, 'Tracing the Roots of American Legal Education: A Nineteenth-Century German Connection', 51 *Rabels Zeitschrift für ausländisches und internationales Privatrecht* 313, 318–22, 326–31 (1987).

Juryman', he was among the first to consider jury research and explore the concept of 'mass consciousness'.[71]

There was other important pioneering work in which psychologists applied their research to areas within law. This included publications by Alfred Binet (1857–1911), the French developer of a standard intelligence test, on witness observation and Carl Jung (1875–1961), the Swiss founder of the analytical school of psychology, on psychological diagnoses of criminal acts.[72] Textbooks on psychology since the 1920s have discussed issues and research interests at the interface between psychology and law. The availability of these textbooks has facilitated teaching legal psychology topics, thus helping to establish the discipline's conceptual boundaries and identity.

The psycho-legal field has been expanding at an impressive rate since the mid-1960s, especially in North America, the late 1970s in the United Kingdom, the early 1980s in Australia, and the 1990s in continental Europe, particularly in the Netherlands, Germany and Spain. A few of legal psychology's contributions have dealt with eyewitness testimony (in part by children), jury decision making, judicial sentencing, expert witnesses, detecting lies (including false memory) and police procedures.[73]

5.6   Sociology of Law

Comparative sociology of law (as with political science) has its origins in the early modern and subsequent European classifications of legal institutions described in section 4. Most of the scholars named there are relevant for comparative sociology of law. For instance, Durkheim wrote, 'Comparative sociology is not a particular branch of sociology; it is sociology itself'.[74] This seems self-evident in that the gold standard of the scientific method in the social sciences rests in the comparison of experimentally allocated groups. For sociology of law—even more so for some other social sciences related to law—the challenges of attaining this standard are great. There are statistical ways to simulate

---

[71]   Hugo Münsterberg, *On the Witness Stand: Essays on Psychology and Crime* (Garden City, NY: Doubleday, Page & Co. 1908); Hugo Münsterberg, *Psychology and Social Sanity* 181–202 (Garden City, NY: Doubleday, Page & Co. 1914). In a jury-like experiment pitting a male group versus a female group, Münsterberg found that the perception accuracy of the male group improved from 52 to 78 percent after discussion, but that there was no such improvement among the women. Ibid., *Psychology* 189–202. 'It is evident that this tendency of the female mind must be advantageous for many social purposes. The woman remains loyal to her instinctive opinion. Hence we have no right to say that the one type of mind is in general better than the other. We may say only that they are different, and that this difference makes the men fit and the women unfit for the particular task which society requires from the jurymen.' Ibid. 198.

[72]   Kapardis (note 69) 1228. Kapardis also lists James McKeen Cattell (1860–1944), an American, Sigmund Freud (1856–1939), the founder of psychoanalysis, and the Russian neuropsychologist Alexandr Luria (1902–77). Ibid.

[73]   Ibid. 1228–33; see Ruth Horry et al., 'Comparative Legal Psychology: Eyewitness Identification', in this volume, ch. 7. Forensic psychology, the provision of psychological information to the court, also involves many psychologists with the law. Ironically, 'comparative psychology' does not so much undertake cross-national studies as rather compare the human species to animals.

[74]   Émile Durkheim, *The Rules of Sociological Method* 139 (Chicago: University of Chicago Press, Sarah A. Solovay and John H. Mueller trans., 8th edn, 1938); see note 41 and accompanying text; Roger Cotterrell, 'Sociology of Law', in Clark (ed.) (note 9) 3, 1413–15.

scientific comparison using the data that scholars and institutions produce, including from experiments and quasi-experiments, but the task is still difficult.[75]

Roger Cotterrell describes several important examples of comparative sociology of law from the nineteenth and twentieth centuries as well as methodological issues that comparatists face.[76] The importance of comparison has increased in the context of globalization. Cotterrell asks whether researchers should be looking for similarities or differences among legal systems, and what should be the appropriate level of inquiry in the reality of legal pluralism.[77] Lawrence Friedman in the 1970s argued that scholars could classify legal systems according to their internal legal culture, which includes the attitudes and values of judges, lawyers, and other legal actors toward a task such as lawmaking or adjudication that relies on reasoning or some other basis of legitimacy. He considered two variables. First, when a legal system requires reasoning premised on legal propositions, it is a closed system; when propositions may be non-legal, the system is open. Second, some systems regard legal propositions as fixed and timeless; others accept change as normal.[78]

Using these two variables, Friedman derived four types of reasoning associated with law. First, closed systems, such as those based on sacred law, formally reject the idea of change. What change does occur must be based on legal fictions. Second, a legal science system such as that in Germany is closed but it permits change by simply adding legal rules or deriving new legal principles. Third, traditional or customary law systems do not accept explicit change but are open to new norms based on shifting behavioral patterns. Fourth, a system permitting change by looking outside the stock of legal propositions includes what Weber called substantive rationality. This could be revolutionary legality, such as that in socialist Russia, or welfare legality, which looks to ethical imperatives or utilitarian principles.[79]

Today, there is renewed interest in comparative socio-legal studies—often taking a sociological focus—as illustrated in the fine summary of the field by Annelise Riles. More of this effort than in the past originates outside Europe and North America or, at least, takes the legal systems of Asia, Africa and Latin America as objects of investigation.[80]

6   THE SPREAD OF COMPARATIVE LAW AND SOCIETY ACTIVITIES WORLDWIDE

6.1   Early Developments

Historically, Europe is the origin of most comparative law and socio-legal activity. Of the two subject matters, comparative law is the older field due in part to the traditional

---

[75]   See Clark (ed.) (note 9) 1, xxiv (listing many entries exploring these methodological issues by topic).

[76]   Cotterrell, 'Comparative Sociology of Law', in this volume, ch. 2.

[77]   Ibid. sec. 6.

[78]   Lawrence M. Friedman, *Law and Society: An Introduction* 76–81 (Englewood Cliffs, NJ: Prentice-Hall 1977).

[79]   Ibid. 80–86; Clark (note 18) 227.

[80]   Annelise Riles, 'Comparative Law and Socio-Legal Studies', in Reimann and Zimmerman (note 17) 775–813.

importance of law as a faculty (in reality two faculties—Roman law and canon law) at European universities. In addition, most law graduates took jobs working in local and regional secular government that had its own customary systems of law.[81] By the second half of the nineteenth century, there were a few national organizations (some sponsoring scholarly journals) of comparative law, which increased in number during the early twentieth century along with international meetings of scholars. During this same period, there emerged national organizations with international congresses in most of the social science disciplines discussed in section 5. Some of these scholars, as illustrated, had an interest in law.

The founders of sociological jurisprudence, the next step in this development, distinguished themselves from social scientists interested in the rise of modernity by their concern with using science and empiricism to transform legal education and practice.[82] One might begin with the late work of Rudolf von Jhering (1818–92), who abandoned the German Pandectists' jurisprudence of concepts for a theory of law more suited to the pragmatic needs of the rising industrial society, a jurisprudence of interests (*Interessenjurisprudenz*).[83] Jhering directly influenced the legal realist statements of Oliver Wendell Holmes Jr. (1841–1935) and the sociological jurisprudence of Roscoe Pound (1870–1964) in the United States.[84] Pound rejected legal formalism and argued that 'law in action', not 'law in the books', formed the basis for law and legal institutions. Lawyers should strive toward a concept of social justice or social interests informed by the insights of sociology. Pound was also America's most distinguished comparatist during the first half of the twentieth century.[85] The Austrian Eugen Ehrlich (1862–1922) and Polish-Russian Leon Petrażycki (1867–1931) wrote that informal and unofficial mechanisms of social control affected legal institutions and framed legal behavior. Social forms of law—intuitive law or living law—preceded the state and jurists should understand them through empirical methods.[86]

Legal realism began in German-speaking countries as the free law school (*Freirechtsschule*). Ehrlich, Ernst Fuchs (1859–1929) and Hermann Kantorowicz (1877–1940) were the principal protagonists. Free law reflected social interests and popular customs that influenced legal decision makers in their work as judges and administrators in resolving

---

[81]   See sections 3.6, 4.

[82]   Reza Banakar, 'Sociological Jurisprudence', in Clark (ed.) (note 9) 3, 1409.

[83]   Mario G. Losano, 'Jhering, Rudolf von', in Clark (ed.) (note 9) 2, 839–40; see Rudolf von Jhering, *Der Kamp ums Recht* (Vienna: Manz 1872, John J. Lalor trans. as *The Struggle for Law*, Chicago: Callaghan 1879); Rudolf von Jhering, 1–2 *Der Zweck im Recht* (Leipzig: Breitkopf & Härtel 1877, 1883, Isaac Husik trans. vol. 1 as *Law as a Means to an End*, Boston: Boston Book 1913).

[84]   Merryman et al. (note 21) 530–31; Konrad Zweigert and Kurt Siehr, 'Jhering's Influence on the Development of Comparative Legal Method', 19 *American Journal of Comparative Law* 215, 225–6 (1971).

[85]   Clark (note 2) 605–07; see Roscoe Pound, 'Law in Books and Law in Action', 44 *American Law Review* 12 (1910); Roscoe Pound, 'The Scope and Purpose of Sociological Jurisprudence', 25 *Harvard Law Review* 489 (1912) (part 3).

[86]   Banakar (note 82) 1409–10; see Clark (note 2) 605–07; Elizabeth Hayden, 'Petrażycki, Leon', in Clark (ed.) (note 9) 3, 1107–08; A Javier Treviño, 'Pound, Roscoe', in Clark (ed.) (note 9) 3, 1160–61.

disputes and applying legislative norms. They were social engineers who considered justice and social well-being. In France, François Gény (1861–1959) also supported judicial creativity through interpretation he called free scientific research.[87] In the United States, legal realism was a reaction against doctrinal formalism, especially the type taught in US law schools through the case method initiated at Harvard in the 1870s. As with free law, legal realism emphasized process (usually judicial process) and accepted indeterminacy. Law professors could use empirical social sciences to explain legal processes and a few, such as Karl Llewellyn (1893–1962) and W. Underhill Moore (1879–1949) successfully carried out significant research. Llewellyn was also an important comparatist. Nevertheless, the realism enterprise in its ambitious form failed since lawyers and judges believed the work was irrelevant to their tasks and it did not provide a normative basis to defend democracy against the threats of totalitarianism.[88]

6.2   Post-World War II

The sustained combination of the two subject matters—comparative law and socio-legal research—began following World War II.[89] The economic and cultural forces of globalization after 1990 have nurtured the increasing importance of this cooperation.[90] In this section, I treat the spread of comparative law and society activities worldwide and then, in section 7, the supportive role of postwar international organizations.

The United States emerged from the war as the world's leading economic and political power. Consistent with this new status, American comparatists—both scholars and practicing lawyers—engaged more actively in the exportation of American law and legal institutions. Some of this interest stemmed from American military occupation, such as that in the late 1940s and 1950s in Germany, Japan and South Korea. One can see the impact in public law, especially constitutional law, and in institutions such as judicial review. During the cold war contest with communism in the 1960s and 1970s, the US government and some American foundations with law and development programs supported the battle in developing nations, many newly independent as part of the United Nations' effort toward decolonization. These programs sought to implant certain American legal features such as active teaching in law schools, or social engineering for lawyers and judges, as a spur to economic and political development. In the 1990s, the American Bar Association's

---

[87]   Mathias W. Reimann, 'Free Law School', in Clark (ed.) (note 9) 2, 605–06; see Judith Boardman, 'Fuchs, Ernst', in Clark (ed.) (note 9) 2, 606–07; Johannes Feest, 'Ehrlich, Eugen', in Clark (ed.) (note 9) 1, 471–2; Stanley L. Paulson, 'Kantorowicz, Hermann', in Clark (ed.) (note 9) 2, 876–7.

[88]   James E. Herget, 'Realism, American Legal', in Clark (ed.) (note 9) 3, 1270–72; see Clark (note 70); Ajay K. Mehrota, 'Llewellyn, Karl N.', in Clark (ed.) (note 9) 2, 966–7. Llewellyn was familiar with German law and had lectured in German universities. His book, *The Case Law System in America* (Chicago: University of Chicago Press, Michael Ansaldi trans., 1989) was a translation of the original German version, *Präjudizienrecht und Rechtsprechung in Amerika* (Leipzig: J. Weicher 1933).

[89]   For an assessment of the situation at the beginning of this period, see Julius Stone, *Law and the Social Sciences in the Second Half Century* (Minneapolis: University of Minnesota Press 1966).

[90]   See, e.g., Brian Z. Tamanaha, *A General Jurisprudence of Law and Society* xvii, 107–11, 120–30, 195–200, 230–36 (Oxford: Oxford University Press 2001).

CEELI program, 'promoting the rule of law', provided thousands of advisers to help write constitutions and laws in Russia, its former republics, and a few other developing nations. Most of this work was not informed with an adequate awareness of the social, political and cultural consequences of legal transplantation.[91]

With the founding of the *American Journal of Comparative Law* in 1952, however, an important medium was available to disseminate the comparative research that did utilize a social or cultural perspective. Pound wrote the introduction to the *Journal*'s first issue.[92] Volume 1, for instance, included two articles on collective labor bargaining in France and Germany.[93] As already described in section 1.2, the *Law & Society Review* began in 1966 with some articles on foreign and comparative investigation.[94] Today, both journals are the pre-eminent peer-reviewed outlets in the world for scholarship in their respective fields.[95]

In addition to journals and their supporting organizations, a few US universities (for instance, California Berkeley and Irvine, New York Buffalo, NYU, Northwestern, Princeton and Wisconsin) have established law and society research centers or graduate degree programs. American foundations, such as Russell Sage, Ford and Walter Meyer, support some of these activities. The National Science Foundation in 1971 established a law and social science grant program. An increasing number of colleges and universities offer one or more courses on law and society, some of which have a comparative element, and a few have departments or programs at times including criminology. Globalization, including how it relates to law, is a popular theme.[96]

Canada also has an active law and society community, which naturally takes on a comparative dimension due to the importance of the French-speaking province of Québec with its French civil-law-influenced legal system. The prominence of First Nations peoples in Canadian politics and cultural life further distinguishes some of its research.[97]

---

[91]   David S. Clark, 'Development of Comparative Law in the United States', in Reimann and Zimmerman (note 17) 175, 204–05.

[92]   Roscoe Pound, 'Introduction', 1 *American Journal of Comparative Law* 1–10 (1952); see notes 84–5 and accompanying text.

[93]   Heinrich Kronstein, 'Collective Bargaining in Germany: Before 1933 and after 1945', 1 *American Journal of Comparative Law* 199–214 (1952); Charles A. Reynard, 'Collective Bargaining and Industrial Peace in France', 1 ibid. 215–32.

[94]   See note 15 and accompanying text.

[95]   Clark (note 91) 177; David O. Friedrichs, 'United States', in Clark (ed.) (note 9) 3, 1534–5. There are currently 17 other US law journals with 'comparative' in the title, and many times that number with 'international', 'transnational' or 'global' in the title, that also publish comparative law research. Friedrichs mentions additional major US law and society journals: *Crime, Law and Social Control*; *Journal of Legal Studies*; *Law & Social Inquiry*; *Law and Human Behavior*; *Law and Policy*; *Legal Studies Forum*; *Research in Law, Deviance and Social Control*; and *Studies in Law, Politics and Society*. Ibid. 1535.

[96]   Friedrichs (note 95) 1535–8; Christopher L. Eisgruber, 'Program in Law and Public Affairs', in Clark (ed.) (note 9) 3, 1197; Howard S. Erlanger, 'Institute for Legal Studies', in Clark (ed.) (note 9) 2, 784; Christine B. Harrington, 'Institute for Law and Society', in Clark (ed.) (note 9) 2, 782–3; Robert A. Kagan, 'Center for the Study of Law and Society', in Clark (ed.) (note 9) 1, 165–6; Lynn Mather, 'Baldy Center for Law and Social Policy', in Clark (ed.) (note 9) 1, 115–16; Christopher Zorn, 'NSF Law and Social Science Program', in Clark (ed.) (note 9) 2, 1073. A list of academic programs and research institutes is at Law and Society Association, Related Links, http://www.lawandsociety.org/links.htm.

[97]   W. Wesley Pue, 'Canada', in Clark (ed.) (note 9) 1, 155–7.

After North America, Europe is the region with the second most vigorous law and society movement. The importance of the European Union for its 27 member states adds a natural comparative law aspect to research about issues within the EU's supranational legal system.[98] Scholars in France, Germany, Italy, the Netherlands (and Flanders), Scandinavia and the UK have produced substantial research for much of the postwar period. This continues the traditional European strength in comparative legal and socio-legal scholarship from the eighteenth and nineteenth century traced in section 4. Section 5 provided many examples of this European tradition in the twentieth century, organized by disciplines related to law.[99]

As in Germany and Italy, law and society research came to an abrupt end in Austria with the rise of National Socialism. Before that time, Austria had more than its share of major scholars such as Ehrlich and lost the legal sociologist Hans Zeisel (1905–92), who emigrated to the US in 1938. Since the 1970s, however, there has been an increase in law and society studies.[100] There is also significant socio-legal investigation, particularly in criminology, in Belgium, Spain and Switzerland.[101]

Little known in the West, Japan has a history in socio-legal scholarship dating from the early twentieth century at a time when it had only recently transplanted European civil law. It leads this field in Asia, which taken together ranks third as regions active in law and society. Izutaro Suehiro (1888–1951) began Japanese interest in this area after he studied in the US (1918–20) and met Ehrlich in Switzerland in 1920. He incorporated Ehrlich's 'living law' concept into a property law treatise, established a research group and set up a counseling center at Tokyo Imperial University for indigent people so that his law students would learn about living law. He was a founding member, along with Takeyoshi Kawashima (1909–92), of the Nihon Ho Shakai Gakkai (Japanese Association of Sociology of Law) in 1947. Today, it has 900 members, second largest behind the Law and Society Association in the US. It also has the oldest journal, *Ho Shakaigaku* (Sociology of Law), published since 1951. Much of the socio-legal research is comparative since Japanese scholars rely on European and North American scholarship for insight. This work challenges the assumption that a capitalist economy and liberal political system

---

[98]   For the combination of comparative law with law and society, see, e.g., Ulrich Drobnig and Manfred Rehbinder (eds), *Rechtssoziologie und Rechtsvergleichung* (Berlin: Duncker und Humblot 1977); Thomas Raiser, *Rechtssoziologie: Ein Lehrbuch* 11, 327–9 (Frankfurt am Main: Alfred Metzner Verlag 1987). The development of comparative law in Europe is comprehensively treated by several authors in Reimann and Zimmerman (note 17) 35–174, 215–36.

[99]   Anne Boigeol and Alain Bancaud, 'France', in Clark (ed.) (note 9) 2, 598–601; Anthony Bradney, 'United Kingdom', in Clark (ed.) (note 9) 3, 1529–33; Vincenzo Ferrari, 'Italy', in Clark (ed.) (note 9) 2, 830–32; John Griffiths, 'Netherlands and Flanders', in Clark (ed.) (note 9) 2, 1060–62; Ole Hammerslev, 'Scandanavia', in Clark (ed.) (note 9) 3, 1343–5; Doris Lucke, 'Germany', in Clark (ed.) (note 9) 2, 643–7.

[100]   Johann J. Hagen, 'Austria', in Clark (ed.) (note 9) 1, 109–10; D.H. Kaye, 'Zeisel, Hans', in Clark (ed.) (note 9) 3, 1599–600; see Ferrari (note 99) 831.

[101]   María Isabel Garrido Gómez, 'Spain', 3 ibid. 1424–5; Christine Rothmayr, 'Switzerland', 3 ibid. 1447–8; Veerle van Gijsegem, 'Belgium', 1 ibid. 120–21. Embryonic socio-legal research exists in Greece. Aspasia Tsaoussis, 'Greece', 2 ibid. 676–7. Suppressed or state-sponsored scholarship was characteristic of Hungary, Poland and Russia until 1989, when research possibilities increased. Adam Czarnota, 'Poland', 3 ibid. 1119–20; András Sajó, 'Hungary', 2 ibid. 722–3; Anita Soboleva, 'Russia', 3 ibid. 1333–5.

require the development of an autonomous legal system with an independent judiciary and vigorous private attorneys.[102] The Japanese experience is an obvious model for East Asian countries.

Korea and Taiwan are examples of Japanese influence, often unacknowledged, since they were an unwilling part of the Japanese Empire until 1945. In particular, democratization movements in the 1980s stimulated socio-legal scholarship.[103] In Southeast Asia, Indonesia and Thailand have rudimentary law and society developments, often supported by non-governmental organizations that have more visibility with increasing liberalization of the media. Human rights, judicial reform and land reform are topics of concern.[104] In South Asia, India received attention in the 1960s and 1970s from US law and development researchers, who worked together with Indian law professors to try to reform legal education. US public interest lawyers worked with the Indian government after the Bhopal disaster in 1984 and restructuring efforts continued in legal education to make it more relevant to Indian reality through clinical training.[105] In China, after some early experience with sociological jurisprudence during the republican period, the People's Republic only permitted Marxist critical theory until the mid-1980s when it allowed law and development conferences and research. Today, there are a few research institutes and some law schools with a law and society focus. Studies cover peasant legal consciousness, administrative litigation and the cultural attitudes necessary for legal transplantation, among other issues.[106]

In Israel, the 1990s saw many graduates from US universities, who became professors or activist lawyers, bring legal realist and socio-legal ideas into their research on Israeli society and particularly its relationship with Palestine. In addition, critical studies are influential, including those dealing with the British post-colonial legacy, as well as cultural, identity and legal consciousness research.[107] There is also an emerging socio-legal research agenda in Turkey.[108]

In Latin America, the fourth region, there has been a small group of socio-legal scholars, whom the law and development efforts of the 1970s initially supported. This number increased during the decades of transition from military regimes to political democracy and market capitalism. Argentina, Brazil, Chile, Colombia and Mexico have the most participants. Investigation often takes on issues with important political interest, such as access to justice, criminal justice, human rights and the legal profession. In countries with a large indigenous population, legal pluralism, customary law and legal culture are also significant.[109] The Chicago School of law and economics has had a significant impact on

---

[102]   Masaji Chiba, 'Kawashima, Takeyoshi', 2 ibid. 878–9; Setsuo Miyazawa, 'Japan', 2 ibid. 835–7.

[103]   Jou-juo Chu, 'Taiwan', 3 ibid. 1451–2; Dae-Kyu Yoon, 'Korea', 2 ibid. 891.

[104]   Kobkun Rayanakorn, 'Thailand', 3 ibid. 1477–8; Emmy Yuhassarie, 'Indonesia', 2 ibid. 735.

[105]   Jayanth K. Krishman, 'India', 2 ibid. 732–3.

[106]   Ji Weidong, 'China', 1 ibid. 178–9.

[107]   Ronen Shamir, 'Israel', 2 ibid. 830; see Nadera Shalhoub-Kevorkain, 'Palestine', 3 ibid. 1091–2.

[108]   Dicle Kogacioglu and Ziya Umut Turem, 'Turkey', 3 ibid. 1528.

[109]   María Inés Bergoglio, 'Argentina', 1 ibid. 92; Maria da Gloria Bonelli, 'Brazil', 1 ibid. 131–3; Héctor Fix-Fierro, 'Mexico', 2 ibid. 1020–21; Césa A. Rodríguez-Garavito, 'Cololmbia', 1 ibid. 207–08.

legislation and government policy in Chile, and some law schools there now have a course on that subject.[110]

In 2006, researchers created the Law and Society Association of Australia and New Zealand to foster socio-legal investigation, in part by holding annual meetings. This entity joined existing bi-national organizations for criminology and for psychology and law.[111]

South Africa is the only country in Africa with a significant law and society presence. Most of the investigation prior to 1990 dealt with apartheid, but since democratization, it typically concerns human rights, courts, criminology and constitutionalism.[112]

6.3   National Organizations

Almost all of the countries mentioned in section 6.2 with significant socio-legal activity have one or more national organizations for law and society and for comparative law. Many of these support a journal, primarily with a national subscription. The pre-eminent peer-reviewed journals with a worldwide circulation are the *American Journal of Comparative Law* and the *Law & Society Review*.[113] There are also specialist law journals in the United States for criminology, anthropology of law, law and economics, law and politics, and legal psychology.[114] In addition, many countries host research institutes that support comparative law and society scholars and their investigation. Nevertheless, as one would suspect, the majority of researchers work as professors at universities in a social science or law department.[115]

The Law and Society Association, although founded in the United States, serves today as a quasi-international organization for socio-legal studies. As the first editor of its *Review* noted, the Association's intent was to be open to all social sciences interested in law.[116] Nevertheless, the practice developed of generally ignoring criminology and law

---

[110]   Iñigo de la Maza, 'Chile', 1 ibid. 178. Political circumstances in Peru have impeded most law and society investigation, although there is a clearinghouse for information on law and society in Latin America. Raquel Z. Yrigoyen-Fajardo, 'Peru', 3 ibid. 1106–07; AlertaNet, Home Page, http://www.alertanet.org.

[111]   Ellen Berah and Ian Freckelton, 'Australian and New Zealand Association of Psychiatry, Psychology and Law', in Clark (ed.) (note 9) 1, 107–08; Peter Grabosky, Australian and New Zealand Society of Criminology, in Clark (ed.) (note 9) 1, 108–09; Law and Society Association of Australian and New Zealand, Home Page, http://www.lsaanz.org.

[112]   Catherine Albertyn, 'South Africa', in Clark (ed.) (note 9) 3, 1421–2. NGO cause lawyers in Egypt have attempted to reform the legal system. Baudouin Dupret, 'Egypt', in Clark (ed.) (note 9) 1, 470–71.

[113]   See notes 92–5 and accompanying text. Several of the national law and society associations are described in Clark (ed.) (note 9) 1–3.

[114]   A partial list would include (ordered by subject and initial year): *Criminology* (1963); *Criminology & Public Policy* (2001); *Crime and Justice: A Review of Research* (1979); *PoLAR: Political and Legal Anthropology Review* (1973); *Journal of Law & Economics* (1958); *Antitrust Law & Economics Review* (1967); *Journal of Legal Economics* (1991); *American Law and Economics Review* (1999); *Journal of Law & Politics* (1983); *Law & Psychology Review* (1975); *Psychiatry, Psychology and Law* (1994). See note 95 for additional law and society journals and note 62 and accompanying text for more law and economics journals.

[115]   The number of national scholarly organizations and research institutes is too large to detail here. Many are described in Clark (ed.) (note 9) 1–3; Reimann and Zimmerman (note 17) 35–236.

[116]   See note 13 and accompanying text.

Table 1.1   Distribution of Law and Society Association scholars, by country (2011)

Country	Number of members
Canada	71
Europe	
United Kingdom	49 (5 from Scotland)
Netherlands	22
Germany	18
Switzerland	11
Ireland	7
Portugal	5
Poland, Slovenia	3 each
Denmark, France, Spain, Sweden	4 each
Italy, Norway	2 each
Austria, Czech Republic, Russia	1 each
Asia	
Japan	47
Israel	17
Korea, Taiwan	8 each
China	4
Iran	3
Singapore, Turkey	2 each
Bangladesh, India, Indonesia, Malaysia, Saudi Arabia	1 each
Latin America	
Mexico	6
Argentina, Chile	5 each
Brazil, Colombia	4 each
Venezuela	2
Australasia	
Australia	27
New Zealand	1
Africa	
South Africa	6
Nigeria	1

and economics, which in any case grew within their own organizations.[117] Table 1.1 illustrates the international character of the Association and provides a rough surrogate for the national distribution of law and society scholars. In 2011, the Association had about 1,600 members, 20 percent of whom live outside the US. Ninety members specifically listed comparative law as an interest.[118]

The American Society of Criminology is another quasi-international organization.

---

[117]   Abel (note 15) 6–7, 11, 14, 17.
[118]   Law and Society Association, *Membership Directory* (2011). The proxy is rough due to the nature of the Association. As noted, it does not have many members specializing in criminology or law and economics. In addition, it is monolingual, inflating the relative attractiveness of the forum for scholars from English-speaking countries.

Among its almost 4,000 members, 50 countries are represented and the United Nations has granted it special consultative status.[119] The Society's international division has published the *International Journal of Comparative and Applied Criminal Justice* since 1977.[120] While criminology is the oldest of the social sciences interested in law, law and economics as an institutional force is the newest. The American Law and Economics Association, founded in 1991, also has a broad geographical representation in its membership and attendance at its conferences.[121] Intermediate in age is the American Psychology-Law Society, founded in 1968, with currently about 3,000 members. It supplies an international dimension by cooperating with the European Association of Psychology and Law and the Australian and New Zealand Association of Psychiatry, Psychology and Law to hold international congresses. The Fourth International Congress on Psychology and Law in Miami (2011), for instance, had 1,000 registrants, 22 percent of whom came from 19 countries other than the United States.[122]

7   THE ROLE OF INTERNATIONAL ORGANIZATIONS

7.1   Comparative Law

The successful international institutionalization of comparative law preceded that of law and society, broadly defined to include all the disciplines discussed in this chapter. Thus, the constitutive meeting for the Académie international de droit comparé occurred in Geneva in 1924. Its first international congress of comparative law took place at the Peace Palace (The Hague) in 1932. National committees (usually comparative law entities) from 31 countries sent 305 delegates. The Académie has continued to hold international congresses every four years (except during World War II) and has membership for individuals and national committees.[123]

From 1949 to 1951, American and European comparatists made concerted efforts to place comparative law studies on a firmer institutional basis. In 1949, UNESCO sponsored a conference of experts in Paris, which recommended the creation of the International Committee for Comparative Law. This was part of an UNESCO-funded program to develop international institutes of social science. The Committee admitted a

---

[119]   Chris Eskridge, 'American Society of Criminology', in Clark (ed.) (note 9) 1, 63–4; see American Society of Criminology, History, http://www.asc41.com/History.html (founded in 1941).

[120]   IJCACJ, Home Page, http://www.ijcacj.com; see note 61 and accompanying text.

[121]   Daniel L. Rubinfeld, 'American Law and Economics Association', in Clark (ed.) (note 9) 1, 59–60.

[122]   Ellen Berah and Ian Freckelton, 'Australian and New Zealand Association of Psychiatry', in Clark (ed.) (note 9) 1, 107–08; Graham Michael Davies, 'European Association of Psychology and Law', in Clark (ed.) (note 9) 1, 510; Gary L. Wells and Lisa Hasel, 'American Psychology-Law Society', in Clark (ed.) (note 9) 1, 60–61; American Psychology-Law Society, Home Page, http://www.ap-ls.org (select Conferences). The first international congress (1999) was a similar cooperative endeavor held in Dublin with 600 registrants from 27 countries. Kapardis (note 69) 1228–9.

[123]   David S. Clark, 'American Participation in the Development of the International Academy of Comparative Law and its First Two Hague Congresses', 54 *American Journal of Comparative Law* 1–21 (Supp. 2006).

national committee if it was satisfied that it was representative of those entities or persons engaged in comparative law in that country.

By 1952, the Committee had accepted 20 members, including the United States. A Council and Bureau conducted the Committee's business. Each national committee had one delegate to the Council, which elected the rotating members of the seven-member Bureau. The Bureau took on an organizational element from the United Nation's Security Council: it had three permanent members—France, the United States and the United Kingdom. The American Foreign Law Association (AFLA) undertook the task in 1950 to become the United States 'national' committee to the International Committee, whose agenda was primarily scholarly and involved sponsoring conferences and book publication. Since the AFLA was largely a body of practicing lawyers from the northeast, it needed to broaden its membership (about 170 in 1950) to include both more law professors and more residents from beyond the eastern seaboard. In 1951, it organized chapters in Chicago and Miami, and by 1952, it listed 38 law professors out of a total membership of 253. Both Germany and the United Kingdom in 1950 also created national committees for comparative law.

Many of the law school affiliated members of the AFLA believed that comparative law needed an organization, principally of law school sponsors, that could support a quality journal dedicated to the subject, similar to those existing in France, Germany, the UK and Italy. Since the US did not have a funded institute or center of comparative law like that in Berlin or Paris, Americans would need to invent the functional equivalent. That entity would be the American Association for the Comparative Study of Law, which held its first meeting in 1951 and changed its name in 1992 to the American Society of Comparative Law (ASCL). Today the ASCL publishes the *American Journal of Comparative Law* and holds annual and other meetings, often with sessions that take a social science perspective.[124]

7.2 Law and Society

Law and society has internationalized along a similar pattern, sometimes affiliating with UNESCO. First, the Société internationale de criminologie, established in 1950, has consultative status at UNESCO as well as the Council of Europe. Like the Académie international de droit comparé, it uses French at its meetings and publications in addition to English, and Spanish as well. While the Académie sponsors world conferences every four years, the Société has its conferences every three years, with the 16th world congress in Japan in 2011.[125]

Second, the International Sociological Association (ISA), founded in 1949 under UNESCO auspices, established the Research Committee on Sociology of Law in 1962. The Research Committee has its own members and holds annual international meetings, sometimes in conjunction with the ISA or the Law and Society Association. Since 1989,

---

[124]   Clark (note 91) 205–09; David S. Clark, 'American Society of Comparative Law', in Clark (ed.) (note 9) 1, 61–3.
[125]   Tony Peters, 'International Society for Criminology', in Clark (ed.) (note 9) 2, 807–08; ISC-SIC, Home Page, http://www.isc-sic.org; see note 123 and accompanying text.

the Research Committee has been responsible for the research and teaching activities at the International Institute for the Sociology of Law in Oñati, Spain.[126]

Third, the International Political Science Association, on the initiative of several American political scientists in 1964, set up the Research Committee for Comparative Judicial Studies. Today it holds annual meetings in different countries and has 200 members from 30 countries.[127]

Fourth, in 1978 the International Union of Anthropological and Ethnological Sciences established the Commission on Folk Law and Legal Pluralism. The Commission has 350 members, holds conferences around the world and promotes teaching and research on its subject matter.[128]

Beyond these international organizations, several regional entities in Europe hold regular meetings and publish journals or coordinate law and society investigation.[129] On a smaller scale, similar entities exist in Latin America.[130] We have also seen examples of cooperation between scholars in Australia and New Zealand.[131] Finally, since the 1990s, some international governmental organizations have taken an interest in research and policy implementation related to drugs and crime, civil society or law and development. Both the United Nations and the World Bank provide examples.[132]

8   ASSESSMENT OF THE ENTERPRISE

Since law and society first developed its institutional apparatus in the United States in the 1960s, it might be enlightening to examine how some of the early members have reflected on the field's original promise and achievement since then. Their views vary widely. Richard Abel, for instance, having served as both president of the Law and Society Association and editor of its *Review*, wrote about his impressions in 2010. At the beginning, he explains, the consensus of the Association's leaders was that social science should

---

[126]   Johannes Feest, 'ISA Research Committee on Sociology of Law', in Clark (ed.) (note 9) 2, 825–6; Johannes Feest, 'International Institute for the Sociology of Law (Oñati)', in Clark (ed.) (note 9) 2, 806–07.

[127]   Michael C. Tolley, 'IPSA Research Committee for Comparative Judicial Studies', in Clark (ed.) (note 9) 2, 824–5.

[128]   Keebet von Benda-Beckmann, 'IUAES Commission on Folk Law and Legal Pluralism', in Clark (ed.) (note 9) 2, 832–3.

[129]   See André-Jean Arnaud, 'European Network on Law and Society', in Clark (ed.) (note 9) 1, 515–16; Gerrit De Geest, 'European Association of Law and Economics', in Clark (ed.) (note 9) 1, 509–10; Davies (note 122). The ministries of justice of the five Scandinavian countries established an entity with a similar mission. Kauko Aromaa, 'Scandinavian Research Council for Criminology', in Clark (ed.) (note 9) 3, 1345–6.

[130]   Raquel Z. Yrigoyen-Fajardo, 'Latin American Network on Law and Society', in Clark (ed.) (note 9) 2, 921–2; Raquel Z. Yrigoyen-Fajardo, 'Red Latinoamericana de Antropología Jurídica', in Clark (ed.) (note 9) 3, 1277.

[131]   See notes 111, 122 and accompanying text.

[132]   See, e.g., Frank Höpfel, 'United Nations Office on Drugs and Crime', in Clark (ed.) (note 9) 3, 1533–4; Richard Messick, 'World Bank Thematic Group on Law and Justice Institutions', in Clark (ed.) (note 9) 3, 1594–5.

help law promote a liberal political agenda and make law more effective.[133] By the 1980s, this agenda was supplemented if not replaced by law and economics and critical legal studies. Most economists interested in law had not found the Association sympathetic to their work, so they developed their ideas within their own organizations and journals. Abel attributes the success of economic analysis of law in influencing judges and policy makers to the shift in national American politics toward conservative positions and support.[134] Critical legal studies, some based on race, gender or sexual orientation, was the other development that confronted the perceived failure of legal liberalism. The 'cultural turn' in research followed with an emphasis on cultural identities, language and signs, and the plurality of meaning.[135] While the critical approaches could tend toward nihilism, cultural approaches typically were committed to a moral evaluation of modern legal systems. However, both argued in general for a radical response (often deconstruction) to the status quo.[136]

Abel is not optimistic about law and society's future.

> In this reactionary political environment, [law and society] was rapidly overshadowed by [law and economics], which had many advantages . . .. Armed with neoclassical theory and a scientific-sounding vocabulary, law professors confidently engaged in economic analysis . . .. By necessity, [law and society] was a big tent, methodologically and theoretically: quantitative and qualitative, positivist and hermeneutic. Some of its choices contributed to [law and society's] marginality: avoiding the often esoteric behavior of economic institutions; studying down (the objects of legal domination) rather than up (those wielding law's power). And the jurisdictional contest was unequal: [law and economics] was lavishly funded, often by conservative foundations . . .. The transformed political environment also may help explain the 'cultural turn' taken by [law and society] (following several of its parent social sciences).[137]

Abel seems to put the declining relevance of law and society research on American political and social culture rather than on the researchers themselves. He explains the rise of law and economics on financial and political support and the false consciousness of the American public.[138]

> Americans who once defined themselves by political ideologies now do so by consumer preferences: how they look, what they wear, the foods they eat, the music they listen to, the soaps they watch, the sports they play, the teams they cheer. (Slackers are just the mirror image, limiting their resistance to not doing or buying. Sartre's committed intellectual has been displaced by the resolutely apolitical hipster.) Americans are fascinated by the peccadilloes of the moment's

---

133   Abel (note 15) 2–3, 4, 11. Law and society 'sought to guide liberal reforms: ending race and sex discrimination, rehabilitating criminals, alleviating poverty, understanding Supreme Court decision making, rendering laws more effective'. Ibid. 16.

134   Ibid. 11, 16–17; see Faust (note 64) and accompanying text.

135   Abel (note 15) 8–9, 11, 13, 15, 17–19; see Gad Barzilai, 'Cultural Identities', in Clark (ed.) (note 9) 1, 360–63; Andrew Valls, 'Critical Race Theory', in Clark (ed.) (note 9) 1, 353–5; Stephanie M. Wildman, 'Critical Feminist Theory', in Clark (ed.) (note 9) 1, 348–50. For their relation to comparative law, see Ugo Mattei, 'Comparative Law and Critical Legal Studies', in Reimann and Zimmerman (note 17) 815–36.

136   Abel (note 15) 15–16; see Stephen C. Hicks, 'Deconstruction', in Clark (ed.) (note 9) 1, 391–3.

137   Abel (note 15) 17.

138   Ibid. 8, 11, 17–19.

celebrities, the fodder of the tabloids and late-night talk shows . . ., today's bread and circuses. Voters are influenced more by politicians' images and lifestyles than their policies (for good or bad, *vide* Obama and Palin). Facebook and Twitter have encouraged entire generations to regress to adolescence, obsessing about the quotidian trivialities of their circle of friends. The cyber-savvy play in the ether. Popular literature has deteriorated into a narcissistic baring of secrets. Whereas feminists taught us to expand the political to include the personal, contemporary politics has collapsed into the black hole of solipsism. Instead of remaking the world—a collective project directed outward—we are obsessed with individual self-improvement.[139]

Is this critique relevant for other parts of the world? Austin Sarat believes it is generally applicable to the West and perhaps worldwide in those places that are industrializing. There is a decline in the 'social as central to the logic of governance', by which he means that the 1960s and 1970s were the high point of a belief in effective government intervention to correct social problems. Social liberalism saw a fusion of law, social science and government. By the 1980s, there began a decline in confidence in legal institutions and reform programs and, as a result, growing support for reconfiguring government. Empirical research on law, and sociology in particular, suffered a loss of prestige.

Sarat argues, however, that law and society research has 'vitality amidst fragmentation'. For the latter—particularity, multiplicity and ambiguity are central virtues of post-realist research that can, nevertheless, lead to a crisis of self-understanding. At the same time, the field has institutionalized itself, as evidenced by the increasing number of relevant professional organizations, journals, book series, research institutes and interdisciplinary programs at universities.[140]

Other researchers have a sanguine view of the future. Such would seem to be the case for law and economics scholars who, as Abel comments, have had notable success.[141] Lawrence Friedman, past president of both the Law and Society Association and the ISA Research Committee on Sociology of Law, believes that the other socio-legal fields have also contributed a body of worthwhile research, much of which is rooted in social theory that in principle can test hypotheses.[142]

Although early law and society researchers were interested in affecting public policy, while a few had overt ideological (including neo-Marxist) programs, many social scientists today reject efforts to promote specific policies, whether they describe them as social justice or economic equality. They believe that research should be conducted in an objective and disinterested manner, reporting findings without recommending policies to legal officials. The comparative dimension here often is associated with globalization issues.[143] In response, others contend that ideological agnosticism, whether in comparative law or

---

[139]   Ibid. 17–18.

[140]   Austin Sarat, 'Vitality amidst Fragmentation: On the Emergence of Postrealist Law and Society Scholarship', in Austin Sarat (ed.), *The Blackwell Companion to Law and Society* 1, 4–8 (Malden, MA: Blackwell Publishing 2004); see Bryant Garth and Joyce Sterling, 'From Legal Realism to Law and Society: Reshaping Law for the Last Stages of the Social Activist State', 32 *Law & Society Review* 409–71 (1998).

[141]   See, e.g., Robert Ashford, 'Socioeconomics', in Clark (ed.) (note 9) 3, 1405–08.

[142]   Lawrence M. Friedman, 'Preface', in Clark (ed.) (note 9) 1, lxv–lxvi; Friedman (note 12) 923–4; see notes 78–9 and accompanying text.

[143]   Friedrichs (note 95) 1536–8; see Dragan Milovanovic, 'Critical Criminology', in Clark (ed.) (note 9) 1, 345–8; Parisi (note 62) 451; Sarat (note 140) 7–8.

law and society studies, is impossible.[144] An admirable attempt to achieve balance in this debate is the recent comparative law and society reader by Friedman and colleagues.[145]

9   CONCLUSION

Comparative law and society is a challenge to the dominant legal theory prevailing today in most countries among politicians and legal professionals. The clearest challenge comes from comparatists who emphasize legal pluralism as a fundamental reality of social life.[146] Legal pluralism contests the established theory, which postulates four premises that seem self-evident and necessary. The dominant legal theory is most firmly entrenched in Europe and Westernized nations, but is also strong in East Asia including China. Those four premises, taught to legal professionals and repeated for the benefit of the public, are nationalism, statism, monism and positivism.

Nationalism as it relates to law took hold in its modern form in two major waves. The first occurred after the American and French revolutions and dramatically reshaped the legal landscape of Europe and the Americas in the nineteenth century. The second wave happened after World War II in conjunction with the United Nations' mandate for decolonization. Since 1945, under the principle of self-determination more than 80 former colonies have gained their independence. Some of these new political units were the result of splitting or reformulating former legal structures and others emerged from consolidation. However, all emphasized what was special about the people within them and different about other people. This singularity, tied to citizenship, could coincide with language, ethnicity, culture (or history), religion, climate, geography or other features. Nationality demanded symbols to further unity: a flag, a song, a seal, the pledge of temporal allegiance, perhaps a bird, tree, flower or motto, possibly a currency or state religion.

Statism suggests that the state should have a monopoly over sovereignty and its implementation through jurisdiction. In traditional Enlightenment terms, this includes jurisdiction to legislate, administer and adjudicate. Statism supports nationalism and is hostile toward legal pluralism.[147] The latter maintains that individuals may have multiple

---

[144]   See, e.g. Horatia Muir Watt, 'Globalization and Comparative Law', in Reimann and Zimmerman (note 17) 579–607.

[145]   Lawrence M. Friedman, Rogelio Pérez-Perdomo and Manuel A. Gómez (eds), *Law in Many Societies: A Reader* (Stanford, CA: Stanford University Press 2011).

[146]   See, e.g., Masaji Chiba, *Legal Pluralism: Toward a General Theory through Japanese Legal Culture* (Tokyo: Tokai University Press 1989); Glenn (note 28); M.B. Hooker, *Legal Pluralism: An Introduction to Colonial and Neo-Colonial Laws* (Oxford: Clarendon Press 1975); Menski (note 21); Brian Z. Tamanaha, *A General Jurisprudence of Law and Society* (Oxford: Oxford University Press 2001); Warwick Tie, *Legal Pluralism: Toward a Multicultural Conception of Law* (Aldershot, UK: Ashgate 1999); Vittorio Olgiati, 'Pluralism, Legal', in Clark (ed.) (note 9) 3, 1116–18.

[147]   Legal pluralism and federalism are not the same. Federalism constitutionally divides sovereignty between a central governing authority and constituent political units. Although a person might live within a state or province and be subject to its law as well as that of the central government, statism is still secure because a subunit's authority and jurisdiction must defer to the superior position of the national government. See G. Alan Tarr, 'Federalism and Subnational Legal Systems: The Canadian Example of Provincial Constitutionalism', in this volume, ch. 9.

obligations or loyalties or in essence live outside official state authority. Legal pluralism characterized all legal systems prior to the rise of nationalism described above. It reflected the more complicated legal universe in which people lived, especially salient during colonialism.

Monism in law is similarly hostile to legal pluralism. Monism holds that there exists the possibility of a single, internally coherent, legal system. Thus, it is supportive of both nationalism and statism so long as the level of concern is the state. However, in the modern nation-state system of independent (and equal) sovereign countries, how can law, binding upon a particular state, exist beyond that state? How can there be international law? The *universal* monist response, as in France, is that the state will incorporate international legal norms and jurisdiction into its national legal system without exception. Consequently, the state is in reality a subunit of the larger international legal system. The more common *national* monist response, as in the United States (with its supreme Constitution) and even more strikingly in the United Kingdom (with its parliamentary supremacy), is essentially dualist. There exist two distinct legal systems, one national and the other international. The former will usually incorporate valid international law into its state system as politically convenient, but in case of a direct conflict between an international norm and the supreme national law, the latter prevails.

Finally, there is positivism. Positivism in law is the philosophical (or jurisprudential) view that purported norms or institutions that the state does not create or recognize as law (or 'legal') are not law. This is the only or dominant theory taught to those who become legal professionals in most of the world. It excludes a meaningful role for natural law,[148] historical jurisprudence or sociological jurisprudence, even in the face of strong religious influence, ethnic and cultural cohesion, or community institutions and processes such as juries.

The strength of this dominant legal theory and its four elements works against the relevance of comparative law in the *Weltanschauung* of most legal professionals. Their legal education is oriented toward national law, perhaps a bit of international law, and likely no foreign or comparative law. This generalization has less validity today in European countries that are members of the European Union, but even among those nations, some governments make little effort to implement proper education about foreign legal systems. In the rest of the world, nationalism in law is a strong force.[149]

Nevertheless, there have been developments since the 1990s that are encouraging for the understanding of foreign legal systems and the study of comparative law. Economic and cultural globalization is one such obvious development. Small segments of legal professionals in most countries occupy themselves with servicing and dealing with the effects

---

[148] I am not arguing that natural law, in its Western forms, is a necessary improvement over positivism. It does avoid the excesses of nationalism and some forms of arbitrariness found in authoritarian statism. It also furthers the comparative law objective of harmonization or legal unification that some comparatists support.

[149] For instance, in the United States during 2010 and 2011, legislators in half of the US states proposed (and in two states adopted) bills or state constitutional amendments designed to restrict the use of international law and foreign laws by state (and sometimes federal) courts. Aaron Fellmeth, 'International Law and Foreign Laws in the U.S. State Legislatures', 15 *ASIL Insights* no. 13 (26 May 2011), http://www.asil.org/insights110526.cfm.

of globalization. A larger group, including judges and government administrators, have occasion to handle foreign and comparative law issues. This involves both transnational transaction work and transnational litigation and arbitration. A few law schools have even promoted themselves as global institutions aware of and supportive of this international legal integration.

Another encouraging trend is the increased interest among legal scholars and researchers in social science disciplines about legal norms, professionals, institutions, processes and culture. Most of this work is 'academic', which in most societies means that it will have little or no impact on the people who do most law jobs. Nonetheless, it offers promise that some small percentage of people will come to appreciate the variety and benefit of legal pluralism. Just as biodiversity is a measure of the health of ecosystems, legal diversity is recognition of the variability and richness of human culture.

Beyond that, there is the eminently practical import of examining differences to learn how better to solve one's own particular legal issues. Most of the other chapters in this volume provide illustration of this point.

FURTHER READING

Clark, David S. (ed.) (2007). 1–3 *Encyclopedia of Law and Society: American and Global Perspectives*. Thousand Oaks, CA: Sage.

Cotterrell, Roger (2008). *Living Law: Studies in Legal and Social Theory*. Aldershot, UK: Dartmouth Publishing Co.

Freeman, Michael (ed.) (2006). *Law and Sociology*. Oxford: Oxford University Press.

Friedman, Lawrence M. and Rogelio Pérez-Perdomo (eds) (2003). *Legal Culture in the Age of Globalization: Latin America and Latin Europe*. Stanford, CA: Stanford University Press.

Friedman, Lawrence, Rogelio Pérez-Perdomo and Manuel Gómez (eds) (2011). *Law in Many Societies: A Reader*. Stanford, CA: Stanford University Press.

Glenn, H. Patrick (2010). *Legal Traditions of the World: Sustainable Diversity in Law*, 4th edn. New York: Oxford University Press.

Likosky, Michael (ed.) (2002). *Transnational Legal Processes: Globalisation and Power Disparities*. London: Butterworths LexisNexis.

Menski, Werner (2006). *Comparative Law in a Global Context: The Legal Systems of Asia and Africa*. Cambridge: Cambridge University Press, 2nd edn.

Merryman, John Henry, David S. Clark and John Owen Haley (2010). *Comparative Law: Historical Development of the Civil Law Tradition in Europe, Latin America, and East Asia*. New Providence, NJ: Matthew Bender & Co.

Mertz, Elizabeth (ed.) (2008). *The Role of Social Science in Law*. Aldershot, UK: Ashgate.

Reimann, Mathias and Reinhard Zimmerman (eds) (2006). *The Oxford Handbook of Comparative Law*. Oxford: Oxford University Press.

Sarat, Austin (ed.) (2004). *The Blackwell Companion to Law and Society*. Malden, MA: Blackwell Publishing.

Sarat, Austin (ed.) (2008). *Law and Society Reconsidered*. Amsterdam: Elsevier.

Zweigert, Konrad and Hein Kötz (1998). *Introduction to Comparative Law*. Oxford: Oxford University Press, Tony Weir trans., 3rd edn.

PART I

METHODS AND DISCIPLINES

2 Comparative sociology of law
*Roger Cotterrell**

1 INTRODUCTION

1.1 The Scope of Comparison

Comparison seems basic to understanding. Deciding what is similar or different as between two or more things makes it possible to give them *identity* within a larger framework; to recognise their particular place in an *environment* of the familiar and the unfamiliar. Comparing happens all the time, but often unsystematically—by observing, recognising and differentiating impressionistically.

Sometimes comparison is a way of *seeking similarity*. To find that something newly discovered is, in important respects, the same as what one already knows can be very reassuring. It affirms knowledge already possessed, suggesting that that knowledge has a wider application than had previously been realised. Comparison undertaken for this purpose tends to validate existing understandings. There might even be an incentive to work towards removing remaining perceived differences and emphasising commonalities. The tendency may be to see apparent differences as superficial, temporary or based on misunderstandings that can be removed.[1]

However, sometimes the aim of comparison is to *appreciate difference*, to value it specially, because it can be salutary to realise that things—for example, legal and social ideas and arrangements—do not have to take the forms that are already familiar to the observer. In appreciating difference, it becomes possible to see that the world and its experiences can be ordered and understood in many different ways. Familiar ways are not necessarily confirmed as the best. One can learn from others, or just see that 'the best' may be relative to time and place; an aggregate of components subject to different cultural interpretations. However, being forced to recognise difference can be disturbing for those who do not wish to have their familiar conceptions challenged.

Open-minded comparison will privilege neither similarity nor difference. Nevertheless, comparison that goes beyond merely gathering impressions, and is intended to be self-conscious, rigorous and systematic in its methods, is 'demanding and difficult'.[2] The aim, at least, is to avoid comparison becoming, as the anthropologist Edmund Leach

---

* Anniversary Professor of Legal Theory, Queen Mary University of London.

[1] The comparatist Édouard Lambert (1866–1947) saw comparative law as a 'unifying force' to efface progressively 'the accidental diversity that prevails among legal systems located in countries of similar development and economic condition'. Quoted in Andrew Huxley, 'Introduction', in Huxley (ed.), *Religion, Law and Tradition: Comparative Studies in Religious Law* 1, 7 (London: Routledge Cavendish 2002).

[2] David Nelken, 'Comparative Sociology of Law', in Reza Banakar and Max Travers (eds), *An Introduction to Law and Social Theory* 329, 331 (Oxford: Hart 2002).

(1910–89) thought it could be, 'a matter of butterfly collecting, . . . arranging butterflies according to their types and sub-types' which 'merely asserts what you already know in a slightly different form'.[3]

The objective, on this view, should not be merely to juxtapose and classify cases or to highlight the exotic. It should be to allow generalisation to be made about relationships between items compared, so that the knowledge obtained can be applied to further comparisons, or turned into statements of general import. Comparison in this sense aims at broadening perspectives on experience—going beyond studies confined to 'the local', whether the local means a single society or part of a society, or a single legal system. One might say that the objective is to be able to *theorise* in some way about the objects compared, taken together.

Comparative lawyers have tended to avoid sustained discussion of theory,[4] but they have often justified comparative legal research on the basis that it aspires to develop a scientific view that can free legal knowledge from its confinement to particular legal jurisdictions.[5] The aim is to build from local legal knowledge gradually towards a more universal knowledge of law; one whose validity transcends national jurisdictional limits. However, as the ambition of legal comparison has been extended, the idea of the local covers an ever-larger range and the effort to transcend it becomes more expansive. Eventually, the entirety of European law and European legal perspectives—the original focus of comparatists' attention[6]—itself begins to appear as a local legal environment whose limited perspectives are to be broadened by comparison further afield. The result should be 'a self-critical questioning of dominant Western assumptions about the nature of law itself'.[7] Thus, on this view, through an ever-widening legal outlook, comparative law might begin to shape a science of law appropriate for an interdependent world.[8]

---

[3]   Quoted in Geoff Payne, 'Comparative Sociology: Some Problems of Theory and Method', 24 *British Journal of Sociology* 13, 15–16 (1973).

[4]   See Geoffrey Samuel, 'Comparative Law and Jurisprudence', 47 *International and Comparative Law Quarterly* 817 (1998); Samuel, 'Epistemology and Comparative Law: Contributions from the Sciences and Social Sciences', in Mark Van Hoecke (ed.), *Epistemology and Method in Comparative Law* 35 (Oxford: Hart 2004). For a survey of theoretical issues, see Van Hoecke, 'Deep Level Comparative Law', ibid. 165.

[5]   Cf. Lawrence Friedman, 'The Law and Society Movement', 38 *Stanford Law Review* 763, 767 (1986) ('Law is the only social process studied in universities that completely lacks any reasonable claim to universality').

[6]   See e.g. Christophe Jamin, 'Saleilles' and Lambert's Old Dream Revisited', 50 *American Journal of Comparative Law* 701, 716 (2002), noting Édouard Lambert's early claim that only continental Europe is the appropriate arena of comparison. The specifically European focus (now reaching out to UK law) is still clearly present today in projects to develop a common European private law.

[7]   Werner Menski, *Comparative Law in a Global Context: The Legal Systems of Asia and Africa* xii (Cambridge: Cambridge University Press, 2nd edn, 2006).

[8]   See Horatia Muir Watt, 'Globalization and Comparative Law', in Mathias Reimann and Reinhard Zimmermann (eds), *Oxford Handbook of Comparative Law* 579 (Oxford: Oxford University Press 2006).

1.2   Comparatists and Sociology

The widening of comparative law's ambition has been paralleled by a growing sense that it must find means of comparing not only legal rules, technical reforms, legal institutions and professional legal practices but also the variety of socio-legal contexts that shape law's meaning and practical significance. Comparatists have long recognised potential links between their subject and sociology of law[9] and some have argued for its development as part of an integrated social science.[10] An eminent early scholar of comparative law, Max Rheinstein (1899–1977), went so far as to declare that 'comparative law is synonymous with sociology of law' insofar as comparative legal scholarship focuses on the functional comparison of legal rules and on the 'social function of law in general'.[11] In fact, sociology of law hardly existed in 1938 when Rheinstein wrote those words so it was understandable that ambitious and imaginative comparatists might seek then to harness the possibilities of this new social scientific enterprise as part of comparative law's established field.

However, sociology of law developed very rapidly as a field of empirical research from the middle of the twentieth century and, in the decades after Rheinstein argued for a unity of comparative law and sociology of law, these research enterprises drifted apart. They generally continued to affirm mutual respect and (with some caveats) the considerable value of each other's projects, but each set its own distinct agendas and rarely engaged seriously with the other's literature.[12] In recent years, however, the position has changed again and there has been much interaction between comparative lawyers and legal sociologists, with leading figures in both fields encouraging this co-operation.[13]

Unsurprisingly, on the sociological side, the field of *comparative* sociology of law—which aims to compare socio-legal experience between different national legal systems or legal cultures—presents the strongest prospects for direct engagement with comparatists' juristic concerns. This chapter seeks to explain the character and purposes of comparative sociology of law, some important problems of method which it faces (and which often mirror those of comparative law), and various forms that research in it can take.

---

[9]   Jean Carbonnier, 'L'apport du droit comparé a la sociologie juridique', in Société de Législation Comparé, *Livre du Centenaire de la Société de Législation Comparé: Un Siècle de Droit Comparé en France (1869–1969)* 75 (Paris: Librairie Générale de Droit et de Jurisprudence 1969); Konrad Zweigert, 'Quelques reflexions sur les relations entre la sociologie juridique et le droit comparé', in 1 *Aspects nouveaux de la pensée juridique: Recueil d'études en hommage à Marc Ancel* 81 (Paris: Pedone 1975) (preface by René Cassin).

[10]   Jerome Hall, *Comparative Law and Social Theory* (Baton Rouge: Louisiana State University Press 1963); see Roger Cotterrell, *Law, Culture and Society: Legal Ideas in the Mirror of Social Theory* 132–4 (Aldershot: Ashgate 2006) (for commentary).

[11]   Max Rheinstein, 1 *Collected Works: Jurisprudence and Sociology, Comparative Law and Common Law (USA)* 296, 298, 301 (Tübingen: J. C. B. Mohr 1979).

[12]   See Cotterrell (note 10) ch. 8.

[13]   See e.g. Esin Örücü and David Nelken (eds), *Comparative Law: A Handbook* (Oxford: Hart 2007); Pierre Legrand and Roderick Munday (eds), *Comparative Legal Studies: Traditions and Transitions* (Cambridge: Cambridge University Press 2003); Andrew Harding and Esin Örücü (eds), *Comparative Law in the 21st Century* (London: Kluwer 2002); David Nelken (ed.), *Comparing Legal Cultures* (Aldershot: Dartmouth 1997); David Nelken and Johannes Feest (eds), *Adapting Legal Cultures* (Oxford: Hart 2001).

1.3   Subjecting Sociology of Law to Cross-national Comparison

Because sociological perspectives, like all social scientific views, are coloured by the time and place in which they arise it may also be rewarding to consider, on a comparative basis, the different orientations and paths of development of sociology of law in different countries.[14] Choices of research questions and of methods; emphases adopted in interpreting results; the uses made of research—all of these can be influenced significantly by different national contexts in which research enterprises spring up. Should this affect the way one makes transnational or cross-cultural comparisons of research findings? Comparisons can be made of findings obtained in different countries, relating to different legal systems, or reporting different practices or experiences of law. Nevertheless, one can argue that other comparisons (perhaps less obvious) should also be made: comparisons of the *different environments in which research findings have been obtained*. Scholars can and should study the specific conditions that shape the character of socio-legal research in different times and places. They need to understand these conditions if cross-national comparison is to be genuinely enlightening.

A comparative sociology of (different national traditions of) legal sociology may seem an intimidating idea if only because of its reflexivity: how far can social scientists study their own practices? However, it can offer illuminating lines of inquiry. Comparisons of research need to take account of local contexts that shape the *aims* of study, the *concepts* used in research and the *emphases* in interpreting findings. A few pointers for inquiry here will have to suffice and in the final parts of this chapter, I try to illustrate the approach, especially by considering a single case study of comparative socio-legal research. The Greenland 'juridical expedition' of 1948–9, an apparently very successful pioneer empirical socio-legal research project, led to sweeping law reform and influenced the development of an entire country. Its story, little known outside Scandinavia, well illustrates how the purposes, politics, methods and results of comparative sociology of law may interrelate in ways that depend greatly on particular historical conditions.

2   COMPARING SOCIETIES

2.1   Macro-comparison

The term 'comparative sociology' might seem odd. Sociologists have often proclaimed their discipline to be a science. As such, like any science, it seeks abstract knowledge, generalisable beyond specific contexts.[15] At least, science should address phenomena that can be conceptualised in ways that transcend any particular national context. We do not usually speak of French, British or comparative chemistry—just chemistry. Yet scientific method involves comparing cases to produce knowledge. So, must sociology *always* be

---

[14]   For preliminary resources for such a study, see Vincenzo Ferrari (ed.), *Developing Sociology of Law: A World-wide Documentary Survey* (Milano: Giuffrè 1990); Renato Treves and J. F. Glastra Van Loon (eds), *Norms and Actions: National Reports on Sociology of Law* (The Hague: Martinus Nijhoff 1968).
[15]   Irving L. Webber, 'Sociology: Parochial or Universal?' 60 *Social Forces* 416, 418–19 (1981).

comparative because, usually lacking the means to conduct social experiments, it must seek understanding by comparing social phenomena as they appear in different times and places?[16] From such comparisons general concepts are drawn—concepts such as 'society', 'class', 'capitalism', 'social structure', 'social networks', 'social action' or 'social relations'. All of these refer to very general, almost universal ideas applicable in an indefinite range of contexts to organise or interpret empirical research, or to make sense of particular historical conditions.

Sociology typically seeks to generalise about the nature of social life based on specific studies in particular times and places. Though much sociological research is descriptive, aimed at clarifying and presenting observations of a certain social environment—for example, some aspect of American society today—the ultimate objective is usually to generalise about 'the social' in a broader sense. To this extent, sociology is a subject in which *theory* is indispensable. Sociology should theorise about the nature of social phenomena in general, based on empirical studies, and should try to illustrate and apply these theories in further research.

Thus, sociology typically addresses such questions as: (1) how is social order possible and maintained, and under what conditions does it break down; (2) what processes determine (and have, in the past, determined) how societies change or remain unchanged in various respects; or (3) how are societies in general structured in terms of power, authority, kinship systems, or networks of co-operation? Sociology's focus is not necessarily on national political societies treated as unities but inevitably much research is located in such societies and relates to them, frequently confining all its conclusions to a national context and addressing specific social issues or experiences in it. Sociologists (like legal scholars) often find it easiest and most rewarding to concentrate on the 'home' environment—the society (or legal system) that is their own, which may be most familiar and within easiest reach.

For these reasons most sociological research, while using comparisons, is not comparative sociology as such—that is, it does not compare social phenomena from two or more distinct national political societies.[17] Nevertheless, the broadest theoretical ambitions in sociology have almost always pushed it towards cross-national ('macro-comparative') study. The classic sociological theorists of the late nineteenth and twentieth centuries produced work that was usually comparative in this way. Max Weber (1864–1920), studying the nature and development of capitalism and the social forms accompanying it in the West, was led to wide-ranging comparative studies, especially in the sociology of religion but also, for example, in relation to law.[18] Émile Durkheim (1858–1917) and his followers, developing sociology as a new science in France, drew widely on accounts of various ancient and tribal societies as well as studies of social conditions in Europe. One of the best known Durkheimian studies of legal development—one whose influence remains

---

[16] As argued in Malcolm Feeley, 'Comparative Criminal Law for Criminologists: Comparison for What Purpose?' in David Nelken (ed.), *Comparing Legal Cultures* 93, 96–9 (Aldershot: Dartmouth 1997).

[17] Payne (note 3) 13; Kenneth A. Bollen, Barbara Entwisle and Arthur S. Alderson, 'Macrocomparative Research Methods', 19 *Annual Review of Sociology* 321, 323 (1991).

[18] Max Weber, 2 *Economy and Society: An Introduction to Interpretive Sociology* ch. 8 (Ephraim Fischoff et al. trans., Berkeley: University of California Press 1978).

powerful to this day—is Marcel Mauss's essay on the nature of gift relationships as an embryonic form of contractual ties,[19] a study in which Mauss drew his material from many different societies.

2.2   Evolution and Development

While Durkheim usually avoided evolutionary assumptions (the idea that different societies might be located at different 'stages' of development), these assumptions undermined the macro-comparative research of some of his followers and foreshadowed problems that still haunt comparative sociology of law. In such evolutionary approaches, 'data from primitive or ancient societies were fitted to the procrustean bed of a certain "stage" of social evolution . . . .. The methodology was basically argument by illustration: a given bit of ethnographic data was selected . . . to demonstrate some aspect of a "law" of evolution'.[20] The temptation is to try to locate societies on a single developmental map. However, seemingly 'less developed' societies need analysing in their own terms, not in relation to what (according to some developmental model) they may, should, or perhaps cannot become.

Scholars still contribute to evolutionary and developmental theory,[21] sometimes based on careful efforts at cross-national comparison, but sometimes not. This theory generally makes no claim that any one stage of development must lead to another. Yet there is usually a clear indication of the stage that the theorists assume they and their readers are living in—whether marked by modernity, post-modernity, societal complexity, subsystem differentiation, the prevalence of a specific kind of legal system or legal thought, or some other feature.

In general, however, the age of the grand comparative theorists who sought to identify 'modern' society by reference to its antecedents has passed. Systematic comparison of whole societies seems too complex a task now; the materials for national comparisons are too vast, the variables too numerous, and the conceptual frameworks available too contested to make it possible to pursue any longer the great comparative ambitions of the Durkheimians, Weber, Karl Marx (1818–83), or their predecessors such as Montesquieu, Maine, Comte or Spencer. They had compared national societies to try to specify for their own times what seemed truly distinctive about 'society' as they experienced it and as contrasted with the different kinds of social order of the past.

If comparison is a means of broadening perspectives—going beyond experience of the

---

[19]   Marcel Mauss, *The Gift: The Form and Reason for Exchange in Archaic Societies* (W. D. Halls trans., London: Routledge 1990).
[20]   Robert Marsh, *Comparative Sociology: A Codification of Cross-Societal Analysis* 22 (New York: Harcourt, Brace and World 1967), quoted in Payne (note 3) 14–15.
[21]   See e.g. Talcott Parsons, *The Evolution of Societies* (Englewood Cliffs: Prentice-Hall 1977); Niklas Luhmann, *Social Systems* (John Bednarz Jr. trans, Stanford: Stanford University Press 1995); Roberto Mangabeira Unger, *Law in Modern Society: Toward a Criticism of Social Theory* (New York: Free Press 1976), Philippe Nonet and Philip Selznick, *Law and Society in Transition: Toward Responsive Law* (New Brunswick: Transaction 2001). For a notable early study in comparative sociology of law using Human Relations Area files to suggest evolutionary legal development, see Richard D. Schwartz and James C. Miller, 'Legal Evolution and Societal Complexity', 70 *American Journal of Sociology* 159 (1964).

local—there is no reason why that broadening cannot be in terms of historical perspective: comparison might sometimes show parallel historical developments in different societies. Nevertheless, it would be dangerous to imagine that one may glimpse the past or future of a particular society in the present conditions of another.[22]

3   SOCIOLOGY AND COMPARATIVE METHODS

3.1   Sociology as a Methodological Resource

Sociology's aspiration to be a *theoretical* study is still the main basis of its potential to make a distinctive contribution to comparative study of law. If the ambitions of worldwide developmental comparison have been scaled down, other aspects of sociology's concern to build rigorous social theory remain very relevant for comparative legal inquiry. Comparative law needs to address important questions about its methods but, as noted earlier, it has not usually sought to engage in depth with relevant theory. Sociology has the potential to provide useful theoretical input to refine the methods of comparative legal study, especially in taking account of the variety of social or cultural contexts of law.

Positivism, instrumentalism, functionalism and cultural interpretation have all offered 'off the peg' methods or orientations for comparatists, each of these having been explored more fully in theoretical debate in fields beyond comparative law itself.

Positivism, long established in legal scholarship at large, simplifies the task of comparison mainly to a consideration of official rules and processes—law as explicitly posited or recognised by the agencies of the state. Instrumentalism, fuelled by legal realism and perhaps more indirectly by pragmatic philosophy and tendencies in social scientific thought, embodies an assumption that law is a tool to achieve intended governmental aims or serve citizens' interests whatever the cultural context. Comparative legal study guided by an instrumental outlook takes as its test of success the usefulness of law for chosen purposes—often a comparative search for legal 'best practice'.[23] The tendency will be to focus on the skills and techniques appropriate to use legal instruments effectively. However, a more critical approach might ask how and when different sectors of society can use law as a tool to achieve their aims. Questions of power operating in and through law are ones which sociology of law addresses.

Functionalism (the claim that legal ideas and practices should be judged and compared not in terms of their form but by reference to the tasks that they serve in any given context) has achieved widespread acceptance in comparative law even though the nature and problems of this approach are rarely discussed in depth.[24] Beyond comparative law,

---

[22]   See also Bollen et al. (note 17) 337–8.

[23]   Cf. David Nelken, *Comparative Criminal Justice* 22–3 (London: Sage 2010).

[24]   For critical discussion see Ralf Michaels, 'The Functional Method of Comparative Law', in Mathias Reimann and Reinhard Zimmermann (eds), *Oxford Handbook of Comparative Law* 339 (Oxford: Oxford University Press 2006); Michele Graziadei, 'The Functionalist Heritage', in Pierre Legrand and Roderick Munday (eds), *Comparative Legal Studies: Traditions and Transitions* 100 (Cambridge: Cambridge University Press 2003).

however, the sociological literature on functional methods is very extensive.[25] Insofar as issues about functionalism have arisen in comparative law, debate on them has often been sidelined. Some might suggest that because others have rigorously addressed these issues elsewhere, comparatists could avoid theoretical discussions that would go far beyond anything of specifically legal concern. To this extent, the literature of social science may incidentally provide a 'parallel' legitimacy for comparatists' use of functional methods.

Sociology offers other methodological resources that have been refined in its theoretical debates. One of these is the notion of legal culture. 'Culture' is often seen as a central idea of anthropology, rather than sociology, but in recent decades the concept of legal culture has been debated and refined especially by sociologists of law. In the work of Lawrence Friedman[26] and, above all, David Nelken[27] it has been presented as a primary template for comparative sociological study of legal phenomena. At the same time, legal culture has become a major focus for comparatists too.[28] The idea usually refers to a range of distinctive characteristics of law or legal experience observed in a certain time and place. These characteristics (taken as an aggregate or set of cultural patterns) can then be confronted with a different aggregate or patterning observed elsewhere, for example in another national setting or region. At its strongest, the concept offers a provisional framework for presenting striking, often puzzling contrasts between observed phenomena—for example between certain 'clusters' of legal practices or experiences of law in one country, say France, and seemingly parallel clusters in another.

3.2   Studying Socio-legal Experience 'from the Inside'

Probably it is best *not* to view the concept of legal culture as a means of developing causal explanations of similarities and differences in socio-legal conditions.[29] Often there are

---

[25]   The classic defence and refinement of functional methodology in sociology is in Robert K. Merton, *On Social Structure and Science* chs 6–7 (Chicago: University of Chicago Press 1996).

[26]   Lawrence M. Friedman, 'Legal Culture and Social Development', 4 *Law and Society Review* 29 (1969); Friedman, *The Legal System: A Social Science Perspective* (New York: Russell Sage Foundation 1975); Friedman, 'Legal Culture and the Welfare State', in Gunther Teubner (ed.), *Dilemmas of Law in the Welfare State* 13 (Berlin: Walter de Gruyter 1986); Friedman, 'The Place of Legal Culture in the Sociology of Law', in Michael Freeman (ed.), *Law and Sociology: Current Legal Issues 2005* 185 (Oxford: Oxford University Press 2006).

[27]   David Nelken, 'Understanding/Invoking Legal Culture', 4 *Social & Legal Studies* 435 (1995); Nelken, 'Using the Concept of Legal Culture', 29 *Australian Journal of Legal Philosophy* 1 (2004); Nelken, 'Comparing Legal Cultures', in Austin Sarat (ed.), *Blackwell Companion to Law and Society* 113 (Oxford: Blackwell 2004); Nelken, 'Rethinking Legal Culture', in Michael Freeman (ed.), *Law and Sociology: Current Legal Issues 2005*, at 200 (Oxford: Oxford University Press 2006); see Chapter 15 of this volume.

[28]   See e.g. Vivian Grosswald Curran, 'Cultural Immersion, Difference and Categories in US Comparative Law', 46 *American Journal of Comparative Law* 43 (1998); Mark van Hoecke and M. Warrington, 'Legal Cultures, Legal Paradigms and Legal Doctrine: Towards a New Model for Comparative Law', 47 *International and Comparative Law Quarterly* 495 (1998); Pierre Legrand, *Fragments on Law-as-Culture* (Deventer: W. E. J. Tjeenk Willink 1999); Roger Cotterrell, 'Comparative Law and Legal Culture', in Mathias Reimann and Reinhard Zimmermann (eds), *Oxford Handbook of Comparative Law* 709 (Oxford: Oxford University Press 2006).

[29]   Cotterrell (note 10) ch. 5.

far too many variables in play within the aggregates or 'clusters' identified as examples of legal cultures, and the relations between these variables may be very hard to isolate. Instead, one should see legal culture as a multi-faceted view of legal experience presented especially through the perceptions, words and actions of those participating in it.

The best way to explore culture (legal or otherwise) may be by means of techniques that anthropologists have long advocated. Thus, Clifford Geertz's famous term 'thick description' refers to an idea of highly detailed, intricate description of particularities, emphasising personal experience of a culture 'from the inside', or through a kind of empathy allowing sensitive, rich appreciation of the outlook of those living in a particular environment.[30]

Comparatists have suggested similar ideas, founded on the same assumptions about the kinds of understandings of culture that can be most valuable. Thus, Vivian Curran refers to 'cultural immersion' as an appropriate means of gaining knowledge of the cultural contexts (interests, beliefs, values, allegiances, traditions and so on) of lawyers' practice and citizens' legal experience.[31]

Disciplinary lines between anthropology and sociology now seem blurred, especially as regards research on law, but if sociology has a special contribution to make it should come, here as elsewhere, from its effort to refine theoretical perspectives, including perspectives on research methods. The turn to anthropological models properly directs attention to the possibilities and challenges of ethnographic techniques, and the benefits of anthropologists' long experience in using these. Sociology's special resources for studying culture may lie mainly in its longstanding debates as to how to compare data and subjective accounts produced in different cultural environments. What makes such data and accounts 'valid', what makes them comparable, how can one generalise from such particularities?

There are no straightforward solutions to these problems[32] but it is worth mentioning in this context the heritage of sociological thought built on Max Weber's idea of an 'interpretive sociology'.[33] This aims to conceptualise the subjective meaning of social action—that is, the meaning which it has for those participating in it—by studying how social life is built on regularly occurring types of action to which meaning can be provisionally attributed. Weber's specific method of ideal (or pure) types is also helpful. These ideal types are deliberately constructed models of social action and social institutions created purely as analytical tools.

These models can incorporate observable patterns of cause and effect as well as interpretations of the subjective elements of meaning attached to social action by those involved in it. Ideal types—whether of 'capitalism', 'legal rationality', 'bureaucracy' or any other social phenomenon—provide an abstract template against which empirical, historically specific data can be compared and in relation to which such data can be organised. So an ideal typical model of, say, 'litigiousness' could provide a kind of abstract yardstick against which empirical evidence from different contexts (for example, several different

---

[30] Clifford Geertz, *The Interpretation of Cultures: Selected Essays* ch. 1 (New York: Basic Books 1973).

[31] Curran (note 28).

[32] For a full discussion, see Nelken (note 23).

[33] For recent general discussion, see Sven Eliaeson, *Max Weber's Methodologies: Interpretation and Critique* (Cambridge: Polity 2002).

societies) could be judged. The ideal type method is only one effort to solve the problem of comparing patterns of social life that necessarily incorporate subjective experiences, but its existence indicates sociology's commitment to refining theoretically methods of comparing social (including legal) phenomena in all their complexity.

4   SOME PROBLEMS OF COMPARATIVE SOCIOLOGY OF LAW

4.1   Qualitative and Quantitative Studies

Difficulties in comparative sociology of law vary, partly depending on whether research is mainly qualitative in approach (as proposed above, for example, as perhaps the most satisfactory way of studying law in culture) or mainly quantitative (as in much socio-legal research aiming at precise cross-national comparisons). *Qualitative* research may build up, through elaborate description and interpretation, intricate portrayals of legal experience in different environments. However, there may be so many variables to compare—so many components of the rich pictures offered—that comparison remains an unsystematic juxtaposition of these pictures, even if presented with much detail. The method may be better suited to appreciating difference than identifying precise similarities between the legal environments compared.

Where comparative study seeks similarity (or presupposes the value of doing so) or sets out to ask specifically why similarity does not exist, it is often organised *quantitatively*— for example through systematic comparisons of litigation rates, the extent of delay in the administration of justice, crime rates, levels of punitiveness (perhaps measured by rates of imprisonment) or effectiveness (using various measures) in criminal justice systems. Quantitative research often seeks causal explanations[34] (for example, why has a development occurred here, but not there; why have similar developments occurred here *and* there despite other differences between the countries compared?).

Comparative sociological research has sometimes aimed to show 'convergence' (different lines of historical development leading to similar conditions), or 'universals' (features present in all the societies that can be compared), or even to identify 'best practice' between countries or legal systems.[35] Seen in this way, some aims of comparative sociology of law directly parallel those of comparative law. A major impetus for research in comparative law exists in efforts to unify or harmonise law across national jurisdictional boundaries (for example in developing a common European private law), or to find optimal legal solutions to common problems based on comparative research.

4.2   Translation and Commensurability

Equally, some difficulties of comparison arise in similar ways in both research fields. For example, comparatists have worried about problems of translating legal ideas. Does the

---

[34]   Edgar Kiser and Michael Hechter, 'The Role of General Theory in Comparative-Historical Sociology', 97 *American Journal of Sociology* 1 (1991); Bollen et al. (note 17) 335.
[35]   Nelken (note 23) 19, 22, 28 and 75.

concept of 'good faith' mean the same thing in German or European law as it means when imported into English law?[36] In comparative sociology of law, researchers sometimes take familiar concepts for granted as a basis for comparison, with insufficient recognition that their meaning can vary significantly between legal systems, or that they carry with them assumptions rooted in particular socio-legal environments.

As David Nelken has carefully explained in relation to many concepts used in Anglo-American comparative criminal justice research, it is unwise to assume stable trans-cultural or transnational meanings. 'Pragmatic' as a valuation, 'delay' as a phenomenon in the administration of justice, and concepts of 'due process', 'judicial independence' and 'effectiveness' can all present problems in this way, as can the concept of 'criminal justice' itself.[37] Ideas of 'legality' or the 'rule of law' or 'human rights' similarly tend to import particular, culturally specific meanings. There are numerous other ideas invoked in comparative sociology that are similarly as problematic.[38]

Comparatists have sometimes tried to avoid these translation problems by adopting a narrow legal positivism. If one compares as little as possible—for example just specific legal *rules* or *procedures*, but not their social contexts, cultural reference-points or wider conceptual settings—the problems might be reduced. However, the comparisons would become arid and formalistic, merely technical. This would discard the whole purpose of broadening comparative law to make it more socially realistic and meaningful in context.

Another approach might be the dramatic one of effectively *abolishing* comparison from comparative law and, following Alan Watson's lead,[39] focusing on the study of legal trans-plants, or borrowings—the importation or imposition of legal ideas or practices from one legal system into another. In this way, 'external', 'foreign' legal phenomena would tend to become objects of study only as far as they are incorporated in a particular legal system. The focus of study would thus be on the latter. In such an approach, comparative legal analysis largely dissolves back into the study of national legal systems together with the transnational relations and doctrinal elements that influence the development of those systems. A similarly bold approach could be to declare that transcultural comparative legal study, insofar as it aims to measure similarity and difference, is *impossible* because one cannot successfully accomplish translation between legal cultures in this context and legal understandings are necessarily confined within their own legal culture.[40]

---

[36]   See Gunther Teubner, 'Legal Irritants: Good Faith in English Law or How Unifying Law Ends Up in New Divergences', 61 *Modern Law Review* 11 (1998), arguing that meanings are likely to diverge because they are rooted in different legal discourses.

[37]   Nelken (note 23) 4, 8, 24, 26, 42–3 and 86. See Stewart Field and David Nelken, 'Early Intervention and the Cultures of Youth Justice: A Comparison of Italy and Wales', in Volkmar Gessner and David Nelken (eds), *European Ways of Law: Towards a European Sociology of Law* 349, 368–70 (Oxford: Hart 2007), discussing different cultural understandings of 'success' in approaches to youth justice.

[38]   See e.g. Bollen et al. (note 17) 343. Even the idea of 'law' itself may be hard to translate reliably in some comparative research.

[39]   Alan Watson, *Legal Transplants: An Approach to Comparative Law* ch. 1 (Athens: University of Georgia Press, 2nd edn, 1993); for critical commentary, see Cotterrell (note 10) 109–16.

[40]   Pierre Legrand, proceeding from such premises, sees comparison not as a matter of such measures of similarity and difference but as 'a gesture . . . which reaches towards the other . . . as an affirmation of alterity' and alterity as 'something ungraspable, something unnamable'. Legrand,

Comparative sociology of law, however, has never adopted such ultimately negative 'give-it-up' approaches to the task of comparison. It cannot do so because it has no equivalent of the jurisdictional closure that a jurist might use to mark off a discrete, internally integrated legal realm. Lawyers may ultimately be able to declare that the law in a specific legal system (or perhaps in a particular legal culture or legal tradition) is necessarily the whole of their field and their legal understanding, because it is 'officially' defined as juristically distinct and autonomous—a particular jurisdiction or set of jurisdictions which lawyers serve or profess to know. Nevertheless, social phenomena (including legal phenomena) cannot be so limited from a *sociological* viewpoint within officially defined jurisdictions. 'Methodological nationalism' is ceasing to be an option.[41] In a globalising world, intricate economic, financial, ethnic, religious, kinship, communication and other networks cross national boundaries. In fact, lawyers' jurisdictional self-limitations will increasingly not work either, as the boundaries of legal jurisdiction become more porous.

Beyond these common difficulties for comparatists and legal sociologists are others more specific to social science. Quantitative sociology of law faces problems in tracing causal linkages and controlling variables[42] as well as finding measures that can be applied uniformly to produce data for different countries. It has to confront problems in sample selection, in the use of secondary data, in the reliability of local informants and in the relative availability, coverage or quality of published information for different countries or legal systems.[43] Equally problematic can be the choices national reporters make or the emphases they adopt in presenting data and the challenges foreign researchers face by personally gathering information abroad. Where comparable quantitative data for different countries can be obtained, it may not be possible to control for all 'external interventions' (for example, particular government decisions), unrelated to the topic of the research, that can affect data.[44]

Nelken distinguishes three approaches a scholar might take in conducting research in a foreign environment: 'researching there' (making relatively short research visits); being 'virtually there' (relying on local experts' reports); or 'living there' (conducting ethnography as an established resident). Each presents its own problems of accessing, translating and assessing information.[45]

'The Same and the Different', in Pierre Legrand and Roderick Munday (eds), *Comparative Legal Studies: Traditions and Transitions* 240, 311 (Cambridge: Cambridge University Press 2003); see Legrand, 'Paradoxically, Derrida: For a Comparative Legal Studies', 27 *Cardozo Law Review* 631, 701 (2005).

[41]   Ulrich Beck and Natan Sznaider, 'Unpacking Cosmopolitanism for the Social Sciences: A Research Agenda', 57 *British Journal of Sociology* 1 (2006).

[42]   See Kiser and Hechter (note 34) for a full discussion of these problems in comparative sociology.

[43]   Bollen et al. (note 17) 342–6.

[44]   See Nelken (note 23), especially at 59–66 discussing Michael Cavadino's and James Dignan's comparative studies of punitiveness in their *Penal Systems: A Comparative Approach* (London: Sage 2006) and 'Penal Policy and Political Economy', 6 *Criminology and Criminal Justice* 435 (2006).

[45]   David Nelken, 'Doing Research into Comparative Criminal Justice', in Reza Banakar and Max Travers (eds), *Theory and Method in Socio-Legal Research* 245, 249–56 (Oxford: Hart 2005).

4.3   The Meaning of 'Sociology' in Comparative Sociology of Law

A further complication (but also, in my view, a strength) of comparative sociology of law may lie in its sociological openness. What makes research 'sociological'? Some writers treat sociology of law as a sociological sub-discipline, a branch of the easily recognised professionalised academic discipline of sociology, with its long-established career paths, distinct university departments, and general and specialist journals and associations. Nevertheless, in many ways it is more realistic to see sociology of law as existing outside this orbit of professionalised academic sociology.[46]

From its beginnings, sociology of law was produced by scholars who did not necessarily see themselves as professional sociologists (often they were jurists), and its development ran in parallel with (rather than as an offshoot of) general sociology. Neither Durkheim nor Weber, major contributors to sociology of law, saw this research field as a limited sociological specialism. Both considered the study of law as central to sociology's ambitions, far more than a specialised arena in which to apply general sociological ideas.[47] Equally, sociology of law has not become an established specialism of academic sociology, but remains a research field (typically referred to as law and society research, or socio-legal studies) contributed to by scholars of many disciplines, who do not see it as confined by disciplinary prerogatives.

In the light of its history and present organisation, sociology of law is best seen as a *transdisciplinary* field. In other words, it is unified not by any disciplinary allegiance (though the established theoretical and methodological traditions of sociology are inevitably of great importance) but by a commitment to the *systematic* and *empirically grounded* study of law as a *social* phenomenon,[48] a study to which many knowledge fields contribute.

5   COMPARATIVE SOCIOLOGY OF LAW IN ITS CONTEXTS OF RESEARCH

5.1   The Range of Research

The sense of increasing interdependence between countries, which encourages the broadening of comparative lawyers' ambitions, no doubt also promotes comparative sociology of law. Certainly, a great deal of research on 'foreign' socio-legal phenomena now occurs. More than a decade ago, two sociologists noted that 'the "leading" US sociological journals rarely publish articles by or on non-US subjects'.[49] That hardly seems true now for leading socio-legal journals. In recent years the Law and Society Association, the leading

---

[46]   Roger Cotterrell, *Living Law: Studies in Legal and Social Theory* 30–34 (Aldershot: Ashgate 2008).

[47]   Wolfgang Schluchter, 'The Sociology of Law as an Empirical Theory of Validity', 2 *Journal of Classical Sociology* 257 (2002).

[48]   Cotterrell (note 10) 54–8.

[49]   William G. Martin and Mark Beittel, 'Toward a Global Sociology? Evaluating Current Conceptions, Methods and Practices', 39 *Sociological Quarterly* 139, 155 (1998).

professional organisation of legal sociologists in the United States, has made a determined effort of outreach to non-US scholars[50] and its journal, the *Law and Society Review*, publishes many studies relating to non-US subjects, though not all can be considered genuinely comparative.

Some are studies in one country with a certain amount of discussion relating the findings to previous studies in other countries.[51] In the period since 2008, such papers have reported, for example, studies in Kenya, Thailand, Mexico, Argentina, Russia, China (and Hong Kong), Israel, India, Australia, Quebec, Turkey and Ghana. Other articles (but significantly fewer) explicitly set out to test general transnationally applicable hypotheses through one or more specific national studies.[52] A very few other papers make direct quantitative comparisons of data from more than one country. And a handful of other studies considers inherently transnational socio-legal phenomena (for example the WTO or the European Union). A glance at the British *Journal of Law and Society* shows a similar pattern as regards the testing or illustration of transnationally applicable hypotheses, but more attention to transnational socio-legal phenomena and fewer specific studies of foreign (that is, non-UK) topics. Authors of articles in both journals tend (following Nelken's terminology) to be scholars 'researching there' or 'virtually there', rather than 'living there', though in some cases they clearly have a personal tie to the countries that are the focus of their research and, where these are Anglophone Western countries, the writers may be based at universities in them.

Admittedly, such a brief glance at the range of journal papers amounts largely to what was castigated at the beginning of this chapter as 'impressionistic' comparison. Nevertheless, it can provoke reflection on conditions that have shaped and will continue to shape comparative sociology of law. How far scholars are able to reach with their comparative research will often depend on their language skills or the resources available to pay for translators and local informants, as well as grants for travel, subsistence, technical aid and study facilities. Access to sources of influence to facilitate interviews with officials and acquisition of data may be very important. Rich and powerful countries can usually, for obvious reasons, provide more resources and access for their own comparative socio-legal researchers than can poorer countries.

Some countries may have an interest in facilitating comparative research in particular foreign regions rather than in others. Funding agents or facilitators may set agendas for the kind of research to be done. No less important are official (government) views as to how far socio-legal research in general is practically important. Moreover, non-governmental attitudes (for example, in the established national cultures of legal or social scientific scholarship in universities) on such matters may powerfully shape research patterns. Many other factors also operate.

All of this is to emphasise that while comparative sociology of law may be producing

---

[50]   A development strongly advocated in the 2002 presidential address to the society: see Lynn Mather, 'Reflections on the Reach of Law (and Society) Post 9/11: An American Superhero?' 37 *Law and Society Review* 263 (2003) and the commentaries on this paper in ibid.

[51]   In some cases, the author's foreign-US comparisons may simply be dictated by a felt need to relate the foreign material directly to US readers' local concerns.

[52]   Bollen et al. (note 17) 335 refer to this as 'parallel demonstration' of theory, 'a case illustration or the illustrative application of a theory to two or more cases'.

an increasingly rich tapestry of knowledge, despite all the problems of method discussed earlier, it cannot be a politically, economically and culturally innocent enterprise. It reflects many complex conditions that determine where, why and how scholars undertake it. These conditions determine who does it, under what circumstances, and with what presuppositions about the kind of knowledge that is to be obtained.

5.2 National Conditions of Research

Some commentators might argue that, ultimately, the conditions of research are much less fundamental than the results of research. After all, even if conditions tilt the ways in which comparative research is done, some research is better than no research, and the use to which findings are put is not necessarily limited by the conditions of their production. Nevertheless, in a world of finite resources, some matters become topics for well-resourced research while others are not funded. This applies also to socio-legal research limited within particular national jurisdictions—some legal systems are the focus of far more research than others are. However, as long as the findings of such nationally limited research relate only to the jurisdiction in which the research has been funded and carried out, their validity as a contribution to national socio-legal self-understanding may not be fatally compromised. The position in comparative socio-legal research is different. When attention is focused on some countries and legal systems far more than others and some are (thanks to this attention) better understood—and perhaps better appreciated—than others, the imbalance might undermine the process of comparison. How should one balance perceptions of similarity and difference? Will there be a tendency always to privilege the *familiar* (made more familiar through extensive research) and to marginalise the *different* (made stranger because of little research and as a result, perhaps, little understood)?

It seems clear that sociology of law—in the form of empirical socio-legal research—is most extensively developed in the Anglophone common law world. Nothing matches, in other countries, the scale of research in the United States, where distinct cultural and political conditions have favoured its growth.[53] From a non-US perspective, the prominence of law in the national culture of the United States is remarkable. This, together with a tradition of pragmatist, instrumental legal thought which encouraged an acceptance that social science might make law a more efficient tool of government, went along with twentieth-century political ambitions to use law for social reform purposes (especially in such areas as race and sex discrimination and combating poverty and urban deprivation).

Weaker echoes of these forces promoting socio-legal research have operated in other countries. Elsewhere in the common law world, if law is less culturally central than in the US, there is nevertheless a tendency to view it pragmatically as a regulatory tool rather than in terms of the juristically refined conceptual structures of continental European code-based systems. In Britain and some Scandinavian countries socio-legal research developed largely as a servant of the emerging welfare state and of aspirations towards

---

[53] Bryant Garth and Joyce Sterling, 'From Legal Realism to Law and Society: Reshaping Law for the Last Stages of the Social Activist State', 32 *Law and Society Review* 409 (1998).

social change. Elsewhere, governments could accept it as a means of acquiring systematic information about public opinion and about the nature and problems of society to be regulated by law. Perhaps surprisingly, only limited retrenchment in sociology of law has occurred as welfare states have faltered and the optimistic idea of law as an instrument of social change has lost much of its mid-twentieth century lustre in Western societies.

In a significant number of continental European countries, the institutionalisation of sociology of law appears to have been the result of the efforts of a few well-placed individuals able to show its potential at an opportune time. Here, just one instructive case will be mentioned, that of Per Stjernquist in Sweden.[54] Stjernquist, a member of a well-connected academic family with links to government as part of the small Swedish cultural and political elite, initially practised as a local judge and developed an interest in social anthropology. Appointed as a professor of civil law at Lund University, he found that his wish to develop teaching in sociology of law was not supported by the law faculty. The popular programme he introduced in 1963 (the first in Sweden) was taught to administrative sciences students, and only later offered to law students. Eventually a chair of sociology of law was created for him at Lund by government decision, but outside the law faculty, which continued to deny any need for the subject. Thus, Stjernquist's chair in sociology of law, unique in Sweden but paralleled by comparable posts elsewhere in Scandinavia, was created by purely governmental initiative against very strong juristic opposition. But such a lonely, isolated development, with 'no supporters among influential [academic] social circles' and initially closely 'attached to the perspectives of legislators and administrators',[55] contrasts sharply with the broad socio-legal movements in some common law countries, and certainly with the vast US growth in this research area.

5.3   A Case Study: The 'Juridical Expedition'

The most general point to draw from the Swedish illustration is that particular national conditions may powerfully shape orientations of research. Cross-national socio-legal comparisons should consider not only the comparability of research topics and findings, but also the *culture of research*. This may be no more or less impenetrable, as a focus of inquiry, than legal culture. 'Cultural immersion', to use Curran's term, may well be an appropriate means of studying it, so that research reports, data and accounts are read as reflecting the contexts of their production. Some cultures of research in a particular time and place may seem unique so that using their findings in comparative study requires care. Nevertheless, even considering apparently unique cases can provide useful insight.

Here then is one such case. In 1948, the government of Denmark commissioned three young Danish lawyers to travel to Greenland to conduct research intended to contribute to the modernisation of the country in preparation for the ending of its dependent

---

    [54]   Per Stjernquist, *Organized Cooperation Facing Law: An Anthropological Study*, Appendix 1 'The Introduction of Sociology of Law in Sweden' (Stockholm: Almqvist & Wiksell 2000); see Roger Cotterrell, 'Per Stjernquist 1912–2005', 48 *Socio-Legal Newsletter* 9 (Spring 2006), available at http://www.slsa.ac.uk/images/slsadownloads/newsletters/48%20spring%202006.pdf.
    [55]   Stjernquist (note 54) 66, 67, also noting that these research orientations were a direct consequence of the way the subject had been established institutionally in Sweden.

colonial status and its integration as a Danish province. The assigned task of the 'juridical expedition' (*juridiske ekspedition*) was to discover and describe existing Greenlandic customary law in the civil and criminal law fields and to clarify how far Danish law could be introduced in Greenland as a law in common for Danes and Greenlanders.[56] The researchers studied anthropological works, literature on Greenland communities, census papers and administrative reports, and spent 16 months travelling in western Greenland, studying local records and interviewing local informants of many kinds about dispute processing and communal organisation and problems. One of the researchers, Agnete Weis Bentzon, wrote later: 'We were indeed innocent anthropologists . . .. We wanted to describe and understand Greenlandic customary law in its cultural context at the same time as we wanted to compare the Greenlandic conception of law with the Danish law'.[57]

The aim was comparative socio-legal research—to relate the jurists' existing socio-legal understandings of *Danish* law[58] to their *Greenlandic* findings—and the politics underlying this aim were somewhat complex. While the overall objective was modernisation of Greenland society, the researchers, like the government officials with whom they had close contact, were convinced 'that the Greenlandic population had to be actively involved in this development to make it successful . . .. [I]ntroducing a legal system that did not allow for norms and customs prevailing among the population subject to the system was doomed to fail'.[59]

Several legal developments followed directly from the findings of the juridical expedition[60] but the most notable was surely the creation of the Greenland Criminal Code of 1954, drafted by Verner Goldschmidt, the criminal law specialist of the expedition. Among the code's distinctive features was (1) its long list of 'measures' (extending far beyond typical penal sanctions and including a very wide range of rehabilitative, educational or therapeutic options), (2) the strong emphasis on individual treatment of offenders, and (3) the very extensive discretion given to courts in deciding on appropriate measures in relation to any particular offence.[61]

The code's approach to crime and disorder reflected the special needs of a society in which close interpersonal co-operation, social harmony and reintegration were essential for survival. As the creation of larger urban centres occurred, these ideas weakened 'and changes in the Greenlandic population were faster than expected' but the 'general impression, confirmed by a . . . survey in 1998, is that the Greenlandic population accepted the principles of the . . . code'.[62] These principles, combining modern conceptions of criminal

---

[56]   Agnete Weis Bentzon and Torben Agersnap, 'Verner Goldschmidt: Danish Sociologist of Law and Culture', 43 *Acta Sociologica* 375, 376 (2000).

[57]   Agnete Weis Bentzon, 'JUREX Reconsidered: A Confessional Tale about the Juridical Expedition (Jurex) to Greenland in 1948–9 and the Greenlanders' "Customary Law"', in Henrik Garlik Jensen and Torben Agersnap (eds), *Crime, Law and Justice in Greenland* 97, 98, 103 (Copenhagen: Copenhagen Business School 1996).

[58]   See Verner Goldschmidt, 'The Greenland Criminal Code and Its Sociological Background', 1 *Acta Sociologica* 217, 217 (1956).

[59]   Bentzon (note 57) 108.

[60]   On reforms in the administration of justice, see Agnete Weis Bentzon, 'The Structure of the Judicial System and its Function in a Developing Society', 10 *Acta Sociologica* 121 (1966).

[61]   See Goldschmidt (note 58).

[62]   Bentzon and Agersnap (note 56) 378.

offences with flexible discretionary responses to offending became established in a context of rapidly accelerating socio-economic change.[63]

How successful was this project as comparative sociology of law? The members of the juridical expedition were, in Nelken's terms, mainly 'researching there' as foreigners, relating the knowledge they acquired at first-hand to their existing Danish socio-legal understandings. To achieve the aim of producing legal solutions that could suit both Greenlanders and Danes present in Greenland such a comparison and integration of different socio-legal experiences was essential. They relied on translators but also learned Greenlandic, which Goldschmidt spoke 'fairly well'.[64] In some respects, their extended stay, coupled with Goldschmidt's longer professional involvement with Greenland, might draw their research methods within range of Nelken's 'living there' category. It was certainly a substantial and intricate engagement with the foreign socio-legal environment.

At the same time, as Weis Bentzon notes, the trio of lawyers were 'collaborators', hired by government to make a specific study, but also saw themselves as 'advocates' for the local populations.[65] Their work was informed by a political agenda requiring, as they saw it, a fine balance between seeking similarity (a uniform law for a modernising society) and appreciating difference (the special socio-legal needs and expectations of Greenlandic communities). However, one commentator suggests that their compromise over legal modernisation in the face of social and political change was a reason why their report remained unpublished, despite the implementation of many of its legal ideas.[66]

Nevertheless, as a demonstration of sociology of law's 'immediate usefulness' for law reform this research seems an amazing success story. Goldschmidt's case might be summarised as 'researched there, proposed reforms, drafted code, saw it enacted and put into effect (with relatively minor amendments)'—an achievement many scholars might envy.

This case study also illustrates many difficulties of comparative sociology of law that I mentioned earlier. How far could one integrate the Greenlandic research into a broader comparative sociology of law? Is the politics that underlies it separable from the research's emphases and interpretive choices? Is such a direct relation between research and practical outcomes a feature of: (1) *a particular kind of society* (liberal post-war Denmark); (2) with *a small political-intellectual elite* (facilitating integration of research into the political process—as perhaps was envisaged with Stjernquist's Swedish development of sociology of law); (3) *at a certain time* (with pressures on Denmark to decolonise); and (4) with access for researchers facilitated by a *specific political-cultural relation* between the country studied (Greenland) and the one from which research initiatives arose

---

[63]   See Elaine J. Schechter, 'The Greenland Criminal Code and the Limits to Legal Pluralism', 7 *Inuit Studies* 79 (1983), arguing that modern European legal conceptions (rather than Greenlandic customary law) increasingly dominated in practice. However, the drafters may have intended the code's flexibility to allow this as socio-economic change occurred. On the continuing existence of diverse legal cultures, see Hanne Petersen, 'Legal Cultures in the Danish Realm: Greenland in Focus', in Kirsten Hastrup (ed.), *Legal Cultures and Human Rights: The Challenge of Diversity* 67 (Hague: Kluwer Law International 2001).

[64]   Bentzon and Agersnap (note 56) 377; Bentzon (note 57) 100.

[65]   Bentzon (note 57) 109.

[66]   Petersen (note 63) 67, 69.

(Denmark)? An ever-broadening comparative sociology of law will need to examine matters such as these to consider how far scholars can effectively integrate bodies of research on a cross-national basis.

6 GLOBALISATION AND THE AIMS OF COMPARISON

The aim of the juridical expedition's research seems straightforward—to inform legal change in a context of 'modernisation'. One could make comparisons with 'law and development' projects in other countries. However, all such projects should be considered in the cultural contexts in which they occur, including those of the culture of research itself. Perhaps only very special conditions allow findings of comparative sociology of law to be translated directly into legal reforms acceptable (as perhaps they were in the Greenland case) both to those promoting them and to those subject to their effects. Goldschmidt wisely saw that the Greenland Code would need changing as society changed and he argued that the law itself should provide procedures for its own critique and reform based on socio-legal research.[67] Law and research should exist in dialectic relation and legislative ambitions should be modest. Nevertheless, how far can comparative studies of law cope with rapid and wide-ranging social, cultural and economic change affecting socio-legal environments?

This question is very relevant in the contexts of globalisation. For present purposes it is not necessary to try to pin down this vague, permanently debated concept but only to note that it is always associated with an increasing scale, intensity and speed of cross-national influences (economic, cultural, political, legal) and with challenges to the assumed adequacy of purely national foci of analysis (for example, national societies, nation states, national sovereignty and national jurisdiction). These national foci remain very important; none has been rendered in any way insignificant. Yet, it seems important to reconsider all of them in a larger transnational context. Thus, comparison of legal systems and national societies in a framework of developing transnational ties (and other ties not defined by nation states) seems imperative.

One form of this comparison often entails *seeking similarity*. In comparative legal studies, harmonisation projects associated with aspirations to develop a common European private law are an example. Some other approaches to comparison outside national frameworks clearly favour *appreciating difference*, as in efforts to defend and legitimise plural forms of law (legal pluralism) within nation states to mirror a growing recognition of cultural diversity in national societies.[68] Such developments reflect especially the aspirations of communities in nation states to define and preserve a cultural identity (based on shared traditions, beliefs or values, allegiances or material interests) at least relatively distinct from national identity.

---

[67] Goldschmidt (note 58) 248, 251.
[68] See e.g. Ralph Grillo, Roger Ballard, Alessandro Ferrari, André J. Hoekema, Marcel Maussen and Prakash Shah (eds), *Legal Practice and Cultural Diversity* (Farnham: Ashgate 2009); Rubya Mehdi, Hanne Petersen, Erik Reenberg Sand and Gordon R. Woodman (eds.), *Law and Religion in Multicultural Societies* (Copenhagen: DJØF Publishing 2008); Prakash Shah, *Legal Pluralism in Conflict: Coping with Cultural Diversity in Law* (London: Glass House Press 2005).

Scholars advocate and pursue the comparative study of law in all of these contexts, whether transnational or intra-national, with the aim of bringing about legal change. However, it remains necessary to ask how the relevant cultures of research and a displacement of national reference-points may affect these research ambitions.

Some writers argue that globalisation intensifies problems of comparative method in sociology. 'Insofar as the conception of separate national societies linked by markets and interstate relations is dislodged in favour of a global world of social relationships, . . . it becomes impossible to meet the formal requirements of discrete and isolated [national] cases necessary for the comparative method'.[69] What is to be compared? If national societies no longer provide obviously distinct units for comparison, the coherence of the idea of 'society' itself is put in issue; thus, new concepts are needed.[70]

One response to challenges of globalisation might be to deny that national structures (such as legal systems) and national societies are inadequate units for comparison, but to recognise that comparison will often find *convergence* between them which might then be identified as evidence of globalising forces. Another approach might be to *assume* globalising forces operate and to ask how far they are empirically identifiable in the circumstances of particular societies or legal systems.[71] Nevertheless, there is no way of creating an 'objective' concept of 'globalising forces'. There will be a range of perspectives[72] reflecting different local cultures of research.

Surely, this matter of diverse perspectives is relevant to both comparative law and comparative sociology of law. There is certainly a tendency to portray transnational phenomena in comparative research as if there was only one objective way to view them. Some legal sociologists claim that there is a single emerging 'modern legal culture',[73] rather than competing views of modernity. Again, some scholars see a particular, definable style of regulating through law to be establishing itself on the world stage,[74] rather than a range of political and cultural clashes around the idea of 'law' and its uses in social life; clashes often accompanied by much misunderstanding. Some comparatists see the drafting of a common European private law as primarily a technical matter in which they can assume a common culture,[75] rather than a task demanding much reflection on the great diversity of intersections of law and culture.

---

[69]   Martin and Beittel (note 49) 153; see Daishiro Nomiya, 'The Demise of Comparative Sociology? Globalization and its Shadow', 16 *International Journal of Japanese Sociology* 35 (2007).

[70]   Beck and Sznaider (note 41); William I. Robinson, 'Beyond Nation-State Paradigms: Globalization, Sociology, and the Challenge of Transnational Studies', 13 *Sociological Forum* 561 (1998).

[71]   See Nomiya (note 69). The idea of a 'diffusion' of legal ideas might be seen as one way of conceptualising in comparative law terms some specifically legal effects of these globalising forces. Cf. William Twining, *General Jurisprudence: Understanding Law from a Global Perspective* ch. 9 (Cambridge: Cambridge University Press 2009).

[72]   Beck and Sznaider (note 41) 18.

[73]   Lawrence M. Friedman, 'Is There a Modern Legal Culture?', 7 *Ratio Juris* 117 (1994); Friedman, 'One World: Notes on the Emerging Legal Order', in Michael Likosky (ed.), *Transnational Legal Processes: Globalization and Power Disparities* 23 (London: Butterworths LexisNexis 2002).

[74]   R. Daniel Kelemen and Eric C. Sibbitt, 'The Globalization of American Law', 58 *International Organization* 103 (2004).

[75]   See e.g. O. Lando, 'Why Codify the European Law of Contract?' 5 *European Review of Private Law* 526, 529–30 (1997) ('The peoples of Europe share the legal values of a Christian

More generally, as noted earlier, in comparative sociology of law there are many problems of translating concepts and difficulties in acquiring comparable data. In one sense, one can also see these as consequences of the understandable attempt to find a common 'objective' viewpoint—a 'view from nowhere'—to organise comparative research. However, almost inevitably, comparative sociology of law is faced with comparisons where similarity and difference cannot be measured on absolute scales. Comparisons often give different results depending on standpoint or perspective.[76]

Comparative study has to find ways to be useful in a world that is becoming interdependent with information flows and economic and financial networks, but is also strongly fragmented by local demands for distinct cultural identity and communal identity and solidarity. That usefulness will depend ultimately on the ability of comparative socio-legal research to operate with a range of perspectives. It will need to maintain a degree of reflexivity about its methods and a constant awareness of the historical contexts in which research projects and traditions develop. It will have to refuse to deal in absolutes and in declarations of context-free objectivity.

Its methods will involve, above all, the patient *negotiation* of *provisional* meanings and a sensitive intercultural *dialogue*[77] across diverse socio-legal environments. The foreign observer may sometimes see these environments as incomprehensible, but (equally dangerously) may sometimes too quickly and easily 'understand' them. To avoid these consequences, comparison has to become, in its most productive form, the endless conversation that philosophy was once claimed to be.[78]

FURTHER READING

Bollen, Kenneth A., Barbara Entwisle and Arthur S. Alderson (1993). 'Macrocomparative Research Methods', 19 *Annual Review of Sociology* 321–51.

Cotterrell, Roger (2006). *Law, Culture and Society: Legal Ideas in the Mirror of Social Theory*. Aldershot, UK: Ashgate Publishing.

Cotterrell, Roger (2006). 'Comparative Law and Legal Culture', in Mathias Reimann and Reinhard Zimmermann (eds), *Oxford Handbook of Comparative Law* 709–37. Oxford: Oxford University Press.

Cotterrell, Roger (2007). 'Is it So Bad to be Different? Comparative Law and the Appreciation of Diversity', in Esin Örücü and David Nelken (eds), *Comparative Law: A Handbook* 133–54. Oxford: Hart.

Freeman, Michael (ed.) (2006). 8 *Law and Sociology: Current Legal Issues*. Oxford: Oxford University Press.

Kalberg, Stephen (2007). 'A Cross-National Consensus on a Unified Sociological Theory? Some Inter-Cultural Obstacles', 10 *European Journal of Social Theory* 206–19.

Nelken, David (ed.) (1997). *Comparing Legal Cultures*. Aldershot, UK: Dartmouth Publishing.

Nelken, David (2002). 'Comparative Sociology of Law', in Reza Banakar and Max Travers (eds), *An Introduction to Law and Social Theory* 329–44. Oxford: Hart.

Nelken, David (2010). *Comparative Criminal Justice: Making Sense of Difference*. London: Sage.

Nelken, David and Johannes Feest (eds) (2001). *Adapting Legal Cultures*. Oxford: Hart Publishing.

---

society and of a market economy which is under governmental control').

[76] See H. Patrick Glenn, 'Are Legal Traditions Incommensurable?', 49 *American Journal of Comparative Law* 133 (2001), arguing that, while comparison cannot be based on absolute measures of similarity and difference, it can always be made in terms of the criteria supplied by the cases compared.

[77] Cf. Christoph Eberhard, 'Towards an Intercultural Legal Theory: The Dialogical Challenge', 10 *Social & Legal Studies* 171 (2001).

[78] Richard Rorty, *Philosophy and the Mirror of Nature* 389–94 (Oxford: Basil Blackwell 1980).

Villegas, Mauricio García (2006). 'Comparative Sociology of Law: Legal Fields, Legal Scholarships, and Social Sciences in Europe and the United States', 31 *Law & Social Inquiry* 343–82.

Watt, Horatia Muir (2006). 'Globalization and Comparative Law', in Mathias Reimann and Reinhard Zimmermann (eds), *Oxford Handbook of Comparative Law* 579–607. Oxford: Oxford University Press.

3   Comparative criminology
*Francis Pakes**

1   INTRODUCTION

Although occasionally seen to be a fringe endeavour within the field of criminology, it is nevertheless clear that comparative research is an important part of the study of criminology and criminal justice. The term 'comparative criminology' at present is associated with a certain type of research that implicitly or explicitly seeks to relate experience from one criminal justice context to another. We can see that through some textbooks (e.g., Dammer and Albanese 2010; Pakes 2010a) and the emergence of a separate comparative criminological methodology (e.g., Pakes 2010b). It is an area with an identifiable body of knowledge and with its own history and stories of success.

John Howard (1726–90) carried out notable early comparative work in the area of prisons in the late eighteenth century. He visited many prisons in Great Britain and in mainland Europe and wrote detailed accounts of what he saw. Having been briefly imprisoned himself in northern France, this life experience may well have ignited a humanitarian spark that led to such seminal work. Like many others, Howard's comparative work had a strong normative component, appalled as he was by his own brief experience of prison life but also because of the poor conditions that he witnessed in Great Britain. Where he saw more favourable conditions, such as in gaols in Belgium and the Netherlands, he used that information in political activity to attempt to replicate such conditions in Great Britain (Howard 1777). Besides Howard's efforts to persuade a House of Commons select committee of the merits of radical changes to prisons and prison conditions, he was also a researcher and a humanitarian and his accounts remain relevant to this day.

Howard's work comprises comparative criminology and criminal justice in a nutshell. During his frequent journeys, he encountered many of the issues that continue to face comparative researchers today, such as issues of language difference, access to information, and the general problems that eighteenth-century travels inevitably brought. However, he wrote with purpose. Rather than thinking of comparative research as a purely intellectual exercise, he clearly coupled it with a powerful imperative for change. Howard made that point from the outset: 'the journies were not undertaken for the traveller's amusement, and the collections are not published for general entertainment, but for the perusal of those who have it in their power to give redress to the sufferers' (Howard 1777: 6). Clearly, therefore, comparative criminological research as an impetus for change is well over 200 years old.

This chapter is organised along two broad themes. The first is concerned with the aims and methods of comparative research. Within this theme, I will consider broad orientations involving comparison of relativism and positivism, case studies, focused

---

*   Reader in Comparative Criminology, University of Portsmouth.

comparisons and other ways in which scholars can carry out comparative research. Finally, I examine the roles that the comparative researcher can assume along with their associated strengths and weaknesses.

The second theme involves two substantive issues. The first is the issue of establishing crime rates, a key concern in comparative criminology. Second, I examine the role and nature of globalisation in relation to comparative criminological research. We shall discover that globalisation's impact on comparative criminology is varied, substantial, and at times surprising. I conclude by providing some thoughts about the future of comparative research in criminology and criminal justice.

2   WHAT IS COMPARATIVE CRIMINOLOGY?

Attempts to define comparative criminology can easily descend into vacuous exercises. Émile Durkheim (1895) was of course correct when he argued that all sociology is essentially comparative and the same is true for criminology. We always seek to understand something in terms of something else. However, that complicates setting apart comparative criminology as a separate and identifiable field. Piers Beirne and David Nelken provide an often-used definition of comparative criminology as 'the systematic and theoretically informed comparison of crime in two or more cultures' (1997: xv). However, even such a broad definition of comparative criminology may be too narrow if it excludes case studies that look at a single case or context. Case studies can be truly comparative in situations in which the comparison will be implicit. One might then say that case studies are proto-comparative, since they allow subsequent explicit comparisons. Consequently, case studies of 'foreign' criminal justice systems could fit under the comparative umbrella where it is clear that they attempt to inform readers about situations in a particular context with which they may not be familiar. Thus, the very aim of comparison pulls case studies under the comparative criminology banner. In addition, Beirne and Nelken refer to the object of study as 'crime', whereas one might argue that it should also include responses to crime, informal and formal. We should look beyond crime to other forms of deviance and harmful behaviour, a point that I will expand on later in this chapter.

3   WHY DO COMPARATIVE RESEARCH?

Scholars carry out comparative research for many different reasons, and for many comparative endeavours these reasons overlap and cannot be clearly distinguished. The first reason may be intellectual curiosity, but usually a mixture of intellectual and pragmatic or instrumentalist reasons will inspire research. The most straightforward reason is to learn from others. The field of criminal justice has its share of success stories that have stimulated global interest. These include zero-tolerance policing in New York, restorative justice from New Zealand and community policing in Japan. Where promising developments occur, there tends to be a pull towards researching it from a comparative perspective.

Comparative scholars face a dual task in assessing these. The first question to answer is whether the reality lives up to the surface impression. This is usually far from easy as the cause and effect of any intervention are difficult to establish. Criminological research is often at best quasi-experimental; it is rare that truly controlled experiments can take place. That makes the evaluation of many initiatives, from policing to sentencing to informal conflict resolution and crime prevention, notoriously difficult.

The second step is even more fraught with difficulty: it involves assessing whether an initiative that is successful in one context can be as successful in another. There are many reasons why we should be sceptical of the ease of such policy transfers or transplants. The success of certain modes of interacting with juveniles, suspects, offenders or citizens in general will be culturally determined to some extent. That makes the wholesale lifting of arrangements from one context into another hazardous. There is the added risk that such endeavours are guided by implicit neo-colonial or ethnocentric attitudes. These are premised on the idea that what was good in a developed Western society should be as successful elsewhere, disregarding local culture, tradition and already-existing means of dealing with similar situations. That raises issues of cultural dominance and hegemony, although there are examples such as the aforementioned restorative justice in New Zealand where family group conferences take place that are modelled on informal conflict resolution in the native Maori culture. They are associated with the indigenous Maori way of resolving issues associated with misbehaving youngsters. This mechanism attempts to be inclusive for the young person and reparative for families and local communities as well as empowering for the victim.

David Nelken (2010) warns us of the conceptual limitations of this 'shop around' approach to comparative inquiry, 'seeing only what is useful for us is a poor way of acknowledging and engaging with the "other"' (2010: 13). Nevertheless, cross-cultural comparison will start from somewhere and how you look at arrangements in a certain place will be coloured and textured by the tacit assumptions that one derives from settings that are more familiar. As Nelken (2010) explains, someone from India will find Italian criminal justice relatively efficient: someone from Denmark probably less so.

It is one conceptual step further to study the very process of how policies travel from one place to another. Trevor Jones and Tim Newburn (2007) distinguish policy transfer, the conscious process of 'taking' policies from elsewhere to adopt them domestically, from policy diffusion, the more intractable set of processes that give certain developments a global reach. This is sometimes in the form of a label, such as 'three strikes and you're out', which is now a banner under which scores of initiatives in many places are placed, quite often places where baseball, the sport that is the origin of the metaphor, is hardly played, if at all. We can research why certain ideas have travelled well, for instance the criminalisation of cannabis, whereas others fail to catch on elsewhere (e.g., Andreas and Nadelmann 2006).

Jones and Newburn (2007) explain that policy transfer in criminal justice often does not take the form of mindless wholesale shopping for detailed arrangements to bottle and take home. Instead, recipients mould the arrangements to the local context so that what is actually imported may well be quite far removed from the original blueprint. There is no doubt that zero-tolerance policing outside of New York City is often very different from the original. The same is true for family group conferences from New Zealand where the appeal of 'purity' and inclusivity are important aspects in the justice system. In fact, these arrangements have inspired activities elsewhere frequently in diluted or altered form.

Thus, policy transfer in practice is often the transplant of generalised notions and intentions rather than of precise arrangements and procedures.

Apart from the instrumentalist aim of deciding what works elsewhere and assessing whether it is applicable at home, there is the further aim of rigorously testing social theory. Criminology is much concerned with identifying causes of crime, such as personal variables (for instance, intelligence or personality factors), social variables (such as family factors or peer groups), and societal trends (for example, economic circumstances, equality, or poverty). The quality of such research improves by adding a comparative perspective to establish whether relationships between variables hold true in differing contexts. Comparative research can cast doubt on what some assume is universal knowledge, for instance the relation between adolescence and crime. Maureen Cain (1995) produced data that cast doubt on the universality of that relation. Thus, comparative research can serve a valuable debunking role.

A third aim of comparative research, perhaps a purer form of intellectual inquiry, seeks to understand arrangements and phenomena in their own terms and context. Such research would often be ethnographic in nature and involve sustained immersion in the context or culture one is studying. The goal is not to arrive at ostensive universal knowledge but to contextualise findings in a certain time and place. Many of criminology's most celebrated works involve ethnography, such as Jock Young's *The Drugtakers* (Young 1971). The argument is that we cannot fully appreciate the meaning of crime if we fail to understand where it happens. Frequently, this type of research intends to highlight the lived experience of individuals, examine their 'sense making' and from there reach a deeper and richer understanding of the meaning of the behaviour that has been labelled as criminal.

Ethnography does not need to involve criminals, but can also examine police officers, prisons or other social or occupational contexts. The leitmotiv of such research is frequently one of difference. It is not assumed that drug dealers in Oslo are essentially the same as those in Oldenburg or that police officers in Seattle are doing essentially the same job as those in Sierra Leone. Rather, scholars expect different results, but perhaps over several studies, communalities may emerge and so ethnographic research is in principle certainly able to cement knowledge that transcends time and place even though context, locality and difference are often emphasised. In essence, comparative research will often yield a blend of similarity and difference (Pakes 2010b); ethnographic research typically celebrates the latter.

Nelken (2010) encourages the comparative researcher to move beyond ethnocentrism and relativism. Ethnocentrism is a hurdle in many comparative studies. The tendency to regard arrangements at home as obvious, necessary and natural and to look at arrangements elsewhere with a lens identifying deviations from the domestic 'norm' is common. After all, as Nelken says, what is good for us is not necessarily good as such. Arrangements in criminal justice are set in wider social and cultural contexts. That might invite a temptation towards 'relativism', the idea that our social world can only be locally understood, that all cultures are unique, and that to strive for universal or even transferable knowledge is an *idée fixe*, a fallacy of methodological positivism. That position is probably too strong. It is not the case that we simply cannot learn from 'others', but in doing so, we must not be too hasty to proclaim universal truths. We must be sensitive to the fact that even oft-assumed universal knowledge is set in time and place.

4   THE COMPARATIVE METHOD

Any discussion about a discipline's aims inevitably invites discussion about method: the 'why' of research has pertinent implications for the 'how'. In this section, I examine case studies, focused comparisons and so-called multi-studies (Heidensohn 2008), such as the International Crime Victim Survey.

Case studies in social science have a long history but, as mentioned earlier, some question whether they are a true 'comparative' method. It is important to appreciate what exactly a good case is, how one selects it and what one can learn from the case study. John Cresswell (2007) argues that a case study involves the investigation of a bounded or self-contained system. It seeks to provide an in-depth understanding of a subject within its real life context. Case studies can utilise evidence from a range of sources, such as official government data, researcher observations, explorative and focused interviews, as well as historical data and media coverage. Case studies tend to be indicative, which means that they are perhaps best suited to raising questions rather than answering them. They are more likely to spur further research if the findings merit that.

However, even an individual case study can have profound theoretical impact. That is particularly true of so-called deviant cases. A deviant case is one that challenges received wisdom regarding the relation between certain variables. Japan provides an illustration. It is a densely populated highly industrialised society, which did not experience a dramatic rise in crime between 1960 and 1990. Conversely, in most Western societies the crime rate jumped substantially (Leishman 1999; Garland 2001). The study of Japan provokes the Western researcher to discover what variables might have been responsible for the Japanese situation. A deviant case, therefore, may cast doubt on what some assume to be a universal relationship (Pakes 2010a). Another justification for selection would include its representativeness, the case that represents (is a regular or typical example of) a larger category. An archetypical illustration would be the case that generates a category. Therefore, to study the archetypical example of adversarial justice would lead one to study judicial arrangements and procedures in England and Wales, for instance.

Typical research designs in comparative criminal justice involve focused comparisons, the comparison of two or a few cases. This often involves a comparison between the context with which the researcher is most familiar against another, less familiar setting. David Downes's comparison of penal policy in England and Wales and the Netherlands is such a comparison (1988). He sought to explain why prison rates in England and Wales were rising for decades after World War II, whereas those in the Netherlands were consistently going down at the same time. Hanns von Hofer's (2003) comparison of prison rate developments in the Netherlands, Finland and Sweden is another example, a focused, in-depth comparison of a small set of cases with emphasis on cultural, historical and legislative differences among the countries studied. At the same time, Von Hofer did arrive at conclusions that applied across the three settings, namely that the prison rates had less to do with levels of crime but more with the political will to not respond to any popular punitivist appeals to the legislators or judges who sentenced those convicted.

Individual cases studies and focused comparisons share an important characteristic. That is, the comparatist will inevitably have an impact on the findings. When sustained immersion in another culture or context is required, it is impossible to expect that the background, skills, expectations and interactions of that individual would not colour her experience. That is particularly evident when we consider possible limitations. Some of these are language, meaningful access, cultural literacy and ethnocentric bias (Leishman 1999). Although these are related, it is useful initially to treat them separately.

The difficulties of language stretch beyond the fact that the researcher may not speak the native language of the jurisdiction studied. Even when the British researcher ventures over the pond to the United States, for instance, issues of language and semantics can be highly pertinent. These link to issues of terminology as well as differences in discourse. One should be careful to consider that something that one says may not mean the same thing as in the scholar's homeland. Of course, language problems are compounded by unfamiliarity with the language spoken elsewhere. Without adequately speaking the language of the group or culture to be studied, one needs to rely on interpreters, who, indeed, may interpret, filter or otherwise affect the input received. One is likely to miss bits of information such as informal conversations, popular media references, or even clues such as the meaning of graffiti in public spaces. The risk of missing essential data to verify or challenge the information provided by cooperative hosts is therefore substantial.

The dynamic notion of language also comes into play. If the researcher relies on the English language, she will find willing speakers of varying levels of proficiency in most countries. However, these people may not properly represent the population as a whole. Keen and fluent speakers of English as an additional language are more likely to be younger, better educated, Internet aware and internationally oriented. An inability to speak a native language may reduce meaningful access to individuals without such characteristics. That may well introduce an unintended bias into the research. Moreover, language is fluid. Some young people in Greece use 'Greeklish', and computer talk worldwide occurs in Techlish, a lingua franca that is dominated by English but in a simplified form relying more heavily on abbreviations and technical jargon. Moroccan youngsters in the Netherlands frequently speak a hybrid of Dutch combined with English and Arabic influences that deviates in both vocabulary and grammar from Dutch. Consequently, when we talk of 'speaking the language', we already introduce an oversimplification.

It is clear that issues of language can become issues of access but the challenges of access are not just of a linguistic nature. Criminology and criminal justice offer specific access challenges. That relates to the closed nature of many of its institutions such as prisons, police custody and forensic psychiatric hospitals as well as immigration deportation centres. The criminal justice professions, perhaps in particular the police, can be quite impenetrable for research, certainly more in certain contexts than in others. Where academic scholars carry out research, then often academics in the comparing context are involved. Similarly, where police officers seek to gain knowledge from abroad, an official visit to the host police force will be a central part of the project. Access therefore is almost inevitably selective and issues of language, profession and the desire to seek to work with likeminded individuals may both introduce and solidify bias.

What Frank Leishman (1999) calls cultural literacy covers a sociological world of notions, knowledge, discourses and assumptions. In essence, comparative research is about understanding differential customs. It is about making sense of difference, not simply detecting it. We need to be well versed in another culture before we can even begin to make sense of it with the rigour required for criminological inquiry.

Ethnocentric bias is an important concept to highlight here. Ethnocentrism has a long history within comparative research. It refers to the tendency of interpreting human behaviour through the lens of one's own background. Although certainly not necessary, often ethnocentrism carries a normative element: one may call arrangements elsewhere 'primitive', for instance. At the same time, researchers may oversimplify and celebrate arrangements elsewhere, perhaps uncritically. Looking at these four elements, they often amplify each other and make comparative research a methodologically hazardous undertaking.

Adequately to consider the value of comparative research we need to assess the person who undertook it. A researcher's strengths and weaknesses will make certain research roles more or less appropriate. Frances Heidensohn (2008) identifies a set of roles that the comparative researcher can adopt and emphasises the importance of critical reflection upon one's own role in comparative research. In British criminology, an important group of comparatists are refugees. In prior decades, these individuals, who often left continental Europe due to the threat of Nazism, gave criminology in the UK much impetus. They include Karl Mannheim (1893–1947) and Sir Leon Radzinowicz (1906–99).

A second category is 'rendezvousers'. Their research method involves short visits to their object of study, which would be informative, but cannot serve as a substitute for long-term immersion. Reformers like John Howard travelled abroad to seek information or inspiration to bring about change at home. Heidensohn also refers to armchair travellers benefiting from the information landscape where local information is available globally. They do their research without the necessity of visiting the local context. Finally, Heidensohn discusses global theorists who seek to develop and test theories that transcend local contexts.

Clearly, researchers are not always free to choose their role. Certainly in the case of refugees, it is more a case of having a role thrust upon them. In a similar vein, one does not necessarily pick cases for comparison for purely academic reasons. The world of comparative research certainly seems richly filled with examples where choices were made because of opportunity or convenience. That of course should not disqualify any research. The challenge is to scrutinise it closely and evaluate its findings on its merit. Lucia Zedner (1995) captured the essence of engaging in comparative criminology most persuasively:

> Doing comparative research rarely entails selling one's home and tearing up one's passport, forever to live among the drug dealers of Delhi or the detectives of Düsseldorf. Neither can one, with credibility at any rate, write about continental criminal procedure without stepping outside the ivy-clad walls of an Oxford College. Rather the research process entails developing a general theoretical (but distant) understanding at home-base, punctuated by a series of forays (often of increasing duration) into the terrain of study. This itinerary is matched by an intellectual journey which takes one from the perspective of global structures to the minutiae of local detail and back and forth over the course of the research in a 'sort of intellectual perpetual motion' (Geertz 1983: 235). While periods of fieldwork provide for immersion in local culture (of the court, the prison, the police station), the journeys between make possible an intellectual distancing. Once more library-bound, the researcher can engage in the detached reflections and distanced evaluation that are the very stuff of comparison. (1995: 19)

5   UNDERSTANDING CRIME IN A COMPARATIVE CONTEXT

Criminology is a strange beast according to Tim Newburn (2007). It is a parasitic endeavour, argues Stanley Cohen (1985), as it leans and feeds on other sciences. Some call it a rendezvous subject, not an area with a clearly demarcated subject matter but rather a platform where scholars of many different disciplines and inclinations meet to study 'the question of crime'. Ian Loader and Richard Sparks (2010) explain that the question of crime goes beyond studying the causes and manifestations of crime. We cannot study crime without considering the procedures by which it is defined, and the politics and debates about criminal justice, risk, order and safety. That makes the area difficult to pinpoint, as well as ever changing due to transformations in criminal definitions, public understandings and penal policies.

There is a global preoccupation with counting crime (Young 2004). This obviously can serve important purposes from both a policy and a scholarly perspective. Comparative crime rates may tell us important things about the relation between crime rates and other variables, such as penalties, socio-economic circumstances, levels of urbanisation, democracy or civic participation. It might seem that counting crime is a straightforward endeavour, but there are many complications. First, where would one look for the relevant statistics? The first point of call might be officially compiled criminal statistics. However, while the compilation and use of statistics is an imprecise science in the first place, it is much more fraught with difficulty in a comparative context.

Criminal statistics, whether compiled by the police, courts or government departments, are often compiled for pragmatic, operational or political reasons. That means that we cannot always trust them for the purpose of scholarly inquiry. More mundane is the consideration that official statistics will fail to detect many criminal acts, often due to non-reporting of crime. There are many reasons why victims or other interested parties would not go to the police: they may not trust the police, may not think the police will do something about it, or believe that what has happened does not constitute a crime. In areas such as stalking and even sexual offences, this latter reason is common.

Criminologists often state that criminal statistics for murder and manslaughter are the most reliable, since these cases are much less likely to be overlooked, not reported or not investigated. In contrast, whether citizens report crimes like theft is questionable if they do not see a benefit in doing so. The United Nations compiles data on murder rates in many countries, both in absolute numbers and per 100,000 citizens. Murder rates are particularly high in many countries in Central America and the Caribbean, including Honduras, Belize and Jamaica, with several dozen murders per 100,000 population. Murder rates are also relatively high in South Africa and Lesotho. Low murder rates (less than one per 100,000) occur in several European countries, including Sweden and Switzerland, but also in the Middle East in nations such as Oman, Bahrain and Egypt.[1] However, even with murder statistics there are several issues to consider. The UN data consist of intentional homicides, which may exclude death by dangerous driving as well as corporate manslaughter. Statistics may not include other types of homicide, such as infanticide or euthanasia. The data may also not reflect honour killings, which often occur without the knowledge of, or most disturbingly with the tacit support of, local or national authorities.

---

[1]   See United Nations Statistics Division, 'Intentional Homicide, Rate per 100,000 Population', http://data.un.org (see Databases: Crime).

Globalisation may have generated other categories, such as the murder or unintentional death of illegal immigrants or those in transit between countries. These events may well escape official attention. In addition, such statistics also frequently fail to capture state-organised crimes, ranging from death squads to police brutality or 'disappearances'. The fact that such statistics are normally compiled at the level of nation states can leave big gaps in the recording of deaths. These could include immigrants in boats seeking entry into Europe or Australia who perish. Such deaths fall outside familiar and perhaps too-narrow conceptions of murder or manslaughter, but must focus our thinking about borders, policy, globalisation and the value of the lives of illegal immigrants (see, e.g., Pickering 2011).

This tells us something fundamental about official statistics beyond the obvious truth that they are often unreliable due to under-recording. They can be profoundly political in what they show and what they hide. For these and other reasons, scholars see victimisation surveys as more reliable. These large-scale surveys include thousands of citizens, randomly selected for inclusion, typically administered in person or via telephone. They ask a host of questions about having been the victim of a crime and often specify whether that occurred within the last year, or the last five years or some other period. That way, surveyors build a picture of crime in society using a representative sample of the population. The British Crime Survey is a good example, whereas the International Crime Victim Survey (ICVS)[2] takes places in dozens of countries all over the world. It also separately includes 33 major cities (Van Dijk et al. 2008).

The outcomes of the ICVS are certainly informative and come with a good degree of precision. Overall, the 2008 publication summarised that an estimated 16 percent of the populations in the 30 nations participating have been victims of at least one of ten common crimes in 2003 or 2004. High-scoring countries include Ireland, England and Wales, New Zealand and Iceland. Lower rates of victimisation occurred in Spain, Japan, Hungary and Portugal. Most of the countries show a distinct downward trend in the level of victimisation since 1995 or 2000. Theft of personal property has the highest victimisation rate of the ten common crimes under investigation. Almost 4 percent of the persons surveyed in the 30 countries and 6 percent in the major cities were victims of theft during the two-year period. On average, 1.8 percent of households in the 30 countries saw their houses burgled in the course of the prior year. On average, 1 percent were victimised by robbery in the 30 countries, with 2.4 percent in the main cities. This split between 1.4 percent in the selected cities in developed countries and 6.1 percent in developing countries (Van Dijk et al. 2008).

The survey also addressed non-conventional crimes. To illustrate, over one in ten of the people surveyed were victims of consumer fraud in the course of one year. Estonia, Greece and Bulgaria stand out in this regard with rates of over 20 percent. At the other end of the scale, Japan has less than a 2 percent level of victimisation. The survey found that the level of experiences with bribe taking or bribe seeking by public officials (street-level corruption) remains very low, 1 percent or less in industrialised countries. However, public officials seeking bribes are comparatively common in Greece and in the countries in East Central Europe that have recently joined the European Union (Van Dijk et al. 2008).

---

[2] See The 2004/05 International Crime Victims Survey, http://rechten.uvt.nl/icvs.

Several limitations are clear from the outset. Only crimes for which there is an identifiable victim will become known through victimisation surveys. Many offences, which produce a tremendous amount of social harm, therefore are usually not identified. This may include drug trafficking, environmental offences and various types of fraud. This is a serious limitation. I already alluded to the problem that what is defined as a crime in a jurisdiction and what is understood as a crime by respondents may be two different things. Victimisation surveys, furthermore, are usually unable to shed light upon crime in closed environments. In addition, the so-called crimes of the powerful are unlikely to surface via victimisation surveys.

Specific to comparative work is the fact that criminal definitions differ across jurisdictions. Definitions of common crimes such as murder and manslaughter differ from country to country, but there are other significant criminalisations, such as adultery, a crime in many Middle Eastern countries, but not elsewhere. Less visible jurisdictional differences involve offences that officials deal with via the penal code in some jurisdictions but via civil or administrative processes elsewhere. For instance, in relation to synthetic drugs, what is not a crime today may well be a crime tomorrow. This highlights that crime is not a natural category, but a social construct, and that definitions and understandings of crime differ and evolve over time.

Take the case of corruption. In many places, from Nigeria to the Philippines, it is common for people to pay small bribes to get proper service out of civil servants or other officials (Pakes 2010a). Citizens often see these situations as inevitable inconveniences and perhaps not so much as crimes. That may have lowered the reporting rate as well as the potential concern that paying bribes may have given the respondent a sense of complicity.

Two further issues with victimisation surveys are conceptual in nature. The first is the reflection of the very nature of crime. We often think of crime as specific instances of behaviour. However, when we look at stalking, bullying and antisocial behaviour, for example, they are fact patterns of repeated behaviour that become the essence of criminal definitions. That has implications for counting; one might say that trying to count them in fact represents misunderstanding them, since such patterns of behaviour simply do not lend themselves to any mechanical tallying process.

Perhaps more important, we must interrogate the desire to count, and we must question the tacit assumption that counting crime somehow is the inevitable step towards understanding it. Counting in a comparative context requires standardisation of definitions and methods, and therein lays a danger that we seek to hold standard views on crimes elsewhere that simply do not fit the social fabric. Young (2004) dismisses this as voodoo criminology. Heidensohn is also quite explicit in denouncing this tendency to count:

> These studies seem sometimes to be pursuing a holy grail that we were all taught long ago to be sceptical of: the perfect, accurate measure of crime, and in the case of cross-cultural comparisons, the precise measure that can be applied across the board to crime around the world. But there are surely serious problems of positivistic oversimplication going on here? A further issue is that the standardised may not catch the interesting, complex facets of the crime problem. (2008: 211)

Thus, the argument goes, bean counting may not actually capture the essence of crime. The real meaning of crime may not lie in the frequency of it but in other aspects of meaning, culture, emotion and society. As Pakes (2010a: 39) argues: 'counting crime is not the same as understanding crime. Crime is both a local and a global phenomenon, and we cannot strip either the local context or the global picture away if we want to truly understand it'.

In addition to the more analytic efforts to understand crime, quantitatively much of the most inspiring work in criminology is heuristic, investigative, and therefore qualitative in nature. It often relies on ethnography and rather than presenting us with reductionist data, it provides a holistic picture that may change the way we think about offending behaviour and those who engage in it. It is deeply concerned with meaning.

We can for instance contrast the work on comparing prison rates with work that examines what actually goes on inside prisons. Roy Walmsley (2008) regularly compiles prison rates for most of the world's countries and territories. These prison data are informative and allow us to gain a global grasp on the number of people detained worldwide. There is therefore no doubt as to the value of such information. First, we can see that from a global perspective prison rates are strongly regionalised. They are low in West Africa and in Southeast Asia, with on average 33 and 53 prisoners per 100,000 population respectively. Compare that to the Caribbean with an average prison rate of 324 prisoners per 100,000 inhabitants. The highest prison rates, however, are to be found in the United States with 756 and the Russian Federation with 629 prisoners per 100,000 population. In Europe, prison rates are highest in the former Soviet republics. Those for the Baltic states of Estonia, Latvia and Lithuania are respectively 259, 288 and 234 per 100,000 people. In many European countries, the ratio remains under 100 per 100,000 inhabitants. That includes France (96), Germany (95), Ireland (76), Sweden (74), Finland (64) and Denmark (63) (Walmsley 2008).

At the same time, however, we must realise that cold numbers only say so much. They are compiled by different agencies and counting rules may differ among them. It is uncertain whether all individuals that the state incarcerates under various labels are actually included. This particularly applies to the People's Republic of China where perhaps several hundred thousand people are held in administrative detention, without trial or conviction, and with little legal protection. Counting typically assumes that 'a prison is a prison'. We, of course, know that there is a spectrum ranging from open prisons to supermaximum security facilities. Although counting is often relatively easy, we must not lose sight of the fact that it is both more interesting and more important to examine what goes on in prisons, who is being held, and how imprisonment comports with wider social and penal objectives.

Sharon Shalev (2009) has done a particularly good job of investigating so-called supermax prisons in the US. She looked at the issue of isolation, justified by notions of dangerousness for an increasing number of inmates in US prisons. She examined a wide range of variables such as the culture among prison officers, the physical layout of prisons and prison cells, and personal interactions (or more often, a lack of them) among inmates and between inmates and prison officers. She highlights the intense and sustained sensory deprivation that inmates suffer and asks pertinent questions about the fairness of this development.

Arguably, Shalev's work is not strictly comparative. However, it highlights important developments in imprisonment that comparative number crunching would not be able to uncover. Instead, what is required is a modern day John Howard type of enterprise where researchers visit prisons, meet inmates, and examine the interactions of design, protocol, culture and discourse within prison walls. That does illustrate the core of comparative work, but it suggests that at its best comparative and 'mainstream' criminological inquiry may well become the same.

6   GLOBALISATION AND COMPARATIVE CRIMINOLOGY

Comparative research thrives on difference. It is rewarding and exciting when the patterns of life, the stories we live by, and the structures of society can be demonstrated to be rooted in time and place. It highlights the human spirit, the ability of people to find meaning and develop culture in a great many different ways. Early anthropological work often celebrated difference. With that came an assumption that human relations were fluid, changeable, contradictory and only properly understood within its local context. Variety was and probably is the spice of comparative life.

Diversity may come with isolation. We can expect to see the most difference in societies that have not had much interaction with other cultures. In some sense, interaction leads to contamination. Some of the pureness of culture is lost when that 'splendid isolation' is no longer maintained. Some of the more romantic endeavours in comparative research could be conceptualised as a quest for purity. These days purity is hard to find. Instead, the researcher is more likely to be overwhelmed by interconnections. Rather than trying to look underneath that web of interrelations as if it only forms a distraction, one should examine the layers of connectivity. This characterises much comparative research today.

Scholars often allude to globalisation, but are not very successful in succinctly explaining it. Nikos Passas provided the following description:

> Globalisation refers to a set of contradictory processes and dynamics resulting in the transformation of the world order through the multiplication and intensification of linkages and interconnectedness. Capital, goods, services, people and ideas cross borders with increasing speed, frequency and ease. Actions in one country have consequences and significance in distant places. Local events and destinies can hardly be interpreted and understood without looking beyond national boundaries. The world is being reconstituted as 'one place' with global communications and media, transnational corporations, supranational institutions, integrated markets, and a financial system that trades 24 hours a day. (1999: 405)

Comparative criminology has been slow in embracing globalisation (Aas 2007), but it is clear that globalisation affects many facets of both crime and responses to crime. Consider Passas's compelling description. He refers to globalisation as contradictory. We indeed see that the flow of globalisation is not all one-way traffic. The vision of the 'world of one locus' seems to invite social science at a global level, but the fact that globalisation accounts for movements and counter-movements makes that less likely. It is important to bear in mind that globalisation is not like a tsunami sweeping all before it. Rather, the dialectic of developments and counter-developments produce turbulence and in that maelstrom surprising things can happen. It is important that comparative researchers therefore are ready to face the unexpected.

One of the most obvious manifestations of globalisation is transnational crime made easier through the ease of travel, porous borders and a high demand for illegal goods. The smuggling of drugs is perhaps the quintessential transnational crime. This is most unambiguously the case for heroin. Heroin has a global market but is manufactured in only a small number of areas in the world. That inevitably brings about a lively global trade set against periodic law enforcement efforts to curb cultivation and trade.

The picture of transnational drug crime and drug control becomes more intriguing when we step back to consider the criminalisation of heroin. Patterns of globalisation are highly apparent when we look at the processes that have led to the almost worldwide prohibition of heroin. This is a relatively recent phenomenon, with international drug treaties only making an appearance in the early twentieth century. Peter Andreas and Ethan Nadelmann (2006) discuss this as the result of so-called global prohibition regimes. Prohibition in the US was followed by decades of aggressively pursuing prohibition elsewhere. This reveals the cultural and economic dominance of the US, but also of Europe, since countries virtually everywhere followed suit regardless of whether heroin was considered a local issue at all. In a non-globalised world where prohibition was not dominated by the West, we instead might have seen a very different state of affairs:

> Some Asian states, for example, might have opted for a different global regime that legitimized the use of opium, some African and Asian states for a regime legitimizing cannabis, many Muslim states for a regime prohibiting alcohol, and some Latin American states for a regime that sanctioned coca. Just as the global prohibition regimes against piracy and the slave trade reflected the desire and capacity of Britain and other European powers to impose their norms on the rest of the world, so the global drug prohibition regime reflected the desire and capacity of the United States to impose its drug-related norms on the rest of the world. (Andreas and Nadelmann 2006: 45)

The assessment of what globalisation does to crime may become even more complicated if we consider harmful conduct on the fringe of legality. Global prohibition regimes emerge through a desire to have uniformity in norms and laws. At the same time, disparities in governance may offer opportunities to organised crime as well as legitimate business and state actors. Passas calls these criminogenic asymmetries. These are structural discrepancies, mismatches and inequalities in the realms of economy, law, politics and culture. Passas uses the example of toxic waste. Many developing countries do not have strong legislation on toxic waste and other environmental issues. If laws exist, they are less likely to be rigorously enforced either because of capacity issues or because of bribery and corruption. That creates opportunities for those looking cheaply to dispose of toxic waste: dump it in places where either it is not illegal, or where the authorities are highly unlikely to investigate it (Moyers 1990).

Thus the combination of globalisation and global asymmetries create criminal opportunities, perhaps particularly for state crime, corporate crime and other 'crimes of the powerful'. Nevertheless, we must use the term 'criminal' advisedly. After all, many of these harmful activities occur just because they may not be strictly criminalised in developing countries. It highlights the fact that a too rigid adherence to official definitions of crime may obscure the very phenomena that in fact are most important to study. It is therefore not surprising that a shift has occurred away from a narrow legalistic approach to comparative criminology towards one that is oriented towards harm and harmful behaviour rather than slavishly following legal definitions.

All these processes have profound implications for comparative criminology both in terms of what we study but also in terms of how we choose study it. It is clear from the above that we have identified new objects of study. We should no longer think of transnational crime as crime that just happens to cross borders. Instead, transnationality is its defining feature and we need a conceptual apparatus to come to terms with that. We need to appreciate that much of human agency is not as bound by time and place as it once was. Financial crime, computer hacking and the spreading of objectionable materials can be done with our fingertips on a computer keyboard anywhere in the world. That should change our view not only of these types of crimes but of many others as well. The study of crime has become to an extent the study of transnationality.

In addition, the study of criminal justice would be too narrow if it simply considered national legislation. Nations are guided and constrained by international treaties and by supranational bodies such as the European Union. Their policymaking is influenced by soft or not-so-soft diplomacy, often supported by financial, military or symbolic incentives. As we saw in the case of global prohibition regimes, we must study the emergence of supranational governance development. However, we should also question and where required problematise it.

Passas, as have others, notes further consequences of globalisation. Globalisation brings about fear—being swamped by strangeness and strangers, losing ways of life or losing control over local destinies. That brings about the very counter-movements that I mentioned earlier. We see these counter-movements particularly in Western Europe where strong societal and political movements seek to limit immigration, in particular from the point of view that immigration would jeopardise cultural tradition and stability. In various nations, such as the Netherlands, Denmark, France and Sweden, these movements seem to be gathering force by bringing about increasingly restrictive immigration policies. One cannot understand such movements without appreciating globalisation.

Juliet Stumpf (2006) has identified a set of processes that contribute to these movements that she calls 'crimmigration'. 'Immigration law today is clothed with so many attributes of criminal law that the line between them has grown indistinct', she argues (2006: 376). This refers to the increased criminalisation of migration, the parallels between deportation and criminal penalties, and criminal sanctions replacing civil measures in dealing with immigration issues, so that immigration law and criminal law increasingly have become doppelgangers. This is another example that shows that comparative criminology should not stay too close to criminal law, since some of its functions actually pass to other systems of law.

7   CONCLUSION

The history of comparative criminology research has ranged from the intrepid travels of John Howard in his tour of domestic and foreign prisons to the complex networks of research and inquiry that brought us the International Crime Victims Survey. It is alive and well with a rich history, a strong present and an exciting future. Nevertheless, it is clear that globalisation has changed comparative criminology in many ways. For one, comparative research has become much more explicitly transnational. The field has moved beyond limiting itself to comparing and contrasting distinct and self-contained states of affairs to become more sensitive to the investigation of the impact of globalisation. That includes the analysis of the travel of goods, people and ideas, global processes of criminalisation, and international efforts to fight crime and to use criminal legislative frameworks and a myriad of other strategies to combat undesired consequences of globalisation.

It has brought about a shift away from crime towards harm, and a similar shift away from narrow conceptions of criminal justice to wider processes of national and transnational coercion and control. There is no doubt that that has revitalised the field. It now addresses today's big questions about fairness and justice in light of global challenges of inequalities. Rather than a fringe endeavour, comparative criminology once more finds itself on the very cutting edge of criminology, perhaps even of social science as a whole.

REFERENCES

Aas, Katja Franko (2007). *Globalization and crime*. London: Sage.

Andreas, Peter and Ethan Nadelmann (2006). *Policing the globe: Criminalization and crime control in international relations*. New York: Oxford University Press.

Beirne, Piers and David Nelken (eds) (1997). *Issues in comparative criminology*. Aldershot, UK: Ashgate.

Cain, Maureen (1995). 'Labouring, loving and living: On the policing of culture in Trinidad and Tobago', in Lesley Noaks, Mike Maguire and Michael Levi (eds), *Contemporary issues in criminology* 84. Cardiff, UK: University of Wales Press.

Cohen, Stanley (1985). *Visions of social control: crime, punishment, and classification*. Cambridge, UK: Polity Press.

Cresswell, John W. (2007). *Qualitative inquiry and research design: Choosing among five traditions*. London: Sage.

Dammer, Harry R. and Jay S. Albanese (2010). *Comparative criminal justice systems* New York: Wadsworth-Thomson Press, 4th edn.

Downes, David (1988). *Contrasts in tolerance: Post-war penal policy in the Netherlands and England and Wales*. Oxford, UK: Clarendon Press.

Durkheim, Émile (1895). *The rules of sociological method*. New York: Free Press.

Garland, David (2001). *The culture of control: Crime and social order in contemporary society*. Chicago: University of Chicago Press.

Geertz, Clifford (1983). '"From the native's point of view": On the nature of anthropological understanding', in Geertz (ed.) *Local knowledge: Further essays in interpretive anthropology* 55–71. New York: Basic Books.

Heidensohn, Frances (2008). 'International comparative research in criminology', in Roy D. King and Emma Wincup (eds), *Doing research on crime and justice* 199–229. Oxford: Oxford University Press, 2nd edn.

Howard, John (1777). *The state of prisons in England and Wales, with preliminary observations, and an account of some foreign prisons*. Manchester: ECCO.

Jones, Trevor and Tim Newburn (2007). *Policy transfer and criminal justice: Exploring US influence over British crime control policy*. Maidenhead, UK: Open University Press.

Leishman, F. (1999). 'Policing in Japan: East Asian archetype?', in R.I. Mawby (ed.), *Policing across the world: Issues for the twenty-first century* 109. London: UCL Press.

Loader, Ian and Richard Sparks (2010). *Public criminology?* London: Routledge.

Moyers, Bill D. (1990). *Global dumping ground: The international traffic in hazardous waste*. Washington, DC: Seven Locks Press.

Nelken, David (2010). *Comparative criminal justice: Making sense of difference*. London: Sage.

Newburn, Tim (2007). *Criminology*. Cullompton, UK: Willan Publishing.

Pakes, Francis (2010a). *Comparative criminal justice*. Cullompton, UK: Willan Publishing, 2nd edn.

Pakes, Francis (2010b). 'The comparative method in globalised criminology', 43 *Australian and New Zealand Journal of Criminology* 17–30.

Passas, Nikos (1999). 'Globalization, criminogenic asymmetries and economic crime', 1 *European Journal of Law Reform* 399–424.

Pickering, Sharon (2011). *Women, borders, and violence: Current issues in asylum, forced migration and trafficking*. New York: Springer.

Shalev, Sharon (2009). *Supermax: Controlling risk through solitary confinement*. Cullompton, UK: Willan Publishing.

Stumpf, Juliet (2006). 'The crimmigration crisis: Immigrants, crime, and sovereign power', 56 *American University Law Review* 367–419.

Van Dijk, Jan, John van Kesteren and Paul Smit (2008). *Criminal victimisation in international perspective: Key findings from the 2004–2005 ICVS and EU ICS*. The Hague: Boom Juridische Uitgevers.

Von Hofer, Hanns (2003). 'Prison populations as political constructs: The case of Finland, Holland and Sweden', 4 *Journal of Scandinavian Studies in Criminology and Crime Prevention* 21–38.

Walmsley, Roy (2008). *World prison population list*. London: King's College, 7th edn.

Young, Jock (1971). *The drugtakers: The social meaning of drug use*. London: MacGibbon & Kee.

Young, Jock (2004). 'Voodoo criminology and the numbers game', in Jeff Ferrell, Keith Hayward, Wayne Morrison and Mike Presdee (eds), *Cultural criminology unleashed* 13–28. London: Glass House.

Zedner, Lucia (1995). 'Comparative research in criminal justice', in Lesley Noaks, Mike Maguire and Michael Levi (eds), *Issues in contemporary criminology* 8. Cardiff, UK: University of Wales Press.

4 Comparative anthropology of law
Elizabeth Mertz and Mark Goodale*

1 INTRODUCTION AND DEFINITIONS

1.1 Legal Anthropology as a Subfield of Anthropology

Like other subfields of sociocultural anthropology, the anthropology of law is an inherently comparative area of study. As the American Anthropological Association has explained, sociocultural anthropology examines 'social patterns and practices across cultures, with a special interest in how people live in particular places and how they organize, govern, and create meaning'.[1] The anthropology of law—also known as legal anthropology—focuses in particular on legal systems, law, and law-like social phenomena across cultures. In recent years, anthropology's emphasis on 'particular places' has expanded to new kinds of locations (for example, virtual or global) in which human interaction now takes place. For legal anthropologists, this also entails attention to the many forms in which legal regulation occurs—from momentary encounters to interactions structured around institutions and texts.

Like most social science fields, the anthropology of law embraces a variety of schools of thought regarding goals, theories, epistemologies and, sometimes, even methods. Scholars in this area nevertheless share a commitment to intensive and rigorous field methodologies requiring extensive involvement in the communities and social fields under study. The results of these studies frequently take the form of 'ethnographies', written reports of fieldwork that include substantial detail as to everyday practices and beliefs. In addition, legal anthropologists share another general foundational precept of their discipline, which requires that fieldworkers attempt to bracket their own categories and presumptions to some degree, so as to generate a more accurate picture of their informants' lived experiences. To the degree that there are unavoidable effects on field research of anthropologists' own positions vis-à-vis their informants, ethnographers have worked to develop 'reflexive' accounts of those effects as well.

1.2 Growth in Anthropological Research on Law

Legal anthropology is a recognized subdiscipline of anthropology in the United States, with its own distinct section, the Association of Political and Legal Anthropology

*   Elizabeth Mertz is the John and Rylla Bosshard Professor of Law, University of Wisconsin-Madison and a Senior Research Professor at the American Bar Foundation.
    Mark Goodale is an Associate Professor of Conflict Analysis and Anthropology, George Mason University and MS Program Coordinator at its Institute for Conflict Analysis and Resolution.
[1]   See American Anthropological Association, 'What is Anthropology?', http://www.aaanet.org/about/whatisanthropology.cfm.

(APLA).[2] A subgroup under the umbrella organization of the American Anthropological Association, APLA recruits a steady stream of younger anthropologists and runs its own journal, *PoLAR: Political and Legal Anthropology Review*.[3] New generations of anthropologists continue to conduct research on law and legal processes, and to self-identify as legal anthropologists. Indeed, the anthropology of law has arguably become more central to the discipline of anthropology as a whole in recent decades, especially in light of growing general interest among anthropologists in topics that fit squarely within the legal anthropological tradition. Examples of such topics include the state and governance in colonial, postcolonial and post-socialist societies; human rights; war, violence and post-conflict processes; global legal processes; and transnational (often legal) institutions.

In the first two decades of a new millennium, this growth in overall anthropological interest is evident in the scholarship of anthropologists from around the globe. It can be seen in the stated interests and topics listed by formal associations of professional anthropologists from many parts of the world, even when these associations do not have sections devoted to particular subfields such as legal anthropology. A brief survey of these associations' websites reveals a pervasive shared concern with legal anthropological questions. In India, for example, anthropological seminars and conferences have focused on tribal rights to natural resources; on women, HIV/AIDS and human rights; and on state policies vis-à-vis NGOs.[4] The Australian Anthropological Association's 'E.Publications' list has included topics such as bureaucracy, governance and the state; police culture; Aboriginal Land Councils and Native title representative bodies; and anthropologists as expert witnesses.[5] The Pan-African Anthropological Association (PAAA) publishes *The African Anthropologist*,[6] which announced an ongoing resurgence of African anthropology that reconceived the anthropological project in response to critiques of its colonial roots;[7] classic legal anthropological topics such as the state and violence against women are part of this newly emerging African anthropological agenda.[8] As we will see, along with some predictable divergences in perspective and emphasis, we also find considerable overlap around the world in shared anthropological concerns with law, legal institutions and law-like processes.

---

[2]   See APLA, Home Page, http://www.aaanet.org/sections/apla/index.htm.

[3]   See Wiley Online Library, *PoLAR*, http://onlinelibrary.wiley.com/journal/10.1111/%28ISSN%291555-2934.

[4]   See Indian Anthropological Association, Events, http://www.indiananthropology.org/Events4.asp. The legal focus of some of these events is evident in specific sessions addressing issues such as 'draft national policy on tribes' and 'revisiting constitutional provisions'.

[5]   See Australian Anthropological Association, AAS Electronic Publications, http://www.aas.asn.au/aas_workingpapers.php.

[6]   See CODESRIA, The African Anthropologist, http://www.codesria.org/spip.php?rubrique66&lang=en.

[7]   Paul Nchoji Nkwi, 'Editorial: Resurgence of Anthropology at African Universities', 14 *The African Anthropologist* v–vii (2007).

[8]   O.M. Njikam Savage, 'Reflections on the Challenges of Anthropology in Contemporary Times and Future Prospects: The Douala Experience', 14 *The African Anthropologist* 101–07 (2007).

2 HISTORY

2.1 Early Scholarship: Comparative and Evolutionary Approaches

It is difficult to say with any certainty when the anthropology of law began; scholars were conducting what today would be classified as anthropological studies of law and legal systems long before there was any self-consciousness of 'legal anthropology' as a distinct and legitimate sphere for research and writing. Some might even point as far back as the fifth century BCE in Greece (Herodotus) or eighteenth-century France (Baron Charles-Louis de Montesquieu, 1689–1755) in tracing the roots of comparative anthropological scholarship on law and political systems.[9] Another notable early writer in this area was Friedrich Karl von Savigny (1779–1861), the German legal scholar whose 1814 anti-codification pamphlet, *The Vocation of Our Time for Legislation and Jurisprudence*, made the argument that law and legal institutions are the unique expressions of a people's culture and history and cannot be understood apart from them.[10]

Nevertheless, within the European and US traditions, the mid-nineteenth century marked the high point of what one can call proto-legal anthropology. Within twenty years of each other, four anthropological studies of law and legal institutions were published that had, collectively, a profound influence on a growing body of theory about the origins and nature of human societies. In 1861, Johann Jakob Bachofen (1815–87), a Swiss scholar, published his seminal *Mother Right: An Investigation of the Religious and Juridical Character of Matriarchy in the Ancient World*.[11] Bachofen drew from a wide range of comparative materials in order to argue that human institutions, including law and morality, were originally conceived within matriarchies.

In this same year, Henry Maine (1822–88) published *Ancient Law*, another landmark study.[12] Like Bachofen, Maine used a wide range of information about different societies and historical epochs—in this case attempting to prove that cultural evolution is universally marked by a progression from *status*, based on kinship, to *contract*, which emerges with the rise of larger and more complex societies. John McLennan's (1827–81) *Primitive Marriage* (1865) made an even more explicit link between anthropological studies of law and evolutionary theories of society, basing his argument for female-centered social rules

---

[9]   On the comparative and ethnographic character of Herodotus' writings about political-legal systems and society, see Rosalind Thomas, *Herodotus in Context: Ethnography, Science, and the Art of Persuasion* (Cambridge: Cambridge University Press 2000). British social anthropologist Alan Macfarlane makes the case for Montesquieu's crucial role in the development of social thought regarding politics and law. Alan Macfarlane, *The Riddle of the Modern World: Of Liberty, Wealth, and Equality* (Basingstoke: Macmillan 2000). See Macfarlane's lecture on Montesquieu and Social Anthropology (2007), http://www.youtube.com/watch?v=kfDHUqL0Rqc.

[10]   Frederick Charles von Savigny, *Of the Vocation of Our Age for Legislation and Jurisprudence* (London: Littlewood, Abraham Hayward trans. 1831, reprinted Union, NJ: The Lawbook Exchange 2002, German orig. 1814).

[11]   Johann Jakob Bachofen, *Das Mutterrecht. Eine Untersuchung über die Gynaikokratie der alten Welt nach ihrer religiösen und rechtlichen Natur* (Stuttgart: Verlag von Krais & Hoffmann 1861).

[12]   Henry Sumner Maine, *Ancient Law: Its Connection with the Early History of Society, and its Relation to Modern Ideas* (London: John Murray 1861).

on the effects of selective pressures that purportedly resulted from early conditions of material scarcity.[13] Indeed, McLennan carried on a regular correspondence with Charles Darwin (1809–82), whose *Origin of Species* had been published in 1859.[14]

Finally, the American lawyer Lewis Henry Morgan (1818–81), who was himself influenced by Bachofen, published his famous work *Ancient Society* in 1877, which established the relationship between law, cultural evolution and comparative research.[15] The shift to evolutionary models in these early works itself marked a turn toward historical context and away from abstract, timeless analyses of 'social contract' or sovereignty, which were not adequate to understanding the complexity and variability found in actual societies. This convergence in understanding emerged despite otherwise stark theoretical and political differences between scholars such as Maine and Morgan.

Most contemporary anthropologists of law would not accept the validity of the armchair methodologies employed by these earlier scholars, nor, in most cases, the unilineal evolutionary conclusions reached throughout these important early works. Particularly problematic under current anthropological approaches would be older evolutionary models that erroneously viewed modern Western society as the pinnacle of an evolutionary development whose earlier stages were exemplified by contemporaneous so-called 'primitive' societies. Nevertheless, the nineteenth-century scholars established one important foundation that connects their work with much contemporary research and theorizing in legal anthropology: the requirement that researchers study and analyze law in its cultural and historical contexts.

2.2   Beginnings of Legal Ethnography and Theories of Structural-functionalism

Despite the fact that Morgan spent time with the Iroquois in upstate New York and then used his experiences in his first writings, he was arguably not the first legal ethnographer. The bulk of his most important work, *Ancient Society*, was derived from his comparative reading and analysis in ancient history rather than from what today would be recognized as ethnographic research. On the other hand, the canonical view that Bronislaw Malinowski (1884–1942) was the first ethnographer of law (rather than Morgan) is perhaps growing less persuasive, in light of changing views within anthropology during the last twenty years on what constitutes ethnography, fieldwork, and the locations where anthropological knowledge is produced.

Yet Malinowski, a Polish-born British social anthropologist, nonetheless transformed the anthropological study of law both theoretically and methodologically.[16]

---

[13]   John F. McLennan, *Primitive Marriage: An Inquiry into the Origin of the Form of Capture in Marriage Ceremonies* (Chicago: University of Chicago Press 1970, orig. 1865).

[14]   Charles Darwin, *On the Origin of Species by Means of Natural Selection* (London: John Murray 1859).

[15]   Lewis H. Morgan, *Ancient Society: Researches in the Lines of Human Progress from Savagery through Barbarism to Civilization* (New York: Henry Holt & Co. 1877).

[16]   Rhoda Metraux, 'Bronislaw Malinowski', in David L. Sills (ed.), 9 *International Encyclopedia of the Social Sciences* 541–9 (New York: Macmillan 1968); George Peter Murdock, 'Bronislaw Malinowski', 45 *American Anthropologist* 441–51 (1943); George W. Stocking, Jr., 'From Fieldwork to Functionalism: Malinowski and the Emergence of British Social Anthropology', in George

Malinowski broke with the great armchair polymaths of the nineteenth century by demanding that any scientific study of law be done, not through the extremely detailed comparativism that had defined the field until that time, but through the application of three innovative methods. These were: (1) participation in the day-to-day life of the people in order to gain deeper understanding of their culture and institutions; (2) long-term residence to get a sense of patterns over time; and (3) mastery of the local language sufficient to conduct research without using translators. Using these ethnographic methods in the Trobriand Islands (1915–18), Malinowski developed a theory of law that moved away from the cultural evolutionary approach of the nineteenth century and instead focused on how sanctions within society functioned in relation to wider social relations.[17]

As Laura Nader notes in her own general overview of legal anthropology, Malinowski's work 'foreshadow[ed] a generation of anthropological research on how order could be achieved in societies lacking central authority, codes, and constables'.[18] This focus moved legal anthropology away from Western-based equations of law with formal institutional 'legal' structures, and toward a more functionally based interest in *social ordering and control*, however achieved, across different societies. In espousing functionalism, Malinowski brought anthropology closer to then-current French sociology, particularly as in the functionalist approach to law espoused by Émile Durkheim (1858–1917)[19]— although Malinowski also notably departed from Durkheim's more sociological formulation in his focus on individual biological needs.

A.R. Radcliffe-Brown (1881–1955), a contemporary of Malinowski, was also an early ethnographer who contributed to a theory of law based on ethnographic fieldwork.[20] However, whereas Malinowski adopted what one can understand as an ethnojurisprudence in arguing that all societies embed social control within wider social relations, Radcliffe-Brown developed a more formal definition of law that required the existence of political institutions capable of enforcing sanctions.[21] Because some societies, like the Andaman Islanders and the Trobrianders, lacked these structural entities, Radcliffe-Brown concluded that some societies lacked law. In this, he perhaps unintentionally evoked the legacy of legal evolutionary theory; however, as time passed, it was to be Malinowski, not Radcliffe-Brown, who had the more palpable influence on later anthropologists of law in this regard.

W. Stocking, Jr, *After Tylor: British Social Anthropology 1888–1951* (Madison: University of Wisconsin Press 1995).

[17]   Bronislaw Malinowski, *Crime and Custom in Savage Society* (London: Routledge & Kegan Paul 1926).

[18]   Laura Nader, *The Life of the Law: Anthropological Projects* 85 (Berkeley: University of California Press 2002).

[19]   Émile Durkheim, *The Division of Labor in Society* (New York: Free Press 1997, French orig. 1893).

[20]   Meyer Fortes, 'Radcliffe-Brown's Contributions to the Study of Social Organization', 6 *The British Journal of Sociology* 16–30 (1955).

[21]   A.R Radcliffe-Brown, *The Andaman Islanders* (New York: Free Press 1964); A.R. Radcliffe-Brown, *Structure and Function in Primitive Society* (New York: Free Press 1965). For a seminal anthropological work that developed a functionalist view of political systems, see Meyer Fortes and E.E. Evans-Pritchard (eds), *African Political Systems* (London: Oxford University Press 1940).

2.3   Law, Culture and Legal Pluralism

For the next thirty years, scholars worked to refine and expand parameters for the anthropological study of law. Central concerns included questions about the nature of law, the relationship of law to other social institutions, and the proper ways to access law as an object for research. An important early example of this was the pioneering collaboration between the anthropologist, E. Adamson Hoebel (1906–93), and the legal scholar, Karl Llewellyn (1893–1962). This association was perhaps less unusual than it might seem because during the first part of the twentieth century legal realists like Llewellyn had been openly searching for non-jurisprudential techniques to use in analyzing the indeterminacy of law and its social content—and anthropologists of law had already been studying these topics.

In *The Cheyenne Way*, Hoebel and Llewellyn utilized the legal realist *case method*— which had entered American jurisprudence and legal education via the German historical jurisprudence of von Savigny—in order to distill the essence of the Cheyenne 'way' of life, as expressed in Cheyenne law.[22] To do this, the scholars focused on what they called 'trouble cases', meaning conflicts resolved in public forums. They argued that trouble cases were a better window into the core of local legal principles than were other possible types of law (that is, administrative or regulatory); this assumption was to become methodologically conventional for many legal anthropologists even as theoretical frameworks shifted.

The general idea that law reflects culture continued as a major theme in legal anthropology, eloquently crystallized later in the work of Clifford Geertz (1926–2006) and his followers.[23] Fieldwork conducted in the 1950s by noted legal anthropologists such as Elizabeth Colson and Leopold Pospíšil expanded the scope of research into disputed cases, asking wider questions about how resolution of these cases was tied to the overall structure of societies.[24]

During the 1940s and 1950s, the anthropology of law emerged as a distinct subdiscipline within American cultural and British social anthropology. Two major figures from this time, Max Gluckman (1911–75) and Paul Bohannan (1920–2007), each pursued ethnographic studies of law and social control that eventually led to quite distinct theoretical positions, and to a debate over the terms within which legal anthropologists should represent local legal categories and concepts. Gluckman maintained that legal categories from Western jurisprudence could be used when abstracting from research findings on indigenous legal ideas and practices; he felt that without the use of general and abstract categories, comparative legal anthropology would not be possible.[25] Bohannan, on the

---

[22]   Karl Llewellyn and E. Adamson Hoebel, *The Cheyenne Way: Conflict and Case Law in Primitive Jurisprudence* (Norman, OK: University of Oklahoma Press 1941).

[23]   Clifford Geertz, *Local Knowledge: Further Essays in Interpretive Anthropology* (New York: Basic Books 1983).

[24]   See, e.g., Elizabeth Colson, *Tradition and Contract: The Problem of Order. The 1973 Lewis Henry Morgan Lectures, University of Rochester* (Chicago: Aldine 1974); and Leopold Pospíšil, *Anthropology of Law: A Comparative Perspective* (New York: Harper & Row 1971).

[25]   Max Gluckman, *The Judicial Process among the Barotse of Northern Rhodesia* (Manchester: Manchester University Press 1955).

other hand, expressed the relativist position that indigenous legal categories were largely irreducible; thus, the legal anthropologist's task was to explain local legal categories in their own terms.[26] The Gluckman–Bohannan debate, which extended through the 1960s, served to expand theory in legal anthropology. It also prefigured many of the later controversies within anthropology more generally over issues of representation and epistemology.

In addition, the 1940s and 1950s were important for the anthropology of law for another quite different reason. During what would be, in retrospect, the waning years of colonialism, the research conducted by many legal anthropologists had either direct or indirect links with colonial institutions and their purposes. Colonial administrators frequently established dual legal systems, in which some matters were adjudicated using the colonial power's law, while other matters would be handled under 'customary law'. Legal anthropologists would later understand this kind of situation, where two or more legal systems coexist within the same region, as a form of 'legal pluralism'.

'Customary law' was supposedly the indigenous system that predated colonial intervention. However, key aspects of the indigenous system were often much changed in the translation in colonial contexts, as was the distribution of power. In validating certain versions of 'customary law', colonial administrators drew upon ethnographic information provided by anthropologists. While some might debate whether or not legal anthropologists at this time directly aided the colonial enterprise, it is clear that (especially for the colonial powers pursuing policies of indirect rule, like the British in West Africa and the Dutch in parts of Indonesia), the information gleaned from on-the-ground studies was a substantial help to colonial administrators. Although many anthropologists of the time were clearly aware of the influence of colonialism on the indigenous practices they studied, it was not until later that legal anthropologists turned the spotlight on this part of the picture and developed more self-conscious analyses of 'customary law' and the role of colonial powers in co-constructing 'tradition'.[27]

2.4 From Law to Disputing

During the 1960s and early 1970s, the anthropology of law underwent a major shift in focus. By that time, anthropologists had nearly exhausted the usefulness of researching the nature of law as such, the characteristics of legal systems in comparative perspective and other issues within ethnological jurisprudence.[28] During the mid-1960s, Nader and other anthropologists moved still more decisively outside of the formal boundaries of law and legal institutions to study disputes as part of wider social and cultural processes. In a remarkable feat of legal anthropological coordination, the Berkeley Village Law Project

---

[26] Paul Bohannan, *Justice and Judgment among the Tiv* (London: International African Institute and Oxford University Press 1957).

[27] See, e.g., Sally Falk Moore, *Law as Process: An Anthropological Approach* (New York: Routledge 1986); John Comaroff and Jean Comaroff, *Of Revelation and Revolution: Christianity, Colonialism, and Consciousness in South Africa* (Chicago: University of Chicago Press, vol. 1, 1991); Martin Chanock, *Law, Custom and Social Order: The Colonial Experience in Malawi and Zambia* (Cambridge: Cambridge University Press 1985).

[28] Pospíšil (note 24).

sent researchers into the field across a wide range of regions over a twenty-year period. The Project was launched, in part, to demonstrate the possibilities of the paradigmatic shift from rules to disputing, but also to develop new questions about the relationship between dispute processes and the state—and, as Nader explains in her history of this time, to explore the connections between agency, power relationships and the resolution of disputes.[29] A concern with agency can also be seen in work by noted legal anthropologist Jane Collier. She analyzed Zinacanteco law as a resource on which individuals drew in pursuing their own strategies and goals.[30]

The focus on dispute brought with it interest in *processual models* for studying law, a direction articulated with clarity in books such as *Rules and Processes* by John Comaroff and Simon Roberts[31] and *Law as Process* by Sally Falk Moore.[32] Along with the concern with law as process came more emphasis on its distinctively local character, a point on which anthropologists with otherwise different perspectives converged. Moore introduced the influential concept of the 'semi-autonomous field', urging anthropologists to consider the ways in which local subgroups within societies developed their own partially autonomous legal dynamics.[33] In *Local Knowledge*, Geertz argued that there are dramatically divergent local 'sensibilities' beneath the conceptualizations of 'fact' and 'law' across different cultures.[34] Lawrence Rosen demonstrated the underlying cultural logics at work as participants in legal proceedings 'bargained for reality'.[35]

The late 1970s and early 1980s also marked a transition in the anthropology of law, especially in the United States, in another way: researchers 'came home', employing methods developed for research in non-Western locations to study law and culture in Western societies (encroaching on areas of the world that were the traditional domain of sociologists, legal scholars and political scientists). Sally Merry, for example, studied conceptions of urban danger as they reflected and reinforced ethnic divisions in a major US metropolis, and then later explored the topic of working-class legal consciousness in the United States.[36] Carol Greenhouse conducted ethnographic fieldwork in a Georgia community and found that religion, alongside local ideas about insiders and outsiders, played a crucial role in how some US citizens utilized (or chose not to utilize) the legal system.[37] In addition, Laura Nader studied the responses of American consumers who had suffered

---

29   Nader (note 18).
30   Jane Fishburne Collier, *Law and Social Change in Zinacantan* (Stanford: Stanford University Press 1973).
31   John Comaroff and Simon Roberts, *Rules and Processes: The Cultural Logic of Dispute in an African Context* (Chicago: University of Chicago Press 1981).
32   Moore (note 27).
33   Sally Falk Moore, 'Law and Social Change: The Semi-Autonomous Social Field as an Appropriate Subject of Study', 7 *Law & Society Review* 719–46 (1973).
34   Geertz (note 23).
35   Lawrence Rosen, *Bargaining for Reality: The Construction of Social Relations in a Muslim Community* (Chicago: University of Chicago Press 1984).
36   Sally Engle Merry, *Urban Danger: Life in a Neighborhood of Strangers* (Philadelphia: Temple University Press 1981); Sally Engle Merry, *Getting Justice and Getting Even: Legal Consciousness among Working Class Americans* (Chicago: University of Chicago Press 1990).
37   Carol Greenhouse, *Praying for Justice: Faith, Order, and Community in an American Town* (Ithaca, NY: Cornell University Press 1986).

'little injustices', but were forced to seek alternatives to the formal legal system because it denied them access.[38]

Of course, legal anthropologists continued to work outside their own—usually Western—countries, and to produce works of importance.[39] At the same time, this shift toward the study of problems within major industrialized nation-states signaled the emergence of an important trend, one that would have a lasting impact on the anthropology of law. Additionally, whether by coincidence or not, at the moment when legal anthropological research was moving into geographical areas that had been more the province of sociology and other cognate disciplines, a formal interdisciplinary movement dedicated to the study of 'law and society' was beginning to gain momentum after its initial emergence in the mid-1960s.[40] The research and writing of legal anthropologists appeared in the movement's journal, the *Law & Society Review*,[41] and legal anthropologists eventually assumed positions of influence with the Law and Society Association (LSA).[42]

2.5 Power, History and the Language(s) of Law

The 1980s were a time of critical self-reflection within anthropology, though more so in the United States than elsewhere. What one can understand as a postcolonial malaise within anthropology that had set in during and after the Vietnam War—and which was partly alleviated through the rise of Marxist anthropology and political economy more generally—contributed to an intellectual climate in which the role of anthropology was reconsidered and partly reconstituted. Trenchant commentary from non-Western scholars on the implicit racism found in Western discourses—including those of anthropology—forced a painful re-examination of anthropological research and writing.[43] As a result, the discipline opened itself to the influence of social and literary critiques drawn from outside the social sciences and explored with renewed energy questions of consciousness, history and 'power', which was now invested with a less structural meaning.

Anthropologists of law were well placed to participate in this series of shifts, especially since law had always been a means through which power had been exercised and, at times, resisted. Likewise, because of the earlier movement toward the anthropological study of law and society within industrialized nations, many legal anthropologists had already broadened their research to include the use of historical sources to complement more

---

[38] Laura Nader, 'Little Injustices: Laura Nader Looks at the Law' (Boston: The Public Broadcasting Associates, 60 min. videocassette, 1981).

[39] See, e.g., Comaroff and Roberts (note 31); Sally Falk Moore, *Social Facts and Fabrications: Customary Law on Kilimanjaro, 1880–1980* (Cambridge: Cambridge University Press 1986).

[40] See The Law and Society Association, Home Page, http://www.lawandsociety.org.

[41] See note 40 (select the *Review*'s link at left).

[42] Their influence can also be seen in the allocation of the LSA's Kalven Prize for lifetime achievement, which has been given to or shared by an anthropologist in seven out of the past 15 years the Prize was awarded. The anthropologists on the Kalven Prize list as of 2011 include Laura Nader, Jane Collier, Sally Falk Moore, Sally Engle Merry, Jean Comaroff, John Comaroff and Carol Greenhouse.

[43] See, e.g., Edward Said, *Orientalism* (New York: Pantheon 1978); Gayatri Chakravorty Spivak, Donna Landry and Gerald M. MacLean (eds), *The Spivak Reader: Selected Works of Gayatri Chakravorty Spivak* (New York: Routledge 1996).

time-restricted ethnography. These two factors combined to bring legal anthropology to the leading edge of social research and theory, and made history and power ordering foci for a new generation of anthropologists.[44] As Carol Greenhouse, Barbara Yngvesson and David Engel explain, this initiated a shift from disputes as a unit of analysis to 'the systems of knowledge and power that frame disputes and connect them to social relations'.[45] It also focused new attention within legal anthropology—and anthropology more generally—on the study of the state and of colonialism itself.

A parallel response to the postcolonial crisis in anthropology involved a reflexive, postmodern critique. Anthropologists taking this route urged a more self-conscious consideration of the entailments of ethnographic writing and the position of the anthropologist vis-à-vis anthropological subjects. From outside the United States, the writings of scholars from subaltern studies and other fields drew pointed attention to the erasure of indigenous voices that had occurred and continued to occur in Western scholarship.[46] Concern with positionality pointed legal anthropologists to consider how the politics of identity in general are constructed in, through or in spite of law—and how imposition of law can also flatten or obliterate alternative viewpoints, frequently those of the disempowered or marginalized. Legal anthropologists went on to use postmodern perspectives to track the impact of law on identity and rights claims at an international or global level.[47]

Another important development within legal anthropology during the 1980s was the emergence of legal language as a topic for ethnographic research. This was related to the concomitant rise of power as a theme, because the same body of social theory that redefined and then elevated power as a central issue for social research also focused on language and discourse, arguing that language was the key medium through which relationships of power were mediated—particularly in legal settings.[48] Legal discourse studies made important contributions both within anthropology and within the interdisciplinary law and society community; it would be accurate to describe this area as a distinct tradition within the subdiscipline of legal anthropology, one that continued through the 1990s.[49]

---

[44]   June Starr and Jane Collier (eds), *History and Power in the Study of Law: New Directions in Legal Anthropology* (Ithaca, NY: Cornell University Press 1989).

[45]   Carol J. Greenhouse, Barbara Yngvesson and David M. Engel, *Law and Community in Three American Towns* (Ithaca, NY: Cornell University Press 1994).

[46]   See note 43. See also Partha Chatterjee, *The Nation and its Fragments: Colonial and Postcolonial Histories* (Princeton: Princeton University Press 1993); Rahajit Guha, *A Subaltern Studies Reader, 1986–1995* (Minneapolis: University of Minnesota Press 1997); Homi K. Babha, *The Location of Culture* (London: Routledge 1994).

[47]   See, e.g., Rosemary Coombe, *The Cultural Life of Intellectual Properties: Authorship, Appropriation, and the Law* (Durham: Duke University Press 1998); Annelise Riles, *The Network Inside Out* (Ann Arbor, MI: University of Michigan Press 2000).

[48]   See, e.g., James Clifford, *The Predicament of Culture: Twentieth-Century Ethnography, Literature, and Art* (Cambridge, MA: Harvard University Press 1988); Susan Gooding, 'Place, Race, and Names: Layered Identities in *U.S. v. Oregon*', 28 *Law & Society Review* 1181–229 (1994).

[49]   William O'Barr, *Linguistic Evidence: Language, Power, and Strategy in the Courtroom* (New York: Academic Press 1982); Elizabeth Mertz, 'Legal Language: Pragmatics, Poetics, and Social Power', 23 *Annual Review of Anthropology* 435–55 (1994). For later scholarship in the area, see John Conley and William M. O'Barr, *Just Words: Law, Language, and Power* (Chicago: University of Chicago Press 1998); Susan Hirsch, *Pronouncing and Persevering: Gender and the Discourses of Disputing in an African Islamic Court* (Chicago: University of Chicago Press 1998);

3 CURRENT AND FUTURE DIRECTIONS

3.1 The Integrative Study of Law across Cultures

The period from 1990 through the present has seen the development of an increasingly complex and integrative approach to studying law within legal anthropology. Where earlier anthropologists spent energy debating whether cultural ideas or social power were primary in shaping legal developments, the newer generation recognized the importance of both—and set about studying the complicated picture that emerged from this recognition. In a similar spirit, legal anthropologists sought to move beyond the division between studying local dynamics and studying wider—even global—patterns. Their long-standing familiarity with cross-cultural analysis (and attendant dilemmas) has provided a disciplinary advantage in efforts to decipher global legal patterns as they play out in local settings.

However, as some of the focus has shifted toward globalization, legal and other anthropologists have had to develop new methods, integrating the 'gold standard' approach provided by long-term fieldwork with new, creative means for tracking the flow of legal developments across the world. From this global perspective, anthropologists have also been able to offer critiques of the spread of Western-influenced legal forms and ideologies—including ideological approaches to conflict, consensus and context in legal settings. Finally, all of these trends in legal anthropology have contributed to growing awareness of the dynamics surrounding the imposition of power, and resistance to power, that surround law at the nexus of local and larger patterns. Some have urged a new 'engaged' anthropology that situates anthropologists more actively within these dynamics. In the following sections we will examine each of these themes, which together point toward future directions for research in legal anthropology.

3.2 Complex Visions of Law: The Dialogue with Critical and European Social Theory and Semiotics

In her Huxley Memorial Lecture, 'Certainties Undone: Fifty Turbulent Years of Legal Anthropology, 1949–1999', Sally Falk Moore identified three major approaches to law within legal anthropology: law as culture, law as domination and law as problem-solver.[50] In addition to their roots in anthropological research, these diverse conceptualizations draw from different strains of European social theory. One could look to Durkheim and Max Weber (1864–1920) for idealist threads, to Karl Marx (1818–83) and his followers for a materialist emphasis on power and the role of economic factors, and to Weberian

Elizabeth Mertz, *The Language of Law School: Learning to 'Think Like a Lawyer'* (Oxford: Oxford University Press (2007); Kwai Ng, *The Common Law in Two Voices: Language, Law and the Post-Colonial Predicament in Hong Kong* (Stanford: Stanford University Press 2009); Susan Philips, *Ideology in the Language of Judges: How Judges Practice Law, Politics, and Courtroom Control* (New York: Oxford University Press 1998); Justin Richland, *Arguing with Tradition: The Language of Law in Hopi Tribal Court* (Chicago: University of Chicago Press 2008).
   [50]   Sally Falk Moore, *Law and Anthropology: A Reader* (Oxford: Blackwell 2004).

analyses of modernity for rationalist and functionalist visions of law.[51] (Of course, this would oversimplify the work of all three theorists considerably.) The sometimes-fierce divisions within anthropology between adherents of these approaches through the 1970s have eased to some degree now, producing interestingly nuanced accounts of how culture and power intertwine in the workings of law.

Here again we can recognize debts to European social theorists such as Michel Foucault (1926–84), Antonio Gramsci (1891–1937), Jacques Derrida (1930–2004), Jürgen Habermas and Pierre Bourdieu (1930–2002)—but legal anthropologists have made a distinctive contribution in their ethnographically grounded accounts of the complex dynamics at work. As part of this integrative vision, legal anthropologists have also incorporated semiotic and linguistic perspectives so that they can analyze the interplay of legal and other discourses that so often bring law to life on the ground.[52] Susan Hirsch, for example, shows how litigants draw on the discourses of Islamic law, Swahili ethics, spiritual health and state law in negotiating deeply gendered marital disputes in a Kenyan court.[53] Charles Briggs and Clara Mantini-Briggs dissect the discourses surrounding the prosecution of a young indigenous woman for infanticide in Venezuela.[54] These analyses take culture, power, language, material resources and politics quite seriously as they work toward an anthropology of law that is adequate to the complex world it seeks to understand.

3.3   The Globalization of Law and of Anthropological Methods

During the 1990s and into the beginning of the new century, legal anthropologists have also turned their attention to much larger research frameworks in order to study the relationship between globalization, transnationalism and law's currents—following paradigm-shifting work along these lines within anthropology more generally by scholars such as Arjun Appadurai.[55] This research led to contributions to the growing body of critical globalization studies, sometimes drawing on postmodern approaches.[56] It also moved legal anthropologists further in the ongoing task of finding methods and models for studying the many-leveled links between local and larger legal processes.

Some scholars have focused on the impact of law in shaping and responding to the movement of people, capital, and cultural ideologies across national boundaries. Susan Coutin, for example, studied how Salvadoran immigrants to the United States negotiated their identities in the United States in light of legal developments in both El Salvador and

---

[51]   For an overview see, e.g., Stewart Macaulay, Lawrence M. Friedman and Elizabeth Mertz, *Law in Action: A Socio-Legal Reader* 186–95 (New York: Foundation Press 2007).

[52]   John Bowen, *Islam, Law, and Equality in Indonesia: An Anthropology of Public Reasoning* (Cambridge: Cambridge University Press 2003).

[53]   Hirsch (note 49).

[54]   Charles Briggs and Clara Mantini-Briggs, '"Bad Mothers" and the Threat to Civil Society: Race, Cultural Reasoning, and the Institutionalization of Social Inequality in a Venezuelan Infanticide Trial', 25 *Law and Social Inquiry* 299–354 (2000).

[55]   Arjun Appadurai, *Modernity at Large: Cultural Dimensions of Globalization* (Minneapolis: University of Minnesota Press 1996).

[56]   William Maurer, *Recharting the Caribbean: Land, Law, and Citizenship in the British Virgin Islands* (Ann Arbor: University of Michigan Press 1997); Riles (note 45).

the US, while Yngvesson examined the process of transnational adoption.[57] Others have focused on the local impacts of multiple layers of law and legal discourse, from international human rights discourses to national and local law—often finding that the consequences of law on the ground differ significantly from stated or intended goals.[58] There is also renewed interest in the ways that both old and new methodologies can be used to track law through its transnational and multi-scalar articulations.[59] Anthropologists whose research questions require them to follow movements of legal developments beyond local boundaries are experimenting with 'multi-sited' methods; these methodologies work across multiple locations while still attempting to retain the anthropological requirement of significant engagement with the local fields under study.[60]

3.4 Rethinking Conflict, Consensus and Context

The move to a global level clearly requires some new approaches to theorizing the contexts of law. Legal anthropologists studying global processes have documented and critiqued the export of Western legal models to other parts of the world. Nader, for example, has sharply criticized the export of US-derived 'harmony' models to other parts of the world.[61] Legal technologies such as alternative dispute resolution (ADR), including mediation, can act to further disempower already marginalized people and to silence disputes whose full expression might further the ends of justice. Western legal exports are also frequently insensitive to local contexts, and anthropologists are uniquely positioned to analyze the results of this insensitivity.

3.5 Law, Resistance and 'Engaged' Anthropology

A continuing challenge for legal anthropologists charting the seemingly unstoppable imposition of elite and capitalist power and law across the world has been to find modes of analysis that do not minimize the impact of global capitalism yet also acknowledge points of resistance and local autonomy. Anthropologists who have led the way in this regard include John and Jean Comaroff, Susan Coutin, and Mindie Lazarus-Black; the work of political scientist James Scott is also frequently cited on this point.[62] All of the

---

[57] Susan Coutin, *Legalizing Moves: Salvadoran Immigrants' Struggle for U.S. Residency* (Ann Arbor: University of Michigan Press 2000); Barbara Yngvesson, 'Placing the Gift Child in Transnational Adoption', 36 *Law & Society Review* 227–56 (2002).

[58] Mark Goodale, *Surrendering to Utopia: An Anthropology of Human Rights* (Stanford: Stanford University Press 2009); ibid., 'The Globalization of Sympathetic Law and Its Consequences', 27 *Law and Social Inquiry* 401–15 (2002).

[59] See June Starr and Mark Goodale (eds), *Practicing Ethnography in Law: New Dialogues, Enduring Methods* (New York: Palgrave/St. Martin's Press 2002); Mark Goodale and Sally Engle Merry (eds.), *The Practice of Human Rights: Tracking Law between the Global and the Local* (Cambridge: Cambridge University Press 2007).

[60] Sally Engle Merry, 'Crossing Boundaries: Methodological Challenges for Ethnography in the Twenty-First Century', 23 *Political and Legal Anthropology Review* 127–34 (2000).

[61] Nader (note 18).

[62] Comaroff and Comaroff (note 27); Coutin (note 57); Mindie Lazarus-Black, *Legitimate Acts and Illegal Encounters: Law and Society in Antigua and Barbuda* (Washington, DC: Smithsonian

themes discussed in this section come together in attempts to resolve this issue; integrative approaches are necessary to map the complex confluence of dynamics involved, while awareness of global patterns—as well as rethinking notions of conflict and context—are also frequently required.[63]

In addition, legal anthropologists have not been simply interested in the relationship between global flows, power and law as a matter of intellectual urgency. Rather, scholars have increasingly explored the ways in which their research findings could form part of wider strategies of resistance to injustice, both through the use of law and legal institutions where appropriate, but also by challenging law when it serves as a foundation for domination. The rise of a more engaged legal anthropology has been partly reflected in the emergence of the anthropology of human rights as an area for research and, at times, in activism by anthropologists concerned with the plight of indigenous populations, cultural minorities and other oppressed populations. On the one hand, there have been some challenges to the perceived dominance of 'power'[64] as an explanatory mechanism in studies of law and its language. On the other hand, some have argued for an epistemology in which the social scientific study of law is linked to law's capacities for resistance and emancipation, thus keeping power as a central focus.

3.6   Directions for Future Research

It seems likely that these themes will remain important foci for future work in legal anthropology. As globalization continues to expand, integrative models and methods emanating from legal anthropology represent a cutting edge for social scientists seeking to track the multi-layered flow of power and legal forms across cultures and societies.[65] At the same time, the analytical categories of 'power' and 'context' in legal anthropology will require further development, taking into account critiques that argue against overly determinist or simplistic models. Anthropologists studying law and politics in the global north are also bringing their characteristic ethnographic vision to issues more typically studied by sociologists, such as crime and bureaucracy.[66] Moreover, there will undoubtedly be a continued push toward an engaged anthropology, 'reinventing' anew a time-honored

---

Press 1994); see James C. Scott, *Weapons of the Weak: Everyday Forms of Peasant Resistance* (New Haven, CT: Yale University Press 1985); id., *Domination and the Arts of Resistance: Hidden Transcripts* (New Haven: Yale University Press 1990); id., *Seeing Like a State: How Certain Schemes to Improve the Human Condition Have Failed* (New Haven: Yale University Press 1998).

[63]   Mindie Lazarus-Black and Susan Hirsch (eds), *Contested States: Law, Hegemony, and Resistance* (New York: Routledge 1994).

[64]   See Marianne Constable, *Just Silences: The Limits and Possibilities of Modern Law* (Princeton, NJ: Princeton University Press 2005).

[65]   For example, ethnographies examine how immigrants can challenge yet live in the shadow of laws governing citizenship and migration. See, e.g., Susan Bibler Coutin, *Nations of Emigrants: Shifting Boundaries of Citizenship in El Salvador and the United States* (Ithaca, NY: Cornell University Press 2007); Ruth Mandel, *Cosmopolitan Anxieties: Turkish Challenges to Citizenship and Belonging in Turkey* (Durham, NC: Duke University Press 2008).

[66]   See thematic sections on these topics in 34 *PoLAR: Political and Legal Anthropology Review* 6–94 (2011) (bureaucracy); 32 ibid. 47–85, 105–23; Association for Political and Legal Anthropology, 'Spillover' Conversations, http://aaanet.org/sections/apla/spillover.html (PoLAR's open access webpage).

concern in anthropology.[67] As legal anthropologists work in new ways with indigenous peoples and others affected by current legal trends, they will have to move into a more complicated engagement with issues such as international human rights, the role of the state and responding to violence and war.[68] Here theory, ethnography, method and legal practice come together in an exciting nexus in which all can be enriched.

FURTHER READING

Donovan, James (2008). *Legal Anthropology: An Introduction*. Lanham, MD: AltaMira Press.

French, Jan (2009). *Legalizing Identities: Becoming Black or Indian in Brazil's Northeast*. Chapel Hill: University of North Carolina Press.

French, Rebecca (1996). 'Of Narrative in Law and Anthropology', 30 *Law & Society Review* 417.

Greenhouse, Carol, Elizabeth Mertz and Kay Warren (eds) (2002). *Ethnography in Unstable Places: Everyday Lives in Contexts of Dramatic Political Change*. Durham, NC: Duke University Press.

Griffiths, John (1986). 'What is Legal Pluralism?' 24 *Journal of Legal Pluralism* 1–55.

Just, Peter (1992). 'History, Power, Ideology, and Culture: Current Directions in the Anthropology of Law', 26 *Law & Society Review* 373–412.

Merry, Sally Engle (1988). 'Legal Pluralism', 22 *Law & Society Review* 869–96.

Merry, Sally Engle (1992). 'Anthropology, Law, and Transnational Processes', 21 *Annual Review of Anthropology* 357–79.

Roberts, Simon (1979). *Order and Dispute: An Introduction to Legal Anthropology*. New York: St Martin's Press.

Strathern, Marilyn (2001). 'The Patent and the Malanggan', 18 *Theory, Culture and Society* 1–26.

Wilson, Richard A. (ed.) (1997). *Human Rights, Culture and Context: Anthropological Perspectives*. London: Pluto Press

---

[67] Dell Hymes (ed.), *Reinventing Anthropology* (New York: Pantheon 1972).

[68] For example, anthropologists have debated the role of anthropological knowledge in 'the war on terror' and actual ground war through the 'human terrain system'. David Price, 'Past Wars, Present Dangers, Future Anthropologies', 18 *Anthropology Today* 3–5 (2002); Jeffrey Sluka, 'Curiouser and Curiouser: Montgomery McFate's Strange Interpretation of the Relationship between Anthropology and Counterinsurgency', 33:S1 *PoLAR: Political and Legal Anthropology Review* 99–115 (2010); American Anthropological Association, American Anthropological Association Executive Board Statement on the Human Terrain System Project (31 Oct. 2007), http://www.aaanet.org/about/Policies/statements/Human-Terrain-System-Statement.cfm.

5 Comparative law and economics: accounting for social norms

*Francesco Parisi and Barbara Luppi**

1 COMPARATIVE LAW AND ECONOMICS[1]

Unlike prior methodological trends in comparative law, the methodology of comparative law and economics is here to stay.[2] The findings of comparative law and economics are increasingly influential among academics and policymakers alike. It is probably the most successful example of the recent expansion of law and economics into areas that were once considered beyond the realm of economic analysis. In an historical perspective, law and economics has affected legal studies beyond its planned ambitions. The introduction of economics into the study of law has irreversibly transformed traditional legal methodology. Contrary to the Langdellian law school tradition, which developed a self-contained framework of case analysis and classification, law and economics examined legal rules as a working system. Economics complemented legal analysis, by providing the analytical rigor necessary for the study of the vast body of legal rules present in a modern legal system.

As pointed out by Francesco Parisi and Barbara Luppi (2012), comparative law and economics has also attracted several criticisms and generated academic skepticism. The critiques point to the many misuses of economic analysis in comparative law. In Section 1 of this chapter, we wish to shed some light on the multi-faceted structure of the comparative law and economics method, providing an assessment of the debate on the merits of this methodology.

1.1 Theory

Much of the work in comparative law and economics builds on the findings of comparative law by identifying interesting legal issues and analyzing them using an economic framework. Comparative law provides a very fertile ground for the economist in searching for interesting issues to analyze. The fact that legal systems choose different solutions to common legal problems indicates that there is no single best rule to resolve the issue in

* Francesco Parisi is the Oppenheimer Wolff and Donnelly Professor of Law, University of Minnesota and a Professor of Economics, University of Bologna. He is also co-series editor of the Elgar Research Handbooks in Comparative Law.

Barbara Luppi is a Research Scholar in the Department of Political Economy, University of Modena and Reggio Emilia.

1   This section is drawn from Parisi (2007) and Parisi and Luppi (2012).

2   The methodology of comparative law and economics has been at the same time influential and controversial. For a survey of the literature, see De Geest (2009); De Geest and van den Bergh (2004); Mattei (1997).

question. In situations like these, economics provides valuable techniques for assessing the comparative advantages and effects of alternative legal rules.

Methodologically, comparative law and economics applies the conceptual apparatus and empirical methods of economics to the study of comparative law and legal systems. The primary hypothesis advanced by positive economic analysis of law is the notion that efficiency shapes the rules, procedures and institutions of the common law. The efficiency hypothesis provides an interesting lens for historical and comparative legal analysis, especially with respect to judge-made law.[3] According to this positive approach, wealth maximization becomes an explanation of the development of the (common) law. According to the law and economics approach, individuals are assumed to be rational, meaning they aim to maximize their wealth.[4] Law and economics focuses on law as an instrument for affecting the relative prices attached to alternative individual actions. The change of a rule of law modifies the relative price structure and thus the constraint of the optimization problem, affecting human behavior. Wealth maximization, which legal rules promote or constrain, serves as a paradigm for the analysis of law.

While positive approaches to law and economics provide a descriptive statement of a law's incentive effects,[5] normative approaches take the analysis one step further and attempt to identify and select policy goals through economic analysis and to provide a prescriptive statement as to what the law should be.[6] The normative school posits that market failures require legal intervention and that economic analysis is the best method for identifying market failures and selecting a law to remedy the resulting harms. Within the normative approach, we find important methodological differences amongst scholars. Since normative analysis is concerned with identifying and comparing laws based on their efficacy, it may be helpful first to identify factors these researchers use to measure and determine each law's respective value. The variable chosen to measure and improve law is called the maximand. Policymakers and economists have a bevy of options at hand, the three most common being wealth, utility and happiness.[7] Additionally, the law and

---

[3] The basic intuition on which the efficiency hypothesis rests is that inefficient rules impose greater costs on the parties than do efficient rules, thereby making the stakes in a dispute higher (Priest 1977). In recent years, a new generation of literature, developed at the interface of law, economics and public choice theory, has provided an alternative hypothesis regarding the evolution of the common law. For example, Fon and Parisi (2003) built upon existing literature on the evolution of judicially created law, considering a model of legal evolution in which judges have varying ideologies and propensities to extend the domain of legal remedies and causes of action. See also Parisi and Fon (2009).

[4] In the early years of law and economics, legal scholars had not immediately accepted the objective of wealth maximization as an ancillary paradigm of justice. Although many differences dissipated gradually over time, two objections are still affecting the lines of the debate. The first objective points out the need to specify an initial set of individual entitlements or rights as a prerequisite for operationalizing wealth maximization. The second focuses on the theoretical difficulty of defining efficiency as an ingredient of justice vis-à-vis other social goals. Guido Calabresi (1980) claims that an increase in wealth cannot constitute social improvement unless it is allowed to reach some other goal, such as equality.

[5] The so-called Chicago School, whose foundations relied on the work carried out by Richard Posner in the 1970s, was heavily involved in developing the positive approach to law and economics.

[6] See Parisi (2004) for a detailed discussion of the alternative schools in law and economics.

[7] Wealth is the easiest category to measure and the paradigm of wealth maximization is therefore preferred for implementation in a policy setting. For example, remedies based on pecuniary

economics methodology requires the adoption of a criterion for the aggregation of individual preferences into social preferences.[8]

The functional school approaches law and economics in a very different manner than both the normative and positive schools and it rejects many of their initial assumptions. The functional approach looks to the revealed choices and preferences of individuals interacting with law as the fundamental criterion for the evaluation of a law's efficacy. When individuals have a choice between two different legal schemes (such as liquidated damages versus court-imposed damages), a market for the selection of legal rules arises. When rational participants are given the choice between legal schemes in a market format, they will choose the law that provides them with the most benefit. Functionalist scholars, therefore, focus on 'sources of law' for analysis rather than substantive legal alternatives. In recent years, scholars of the functional school in law and economics have directed their attention to the study of law as a product. These contributions are of great theoretical and practical importance.[9] Through comparative analysis, functional scholars identify both political failures in the formation of law and market failures that individuals correct through selection of different legal schemes. From that standpoint, scholars in the functional school are less interested in maximizing aggregate wealth, utility or happiness, but instead attempt to develop meta-rules that foster the free individual choice of different legal schemes to create a market-like mechanism in the creation and selection of legal rules.

---

damages are easier to calculate than remedies based on loss of utility or happiness. In contract law, the adoption of a wealth measure allows researchers to determine wealth distribution between parties and the default pecuniary consequences induce parties to fulfill contractual obligations unless it becomes more efficient to breach. Wealth, however, only captures one dimension of social welfare and one cannot use it as a reliable proxy for social well-being in all areas of the law. For example, in criminal law, the damages caused by crimes cannot be evaluated correctly based on wealth transfer. A thief causes a loss that is often equivalent to the benefit that the thief gains. Thus, the new wealth effects of a theft are often zero. Other factors, however, affect the policy choice to prosecute theft.

[8]   The Pareto criterion constitutes the simplest method of aggregating social welfare. An optimal Pareto allocation maximizes the well-being of one individual while keeping the well-being of other individuals constant. Alternatively, the Pareto criterion rejects policy that would harm one individual regardless of the net gain for all other relevant parties.

However, the Pareto criterion may not be the correct variable to use because it does not capture cardinal preferences or the intensity with which society benefits from the policy change. Other aggregation methods are the Kaldor-Hicks criterion, which uses a linear summation method for aggregating social utility that captures cardinal preferences, or the Nash criterion, which uses a non-linear multiplication. In the Kaldor-Hicks aggregation, a policy change is efficient if the gainers gain more than the losers lose. Contrary to the Pareto and Kaldor-Hicks criteria, the Nash aggregation criterion rejects the notion that social welfare maximization requires purely the maximization of total payoffs. The Nash function judges the overall well-being of society in relation to its weakest member and measures aggregate wealth, utility or happiness, taking into account relative disparities amongst society members.

[9]   In a recent volume, Parisi (2011) collects original contributions from several scholars who have been protagonists in this trend in the literature. The contributions offer a sampling of the functionalist approach with a comparative evaluation of the alternative sources of law, focusing on the characteristics of specific instruments of legal intervention and on broader topics such as conflict of law, federalism, regulatory competition, and law and development.

1.2   Empirical Testing

Normative, positive and functional theorists attempt to formulate hypotheses that provide a testable prediction. Empirical law and economics applies econometric analysis, involving statistical methods and other research tools, to economic theory.[10] Analysts need empirical data to test theoretical hypotheses. They will select a method for gathering the data set that best fits their hypothesis. One of the main problems affecting empirical analysis relates to the availability and quality of the data. Data can be collected either at the macro level, that is, at an aggregate level (such as a country or regional level) or at the micro level, that is, at the single unit of observation (either the consumer or the firm). Microeconomic data are crucial to measuring the reaction of an economic agent (a consumer or a firm) to exogenous changes in economic policy and legislation. For example, the researcher can use them to estimate the consumer's sensitivity to the introduction of a tax or the change in a tortfeasor's level of precaution if courts impose a stricter liability rule. Microeconomic data are essential to calibrate economic policies and estimate the impact of legislation changes on individual choices. However, microeconomic data are difficult to collect and are less reliable than other data, since they are more vulnerable to measurement errors.

Researchers frequently use cross-country comparisons to validate theoretical results with empirical testing. For example, they may calibrate economic analysis to capture specific country responsiveness to exogenous changes of the law. Researchers have constructed cross-country data sets to test the efficiency hypothesis for the common law, since they can compare common law and civil law countries.[11] When constructing a data set, scholars may face the problem of a scarcity of data and may encounter difficulties finding variables that correctly measure the phenomenon under analysis.[12] To estimate the role of legal families on the effectiveness of financial systems, Rafael La Porta and colleagues (1998) constructed a unique measure, classifying each country based on the origin of its legal system, distinguishing between civil law and common law countries.

Empirical works aim at testing theoretical models based on real world data, in order to evaluate the ability of theory to predict real world phenomena. Methodologically, empirical analysis tests for the presence of significant relationships between variables identified by theoretical models. It allows researchers to calibrate their models for the estimation of agents' reactions to (exogenous) changes in the relevant variables driving economic or social phenomena, such as a change in the law, the quality of legal enforcement, the economic determinants of markets or an economic policy. La Porta and co-authors (1997, 1998) found that the legal system adopted in many developing countries often

---

[10]   See Greene (2002) for a detailed discussion on econometric methodology.

[11]   La Porta, Lopez de Silanes, Shleifer and Vishny (1997, 1998) proposed the first empirical analysis of the common law efficiency hypothesis. They examined the role of the origin of a country's law on the effectiveness of its financial systems, focusing on a subset of specific rules, such as investor protections against expropriation by insiders and the quality of legal enforcement.

[12]   For example, in La Porta, Lopez de Silanes, Shleifer and Vishny (1997) macroeconomic data are employed in the absence of microeconomic data for the access to credit of individual firms, such as an individual firm's bank debt or commercial debt. The effectiveness of each financial system has been proxied by three macroeconomic variables.

shares a legal origin with its respective European colonizer, which imposed the same or a similar legal system through occupation and colonization. Their empirical work establishes that legal origin significantly affects legal protections for investors and the quality of enforcement. In particular, common law countries protect both shareholders and creditors more than civil law countries and have better enforcement quality. Additionally, civil law countries have weaker investor protections and less developed capital markets compared to common law countries. They interpret this evidence as support for the common law efficiency hypothesis.

The evolution of a phenomenon over time is another relevant dimension in empirical studies. Time series studies provide useful empirical data by quantifying a change in a variable over a historical period. For example, a researcher could compare how a legal system evolves towards efficiency. While time series studies may not suffer from some of the pitfalls of cross-country comparisons, they can easily be affected by extraneous variables. The level of efficiency achieved in a jurisdiction may experience a drop because the policymaker reduces the amount of resources channeled to the courts in a period of severe recession, regardless of the prevailing judicial orientation in the application of the law. Statistical techniques are available for isolating the effects of multiple variables (for example, by looking at how judicial orientation on the application of a specific rule has changed over time in jurisdictions where financial resources to courts were not modified) to provide more accurate estimates of the effects of specific explanatory variables. By doing so, the researcher limits the number of hidden extraneous variables that might affect the data. Panel data measure changes across jurisdictions and over time. This can help isolate some of these extraneous variables. For instance, if the same drastic net decrease in the use of a specific exception to a rule happened in two jurisdictions with substantially different financial resources during the same period, we could conclude that some alternative variable was skewing the data.[13]

Mapping the theoretical hypothesis onto the real data set is a crucial aspect of statistical methodology. In the illustrative example used here, this means that the common law efficiency hypothesis should be interpreted based on the available data. Anthony Niblett and colleagues (2010) adopt two alternative views of efficiency. Under a strict view of efficiency, convergence requires only the application of the economic loss rule, while under a broader view of efficiency, generally recognized exceptions are accepted for evaluating convergence towards efficiency.[14]

Empirical testing of a hypothesis sometimes leads to findings that run contrary to conventional economic theories. A variety of constraints and incentives affect human

---

[13]   Niblett, Posner and Shleifer (2010) investigate the evolution of the common law efficiency hypothesis over time. The authors focus their attention on a subset of cases relative to the application of the economic loss rule in construction disputes. They constructed a panel data set of 461 state court appellate decisions from 1970 to 2005. To evaluate the efficiency of the common law system in business law, they tallied the use of exceptions to the economic loss rule by appellate courts in tort claims. They identified two categories of exceptions: 'generally recognized exceptions' (that is, those widely accepted in the majority of jurisdictions), and 'idiosyncratic exceptions' (that is, those applied only to a limited number of cases or by a few jurisdictions).

[14]   Contrary to La Porta, Lopez de Silanes, Shleifer and Vishny (1997, 1998), Niblett, Posner and Shleifer (2010) find the evidence to be unsupportive of the common law efficiency hypothesis in the field of business law.

behavior; law is only one of them. Economics provides a method for understanding the incentive effects of alternative laws, while other instruments may help us understand other constraints and incentives found throughout society. Therefore, the interaction between economists and other theorists becomes crucial. Scholars from the disciplines of sociology and anthropology utilize their tools to explain how law and norms interact, the study of which is termed 'law and society'. Those scholars might study how laws could affect different communities where non-legal norms already address the behavior. In Section 2, we will explore these important interactions, with special attention to social norms.

2 ACCOUNTING FOR SOCIAL NORMS: EXPERIMENTAL AND EMPIRICAL EVIDENCE

Recent comparative law and economics literature utilizes quantitative methods to evaluate the effectiveness of alternative laws and legal institutions. The effectiveness of the law critically hinges upon compliance. Legal policymakers announce the consequences of a violation of law by threatening sanctions or promising rewards. The extent to which sanctions or rewards are actually imposed depends on the level of legal enforcement. Legal policymakers create incentives for compliance by selecting the severity of legal sanctions or the magnitude of rewards and by setting levels of legal enforcement.

Deterrence theory assumes that higher expected punishments (the combination of severity and probability of punishment) produce higher deterrence. Enforcement is generally imperfect since not all behavior is observed; hence, sanctions and rewards are administered with uncertainty. The expected legal sanction (reward) affects individual private incentives through a change in expected costs (benefits) of legal compliance. Deterrence theory assumes that individuals make a calculated and rational decision, weighing the pros and cons of specific activities under the law. Note however that many acts are committed under exceptional circumstances and contingent factors may overshadow a rational calculation of costs and benefits.

Whether through threats or promises, the effects of the law depend on the actual level of enforcement. Legal theorists believed that a law without enforcement was equivalent to a law without a sanction (*lex imperfecta*) and was doomed to be ineffective. However, recent legal and economic literature has shown that the effects of a law are not limited to the creation of incentives through the enforcement of legal sanctions. Law conveys social values to society. According to expressive law theories and focal-point theories of law (Cooter 1998, 2000; McAdams 2000a, 2000b), law plays an expressive role in society. To the extent that the values expressed by the law are internalized, private enforcement and compliance become possible even in the absence of central legal enforcement. Self-compliance stems from the internalization of the rule and the resulting first-party enforcement.

Individual values and social norms of conduct influence human behavior. Personal values represent an individual's expressed value judgments, identifying what someone should and should not be allowed to do. Individuals willfully behave according to their personal values and impose sanctions on violators of private norms. Personal values and norms provide private incentives to individuals, affecting the payoff associated with a given behavior. Alternatively, social norms identify frequency distributions of individual values and norms in the population, indicating private values and norms more frequently adopted by individuals in the population. Hence, the exogenous restrictions imposed by legal rules may not be the only driving force behind individual behavior; private and social norms also substantially influence an individual's choices.

This chapter examines the determinants of self-compliance with rules in the absence of legal enforcement. Self-compliance with the law refers to the effects of first-party enforcement, where individuals withhold action because of their preference for law-abiding behavior, even if the rule lacks external enforcement. Current legal and economic theory adopts the term 'first-party enforcement' to refer to situations where the subject of the law faces a conditional cost in case of violation of the law in the form of guilt or shame. These conditional costs stem from an honor system of 'upright conduct', in which compliance with the rules stands as an ethical imperative.

Unlike the direct incentives created through second-party and third-party enforcement (for example, legal sanctions, financial rewards or reputational sanctions), the degree of internalization and self-compliance with law varies extensively across individuals. Furthermore, the interaction of social norms and legal rules influences human behavior in a complex and non-linear way. Law gives incentives to individuals that do not add linearly to private moral incentives provided by internalized norms. Legal rules reflect the social values and opinions of the population when they coincide with prevailing social norms. Legal rules reflecting social values and norms receive public support that reinforces underlying individual opinions in the population.

Law plays an expressive role in society (Cooter 1998, 2000), in the sense that it supports pre-existing opinions in the population. We will discuss in detail the concept of expressive law in Section 2.1. However, legal rules may not necessarily coincide and may conflict with private norms. In these cases, legal rules may trigger opposition. Individuals may choose to openly violate the legal rule through civil disobedience. They may also express their public dissent to others, triggering a wave of protest against a newly introduced legal rule. Civil disobedience and protest may trigger support for social values and norms contrary to existing legal rules and induce crowding-out effects on individual incentives. These forms of protest are also called 'countervailing norms' and will be discussed in Section 2.2.

An extensive research program in empirical and experimental law and economics has tried to identify types of interactions between legal and social norms. Psychological research attempts to identify the factors that affect the individual's degree of self-compliance with the law. An individual's level of education, religion, understanding of the rule, ability to exercise self-control and attitude towards society may each affect the degree of self-compliance of that individual with the law. Recent research developments in psychology, economics and law have studied the importance of behavioral and psychological traits on the effectiveness of deterrence, pointing out the need for a deeper understanding of the interaction of social and psychological factors and their effect on levels of self-compliance.

The psychological literature has investigated the deterrence issue, reaching consensus on a number of stylized facts. When a punishment (whether a fine, a freedom restriction or a generally negative consequence) is imposed on a human behavior, it produces a reduction in that particular behavior. This behavior tends to reappear when the punishment is removed. The effectiveness of the punishment depends on several factors, such as the severity of the punishment or the certainty (probability) of the punishment. Also relevant is whether the punishment is associated with a stimulus or only with the actual materialization of the targeted behavior. Individuals tend to adapt to the punishment, thereby reducing its effectiveness over time. Psychological evidence suggests that individuals do not always make rational choices in many areas of human behavior. Criminal activity often occurs in the presence of deviating behaviors such as drug and alcohol abuse. Smoking, alcohol abuse and drug use can be partially explained by the presence of bounded rationality, lack of willpower or more complex factors such as addiction. Evidence from the literature in psychology suggests that the application of incentive protocols to population-based policies with regard to health habits may have stronger effects than policies based on deterrence. By exploiting the intuition of the incentive mechanism examined by economic theory, incentive protocols are flexible and more manageable than fixed regulations and preserve freedom of choice (Sindelar 2008).

According to psychological research, the introduction of a punishment changes each individual's perception of the environment in which he or she operates. Concerning economic theory, Uri Gneezy and Aldo Rustichini (2000) suggested that we may interpret the environment (either real or experimental) as an incomplete contract. The introduction of a punishment or reward, contingent on performance or compliance, into an incomplete contract reshapes the individual's perception of that contract, and different individuals will reorient in different ways. This informational effect is added to the direct incentive effect, and may reduce or substantially alter the effectiveness of the punishment introduced, depending on the overall trends in adaptation. For example, Gneezy and Rustichini (2000) presented a field study in day-care centers where a fine was introduced that penalized parents who arrived late to pick up their children. The authors found that deterrence theory was violated and that the introduction of a fine actually increased the frequency of the unwanted behavior. Therefore, deterrence theory may be undermined when the complexity of the environment is not fully considered. The consequence of a delayed pickup of a child was not specified in the contract between the parents and the day-care center. The contract was incomplete and parents acted based on their own belief regarding the occurrence of arriving late. The introduction of the fine, therefore, modified the environment. The authors offered an additional explanation based on social norms. In the absence of the fine for late pickup, parents could have interpreted the teachers' behavior as a 'generous, non-market activity'. Parents obeyed an ethical imperative, believing that they should not take advantage of the teachers' patience by arriving late. The introduction of the fine may have changed the social norm by allowing the parents to perceive the fine as a price for tardiness. Parents may feel less guilty when tardy since they have compensated the teacher (whose actions are no longer generous, non-market activity) by paying the fine.

2.1   Expressive Law

Law and economics scholars have conducted an in-depth analysis of the role of social norms in deterrence theory while recognizing that the concept of the social norm is also at the core of sociological theory. According to James Coleman (1990: 293), 'a norm concerning a specific action exists when the socially defined right to control the action is held not by the actor but by the others'. Coleman states that the authority of the others is created by social consensus, giving members of the community the power to enforce the norm by an external sanctioning system. When the norm is internalized, an inner sanctioning system is triggered. This sanctioning system represents a form of first-party enforcement and may lead to self-compliance.[15]

Individual values and social norms of conduct, therefore, influence human behavior. Personal values represent the value judgments expressed by an individual, identifying what she should and should not be allowed to do.[16] Individuals are willing to behave according to their personal values and to impose sanctions on violators of private norms. Personal values and norms provide private incentives to individuals, affecting the payoff associated with their behavior. Social norms identify frequency distributions of individual values and norms in the population, indicating private values and norms adopted more frequently by individuals in the population.

In first-party enforcement, internalization and personal ethics play a critical role. In second-party enforcement, face-to-face interactions instead become the crux, while third-party enforcement requires the involvement of communities. Expressive law literature has thus far focused on the role of law in affecting incentives through second- and third-party enforcement.

Economic research aims to isolate the effects of law on first-party enforcement, identifying the main factors that influence the attitude of individuals towards the law and their willingness to comply in the absence of legal sanctions and second-party and third-party enforcement. Empirical and experimental testing evaluates and compares the effective relevance of these factors on observed behavior. As shown in the existing literature, when social norms and legal rules interact, they influence human behavior in a complex and non-linear way. Law gives incentives to individuals that do not add linearly to private moral incentives provided by social norms. In fact, legal rules do not necessarily coincide and may even conflict with private norms.

Legal rules reflecting social values and norms receive public support that reinforces underlying individual opinions in the population. Law, therefore, plays an expressive role in the society (Cooter 1998, 2000), in the sense that it supports pre-existing opinions in the population. Law may more effectively influence individual behavior when legal rules are aligned with the prevailing social values and norms. People tend to comply more effectively with law when legal rules express values in line with existing social values. People then perceive law as 'legitimate' and those subject to the law tend to accept the need to act in accordance with the dictates of the lawmaking authority. According to Tom Tyler (1990: 25), legitimacy identifies an 'acceptance by people of the need to bring their behavior into line with the dictates of an external authority'. The perception of the legitimacy of law significantly influences an individual's compliance with law. Further, Robert Cooter (1998, 2000) identifies alternative ways through which legal rules affect individual behavior. Legal rules express social values that can create, modify or destroy existing social norms. The most fundamental way through which law can affect individual behavior is deterrence. Law can impose sanctions on those individuals who violate the dictates of a specific legal rule. Sanctions do not change the preferences and moral values

---

[15]   Other relevant references for social norm theory are Ullmann-Margalit (1977); Sunstein (1995); Kahan (1998).

[16]   Private and social norms do not control individual behaviour on their own; behavior is also substantially influenced by the exogenous restrictions imposed by legal rules. Legal rules provide private incentives to individuals through the imposition of legal sanctions.

of individuals but instead modify the payoff associated with violating the legal rule. This induces a change of behavioral patterns without causing a preference change. In addition, law can influence behavior through expression. People tend to comply with legal rules, even in the absence of legal sanctions and enforcement, because they respect the law in general and feel obliged and compelled to obey it. Cooter (2000) analyzed the effectiveness of expressive law and showed that it is more effective the greater the alignment with prevailing social values and norms. Expressive law can lead to a reduction in private enforcement costs, since individuals will comply more frequently with the law since it expresses the same values they hold.

Law can directly influence individual preferences and tastes through internalization and gradual adaptation. The internalization of a social norm leads individuals to perceive a moral commitment that associates a psychological cost with violation of the norm. The internalization of the norm occurs only when it produces a Pareto improvement, that is, when a rational individual finds it advantageous to change his preferences relative to the original preferences.

Multiple equilibria may arise in the presence of social norms. In such systems, both interior and corner solutions may exist. Interior solutions identify equilibrium configurations where individuals who comply with the social norm coexist with a positive fraction of individuals in the population violating the social norm. At the equilibrium configuration, each individual gets the same expected payoff from obeying the social norm and from violating it. This condition identifies the optimal proportion of individuals in each category. This implies that in an interior equilibrium, wrongdoers and right-doers coexist.[17] On the contrary, corner solutions are characterized by the entire population converging on compliance with the social norm or, in the opposite case, on violation of it.

Social norms coexist with legal norms. A new law may enact a norm without enforcement. Law enactment without enforcement has no effect on the equilibrium as long as it does not change the individual perception of the social norm and does not affect its internalization. The impact on the prevailing equilibrium depends on the characteristics of the system of social norms. Law may increase the frequency of upholding the norm in the population, thereby reducing the payoff of the wrongdoers and increasing the equilibrium level of the right-doers in the population. In other cases, law may not be enough to induce individuals to invest in norm upholding, thereby having no effect on the prevailing equilibrium. Empirical and experimental research must investigate more deeply the factors that influence the extent to which individuals internalize legal commands and their willingness to comply with law when external incentives are absent.

A system of social norms typically has multiple equilibria. Law can create or select a focal point by expressing values (McAdams 2000b).[18] In the presence of multiple equilibria, law may help coordination to a Pareto-superior equilibrium. Law selects the equilibrium by creating a focal point. The formation of a focal point can create or destroy a social norm, thereby affecting the prevailing equilibrium. Cooter (1998) identifies this as

---

[17]   Analytically, the condition that identifies an interior solution in the presence of social norms requires the expected payoff of wrongdoers to be equal to the expected payoff of right-doers and determines the proportion of wrongdoers and right-doers in the population.

[18]   See McAdams and Nadler (2005) for an empirical test of focal-point theory.

the first function of expressive law. According to the theory of expressive law, law enactment without enforcement may induce voluntary obedience, thereby making the law effective without imposing any sanction. Law enactment without enforcement, however, may fail to induce a sufficiently large shift of behavior on the part of a coordinating group and hence may have no impact on the equilibrium. The establishment of a focal point requires detailed information on the payoff functions of individuals in the population. However, this kind of information is rarely available to lawmakers. In these cases, law may fail to induce coordination on a social norm and can crowd it out.[19]

2.2   Countervailing Norms

Legal rules may diverge from social values and norms. In these cases, legal rules may trigger opposition. Individuals may choose to openly violate the legal rule and engage in civil disobedience. Individuals may also express their public dissent to others, triggering a wave of protest against the newly introduced legal rule. Civil disobedience and protest may trigger support for social values and norms contrary to existing legal rules and induce crowding-out effects on individual incentives. When lawmakers attempt to modify an existing social norm too swiftly through new law, it triggers a backlash and subsequent cascade effect. However, laws contrary to social norms that are introduced incrementally may inspire neither widespread disobedience nor a cascade effect; they eventually achieve the desired change.

Legal philosophers and political theorists have often recognized that law and morality share a common function—both being instrumental in fostering a satisfactory social coexistence. From this recognized common purpose, legal philosophers have also argued, law derives its legitimacy and acceptance in a free society (Cotta 1981). Through this complex interaction, morality generally drives law, while in other situations law is utilized as an instrument of moral suasion. As pointed out by Francesco Parisi and Georg von Wangenheim (2006), when law is utilized to shape social and moral beliefs, it cannot deviate too far from current communal perceptions.[20] Cooter also perceives the avoidance of a conflict between law and morality as crucial, inasmuch as some 'people respect laws that align with morality. Now I consider the possibility that some people's morality requires them to respect law. In other words, I assume that some people believe that they ought to obey the law because it is law' (2000: 1598).

Under each of these views, to preserve the perceived authority of the law, lawmakers must align the law with existing morality. As laws begin to depart from social values, the influence of law on behavior may vanish. Although slight departures from current norms may lead to gradual adaptation and acceptance,[21] new statutes that differ substantially from current opinions may lead to opposition. As pointed out by Parisi and

---

[19]   See, e.g., Frey (1997); Frey et al. (1996).

[20]   For example, criminal law tends to drive the evolution of social norms in the same direction as the law, because it influences mainly human behavior affected by some ambiguity regarding the rightness of the conduct.

[21]   A gradual change of a law may be preferable to radical legislation when the legal norm may pull the social norm in the desired direction in small consecutive steps (Parisi and von Wangenheim 2006).

von Wangenheim (2006) and Emanuela Carbonara and colleagues (2008a, 2008b, 2011), dissent may result from a discrepancy between law and the prevailing social attitude toward the regulated conduct. Dissent can take the form of protest and civil disobedience and can, through a process of hysteresis, lead to reinforcing the contrary social opinion. Parisi and von Wangenheim (2006) examine the effect of legal rules that are distant from current social norms or that lack communal legitimacy. When legal rules and social norms differ substantially, laws may have little effect and fail to meet their goals. In such cases, social norms likely have a countervailing effect on legal rules. Incentives and sanctions introduced by legal systems may not be enough; hence, a greater expenditure of resources might be needed to enforce such legal rules.[22]

The factors considered above—internalization and self-compliance, expressive effect and countervailing effects—can play an important role in determining the effectiveness of the law in shaping individual behavior. Legal scholars that wish to use quantitative methods for the comparative analysis of legal rules and legal institutions should be aware of the possible presence of these factors. When evaluating the effects of a legal rule, comparative law and economics scholars should carefully control for the presence of the effects discussed in this brief survey to avoid reaching false conclusions about the intrinsic merits of the rule.

REFERENCES

Calabresi, Guido (1980). 'About Law and Economics: A Letter to Ronald Dworkin', 8 *Hofstra Law Review* 553–62.
Carbonara, Emanuela, Francesco Parisi and Georg von Wangenheim (2008a). 'Legal Innovation and the Compliance Paradox', 9 *Minnesota Journal of Law, Science and Technology* 837–60.
Carbonara, Emanuela, Francesco Parisi and Georg von Wangenheim (2008b). 'Lawmakers as Norms Entrepreneurs', 4 *Review of Law and Economics* 779–99.
Carbonara, Emanuela, Francesco Parisi and Georg von Wangenheim (2011). 'Countervailing Norms', in Francesco Parisi (ed.), *Production of Legal Rules* ch. 11. Cheltenham, UK and Northampton, MA, USA: Edward Elgar.
Coleman, James S. (1990). *Foundations of Social Theory*. Cambridge, MA: Harvard University Press.
Cooter, Robert (1998). 'Expressive Law and Economics', 27 *Journal of Legal Studies* 585–608.
Cooter, Robert (2000). 'Do Good Laws Make Good Citizens? An Economic Analysis of Internalized Norms', 86 *Virginia Law Review* 1577–1601.
Cotta, Sergio (1981). *Giustificazione e obbligatorietà delle norme*. Milan: Giuffrè.
De Geest, Gerrit (ed.) (2009). *Economics of Comparative Law*. Cheltenham, UK and Northampton, MA, USA: Edward Elgar (vol. 24, Economic Approaches to Law series).
De Geest, Gerrit and Roger van den Bergh (eds) (2004). 1–3 *Comparative Law and Economics*. Cheltenham, UK and Northampton, MA, USA: Edward Elgar (International Library of Critical Writings in Economics series).
Fon, Vincy and Francesco Parisi (2003). 'Litigation and the Evolution of Legal Remedies: A Dynamic Model', 116 *Public Choice* 419–33.
Frey, Bruno S. (1997). 'A Constitution for Knaves Crowds Out Civic Virtues', 107 *Economic Journal* 1043–53.
Frey, Bruno S., Felix Oberholzer-Gee and Reiner Eichenberger (1996). 'The Old Lady Visits Your Backyard: A Tale of Morals and Markets', 104 *Journal of Political Economy* 1297–313.

---

[22]　When a statute promotes a behavior radically different from the prevailing social norm, civil disobedience arises and may cause the statute to be unsustainable. In such cases, the statute would need to be backed by very strong expected sanctions. This occurs under authoritarian regimes, which invest in strong enforcement to support the enactment of statutes deviating significantly from social norms.

Glimcher, Paul W. and Aldo Rustichini. (2004). 'Neuroeconomics: The Consilience of Brain and Decision', 306 *Science* 447–52 (Oct. 15).
Gneezy, Uri and Aldo Rustichini, A. (2000). 'A Fine is a Price', 29 *Journal of Legal Studies* 1–17.
Greene, William (2002). *Econometric Analysis*. Upper Saddle River, NJ: Prentice Hall, 5th edn.
Kahan, Dan M. (1998). 'Social Meaning and the Economic Analysis of Law', 27 *Journal of Legal Studies* 609–22.
La Porta, Rafael, Florencio Lopez de Silanes, Andrei Shleifer and Robert W. Vishny (1997). 'Legal Determinants of External Finance', 52 *Journal of Finance* 1131–50.
La Porta, Rafael, Florencio Lopez de Silanes, Andrei Shleifer and Robert W. Vishny (1998). 'Law and Finance', 106 *Journal of Political Economy* 1113–55.
Mattei, Ugo (1997). *Comparative Law and Economics*. Ann Arbor, MI: University of Michigan Press.
McAdams, Richard H. (2000a). 'An Attitudinal Theory of Expressive Law', 79 *Oregon Law Review* 339–90.
McAdams, Richard H. (2000b). 'A Focal Point Theory of Expressive Law,' 86 *Virginia Law Review* 1649–729.
McAdams, Richard H. and Janice Nadler (2005). 'Testing the Focal Point Theory of Legal Compliance: The Effect of Third-Party Expression in an Experimental Hawk/Dove Game', 2 *Journal of Empirical Legal Studies* 87–123.
Niblett, Anthony, Richard Posner and Andrei Shleifer (2010). 'The Evolution of a Legal Rule', 39 *Journal of Legal Studies* 325–58.
Parisi, Francesco (2004). 'Positive, Normative and Functional Schools in Law and Economics', 18 *European Journal of Law and Economics* 259–72.
Parisi, Francesco (2007). 'Economics, Law and', in David S. Clark (ed.), 1 *Encyclopedia of Law and Society* 451–8. Thousand Oaks, CA: Sage Publications.
Parisi, Francesco (2011). *Production of Legal Rules*. Cheltenham, UK and Northampton, MA, USA: Edward Elgar.
Parisi, Francesco and Vincy Fon (2009). *The Economics of Lawmaking*. Oxford: Oxford University Press.
Parisi, Francesco and Barbara Luppi (2012). 'Quantitative Methods in Comparative Law', in Pier Giuseppe Monateri (ed.), *Methods of Comparative Law* ch. 16. Cheltenham, UK and Northampton, MA, USA: Edward Elgar.
Parisi, Francesco and Vernon L. Smith (eds) (2005). *The Law and Economics of Irrational Behavior*. Stanford, CA: Stanford University Press.
Parisi, Francesco and Georg von Wangenheim (2006). 'Legislation and Countervailing Effects from Social Norms', in Christain Schubert and Georg von Wangenheim (eds), *Evolution and Design of Institutions* 25–55. London: Routledge.
Priest, George L. (1977). 'The Common Law Process and the Selection of Efficient Rules', 6 *Journal of Legal Studies* 65–82.
Sindelar, Jody L. (2008). 'Paying for Performance: The Power of Incentives over Habits', 17 *Health Economics* 449–51.
Schelling, Thomas C. (1980). *The Strategy of Conflict*. Cambridge, MA: Harvard University Press, rev. edn.
Sunstein, Cass R. (1995). *Social Norm and Social Roles*. Chicago: University of Chicago Law School (Coase Lecture Series).
Tyler, Tom R. (1990). *Why People Obey the Law*, New Haven, CT: Yale; reissued by Princeton University Press (2006).
Ullmann-Margalit, Edna (1977). *The Emergence of Norms*. Oxford: Clarendon Press.

6 Comparative law and political economy
*John C. Reitz**

1 THE POLITICAL ECONOMY THESIS

1.1 Employment Law as an Example

In the spring of 2006, riots gripped France. The French government proposed to amend the statutory law concerning employment by introducing a type of employment that could be terminated without any reason ('at-will employment') for young, first-time workers. Most employment in France is covered by statutory protections prohibiting dismissal without substantial reasons. The riots illuminated in a particularly dramatic way how different prevailing ideas about the appropriate degree of state intervention in the market can be in various countries, even as between Western democratic nations with robust legal systems and many common cultural traditions. Americans looked on with growing disbelief as the strikes spread in France because most Americans work under at-will contracts. Many Americans had difficulty seeing how the French rioters, who included not only students, but also union members and retirees, could be so incensed about the introduction of a limited form of at-will employment.[1]

This example illustrates not only national diversity in views over the appropriate level of state intervention in the market, but also how those differences are reflected in substantial and important variations in legal rules. French law regulates employment relationships generally through legislation restricting employee dismissals in most cases to 'cause' (that is, serious breaches by the employee) or such restructuring of the business that it is impossible, even with job retraining, to find a new job within the company for the employee. When dismissals are allowed, French law requires minimum notice periods, except in the most egregious cases of termination for cause.

In the United States, where employment law is primarily a matter of state law, only two states have adopted legislation restricting at-will employment generally. Most states have no general rules limiting at-will employment, though civil service protections may do so for most state and federal government employees, as do academic tenure rules for many

* Edward L. Carmody Professor of Law and Director, LL.M. Program and Visiting Scholars, University of Iowa College of Law. The author would like to thank Jessica Burton, Jinny Huang, Anton Radchenko and Ina Vujica for research assistance and his Iowa colleagues for their comments at a faculty presentation in June 2011.

[1] John C. Reitz, 'Political Economy and Contract Law', in Reiner Schulze (ed.), *New Features in Contract Law* 247, 247–9, 254–5 (Munich: Sellier 2007). The US did witness important public demonstrations in some states during 2011 in opposition to attempts to eliminate public-sector union job protections and bargaining rights, but these were not demonstrations in opposition to at-will employment generally. They were just in support of public unions, which account for a small portion of the overall workforce.

Figure 6.1   Political economy spectrum

teachers. Employment law in the US thus leaves most parties to whatever they can negotiate in the market, which except for the small proportion of unionized workers and some top company officials, tends to be the at-will rule. In this sense, the law concerning employment in the United States is more market-centered than the corresponding rule in France.[2]

The political economy thesis claims that this difference in employment law matches a general and more systematic difference between France and the US, which I refer to as a difference in 'political economy'. The concept of political economy reflects differences in the degree to which each country relies on the state to assure general welfare, whether through regulation or welfare transfers or both. Countries can be arrayed, I argue, on a spectrum according to whether they generally prefer to rely more on state actors to make important decisions about the allocation of resources and provision for the general welfare (a more state-centered political economy) or more on private forces acting in the market (a more market-centered political economy).

The conventional spectrum of national styles of political economy runs from laissez-faire capitalism at the extreme market-centered end, through social democracy in the middle and ultimately to state socialism and the command economy at the extreme state-centered end. It may be true that '[s]ince the end of the 1970s most Western democracies have moved incrementally in a neoliberal direction, emphasizing voluntary exchange, competitive markets, and private contracts rather than political authority and democratic politics'.[3] Nevertheless, this chapter argues that there are still substantial differences among countries with respect to political economy. The political economy thesis asserts that these variations are embedded in assorted political and economic institutions, including the legal system. Institutional structure, I argue, provides the best evidence of the culture that each distinctive political economy represents. Political economy thus refers not only to attitudes and beliefs about state intervention, but also to the institutional structure that reflects and reinforces those attitudes and beliefs.

This chapter will illustrate the thesis primarily with respect to four countries: France, Germany, the United Kingdom and the United States. Section 2 contends (and Figure 6.1 illustrates) that the United States is the most market-centered political economy of any of these countries, France the most state-centered, and the UK and Germany fall in between, but Germany is the more state-centered of the two.

---

[2]   See generally Reitz (note 1). Employment law in many US states is developing a tort of public policy which limits employer discretion to dismiss an employee for certain 'bad' reasons that violate public policy, but the outlines of that tort are still not very clear and, in any event, the tort does not eliminate at-will employment. Ibid. 253–4.

[3]   James G. March and Johan P. Olsen, 'Elaborating the "New Institutionalism"', in R.A.W. Rhodes, Sarah A. Binder and Bert A. Rockman (eds), *Oxford Handbook of Political Institutions* 3, 13 (Oxford: Oxford University Press 2008).

On that basis, the contrast between the US and France with respect to employment law fits the divergence in overall political economies: France, the more state-centered political economy, has the more state-centered employment law, and the US, with the more market-centered political economy, has the more market-centered employment law.[4]

At first blush, the German and British rules on the employment relationship appear quite similar to French law, but there are small variations that fit the differences in the countries' overall political economies.[5] One detail in particular demonstrates that French law is more state-centered than either German or British employment regulation. At the end of World War II, the French government was keeping track of both hiring and dismissals. From 1975 to 1986, the Ministry of Labor required prior authorization for any dismissals related to economic restructuring. Even today, restructuring companies cannot dismiss workers without a written plan, now called a 'plan to preserve employment', which will be enforced to avoid lay-offs if possible.[6]

A recent study of how the legal culture concerning employment developed in Germany, France and the United Kingdom[7] reveals the historical roots of rather different approaches to the use of state power in the employment law of the respective countries. In the period of industrialization, factory owners on the continent of Europe, unlike those in England, 'saw themselves as having "duties as well as the privileges that such a position entails"'.[8] In the nineteenth century, the French government reinforced those attitudes because, already by that time, it was monitoring the hiring and firing of workers and exerting pressure on

---

[4]   Reitz (note 1) 249–54, 257–9 (citations for relevant law in all four countries).

[5]   For example, French and German restrictions on dismissal date back to the end of World War II or even earlier. Reitz (note 1) 251 n.21. By contrast, the British adopted statutory restrictions on dismissals only in the 1970s and 1980s. Ibid. 257. '[P]resent British legislation [on dismissals] is less extensive than that found elsewhere in Europe'. Stephen Hardy, *Labour Law and Industrial Relations in Great Britain* § 285, at 161 (Alphen aan den Rijn: Kluwer Law International 2007). In particular, the tribunals that enforce the law tend to give precedence to employers' rights to manage over employees' rights to job security and rarely grant the remedy of reinstatement. Moreover, the protections do not apply until the employee has worked continuously at least one year. Ibid. §§ 288–9, 293, at 162–3, 165. Both France and Germany restrict fixed-term contracts to prevent employers from undermining the statutory protections against at-will employment, but France's limitations are stricter than Germany's. Compare Jean-Maurice Verdier, Alain Coeuret and Marie-Armelle Souriac, 2 *Droit du travail* 57 (Paris: Dalloz, 15th edn, 2009) (fixed-term contracts allowed only for good reasons and, subject to some exceptions, only for maximum cumulative period of 18 months); Jens Kirchner and Sascha Morgenroth, 'Executive Summary: German Employment and Labour Law', in Jens Kirchner, Pascal R. Kremp and Michael Magotxch (eds), *Key Aspects of German Employment and Labour Law* 1, 12 (Heidelberg: Springer Verlag 2010) (two-year cumulative maximum applies only to fixed-term contracts that are not justified).

[6]   Verdier et al. (note 5) 306–07; Pierre-Yves Verkindt, *Le droit du travail* 141–50 (Paris: Dalloz 2005).

[7]   Beth Ahlering and Simon Deakin, 'Labor Regulation, Corporate Governance, and Legal Origin: A Case of Institutional Complementarity?' 41 *Law and Society Review* 865 (2007) (also covering the development of law concerning corporate governance in these same countries).

[8]   Ibid. 897, quoting David M. Landes, *The Unbound Prometheus* 191 (Cambridge: Cambridge University Press 1969) (noting that these attitudes are also the result of scarcity of labor because continental rural populations continued to have access to agricultural land; English workers did not).

employers to limit the number of jobless to forestall social disruption.[9] French law thus conceptualized state regulation of the employment relationship as part of *ordre public social* and therefore developed the idea that the state assumed responsibility for establishing minimum protections for workers, an obviously state-centered approach.

However, in Germany, under the influence of the conservative jurist Otto von Gierke (1841–1921), labor's obvious subordination to the enterprise was interpreted as a process that made the worker a member of the enterprise community. The German approach is just a shade less state-centered because the communitarian conception of the enterprise provided a reason based on society for imposing the same kind of protections that France imposed based on state interests.[10] England, by contrast, regulated the labor agreement in the eighteenth and nineteenth centuries in an even heavier way than the civil law, using the criminal law to enforce the terms of service contracts. That experience, reinforced by the strong subordination implied in the common law terminology of 'master-servant' for the law of the employment relationship, made organized labor in England reluctant to fight for substantive legal protections. They saw the law as a tool of the employer class; to serve the interests of labor, they preferred to rely on collective bargaining.[11]

In this case, history does not teach that the civil law started out in a more regulatory mode than the common law, but it does reveal the development of distinctive political economies in the labor law of all four countries. In France and Germany, even before industrialization threatened to turn employee discharges into acute social problems, the law had begun to adopt aspects of the modern regulatory approach. This kind of regulation attempts to balance worker and employer interests, with a somewhat more state-centered version in France than in Germany, while in the common law the class bias of the early forms of English regulation led to a de-emphasis on state regulation in favor of voluntarist solutions through collective bargaining. However, in the 1970s and 1980s, the intermediate nature of the British political economy manifested itself, perhaps under the influence of the European Community, as British law largely abolished employment at will, a move the US, however, has not followed.

1.2   The Thesis and Chapter Plan

The political economy thesis asserts, first, that one can generalize meaningfully enough about the level of government intervention in the market to say that each country has an overall political economy and, second, that major differences among legal systems fit or make sense in light of the diversity among political economies of the respective countries. In other words, the political economy thesis claims that each country's legal system tends to manifest a particular level of government intervention that matches the country's overall political economy.

Both the claims about countries' overall political economies and their legal systems involve large generalizations. The problem of generalizing about countries and their legal

---

[9]   Ibid.
[10]   Section 2.3 below shows how well the German approach fitted its strongly corporatist institutional structure.
[11]   Ahlering and Deakin (note 7) 895–96.

systems is a major challenge for comparative law.[12] Drawing on the institutional literature of social science, Section 2 argues that the institutional structure of a country provides the most reliable measure of its overall political economy. Law is part of that institutional structure, and the political economy thesis states simply that it tends to be consistent with the overall institutional structure. Section 2 illustrates what 'institutional structure' and 'political economy' mean by setting out the basis for characterizing the political economies of four countries. Section 3 reviews four more examples of areas of the law in the four countries that support the political economy thesis. These illustrations make the thesis plausible, but obviously many more examples are required to show how pervasively the legal system reflects a country's overall political economy.

The case of employment law clearly involves market regulation. Based on that example, the claim that the legal system reflects the country's political economy may appear tautological. Political economy is about the degree of regulation or welfare and whether it is embodied in laws and regulations. To that extent, the legal system of course reflects the prevailing views about regulation and the thesis may not seem so interesting. More interesting is the way in which aspects of the legal system that are not so obviously regulatory reflect political economy. Section 3 illustrations include, inter alia, abstract review for constitutional challenges to legislation, aspects of civil procedure, remedies for breach of contract, and the contrast between presidential and parliamentary systems of government. In a sense, of course, most law is regulatory—it regulates our relations with other people and institutions. The interesting point of the thesis is that, even when law regulates our participation in non-market systems (such as legal or political systems), it often bears the imprint of the style and degree of regulation that it uses when it regulates our participation in the market.

Although the level of state intervention in the market tends in various countries and times to be the focus of vigorous normative debate, the thesis itself is not a normative one. I do not claim that one nation's political economy is better than another's. This is an important point about the political economy thesis because some of the similar work reviewed in Section 4 has made such a claim. The political economy thesis does not use the term 'market-centered' to mean 'market-friendly' or 'market-supportive'. Law is market-centered with respect to a particular subject if it relegates control functions chiefly to private parties negotiating in a market rather than to state officials. All markets probably need some forms of effective, intelligent state regulation to function well, so on some issues, state-centered law may be more supportive of economic growth than market-centered law.

Nor do I claim that because of a nation's overall political economy it cannot or should not adopt a legal institution or rule that might reflect a different political economy. In fact, as Section 2 shows, it seems clear that every nation's legal system contains elements that do not conform to the overall political economy. The political economy thesis claims only that, on balance, each nation does have a dominant, pervasive or characteristic position on the political economy spectrum and, further, that so many important variations among legal rules and institutions fit the differences in national political economies that each country's

---

[12]   John Reitz, 'Legal Origins, Comparative Law, and Political Economy', 57 *American Journal of Comparative Law* 847 (2009).

distinctive political economy must be considered a major design principle for its legal system. Section 5 discusses the utility of the thesis for comparative law and the further work required. Seeing apparently isolated differences among legal systems as part of systematic variation in political economy may be crucial for outsiders to make sense of the differences and to take seriously law based on political economies very different from their own.

My usage of the term 'political economy' may be a bit different from that of many authors, but it is well within the boundaries of the many meanings the term has had in its long career. As Barry Weingast and Donald Wittman have written:

> For Adam Smith, political economy was the science of managing a nation's resources so as to generate wealth. For Marx, it was how the ownership of the means of production influenced historical processes. For much of the twentieth century, the phrase political economy has had contradictory meanings. Sometimes it was viewed as an area of study (the interrelationship between economics and politics) while at other times it was viewed as a methodological approach. Even the methodological approach was divided into two parts—the economic approach (often called public choice) emphasizing individual rationality and the sociological approach where the level of analysis tended to be institutional.[13]

My use of the term to denote the level of government intervention in the economy represented by the bulk of a nation's institutional structure fits within these traditional meanings. Using the term to focus on types of institutional structure relating politics and economics is not far from Adam Smith's usage because it is but a short step from the science of managing a nation's resources to the chief forms for doing so. I also draw heavily on certain social scientists who use the term to explore questions of the political and economic structure of a country, including different forms of business and financial organization and the applicability of the corporatist, statist, and pluralist models discussed in Section 2.3.[14] My usage is perhaps narrower than most because I use the term to focus on what institutions tell us about the prevailing degree in each country of state intervention in the market.

2   THE CONCEPT OF POLITICAL ECONOMY

As a cultural concept, political economy refers to a mixture of attitudes and beliefs (about the dominant view for the desirable degree of government intervention) and behaviors (the degree to which the government actually intervenes in the market). To say that a country has a specific political economy thus involves a generalization that is problematic on a number of levels. First, how does one combine attitudes and beliefs with behavior

---

[13]   Barry R. Weingast and Donald A. Wittman, 'The Reach of Political Economy', in Barry R. Weingast and Donald Wittman (eds), *The Oxford Handbook of Political Economy* 3 (Oxford: Oxford University Press 2008) (defining it for their purposes as a 'grand (if imperfect) synthesis' of these various usages, which they characterize as the 'methodology of economics applied to the analysis of political behavior and institutions'). See *Oxford English Dictionary*, 'economy' (Glasgow: Oxford University Press, compact edn, 1971).

[14]   See, e.g., Stephen Wilks and Maurice Wright (eds), *The Promotion and Regulation of Industry in Japan* (New York: St. Martin's Press 1991); Kozo Yamamura and Yasakichi Yasuba (eds), *The Political Economy of Japan* (Stanford: Stanford University Press 1987).

in one comparative measure? Second, how can one deal with the variability of political economy? The question of how much government intervention there should be on any given issue may often be in contention in a country and the political support for different levels of intervention may vary substantially over time and with respect to different issues. Different legal rules with the same legal system may therefore reflect different degrees of state intervention. How can we speak meaningfully of a single political economy for any given legal system or country?

Section 2.1 considers a variety of general sources of information about the political economy of a country and its associated institutions, such as historical trends in political and economic thought and general political and economic policies. Section 2.2 contends that institutional structure may provide the best basis for generalizing about national political economies. Section 2.3 then sets out a typology of state structures relating to political economy based on the institutional literature of social science and applies it to the four target countries to justify the positions I have assigned these countries on the political economy spectrum in Figure 6.1.

2.1   General Sources of Information about Political Economy

In view of the difficulties of generalizing, it seems reasonable to consider as much information about a country's political economy and associated institutions as possible. We can start with the history of ideas concerning government intervention in markets. While this is not the place for a detailed intellectual history of political economy, a quick overview of the history of some relevant ideas is suggestive of the differences I have asserted with respect to political economy.

The US has a long tradition of skepticism toward state intervention and trust in markets that is rooted in celebration of individualism and individual initiative. The frontier experience reinforced this tradition.[15] The result was strong support for laissez-faire capitalism in the first century of the country's existence. This support seemed especially reasonable because of the perception that there was a plentiful supply of new land.[16] Continental Europeans, by contrast, have a long tradition of a much more favorable view of the state.[17] All the European countries faced a shortage of virgin lands much earlier and they constantly faced the danger of invasion or domination by neighbors. In such circumstances, it would be understandable if they sought ways to promote social and economic cooperation, to avoid 'winner-takes-all' strategies.

Claus Offe calls the resulting form, a highly regulated market in Europe, 'embedded' capitalism;[18] Harald Baum emphasizes that the result was hostility toward the market and

---

[15]   Robert N. Bellah, Richard Madsen, William M. Sullivan, Ann Swidler and Steven M. Tipton, *Habits of the Heart* 27–51 (New York: Harper and Row 1986).

[16]   Herbert Hovenkamp, *Enterprise and American Law 1836–1937*, at 183–92 (Cambridge, MA: Harvard University Press 1991).

[17]   Gerhard Caspar, 'Changing Concepts of Constitutionalism: 18th to 20th Century', 1989 *Supreme Court Review* 311, 318–19; J.P. Nettl, 'The State as a Conceptual Variable', 20 *World Politics* 559, 567, 570–77 (1968).

[18]   Claus Offe, 'The European Model of "Social" Capitalism: Can It Survive European Integration?', 11 *Journal of Political Philosophy* 437, 443, 439–46 (2003). Offe takes the term

a strong belief in the fairness and ethical superiority of state intervention.[19] G.W.F. Hegel (1770–1831) provided the philosophical basis for the strong or interventionist state by elaborating the concept of the state as the promoter of citizen welfare.[20] Since World War II, German thinking about the market has been dominated by 'Ordoliberalism', which prescribes strong state intervention for the limited purpose of creating fair social and economic conditions for a 'social market economy'.[21] The French continue to have 'greater expectations of the state than do Americans' and 'a favorable view of . . . governmental services'; they 'rely on the state to guarantee [economic security]'.[22] England's intermediate position on the political economy spectrum fits with the fact that it has been the home of both Thomas Hobbes (1588–1679) and John Locke (1632–1704), subject to both liberalism and socialism.

With respect to overall political and economic policies, the principal contrast is between the US on the one hand and the European countries on the other. Thus, for example, all three European countries have a long tradition of intervention in the economy, though by the nineteenth century England had became known for its more liberal approach to trade. Government intervention used to take the form of mercantilism or *dirigisme*. After 1945, it continued in France as *planification* until 2005,[23] a detail that suggests the continuation of a somewhat more state-centered pattern in France than in the UK or Germany. France, Germany and the UK have all had strong leftist parties that have alternated in power since World War II with more market-oriented parties. In the US, socialist political parties have had success only in one or two states and only for a short period. Throughout US history, there has been little state ownership of economic assets,[24] considerable ambivalence toward regulation and recurrent enthusiasm for deregulation.[25] All three of the other countries nationalized important sectors of their economies in the three decades following World War II, perhaps none more than the UK. However, they have all been vigorously

---

'embedded capitalism' from Karl Polanyi, *The Great Transformation* (New York: Rinehart and Co. 1944). The term seems especially fitting in view of the prevalence of corporatist structures on the continent of Europe. See Section 2.3 below.

[19]   Harald Baum, 'Change of Governance in Historic Perspective: The German Experience', in Klaus J. Hopt, Eddy Wymeersch, Hideki Kanda and Harald Baum (eds), *Corporate Governance in Context: Corporations, State, and Markets in Europe, Japan, and the US* 3, 6–8 (Oxford: Oxford University Press 2005).

[20]   Caspar (note 17) 318–19, 325; Nettl (note 17) 570–77.

[21]   David J. Gerber, 'Constitutionalizing the Economy: German Neoliberalism, Competition Law and the "New" Europe', 42 *American Journal of Comparative Law* 25, 25–7 (1994).

[22]   William Safran, *The French Polity* 72, 74 (New York: Pearson Education, Inc., 7th edn, 2009).

[23]   During the post-war period, the French government adopted multi-year national economic plans, which a planning commissariat prepared. Vincent Wright, *The Government and Politics of France* 102 (London: Unwin Hyman, 3rd edn, 1989). They were always more hortatory than mandatory and gradually lost importance after President Charles de Gaulle (1959–1969). In 2005, the last planning commissioners were dismissed. Safran (note 22) 353–6.

[24]   Canda S. Chahyadi, William L. Megginson and Jesus M. Salas, 'Privatisation and Public Enterprises in the USA', in Judith Clifton, Francisco Comín and Daniel Díaz-Fuentes (eds), *Transforming Public Enterprise in Europe and North America* 207–12 (Basingstoke, UK: Palgrave Macmillan 2007) (noting large number of municipally owned electric power companies).

[25]   Caspar (note 17) 329.

privatizing in the last 30 years. By the end of the century, the UK had joined the US in having no significant state-owned enterprises, while France appears to continue to have a greater governmental stake in its economy than Germany.[26] All three European countries provide some form of universal health care. Their economies were characterized by 'mild cartel-like arrangements' during much of the twentieth century, a factor which suggests some considerable hesitancy about unconstrained markets.[27]

All of this information seems consistent with my claims about the differences in the respective political economies of the four target countries, but with the exception of the information about relative levels of state ownership in the economy, this general information differentiates most clearly only between the United States and the other three countries. For better differentiation, we turn to institutional structure.

2.2   The Importance of Institutions

The revival of social science interest in the various ways in which states and their economies are structured, and the ways in which government interacts with society and the economy, has produced an extensive 'new institutionalism' literature. These studies focus on the variation among countries in their 'formally organized institutions that define the context within which politics and governance take place'.[28] Institutions are defined broadly and include both the obvious structures of the political, economic and legal systems, such as courts, legislatures and stock exchanges, but also the formal and informal rules by which they operate, including at least the basic rules of specific areas of law.[29]

---

[26]   William Leon Megginson, *The Financial Economics of Privatization* 8–15, 400–06 (New York: Oxford University Press 2005) (general history of state ownership of economic assets and privatizations). According to Megginson, during the post-war period, France embraced state ownership more enthusiastically than Germany, which preferred a mix of direct ownership and regulation. Right after World War II, the UK nationalized with great enthusiasm, reaching a high of over 20 percent of the economy. Ibid. at 12. By the mid-1970s, many Western European countries had state-owned companies accounting for more than 10 percent of their national output. Ibid.

For estimates of the size of remaining government stakes in France and Germany, both in absolute values and as a percentage of GDP, see Luca Farinola and William L. Megginson, 'Leviathan as Shareholder: The Value of Governments' Stakes', *Privatization Barometer Newsletter* issue no. 4 (Jan. 2006) 25, 28 (figs 1 and 3), at http://www.privatizationbarometer.net/newsletter (select Archive); R.O., 'Remaining Central Government Enterprise Portfolios in Europe' (CESifo DICE Report 2/2006: Database), at http://www.cesifo-group.de (select DICE Database, then Public Sector, then Public Finance-Public Revenues) (France about 7 percent of GDP, Germany a little more than 1 percent). Both sources are based on figures for central government holdings in listed companies only; these estimates therefore understate state holdings for Germany, where lower levels of government also have substantial holdings.

[27]   John Zysman, *Governments, Markets, and Growth* 253 (Ithaca, NY: Cornell University Press 1983).

[28]   March and Olsen (note 3) 6.

[29]   March and Olson define institution as 'a relatively enduring collection of rules and organized practices, embedded in structures of meaning and resources that are relatively invariant in the face of turnover of individuals and relatively resilient to the idiosyncratic preferences and expectations of individuals and changing external circumstances'. Ibid. 3. Another view is that 'they are the "shared beliefs" that impart stability and order to economic interactions'. Ahlering and Deakin

Institutionalists posit that 'institutions create elements of order and predictability. They fashion, enable and constrain political actors as they act within a logic of appropriate action. [They] are carriers of identities and roles and they are markers of a polity's character, history, and vision'.[30] The focus on institutions asserts that states 'matter because their organizational configurations, along with their overall patterns of activity, affect political culture, encourage some kinds of group formation and collective political actions (but not others), and make possible the raising of certain political issues (but not others)'.[31] From this point of view, '[t]he state appears as a network of institutions, deeply embedded within a constellation of ancillary institutions associated with society and the economic system'.[32] The actual effect of institutional structure on state policy remains controversial, but James March and Johan Olsen assert that 'most political scientists probably would grant that the variation in institutions accounts for at least some of the observed variation in political processes and outcomes'.[33]

Institutions may provide help in several ways in the formulation of generalizations about political economy. First, to the extent that they embody a particular level of state intervention or reliance on state officials, they probably reflect a view that was dominant at least at the time the institution was first adopted. Second, by definition, institutions resist change.[34] Third, their continued existence tends to reinforce the views they reflect. They therefore should be a force for stability, contributing to keeping the views they reflect dominant. At any rate, their persistence suggests the continued importance of the views about political economy they represent. Even if societal views have changed, the possibility of 'institutional complementarity', 'lock-in' or 'path dependency'[35] suggests that the political economy they represent remains an important aspect of a country's overall political economy. Finally, while they may be evidence of attitudes and beliefs, institutions themselves are actually the product of behavior, so they combine those two levels of the culture represented by political economy.

These considerations all suggest that paying attention to the political economy expressed by a nation's institutions may provide a more meaningful guide to the country's actual political economy than surveys of mass values and attitudes. In short, a country's institutional structure may provide a reasonably good and much more tangible proxy for the nation's culture with respect to political economy. If many of the country's institutions represent roughly the same degree of state intervention in the market, that fact gives a reasonable basis for characterizing the nation's political economy.

One may object that this method simply substitutes for the problematic task of

---

(note 7) 869, quoting Masahiko Aoki, *Towards a Comparative Institutional Analysis* (Stanford: Stanford University Press 2001).

[30]   March and Olsen (note 3) 4.

[31]   Theda Skocpol, 'Bringing the State Back In: Strategies of Analysis in Current Research', in Peter B. Evans, Dietrich Rueschemeyer and Theda Skocpol (eds), *Bringing the State Back In* 3, 21 (Cambridge: Cambridge University Press 1985).

[32]   Peter A. Hall, *Governing the Economy: The Politics of State Intervention in Britain and France* 17 (Cambridge: Polity Press 1986).

[33]   March and Olsen (note 3) 6.

[34]   See definitions in note 29.

[35]   Ahlering and Deakin (note 7) 869–72. The standard example is the QWERTY keyboard for typewriters and computers. Ibid. 870.

generalizing about a nation's attitudes and behaviors relating to political economy the problematic task of estimating the political economy reflected by numerous disparate institutions. It is a fair point. Reference to institutions does not eliminate the necessity of relying on judgment to aggregate a mass of data. Moreover, it may be unclear in the case of some institutions what political economy they represent. However, the turn to institutions does give us tangible evidence of the culture we seek to characterize, and I have argued that the institutions themselves may represent the most important aspect of that culture.

2.3   A Typology for Institutional Structure

It would be very convenient if social science were to provide a generally agreed upon typology for characterizing each country's distinctive institutional structure. Although scholars have proposed many different typologies, none has met with general acceptance. As in the case of most generalizations, the closer one looks, the less clear the distinctions are.

Nevertheless, all of the most influential typologies seem to suggest at least the tripartite distinction captured by the categories in Figure 6.1 of statism, corporatism and pluralism. As discussed below, these categories correspond roughly to the state-centered end, the middle, and the market-centered end of the political economy spectrum, respectively. Even though there is vigorous debate, for example, about whether corporatism is a useful category and which countries are predominantly corporatist,[36] I nevertheless invoke them as ideal types. The point is not to classify any particular country as pluralist or corporatist, but to point to aspects of institutional structure that make one country more pluralist, more corporatist, or more statist than another. This subsection explains what each of these categories means by showing how they apply to the four target countries. The subsection will close with an argument that this typology is generally consistent with the other most influential systems for classifying political and economic institutions.

Of the four countries, the United States has the highest degree of pluralism.[37] Pluralist representation of interests can work in the US because it is 'a polity in which virtually all scholars agree that there is less structural basis for [state sector] autonomy than in any other modern liberal capitalist regime'.[38] The US provides the classical illustration of interest-group pluralism, in which societal groups interact with the state in a pattern of open competition among privately organized interest groups.[39] This pattern and 'the

---

[36]   See, e.g., Bob Jessop, 'corporatism', in Craig Calhoun (ed.), *Dictionary of the Social Sciences* 242 (Oxford: Oxford University Press 2002) ('one of the most contested concepts in political science and (international) political economy' (ibid.)). '[T]here was a period in the 1970s and early 1980s when corporatism had become a buzzword with so many definitions that it became almost meaningless'. Ibid. 246. For the debate on whether France is corporatist, see note 50 below.

[37]   See David Wilsford, *Doctors and the State: The Politics of Health Care in France and the United States* 56–83 (Durham, NC: Duke University Press 1991) (describing the fragmentation of the American concept of 'state' because of the effects of liberalism). 'Pluralism describes this system, in which, the myth would have it, *all* interests should be able to penetrate the purposely permeable political arena'. Ibid. 69; emphasis in the original.

[38]   Skocpol (note 31) 12.

[39]   Ibid.; Wilsford (note 37) 54.

absence of a politically unified working class, ha[ve] encouraged and allowed US capitalists to splinter along narrow interest lines and to adopt an antistate, laissez faire ideology'.[40]

The US has nevertheless developed some strong state institutions[41] and some corporatist structures,[42] but these are the exception. The preference for open competition among interest groups is inconsistent with the privileged access that characterizes corporatist institutions. The pluralist system provides private interests with many access points to the public policy process. State power is 'everywhere permeated by organized societal interests'.[43] There is no independent state interest; it is really just the sum of private interests. The result hoped for is full democratic control and transparency; the constant danger is 'grid-lock government'. In any event, it is quite difficult for state officials to control the process of policy formation, so decisive state action is possible only when there is a strong societal consensus. Pluralism in the United States thus appears to express and reinforce an anti-state, pro-market ideology.

The three European countries all exhibit a more corporatist structure than the US, but it is an especially characteristic feature for Germany. Scholars who study Germany emphasize the way in which private economic interests form umbrella organizations that play important roles in the determination of state policy.[44] 'Numerous institutions—corporate bodies, foundations, institutes—are organized under public law and carry out important policy functions'.[45] Because these bodies are self-governing, Peter Katzenstein concludes that '[s]tate administration [in Germany] is . . . mediated by the self-government of many social sectors'.[46] A classic example of German corporatism concerns the roles that both labor unions and private professional associations (*Berufsgenossenschaften*) play in setting the standards for toxic chemicals in the workplace.[47]

Political parties in Germany are also more powerful than those in France or the US because of the way they control the workings of government.[48] Corporatist structures enable communication and consensus building in both directions, from society to state officials and from state officials to society. They fit a middle position on the political economy spectrum because they are designed to facilitate consensus through self-governing structures and bargaining among various umbrella groups and with the government, a solution that relies on both private and state actors.[49]

---

40   Skocpol (note 31) 27.
41   Nettl (note 17) 569 (discussing autonomy of certain federal institutions).
42   Robert H. Salisbury, 'Why No Corporatism in America?', in Philippe C. Schmitter and Gerhard Lehmbruch (eds), *Trends toward Corporatist Intermediation* 213 (Beverly Hills, CA: Sage Publications 1979).
43   Skocpol (note 31) 12.
44   Peter J. Katzenstein, *Policy and Politics in West Germany* 23–30 (Philadelphia: Temple University Press 1987); Kenneth Dyson, 'Theories of Regulation and the Case of Germany: A Model of Regulatory Change', in Kenneth Dyson (ed.), *The Politics of German Regulation* 1, 16 (Aldershot, UK: Dartmouth 1992); Hall (note 32) 236; Gerhard Lehmbruch, 'The Institutional Framework of German Regulation', in Kenneth Dyson (ed.), *The Politics of German Regulation* 29, 39–42 (Aldershot, UK: Dartmouth 1992).
45   Katzenstein (note 44) 58.
46   Ibid.
47   Ibid. 32–3.
48   Dyson (note 44); Katzenstein (note 44).
49   Cf. Alan Cawson, 'Conclusion: Some Implications for State Theory', in Alan Cawson (ed.), *Organized Interests and the State* 221, 225 (London: Sage Publications 1985). 'Corporatism seems

There is considerable debate over how corporatist France's interest group structure is.[50] One French institution that is clearly corporatist is the Conseil Economique et Social (CES), an umbrella organization for private interests, which the government is constitutionally obliged to consult in preparing legislation on domestic issues. The CES includes delegates of trade unions, farm groups, business and professional groups, cooperative and mutual societies, nationalized industries, and unaffiliated experts and civil servants.[51] William Safran contends that scholars have increasingly been classifying France as statist because several aspects of the state-interest group interaction in France do not fit the corporatist mold and because France is so different in important ways from the United States.[52] However, Safran argues, France is becoming increasingly pluralistic, although, he concedes, there are still many ways in which certain interest groups may have privileged contacts with state officials. He concludes that '[m]ore often than not, policy making (e.g., on issues such as working conditions, wages, and productivity) is a tripartite affair, involving government, labor, and business'.[53] Scholars usually take these arrangements as hallmarks of corporatism.

To the extent that French political structure falls away from the corporatist model, it looks unlike both Germany and the US. For example, because of ideological fragmentation of its chief interest groups, French corporatist arrangements tend not to provide as significant a check on the autonomy of state actors as German corporatism does.[54] Because France is a unitary state, the national government in France can embody the French state in a way that the German federal government cannot.

Moreover, David Wilsford argues that the French state has 'tactical advantages' to make its policies prevail despite opposition from private interests. These tactical advantages include:

(1)   powers of the executive branch to make law and control the legislature;
(2)   the French president's especially strong powers to control state action;
(3)   the tradition of powerful ministerial staffs, separate from the ministries' functional divisions, that constitute cohesive units serving each cabinet minister for decision-making and policing; and

---

to require a state system which is strong enough to preserve its autonomy from societal interests, yet not strong enough for an independent conception of a transcendent interest to be enforced upon society in a directive mode without the participation of interest organizations'. Ibid.

[50]   John T.S. Keeler, 'Comment on Wilson', 79 *American Political Science Review* 819 (1985); F.L. Wilson, 'French Interest Group Politics: Pluralist or Neocorporatist?' 77 *American Political Science Review* 895 (1983); F.L. Wilson, 'Reply to Keeler', 79 *American Political Science Review* 822 (1985). For a more recent review of the debate, see Safran (note 22) 181–92 (with France's key corporatist characteristics (ibid. 182)).

[51]   Safran (note 22) 183.

[52]   Ibid. 189.

[53]   Ibid. 192.

[54]   'French governments have exercised a certain discretion in giving some interest groups favorable representation in advisory councils and in choosing others as privileged interlocutors . . .. [T]he fragmentation of and competition among interest groups have strengthened the government's power to determine which association is the "most qualified" defender of a particular socio-economic sector.' Ibid. 183. If this is corporatism, it seems to be a more statist version.

(4)   a strong, prestigious, well-trained and socially cohesive central government bureaucracy, staffed at the highest levels almost exclusively by an administrative elite who all
graduated from the same small number of *grandes écoles*.[55]

These structural features push France in the direction of the statist model, in which a
strong state bureaucracy develops state policy with minimal input from non-governmental
groups. It may be wrong to think of France as statist; it has after all a vigorous democracy.
Nevertheless, of the four countries under study, it has the most statist or state-centered
features.

The United Kingdom at various times has also displayed significant features of corporatist organization, including the kind of tripartite agreement between business, labor and
government that typifies corporatism in Germany and France. However, in the UK, these
agreements have proven to be more fragile than they have been in Germany or France.[56]
To the extent the UK falls away from the corporatist model, it falls in a direction opposite
from that taken by France and more in the direction of the United States. It is difficult
to know how to sum up the elements of the UK political structure for the purposes of
placing it on the political economy spectrum. Perhaps one should conclude that forces
that favor the market are precariously balanced against forces that favor the state, making
its political economy swing with the elections and from pressure by the European Union.
Here I treat the UK as a stable intermediate case. It is less market-centered than the US
because of the presence of much stronger political forces with ideological commitments
to state intervention and more corporatist institutional structures. However, the UK does
have a stronger tradition of preferring reliance on the market to reliance on the state than
what we find in Germany and France.

When we compare this contrast among pluralism, corporatism and statism with the
other main typologies on offer, we see that they are quite similar. For example, in his
survey of typologies, Michael Moran says that 'one of the best established classifications
in the literature' is one that contrasts

(1)   Anglo-American capitalism, 'where well organized securities markets not only
dominate capital markets, but also enforce a system of corporate governance which
marginalizes the state';
(2)   Rhineland capitalism, 'where a history of bank domination of capital markets and
elaborate systems of corporate cross-ownership result in the coordination of firm
strategies by networks that unite state and corporate elites'; and

---

[55]   Wilsford (note 37) 38–45. But see Safran (note 22) 189–92 (reviewing critically the application of statism to France and arguing that 'the policy process in France has become more pluralistic
and incremental' (ibid. 192)). Safran recognizes, however, the high status, and common education
of the bureaucratic elites in the *grands écoles*. Ibid. 294–8. He also recognizes that French policy
making does not correspond either to American pluralism or to corporatism, but rather is the result
of an interplay of market decisions, inputs by socioeconomic sectors, and autonomous governmental preferences—these last influenced by partisan considerations. 'The traditional ideology of
Colbertism can be seen in the tendency of the public authorities to control a large part of the credit
machinery; socialism has been reflected in minimum-wage and nationalization policies; . . . and the
"expertocratic" orientation revealed itself in the French approach to economic planning.' Ibid. 353.
[56]   Hall (note 32) 253–4.

(3)   East Asian capitalism, 'where a more recent history of spectacular economic development is attributed in part to the capacity of public bureaucratic
agencies to manage firm investment and disinvestment in the light of strategic
state goals'.[57]

The first category obviously describes a financial analogue to pluralist interest group
representation. It also clearly represents a market-centered political economy. The third
category is noticeably more statist and represents a more state-centered form of political
economy. The middle category's pattern of coordination through networks that unite
state and corporate elites is typical of corporatism, in which the influence of state and
private actors is more evenly balanced, suggesting a position at the middle of the political
economy spectrum. This typology's main difference from the pluralist, corporatist and
statist model concerns how it is applied to specific countries, but the points of contrast
are virtually identical. I would concede, for example, that France's statism may be more
apparent by comparison with Germany than in any absolute sense according to world
standards.

The highly influential 'varieties of capitalism' project of Peter Hall and David Soskice
echoes the distinction between Anglo-American and Rhineland capitalism. It arrays the
nations on a spectrum between the poles of the 'liberal market economy' and the 'coordinated market economy', which corresponds rather well to the poles I have suggested
for political economy if we lop off the truly state-centered end of the spectrum on the
grounds that it is not 'capitalism'.[58] Moreover, those authors distinguish French and
German styles of the coordinated market economy on some of the same bases I have
suggested for labeling Germany more corporatist and France more statist. For example,
they write that 'in Germany, coordination [among firms] depends on business associations and trade unions that are organized primarily along sectoral lines'. By contrast, in
France, because the managers of leading firms attend a few elite schools and typically
work for government before going to the private sector, French firms 'have close ties to
the state and weak ties to the rest of the enterprise. As a result, . . . they are less likely
to pursue the corporate strategies found in Britain or Germany and more likely to look
to the state for assistance'.[59]

Based on the foregoing social scientific analysis of institutional structure, it therefore
seems reasonable to assign the United States to the market-centered end of the political
economy spectrum, Germany to the middle of the spectrum, France somewhat more
toward the state-centered end and the United Kingdom somewhere in between Germany
and the US.

---

[57]   Michael Moran, 'Economic Institutions', in R.A.W. Rhodes, Sarah A. Binder and Bert A.
Rockman (eds), *The Oxford Handbook of Political Institutions* 144, 152 (Oxford: Oxford University
Press 2008) (general survey of typologies).
[58]   Peter A. Hall and David Soskice, 'An Introduction to Varieties of Capitalism', in Peter A.
Hall and David Soskice (eds), *Varieties of Capitalism* 1, 8–9 (Oxford: Oxford University Press
2001).
[59]   Ibid. 34–5.

3   FURTHER EXAMPLES ILLUSTRATING THE THESIS

3.1   Standing to Challenge the Constitutionality of Legislation

Rules of standing govern which parties may raise public law issues in litigation. As they relate to constitutional challenges to legislation, they nicely illustrate the political economy thesis. In both France and Germany, certain designated public office holders or groups of office holders have automatic standing to raise questions in their constitutional courts about legislation on an 'abstract' basis—that is, without the kind of individual interest at stake that occurs when the challenged statute is applied to a specific person. That kind of standing is obviously more state-centered than the US federal constitutional rule, which, generally, allows only parties asserting individual, personal harms in concrete cases to bring constitutional challenges. Note that, although the European model is called 'abstract review', what US law rejects is not necessarily review that is abstract, but rather the automatic standing of designated public officials.

US law in fact stretches the requirements of 'concreteness' in many cases, but only for private parties, not for officials seeking to sue in their official capacity.[60] Not only is the US rule less state-centered in the way it relies primarily on non-state actors to assert constitutional claims in court, it also uses the same logic as Adam Smith's (1723–90) rationale for the market. Smith's thesis was that in a system of buyers and sellers free to pursue their own best interests in market transactions, the operation of the market's 'invisible hand' would yield an allocation of goods and services to their highest use. Similarly, in the US system of constitutional litigation limited to concrete review, the public good of enforcement of the constitutional order is supposed to result from the efforts of private litigants raising constitutional claims for their own personal ends in their own private law suits. The US law of standing thus appears especially market-centric.

The German system is not as state-centered as the French one since it has long made provision for private parties to raise constitutional claims, too, in their own concrete cases. In France, for over 40 years, abstract review at the behest of officials has been the only form of constitutional challenge permitted. Since 2010, however, the French system has supplemented abstract review by adding a system of reference from the regular court systems to the French Constitutional Court, the Conseil Constitutionnel.[61] Nevertheless,

---

[60]   In Germany, the relevant office holders include one-third of the lower house of the legislature. In France, they include 60 senators or 60 representatives. For relevant citations to German, US federal law and French law prior to 2008, see John Reitz, 'Political Economy and Abstract Review in Germany, France, and the United States', in Sally Kenney, William Reisinger and John Reitz (eds), *Constitutional Dialogues in Comparative Perspective* 62 (Basingstoke, UK: Macmillan Press 1999). For a typical federal case refusing to stretch standing for an official party, see *Raines v Byrd*, 521 US 811 (1997). State law may stretch concreteness requirements for private parties even more than federal law by allowing them to assert claims liberally as representatives of the public interest. However, no state makes similar allowances for public officials. See John Reitz, 'Standing to Raise Constitutional Issues as a Reflection of Political Economy', in Richard S. Kay (ed.), *Standing to Raise Constitutional Issues: Comparative Perspectives* 257, 283–6 (Brussels: Bruylant 2005).

[61]   The new French review by court reference was adopted in 2008 by constitutional amendment, adding art. 61-1, which was implemented by a 2009 organic statute that took effect in 2010. Legifrance, Constitution du 4 octobre 1958, art. 61-1, http://www.legifrance.gouv.fr (select La

the French system is still more state-centered than the German system because, unlike the French, the German system grants private parties a right of direct access to the constitutional court if the regular courts refuse to refer the case. Only in France, the most state-centered country under consideration, do state officials completely control whether a constitutional challenge can get to the Constitutional Court.

The British first adopted judicial review of legislation in the 1998 Human Rights Act (HRA), and then only in the restricted form of allowing the higher regular courts to opine that challenged statutes are incompatible with the statutory HRA. This includes the Appellate Committee of the House of Lords, which used to serve as the highest court in the UK and has now become the Supreme Court of the United Kingdom. If the courts are unable to interpret a statute in a way that is compatible, they must still apply the statute, even as they issue their finding of incompatibility. Despite the care taken to preserve at least the letter of parliamentary sovereignty, this form of judicial review is still important.[62]

British standing doctrines in general look similar to or even stricter than US doctrine, usually requiring a concrete interest (called a 'sufficient interest' in British law). However, the UK's intermediate political economy is expressed in the adoption of one element of automatic standing for officials. Under legislation devolving power to the Scottish Parliament, it is 'possible for law officers of the United Kingdom and of the devolved government to make [a] referral' to the Judicial Committee of the Privy Council (now the Supreme Court) concerning the 'validity of devolved legislation, both before it comes into force and post-enactment in a freestanding application absent any concrete dispute'.[63]

3.2   Civil Procedure: Witness Interrogation

There is a significant difference between the way that civil and common law systems bring witness statements before a court and make them part of the record upon which the case is to be decided. In the US and the UK, attorneys for the parties have the chief responsibility for interrogating witnesses at trial. Judges may be authorized to ask questions, as well, but they seldom do, especially in the US, where jury practice tends to color all litigation.[64]

In Germany, judges have the chief responsibility for interrogating witnesses and making the record of their testimony, but the parties' attorneys can ask additional questions and make a record of the court's failure to investigate.[65] The French legal system avoids taking

---

Constitution, then titre VII). Services du Conseil constitutionnel, *Textes Relatifs à la question prioritaire de constitutionnalité: Dispositions organiques* (17 Jan. 2011), at http://www.conseil-constitutionnel.fr/conseil-constitutionnel/root/bank_mm/QPC/dispositions_organiques.pdf.

[62]   Stephen Gardbaum, 'The New Commonwealth Model of Constitutionalism', 49 *American Journal of Comparative Law* 707, 732–9 (2001).

[63]   Joanna Miles, 'Standing in a Multi-Layered Constitution', in Nicholas Bamforth and Peter Leyland (eds), *Public Law in a Multi-Layered Constitution* 391, 398 (Oxford: Hart Publishing 2003) (citing Scotland Act 1998, sec. 33, sched. 6, paras 4 and 34).

[64]   William Burnham, *Introduction to the Law and the Legal System of the United States* 82 (St. Paul, MN: Thompson-West, 4th edn, 2006); Penny Darbyshire, *English Legal System* 108 (London: Sweet and Maxwell, 7th edn, 2007).

[65]   John Langbein, 'The German Advantage in Civil Procedure', 52 *University of Chicago Law Review* 823 (1985).

witness testimony, if possible, but if controverted issues of fact have to be resolved, the court usually appoints an expert, who investigates the issues with the full participation of the parties but without formal rules of evidence or a verbatim transcript. The expert reduces the evidence of relevant witnesses to a written report, which is very difficult for the parties to challenge.[66]

The contrast shows the greater degree of liberalism in the common law tradition of the UK and the US. In effect, these more market-centered common law countries privatize the function of witness interrogation, which in the civil law is primarily the judge's job or, as in France, the job of the judge's agent, the expert. The commanding role of civilian judges in this regard fits their more state-centered political economies: in those systems, the state actors provide the main service of creating the record of witness testimony for the trial. Once again, French law shows its greater state-centeredness through the greater restrictions on the private parties' ability to challenge the investigation by the expert chosen by the judge.[67]

3.3   Contract Remedies

In the common law of the UK and the US, the normal remedy is monetary damages in an amount sufficient to put the plaintiff in the position she would have been in had the defendant not breached the contract. The court will order the breaching party to perform its side of the bargain (an order the common law terms 'specific performance') only if the plaintiff can show that damages would be insufficient to render the non-breaching party whole. Thus, for example, the common law grants specific performance for contracts for the sale of goods only if the goods to be sold are unique, some other aspect of the defendant's contract performance is unique or some of the damages the party has undoubtedly suffered cannot be determined without undue speculation. In the civil law of Germany and France, by contrast, the normal remedy for contract breach is to order the breaching party to perform its contractual promises. The plaintiff has the option to choose monetary damages instead, but in principle, she is not required to accept the substitute remedy of damages.[68]

---

[66]   Richard W. Hulbert, 'Comment on French Civil Procedure', 45 *American Journal of Comparative Law* 747 (1997); Daniel Soulez Larivière, 'Overview of the Problems of French Civil Procedure', 45 *American Journal of Comparative Law* 737, 745 (1997).

[67]   The aversion to regulation and preference for private enforcement of public policies in the US political economy may be linked to some of the civil procedure rules unique to the US that promote private litigation. These include the broad discovery powers for private litigants, narrow privileges, contingent fees, the American rule that generally does not shift attorney fees to the loser, treble damages in antitrust suits, punitive damages and class actions. John Reitz, 'Doubts about Convergence: Political Economy as an Impediment to Globalization', 12 *Transnational Law and Contemporary Problems* 139, 148–51 (2002).

[68]   This subsection is based on Reitz (note 1) 270–71. The principle is clearer in the German code than in the French one, which seems to suggest that specific performance is available only for obligations 'to give', not for those 'to do or not to do'. However, French courts and scholars have come around to the same general principle, and finally in 1972, France adopted a statutory basis for the courts' power to levy fines to enforce specific performance, a power the courts had long timidly asserted on their own. Note that all systems refuse specific performance in some cases, such as those involving close personal relationships or special forms of artistic or intellectual creativity. John P.

There is no claim here that political economy is the single cause of the difference in rules. The common law rule represents the settlement of the 'long jurisdictional struggle' in the late Middle Ages and the early modern period between the English common law courts and the courts of equity.[69] Nevertheless, it is clear that the common law rule is predicated on the presence of markets on which substitute performance of the breached contract can be purchased, while the civil law rule makes sense even if there is no market for substitute performance. In that sense, the common law remedy fits a more market-centered political economy, not because it is less regulatory, but because it literally fits an economy that includes a robust market and relies on the market to limit the state intervention necessary to provide a legal remedy to the bare minimum, a simple order to pay money. The civil law rule is not inconsistent with robust markets, but it is not tied to them, and in that sense is not as market-centered. Moreover, the order to perform the contract may be—depending on the contract—a more complex and deeper form of state intrusion, requiring the enforcement officer, if state enforcement is required, to monitor more complex behavior than simply paying a debt.

The difference in principle in contract remedies may not make much of a practical difference. The victim of a contract breach normally does not want to continue dealing with the breaching party if substitute performance is available and, under either system of contract remedies, victims normally choose the substitute remedy of damages. Nevertheless, the difference is symbolically important and shapes the way lawyers think about contracts and their remedies.

French contract law is in several ways the most state-centered of the versions of contract law under comparison.[70] One striking aspect has to do with the remedy of contract termination. In US, British and German law, one contracting party's breach gives the other party the right to terminate the contract if the breach is serious enough. However, in France, the non-breaching party has no unilateral termination right. If he wishes to be released from his own contract promises, he in principle has to sue to get court authorization. The rule clearly expresses the idea that the French state may have an interest in the continued performance of the contract independent of the parties' interests.[71] The difference may be largely symbolic because all of these countries recognize that one party's serious breach may justify the other party in suspending his performance pending

---

Dawson, 'Specific Performance in France and Germany', 57 *Michigan Law Review* 495 (1959) (for the law up to 1959); Ugo A. Mattei, Teemu Ruskola and Antonio Gidi, *Schlesinger's Comparative Law* 879–85 (New York: Foundation Press, 7th edn, 2009) (for a wealth of citations and the 1972 French statute).

[69] E. Allen Farnsworth, 3 *Farnsworth on Contracts* § 12.4, at 163–4 (New York: Aspen Publishers 3rd. edn, 2004)

[70] One important aspect of French contract law is the persistence of price controls. Price controls are most obviously part of a state-centered political economy, and alone among the four target countries, France has long had and still has a system of price controls, today limited principally to sale of certain commodities, agricultural and residential leases, and nearly all labor wages. Reitz (note 1) 260.

[71] It is revealing that this rule is included in the new Russian Civil Code, adopted in stages in the mid-1990s. However far the Russian political economy may have moved since the fall of communism, and the end of its command economy, it is still undoubtedly a strongly state-centered one. Ibid. 272.

assurances or guarantees that the other side will fulfill his contract obligations. Parties are also free to settle their differences and renegotiate contracts without litigation, so the non-breaching party does not always have to go to court in France. Nevertheless, the rule is more than a formality. Lawyers have to negotiate around it.[72]

3.4   Separation of Powers: Presidential and Parliamentary Systems

Differences in the degree to which distinct versions of presidential and parliamentary systems concentrate lawmaking power also fit variations in political economy. The key to understanding this relationship lies in recognizing that the US system of checks and balances, which rather evenly distributes power to pass legislation among the two houses of the legislature and the president, is profoundly threatening to a more state-centered political economy. The US system promotes legislative deadlock because any one of the three—either legislative house or the president—can block legislation. The president's veto can be overridden by a two-thirds vote in both houses, but that supermajority is difficult to obtain for most legislation.

The risk of deadlock may be acceptable in the American political economy because of the dominant hostility toward state regulation. Better to risk deadlock than to concentrate lawmaking power and run the risk that the state will enact bad regulation. However, in more state-centered political economies, the risk of deadlock is less acceptable because people expect the state to act to secure the common welfare and therefore it must be able to enact a legislative program.

I have argued that the parliamentary system of the United Kingdom, the German parliamentary system that limits votes of no-confidence to those in which the opposition is prepared to form a new government immediately (known as a 'constructive' vote of no-confidence), and the French presidential-parliamentary system represent legislative systems that progressively concentrate power to overcome legislative deadlock. The progressive concentration of power thus fits the increase in state-centered political economy as one moves from Britain to Germany to France.[73]

4   RELATED WORK ON LAW AND POLITICAL ECONOMY

There is a long tradition of exploring the connections between law, on the one hand, and political and economic factors, on the other. This tradition goes back at least to Karl Marx (1818–83) and Max Weber (1864–1920), but those two writers did not attempt to link political and economic structures to specific rules of law, and for a long time, neither

---

[72]   For other differences in contract law that match differences in political economy, see ibid. Reitz argues, for example, that the common law doctrine of consideration, which is unknown in the civil law world, reflects a market-centered political economy. In addition, differences in the regulation of the customer's right to rescind certain types of consumer contracts and in the regulation of standard contract terms reflect the countries' general political economies. Ibid. 261–9.

[73]   John Reitz, 'Political Economy and Separation of Powers', 15 *Transnational Law and Contemporary Problems* 579 (2006).

did any other Western scholars.[74] The best comparative law work focused on specific areas of law has always been alert to the impact of non-legal factors. We find many studies that compare specific areas of law in two or more countries pointing to features relating to political economy, especially the relative tendency toward state intervention in the economy, which helps to explain observed differences.[75] Nevertheless, the implication for comparative law of the revival of interest in the social sciences in evolutionary and institutional analysis has been 'as yet largely unrealized'.[76] Outside of my own work, only two types of attempts have been made to explore more systematically the relationship between national differences in specific areas of law and differences in general political economy.

The first effort was by Mirjan Damaška in his 1986 book, *The Faces of Justice and State Authority*, which argues that the diversity in systems of civil and criminal procedure could be seen as the product of two factors. The first factor has to do with differences in the dominant views within a given country about whether the state should 'manage the lives of people and steer society' or merely 'provide a framework for social self-management and individual self-definition'. The managerial view leads, he contends, to a conception of the administration of justice as primarily concerned with implementation of the state's policies. The more passive view of the state's purposes leads to a conception of the administration of justice as being primarily about resolving disputes.[77] Damaška's second factor concerns whether authority within the state is structured in a hierarchical or coordinate way.

His book is of seminal importance for the political economy thesis. Damaška's first factor, the choice between a policy-implementing process and a process for the resolution of disputes, is essentially the core question for political economy: how interventionist the state should be. His second factor is an aspect of political structure that I would include in the concept of political economy, essentially for reasons Damaška gives: A hierarchically organized bureaucracy fits a policy-implementing state much better than a coordinate organization because the dispersion of power in the coordinate model can too

---

[74]   See, e.g., Maureen Cain and Alan Hunt (eds), *Marx and Engels on Law* (London: Academic Press 1979); Léontin Constantinesco, 3 *Rechtsvergleichung* 362–84 (Cologne: B. Heymanns 1983); Max Weber, *Max Weber on Law in Economy and Society* (Max Rheinstein ed., Edward Shils and Max Rheinstein translators, Cambridge, MA: Harvard University Press 1954) (selections from Max Weber, *Wirtschaft und Gesellschaft* (Tübingen: Mohr, 2nd edn, 1925)); David M. Trubek, 'Max Weber on Law and the Rise of Capitalism', 1972 *Wisconsin Law Review* 720 (1972).

Cf. Mirjan R. Damaška, *The Faces of Justice and State Authority* 6 n.7 (New Haven, CT: Yale University Press 1986). Damaška notes that 'Marx never attempted to link his broad models of socioeconomic structure to formal aspects of the legal process', and dismissed the many subsequent attempts in the Soviet Union to do so, none of which appears to have been translated into English. Ibid.

[75]   E.g., Ronald Brickman, Sheila Jasanoff and Thomas Ilgen, *Controlling Chemicals: The Politics of Regulation in Europe and the United States* (Ithaca, NY: Cornell University Press 1985) (toxic chemical regulation); Joseph B. Board, Jr., 'Legal Culture and the Environmental Protection Issue: The Swedish Experience', 37 *Albany Law Review* 603 (1973); Mark J. Roe, 'A Political Theory of American Corporate Finance', 91 *Columbia Law Review* 10 (1991); Clyde Summers, 'Comparisons in Labor Law: Sweden and the United States', 7 *Industrial Relations Law Journal* 1 (1985).

[76]   Ahlering and Deakin (note 7) 866.

[77]   Damaška (note 74) 11.

easily frustrate state action.[78] Thus, even though he does not mention the term, Damaška uses aspects of political economy in his analysis. Broadly speaking, the current political economy thesis can be seen as an attempt to expand Damaška's approach, both beyond the subjects of civil and criminal procedure and beyond the narrow limits of the specific institutional structure he takes into account.

Another effort to link differences in specific legal rules systematically to elements of political economy has emerged out of the debate over the 'legal origins' literature. This literature applied the empirical methods of comparative economics, including numerical coding or indexing of a wide variety of information about a relatively large number of legal systems and statistical analysis of the correlations among the various features coded. One of the first questions they investigated concerned the correlations among membership in particular legal traditions, the level of protection for corporate shareholders and creditors and the dispersal of share ownership. Subsequent studies applied the technique to a broad list of legal rules and institutions.

Based on these studies, legal origins scholars argue that the common law is better than the civil law, especially the French subgroup of civil law, at fostering economic growth. Although the World Bank has been strongly influenced by the legal origins thesis, all aspects of the legal origins literature, from their coding to their conclusions, and especially the claim of the superiority of the common law for economic development, have been sharply criticized by comparative law scholars.[79] The importance of this literature for the political economy thesis lies in the reactions to the controversy elicited by the legal origins literature.

First, three of the leading legal origins scholars responded to the criticism by modifying the broad claim that the common law promotes economic growth better than the civil law[80] and broadening their interpretation of the term 'legal origins', so that it now stands, they say, for:

> a style of social control of economic life (and maybe of other aspects of life as well). In strong form (later to be supplemented by a variety of caveats), we argue that common law stands for the strategy of social control that seeks to support private market outcomes, whereas civil law seeks to replace such outcomes with state-desired allocations.[81]

Thus, legal origins scholars are coming to focus squarely on what I call political economy, although they do not use that term.

Current work on political economy agrees with the reformulation of the legal origins thesis as it relates to the four countries examined in this chapter. That is, for many

---

[78]   Ibid. 13. Cf. Section 3.4 above using a similar argument for connection between political economy and forms of separation of powers.

[79]   See, e.g., Ralf Michaels, 'Comparative Law by Numbers? Legal Origins Thesis, Doing Business Reports, and the Silence of Traditional Comparative Law', 57 *American Journal of Comparative Law* 765 (2009) (summary of the controversy and introduction to a symposium on that topic).

[80]   Rafael La Porta, Florencio Lopez de Silanes and Andrei Shleifer, 'The Economic Consequences of Legal Origins', 46 *Journal of Economic Literature* 285, 326–7 (2008) (civil law better in conditions of moderate turbulence).

[81]   Ibid. 286.

important issues, the law in the UK and the US (common law nations) tends to reflect a more market-centered political economy than the law in civil law countries like France and Germany.[82] The political economy thesis differentiates according to economic and political variables among members of the same legal tradition, whether from the civil or common law, and this makes for a more nuanced treatment.[83] Nevertheless, the reformulated legal origins thesis highlights significant differences in political economy between the two legal traditions.

Second, a group of scholars in labor law and corporate governance have argued for a reformulation of the legal origins thesis in a way that brings it even closer to the political economy thesis. While rejecting as untenable some of the distinctions the legal origins scholars seek to draw between civil and common law, they argue nevertheless that

> there were, and are, differences between the common law and the civil law, at the level of core concepts and guiding assumptions . . .. Thus in the civil law, the tendency is for freedom of contract to be socially conditioned when, in common law systems, it is , formally, unconstrained . . .. The enduring difference between common law and civil law systems operates at the level of the ingrained assumptions and understandings that are deployed in legal analysis, and in the values they serve to perpetuate.[84]

The differences with regard to contracts correspond broadly to the difference between 'liberal market' and 'coordinated market' systems postulated by the 'varieties of capitalism' literature, as does the 'distinction widely drawn in the corporate governance field . . . between systems based on arms-length or outsider control and those based on direct or insider control'.[85] Building on this institutional typology, these scholars use the concept of complementarity and a fine-grained historical analysis to develop an explanation for the 'evolution of distinctive legal cultures' in the civil and common law related to employment law and corporate governance.[86]

These scholars assert, in essence, that the critical factor explaining variation in employment law among these countries is the timing of industrialization. In brief, they argue that Great Britain's early industrialization occurred before its legal order had adopted modern notions of contract and property, with the result that the contract of employment and the company limited by share capital developed more slowly than on the Continent. There,

---

[82] Reitz (note 12) 857–9. There is great variation in the political economies of common law countries. New Zealand, in particular, appears to be more state-centered than the other Western, developed countries in the common law tradition. Important aspects of its political economy have been changing, sometimes dramatically, but it still seems roughly as state-centered as Germany in some important ways. See Reitz (note 73) 587, 589–90, 597–8, 601–02.

[83] Since the legal origins studies are based on numerical coding systems, the coding may suffice to show distinctions among countries of the same legal tradition, but the legal origins literature has not been looking for those intra-family distinctions.

[84] Ahlering and Deakin (note 7) 901 (citing Katherina Pistor, 'Legal Ground Rules in Coordinated and Liberal Market Economics' 9 (Brussels: European Corporate Governance Institute, ECGI Working Paper Series in Law, Paper No. 30/2005).

[85] Ahlering and Deakin (note 7) 872. See John Armour, Simon Deakin, Priya Lele and Mathew Siems, 'How Do Legal Rules Evolve? Evidence from a Cross-Country Comparison of Shareholder, Creditor, and Worker Protection', 57 *American Journal of Comparative Law* 579, 597–9 (2009).

[86] Ahlering and Deakin (note 7) 889. For the part of their work concerning employer terminations, see Section 1.1.

the nineteenth century codification movements led to a modernization of company and employment law several decades before industrialization. Codification on the Continent also contributed, they contend, to earlier recognition of the claims of organized labor. Then, once that basic pattern in each country was set, it became quite resistant to change because of complementarity.[87]

This discussion, which the authors call 'comparative institutional analysis',[88] is similar to the political economy analysis. Both approaches attempt to relate variation in the shape of the law in specific areas to differences in institutional structure relating to the degree of state intervention. The comparative institutionalists base their investigations on the dichotomy between liberal and coordinated markets from the 'varieties of capitalism' literature, but as we have seen in Section 2.3, this framework tracks the typology I have proposed for the political economy spectrum. Both approaches appear to place the four target countries in about the same positions on the political economy spectrum.[89] Neither discussion assumes that the differences found are immutable. Both are interested in how the divergence may wax and wane over time. The two approaches thus appear to be generally compatible; indeed, the comparative institutionalists' investigation sets the gold standard for careful, thorough comparison of the relevant law and its historical evolution.

Of course, the approaches are not identical. The comparative institutionalists have so far worked mainly on labor and corporate law. Their primary focus has been to criticize the coding on which the earlier legal origins literature is based and to take issue with the explanations that literature offered for how relevant divergence developed between the civil and common law. I have not used coding methods to develop the political economy thesis, though I see no reason why it could not be investigated using defensible coding techniques in multi-country studies. The debate about the reasons for the development of different legal cultures with respect to aspects of political economy may lend insight into how mutable those variations are. However, the political economy thesis has done its work when it has established pervasive and correlated patterns in both the general institutional structure of a country's political and economic systems and in its legal system. Other theories and methodologies can explain how the variations in political economy developed and persist or change. With the comparative institutional scholars, I expect that a 'deeper engagement with historical evidence' will offer the best methodology.[90]

5   SIGNIFICANCE OF THE POLITICAL ECONOMY THESIS

5.1   To Promote Understanding

What is the value of a thesis that does not provide a normative basis for demonstrating what the law should be? I believe that its real value lies in its utility for comparative law.

---

[87]   Armour et al. (note 85) 597–8.
[88]   Ahlering and Deakin (note 7) 903.
[89]   Ahlering and Deakin (note 7) only treat France, Germany and the United Kingdom, but Armour et al. (note 85) also treat the United States.
[90]   Ahlering and Deakin (note 7) 903.

Like any other defensible generalization, it promises to be useful for making sense of and organizing a variety of disparate information about the legal systems to which it applies. More importantly, it should be useful in promoting understanding. Like all comparative study, the political economy thesis may help lawyers better understand their own systems. Many of the examples discussed above involve rules and institutions so firmly fixed in the differing legal cultures and central to the way that the legal systems as a whole function that justifications have not been articulated or seriously debated. Analysis of the underlying political economy thus exposes unarticulated normative justifications related to political economy that one ought to examine openly.

US standing doctrine, for example, has long been in search of an adequate rationale. The comparison of that doctrine to the forms of abstract review common in continental Europe makes the liberal and anti-paternalistic basis for US standing doctrine apparent. By contrast, it helps Americans understand German discussion of abstract review as 'an objective procedure' to vindicate 'objective rights (or law)' (*objektives Recht*), a concept which stands for the state's interest in fulfilling its role to ensure the constitutional legal order.[91]

Political economy also helps to explain an apparent paradox regarding judicial review. Although Europeans long resisted judicial review of legislation for fear it would politicize the judiciary, they ultimately adopted it with abstract review, a form that permits the official plaintiffs to thrust judicial review quickly and directly into political debate, because they can bring a case in the constitutional court as soon as the statute in question has been promulgated (or even before in the case of France). In the US, the constitutionality of a statute cannot usually be tested in court until someone tries to enforce the statute against someone else. The requirement of waiting for a concrete case to arise tends to create a delay between the political debate and the court litigation. US jurists tend to think that the delay helps the public to keep from seeing the court case as nothing more than an extension of the political battle in the legislature, and they worry that abstract review may exacerbate confusion of law and politics. But the more state-centered political economies of France and Germany finally accepted judicial review, at least partly on the basis that the state has the responsibility to provide a constitutional legal order. State actors, however, cannot assure the fulfillment of that duty unless they have a way to ensure that appropriate legal challenges are brought to the constitutional courts. In other words, the more state-based political economies in France and Germany appear to be associated with a more state-based conception of what judicial review is about. Some form of automatic official standing is required in these more state-based political economies.[92]

By demonstrating the link between the design principles for political and economic systems and for law, the political economy thesis helps lawyers from one system make sense of and take seriously legal systems bearing the mark of a very different political economy that clashes strongly with their own. It is easy to dismiss something that appears too different. US lawyers are quick to see problems with abstract review or with judge-led questioning of witnesses. Non-US lawyers, alternatively, are ready to

---

[91]   Reitz, 'Political Economy' (note 60) 80–84.
[92]   Ibid.

see the possible problems with attorney-led questioning or the way that US rejection of abstract review deprives important state actors of a way to test the constitutionality of enacted law. The political economy thesis suggests, not that one country is right and another is wrong, but rather that these differences relate to a much broader policy variation in the appropriate degree of state intervention. By seeing the foreign law as part of a broader pattern, we are less able to dismiss it as irrational or unworthy. This forces us to engage with the foreign rule, to take it seriously, and to give it respect, even if we remain convinced that our political economy makes more sense than the foreign one.

In this way, the political economy thesis serves the most important function of comparative law, facilitating real cross-cultural understanding, not a superficial cultural relativism, but a real appreciation of foreign ideas as rational responses to a different history and a distinct way of balancing competing values. The political economy thesis posits that political economy is a central part of the distinctive legal culture in each country. It constitutes an essential element in the '"ground rules" or shared assumptions [that serve] as aids to the interpretation of the law' or the 'conceptual modes of thought through which legal discourse creates "epistemological maps" . . . that describe and categorize economic and social relations'.[93] This kind of serious, respectful cross-cultural understanding is at the heart of comparative law study,[94] and it is not a luxury good. It is vital for dealing with today's globalized world, in which collisions between differing political economies are becoming ever more important. Unfortunately, the contending parties do not always appreciate the variation in political economy underlying these conflicts.[95]

5.2   Future Lines of Research

The political economy thesis has been advanced primarily with respect to four countries: France, Germany, the United Kingdom and the United States. Nevertheless, even as to these countries, systematic work has so far been limited. The examples presented in this chapter are sufficient to show some good support for the thesis from several different parts of the legal system. Yet more work is needed even for these four countries to substantiate the claim that pervasive variations throughout the legal systems correspond to the overall differences in national political economies. Valid generalizations will require the cumulation of examples and the consideration of counter-examples.[96]

The thesis may also apply much more broadly to many, if not most, other modern legal

---

[93]   Ahlering and Deakin (note 7) at 899 (quoting Geoffrey Samuel, *Epistemology and Method in Law* (Aldershot, UK: Ashgate 2003).

[94]   William Ewald, 'Comparative Jurisprudence (I): What Was it Like to Try a Rat?' 143 *University of Pennsylvania Law Review* 1889 (1995).

[95]   Reitz (note 67). This study examines a conflict between the US and EU over differences in privacy protection regulation concerning personal information gathered in e-commerce, a trade dispute with Japan over Japanese restrictions on large retail stores, which was intended to protect its small- and medium-sized retailers, disputes over extraterritorial applications of US discovery rules and the contest between US and European models for influence over the drafting of the new Russian Civil Code.

[96]   The author intends to publish a book on this subject.

systems. It seems most likely applicable to other developed Western countries with sophisticated legal systems. However, except for an occasional look at countries other than the four on which this chapter has focused,[97] that work is waiting to be done. The applicability of the thesis seems plausible for much of the rest of the world. Models for the modern state and its governing structures have come mainly from Western Europe, and virtually every modern legal system bears influence from either the common law or the civil law or both. In addition, these transplants often have directly emanated from one of the four countries on which I have so far concentrated attention.

Nevertheless, it is also not clear how some of the concepts on which the political economy thesis relies apply to non-European countries. The contrast between pluralist, corporatist and statist polities, which seems serviceable for the United States and Western Europe, may not make sense in other polities.[98] Serious lack of state capacity may affect political economy in some states. It might be especially interesting to see what has happened to law imported from more state-centered political economies into less developed nations that lack the capacity for the state action required to make the state-centered law function. Does it just become dysfunctional, or does it actually change? These are the types of questions that scholars will have to address in extending the political economy thesis beyond the original focus on Western Europe and the United States.

FURTHER READING

Ahlering, Beth and Simon Deakin (2007). 'Labor Regulation, Corporate Governance, and Legal Origin: A Case of Institutional Complementarity?' 41 *Law and Society Review* 865.

Armour, John, Simon Deakin, Priya Lele and Mathew Siems (2009). 'How Do Legal Rules Evolve? Evidence from a Cross-Country Comparison of Shareholder, Creditor, and Worker Protection', 57 *American Journal of Comparative Law* 579.

Brickman, Ronald, Sheila Jasanoff and Thomas Ilgen (1985). *Controlling Chemicals: The Politics of Regulation in Europe and the United States*. Ithaca, NY: Cornell University Press.

Damaška, Mirjan R. (1986). *The Faces of Justice and State Authority*. New Haven, CT: Yale University Press.

Hall, Peter A. and David Soskice (eds) (2001). *Varieties of Capitalism*. Oxford: Oxford University Press.

Reitz, John (1999). 'Political Economy and Abstract Review in Germany, France, and the United States', in Sally Kenney, William Reisinger and John Reitz (eds), *Constitutional Dialogues in Comparative Perspective* 62. Basingstoke, UK: Macmillan Press.

Reitz, John (2001). 'Political Economy as a Major Architectural Principle of Public Law', 75 *Tulane Law Review* 1121–57.

Reitz, John (2002). 'Doubts about Convergence: Political Economy as an Impediment to Globalization', 12 *Transnational Law and Contemporary Problems* 139.

Reitz, John (2002). 'Standing to Raise Constitutional Issues', 50 (Supp.) *American Journal of Comparative Law* 437–61. Reprinted with updating as 'Standing to Raise Constitutional Issues as a Reflection of Political Economy', in Richard S. Kay (ed.), *Standing to Raise Constitutional Issues: Comparative Perspectives* 257–86. Brussels: Bruylant 2005.

Reitz, John (2006). 'Political Economy and Separation of Powers', 15 *Transnational Law and Contemporary Problems* 579.

---

[97]   E.g., Reitz (note 73) (New Zealand's version of separation of powers); Reitz (note 67) (aspects of EU law concerning the privacy of personal information, Japanese regulation of retail stores and the Russian Civil Code).

[98]   For the debate about Japan, see Wilks and Wright (note 14); Yamamura and Yasuba (note 14).

Reitz, John C. (2007). 'Political Economy and Contract Law', in Reiner Schulze (ed.), *New Features in Contract Law* 247. Munich: Sellier.

Reitz, John (2009). 'Legal Origins, Comparative Law, and Political Economy', 57 *American Journal of Comparative Law* 847.

Wilsford, David (1991). *Doctors and the State: The Politics of Health Care in France and the United States.* Durham, NC: Duke University Press.

7 Comparative legal psychology: eyewitness identification

Ruth Horry, Matthew A. Palmer, Neil Brewer and Brian L. Cutler*

1 INTRODUCTION

We focus in this chapter on one important area of legal psychology: eyewitness identification. Following a brief overview of the broader field of legal psychology and the history of eyewitness identification research, we outline the major contributions that psychological science has made to our understanding of eyewitness identification, and review the procedures used to collect and interpret identification evidence in the United States and England and Wales. We conclude with some thoughts about how one might improve the treatment of identification evidence in legal settings in the future.

1.1 Overview of Legal Psychology

Legal psychology has shaped thinking and practice in many areas of the criminal justice system, with psychologists (including researchers, and clinical and forensic practitioners) and legal professionals (including lawyers, judges and police officers) contributing actively to this field. Rather than attempt a detailed review of legal psychology in this short chapter, we introduce—as a starting point for readers interested in a broader treatment—a few brief examples of research issues that have attracted programmatic attention from researchers.

Legal psychology research has had much to say about the interpretation of evidence presented in the courtroom. Numerous studies have examined the way that jurors make decisions, both individually and collectively. For example, research suggests that juror-eligible individuals are better able to process and recall relevant information—and, hence, make better judgments—if they receive judicial instructions before, rather than after, hearing complex evidence.[1] In addition, several studies have found evidence of group

* Ruth Horry is a Postdoctoral Fellow, School of Psychology, Flinders University in Adelaide, South Australia.

Matthew A. Palmer is a Lecturer in the School of Psychology, University of Tasmania.

Neil Brewer is Dean, School of Psychology and Professor of Psychology, Flinders University.

Brian L. Cutler is Associate Dean and Professor, Faculty of Social Sciences and Humanities, University of Ontario Institute of Technology.

[1] Lynne ForsterLee, Irwin A. Horowitz and Martin J. Bourgeois, 'Juror Competence in Civil Trials: Effects of Preinstruction and Evidence Technicality', 78 *Journal of Applied Psychology* 14–21 (1993).

polarization, with the views held by jurors becoming stronger and even extreme as the jury interacts.[2]

The large literature on detecting deception is one of the best-known areas of legal psychology and it, too, is relevant to the interpretation of evidence in court. For example, numerous laboratory and field studies have demonstrated that lay persons and professionals (such as police officers) are only marginally better than chance at detecting lies in face-to-face interactions; however, through training and the use of innovative interviewing techniques, it is possible to enhance deception detection accuracy substantially.[3]

In work spanning the areas of investigative interviewing and false memory, researchers have demonstrated that presenting false incriminating evidence can lead innocent people to not only confess to a crime they did not commit, but also come to believe they are actually guilty.[4] This finding has important ramifications for the interpretation of confessions in police investigations and the courtroom.

Psychology has also shaped understanding of the relationship between mental illness and offending. For example, although we know that people diagnosed with schizophrenia are statistically more likely than non-schizophrenics to commit violent crimes, the risk of an individual with schizophrenia committing a violent crime is still very small (one study has estimated that only 0.02 percent of schizophrenics will be convicted of a serious violent offence in a given year).[5] Psychology has been instrumental in advancing understanding of the development, diagnosis, treatment and management of psychopathy, which has important implications for the legal system in terms of sentencing, predicting violent behavior and evaluating risk of recidivism.[6] More broadly, clinical and forensic psychologists play a critical role in defining and assessing defendants' fitness to stand trial.[7] Some researchers have estimated that approximately one in 15 defendants in the US undergo such an assessment.[8]

These are only a few of many areas of legal psychology, and we encourage interested readers to consult one of the many books that provide a broader coverage.[9]

---

[2]   Reid Hastie, Steven D. Penrod and Nancy Pennington, *Inside the Jury* (Cambridge, MA: Harvard University Press 1983).

[3]   Aldert Vrij, *Detecting Lies and Deceit: Pitfalls and Opportunities* (Chichester, UK: John Wiley & Sons 2008).

[4]   Saul M. Kassin and Katherine L. Kiechel, 'The Social Psychology of False Confessions: Compliance, Internalization, and Confabulation', 7 *Psychological Science* 125–8 (1996).

[5]   Cameron Wallace, Paul Mullen, Philip Burgess, Simon Palmer, David Ruschena and Chris Browne, 'Serious Criminal Offending and Mental Disorder: Case Linkage Study', 172 *British Journal of Psychiatry* 477–84 (1998).

[6]   Robert D. Hare, 'Psychopathy: A Clinical Construct Whose Time Has Come', 23 *Criminal Justice and Behavior* 25–54 (1996).

[7]   Keith R. Cruise and Richard Rogers, 'An Analysis of Competency to Stand Trial: An Integration of Case Law and Clinical Knowledge', 16 *Behavioral Sciences and the Law* 35–50 (1998).

[8]   Ibid.

[9]   See the Further Reading section at the end of this chapter.

1.2 Eyewitness Identification

There is good reason why, of all the different areas of legal psychology, eyewitness iden-tification warrants close examination. Identification evidence has considerable impact on police investigations and the outcome of courtroom trials. It often constitutes a key part of prosecution evidence and is very influential in shaping juror decisions,[10] particularly if the witness is confident in his or her testimony.[11] However, eyewitnesses are often mis-taken, as demonstrated numerous times in laboratory research and field studies involving police investigations.[12] Because eyewitness evidence is persuasive yet unreliable, it is not surprising that false identification is one of the major precursors of wrongful conviction in the United States and United Kingdom. According to The Innocence Project (a non-profit organization dedicated to overturning wrongful convictions and reforming the legal system), mistaken identification has played a role in more than 75 percent of the 290 cases of proven wrongful convictions in the US.[13] Many of these were for serious crimes; the average sentence of exonerated persons is 13 years and DNA evidence has proven the innocence of 17 persons who were awaiting execution.[14] Refining the way that profession-als collect and interpret identification evidence in the legal system has the potential greatly to reduce the number of innocent persons who are wrongly convicted.

Although many might expect identification procedures to be relatively uniform across different locations, this is not the case. One of the aims of this chapter is to give readers an appreciation of the amount of variability that exists in identification procedures not only between countries, but also between different jurisdictions in the US. The other aim is to highlight similarities and differences between the ways that professionals actually collect and interpret identification evidence in different legal settings, and the way that scientific research tells us that it should be collected and interpreted.

2 THE SCIENCE OF EYEWITNESS IDENTIFICATION

2.1 A Brief History of Eyewitness Research

Eyewitness identification research has its foundations in classic psychological research on memory and social influence. An identification test is essentially a recognition

---

[10] Elizabeth F. Loftus, 'Reconstructing Memory: The Incredible Eyewitness', *Psychology Today* 116–19 (December 1974); Fredric D. Woocher, 'Did Your Eyes Deceive You? Expert Psychological Testimony on the Unreliability of Eyewitness Identification', 29 *Stanford Law Review* 969–1030 (1977).

[11] Brian L. Cutler, Steven D. Penrod and Thomas E. Stuve, 'Jury Decision Making in Eyewitness Identification Cases', 12 *Law & Human Behavior* 41–56 (1988).

[12] Brian L. Cutler and Steven D. Penrod, *Mistaken Identification* (New York: Cambridge University Press 1995); Nancy Steblay, Jennifer Dysart, Solomon Fulero and R.C.L. Lindsay, 'Eyewitness Accuracy Rates in Sequential and Simultaneous Lineup Presentations: A Meta-Analytic Comparison', 25 *Law and Human Behavior* 459–73 (2001).

[13] The Innocence Project, Eyewitness Misidentification (2011), http://www.innocenceproject.org/understand/Eyewitness-Misidentification.php.

[14] The Innocence Project, Innocence Project Case Profiles (2011), http://www.innocence-project.org/know.

memory test; a witness must decide whether any of the lineup members presented match his or her memory of the culprit in question. Therefore, eyewitness identification research has been able to take guidance from the substantial recognition memory literature. For example, we know that identification performance—like recognition performance—decreases as the amount of time elapsing between viewing the culprit and the test increases.[15] However, although eyewitness researchers have been able to build on basic memory research, they have also had to consider the influence of numerous situational and social factors that might operate in the context of an identification test. For instance, the fact that the police have called in a witness to attempt an identification may lead the witness to assume that the culprit is in the lineup. This assumption may lead the witness simply to pick the person that best matches her memory of the culprit.[16]

Many researchers have made substantial contributions in terms of building on basic memory research to advance understanding of eyewitness memory. The early foundations of eyewitness research were laid in the late nineteenth and early twentieth centuries, most notably through the work of Hugo Münsterberg and George Arnold in the US and William Stern in Europe.[17] Eyewitness memory research returned to prominence in the 1970s through Elizabeth Loftus's groundbreaking work on false memories for events,[18] Robert Buckhout's well-publicized demonstrations of mistaken identification[19] and Gary Wells's conceptual distinction between *system* and *estimator* variables.[20] System variables are factors within the control of investigators that affect identification accuracy: for instance, the instructions given to witnesses, and the method used to select lineup fillers. Estimator variables are factors outside the control of investigators that affect identification accuracy: for example, the conditions under which persons witnessed the crime, and the characteristics of the witness.

Within the legal profession, there has been a long-standing appreciation of problems associated with eyewitness identification evidence.[21] However, it was during the 1990s that eyewitness research really began to receive broader attention from the legal community. This occurred not due to any particular breakthrough in eyewitness research, but because of substantial advances in DNA testing techniques. These advances led to numerous

---

[15]   Kenneth A. Deffenbacher, Brian H. Bornstein, E.K. McGorty and Steven D. Penrod, 'Forgetting the Once-Seen Face: Estimating the Strength of an Eyewitness's Memory Representation', 14 *Journal of Experimental Psychology: Applied* 139–50 (2008); Hermann Ebbinghaus, *Memory: A Contribution to Experimental Psychology* (New York: Dover 1964, originally published 1895).

[16]   Gary Wells, 'What Do We Know about Eyewitness Identification?', 48 *American Psychologist* 553–71 (1993).

[17]   George F. Arnold, *Psychology Applied to Legal Evidence and Other Constructions of Law* (Calcutta: Thacker, Spink & Co. 1906); Hugo Münsterberg, *On the Witness Stand* (New York: Doubleday, Page & Co. 1908); L. William Stern (ed.), 1–2 *Beiträge zur Psychologie der Aussage* [Contributions to the Psychology of Testimony] (Leipzig: J.A. Barth 1903–06).

[18]   Elizabeth F. Loftus, *Eyewitness Testimony* (Cambridge, MA: Harvard University Press 1979).

[19]   Robert Buckhout, 'Eyewitness Testimony', 231 *Scientific American* 23–31 (1974).

[20]   Gary L. Wells, 'Applied Eyewitness Testimony Research: System Variables and Estimator Variables', 36 *Journal of Personality and Social Psychology* 1546–57 (1978).

[21]   For a review, see Woocher (note 10).

exonerations,[22] some of which received extensive media coverage. A report commissioned by former US Attorney General Janet Reno found that the majority of these wrongful convictions involved mistaken identification.[23] Nowadays, many members of the law enforcement and judicial communities dedicate substantial time and effort to improving practices in the collection and treatment of identification evidence (such as Barry Scheck and Peter Neufeld, founders of The Innocence Project).

Eyewitness identification research has flourished in recent decades. There is now an extensive international community of eyewitness researchers, many based in the US and UK. These researchers collaborate across international borders, publish their findings in a common set of high-quality international journals (for example, *Law and Human Behavior* or *Journal of Experimental Psychology: Applied*), and attend national and international conferences. The journals and conferences are run by various professional organizations such as the American Psychology-Law Society, the European Association of Psychology and Law, and the Society for Applied Research in Memory and Cognition. Eyewitness memory is the subject of numerous journal articles and book chapters, and books and psychology textbooks often examine it. In the next section, we review some of the most important issues that eyewitness researchers have addressed. We discuss several issues that the vast majority of researchers agree on, followed by two issues that eyewitness researchers are still debating.

2.2 Current Scientific Knowledge

Eyewitness researchers have reached a consensus on two crucial issues regarding the construction of lineups. First, they agree that lineups should contain only one suspect. By allowing all positive identifications to be classified as suspect identifications or known errors, single-suspect lineups (versus all-suspect lineups) greatly reduce the chance that an innocent suspect will be falsely identified.[24]

Second, researchers agree that lineups must be unbiased or 'fair'. By this, they mean that the suspect should not stand out relative to other lineup members. The key point here is that lineups should provide a good, but not unreasonably difficult, test of whether the suspect is the culprit. Research suggests that an important first step is to select fillers (the innocent persons who appear in the lineup together with the suspect) that match the physical description of the culprit as given to police investigators by the witness[25] (and

---

[22] Barry Scheck, Peter Neufeld and Jim Dwyer, *Actual Innocence* (New York: Random House 2000).

[23] Edward Connors, Thomas Lundegran, Neal Miller and Tom McEwan, *Convicted by Juries, Exonerated by Science: Case Studies in the Use of DNA Evidence to Establish Innocence after Trial* (Alexandria, VA: National Instiue of Justice 1996); Gary L. Wells, Mark Small, Steven Penrod, Roy S. Malpass, Solomon M. Fulero and C.A.E. Brimacombe, 'Eyewitness Identification Procedures: Recommendations for Lineups and Photospreads', 22 *Law & Human Behavior* 1–39 (1998); Gary L. Wells, Amina Memon and Steven D. Penrod, 'Eyewitness Evidence: Improving its Probative Value', 7 *Psychological Science in the Public Interest* 45–75 (2006).

[24] Gary L. Wells and John W. Turtle, 'Eyewitness Identification: The Importance of Lineup Models', 99 *Psychological Bulletin* 320–29 (1986).

[25] C.A. Elizabeth Luus and Gary L. Wells, 'Eyewitness Identification and the Selection of Distracters for Lineups', 15 *Law & Human Behavior* 43–57 (1991).

hence likely to be easily brought to mind by the witness). Using fillers that do not match the culprit's description (for example, the witness described the culprit as blond, and a blond suspect was placed in a lineup of brunettes) increases the risk that an innocent suspect who resembles the perpetrator will be mistakenly identified. In some cases, it is not feasible or does not make sense to select lineup members who match the description of the culprit (for instance, there is no description, or the suspect does not match the description of the culprit). In these cases, lineup fillers should be similar to the suspect, though precisely what constitutes 'similar' remains a subjective judgment. An extreme hypothetical example of high similarity is a lineup of clones, which would represent a task beyond any witness, regardless of the strength of the witness's memory. Choosing fillers that match the description of the culprit is an effective compromise that yields a better mix of higher correct identification rates from culprit-present lineups and lower false identification rates from culprit-absent lineups compared to the match to suspect strategy.[26]

As an aside, although care must be taken in selecting appropriate lineup fillers, the exact number of fillers included in the more typically used lineups (that is, six, eight, ten or 12) appears to be less critical. In fact, some research suggests that, provided there are at least three plausible fillers, the total number of lineup members does not influence witnesses' propensity to choose from the lineup or the accuracy of their identification decisions.[27]

In terms of the presentation and administration of lineups, many (though by no means all) eyewitness researchers agree on numerous issues regarding the medium of presentation (for instance, live lineups versus photospreads), the use of double-blind lineup administration, the instructions given to witnesses prior to the lineup and procedures for recording information about the witness's identification decision (for example, witness confidence).

First, there is no meaningful evidence that identification performance differs between live lineups and photospreads.[28] Although this is perhaps surprising given the additional cues (such as build, posture or gait) available to witnesses viewing a live lineup, our current state of knowledge suggests that photospreads are no less valid in conducting identification tests than live lineups.

Second, many researchers strongly argue that lineups should use double-blind administration, meaning that the lineup administrator should not know which lineup member is the suspect and which are fillers. Knowing who the suspect is can alter the way that the lineup administrator interacts with a witness, even if the witness and administrator themselves are unaware of this.[29] In turn, this can lead to higher false identification rates compared to double-blind lineups.[30] There are multiple ways of achieving double-blind

---

[26]   Gary L. Wells, Sheila M. Rydell and Eric P. Seelau, 'The Selection of Distractors for Eyewitness Lineups', 78 *Journal of Applied Psychology* 835–44 (1993).

[27]   Glenn J. Nosworthy and R.C. Lindsay, 'Does Nominal Lineup Size Matter?', 75 *Journal of Applied Psychology* 358–61 (1990).

[28]   Brian, L. Cutler, G.L. Berman, Steven Penrod and Ronald P. Fisher, 'Conceptual, Practical, and Empirical Issues Associated with Eyewitness Identification Test Media', in David F. Ross, J. Don Read and Michael P. Toglia (eds), *Adult Eyewitness Testimony: Current Trends and Developments* (New York: Cambridge University Press 1994).

[29]   Sarah M. Greathouse and Margaret Bull Kovera, 'Instruction Bias and Lineup Presentation Moderate the Effects of Administrator Knowledge on Eyewitness Identification', 32 *Law and Human Behavior* 70–82 (2008).

[30]   Ibid.

administration. For example, the administrator can present the images of the lineup members in a randomly determined order on a computer screen that she cannot see, or shuffled in a folder so that the administrator is unaware of the suspect's position in the lineup until after the witness has made a decision.

Third, prior to viewing the lineup, the administrator should instruct the witness that the lineup may or may not contain the culprit, and that if the witness thinks the culprit is not in the lineup, it is appropriate to indicate so. Such instructions are often termed 'unbiased instructions'. Relative to unbiased instructions, biased instructions (which omit the above information) increase the propensity of witnesses to choose someone from the lineup. Although biased instructions can increase the rate of correct identifications from target-present lineups, they also produce a disproportionately large increase in false identifications from target-absent lineups.[31] Thus, on balance, the evidence clearly favours the use of unbiased lineup instructions that clearly indicate that the culprit might not be present in the lineup.

Fourth, immediately after the identification test, the lineup officer should make an accurate record of the witness's response (for instance, if the witness cannot decide between two lineup members then that should be recorded, even if one of the candidates is the police suspect) and the confidence with which that response was made. Recording witness confidence at the time of the identification response is important because there is a wealth of evidence that identification confidence judgments can be influenced by feedback from various sources (such as lineup administrators, other witnesses or attorneys).[32] For example, confirming feedback from a lineup administrator ('Good! You identified the suspect') greatly inflates witnesses' confidence in the accuracy of their decisions. There is debate among researchers about the usefulness of confidence assessed immediately after the identification test for evaluating identification accuracy. However, researchers do agree that confidence judgments influenced by feedback from external sources are not valid indicators of accuracy. (Note that this applies to identification confidence statements made in the courtroom as well.)

Finally, eyewitness researchers recommend that investigators should not have witnesses view a suspect on repeated occasions. This can occur, for example, if investigators ask witnesses to scan a series of mugshots, or to identify a suspect in a show-up (in which the suspect is presented to the witness alone without other persons), prior to viewing a formal lineup. Repeated exposure to a suspect increases the familiarity of that person to the witness, in turn increasing the chances that the witness will identify the repeated suspect regardless of whether the suspect is in fact the culprit.[33]

---

[31]   Roy S. Malpass and Patricia G. Devine, 'Eyewitness Identification: Lineup Instructions and the Absence of the Offender', 66 *Journal of Applied Psychology* 482–9 (1981).

[32]   Carolyn Semmler, Neil Brewer and Gary L. Wells, 'Effects of Postidentification Feedback on Eyewitness Identification and Nonidentification Confidence', 89 *Journal of Applied Psychology* 334–46 (2004); Gary L. Wells and Amy L. Bradfield, '"Good, You Identified the Suspect": Feedback to Eyewitnesses Distorts their Reports of the Witnessing Experience', 83 *Journal of Applied Psychology* 360–76 (1998).

[33]   Kenneth A. Deffenbacher, Brian H. Bornstein and Steve D. Penrod, 'Mugshot Exposure Effects: Retroactive Interference, Mugshot Commitment, Source Confusion, and Unconscious Transference', 30 *Law and Human Behavior* 287–307 (2006).

Not surprisingly, eyewitness researchers are seldom, if ever, unanimous in their rec-ommendations regarding identification testing. While there may be broad agreement on many issues surrounding the collection and interpretation of identification evidence, there are two prominent issues that have divided researchers: the usefulness of witness confi-dence as an indicator of the likely accuracy of identification decisions, and the method that should be used to present lineup members to witnesses.

Many eyewitness researchers have argued that the relationship between eyewitness identification confidence and accuracy is, at best, modest.[34] This implies that the confi-dence expressed by a witness in an identification decision should have little or no bearing on investigators' assessments of the likely accuracy of that decision. However, a growing body of evidence now contradicts this view. This change has largely been due to two advances in the way that the confidence-accuracy relationship is examined. First, when researchers began to look at the confidence-accuracy relationship separately for different types of identification responses, it emerged that confidence and accuracy were correlated more strongly for positive identifications than for lineup rejections (that is, 'culprit is not present' responses) and correct identifications were consistently made with greater confi-dence than incorrect identifications.[35]

Second, whereas earlier work examined primarily the correlation between confidence and accuracy, researchers have now begun to use other statistical techniques to assess different aspects of the confidence-accuracy relationship. For example, calibration reflects the extent to which the subjective probability of accuracy (that is, witness con-fidence) matches the actual probability of accuracy. If calibration is perfect, then deci-sions made with 10 percent confidence will be 10 percent likely to be correct, decisions made with 20 percent confidence will be 20 percent likely to be correct and decisions made with 100 percent confidence will all be correct. Research indicates that confidence and accuracy are well calibrated for positive identifications but not lineup rejections, although positive identifications are typically made with some degree of over-confidence (for instance, decisions made with 90–100 percent confidence are correct approximately 75–90 percent of the time).[36] Note that calibration is a particularly useful approach because it can assist jurors.[37] That is, knowing that positive identifications made with, for example, 90 percent confidence are 80 percent likely to be correct will help jurors

---

[34]   Robert K. Bothwell, Kenneth A. Deffenbacher and John C. Brigham, 'Correlation of Eyewitness Accuracy and Confidence: Optimality Hypothesis Revisited', 72 *Journal of Applied Psychology* 691–95 (1987).

[35]   Siegfried L. Sporer, Steven Penrod, Don Read and Brian Cutler, 'Choosing, Confidence, and Accuracy: A Meta-Analysis of the Confidence-Accuracy Relation in Eyewitness Identification Studies', 118 *Psychological Bulletin* 315–27 (1995).

[36]   Neil Brewer and Gary Wells, 'The Confidence-Accuracy Relationship in Eyewitness Identification: Effects of Lineup Instructions, Foil Similarity, and Target-Absent Base Rates', 12 *Journal of Experimental Psychology: Applied* 11–30 (2006); Nathan Weber and Neil Brewer, 'Confidence-Accuracy Calibration in Absolute and Relative Face Recognition Judgments', 10 *Journal of Experimental Psychology: Applied* 156–72 (2004).

[37]   Peter Juslin, Nils Olsson and Anders Winman, 'Calibration and Diagnosticity of Confidence in Eyewitness Identification: Comments on What Can be Inferred from the Low Confidence–Accuracy Correlation', 22 *Journal of Experimental Psychology: Learning, Memory, and Cognition* 1304–16 (1996).

evaluate identification evidence, whereas knowing that the confidence-accuracy correlation is 0.4 will not.

Overall, the evidence indicates that the confidence-accuracy relationship is more complex than previously thought. It is not a constant. Witness confidence is a useful indicator of accuracy, provided (1) confidence is measured immediately after the test, without the witness being influenced by feedback from external sources, and (2) the witness makes a positive identification from the lineup. Here, it is important to emphasize one fact that all eyewitness researchers agree about: even an identification made with absolute certainty can be wrong. Numerous experiments have demonstrated this under a wide variety of viewing and testing conditions[38] and high-profile criminal cases serve to illustrate the point.[39]

The second major topic of debate among eyewitness researchers is the manner in which administrators should present lineups to witnesses. In police investigations, most lineup presentations occur simultaneously, with the witness viewing all lineup members at once either in a live lineup or photospread. However, many researchers advocate sequential presentation, whereby the witness views one lineup member at a time.[40] The witness must decide whether a particular lineup member is the culprit before moving on to the next lineup member. In some versions of sequential presentation, the witness can only view lineup members once and the procedure finishes when the witness positively identifies someone or she has viewed all lineup members. In other versions, the witness views the entire lineup, regardless of whether and when the witness makes a positive identification.

Numerous studies suggest that sequential presentation dramatically reduces the false identification rate without substantially reducing correct identifications, thereby enhancing overall accuracy.[41] However, more recently, some researchers have argued that this effect emerges only under certain conditions, such as when the lineup is biased (that is, where an innocent suspect stands out as the best match to the culprit) and when the suspect appears relatively late in the order of a sequential lineup.[42] Some researchers argue that they have not yet tested sequential presentation under sufficiently varying conditions, and that the evidence in favour of sequential presentation does not yet warrant recommendations to adopt a wide-scale procedural change.[43]

Although many journal articles have focussed on a comparison of sequential versus simultaneous lineups, perhaps the most critical issue raised in this debate is that neither

---

[38] Ibid.; Sporer et al. (note 35).

[39] *Cotton v North Carolina*, 318 NC 663 (1987); Jennifer Thompson, 'I Was Certain, But I Was Wrong', *New York Times* (18 June 2000).

[40] Nancy K. Steblay, Jennifer E. Dysart and Gary L. Wells, 'Seventy-Two Tests of the Sequential Lineup Superiority Effect: A Meta-Analysis and Policy Discussion', 17 *Psychology, Public Policy, & Law* 99–139 (2011).

[41] Steblay et al. (note 12).

[42] Curt A. Carlson, Scott D. Gronlund and Steven E. Clark, 'Lineup Composition, Suspect Position, and the Sequential Lineup Advantage', 14 *Journal of Experimental Psychology: Applied* 118–28 (2008).

[43] Roy S. Malpass, Colin G. Tredoux and Dawn McQuiston-Surrett, 'Public Policy and Sequential Lineups', 14 *Legal and Criminological Psychology* 1–12 (2009).

sequential nor simultaneous lineups produce ideal accuracy rates.[44] Therefore, enhancing identification accuracy through the development of novel methods of lineup presentation should be a top priority for eyewitness researchers.[45]

3   PROCEDURES FOR COLLECTING EYEWITNESS IDENTIFICATION EVIDENCE

This section contrasts the ways in which eyewitness identification evidence is collected and admitted to trial in the UK (particularly England and Wales) and the US. These countries differ dramatically in terms of the structuring of their policing and judicial systems, although comparatists classify both within the common law tradition. England follows a centralized model, with police powers mandated by the Police and Criminal Evidence (PACE) Act 1984 and accompanying Codes of Practice.[46] The US follows a decentralized model, with thousands of independent law enforcement agencies. Most judicial power is devolved to state courts under the principle of federalism. State constitutions and legislation only bind officials and legal professionals within that state.[47] These organizational differences between England and the US have created stark differences in eyewitness identification procedures.[48] In the following subsections, we review these procedures and consider how well they conform to the recommendations of psychologists.

3.1   Procedures in England and Wales

The PACE Act Codes (hereafter 'the Codes') govern many aspects of policing in England, including eyewitness identification procedures. Officials review the Codes regularly and they are legally enforceable. The Codes specify several permitted methods for collecting identification evidence, including video and live lineups.[49] Ten years ago, most lineups in England were live.[50] However, live lineups were expensive, inefficient and problematic.[51]

---

[44]   R.C.L. Lindsay, Jamal K. Mansour, Jennifer L. Beaudry, Amy-May Leach and Michelle I. Bertrand, 'Sequential Lineup Presentation: Patterns and Policy', 14 *Legal and Criminological Psychology* 13–24 (2009).

[45]   Neil Brewer and Matthew A. Palmer, 'Eyewitness Identification Tests', 15 *Legal and Criminological Psychology* 77–96 (2010); Wells, Memon and Penrod (note 23).

[46]   See UK Home Office, Police and Criminal Evidence Act 1984 (PACE) and accompanying codes of practice, http://www.homeoffice.gov.uk/police/powers/pace-codes (including Welsh translation). The PACE Act Codes apply to all police forces in England and Wales. Throughout this chapter, we will discuss English procedure though the same arguments apply as well in Wales.

[47]   US Department of Justice, *Outline of the U.S. Legal System* (2004), http://www.america.gov/publications/books/outline-of-us-legal-system.html.

[48]   Roy S. Malpass, Stephen J. Ross, Christian A. Meissner and Jessica L. Marcon, 'The Need for Expert Testimony on Eyewitness Identification', in Brian L. Cutler (ed.), *Expert Testimony on the Psychology of Eyewitness Identification* (Oxford: Oxford University Press 2009).

[49]   The Codes do not permit identification from photospreads.

[50]   Yvette Tinsley, 'Even Better than the Real Thing? The Case for Reform of Identification Procedures', 5 *The International Journal of Evidence & Proof* 99–110 (2001).

[51]   Ibid.

These problems led to the development of the video lineup.[52] Digital video clips of thousands of volunteers are stored in large databases, making it fast and easy to select suitable fillers, and cancellation of lineups due to witness non-attendance dropped from 46 to 5 percent.[53] Field studies conducted in England before and after the widespread adoption of video lineups have shown remarkable consistency in the rates at which witnesses identify suspects.[54] Given the obvious benefits of video lineups, the Codes prioritize the use of video lineups over any other identification procedure. Video lineups are now standard procedure across most forces in England.

The Codes provide rules for conducting lineups (whether video or live). Some of these rules conform to current best practices advocated by psychologists. For example, the witness must be cautioned that the culprit may or may not be present in the lineup, the lineup must contain a sufficient number of plausible fillers (specifically, at least eight fillers), and witnesses must not be given any information that could cue them to the identity of the suspect before the lineup (including the decisions of other witnesses). Other rules, however, flout what many researchers would consider best practice recommendations. The Codes do not require double-blind lineup administration, stating only that 'care must be taken not to direct the witness's attention to any one individual image or give any indication of the suspect's identity'.[55] The officer who administers the lineup must not have any other involvement with the case and should therefore have no stake in securing a suspect identification. Yet as long as the officer is aware of the identity of the suspect, there remains a risk of unintentional cueing.[56] Even if there is no cueing, the use of non-blind administration leaves open the possibility of cueing and therefore threatens the credibility of the procedure.

The Codes also state that administrators must choose fillers to resemble the suspect. However, many psychologists argue that officials should choose fillers, in the first instance, to match the witness's description of the culprit, rather than just in terms of similarity to the suspect's appearance.[57] In a description-matched strategy, fillers are matched on all features in the witness's description, but can differ on other features. While this ensures that all lineup members match the witness's description, research does not provide any

---

[52]   Richard I. Kemp, Graham E. Pike and Nicola A. Brace, 'Video-Based Identification Procedures: Combining Best Practice and Practical Requirements When Designing Identification Systems', 7 *Psychology, Public Policy, & Law* 802–07 (2001).

[53]   Graham Pike, Richard Kemp, Nicola Brace, J. Allen and G. Rowlands, 'The Effectiveness of Video Identification Parades', 8 *Proceedings of the British Psychological Society* 44 (2000).

[54]   Daniel B. Wright and Anne T. McDaid, 'Comparing System and Estimator Variables Using Data from Real Line-ups', 10 *Applied Cognitive Psychology* 75–84 (1996); Tim Valentine, Alan Pickering and Stephen Darling, 'Characteristics of Eyewitness Identification that Predict the Outcome of Real Lineups', 17 *Applied Cognitive Psychology* 969–93 (2003); Amina Memon, Catriona Havard, Brian Clifford, Fiona Gabbert and Moray Watt, 'A Field Evaluation of the VIPER System: A New Technique for Eliciting Eyewitness Identification Evidence', 17 *Psychology, Crime, & Law* 711–29 (2011); Ruth Horry, Amina Memon, Daniel B. Wright and Rebecca Milne, 'Predictors of Eyewitness Identification Decisions from Video Lineups in England: A Field Study', 36 *Law & Human Behavior* (2012) (DOI: 10.1007/s10979-011-9279-z).

[55]   Police and Criminal Evidence Act, Code D: Code of Practice for the Identification of Persons by Police Officers § 173 (1984).

[56]   Greathouse and Kovera (note 29).

[57]   Luus and Wells (note 25).

clear specifications of precisely how similar to the suspect the fillers should be in order to produce an appropriately discriminating test. Two studies evaluated the fairness of lineups from real cases from England.[58] While live lineups were biased towards choosing the suspect, video lineups were found to be fairer despite the use of a suspect-matched strategy.

The Codes do not require the witness to provide a statement of certainty following identification. Given the common finding that information encountered after the identification procedure distorts witness confidence,[59] recording confidence immediately is essential if the confidence assessment is to inform any evaluation of the likely reliability of the identification. The Codes state that any comments made by the witness must be recorded, but they do not require officers to ask for a statement of certainty. Anecdotal evidence actually suggests that officers may prevent witnesses making such statements so that the witnesses do not undermine the strength of a suspect identification.[60] There is clearly a need for the Codes to address this shortcoming concerning the assessment of witness confidence, particularly if a witness will be asked later in an investigation—or worse, in court—about the confidence in her identification.

UK police developed the video lineup and it is quite unlike the procedures employed in the laboratory. The process necessitates that each clip is seen individually, one after the other. At first glance, this seems very similar to the sequential lineup developed by psychologists.[61] However, the video lineup procedure used in England requires all witnesses to view the lineup twice and allows unlimited additional passes through the lineup. The sequential lineup procedure was designed to undermine witnesses' abilities to rely on 'relative judgments' (that is, select the person who is the best match to the culprit).[62] Allowing witnesses to return to different faces repeatedly may reinstate that ability, removing any potential benefits of sequential presentation. Analyses of real identifications have shown that witnesses who request additional viewings of the lineup are more likely to choose incorrectly than those who view the lineup only once.[63]

What can we conclude about lineup procedures in England? Video lineups are easier than live lineups to administer. It is easier to create fair lineups with the PACE system than with live lineups due to the large database of available fillers.[64] Clear, legally enforceable guidelines ensure consistency across all police forces in England. However, these rules do not always conform to recommended best practices. Lineups are not required to

---

[58]   Tim Valentine and Pamela Heaton, 'An Evaluation of the Fairness of Police Line-Ups and Video Identifications', 13 *Applied Cognitive Psychology* S59–S72 (1999); Tim Valentine, Niobe Harris, Anna C. Piera and Stephen Darling, 'Are Police Video Identifications Fair to African-Caribbean Suspects?', 17 *Applied Cognitive Psychology* 459–76 (2003).

[59]   Semmler et al. (note 32); Wells and Bradfield (note 32).

[60]   Mark R. Kebbell, 'The Law Concerning the Conduct of Lineups in England and Wales: How Well Does It Satisfy the Recommendations of the American Psychology-Law Society?', 24 *Law & Human Behavior* 309–15 (2000).

[61]   R.C.L. Lindsay and G.L. Wells, 'Improving Eyewitness Identifications from Lineups: Simultaneous Versus Sequential Lineup Presentation', 70 *Journal of Applied Psychology* 556–64 (1985).

[62]   Ibid.

[63]   Memon et al. (note 54); Horry et al. (note 54).

[64]   Kemp et al. (note 52); Valentine and Heaton (note 58); Valentine et al. (note 58).

be double blind, officials need not record witness confidence following the identification and fillers are matched to the appearance of the suspect without necessarily matching the description of the culprit. In a 2007 consultation, the British Psychological Society raised these concerns,[65] yet the revised Codes did not address these issues. Psychologists, therefore, must continue to work with policy makers to improve the quality of eyewitness identification procedures in England.

3.2   Procedures in the United States

In contrast to England, the US has no national, legally enforceable rules on eyewitness identification procedures, leading to huge procedural variation across the country. In a national police survey, most officers reported that they learned about identification procedures from other officers,[66] and the vast majority used only their own judgment to assess lineup fairness.[67] Photospreads were the most common procedure reported, with some police departments also using live lineups.[68] A statewide survey of law enforcement agencies in Texas found that only 12 percent had written policies on eyewitness identification procedures.[69] Written policies, when in place, often fell short of best practice recommendations, with few requiring double-blind administration.[70] Various groups have called for procedural reform in the wake of the US DNA exoneration cases, including the American Psychology-Law Society,[71] the National Institute of Justice (NIJ),[72] the Justice Project[73] and the American Bar Association.[74] The recommendations of these groups differ in some minor ways, but together they cover many key components, including the use of single-suspect lineups and cautionary instructions that the culprit may not be present. Some groups have advocated sequential lineups, while others have remained impartial on that point, given unresolved debates in the psychological literature.

---

[65]   Daniel B. Wright, 'British Psychological Society Submission to the Home Office Consultation on "Modernising Police Powers: Review of the Police and Criminal Evidence (PACE) Act 1984"' (2007), http://www.bps.org.uk (search 'Modernising Police Powers').

[66]   Michael S. Wogalter, Roy S. Malpass and Dawn E. McQuiston, 'A National Survey of U.S. Police on Preparation and Conduct of Identification Lineups', 10 *Psychology, Crime, & Law* 69–82 (2004).

[67]   Ibid.

[68]   Ibid.

[69]   The Justice Project, 'Eyewitness Identification Procedures in Texas' (2008), http://www.the justiceproject.org/wp-content/uploads/texas-eyewitness-report-final2.pdf.

[70]   Ibid.

[71]   Wells et al. (note 23).

[72]   Technical Working Group for Eyewitness Evidence, *Eyewitness Evidence: A Guide for Law Enforcement*, Washington, DC: United States Department of Justice, Office of Justice Programs (1999).

[73]   The Justice Project, 'Eyewitness Identification: A Policy Review' (n.d.), http://www.thejusti ceproject.org/wp-content/uploads/polpack_eyewitnessid-fin21.pdf.

[74]   American Bar Association, Criminal Justice Section, 'American Bar Association Statement of Best Practices for Promoting the Accuracy of Eyewitness Identification Procedures Dated August, 2004', http://adnew.abanet.org/sections/criminaljustice/CR209700/PublicDocuments/ABAEyewitnessIDrecommendations.pdf.

Uptake of these recommendations has been slow. It is more than ten years since the NIJ published its guide, yet few states have reformed their procedures. New Jersey became the first in 2001, when the attorney general mandated the NIJ guidelines statewide. A handful of other states have adopted guidelines or passed legislation, including Illinois, Maryland, New York, North Carolina, Ohio, Vermont, West Virginia and Wisconsin.[75] Others have established advisory groups to review existing procedures, including California and Texas.[76] Some reforms have taken place at local level, including in Denver, Boston and Dallas.[77] However, most states have resisted change despite the role that mistaken identification plays in US wrongful conviction cases. Why has change been so slow? Law enforcement is decentralized in the US, with no single governing body to ensure consistency. There has also been a 'historical lack of communication between scientists and law enforcement'.[78] Researchers usually publish their empirical findings in psychological journals and present them at scientific conferences, which are inaccessible to most people in law enforcement. There has also been a lack of leadership from the higher courts and legislatures.[79]

In addition, there are further challenges for reform. In 2005, the Illinois legislature commissioned the state police to conduct a pilot study to test the effectiveness of the double-blind sequential lineup in the field. Across three local jurisdictions, the double-blind sequential lineup was compared with the (non-blind) simultaneous lineup.[80] At first glance, the results appeared to suggest that the non-blind simultaneous procedure was, in fact, superior to the double-blind sequential procedure. However, the academic community met this study with a furious backlash, citing methodological flaws so severe as to prohibit any meaningful conclusions being drawn from the data.[81] Field experiments are now under way with the cooperation of law enforcement officials and psychologists, which will avoid the pitfalls of the Illinois pilot program.

Those who resist procedural reform argue that there are already legal safeguards in place to protect innocent suspects, including a constitutional right to legal counsel at a post-indictment live lineup,[82] pre-trial motions to suppress identification evidence obtained using suggestive procedures and cross-examination of witnesses at trial. These safeguards, however, are 'starkly inadequate'.[83] Most identification procedures involve photospreads

---

[75]   Supreme Court of New Jersey, 'Report of the Special Master' (2010), filed in *New Jersey v Henderson*, http://www.judiciary.state.nj.us/pressrel (search 'Henderson').

[76]   Ibid.

[77]   Ibid.

[78]   The Justice Project (note 73) 2.

[79]   Ibid.

[80]   Sherri H. Mecklenburg, *Report to the Legislature of the State of Illinois: The Illinois Pilot Program on Double-Blind, Sequential Lineup Procedures* (Springfield, IL: Illinois State Police 2006).

[81]   Daniel L. Schacter, Robyn Dawes, Larry L. Jacoby, Daniel Kahneman, Richard Lempert, Henry L. Roediger and Robert Rosenthal, 'Policy Forum: Studying Eyewitness Identifications in the Field', 32 *Law & Human Behavior* 3–5 (2008); Nancy K. Steblay, 'What We Now Know: The Evanston Illinois Field Lineups', 35 *Law & Human Behavior* 1–12 (2011); Gary L. Wells, 'Field Experiments on Eyewitness Identification: Toward a Better Understanding of Pitfalls and Prospects', 32 *Law & Human Behavior* 6–10 (2008).

[82]   *United States v Wade*, 388 US 218 (1967).

[83]   The Justice Project (note 73) 2.

rather than live lineups,[84] yet the constitutional right to counsel does not apply to photo-spreads. Very few pre-trial suppression motions are successful,[85] for reasons that we will explore later. Cross-examination is not useful for revealing inaccuracies in identification evidence, as even honest witnesses who are certain in their memories may be inaccurate. The best protection for the innocent is to use fair identification procedures.

In conclusion, England and the US differ markedly in their eyewitness identification procedures. All police forces in England must conform to one standard set of rules. No such national, legally enforceable rules exist in the US. There are, however, guidelines published by several different bodies, which have begun to influence policy at state and local levels. At present, procedures in both countries fall short of ideal procedures recommended by psychologists.

Differences in law and legal procedures between England and the US and among the US states and jurisdictions understandably result in variation in the procedures used for eyewitness identification. This may be acceptable from a legal perspective, but this state of affairs makes much less sense from a psychological perspective. There is no reason to think that human memory operates differently among British and US citizens and differently among citizens of New York and New Jersey. On the contrary, it is reasonable to expect that the factors that influence identification accuracy—including procedures for securing eyewitness identifications—are the same among these groups. Indeed, researchers from various continents collaborate on eyewitness research regularly and operate under the implicit assumption that findings are generalizable across populations. Psychologists would hope that the existence of an internationally accepted body of research on eyewitness science should produce a set of best practices that would be applicable across countries. Perhaps continued international collaboration among scientists will eventually lead to such a positive development.

4 EYEWITNESS IDENTIFICATION EVIDENCE IN THE COURTS

4.1 Courts in England and Wales

Following two high-profile cases of wrongful conviction in England, Lord Devlin led an inquiry into eyewitness identification evidence. The Devlin Report,[86] published in 1976, recommended that no trial should proceed based on eyewitness identification evidence alone, as the risks of wrongful conviction were too high.[87] The response of the courts to the Devlin Report, however, was slow and conservative. Devlin's central recommendation, that prosecutors should not try suspects on uncorroborated eyewitness identification, was

---

[84] Wogalter et al. (note 66).

[85] Gary L. Wells and Deah S. Quinlivan, 'Suggestive Eyewitness Identification Procedures and the Supreme Court's Reliability Test in Light of Eyewitness Science', 33 *Law & Human Behavior* 1–24 (2009).

[86] Lord P. Devlin, *Report to the Secretary of State for the Home Department on the Departmental Committee on Evidence of Identification in Criminal Cases* (London: HMSO 1976).

[87] Ibid.

never affirmed by statute or court rule. Graham Davies, an eminent professor of legal psychology in the UK, lamented that 'a promising start with Devlin has been muted by the conservatism of the law lords'[88] and argued that miscarriages of justice would continue to plague the English justice system until this recommendation was carried into law.[89]

Following the Devlin Report, the Court of Appeal attempted to draw a meaningful distinction between good and poor quality identifications.[90] The Court reviewed several cases involving disputed eyewitness identification evidence, and distinguished between poor quality identifications based on a witness's 'fleeting glimpse' and good quality identifications based on longer exposure durations. The Court presented a hypothetical scenario in which a witness was kidnapped and in the presence of the kidnapper over several days. The Court ruled that any identification made by this witness would be high quality, and would be sufficient for a conviction even if uncorroborated. In contrast, a witness who catches a brief glimpse of a handbag thief would provide a poor quality identification. The Court ruled that uncorroborated poor quality identifications should automatically result in the dismissal of the case.

These rulings, known as the *Turnbull rulings*, provide grounds for exclusion of eyewitness identification evidence if based only on a brief observation of the culprit. However, this only applies to uncorroborated evidence, and evidence from other witnesses (even of poor quality) is treated as independent corroborating evidence. In a very high profile case, a court convicted Barry George of murdering the television presenter Jill Dando. Nine witnesses described seeing a man of similar appearance to George in the proximity of the crime several hours before the murder. Eight of these witnesses attended live lineups, conducted a year and a half after the incident. Only one witness made an unqualified positive identification of George. Four witnesses made no identification, one identified a volunteer, and two made tentative identifications of George.[91] At trial, both of the latter witnesses testified to being sure in their identifications of George, despite their misgivings at the time of the lineup.

George appealed his conviction in 2002 based on the inconsistencies of the eyewitness evidence.[92] Amazingly, the Court concluded that 'when the identification evidence is looked at as a whole, it provides compelling evidence that the appellant had been at the scene of the crime at the relevant time'.[93] The Court dismissed that appeal, though George launched a successful appeal in 2007[94] and was acquitted at a retrial in 2008. This case was an embarrassing failure of the English legal system, which highlights the urgent need

---

[88]   Graham M. Davies, 'The Legal Impact of Psychological Research on Eyewitness Testimony: British and American Experiences', 24 *Journal of the Forensic Science Society* 165, 172 (1984).

[89]   Graham M. Davies, 'Mistaken Identification: Where Law Meets Psychology Head On', 35 *The Howard Journal* 232–41 (1996).

[90]   *Regina v Turnbull*, 98 Cr App R 313 (1977).

[91]   One of these witnesses identified George only after discussing the lineup with another witness, who had positively identified George.

[92]   *Regina v George* (2002) EWCA Crim 1923.

[93]   Ibid.

[94]   *George v Regina* (2007) EWCA Crim 2722. The appeal raised considerable questions about the sole piece of forensic evidence presented by the prosecution, a single particle of gunshot residue. George was granted a retrial with the forensic evidence excluded, and was acquitted by a jury based on the eyewitness evidence alone.

for the courts to reconsider the standards by which eyewitness identification evidence is admissible at trial.

Violations of the PACE Act Codes also provide grounds for exclusion. For example, the Codes mandate the use of a video or live lineup whenever a suspect is known and identity is disputed.[95] Identification by any other means, including photographs, can lead to dismissal of a case.[96] Violations of any of the specific rules that govern lineup procedure provide grounds for exclusion[97] and strict enforcement of the Codes by the courts provides strong incentives for police to use fair lineup procedures. However, the courts are inconsistent in their decisions to exclude eyewitness identification evidence.[98] The prevailing view in the courts is that the *Turnbull* guidelines are sufficient to overcome the dangers of a suggestive procedure. In *Regina v Williams*,[99] for example, the police officers presented the suspect to the witness in handcuffs. The Court of Appeal acknowledged that the procedure was extremely suggestive, yet determined that the identification was of good quality, as the witness had had a prolonged opportunity to observe the culprit. Though the Court initially intended the *Turnbull* guidelines to improve the way in which eyewitness identification evidence was used in trial courts, they have backfired. The courts place 'too much faith' in the trial as a means of determining the reliability of eyewitness evidence.[100] They are not enforcing the use of fair identification procedures, reducing the incentives for police to conform to the Codes.

4.2   Courts in the United States

In *United States v Wade* (1967),[101] the federal Supreme Court stated that 'there is grave potential for prejudice, intentional or not, in the pretrial lineup', and ruled that suspects have a constitutional right to counsel during a live lineup. In 1968, the Supreme Court ruled that identifications obtained using 'impermissibly suggestive' procedures might nevertheless be admissible under certain circumstances.[102] In this ruling, the Court showed great insight into some of the risk factors that were later scientifically shown to reduce the reliability of eyewitness identifications, including the use of unfair lineups, prior exposure to mugshots and biased pre-lineup instructions.

However, just a few years later, the Supreme Court issued a ruling that created a precedent regarding the admissibility of identification evidence. In *Neil v Biggers* (1972),[103] the Court ruled that the use of suggestive identification procedures is a violation of the

---

[95]   *Regina v Popat* (1998) EQCA Crim 1035.

[96]   *Regina v Finley*, CLR 50 (England and Wales 1993).

[97]   In *Regina v Kamara* (2000) EWCA Crim 37, two suspects stood in separate lineups containing several of the same volunteers. Under the Codes, a witness may not see any lineup member before a lineup, and multiple lineups must contain different volunteers. These violations of PACE led the Court to quash the conviction.

[98]   Andrew Roberts, 'Eyewitness Identification Evidence: Procedural Developments and the Ends of Adjudicative Accuracy', 6 *International Commentary on Evidence* art. 3.

[99]   *Regina v Williams* (2003) EWCA Crim 3200.

[100]   Roberts (note 98).

[101]   See note 82.

[102]   *Simmons v United States*, 390 US 377 (1968).

[103]   *Neil v Biggers*, 409 US 188 (1972).

suspect's rights only if there is a substantial likelihood of mistaken identification, given the totality of the circumstances. The Court established five criteria (the *Biggers* criteria) for assessing the reliability of a witness's evidence: opportunity to view the criminal; attention paid; accuracy of description;[104] certainty of the witness; and delay between the crime and the identification. The Court reaffirmed the use of these criteria in *Manson v Braithwaite* (1977),[105] and they continue to be the 'law of the land' in the US regarding eyewitness identification evidence.[106]

Gary Wells, a leading eyewitness researcher in the US, has published several papers highlighting serious flaws in the logic of the *Biggers* ruling.[107] The Court suggested a two-inquiry logic. First, was the identification procedure 'impermissibly suggestive'? If so, then is the identification nevertheless reliable? The first prong of the test, establishing that an identification procedure is impermissibly suggestive, is attainable by demonstrating in some fashion that the police or prosecutor—directly or indirectly—led the witness to identify the suspect. One reaches the second and more problematic prong when the prosecutor or judge establishes that the first prong exists. When the official deems the identification procedure impermissibly suggestive, the second prong, the reliability test, is invoked. The Court assumed that one can determine the reliability of a witness independently of the procedures used to obtain the identification by examining the *Biggers* criteria. Yet research shows that this assumption is not valid. Suggestive procedures can distort the memory of a witness, irreparably damaging any chance of obtaining a reliable identification.[108] Of the five *Biggers* criteria, three (opportunity to view, attention paid, certainty) rely upon self-reports of the witness and can be artificially bolstered by suggestive procedures.[109] Wells and Quinlivan argue that using self-report measures to assess reliability 'seems a bit like assigning a student's grade based on his or her self-reports of how hard they studied'.[110]

The *Biggers* criteria were based upon the intuitions of the Supreme Court judges in 1972 and have not been updated to reflect scientific knowledge. Research has shown, for example, that a person's ability to describe a face is not strongly related to her ability to recognize a face,[111] and that confidence is extremely malleable and prone to distortion.[112] The very self-reports that are used to independently evaluate the reliability of the

---

[104]   'Accuracy' was a strange term for the Court to use, as one can only assess that if he assumes that the defendant is guilty. The Court was presumably referring to the consistency between the witness's description and the physical appearance of the suspect.

[105]   *Manson v Braithwaite*, 432 US 98 (1977).

[106]   Wells and Quinlivan (note 85) 1.

[107]   Gary L. Wells and Donna M. Murray, 'What Can Psychology Say About the *Neil v. Biggers* Criteria for Judging Eyewitness Accuracy?', 68 *Journal of Applied Psychology* 347–62 (1983); Amy L. Bradfield and Gary L. Wells, 'The Perceived Validity of Eyewitness Identification Testimony: A Test of the Five *Biggers* Criteria', 24 *Law & Human Behavior* 581–94 (2000); Wells and Quinlivan (note 85).

[108]   Wells and Quinlivan (note 85).

[109]   Ibid.

[110]   Ibid. at 9.

[111]   Gary L. Wells, 'Verbal Descriptions of Faces from Memory: Are they Diagnostic of Identification Accuracy?', 70 *Journal of Applied Psychology* 619–26 (1985).

[112]   Semmler et al. (note 32).

eyewitness identification are prone to distortion by suggestive identification procedures.[113] Legal scholars have argued that the reluctance of the judicial system to inform its decision-making with the scientific literature violates defendants' rights to a fair trial.[114]

The defence has a right to file a motion to suppress eyewitness identification evidence obtained using 'impermissibly suggestive' procedures. However, since the *Biggers* ruling, the burden of proof is on the defence to show that the procedure was suggestive *and* that the risk of misidentification was high. Pre-trial hearings therefore focus on evaluating the reliability of the witness against the *Biggers* criteria and are rarely successful.[115] The criteria are open to interpretation, as they do not specify absolute values for how long the culprit had to be viewed, how much attention had to be paid and so on, for the witness to be deemed reliable. In *Manson v Braithwaite*, two judges dissented, disagreeing almost completely about the witness's standing on each of the *Biggers* criteria.[116] Even in *Biggers*, a substantial delay between the crime and the lineup meant that one could deem the witness 'reliable' on only four of the five criteria.[117] The flexibility of the *Biggers* criteria renders them problematic and does nothing to deter the use of unfair identification procedures.[118]

Change may be on the way, however. In June 2010, the Supreme Court of New Jersey held a plenary hearing to evaluate the validity of the *Biggers* criteria in light of scientific research.[119] Two hundred books and journal articles on eyewitness identification were reviewed, and the Court heard testimony from leading researchers. Its report concluded that the *Biggers* criteria are not valid, and they do not reflect the full range of factors that influence eyewitness memory. A search through the records of New Jersey's appeal courts revealed only *one* case in which a pre-trial hearing to suppress identification evidence was successful.[120] The recommendations were twofold. First, a judge should hold a mandatory pre-trial hearing in every case involving eyewitness identification. These hearings should focus on the fairness of the identification procedure, and the burden of proof should be shifted to the prosecution to prove that the procedures conformed to the NIJ guidelines.[121] In effect, the NIJ guidelines would be treated as legally binding, and violations of the guidelines would render evidence inadmissible. Second, the jury should receive instructions educating them about the full range of factors that could have influenced the reliability of a witness in a given case. These instructions should be tailor-made to the specific needs of each case, and should reflect contemporary scientific knowledge.

Scholars await reactions of judiciaries to this development. The report is unprecedented in that a state supreme court has systematically reviewed the scientific literature

---

[113]   Wells and Quinlivan (note 85).

[114]   Michael R. Headley, 'Long on Substance, Short on Process: An Appeal for Process Long Overdue on Eyewitness Lineup Procedures', 53 *Hastings Law Journal* 681–703 (2001); Andrew Roberts, 'Pre-Trial Defence Rights and the Fair Use of Eyewitness Identification Procedures', 71 *The Modern Law Review* 331–57 (2008).

[115]   Wells and Quinlivan (note 85).

[116]   *Manson v Braithwaite* (note 105).

[117]   *Neil v Biggers* (note 103).

[118]   Wells and Quinlivan (note 85).

[119]   'Report of the Special Master' (note 75).

[120]   Ibid.

[121]   Technical Working Group for Eyewitness Evidence (note 72).

to evaluate its own policies on eyewitness identification evidence. The recommendations of the report would improve the fairness of lineup procedures used on the front line, and would allow lawyers to present eyewitness evidence to jurors in a careful and unbiased manner. However, American courts might ignore this report just as the English judiciary ignored the Devlin report. Even if New Jersey were to pass a statute on the admissibility of eyewitness evidence, it would only be legally binding within that state. Other states might well follow, but ultimately the US Supreme Court would need to interpret the national constitution to ensure uniformity across the entire country.

4.3   Expert Testimony

Another pertinent issue in eyewitness identification is the use of expert witnesses at trial.[122] Lawyers and judges sometimes ask experts to testify about the reliability of eyewitness memory, the factors that affect an eyewitness' ability to encode information into memory, the influence of suggestive identification procedures on the risk of false identification, and the relation between eyewitness confidence and accuracy. Eyewitness experts do not give opinions about the accuracy of specific eyewitnesses. There are tight constraints on expert witnesses in English courts. The 'hearsay rule', which prevents witnesses from testifying (subject to exceptions) on anything outside of their direct experience, prohibits experts from presenting experimental results at trial.[123] Courts have ruled that eyewitness reliability is commonsense knowledge within the understanding of jurors.[124] Instead, the courts rely on instructions given to the jury by the judge. These instructions (known as *Turnbull* instructions) are tailored to the needs of each case, but must address the following points: mistaken witnesses can be convincing; multiple witnesses can be mistaken; and the circumstances of the initial observation (such as exposure duration, distance, lighting, retention interval, and so on) can influence the accuracy of a witness's memory.[125] Failure to deliver adequate *Turnbull* instructions can lead the appellate courts to overturn convictions.[126]

Expert testimony on eyewitness memory is more common in the US than in England, though rules on expert testimony vary between states. Although there are several grounds for judges to deny the admission of expert testimony about eyewitness memory, the single most common reason is that they believe that the content of the testimony is within the common sense of the jury. In other words, there is nothing the expert has to offer that jurors do not already know. Considerable research, however, as discussed in this chapter, has uncovered significant gaps between lay and scientific knowledge about eyewitness memory.[127] If the influence of suggestive identification procedures was wholly a matter of common sense, there would be no need to improve police or judicial procedures. The fact

---

[122]   For a fuller treatment of this topic, see Brian L. Cutler (ed.), *Expert Testimony on the Psychology of Eyewitness Identification* (Oxford: Oxford University Press 2009).

[123]   Davies (note 88).

[124]   *Regina v Turner* (1974) 60 Crim App R 80.

[125]   *Regina v Turnbull* (note 90).

[126]   *Regina v Kamara* (note 97).

[127]   Tanja R. Benton, David F. Ross, Emily Bradshaw, W. Neil Thomas and Gregory S. Bradshaw, 'Eyewitness Memory is Still Not Common Sense: Comparing Jurors, Judges and Law Enforcement to Eyewitness Experts', 20 *Applied Cognitive Psychology* 115–29 (2006).

that many jurisdictions have adopted reforms based on eyewitness research is evidence that eyewitness memory is not a matter of common sense. This widespread basis for rejecting proffers of expert testimony is, therefore, highly problematic.

5 CONCLUSION

In this chapter we have highlighted huge variations in the procedures used to collect eyewitness evidence between the US and England and across jurisdictions within the US. We also identified sizeable gaps between the recommendations of psychologists and the procedures used in the field. Besides the psychological literature, there are key members of the legal community (lawyers, judges, prosecutors and policy makers) who have taken a keen interest in this issue, and who have been working to reform procedures for some time.[128] Indeed, the best hope for achieving procedural reform is to open up new channels of communication between scientists, legal professionals, and law enforcement officials, and to strengthen the ties that are already in place. There is, perhaps, reason to be optimistic. New field studies are under way in the US, involving close collaboration between psychologists and law enforcement personnel. New Jersey's special report[129] was a product of cooperation between the judiciary and scientists, which may have far-reaching consequences for eyewitness evidence in the US. While satisfactory complete reform may still be some way off, the rate of change is increasing and looks set to continue.

FURTHER READING

Brewer, Neil, and Kipling D. Williams (eds) (2005). *Psychology and Law: An Empirical Perspective*. New York: Guilford Press.
Cutler, Brian L. (ed.) (2008). 1–2 *Encyclopedia of Psychology and Law*. Los Angeles: Sage Publications.
Lindsay, R.C.L., David F. Ross, J. Don Read and Michael P. Toglia (2007). 2 *The Handbook of Eyewitness Psychology: Memory for People*. Mahwah, NJ: Lawrence Erlbaum Associates.
Toglia, Michael P., J. Don Read, David F. Ross and R.C.L. Lindsay (eds) (2007). 1 *The Handbook of Eyewitness Psychology: Memory for Events*. Mahwah, NJ: Lawrence Erlbaum Associates.

---

[128] See, e.g., Woocher (note 10).
[129] Report of the Special Master (note 75).

PART II

CORE ISSUES

8 Separation of legislative and executive governmental powers
*Howard J. Wiarda and Jonathan T. Polk**

1   INTRODUCTION

Prior to the Second World War, comparative politics largely focused on the formal and legal aspects of government, including diverse configurations of the executive and legislative body. Analyses generally consisted of case studies, drawn almost exclusively from the United States or Europe, with an emphasis on the constitution and other institutional arrangements of various states. This both reflected the legal background of the discipline at the time and stemmed from the legitimate postwar need, well into the 1950s, to build institutions from the ground up. Woodrow Wilson's *Congressional Government* (1885), an analysis and comparison of the political system of the United States with that of Great Britain, stands as a fine example of the importance and prominence of investigations detailing various institutional configurations for the nascent field of political science, or what at the time might have more properly been called comparative government. The work of Herman Finer (1949), Karl Loewenstein (1957) and Carl Friedrich (1950) further represent foundational texts of the formal-legal approach common to early comparative analysis.

As the war came to a close and a host of new states entered the world political scene, there was a corresponding call for change within comparative politics. Authors such as David Easton (1953) and Roy Macridis (1955) encouraged comparativists to move away from their interest in static institutional analysis, and increasingly focus on the political actors and processes that animated them. Criticized as overly focused on Europe, not genuinely comparative, and unable to make broader, more generally applicable claims, comparativists experienced a rapid change as a host of newly minted PhDs and post-docs entered the field to research the newly formed states (Almond 1990). The behavioral revolution in political science—marked in comparative politics by an increasing interest in newly emerging countries, the importance of political culture, and questions of political and economic development—temporarily led comparativists away from the type of institutional studies that had produced rich descriptions of executive-legislative relations.

The Cold War between the United States and the Soviet Union further fueled the rise of geopolitical interest in the economic and political development of the new states.

*   Howard J. Wiarda is the Dean Rusk Professor of International Relations and Head, Department of International Affairs, University of Georgia. He is also Senior Scholar, Center for Strategic and International Studies, and Woodrow Wilson Center Public Policy Scholar (Washington, DC).

Jonathan T. Polk is Graduate Assistant, Department of International Affairs, Center for the Study of Global Issues, University of Georgia.

Throughout the 1960s, prominent developmentalist theorists such as Walt Rostow (1960), Cyril Black (1966) and A.F.K. Organksi (1965) emerged from this confluence of academic and political interest. The importance of economic growth for financial stability, and its supposed natural counterpart, Anglo-American style liberal democratic government, took precedence for this group of scholars rather than the particulars of institutional arrangements. This first wave of developmental economists were not the only ones to emphasize the social prerequisites for democracy rather than institutions, as both Seymour Martin Lipset (1960) and Karl Deutsch (1963) discussed the importance of education, economic development, social mobilization, legitimacy and other factors for a country's development. Political science, not unlike political and economic development (a problematic point for developmentalists), is often not unilinear in its progression, and by the end of the 1980s and throughout the 1990s institutional analysis began to reappear within the discipline.

After years in the wilderness, a renewed interest in institutions, particularly as independent variables capable of explaining different outcomes, grew out of what came to be called 'new institutionalism' (March and Olsen 1984). The earlier version of institutional scholarship was heavily descriptive, based on cross-national constitution comparison, and generally static. New institutionalism, however, stresses the dynamic, evolving, and interactive aspects of political institutions as they emerge and grow over time (see, e.g., Hall and Taylor 1996; Immergut 1997; Peters 2005). Amidst this revival of institutionalist scholarship, questions of executive-legislative institutional configurations and the subsequent impact of these various arrangements on democratic governance regained prominence, particularly for those interested in the post-Cold War wave of states transitioning to democratic forms of government (for recent examples, see Carey 2005; Kim and Bahry 2008; Svolik 2008; Sing 2010). Scholarly works by von Mettenheim (1997), Frye (1997, 2002), Taras (1997, 2003), Metcalf (2000), Siaroff (2003) and Shugart (2005) are just a few more of a non-exhaustive list demonstrating the growth in the last 25 years of a subfield in comparative politics studying the institutional dynamics of executive-legislative relations.

Comparativist work focused on executive-legislative relations typically addresses three fundamental types of arrangements: pure presidentialism, pure parliamentarism, and systems with a mixture of the two. Executive-legislative relations vary substantially between, as well as within, each of these institutional configurations. Scholars frequently classify regime types according to dispositional properties, such as whether there is a president, a prime minister or both, and, if there are popularly elected, relational properties such as the patterns of executive politics within a given system. But some have argued (Elgie 1998) that this mixture of analysis based on dispositional and relational properties tends to produce conceptual ambiguity as well as exaggerated claims with regard to particular relational properties, making it best to employ dispositional properties alone when classifying regime types. We therefore organize the remainder of the chapter by beginning with a discussion of presidential systems, before moving on to parliamentary democracies, followed by an overview of semi-presidential regimes, which mix both presidential and parliamentary features.[1]

---

[1]   For other recent overviews of comparative executive-legislative relations, see Carey (2005) and Shugart (2006).

The final sections of the chapter explore the potential impact of consociational arrangements and other types of constitutional engineering on democratic consolidation and other aspects of governance. The resurgence of institution-based research in comparative politics has produced a renewed enthusiasm for, and attention to, institutional design as a means of achieving harmonious relations between the various subgroups within a given society. Understanding the implications of different constitutional arrangements and the accompanying patterns of executive-legislative relations is no doubt of paramount importance, particularly for newly emerging democracies in countries with a history of internal conflict. It must, however, also be noted that political institutions are not infinitely variable, but are embedded within particular cultural, social, and historical environments that may limit the range of viable options for policymakers.

Indeed, temporal and geographic analysis of a dataset of the electoral institutions used in all democratic legislative and presidential elections in 199 countries between 1946 and 2000 finds that a similar type of regime (parliamentary, presidential, mixed) and legislative electoral system (majoritarian, proportional, multi, mixed) is frequently found within a given geographical region (Golder 2005). The author goes on to suggest that further research is required to uncover how these patterns emerged, reminding us that the choices available to political elites hoping to change institutional rules to bring about desirable outcomes may be more constrained by the historical trajectory of a given geographical region than it might initially appear (ibid.: 119). Although this chapter focuses on institutional analyses of executive-legislative relations, the study of political culture remains a foundational approach within comparative politics, one which should continue to be brought to bear on questions of institutional dynamics in future scholarship.[2]

2   EXECUTIVE-LEGISLATIVE RELATIONS IN PRESIDENTIAL SYSTEMS

Giovanni Sartori recognizes a regime as presidential 'if and only if, the head of state i) results from popular election, ii) during his or her pre-established tenure cannot be discharged by a parliamentary vote, and iii) heads or otherwise directs the governments that he or she appoints' (Sartori 1994: 84). Within comparative politics, Sartori's definition of presidentialism has become a seminal departure point for subsequent analysis of this regime type. For Juan Linz, individual democratic legitimacy and a rigidly fixed term for the directly elected head of state make up the two key aspects all presidential systems share (Linz 1994: 6). The popular mandate of the executive and its inflexible term limit sharply differentiate presidential regimes from parliamentary forms of government in which executive power flows from and fuses with the legislature, subject to the latter's continued approval. In addition to these major differences in the ways presidential and parliamentary systems structure the relations between the executive and legislative organs of government, there are other institutional features unique to presidencies, such as divided government and non-concurrent elections, which influence executive-legislative relations.

---

[2]   On this point, see Chapter 15 below on Legal Cultures, a field analogous to political culture.

The 112th United States Congress, which began in January 2011, ushered the US back into a period of divided government, a situation that occurs when one political party controls the presidency and another party controls one or both branches of the legislature. This particular configuration of government stems from the US system's separation-of-powers and is only possible within regimes in which the executive and legislative branches are elected independently of one another, with their own source of democratic legitimacy. This stands in contrast with European-style parliamentary democracies in which the source of executive power originates in the legislature, making divided government impossible.

Divided government, relatively rare in the US throughout the early twentieth century, occurred more frequently in the latter half of that century. Does divided government lead to ineffective government and legislative gridlock? This question, one of practical importance to President Barack Obama's administration and citizens of the United States, is one that political scientists have explored in depth. A study by Paul Peterson and Jay Greene (1994) suggests that gridlock is not necessarily the outcome of divided government. The authors identify two types of inter-branch conflict, constituent and partisan. According to their analysis, the latter has been present in the House of Representatives for quite some time and is increasingly present in the Senate. The other type, constituent conflict, arises because the executive has a national constituency and is therefore primarily concerned with national policy, whereas members of Congress are more concerned with distributive implications of national policies for their particular electoral district. Not surprisingly, constituent conflict between the executive and legislative is fiercest surrounding issues of both national and distributive importance. Yet Peterson and Greene (1994) find that conflict between members of Congress and executives of the opposite party did not increase between 1947 and 1990, and that conflict with executive officials of the same party declined. Taken together, this produced an overall drop in executive-legislative conflict. There is some evidence that voters often prefer divided government as a further check and balance between the two branches.

Another key difference between presidential and parliamentary systems is the potential for non-concurrent elections in presidential democracies. Scholars studying the various ways different institutions of presidentialism allow voters to hold governments accountable find that concurrent and non-concurrent elections bring about different types of accountability (Samuels 2004). Electoral sanctioning, for example, is weak in non-concurrent elections but stronger in concurrent elections. Samuels further finds that voters tend to punish presidents more than they do legislators for the same type of performance in office. Overall, the article provides a blueprint for when accountability converges on the type we might expect in parliamentary regimes and when uniquely presidential forms of accountability will manifest themselves.

Turning to broader questions pertaining to presidential forms of government and democratic performance, *Presidents and Assemblies* (Shugart and Carey 1992) explores a range of these matters in an analysis covering up to 46 countries. After separating democratic countries into three types: parliamentary, presidential, and 'other', the authors probe the impact of these different forms of government on democratic survival, finding that, on the whole, presidential democracies are more likely to break down than parliamentary democracies, but that when restricted to just developing nations, presidentialism actually outperforms parliamentarism in survival. Matthew Shugart and John Carey's comparison of presidential systems highlights the differences that exist within presidential forms of government and creates a means of measuring presidential power thought by many to be superior to others available (see, e.g., Metcalf 2000). Their analysis suggests that it is of crucial importance to understand that substantial variation exists within different presidential regimes. More problems arise in systems with strong presidential powers, a large number of weak political parties, and those that hold non-concurrent elections for the presidency and legislature. For new democracies, this reinforces the importance of carefully considering the impact of presidential, electoral and party systems on democratic consolidation.

Looking at 98 countries between 1970 and 2002, José Cheibub (2006) finds that presidential systems create higher incentives for governments to keep budgets under control than parliamentary democracies, which is why the gross domestic product ratio of the central government budget balance was higher in presidential than in parliamentary systems during the period he studied. The ability for voters to clearly recognize and punish the agents responsible for economic policies in presidential systems is, according to the argument, the crucial feature in differentiating presidential from parliamentary regimes. There are, however, differences in the degree to which presidents exert control over the budget process, and importantly, these often hinge on the nature of executive-legislative relations in budget making. For those systems in which the legislature has a relatively strong hand in the creation of the budget, balances tend to be lower, whereas for the regimes in which the president has more control or can veto legislation, budget balances tend to run higher (ibid.). Cheibub's findings appear to corroborate Shugart and Carey's earlier assertion that overly strong presidents, compared to the legislative body, can be particularly problematic for desirable governance outcomes.

Refining pre-existing arguments that presidential regimes are less likely to produce democratic stability than parliamentary forms of government, Scott Mainwaring (1993) argues that the mixture of a multiparty system with presidentialism creates a particularly problematic mixture for democratic stability. None of the 31 democracies in the world that had existed for 25 years or more at the time of his study was a multiparty presidential system. According to Mainwaring, this particular institutional configuration enhances executive-legislative gridlock, is more likely to generate ideological polarization and complicates the coalition building process—all of which undermines institutional stability.

Subsequent research by Matt Golder (2006) takes the work of Mainwaring as its departure point. Working from the premise that legislative fragmentation has a negative impact on the survival of democratic presidential regimes (see Mainwaring 1993; Stepan and Skach 1993), he investigates whether or not presidential elections matter for legislative fragmentation. Both presidential regimes and runoff systems were on the rise throughout the latter part of the twentieth century. In 1978, there were only eight presidential systems compared to 35 in 2000, while runoffs were employed in just over 30 percent of presidential elections in 1950. By 1990, that ratio rose to 69 percent (Golder 2006: 34), making it all the more important to understand their consequences for legislative fragmentation. Golder uses a worldwide dataset in an attempt to reconcile the contradictory findings of previous research, which usually focused on a particular region of the world rather than all of them. His research suggests that the number of presidential candidates is a critical factor in explaining whether presidential elections reduce, increase, or have no effect on the size of a country's party system. When the number of presidential candidates is low, so is legislative fragmentation, but crucially, there is strong evidence that when runoff systems are employed in presidential elections, social heterogeneity increases the number of presidential candidates. These results suggest that the proclivity of new democracies to use runoffs to elect presidents and proportionality for choosing representatives is likely to increase legislative fragmentation, which will place their democratic survival at increased risk.

Allen Hicken and Heather Stoll (2008) are also interested in institutional explanations of variation in the size of party systems, particularly the number of candidates competing in presidential elections. They, however, focus on the degree of authority vested in the executive rather than differences in electoral rules, which had formerly dominated institutional explanations of variation across these party systems. They find a non-linear relationship between the concentration of authority in the executive as opposed to the legislature (what they call horizontal centralization) and the number of presidential candidates. For moderately powerful presidents, increasing executive authority decreases presidential candidates, but for very weak or very strong presidents, an increase in presidential powers increases the number of candidates. Hicken and Stoll find similar, though weaker, results for vertical centralization—the amount of authority concentrated in the national as opposed to subnational government. If the research of Mainwaring, Stepan and Skach, and Golder concerning the deleterious effects of party fragmentation holds true, Hicken and Stoll's findings about the impact of the concentration of authority in the executive, relative to the legislature, on the size of the party system represents yet another contribution to our understanding of this important area of study.

A cornerstone of comparative politics is the belief that the particular historical and cultural contexts of specific regions and countries can bring about perceptible and important variation in the patterns of politics across countries. As mentioned earlier, a worldwide analysis of democratic regime types and electoral systems reveals regional similarities in both institutions (Golder 2005). This section began with classic and general definitions of presidentialism that view presidential terms as fixed and irrevocably mandated by the public. There is also a relatively widespread assumption that political conflict in these systems brings about democratic breakdown. Yet, this might not always be the case, at least not in every region of the world.

Between 1978 and 2003, civilian actors or legislatures attempted to force 40 percent of elected presidents in South America out of office early. Twenty-three percent fell through impeachment by the legislature and by resignations. Presidents personally involved in scandal, lacking a congressional majority, and embracing neoliberal policies were more likely to face challenges to their presidency. Challenged presidents facing large street protests seeking their removal from office were unlikely to endure in office, and the interaction of legislatures empowered by the challenge to the executive and civil society emerged as a surprisingly powerful alliance in these scenarios (Hochstetler 2006). Juan Linz's (1994) argument that the dual legitimacies of presidents and legislatures push South American presidential systems to conflict and breakdown is, on the whole, supported by this complementary research. Yet, Hochstetler's work encourages us to turn a scholarly eye back to the importance of civil society in the ongoing power struggle between executives and legislatures in South America and to explore the applicability of this framework to other regions.

Another recent article focused on Latin American presidencies uses expert survey data to estimate differences between presidents and their parties on various policy dimensions in 18 countries within the region (Weisehomeier and Benoit 2009). As opposed to the multidimensional nature of competition in much of Europe, the authors find that political contestation in Latin America takes place almost exclusively along the left-right political dimension. They also find that presidents in bicameral and proportional representation systems are more likely to maintain positions independent of their parties. Additionally, presidents and their parties are more likely to diverge when legislative elections are non-concurrent and when they differ regarding the importance of a given policy dimension (ibid.).

In many post-communist presidencies, presidential power varies according to the relative bargaining power of the favorite candidate and the uncertainty of the election's outcome (Frye 1997). After drawing upon 24 post-communist systems to test various theories of institutional choice, Timothy Frye holds his preferred model, based on incomplete contracting theory, up to scrutiny through Belarusian, Estonian and Russian cases from the early 1990s. His research supports many assertions commonly found in the rational choice school of institutional design. Even amidst murky transitional systems, political actors know their interests, seek power and design institutions under various levels of uncertainty in such a way as to maximize their interests and hedge their bets in times of great uncertainty.

In concluding the discussion on executive-legislative relations in presidential systems, Linz, Alfred Stepan, and Mainwaring point out a noteworthy trend that has also affected parliamentary regimes. In both, they find a move toward stronger executives. Even in parliamentary forms of government, where power emanates from the legislative body, the importance of the executive has been on the rise.

3   EXECUTIVE-LEGISLATIVE RELATIONS IN PARLIAMENTARY SYSTEMS

Incentives and tactics for citizens, politicians, and parties differ significantly between presidential and parliamentary systems, but the single most important difference is that the executive in the latter is appointed by and dependent on the support of the legislature (Benoit and Laver 2006: 54; Gallagher, Laver and Mair 2006). Prime ministers require the confidence of the legislature for survival in a way that independently elected presidents do not. As discussed above, in presidential systems voters elect the executive and legislative branches of government to fixed terms independently of one another. Prime ministers, however—in some countries called chancellors—are selected by the legislature, which is therefore the only body that can claim to directly represent the voice of the people. In European-style parliamentary systems, the executive branch is composed of the cabinet, which the prime minister heads. As opposed to presidential systems such as the United States, where the president appoints cabinet members who serve at his leisure, cabinet members in parliamentary systems are usually drawn from leading members of parliament. In this institutional configuration, the prime minister is only the first of the team, that is, the *prime* minister (Crepaz and Steiner 2008).

New cabinets must win a parliamentary vote of confidence. Even in countries such as the United Kingdom, in which the monarch appoints the cabinet and an explicit vote is unnecessary, it is still understood that the confidence of Parliament is necessary for the cabinet to come into existence. In most European parliamentary democracies, the vote of confidence actually takes place, usually falling along party lines. In this, we see one major difference in executive-legislative relations between presidential and parliamentary systems. The institutional configuration of parliamentary systems is structured so that executive power flows from the legislature, making the legislative branch much stronger than it is in most presidential systems. Coupled with proportional representation electoral systems that tend to enhance the power of political parties, the importance of a politician working her way through the ranks of the party to attain a leadership position strengthens party discipline much more in parliamentary systems than in presidential arrangements (ibid.).

The importance of political parties and by extension the legislature in Western European democracies is further highlighted by research on control over government portfolios. Within the literature on European parliamentary democracies, it is widely understood that parties control government posts (Budge and Keman 1990; Klingemann et al. 1992; Laver and Budge 1992; Laver and Shepsle 1994). Recent scholarship by Petra Schleiter and Edward Morgan-Jones (2009) explores the extent to which parties control government posts since the democratic transitions of the 1990s introduced a substantial number of new semi-presidential regimes to Europe. Their article provides a principal-agent explanation for variation in 28 parliamentary and semi-presidential regimes of Europe, and finds that in 'parliamentary regimes 96–98 percent of the top government portfolios are controlled by parties' (ibid.: 688). The pre-eminent role of the legislature in parliamentary systems results in 'tight party control over government posts, which serves both the party in parliament and its agents in cabinet because their fates are mutually dependent given the fusion of executive and legislative power and their joint accountability in parliamentary elections' (ibid.: 687).

Scholarship by Kaare Strøm (2000) suggests that parliamentary democracy is widely embraced by politicians and that the scholarly community takes a particularly favorable view of parliamentarism. He argues that this regime type is more conducive to decisional efficiency, in no small part for the institutional configurations enumerated above, and creates more incentives toward effort than within presidentialism. The pressure on legislators to place the interests of their party above their own personal goals within the parliamentary constitutional design provides politicians in these systems with greater incentives than presidential systems to pursue policies geared toward broad, countrywide constituencies rather than narrower, regional subgroups (Shugart 1999). Yet Strøm goes on to argue that parliamentarism is no sure cure for moral hazard and is also prone to problems often associated with informational inefficiencies such as a lack of transparency and clear accountability (2000). Matthew Shugart, for his part, is quick to point out that the nationally oriented parties that help bring about non-parochial policies are frequently in short supply in less developed countries due to disparities in development across regions and income groups. When this is the case, he argues that presidential executives may actually enhance collective-good provision, since being elected nationally, they possess enough power over legislation to counterbalance, to some extent, the narrower inclinations of a legislature whose members remain close to their regional constituencies (1999).

Another substantial difference in executive-legislative relations in presidential and parliamentary democracies is the means by which the legislature may remove the executive leader. Just as parliamentary cabinets require the confidence of parliament at their formation, the fundamental position of power for the legislature in parliamentary regimes means that 'the Prime Minister and his or her cabinet are accountable to any majority of the members of parliament and can be voted out of office by the latter, through an ordinary or constructive vote of no confidence' (Müller et al. 2003: 13). This political action stands in stark contrast to the impeachment process found in presidential systems. A vote of no confidence does not imply illegality; whereas an impeached and convicted president leaves politics disgraced, a prime minister whose cabinet loses a vote of no confidence frequently stays on as a member of parliament. How votes of confidence and no confidence are handled by parliaments varies from country to country. However, it is important to recognize that the ability to call votes of no confidence at almost any point in the existence of a particular government generally enhances the power of the legislature relative to the executive.

4   EXECUTIVE-LEGISLATIVE RELATIONS IN SEMI-PRESIDENTIAL REGIMES

First introduced to political science by Maurice Duverger (1980) and often associated with the French Fifth Republic, the concept of the 'semi-presidential' regime has received scholarly attention as examples of this political system have increased. This is true particularly for countries in Africa and those in Eastern Europe transitioning to democracy after the fall of communism. Using Duverger's initial definition of semi-presidentialism, Shugart (2005) lays out what he sees as the three defining features of the regime type: 'A president who is popularly elected; the president has considerable constitutional authority; there exists also a prime minister and cabinet, subject to the confidence of the assembly majority' (ibid.: 324).[3] This mixture produces what Jean Blondel (1984) and others refer to as a *dual executive*; the popularly elected president is not merely a figurehead, nor is the president an unambiguous chief executive, because the prime minister may not necessarily be directly subordinate to the president. The hybrid regime type combines an executive and legislature that are independently responsible to the electorate—elements of the presidential system—with the hierarchical subordination of the executive to the legislature—found in parliamentary governments—to produce a complicated variety of executive-legislative dynamics.[4]

As opposed to parliamentary systems, where the composition of the cabinet is tightly controlled by political parties, Schleiter and Morgan-Jones's (2009) empirical analysis of 438 governments in 28 European parliamentary and semi-presidential democracies reveals that semi-presidential regimes are much more likely to include non-partisans in the cabinet. The existence of a second principal element other than the legislature—the independently elected president—with potentially different incentives than those of the

---

[3]   Sartori (1994: 132) creates an alternate definition using five essential characteristics.
[4]   For more on the defining characteristics of semi-presidentialism, see Duverger (1980); Shugart (2005).

president's party, limits the importance of co-partisans in the cabinet and increases the utility of adding loyal non-partisans in their place. The authors also present evidence that differences between presidential and semi-presidential systems extend to appointments of top government posts. In the latter regime type, 'one in six prime ministers and a quarter of all foreign ministers escape party control', indicating 'that the choice of the prime minister is an endogenous part of the cabinet formation process, which is negotiated by the government's popularly elected principals like the control of other portfolios' (ibid.: 688).

Building on this research on control of government portfolios, Schleiter and Morgan-Jones (2010) recognize that the prominence of presidents, prime ministers and legislative assemblies relative to the cabinet can vary substantially in semi-presidential regimes. Their 2010 analysis, which uses data on 218 cabinets in 13 Eastern and Western European semi-presidential regimes (1945 to 2005), sets out to explain which actors control government appointments in different situations and why. Bargaining models view the formation of semi-presidential cabinets as the result of a struggle between prime minister and president (Amorim Neto and Strøm 2006: 619). Alternatively, the principal-agent perspective employed by Schleiter and Morgan-Jones (2009, 2010) suggests that parties—negotiating with the president on behalf of the assembly—are the actors empowered by the electorate to form a government (see Protsyk 2005; Shugart 2005). Rather than focusing on the prime minister, a position that is essentially the agent of a political party, this perspective sees the degree of constitutional authority granted to the president and assembly as the primary factor that determines control over semi-presidential cabinets (Schleiter and Morgan-Jones 2010).

Some scholars portray semi-presidentialism as a form of parliamentary government (e.g., Budge and Keman 1990; Laver and Shepsle 1994; Strøm 1990; Warwick 1994) in which presidential influence never outstrips parliamentary control over the cabinet (Amorim Neto and Strøm 2006). Schleiter and Morgan-Jones juxtapose this with their evidence, which suggests that 'presidents can and do under predictable circumstances become the primary principal of semipresidential governments' (2010: 1436).[5] They conclude that one should not think of semi-presidentialism as a modified form of parliamentarism. They also counter Duverger's conclusion that 'although the constitution plays a certain part in the application of presidential powers, this role remains secondary compared to that of other parameters' (1980: 179). Others share the view on the importance of constitutional powers for presidential influence on government (e.g., Linz and Stepan 1996: 278; Siaroff 2003: 303). Schleiter and Morgan-Jones's findings support those such as Protsyk (2005) and Shugart and Carey (1992: 106–30) who argue that a constitutionally empowered president is much more likely to influence semi-presidential government than one lacking much constitutional authority.

Concerned that many post-communist countries around the world have selected semi-presidential constitutions, which she claims to be a relatively unknown and undertheorized regime type, Cindy Skach (2005) seeks to explain when and why this style of government can present challenges to democracy, constitutionalism and the protection

---

[5]   For other arguments contending that either president or parliament can control these types of governments, see, e.g., Lijphart 1999; Pasquino 1997; Protsyk 2005; Sartori 1997; Schleiter and Morgan-Jones 2009; and Shugart, 2005).

of fundamental rights in newly democratizing countries. In an argument similar to that of Schleiter and Morgan-Jones, Skach highlights the importance of the extent of presidential powers—particularly decree, veto and emergency powers—relative to the legislature's limitations on these powers in determining the ease with which presidents can govern without the prime minister or with a handpicked cabinet. At the extremes, semi-presidential systems can ebb over time into constitutional dictatorships, which frequently display 'the packing of the cabinet with non-party, technocratic specialists rather than political party representatives. This technocratization of the cabinet distances it from both citizens, and their political party representatives in the legislature' (Skach 2005: 349).

Skach suggests that the ideal institutional configuration for reducing conflict in semi-presidentialism features a prime minister with a legislative majority and a president from the same party, which she refers to as 'consolidated majority government'. The author contrasts this with a subtype she introduces to the literature: 'divided minority government'. In this unfortunate configuration, 'neither the president nor the prime minister, nor any party or coalition, enjoys a substantive majority in the legislature' (ibid.: 351). This lack of a clear majority facilitates instability within legislative coalitions and encourages presidential intervention and the use of reserved powers. For Skach, the ability to build legislative majorities and integrate the president into an institutionalized party system is key to reducing conflict in semi-presidential regimes. New democratizing countries, however, frequently suffer from weakly institutionalized party systems, presidents that view themselves as above parties, and proportional representation electoral systems that emphasize party representation rather than majorities in the legislature. In situations such as these, semi-presidential constitutions may exacerbate pre-existing tensions within the political system (ibid.: 362).

A potential benefit of semi-presidential regimes is that the direct election of the president could encourage and strengthen democratic practices. There is, however, a danger that increasing the number of elections may fatigue voters and decrease participation levels. An analysis of electoral turnout in parliamentary democracies with a non-hereditary head of state from 1945 to 2006 finds that direct presidential elections decrease turnout in parliamentary elections by about 7 percent (Tavits 2008). Margit Tavits is careful to avoid normative claims about the consequences of decreased turnout in parliamentary elections when separate independent presidential elections also take place. However, she does report to potential constitution designers that: '[s]implifying the representational process by having fewer elected offices and concentrating the decision-making power in these offices makes it easier and therefore more likely for the voter to participate in the democratic process' (ibid.: 52).

Accountability of prime ministers and governments to presidents in semi-presidential systems can often be unclear. Shugart (2005: 333) follows Shugart and Carey (1992) in further delineating between *premier-presidential* and *president parliamentary* subtypes of semi-presidentialism. In the former subtype, the premier and cabinet are accountable to the assembly exclusively, while in the latter they are dually accountable to the assembly and the president. Siaroff (2003), however, follows Sartori (1994) in criticizing these subcategories as hollow. Analyzing executive-legislative dynamics from the perspective of the president, he goes even further than Sartori by rejecting the concept of semi-presidentialism entirely, arguing that it is more accurate and useful to use terms such as parliamentary systems with presidential dominance, parliamentary systems with a presidential corrective, and parliamentary systems with figurehead presidents (Siaroff 2003).

The ongoing and growing debate about semi-presidential and other hybrid regime types within the literature on political institutions indicates the contested nature of mixed political systems and the complications they present in categorizing executive-legislative relations. The rapid expansion of semi-presidential regimes across many post-communist countries presents researchers with a host of new cases for analysis and a pressing need for deeper understanding of the relationship between mixed regimes and the consolidation of democracy.

5   THE PROPER EXECUTIVE-LEGISLATIVE BALANCE FOR DEMOCRATIZATION

In a debate within the pages of the *Journal of Democracy*'s earliest volumes, Juan Linz (1990a, 1990b) and Donald Horowitz (1990) explore the impact of constitutional systems—presidential or parliamentary—on the stability of a democratic regime. In general, proponents of presidentialism point to the direct election of the chief executive as an advantage from the standpoint of democratic participation and emphasize the potential importance of the strong and effective leadership that a president can provide in bringing about desirable governance outcomes. Those that support the parliamentarian system, however, view the concentration of executive power in the presidency as detrimental to democratic practice and point to the possibility of executive-legislative gridlock and stalemate as undesirable qualities of presidentialism from the perspective of governing efficiency.

Drawing from his works on Latin American politics, Linz points to a variety of failed presidential systems in that geographic area. He argues that presidential systems in Latin America have suffered from competing claims to authority from the executive and legislature and that limited options for power sharing and coalition building, along with the fixed terms of the president, increased the probability of democratic breakdown. Horowitz highlights the difficulties parliamentary forms of government have had in the new countries of postwar Asia and parts of Africa. Seymour Martin Lipset (1990), in response to these articles, emphasizes the existence of counter-examples to each author's argument, for instance, interwar failures of democratic parliamentarism in large swaths of Europe and successful democratic presidentialism in parts of Latin America. Suggesting that it is an oversimplification to conclude that presidentialism is inherently unstable because power is concentrated in a single person and that parliamentarism is the more stable because power seems diversified, he argues that '[a] prime minister with a majority of parliament behind him has much more authority than an American president' (1990: 81). Lipset goes on to stress the enduring importance of cultural and economic factors, rather than any particular institutional configuration, in explaining the divergence of Latin American states from the United States on matters of democratic stability and a host of other questions pertaining to democratic development.[6]

---

[6]   Quantitative analysis by authors discussed below provides some support for Lipset's point about the importance of economic factors, in particular.

Building on this debate surrounding the benefits of parliamentary and presidential forms of government for new democratic constitutions, Arend Lijphart (1991, 2004) suggests that parliamentarism, in tandem with an electoral system featuring proportional representation, is best for newly democratic countries, particularly those with deep ethnic cleavages. He argues that the Anglo-American dominance of political science has produced a tendency within the discipline to prefer majoritarian systems like the United Kingdom and the United States. However, this tendency to view majoritarianism and presidentialism as superior in democratic quality and efficiency is largely contradicted by his analysis. Parliamentary proportional representation systems outperform presidential majoritarian regimes with respect to representation, protection of minority interests, voter participation and control of unemployment (1991). The Westminster or majoritarian style of democracy most often uses plurality electoral systems, which tend to produce two-party systems, one-party governments, and much stronger executives in relation to their legislature. The consensus model of democracy, on the other hand, attempts to distribute and share power in a variety of ways throughout a given society. Making use of proportional representation electoral systems, this style of democracy more often produces multiparty systems, coalition governments, and more balanced power between the executive and legislative branches of government via a stronger legislature (Lijphart 1984).

Although the formal separation of executive and legislative branches tends to encourage a balance in executive-legislative power, the existence of the presidency as the most important political office to be won enhances the power of large parties within presidential systems, an advantage that is present for larger parties in legislative elections, even those conducted according to proportional representation electoral formulas. The institutionally induced tendency toward two large parties in presidential systems frequently brings about cabinets almost exclusively composed of members from the governing majority. According to Lijphart, 'presidential systems concentrate executive power to an even greater degree than does a one-party parliamentary cabinet—not just in a single *party* but in a single *person*' (1991: 74).

Using the conversation begun by Linz, Horowitz, Lijphart, Shugart and Carey, Mainwaring, and others as a departure point, several recent studies further our understanding of what contributes to the democratic survival of presidential regimes. As Hochstetler (2006) pointed out in the context of Latin America in particular, several presidents in third wave[7] democracies have resigned or been removed from office, bringing into question the supposed inflexibility of presidential terms. In their study of presidential survival in new democracies between 1974 through 2003, Young Hun Kim and Donna Bahry (2008) find that lack of partisan resources in legislatures, a low share of the first-round vote, an imbalance in presidential power, a declining economy and public mobilization against the incumbent increase presidential instability. Their analysis also reveals,

---

[7]   The political scientist Samuel Huntington created the typology of waves. The first democratic wave occurred in the early nineteenth century with the extension of suffrage to more males and ended with fascism in Europe. The second wave followed the Second World War and peaked in the early 1960s, when military dictatorships replaced some democracies. Finally, the third wave began in the mid-1970s and continues today. See Huntington (1991). See also Hagopian and Mainwaring (2005).

consistent with Hochstetler's (2006) evidence on presidential regimes in Latin America, that across much of the globe, although presidents may fall, democratic governments usually persist, suggesting that presidential and democratic survival are separate from one another and that presidential removal need not necessitate a breakdown in democratic government.

Analysis using a dataset covering 85 countries from 1946 to 2002 presents evidence that presidential democracies are not intrinsically more likely to collapse than parliamentary regimes (Sing 2010). The study's findings highlight the importance of US foreign policy and an effective legislature with sufficient powers of oversight to reduce the military's threat to democratic survival in explaining the breakdown of presidential democracies. The importance of these relatively neglected variables for Sing's results is reminiscent of the call for comparativists to move beyond macro-institutional features in explanations of variation between presidential and parliamentary governance outcomes (Bernhard, Nordstrom and Reenock 2001). Research by Bernhard and his colleagues indicates that institutions alone do not determine democratic survival, but that the interaction of institutions with economic performance is necessary to explain the breakdown of democracies. They test the impact of the combination of party system and parliamentarism and presidentialism with economic performance to explain the likelihood of breakdown across all democracies from the period 1919 to 1995. Their results stress the importance of dispersion or concentration of decision-making power and suggest that majoritarian types of democracy weather economic downturns better than pluralist ones. When economic growth is present, however, they find that pluralist democracies are more likely to endure than majoritarian ones.

According to Milan Svolik (2008), differentiating between consolidated and non-consolidated democracies, a common practice in qualitative analysis of democratic survival, has been less influential in quantitative studies of non-consolidated democracies to their detriment. He sets about addressing this shortcoming as he explores what brings about democratic consolidation and authoritarian reversals in unconsolidated democracies. Svolik finds 'that low levels of economic development, a presidential executive, and a military authoritarian past reduce the odds that a democracy consolidates' (2008: 154). However, these factors do not exert a substantial impact on the risk that a non-consolidated democracy will experience an authoritarian reversal, which comes about primarily because of economic recession.

6   CONCLUSIONS

The debate between presidential and parliamentary regime types rages on, particularly with regard to new democracies in developing or semi-developed countries. In more institutionalized and stable democracies like the US or in Western Europe the issue is no longer so important, but in the developing world it remains a controversial topic. In countries with weak institutions and weak civil society, scholars usually think that a presidential system with power concentrated in the executive provides the glue, the centrality and the cement that holds under-institutionalized countries together. Without that glue, they would likely disintegrate into conflict, division and civil war. In contrast, better institutionalized countries, even in the developing world, with strong consensus and strong civil societies, such as Chile or Uruguay, can afford the 'luxury' of having a more democratic and perhaps less stable parliamentary or semi-presidential regime.

A second and perhaps even more fundamental question in many developing countries is whether these fine points of institutional organization matter very much at all. Of course they do; but by how much? In the developing world, the most important cleavages are likely to be those of class, tribe, clan, ethnicity, poverty, social structure, economic underdevelopment, and so on. In these countries, constitutional or institutional engineering is unlikely to have an immediate effect, certainly not in the short term, on these other more basic cleavages. In their nearly 200 years of independent history, quite a few Latin American countries have had 20, 30, and even 40 constitutions, all beautifully written and often alternating between presidential, semi-presidential, and parliamentary forms. Nevertheless, none of these documents by themselves has ever solved the even more basic problems of poverty, inequality, elite rule, lack of consensus and lack of development in these societies. Hence, the main issue may not be institutional or constitutional, but rather go to problems more fundamental in these societies.

A key issue in the literature (Barry 1975, 2001; Horowitz 2002; Lijphart 2001, 2004), and one illustrative of many of these themes, revolves around the concept of consociationalism. One may define consociationalism as an electoral and civil arrangement that attempts to incorporate and share power throughout the various politically salient subgroups within a given society. This form of civic engineering rests on four principles: (1) a grand coalition as a means of achieving broad representation in political decision making, particularly at the executive level; (2) segmental autonomy in matters of self-interest for the subgroups, for instance schools and culture; (3) proportional representation in the legislature; and (4) veto rights for all subgroups on matters of substantial importance to the subgroup (Lijphart 2004).

As employed by Lijphart, some have suggested consociationalism as an institutional formula for societies with deep ethnic or religious cleavages, such as the Netherlands or Belgium. As for how consociationalism has fared across the world, the record is mixed. First, while these types of arrangements have been largely successful in Western Europe, we must conclude that consociationalism has worked better in the Netherlands than in Belgium. Second, when Lijphart took his consociationalism 'on the road', so to speak, to deeply divided, but semi-developed, middle income countries like Lebanon or South Africa, he encountered challenges to his ideas and institutional suggestions that required modifications in the theory to maintain its utility and applicability (Lijphart 2001). Third, in even less developed, poor, and woefully under-institutionalized countries, where the cleavages are based on fundamental tribal, clan, or ethnic divisions, even consociational power sharing arrangements are sometimes not powerful or robust enough to overcome these deep societal conflicts.

This leaves us with 'Wiarda and Polk's Law': the less developed a country, the less will institutional solutions by themselves assist in solving pressing national problems. So the debate goes on; what matters most? Is it culture or more specifically political culture, is it class or societal cleavage, or is it institutions? The answer is: it depends. It depends on a country's level of development, on the depth and intensity of its societal divisions, on the period of time, on geography and on political culture. In addition, importantly, it depends on a country getting its institutions correct.

REFERENCES

Almond, Gabriel (1956). 'Comparative Political Systems', 18 *Journal of Politics* 391–409.
Almond, Gabriel (1990). *A Discipline Divided: Schools and Sects in Political Science*. Newbury Park, CA: Sage Publications.
Amorim Neto, Octavio and Kaare Strøm (2006). 'Breaking the Parliamentary Chain of Delegation: Presidents and Non-Partisan Cabinet Members in European Democracies', 36 *British Journal of Political Science* 619–43.
Barry, Brian (1975). 'The Consociational Model and Its Dangers', 3 *European Journal of Political Research* 393–412.
Barry, Brian (2001). *Culture and Equality: An Egalitarian Critique of Multiculturalism*. Cambridge, MA: Harvard University Press.
Benoit, Kenneth and Michael Laver (2006). *Party Policy in Modern Democracies*. London: Routledge.
Bernhard, Michael, Timothy Nordstrom and Christopher Reenock (2001). 'Economic Performance, Institutional Intermediation, and Democratic Survival', 63 *Journal of Politics* 775–803.
Black, Cyril (1966). *The Dynamics of Modernization: A Study in Comparative History*. New York: Harper & Row.
Blondel, Jean (1984). 'Dual Leadership in the Contemporary World: A Step towards Executive and Regime Stability', in Dennis Kavanagh and Gillian Peele (eds), *Comparative Government and Politics: Essays in Honour of S.E. Finer* 75. London: Heinemann.
Budge, Ian and Hans Keman (1990). *Parties and Democracy*. Oxford: Oxford University Press.
Carey, John (2005). 'Presidential versus Parliamentary Government', in Claude Ménard and Mary M. Shirley (eds), *Handbook of New Institutional Economics*. Berlin: Springer-Verlag.
Cheibub, José Antonio (2006). 'Presidentialism, Electoral Identifiability, and Budget Balances in Democratic Systems', 100 *American Political Science Review* 353–68.
Crepaz, Markus M.L. and Jürg Steiner (2008). *European Democracies*. New York: Longman.
Deutsch, Karl (1963). *Nation-Building*. New York: Atherton Press.
Duverger, Maurice (1980). 'A New Political System Model: Semi-Presidential Government', 8 *European Journal of Political Research* 165–87.
Easton, David (1953). *The Political System: An Inquiry into the State of Political Science*. New York: Knopf.
Elgie, Robert (1998). 'The Classification of Democratic Regime Types: Conceptual Ambiguity and Contestable Assumptions', 33 *European Journal of Political Research* 219–38.
Elkins, Zachary and John Sides (2007). 'Can Institutions Build Unity in Multiethnic States?' 101 *American Political Science Review* 693–708.
Frye, Timothy (1997). 'A Politics of Institutional Choice: Post-Communist Presidencies', 30 *Comparative Political Studies* 523–52.
Frye, Timothy (2002). 'Presidents, Parliaments, and Democracy: Insights from the Post-Communist World', in Andrew Reynolds (ed.), *The Architecture of Democracy: Constitutional Design, Conflict Management, and Democracy* 81–103. Oxford: Oxford University Press.
Finer, Herman (1949). *Theory and Practice of Modern Government*. New York: H. Holt.
Friedrich, Carl (1950). *Constitutional Government and Democracy: Theory and Practice in Europe and America*. Boston: Ginn.
Gallagher, Michael, Michael Laver and Peter Mair (2006). *Representative Government in Modern Europe*. New York, McGraw-Hill, 4th edn.
Golder, Matt (2005). 'Democratic Electoral Systems around the World, 1946–2000', 24 *Electoral Studies* 103–21.
Golder, Matt (2006). 'Presidential Coattails and Legislative Fragmentation', 50 *American Journal of Political Science* 34–48.
Hagopian, Frances and Scott P. Mainwaring (eds) (2005), *The Third Wave of Democratization in Latin America: Advances and Setbacks*. Cambridge: Cambridge University Press.
Hall, Peter A. and Rosemary C. R. Taylor (1996). 'Political Science and the Three New Institutionalisms', 44 *Political Studies* 936–57.
Hicken, Allen and Heather Stoll (2008). 'Electoral Rules and the Size of the Prize: How Political Institutions Shape Presidential Party Systems', 70 *Journal of Politics* 1109–27.
Hochstetler, Kathryn (2006). 'Rethinking Presidentialism: Challenges and Presidential Falls in South America', 38 *Comparative Politics* 401–18.
Horowitz, Donald L. (1990). 'Comparing Democratic Systems', 1 *Journal of Democracy* 73–9.
Horowitz, Donald L. (2002). 'Constitutional Design: Proposals versus Processes', in Andrew Reynolds (ed.), *The Architecture of Democracy: Constitutional Design, Conflict Management, and Democracy* 15–36. Oxford: Oxford University Press.

Huntington, Samuel P. (1991), *The Third Wave: Democratization in the Late Twentieth Century.* Norman, OK: University of Oklahoma Press.

Immergut, Ellen (1997). 'The Theoretical Core of the New Institutionalism', 25 *Politics and Society* 5–34.

Kim, Young Hun and Donna Bahry (2008). 'Interrupted Presidencies in Third Wave Democracies', 70 *Journal of Politics* 807–22.

Klingemann, Hans-Dieter, Richard I. Hofferbert and Ian Budge (1992). *Parties, Policies and Democracy.* Boulder, CO: Westview.

Landman, Todd (2008). *Issues and Methods in Comparative Politics: An Introduction.* London: Routledge, 3rd edn.

Laver, Michael and Ian Budge (eds) (1992). *Party Policy and Government Coalitions.* Basingstoke: Macmillan.

Laver, Michael and Kenneth A. Shepsle (eds) (1994). *Cabinet Ministers and Parliamentary Government.* Cambridge: Cambridge University Press.

Lijphart, Arend (1969). 'Consociational Democracy', 21 *World Politics* 207–25.

Lijphart, Arend (1984). *Democracies: Patterns of Majoritarian and Consensus Government in Twenty-One Countries.* New Haven: Yale University Press.

Lijphart, Arend (1991). 'Constitutional Choices for New Democracies', 2 *Journal of Democracy* 72–84.

Lijphart, Arend (1999). *Patterns of Democracy: Government Forms and Performance in Thirty-Six Countries.* New Haven, CT: Yale University Press.

Lijphart, Arend (2001). 'Constructivism and Consociational Theory', 12 *APSA-CP* 7–25.

Lijphart, Arend (2004). 'Constitutional Design for Divided Societies', 15 *Journal of Democracy* 96–109.

Linz, Juan J. (1990a). 'The Perils of Presidentialism', 1 *Journal of Democracy* 51–69.

Linz, Juan J. (1990b). 'The Virtues of Parliamentarism', 1 *Journal of Democracy* 84–91.

Linz, Juan J. (1994). 'Presidential or Parliamentary Democracy: Does It Make a Difference?', in Juan J. Linz and Arturo Valenzuela (eds), *The Failure of Presidential Democracy.* Baltimore: Johns Hopkins University Press.

Linz, Juan J. and Alfred Stepan (1996). *Problems of Democratic Transition and Consolidation.* Baltimore, MD: Johns Hopkins University Press.

Lipset, Seymour Martin (1960). *Political Man: The Social Bases of Politics.* Garden City, NY: Doubleday.

Lipset, Seymour Martin (1990). 'The Centrality of Political Culture', 1 *Journal of Democracy* 80–83.

Loewenstein, Karl (1957). *Political Power and the Government Process.* Chicago: University of Chicago Press.

Macridis, Roy (1955). *The Study of Comparative Government.* New York: Random House.

Mainwaring, Scott (1993). 'Presidentialism, Multipartism, and Democracy: The Difficult Combination', 26 *Comparative Political Studies* 198–228.

March, James G. and Johan P. Olsen (1984). 'The New Institutionalism: Organizational Factors in Political Life', 78 *American Political Science Review* 734–49.

Metcalf, Lee Kendall (2000). 'Measuring Presidential Power', 33 *Comparative Political Studies* 661–85.

Mettenheim, Kurt von (1997). *Presidential Institutions and Democratic Politics: Comparing Regional and National Contexts.* Baltimore, MD: Johns Hopkins University Press.

Müller, Wolfgang C. (2000). 'Political Parties in Parliamentary Democracies: Making Delegation and Accountability Work', 37 *European Journal of Political Research* 309–33.

Müller, Wolfgang C., Torbjörn Bergman and Kaare Strøm (2003). 'Parliamentary Democracy: Promise and Problems', in K. Strøm, W.C. Müller and T. Bergman (eds), *Delegation and Accountability in Parliamentary Democracies* 3–32. Oxford: Oxford University Press.

Organski, A.F.K. (1965). *The Stages of Political Development.* New York: Knopf.

Pasquino, Gianfranco (1997). 'Semi-Presidentialism: A Political Model at Work', 31 *European Journal of Political Research* 128–37.

Peters, B. Guy (2005). *Institutional Theory in Political Science: The 'New Instutitionalism'.* New York: Continuum, 2nd edn.

Peterson, Paul E. and Jay P. Greene (1994). 'Why Executive–Legislative Conflict in the United States is Dwindling', 24 *British Journal of Political Science* 33–55.

Protsyk, Oleh (2005). 'Prime Ministers' Identity in Semi-Presidential Regimes: Constitutional Norms and Cabinet Formation Outcomes', 44 *European Journal of Political Research* 721–48.

Rostow, W.W. (1960). *The Stages of Economic Growth: A Non-Communist Manifesto.* Cambridge: Cambridge University Press.

Samuels, David (2004). 'Presidentialism and Accountability for the Economy in Comparative Perspective', 98 *American Political Science Review* 425–36.

Sartori, Giovanni (1968). 'Political Development and Political Engineering', in John D. Montgomery and Alfred O. Hirschman (eds), 17 *Public Policy* 273. Cambridge, MA: Harvard University Press.

Sartori, Giovanni (1994). *Comparative Constitutional Engineering.* New York: New York University Press, 2nd edn.

Sartori, Giovanni (1997). *Comparative Constitutional Engineering: An Inquiry into Structures, Incentives and Outcomes.* Basingstoke, UK: Macmillan.

Schleiter, Petra and Edward Morgan-Jones (2009). 'Party Government in Europe? Parliamentary and Semi-Presidential Democracies Compared', 48 *European Journal of Political Research* 665–93.

Schleiter, Petra and Edward Morgan-Jones (2010). 'Who's in Charge? Presidents, Assemblies, and the Political Control of Semipresidential Cabinets', 43 *Comparative Political Studies* 1415–41.

Shugart, Matthew (1999). 'Presidentialism, Parliamentarism, and the Provision of Collective Goods in Less-Developed Countries', 10 *Constitutional Political Economy* 53–88.

Shugart, Matthew (2005). 'Semi-Presidential Systems: Dual Executive and Mixed Authority Patterns', 3 *French Politics* 323–51.

Shugart, Matthew (2006). 'Comparative Legislative–Executive Relations', in R.A.W. Rhodes, Sarah A. Binder and Bert A. Rockman (eds), *The Oxford Handbook of Political Institutions* 344–65. Oxford: Oxford University Press.

Shugart, Matthew and John Carey (1992). *Presidents and Assemblies: Constitutional Design and Electoral Dynamics*. Cambridge: Cambridge University Press.

Siaroff, Alan (2003). 'Comparative Presidencies: The Inadequacy of the Presidential, Semi-Presidential and Parliamentary Distinction', 42 *European Journal of Political Research* 287–312.

Sing, Ming (2010). 'Explaining Democratic Survival Globally (1946–2002)', 72 *Journal of Politics* 438–55.

Skach, Cindy (2005). 'Constitutional Origins of Dictatorship and Democracy', 16 *Constitutional Political Economy* 347–68.

Stepan, Alfred and Cindy Skach (1993). 'Constitutional Frameworks and Democratic Consolidation: Parliamentarism and Presidentialism', 46 *World Politics* 1–22 (Oct.).

Strøm, Kaare (1990). *Minority Government and Majority Rule*. Cambridge, UK: Cambridge University Press.

Strøm, Kaare (2000). 'Delegation and Accountability in Parliamentary Democracies', 37 *European Journal of Political Research* 261–89.

Svolik, Milan (2008). 'Authoritarian Reversals and Democratic Consolidation', 102 *American Political Science Review* 153–68.

Taras, Ray (ed.) (1997). *Postcommunist Presidents*. Cambridge: Cambridge University Press.

Taras, Ray (2003). 'Executive Leadership: Presidents and Governments, in Stephen White, Judy Batta and Paul G. Lewis (eds), 3 *Developments in Central and Eastern European Politics* 115–32. Durham, NC: Duke University Press.

Tavits, Margit (2007). 'Clarity of Responsibility and Corruption', 51 *American Journal of Political Science* 218–29.

Tavits, Margit (2008). 'Direct Presidential Elections and Turnout in Parliamentary Contests', 62 *Political Research Quarterly* 42–54.

Warwick, Paul V. (1994). *Government Survival in Parliamentary Democracies*. Cambridge, UK: Cambridge University Press.

Wiarda, Howard J. (1999). *Introduction to Comparative Politics: Concepts and Processes*. Belmont, CA: Wadsworth, 2nd edn.

Wiarda, Howard J. (2002). *New Directions in Comparative Politics*. Boulder, CO: Westview Press.

Wiesehomeier, Nina and Kenneth Benoit (2009). 'Presidents, Parties, and Policy Competition', 71 *Journal of Politics* 1435–47.

Wilson, Woodrow (1885). *Congressional Government*. Boston: Houghton, Mifflin.

9 Federalism and subnational legal systems: the Canadian example of provincial constitutionalism

G. Alan Tarr[*]

1 INTRODUCTION

Scholars have long recognized that studying the constitutional architecture of other countries enhances one's understanding of one's own constitutional arrangements by making the familiar and seemingly obvious problematic and contingent. As Kim Scheppele put it: 'One reason [for studying comparative constitutionalism] is that many of the taken-for-granted fixed starting points of our field are actually variables connected to time and space, variables whose variable quality is obscured if we do not know the counterexamples.'[1] With this in mind, this chapter analyzes provincial constitutionalism in Canada in light of American state constitutions and, to a lesser extent, the subnational constitutions of other federal systems. Such a study is valuable substantively, as previous research on Canadian constitutionalism has largely ignored provincial constitutions.[2] In addition, looking at Canadian provincial constitutions from a comparative perspective highlights what is common and what distinctive in subnational constitutions in various federal systems. Finally, by examining Canadian provincial constitutionalism comparatively, this study reveals what these diverse experiences suggest about the role that subnational constitutions play in governance and in guaranteeing rights.

This chapter pays particular attention to developments in Quebec, because the relation between provincial constitutions and rights has been a topic of more than scholarly interest in that province. The idea of a separate, entrenched Quebec constitution has periodically

---

[*] Director of the Center for State Constitutional Studies and Distinguished Professor of Political Science, Rutgers University-Camden. The author began research on this chapter while he was a Fulbright scholar in Ottawa, Canada, and he wishes to acknowledge the generous support of the Fulbright Program. The views expressed in the chapter, however, are exclusively the author's and do not necessarily represent the views of the Fulbright Program. An earlier version of this chapter appeared in 40 *Rutgers Law Journal* 767 (2009); the author gratefully acknowledges the *Journal*'s permission to republish that material.
   [1] Kim Lane Scheppele, 'The Agendas of Comparative Constitutionalism', *Law and Courts: Newsletter of the Law & Courts Section of the American Political Science Association* 5 (spring 2003), available at http://www1.law.nyu.edu/lawcourts/pubs/newsletter/index.html.
   [2] There are only a few isolated studies of Canadian provincial constitutions, and these tend to be province-specific. See, for example, Gerald Baier, 'Canada: Federal and Sub-national Constitutional Practices', in Michael Burgess and G. Alan Tarr (eds), *Constitutional Dynamics in Federal Systems: Sub-National Perspectives* 174–92 (Montreal: McGill-Queen's University Press 2012); James T. McHugh, 'The Quebec Constitution', 28 *Quebec Studies* 3 (1999); Campbell Sharman, 'The Strange Case of a Provincial Constitution: The British Columbia Constitution Act', 17 *Canadian Journal of Political Science* 87–108 (March 1984); Nelson Wiseman, 'Clarifying Provincial Constitutions', 6 *National Journal of Constitutional Law* 2 (1995).

been a subject of political debate, leading to the enactment of 'An Act Respecting the Exercise of the Fundamental Rights and Prerogatives of the Quebec People and the Quebec State' in 2000.[3] The introduction of Bill 196 in the Quebec National Assembly in 2007, proposing a constitution for Quebec, suggests that the province is continuing to explore subnational constitutional possibilities.[4]

A preliminary terminological point deserves mention. Although the term 'subnational' is generally used to denote the constitutions of constituent units in federal systems, its use in the Canadian context is problematic, because a Quebec Constitution would be the constitution of a nation, albeit one situated within the borders of Canada.[5] However, rather than invent an entirely new vocabulary, this chapter employs the term 'subnational' even in the Canadian context. With this caveat, let us turn to Canadian provincial constitutionalism.

2   THE DISTINCTIVENESS OF CANADIAN PROVINCIAL CONSTITUTIONALISM

Like most scholars of comparative constitutionalism or comparative federalism, I began as a student of constitutionalism and federalism within my own country, the United States. When my focus shifted from American state constitutions to subnational constitutions in other federal systems, I decided to examine Canadian provincial constitutions. After a fruitless search for the texts of these constitutions, I concluded that Canada did not have subnational constitutions. This conclusion was premature: Canadian provinces are not literally 'constitution-less'. There are elements of provincial constitutions in Part V, in Section 133, and in other provisions of the Constitution Act of 1867.[6] One finds other elements in the Canadian Charter of Rights and Freedoms, adopted in 1982: for example, Section 5 of the Charter mandates that the provincial legislature must sit at least once every twelve months.[7] Still other elements are in ordinary provincial statutes, such as electoral laws, bills of rights, and so on. Indeed, some provincial laws are even denominated by the term 'Constitution'—for example,

---

[3]   Act Respecting the Exercise of the Fundamental Rights and Prerogatives of the Quebec People and the Quebec State, R.S.Q. c. 20.2 (2000).

[4]   In 2007, a Parti Québécois member of the National Assembly, Daniel Turp, introduced Bill 196, a proposed Quebec Constitution, which did not pass the first reading. The bill's text is at http://www.assnat.qc.ca/en/travaux-parlementaires/projets-loi/projet-loi-196-38-1.html.

[5]   On Canada as a dual-nationality federation, see Peter H. Russell, *Constitutional Odyssey: Can Canadians Become a Sovereign People?* (Toronto: University of Toronto Press 1993), and David M. Thomas, *Whistling Past the Graveyard: Constitutional Abeyances, Quebec, and the Future of Canada* (Toronto: Oxford University Press 1997). Quebec has denominated its provincial legislature the National Assembly.

[6]   For example, Section 133 guarantees that debate in the Quebec National Assembly may be conducted in French or English, that pleadings in Quebec courts may be conducted in either language, that the records and journals of the Quebec National Assembly must be in both French and English, and that the laws enacted by that Assembly be published in both languages. For how this provision has frustrated efforts by Quebec to elevate French to a special status within the province, see *Attorney General of Quebec v. Balikie*, 2 S.C.R. 1016 (1979).

[7]   Canadian Charter of Rights and Freedoms s. 5.

the British Columbia Constitution Act.[8] In addition, unwritten elements of provincial constitutions, such as responsible government, are enshrined in constitutional conventions.[9]

From a Canadian perspective, this approach to subnational constitutionalism does not seem unusual. After all, the federal constitution, like its provincial counterparts, is not enshrined in a single document. Jurists assert that according to Section 52 of the Constitution, at least 26 documents are part of the 'supreme law of Canada'.[10] Moreover, much that is of constitutional dimension is enshrined in unwritten practices (constitutional conventions) rather than in constitutional text. Still, from a comparative federalism perspective, the Canadian approach is distinctive: the state constitutions in the most immediately comparable former British colonies, the United States and Australia, are written documents separate from the federal constitutions. In addition, given the close historical connection between constitutional government and popular sovereignty, it is striking that there are no provincial constitutional arrangements that are adopted by the people of a province directly, rather than through their representatives, and no provincial constitutional arrangements that are changeable by the people of a province directly.

This is not to suggest that Canada's approach to subnational constitutionalism is idiosyncratic. Some federal systems—Belgium, Nigeria and India, for example—do not have separate subnational constitutions.[11] Moreover, some federal or quasi-federal systems, such as South Africa, allow subnational constitutions but either actively discourage their creation or permit constituent units only minimal discretion in designing their political arrangements. Nevertheless, finding Canada in this company is somewhat surprising. The practice of allocating very limited constitutional space to constituent units is most common in centralized federations, such as Nigeria and Malaysia, or in federations seeking to forge a single national identity and discourage diversity, such as South Africa and India.[12] Neither description applies to Canada.

---

[8]   See Campbell Sharman, 'The Strange Case of a Provincial Constitution: The British Columbia *Constitution Act*', 17 *Canadian Journal of Political Science* 87 (1984). Sharman notes, however, that 'there is no indication in format or wording that the Act is anything more than an ordinary act of the legislature'. Ibid.: 97.

[9]   In Canada, 'constitutional conventions' refers not to gatherings of delegates elected to devise or revise constitutions but to long-standing practices that have assumed a constitutional dimension. For the British roots of Canadian constitutional conventions, see Geoffrey Marshall, *Constitutional Conventions: The Rules and Forms of Political Accountability* (Oxford: Clarendon 1984). Canadian scholars also highlight constitutional 'abeyances' that pass over and thus obscure what might otherwise be points of contention. See Michael Foley, *The Silence of Constitutions: Gaps, 'Abeyances', and Political Temperament in the Maintenance of Government* (London: Routledge 1989). Both 'constitutional conventions' and 'abeyances' point to extra-textual elements in the Canadian constitutional tradition.

[10]   Section 52 refers to a list found in the Schedule to the Constitution Act of 1982. See Rainer Knopff and Anthony Sayers, 'Canada', in John Kincaid and G. Alan Tarr (eds), *Constitutional Origins, Structure, and Change in Federal Countries* 106 (Montreal: McGill-Queen's University Press 2005) (vol. 1 in the series *A Global Dialogue on Federalism*).

[11]   One Indian state, Kashmir, does have its own constitution.

[12]   'Constitutional space' refers to the range of discretion available to subnational constitution-makers. Subnational constitutional space would seem to include, though it might not be limited to, the following:

Pointing out Canada's distinctive approach to provincial constitutionalism of course invites the so-what question: does it really matter that Canada has chosen not to authorize free-standing, written provincial constitutions? Certainly one can defend or criticize that choice, but one can hardly deny its importance: choices in constitutional design have consequences. The consequences become clear when one compares the Canadian and American approaches to four issues: entrenchment, the locus of authority for the interpretation of subnational law, the political role played by subnational constitutions, and subnational constitutional change.

3   ENTRENCHMENT

A major function of a written constitution is to entrench limitations on government. Some limitations may be designed to protect rights and are characteristically enshrined in bills or charters of rights. The federal Charter of Rights and Freedoms, which imposes restrictions on both federal and provincial governments in Canada, is an obvious example. Yet entrenched provisions other than rights guarantees can also indirectly help safeguard rights. For example, constitutionalizing popular government and a system of checks and balances may prevent those in power from abusing their authority—what Alexander Hamilton likely had in mind when in *Federalist No. 84* he claimed that 'the Constitution is itself, in every rational sense, and to every useful purpose, A BILL OF RIGHTS'. Constitutionally entrenched requirements may advance the right of popular government, as well as personal rights. Looking to the American experience, during the mid-nineteenth

---

a.   the power to draft a constitution;
b.   the power to amend that constitution;
c.   the power to replace that constitution;
d.   the power to set goals of government;
f.   the power to define the rights that the constituent unit will protect
g.   the power to structure the governmental institutions of the constituent unit, including whether the legislature shall be bicameral or unicameral;
h.   the power to define the process by which law is enacted in the constituent unit;
i.   the power to create offices;
j.   the power to divide powers among the governmental institutions of the constituent unit;
k.   the power to determine the mode of selection for public officials of the constituent unit;
l.   the power to determine the term of office and the mode of and bases for removal of officials of the constituent unit prior to the completion of their term of office;
m.   the power to establish an official language;
n.   the power to institute mechanisms of direct democracy;
o.   the power to create and structure local government;
p.   the power to determine who are citizens of the constituent unit; and
q.   the power to establish qualifications for voting for officials of the constituent unit.

For a detailed discussion of the concept, see Michael Burgess and G. Alan Tarr, 'Introduction: Sub-national Constitutionalism and Constitutional Development', in Burgess and Tarr (note 2) 3–40; Robert F. Williams and G. Alan Tarr, 'Subnational Constitutional Space: A View from the States, Provinces, Lander, and Cantons', in G. Alan Tarr, Robert F. Williams and Josef Marko (eds), *Federalism, Subnational Constitutions, and Minority Rights* (Westport, CT: Praeger 2004).

century, provisions were inserted in American state constitutions to require that the titles of legislative bills reflect their contents, that bills address only a single subject, that they be given multiple readings before passage, and so on.[13] These regulations of the legislative process were designed to promote greater transparency in government and, thereby, to encourage greater accountability to voters. Beginning in the late nineteenth century, requirements were inserted in American state constitutions for balanced operating budgets, and in the late twentieth century for other limitations on state taxing and spending.[14] These amendments reflected a perception that representatives could not be trusted to tax and spend in ways consistent with the wishes of their constituents and that effective popular government therefore required restrictions on their actions.

What is striking about these limitations imposed on the process and substance of state legislation in the United States is that they are state constitutional restrictions, without precedent or parallel in the federal Constitution. The restrictions also vary considerably from state to state—Colorado, for example, in 1992 adopted a 'Taxpayers' Bill of Rights' that restricted tax increases and imposed onerous requirements on their enactment.[15] Having separate state constitutions, with provision for a popular role in the amendment or revision of those constitutions, has enabled citizens within the various states to devise their own processes of government, and having written, entrenched constitutions enabled them to make their choices effective as restraints on those holding political office.

Let us turn back to express guarantees of rights. Even if rights guarantees are entrenched in the federal constitution, there are reasons why constituent units may wish to safeguard rights beyond those protected in that document. One reason has to do with timing: constituent units may be constitutionalizing rights guarantees at a different point in time. In the United States, for example, the federal Bill of Rights was adopted in 1791 and reflected the rights understanding dominant in the late eighteenth century. Over time, as understandings of rights shifted, states acted to secure social and economic rights not contemplated in the federal Bill of Rights. For example, the New York Constitution guarantees a right to housing, the New Jersey Constitution a right to collective bargaining, the Montana Constitution a right of access to governmental information, and 17 states a right to gender equality.[16] In addition, constituent units may wish to safeguard rights that are of particular concern to their residents. Again, drawing on the experience of the American states, New Mexico has mandated that teachers be prepared to instruct students proficient in either English or Spanish. Hawaii has an entire Article of its constitution devoted to the concerns of native Hawaiians, and Montana 'recognizes the distinct

---

[13]   See G. Alan Tarr, *Understanding State Constitutions* 118–21 (Princeton, NJ: Princeton University Press 1998).

[14]   Ibid.: 157–61.

[15]   Colorado Constitution art. X, § 20.

[16]   New York Constitution art. XVIII, § 1; New Jersey Constitution art. I, § 19; Montana Constitution art. II, § 9. On gender equality, see G. Alan Tarr and Mary Cornelia Porter, 'Gender Equality and Judicial Federalism: The Role of State Appellate Courts', 9 *Hastings Constitutional Law Quarterly* 919–73 (summer 1982); Linda J. Wharton, 'State Equal Rights Amendments Revisited: Evaluating their Effectiveness in Advancing Protection against Sex Discrimination', 36 *Rutgers Law Journal* 1201–93 (summer 2005).

and unique cultural heritage of American Indians and is committed in its educational goals to the preservation of their cultural integrity'.[17]

It should be emphasized that differences between federal and subnational rights guarantees are not limited to the United States. For example, in Germany the *Land* constitutions that preceded the adoption of the Basic Law tended to include 'the whole array of political and social provisions, including basic human rights'.[18] Those drafted after the adoption of the Basic Law focused on organizational principles, because social concerns and rights guarantees had already been dealt with in the Basic Law. Finally, the *Land* constitutions drafted since 1990 have reflected 'modern values', seeking to guide political practice through the inclusion of social rights and state goals. This social democratic emphasis is particularly evident in the constitutions of those *Länder* that became part of a united Germany following the collapse of the German Democratic Republic.[19]

As the Quebec Charter of Rights shows, differences between federal and subnational rights protections are a feature of Canadian federalism as well. Unlike the federal Charter of Rights and Freedoms, the Quebec Charter does not limit its focus to civil and political rights. It also safeguards social and economic rights, such as rights to housing, to education, to information and to social assistance.[20] Even in its treatment of 'first-generation' rights, it diverges from the federal Charter (which it preceded), by including distinctive provisions relating to rights to one's dignity and reputation, to privacy, to property and to professional secrets.[21]

Yet, given the system of subnational constitutionalism in Canada, the status of the guarantees found in the Quebec Charter of Rights (and hence their efficacy) remains problematic. In the United States and in Germany, the two examples used above, the rights guaranteed by state and *Land* constitutions operate as substantial checks on government action. They enjoy a status superior to ordinary legislation, they are enforceable in the courts and they cannot be changed without the extraordinary procedure of constitutional amendment. Thus, the entrenchment of rights protections ensures durability and enforceability. In contrast, the Quebec Charter of Rights is merely a statute enacted by the National Assembly. It is in legal theory not superior to other enactments and therefore subsequent inconsistent legislation could presumably supersede it. To its credit, the Quebec Charter of Rights recognizes the issue posed by non-entrenchment and seeks to deal with it. Section 52 provides that no provision of any other act passed by the Quebec National Assembly may derogate from the Charter's provisions, unless such act expressly states that it applies despite the Charter. This doubtless has moral force, but its legal force is more problematic:

---

[17]   New Mexico Constitution art. XII, § 8; Hawaiian Constitution art. XII; Montana Constitution art. I, § 2, para. 2.

[18]   Arthur B. Gunlicks, 'State (*Land*) Constitutions in Germany', 31 *Rutgers Law Journal* 981 (summer 2000).

[19]   Ibid.: 986–7; see generally, Peter E. Quint, *The Imperfect Union: Constitutional Structures of German Unification* 73–99 (Princeton, NJ: Princeton University Press 1997).

[20]   On the right to education, see Quebec Charter of Human Rights and Freedoms, R.S.Q., c. C 12, pt. I, ch. IV, c. 6, s. 41 (1975); on informational rights, see ch. IV, c. 6, s. 44; and on social assistance, see ch. IV, c. 6, s. 45.

[21]   On the right to dignity and reputation, see ibid. ch. I, c. 6, s. 5; on the limited right to property, see ch. I, c. 6, s. 6; and on the right to professional secrets and non-disclosure of confidential information, see ch. I, c. 6, s. 9.

how can legislators restrict the power to legislate of their successors through the enactment of a piece of ordinary legislation, even one of constitutional dimension?[22]

4 THE LOCUS OF AUTHORITY FOR THE INTERPRETATION OF SUBNATIONAL LAW

We turn now from the creation of guarantees of constitutional rights to their interpretation and enforcement. In Canada, the authoritative interpreter of provincial law, as of federal law, is the Supreme Court of Canada, whose members the Governor General appoints on recommendation of the Prime Minister. For cases that do not reach the Supreme Court, the definitive interpretation usually comes from the courts of appeals of the various provinces, whose members the Governor General likewise appoints on the recommendation of the Prime Minister. Thus, the ultimate resolution of questions of provincial law resides with judges who are appointed by the federal government—without formal provincial input and who receive their salaries from the federal government—in short, with federal officials.

Canada's centralization of judicial authority is not unusual. The constituent units in all federal systems choose their own legislators and executives, but the same does not necessarily hold true for judges. Some federations—India and South Africa, for example—dispense with subnational courts altogether, opting for a single court system. Others, such as Brazil and Nigeria, provide for lower state courts but not for a full hierarchy of state courts paralleling the federal hierarchy. In addition, most federal systems lodge the final interpretation of both the federal constitution and subnational constitutions in the federal supreme court or constitutional court.[23]

One can see the alternative to this centralization of interpretive authority by contrasting Canada's approach with that of the United States. In the United States, the ultimate interpreter of state (subnational) law, including the state's constitution, is the state supreme court. The justices of that court are chosen within the states, according to procedures established by state constitutions; they are paid from the state treasury and they hold their office during terms prescribed by state constitutions. Thus, if a case does not raise a 'federal question' (that is, a matter of federal law) and is resolved on 'independent and adequate state grounds' (exclusively on the basis of state law), then the decision of the state supreme court is final and cannot be appealed to the United States Supreme Court.

The implication of this decentralization of interpretive authority for the protection of rights becomes apparent when one examines the so-called new judicial federalism in

---

[22] A number of jurisdictions have begun to examine an alternative approach to rights protection, often referred to as the 'parliamentary rights model'. See Janet L. Hiebert, 'Parliamentary Bills of Rights: An Alternative Model?' 69 *Modern Law Review* 9–28 (2008); Julie Debeljak, 'Rights Protection without Judicial Supremacy: A Review of the Canadian and British Models of Bills of Rights', 26 *Melbourne University Law Review* 285–324 (2002); Mark Tushnet, 'Weak-Form Judicial Review and "Core" Civil Liberties', 41 *Harvard Civil Rights-Civil Liberties Law Review* 1–22 (winter 2006).

[23] For information on the court systems of various federal countries, see Kincaid and Tarr (note 10).

the United States. The new judicial federalism involves the increased reliance by state judges on state declarations (bills) of rights to secure rights unavailable under the US Constitution.[24] This phenomenon originated in the early 1970s in reaction to personnel shifts on the US Supreme Court that seemed to threaten that the Court would abandon its liberal activism and erode the gains made by civil libertarians during the chief justice-ship of Earl Warren (1953–69). In particular, there was concern that the Supreme Court under Warren's successor, Chief Justice Warren Burger (1969–86), would narrow the rights available to defendants in criminal cases and look less sympathetically at the civil rights claims of African Americans. To safeguard the gains they had made under Chief Justice Warren and to pursue further objectives, civil-liberties groups that had previously sought Supreme Court review began to litigate their constitutional claims in state courts rather than in federal courts, framing their constitutional arguments in terms of state constitutional rights.

Several factors made this change in approach attractive to civil-liberties groups. For one thing, state declarations of rights included guarantees not found in the federal Constitution. For example, some state constitutions expressly protected privacy rights, others specifically prohibited race and gender discrimination, still others guaranteed a right to a legal remedy and some guaranteed positive rights. Thus, state constitutions offered the possibility of extending rights protections beyond those recognized by the Warren Court. In addition, even when state guarantees were analogous to those found in the federal Bill of Rights—for example, state guarantees of freedom of speech and of religious liberty—often they were framed in distinctive language, and these textual differences could provide the basis for interpretations diverging from those emanating from the US Supreme Court. In addition, state guarantees might have different generating histories or reflect different values that could likewise provide a basis for rulings that afforded more expansive protections than those based on the federal Bill of Rights. Most importantly, under the doctrine of 'independent and adequate state grounds,' one could not appeal rulings based solely on state law to the Supreme Court. This meant that rights-enhancing state rulings, if based on rights guarantees in state constitutions, would be insulated from reversal by a more conservative Supreme Court.

If the new judicial federalism began as a tactical response to political shifts on the Supreme Court, it no longer has that character. Rather, over time the new judicial federalism, now decidedly middle-aged, has become institutionalized in American federalism.[25] State courts throughout the nation regularly rely on state declarations of rights to resolve disputes, and although particular rulings may be controversial—for example, the California Supreme Court's ruling that banning same-sex marriage violated the state constitution—the controversy centers on whether the judges properly interpreted the state constitution. Judicial reliance on state law is now fully

---

[24]   There is a vast literature on the new judicial federalism. For a summary discussion, see G. Alan Tarr, 'The Past and Future of the New Judicial Federalism', *Publius:* 24 *The Journal of Federalism* 63–79 (spring 1994). For a comprehensive review of pertinent cases, see Jennifer Friesen, *State Constitutional Law: Litigating Individual Rights, Claims and Defenses* (Newark, NJ: LexisNexis, 4th edn, 2006).

[25]   Robert F. Williams, *The Law of American State Constitutions* ch. 5 (New York: Oxford University Press 2009).

accepted.[26] Moreover, over time there has emerged a distinctive state constitutional jurisprudence and a focus on state constitutional issues, such as tort reform and environmental rights, which do not reflect disappointment about the rulings emanating from the nation's capital.[27]

One can best appreciate the relevance of this American experience for thinking about subnational constitutions and the protection of rights by engaging in a simple thought experiment: could a new judicial federalism arise in Canada? Assuredly, the federal Charter of Rights and Freedoms protects against both federal and provincial violations of fundamental rights, and it is likely that these guarantees, like their analogues in the US Bill of Rights, will continue to play the paramount role in safeguarding rights. Nonetheless, some of the preconditions for a Canadian new judicial federalism seem in place.

Quebec has adopted its own Charter of Rights, and other provinces as well have enacted analogous human rights laws. Moreover, the Quebec Charter seems to exhibit several of the same characteristics that promoted the development of a distinctive state civil-liberties jurisprudence. American state judges grounded their innovative rulings in guarantees that they found exclusively in state declarations of rights, and certainly, Quebec's protections of social and economic rights have no analogue in the Charter of Rights and Freedoms. American state judges also emphasized the distinctive wording of state constitutional protections, and to some extent, one finds this textual distinctiveness in the Quebec Charter as well. American state judges further relied on the distinctive generating history of state guarantees to justify divergent interpretations, and the fact that the Quebec Charter preceded the federal Charter indicates that it did not merely copy federal guarantees. Finally, American state judges grounded rulings in the distinctive values found within their states, and obviously, Quebec can claim a more distinctive set of values than can any American state.

Why, then, has a new judicial federalism not developed in Canada, and why is it unlikely to do so? In part, the answer lies in the non-entrenched character of provincial charters of rights. However, beyond that, it lies in the structure of the Canadian judiciary and the locus of interpretive authority. In the United States, having different authoritative interpreters for federal law and state law encouraged different interpretations of those two bodies of law. Perhaps unsurprisingly, the converse is also true. In Canada, the same judges serve as authoritative interpreters of both federal and provincial law, and this

---

[26]   This ruling—*In re Marriage Cases*, 183 P.3d 364 (2008)—was overturned in November, 2008, with the popular ratification of an amendment to the California Constitution (Proposition 8) that defined marriage as the union of one man and one woman. That amendment was subsequently struck down by a federal district court on federal constitutional grounds in *Perry v Schwarzenegger*, 704 F. Supp. 2d 921 (N.D. Cal. 2010), and that ruling is currently being appealed in the federal courts.

[27]   See Robert F. Williams, 'Tort Reform and State Constitutional Law', 32 *Rutgers Law Journal* 897–905 (summer 2001); Victor E. Schwartz and Leah Lorber, 'Judicial Nullification of Civil Justice Reform Violates the Fundamental Federal Constitutional Principle of Separation of Powers: How to Restore the Right Balance', 32 *Rutgers Law Journal* 907–75 (summer 2001); Barton H. Thompson, Jr., 'The Environment and Natural Resources', in G. Alan Tarr and Robert F. Williams (eds), *State Constitutions for the Twenty-first Century: The Agenda of State Constitutional Reform* 307–40 (Albany, NY: State University of New York Press, 2006).

encourages similar interpretations of those bodies of law. Put differently, Canadian judges have tended to assimilate federal and provincial charters rather than emphasizing the differences between them and drawing legal conclusions from those differences. In addition, as Sébastien Grammond has suggested, 'the Supreme Court's position at the apex of the Canadian judiciary may induce it to prefer uniform solutions based on norms applicable throughout the country'.[28] Also, the federal judges' greater familiarity with and reliance upon the federal Charter of Rights and Freedoms may discourage them from vigorously reviewing challenges rooted in protections not found in that Charter, such as the social and economic guarantees of the Quebec Charter.[29] This may explain why the Supreme Court of Canada has not undertaken aggressive enforcement of the unfamiliar social and economic rights provisions found in the Quebec Charter of Rights.[30]

In sum, federalism may permit constituent units to enshrine in bills or charters of rights those guarantees that they find most important. Nevertheless, this does not ensure that those rights will have practical effect. As the comparison of the American and Canadian experiences shows, the structure and jurisdiction of the judiciary can be crucial in vindicating (or not vindicating) those rights valued by minorities concentrated in particular constituent units.

5   THE POLITICAL ROLE OF SUBNATIONAL CONSTITUTIONS

Subnational constitutions serve important political purposes, regardless of the content of the documents. They may be instruments of conflict management during periods of political instability, as was the case in KwaZulu Natal during the transition from apartheid to democracy in South Africa, and in the southern Sudan.[31] The process of subnational constitution making itself can provide opportunities for political involvement and thus contribute to political socialization.[32] It may also help forge a sense of common political identity.

---

[28]   Sébastien Grammond, 'Canadian Federalism, Cultural Diversity, and Conceptions of Fundamental Rights', in J.M. Castellà Andreu and Sébastien Grammond (eds), *Diversidad, Derechos Fundamentales y Federalism: Un Diálogo entre Canadá y España* 43 (Barcelona: Atelier 2010).

[29]   This was a problem in the early years of the new judicial federalism as well, as state judges were far more familiar with the federal Bill of Rights than with their own declarations of rights.

[30]   Grammond (note 28) 41–6.

[31]   For discussion of how the processes of national and subnational constitution making in South Africa served these purposes, see Jonathan L. Marshfield, 'Authorizing Subnational Constitutions in Transitional Federal States: South Africa, Democracy, and the KwaZulu-Natal Constitution', 41 *Vanderbilt Journal of Transnational Law* 585–638 (March 2008). On subnational constitution making in the Sudan, see Christina Murray and Catherine Maywald, 'Subnational Constitution-Making in Southern Sudan', 37 *Rutgers Law Journal* 1203–34 (summer 2006).

[32]   Subnational constitution making may also lead to the emergence of a new cohort of political leaders. For example, when a constitutional convention was called in Montana to draft a new state constitution in 1972, members of the state legislature were barred from serving as delegates. One consequence was that women who had previously been confined to supportive or less visible political roles had the opportunity to serve as delegates. Thus, whereas in 1972 the two houses of the Montana Legislature included only five women, the constitutional convention the same year

However, these instrumental purposes pale in comparison with the fundamental purpose of subnational constitution making. Perhaps the basic political right, particularly for internal nations within multi-national countries, is the right of self-determination— the power to determine the fundamental character, membership, and future course of their political society. This right of self-determination is inevitably limited when nations are constituent members of a larger political entity, but it is not effaced.

Bill 196 clearly reflects this understanding, subordinating particulars of institutional design to the broader purpose of 'entrench[ing] the fundamental values of Quebec in a Quebec Constitution'.[33] The Bill acknowledges the identity of Quebecers as a French-speaking nation and affirms that 'it is the prerogative of the Québec nation to express its identity through the adoption of a Québec Constitution'. It bases this prerogative on the 'inalienable right [of a nation] to freely choose its political system and determine its legal status'. Whatever one's assessment of the wisdom or prudence of such declarations, they certainly underscore the importance of a subnational constitution as a vehicle for asserting and exercising the political rights of minorities in federal systems.

Two points about the political role of subnational constitutions should be highlighted. First, although subnational constitutions may provide an opportunity for articulating a constituent unit's self-understanding and its view of the character of the federation, they are not the only means for doing so. In a system without separate subnational constitutions, other documents may likewise serve this function. In the Quebec case, the Charter of the French Language to some extent already serves the purpose of providing a definitive statement of political and social identity, what defines Quebec as a nation.[34] Thus, the Preamble of the Charter affirms that in Quebec 'the French language, the distinctive language of a people that is in the majority French-speaking, is the instrument by which that people has articulated its identity'. The political, social and economic structures of the Quebec polity thus become mechanisms to support and enhance that national identity. To put it differently, aims precede and give direction to institutional arrangements, the same prioritizing as found in Bill 196.

Second, the right of self-determination is inevitably limited within multi-national federations, as indeed it is within federations more generally. Federal law circumscribes the constitutional space available to subnational constitution makers, and federal systems have devised two non-exclusive approaches for ensuring that constituent units do not exceed the constitutional space available to them.[35] They may seek to minimize the occasions for conflict prior to the exercise of choice by subnational constitution makers, and they may create mechanisms for federal review of the choices made by those constitution makers.

One way to minimize conflicts is for the federal constitution to give the federal government some control over the content of subnational constitutions at the time they are being created. For example, the United States Constitution implicitly confers on Congress the

---

included 19, and several female delegates used their convention experience as a stepping-stone to political careers within the state. See Larry M. Elison and Fritz Snyder, *The Montana State Constitution: A Reference Guide* 10–11 (Westport, CT: Greenwood Press, 2008).

[33]   Bill 196, Quebec Constitution (note 4); see text at note 4.

[34]   Charter of the French Language, R.S.Q. c. C-11, available at http://www.canlii.org/en/qc/laws/stat/rsq-c-c-11/latest/rsq-c-c-11.html.

[35]   See Williams and Tarr (note 12) 6–11.

power to impose such conditions. In empowering Congress to admit new states to the Union, it in effect gives Congress the power to establish the conditions under which it will admit them.[36] Moreover, in countries in which the national legislature has responsibility for crafting the functional equivalent of the subnational constitution, such scrutiny is built into the ordinary process of legislation. This is true, for example, in quasi-federations such as China, Italy and Spain.[37] In addition, Switzerland requires that the Federal Parliament guarantee that cantonal constitutions are consistent with federal law. This mandate has had real force: in the late nineteenth century, the Parliament rejected several cantonal constitutions that failed to provide equal political rights.[38] In addition, in South Africa the Constitutional Court reviews proposed provincial constitutions and proposed amendments to those constitutions before they take effect.

Another mechanism used to minimize conflicts between federal and subnational constitutions is to prescribe the contents of the subnational constitutions in the federal constitution. This may obviate the need for separate subnational constitutions altogether, as in Nigeria and India. Alternatively, it can dramatically restrict the range of choice available to subnational constitution makers. This has been the Canadian approach. Likewise important are the supremacy clauses one finds in many federal constitutions, which confirm that federal law is superior to state law, so that in cases of conflict, valid federal enactments—be they constitutional provisions, statutes or administrative regulations—prevail over state enactments, including state constitutional provisions. This, of course, limits subnational constitutional space: consider, for example, how Section 23 of the Canadian Charter of Rights and Freedoms limits provincial policy with regard to minority-language schools. It also may deter subnational constitution makers from proposing some provisions that they would have wished to adopt. Likewise important may be the lists of competences awarded either exclusively or concurrently to the federal government. The broader the range of competences granted exclusively to the federal government, the fewer the opportunities available to subnational units to address matters in their constitutions or statutes.

---

[36]   The main provision dealing with the admission of new states is art. IV, § 3 of the US Constitution. Further constitutional support for congressional conditions on admission is provided by art. IV, § 4 of the US Constitution, which directs the federal government to 'guarantee to each State in the Union a Republican Form of Government'. In addition to imposing conditions on prospective states, Congress also supervised the constitutions that southern states adopted in the aftermath of the Civil War, requiring an acceptable constitution as a condition for 'readmission' to the Union. However, the effects of these congressional efforts were short lived. Most Southern states repudiated their Reconstruction constitutions as soon as they could, typically replacing them with documents that by the late nineteenth century entrenched white political control, and Congress did nothing to prevent this undermining of republican government. See Don E. Ferenbacher, *Constitutions and Constitutionalism in the Slaveholding South* (Athens, GA: University of Georgia Press 1989); Kermit L. Hall and James V. Ely, Jr. (eds), *An Uncertain Tradition: Constitutionalism and the History of the South* (Athens, GA: University of Georgia Press 1989).

[37]   See Eduardo J. Ruiz Vieytez, 'Federalism, Subnational Constitutional Arrangements, and the Protection of Minorities in Spain', in Tarr, Williams and Marko (note 12) 133–54; Francesco Palermo, 'Asymmetric "Quasi-Federal" Regionalism and the Protection of Minorities: The Case of Italy', in Tarr, Williams and Marko (note 12) 107–32.

[38]   Giovanni Biaggini, 'Federalism, Subnational Constitutional Arrangements, and the Protection of Minorities in Switzerland', in Tarr, Williams and Marko (note 12) 220.

Complementing strategies for preventing disputes over subnational constitutional space are mechanisms for policing or resolving disputes when they arise. One widely used mechanism for policing constitutional boundaries is federal review of subnational constitutional provisions. Such review can occur before the provisions take effect, as in South Africa, or during the course of ordinary litigation, as in the United States. In most federal systems, the federal judiciary exercises this responsibility, but this is not the only possible approach. The constitution of the Russian Federation, for example, authorizes the president of the Federation to suspend the acts of subnational executives if he believes them in violation of the federal law or human rights. The Justice Ministry also has the power to revoke regional laws that are in violation of the Federation Constitution, and even before the accession of President Vladimir Putin, it had used that power to revoke nearly 2000 regional laws and constitutional provisions.[39]

In sum, the power to define oneself constitutionally is perhaps the fundamental political right, and the creation of subnational constitutions provides an opportunity to exercise that right. Yet the autonomy of constituent units is limited in a federal system, and this holds true even if the units coincide with internal nations in a federation. A federation may limit this autonomy either by prescribing the contents of subnational constitutions, in whole or in part, or by policing what constituent units place in their constitutions. Canada employs a combination of these two approaches. It prescribes much of the content of subnational constitutions in federal constitutional documents and constitutional conventions, and it provides for federal judicial review of provincial enactments, including enactments of constitutional dimension. Beyond that, as noted previously, it provides for the authoritative interpretation of provincial law by federal judges.

6   SUBNATIONAL CONSTITUTIONAL CHANGE

As important as the power to create one's own fundamental law is the power to change it, to alter or replace that law in response to changes in conditions, in political outlook, or even in identity and self-understanding. This option of constitutional renewal is crucial at both national and subnational levels. Yet constitutional change in federations is complicated and often contentious, because of the potentially conflicting interests of the federation and its constituent units or conflicts among the constituent units. Devising procedures for amending the federal constitution may itself generate conflict, because decisions about who can change the terms of the federation agreement may themselves depend on contested understandings about who the parties to that agreement are and what the nature of the federation is. Canada is a case in point, with debate continuing about whether the federation is rooted in two founding nations or in provincial equality.

---

[39]   Constitution of the Russian Federation art. 85, § 2. The estimate of subnational laws invalidated was supplied by State Prosecutor Yuri Skuratov, quoted in 'Constitution Watch', 7 *Eastern European Constitutional Review* 32 (winter 1998). Indeed, President Putin identified harmonization of the constitutions and laws of the Federation's constituent units with those of the Federation as a major element in his federalism initiative. See Mark A. Smith, 'Putin: An End to Centrifugalism?' in Graeme P. Herd and Anne Aldis (eds), *Russian Regions and Regionalism: Strength through Weakness* 27–8 (London: Routledge Curzon 2001).

Whatever the resolution of such fundamental issues, in practice the provisions for amending federal constitutions are usually designed to provide some protection for the continued existence and autonomy of constituent units. Thus, it is common for constitutional changes in federations to require the approval of both the national legislature and a large proportion of constituent units, either for all amendments or at least for those of particular importance to the constituent units. In addition, federal constitutions may grant extraordinary protection to the territorial integrity of existing constituent units and to their participation in the processes of the federal government. For example, the United States Constitution forbids tampering with either state borders or the equal representation of states in the Senate not only by congressional legislation but also by the ordinary processes of constitutional amendment.[40]

Although one might view provinces, states and cantons as made up of local units of government, one does not usually understand these constituent units as mini-federations of local units.[41] As a result, the concerns that complicate the system of constitutional amendment at the federal level typically do not apply at the subnational level. Thus, constitutional amendment at the subnational level tends to be easier and more 'popular'.[42] Often, there are more mechanisms for constitutional change available at the subnational level—in Florida, for example, there are five separate procedures for proposing state constitutional amendments, including proposal by a constitutional convention, by the legislature, by the Constitutional Revision Commission, by the Taxation and Budget Reform Commission, or by the initiative.[43] Constituent units tend to make greater use of alternatives to legislative proposal, such as conventions or constituent assemblies (for example, in Argentina, Mexico, the United States and Switzerland) and referenda (for example, in Australia, Germany, Mexico, Russia, Spain, Switzerland and the United States). Even within a single federation, the constituent units of a federation may establish different mechanisms for amending their constitutions, although in general there is a greater tendency to involve the populace directly in the proposal or ratification of constitutional changes (for example, in Brazil, Mexico, Switzerland and the United States). Although there may be notable exceptions, overall it appears that subnational constitutions are amended more frequently than are their federal counterparts.

In Canada, the process of provincial constitutional change is complicated by two factors. First, insofar as provincial constitutional provisions are contained in provincial legislation, no special procedure is required for their amendment—the entrenchment issue once again. Second, insofar as components of provincial constitutions are contained in federal constitutional documents, the mechanisms for constitutional change must be

---

[40]   United States Constitution art. IV, § 3, para. 1; art. V.

[41]   This is in fact possible. For example, in some Mexican states the approval of more than half the municipal councils is required before a change may be made to the state constitution. See Juan Marcos Gutiérrez González, 'United Mexican States', in Kincaid and Tarr (note 10) 215.

[42]   The analysis of modes of subnational constitutional change relies on Anne Twomey, 'The Involvement of Sub-national Entities in Direct and Indirect Constitutional Amendment within Federations', unpublished paper delivered at the Seventh World Congress of the International Association of Constitutional Law (2007), available at http://www.iacl-aidc.org/?page_id=62 (select workshop report, then Twomey paper).

[43]   See Florida Constitution art. XI.

prescribed at the federal rather than the provincial level. Section 45 of the Constitution Act of 1982 is designed to deal with this, mandating that '[s]ubject to section 41, the legislature of each province may exclusively make laws amending the constitution of the province'.

This resolution of the issue of subnational constitutional change deserves close analysis. The Section 45 delegation of the amending power to provincial legislatures assimilates the procedures for provincial constitutional change, regardless of the location of the provision to be amended. Whether one finds the provincial constitutional provision in federal constitutional documents or in provincial statutes, the same procedure for change—that is, an enactment by the provincial assembly—suffices. Still, the Section 45 delegation of power is not a complete delegation. There are some potential changes at the provincial level, identified in Section 41, which would have implications beyond the borders of the province.[44] These changes require the concurrence of the federal Parliament and the legislative assemblies of the various provinces. This recognition that some political arrangements within a single constituent unit may affect the federation as a whole is hardly unusual—consider, for example, the homogeneity clauses of the Austrian and German constitutions or the guarantee of a republican form of government in the United States Constitution.[45] Nonetheless, the Section 45 delegation confirms that some constitutional matters relating to provinces found in the federal constitution do not have federal implications, and that therefore their inclusion in the federal constitution is a matter of choice—or possibly historical accident—rather than necessity.

Comparison of Section 45 with the provisions governing the amendment of the federal constitution shows that Canada has made it easier to amend provincial constitutions than to amend the federal constitution. This is consistent with how many other federal systems have treated amendment of subnational and federal constitutions. Yet what seems like an enhancement of provincial power in Section 45—authorizing the provincial legislature unilaterally to amend the provincial constitution—may also be a restriction on provincial authority. By lodging the power of amendment 'exclusively' in provincial legislatures, Section 45 may preclude provinces from devising alternative mechanisms for amending those components of their constitutions found in the federal constitution.[46] If

---

[44]   These include: '(*a*) the office of the Queen, the Governor General and the Lieutenant Governor of a province; (*b*) the right of a province to a number of members in the House of Commons not less than the number of Senators by which the province is entitled to be represented at the time this Part comes into force; (*c*) subject to Section 43, the use of the English or the French language; (*d*) the composition of the Supreme Court of Canada; and (*e*) an amendment to this Part'. Part V of the Constitution Act, 1982, being Schedule B to the Canada Act 1982, ch. 11, sec. 41 (UK).

[45]   For a particularly insightful discussion of how this operates in the Austrian context, see Anna Gamper, 'The Principle of Homogeneity and Democracy in Austrian Federalism: The Constitutional Court's Ruling on Direct Democracy in Voralberg', 33 *Publius: The Journal of Federalism* 45–58 (winter 2003).

[46]   A provincial legislature can impose upon itself 'manner and form' requirements with regard to the amendment of a provincial constitution, so it may be able to establish a supermajority requirement for constitutional amendments. If, however, a provincial legislature decided to provide for amendment by referendum, it would be necessary to decide whether this decision was merely a 'manner and form' regulation (and hence constitutional) or a delegation of a power assigned exclusively to the legislature.

this is true, it is despite the fact that Section 45, by delegating this authority to provinces, acknowledges that the federal government has no stake in whether or how those provisions are amended. Certainly, Section 45's authorization of amendment of provincial constitutions by provincial assemblies stands in marked contrast to the special procedures established by the federal constitution for the amendment of many of its own provisions. The absence of supermajority requirements or popular ratification procedures for provincial amendments may suggest that provincial constitutions are viewed as different in dignity from the federal constitution. They are more akin to ordinary statutes than to fundamental law.[47]

7 CONCLUSION

Subnational constitutions have considerable potential as vehicles for safeguarding the rights of geographically concentrated minorities and the rights of internal nations within multi-national federations. These rights include primarily political rights, particularly the rights (within parameters established by the federation) to affirm one's own identity, to set one's own social and political goals, and to devise those institutional arrangements best suited to the achievement of those goals. These matters are typically enshrined in the subnational constitution, the fundamental law of the constituent unit. This act of political creation is not typically a one-time endeavor. The subnational constitution also establishes procedures whereby, as conditions or views change, subsequent generations can engage in constitutional re-creation, amending or altogether revising the constitutional arrangements under which they choose to live. Moreover, those living under subnational constitutions in a wide variety of federations have not been reluctant to exercise the constitution changing power lodged in them.

Subnational constitutions can also protect the right of groups to maintain their own distinctive identities, through provisions dealing with such bulwarks of identity as religion, language and ethnicity. In most federations, federal rights guarantees restrict both federal and subnational governments, thereby circumscribing the range of discretion available to constituent units. These federal guarantees serve as a baseline, safeguarding basic rights for all and ensuring that assertions of identity do not lead to oppression of those who do not share the identity. Nevertheless, local conditions and values may lead particular constituent units to use their subnational constitutions to go beyond the federal minimum. This is demonstrated by subnational provisions establishing official languages in various Ethiopian states, by provisions safeguarding the language rights of minority populations in some German *Länder*, and by provisions acknowledging the rights of native peoples concentrated in the constituent unit, as in Mexico.[48]

---

[47]   The absence of supermajority requirements or popular ratification, alternatively, could simply reflect Canadian political culture, which has shown a distrust of referenda and unmitigated popular sovereignty. See John Dinan, 'Patterns of Subnational Constitutionalism in Federal Countries', 39 *Rutgers Law Journal* 837–61 (summer 2008).

[48]   On Ethiopia, see Yonatan Tesfaye Fessha, 'Institutional Recognition and Accommodation of Ethnic Diversity: Federalism in South Africa and Ethiopia' 399–406 (unpublished Ph.D. dis-

Finally, subnational constitutions provide a vehicle whereby those within a constituent unit can determine what rights they deem most essential and give constitutional recognition and protection to those rights. In federations in which there are both federal and subnational bills of rights, doubtless there will be considerable overlap between federal and subnational guarantees. Yet this overlap need not be complete. Within a federation, there may well be different views about the constitutionalization of, for example, social or economic rights. Local circumstances and values may dictate that particular rights are given constitutional protection in some constituent units but not in others. In addition, there may be disagreement about what 'reasonable limits' on rights 'can be demonstrably justified in a free and democratic society'.[49] In the United States, jurists often describe the federal Bill of Rights as a floor rather than a ceiling. It establishes a standard, below which constituent units cannot go, but it does not otherwise limit state initiatives in expanding rights—they can build on that floor.

Yet nothing guarantees that this building project will occur. As this chapter shows, the opportunities that constituent units enjoy for identifying and promoting rights depend on political circumstances within their federations. Even when such opportunities exist, constituent units may fail to take advantage of the constitutional space available to them.[50] Given the constitutional choices made by Canada with regard to provincial constitutionalism, the challenge for citizens of Quebec is to determine what opportunities exist for provincial initiatives aimed at extending and securing rights. This challenge exists for the people of many other subnational units around the world.

FURTHER READING

Burgess, Michael and G. Alan Tarr (eds) (2012). *Constitutional Dynamics in Federal Systems: Sub-National Perspectives*. Montreal: McGill-Queen's University Press.

Dinan, John (2008). 'Patterns of Subnational Constitutionalism in Federal Countries', 39 *Rutgers Law Journal* 837–61.

Foley, Michael (1989). *The Silence of Constitutions: Gaps, 'Abeyances', and Political Temperament in the Maintenance of Government*. London: Routledge.

Friesen, Jennifer (2006). *State Constitutional Law: Litigating Individual Rights, Claims and Defenses*. Newark, NJ: LexisNexis, 4th edn.

Gamper, Anna (2003). 'The Principle of Homogeneity and Democracy in Austrian Federalism: The Constitutional Court's Ruling on Direct Democracy in *Voralberg*', 33 *Publius: The Journal of Federalism* 45–58.

Grammond, Sébastien (2010). 'Canadian Federalism, Cultural Diversity, and Conceptions of Fundamental Rights,' in J.M. Castellà Andreu and Sébastien Grammond (eds), *Diversidad, Derechos Fundamentales y Federalism: Un Diálogo entre Canadá y España* 29–46. Barcelona: Atelier.

Gunlicks, Arthur B. (2000). 'State (*Land*) Constitutions in Germany', 31 *Rutgers Law Journal* 971–98.

---

sertation, University of the Western Cape 2008), available at the Electronic Thesis and Dissertation Library, http://etd.uwc.ac.za, and on file with the Center for State Constitutional Studies, Rutgers University-Camden. On Germany and the protection of language rights of minorities within particular *Länder*, see Norman Weiss, 'The Protection of Minorities in a Federal State: The Case of Germany', in Tarr, Williams and Marko (note 12) 80–81. On Mexico, where the Oaxaca Constitution extended protections for native people before the federal constitution, see Gutiérrez González (note 41) 214.

49   Canadian Charter of Rights and Freedoms art. I.
50   For discussion of this point, see Williams and Tarr (note 12).

Kincaid, John and G. Alan Tarr (eds) (2005). *Constitutional Origins, Structure, and Change in Federal Countries*. Montreal: McGill-Queen's University Press.

Marshfield, Jonathan L. (2008). 'Authorizing Subnational Constitutions in Transitional Federal States: South Africa, Democracy, and the KwaZulu-Natal Constitution', 41 *Vanderbilt Journal of Transnational Law* 585–638.

Murray, Christina and Catherine Maywald (2006). 'Subnational Constitution-Making in Southern Sudan', 37 *Rutgers Law Journal* 1203–34.

Russell, Peter H. (1993). *Constitutional Odyssey: Can Canadians Become a Sovereign People?* Toronto: University of Toronto Press.

Sharman, Campbell (1984). 'The Strange Case of a Provincial Constitution: The British Columbia Constitution Act', 17 *Canadian Journal of Political Science* 87–108.

Tarr, G. Alan (1998). *Understanding State Constitutions*. Princeton, NJ: Princeton University Press.

Tarr, G. Alan, Robert F. Williams and Joseph Marko (eds) (2004). *Federalism, Subnational Constitutions, and Minority Rights*. Westport, CT: Praeger.

Thomas, David M. (1997). *Whistling Past the Graveyard: Constitutional Abeyances, Quebec, and the Future of Canada*. Toronto: Oxford University Press.

Williams, Robert F. (2009). *The Law of American State Constitutions*. New York: Oxford University Press.

10 Judges, their careers, and independence
Carlo Guarnieri*

Modern political systems entrust judges with the function of adjudicating disputes arising from the application of recognized legal norms. In constitutional democracies, judges enjoy strong guarantees, regulated by ordinary statutes, organic laws, constitutional norms and often supported by settled practices. However, although within a set of common principles, comparatists can single out different legal traditions—with significant implications for the status of judges.

1 JUDICIAL IMPARTIALITY AND INDEPENDENCE

One cannot analyze the status of the judge without taking into consideration its institutional function: adjudication. Adjudication is a type of dispute resolution that relies on an independent, third-party facilitator: an externally appointed judge.[1] Therefore, the freedom of action of the parties to the dispute is limited. They must comply with the judge's decision, even though they have no control over the choice of judge, whom the state imposes. In general, judicial proceedings are much more effective than other proceedings—such as mediation or arbitration—because they do not need the consent of both parties to achieve a resolution of the dispute. However, one should weigh this effectiveness against the risks for the disputing parties who must relinquish much more control over the proceeding. Judicial proceedings are usually initiated without mutual consent, as legal disputes are triggered by the action of one party against another. In some cases, for example in criminal proceedings, a public prosecutor acting on behalf of the state can initiate proceedings, not only against the will of the accused, but also without the consent of the victim.

For these reasons, judges are inherently in a difficult position. They must resolve cases without the main element that makes the procedural triad an effective means of resolving disputes in other proceedings: the willingness of the participants to submit to both the proceedings and the involvement of the third party. This missing element constitutes a crisis of consensus that is always latent in the judicial process.[2] To address this weakness, the judicial process tends to include several principles creating the appearance of and reinforcing judicial impartiality. The most important are: (1) the prohibition against ad hoc justice, which means that the dispute must be resolved by a judge having pre-existing jurisdiction over the general subject matter; (2) the adversary principle (*et audi alteram*

---

* Professor of Political Science, University of Bologna.
[1] Martin Shapiro, *Courts: A Comparative and Political Analysis* (Chicago: The University of Chicago Press 1981).
[2] Shapiro (note 1) 8–17.

partem), which establishes the right of both parties to be heard by the judge; and (3) the principle of judicial passivity (*ne procedat judex ex officio*), which forbids the judge from initiating proceedings independently.[3] Another element that reinforces the appearance of judicial impartiality is the fact that judicial decisions tend to be bound by a system of statutory legal norms and, in some cases, judicial precedents. This reliance on pre-existing norms aims to temper the disappointment of the losing party and prevent the judge from appearing personally responsible for the decision.

Above all, the need to guarantee judicial impartiality implies that judges must be independent of the disputing parties and protected from their interference. Such independence is a necessary condition for safeguarding at least the appearance of judicial impartiality, as any judge who is dependent in some way on one of the parties cannot be, and especially cannot appear to be, impartial. In the political development of Europe, the incorporation of judges into the machinery of the state and the superiority of government-appointed judges over other types of judges—for example, feudal or city judges—have largely guaranteed judicial independence from the parties in dispute, at least in the case of private citizens. However, the incorporation of the judge into the state organization creates the need to redefine judicial impartiality when one of the parties is the state itself or one of its representatives. In this case, only by defining judicial independence in relation to the state[4] can the judge act as an impartial third party in disputes between the state and citizens (for instance in criminal trials or administrative law cases). Judges can then become an effective check on the way public functions are performed, since guarantees of independence allow judges to resolve such disputes and interpret the relevant laws without coming under pressure from the state.

This last element explains why the protection of judicial impartiality through strong guarantees of judicial independence became one the most important traits of constitutionalism. Since one of the main objectives of constitutionalism is to limit the arbitrary exercise of government power and to make it legally accountable,[5] submitting the performance of public functions to the scrutiny of an independent body becomes an effective and essential check on the exercise of political power. It ensures the supremacy of the law and is a fundamental step in building a constitutional state.

Even though some degree of judicial independence exists in all constitutional regimes, there are important differences among countries, particularly between civil law and common law countries.[6] Historically, judges in civil law countries have enjoyed less independence and their role has tended to be far less politically significant. In those states, the monarchy brought about the centralization of political authority, including the judicial function, to which judges were initially subordinated. The constitutionalization of political power and the consequent development of judicial guarantees of independence partially weakened this relationship, but the organizational integration of the judiciary

---

[3]   Mauro Cappelletti, *The Judicial Process in Comparative Perspective* (Oxford: Clarendon Press 1989).

[4]   Shapiro (note 1) 19–20.

[5]   Giovanni Sartori, *The Theory of Democracy Revisited* (London: Chatham House 1987).

[6]   John H. Merryman and Rogelio Pérez-Perdomo, *The Civil Law Tradition* (Stanford: Stanford University Press, 3rd edn, 2007); Raoul C. Van Caenegem, *Judges, Legislators and Professors* (Cambridge: Cambridge University Press 1987).

into the structure of public administration was maintained, if not strengthened. The decline of the monarchy in the nineteenth century did not radically alter the situation; it merely transferred the power to exert influence over the judiciary to a parliamentary or presidential executive.

The situation in Anglo-Saxon countries is different. In England, the centralization of political authority resulted in the hegemony of one institution, Parliament. However, the political context of such a development is more polycentric: the political branches do not monopolize the creation of legal norms since an important role has always been reserved for judicial decisions. As a result, English judges have been able to maintain some autonomy in relation to parliamentary statutes. In addition, common law principles that judges developed still remain one of the basic elements of English law. In the United States, a written constitution combined with judicial review of legislation has ensured from the outset that the judiciary would not be subordinate to the political branches. On the contrary, following the rules laid down by the Constitution, the American judiciary has emerged as an equal power to the legislature and the executive, and its main task has been to balance lawmaking power in a constitutional system of checks and balances.

Summing up, in any constitutional state whose foremost objective is to safeguard the rights of citizens, judicial independence is primarily aimed at guaranteeing and supporting judicial impartiality in the adjudication process. Consequently, its main point of reference must be the state and its institutions, particularly the executive, which directly or indirectly is most often a party to such adjudication. However, with the introduction of judicial review of legislation, the legislature also becomes a point of reference for judicial independence. Jurists consider the judiciary a power on the same level as the legislative and the executive: it becomes a veritable Third Branch, as jurists often refer to it in the United States.[7]

2   JUDICIAL INDEPENDENCE: ITS CONTENT

Although guarantees of independence—or institutional independence—are designed to protect judges from improper pressures, they cannot assure their independent behaviour. In fact, complete judicial autonomy is difficult to conceive, because judges cannot be completely isolated from their environment. Therefore, we should distinguish between institutional independence and independence on the bench. Although the first is the necessary condition of the second, they do not coincide.[8]

Since 1990, the influence of the international environment has been especially significant in the field of judicial independence as in other areas. Jurists view the independence of courts and judges as indispensable elements of the right to a fair trial, which they consider an essential component of the Rule of Law and guaranteed by the most important universal and regional conventions regarding civil and political rights. The jurisprudence of the supervisory bodies set up under these conventions has had a significant impact

---

[7]   Pasquale Pasquino, *Uno e trino: Indipendenza della magistratura e separazione dei poteri* (Milan: Anabasi 1994).

[8]   Peter H. Russell, 'Toward a General Theory of Judicial Independence', in Peter H. Russell and David M. O'Brien (eds), *Judicial Independence in the Age of Democracy* 1–24 (Charlottesville: University Press of Virginia 2001).

on the setting of national judiciaries.[9] Moreover, a range of other instruments, although technically non-binding, have been widely endorsed and have influenced in a softer but no less effective way the strengthening of judicial guarantees of independence. In the last 25 years, the United Nations and the Council of Europe have been the most active in this field. Principle five of the 1985 Basic Principles on the Independence of the Judiciary of the United Nations states in a sweeping way that 'the judiciary shall decide matters before them impartially, on the basis of facts and in accordance with the law, without *any* restrictions, improper influences, inducements, pressures, threats or interferences, direct or indirect, from *any* quarter or for *any* reason' (emphasis added).[10] One can find similar provisions in the recent 2010 Recommendation by the Committee of Ministers of the Council of Europe on 'judges: independence, efficiency and responsibilities'.[11]

Broadly speaking, all democratic constitutional systems approach judicial independence in similar terms: in principle, judges are subordinate only to the law. However, differences emerge when considering the status that judges enjoy and, above all, the way their guarantees of independence work in practice. The most significant elements concern appointments, salary, transfers, disciplinary proceedings and career patterns, with the last factor being the most important variable characterizing the organizational structure of the judiciary. All of them determine the position of individual judges in relation to their colleagues and those responsible for decisions affecting their professional life. Taken as a whole, one can use these elements to assess the extent of both internal and external judicial independence. While external independence refers to the relations between the judiciary and other branches of government, internal independence focuses on guarantees aimed at protecting individual judges from undue pressures from within the judiciary: fellow judges and, above all, superiors.[12] Although not always considered in full, the role played by organizational hierarchies is crucial for understanding the internal dynamics of the judiciary, which in turn affect the actual degree of judicial autonomy. Here still relevant is the distinction between the common and civil law traditions, as they create two alternative models of judicial organization.

3   JUDICIAL INDEPENDENCE IN COMMON LAW COUNTRIES

3.1   United Kingdom

The English judicial system was founded on a strict association among legal professions.[13] Recruited almost exclusively from practising barristers (that is, lawyers entitled to practise

---

[9]   Guy Canivet, Mads Andenas and Duncan Fairgrieve (eds), *Independence, Accountability, and the Judiciary* (London: British Institute of International and Comparative Law 2006).
[10]   Endorsed by UN General Assembly resolutions 40/32 of 29 November 1985 and 40/146 of 13 December 1985.
[11]   Recommendation CM/Rec(2010)12, available at Council of Europe, https://wcd.coe.int/wcd/ViewDoc.jsp?id=1707137&Site=CM.
[12]   Shimon Shetreet, 'Judicial Independence: New Conceptual Dimensions and Contemporary Challenges', in Shimon Shetreet and Jules Dechênes (eds), *Judicial Independence: The Contemporary Debate* 637–8 (Dordrecht: Nijhoff 1985); Russell (note 8).
[13]   John S. Bell, *Judiciaries within Europe: A Comparative Review* 298–349 (Cambridge: Cambridge University Press 2006).

as an advocate, particularly in the higher courts) with numerous years of experience, the bar has dominated the professional judiciary. The move from private practice to the bench is the most typical career path for an English judge. This approach, as a transplant, travelled to some extent into the American and other common law systems, and results in a form of professional mobility that is largely unknown in continental Europe.[14]

The United Kingdom does not have a single unified legal system. Since 1998, there have been significant efforts to devolve legal authority to subnational units. Thus, as far as the judiciary is concerned, England and Wales have one system, Scotland has another, and Northern Ireland has a third system. The formal power to appoint most judges is vested in the crown. Traditionally, the Lord Chancellor played the central role in their appointment, but recently Parliament radically reformed that role.[15] The Constitutional Reform Act 2005[16] has introduced a significant number of changes to the ways in which judges are appointed, managed and disciplined. The reform created a Judicial Appointment Commission, whose job is to recommend names for the Lord Chancellor de facto to appoint to any judicial post in England and Wales, excluding lay magistrates.[17] The Commission (with 15 members), instituted in 2006, is an independent body, chaired by a lay person and composed of five judges—taken from the different levels of courts—plus a solicitor, a barrister, a lay judge, a tribunal member and five lay members who have not practised law. The commissioners are selected by a complex process involving the Lord Chancellor, the Lord Chief Justice—who presides over the Court of Appeal and is considered the head of the judiciary—the Judges' Council, and others. The Lord Chancellor can accept or reject proposals of the Commission or ask for reconsideration, but cannot appoint judges whose names the Commission has not recommended.

Professional judges have traditionally been recruited exclusively from among the smallest group within the UK legal profession, barristers (or advocates in Scotland), and their salaries have always been considered adequate to attract high quality professionals. Therefore, the judiciary has come from an elite group, currently numbering approximately 12,000 in England and Wales. In the 1970s, the judiciary began to open itself up incrementally to solicitors, who are far more numerous (more than 100,000) than barristers. However, solicitors have remained a smaller segment of the judiciary and are mostly confined to its lower ranks. The Courts and Legal Services Act 1990[18] made it possible for solicitors to qualify as advocates in the higher courts under certain conditions. Thus, in principle, solicitors can now reach the higher ranks of the judiciary, but the number of solicitor-advocates in the higher courts has grown very slowly, and the same is true of their

---

[14]   In England, non-professional judges play an important role in the administration of justice. There are almost 30,000 lay magistrates in England and Wales who are not required to have any formal legal education and do not receive remuneration, although they adjudicate the majority of criminal and civil cases.

[15]   Bell (note 13) 310–11. Since 2009, the Supreme Court of the United Kingdom has taken over the unifying role of review from the subnational judiciaries that the law lords in the House of Lords used to perform.

[16]   Available at The National Archives, http://www.legislation.gov.uk/ukpga/2005/4/contents.

[17]   The Judicial Appointments Board for Scotland makes most appointments of Scottish judges and the Northern Ireland Judicial Appointments Commission makes those appointments in Northern Ireland.

[18]   Available at The National Archives, http://www.legislation.gov.uk/ukpga/1990/41/contents.

appointment to the judiciary. This is due at least in part to the fact that a prolonged advocacy qualification is necessary before judicial appointment, with judges generally recruited after at least seven to ten years of advocacy. As a result, the average age of appointment to the professional judiciary in the UK is far older than the age of judges on the Continent. As for the future, it is still too early to assess the impact of the 2005 reform.

Historically, the English judiciary did not have a formal career structure, and the notion of a judicial career was virtually unknown. When specific vacancies occurred, the crown appointed individuals (on the Lord Chancellor's recommendation) according to the skills needed for the particular judicial office. Moves from one position to another were possible, but the system did not openly encourage individual aspirations for advancement. However, since the early 1970s, some type of a career pattern has slowly taken shape. The principle has emerged whereby judges already serving in lower courts are eligible for appointment to higher jurisdictions and professional full-time judges tend to be chosen from among the ranks of part-time judges. The UK system now appears to be moving closer to the model found in civil law countries, although some significant differences remain. Judicial promotions occur in much the same way as initial appointments and do not follow predetermined patterns. More importantly, judges do not undergo any systematic evaluation, as do their European civil law counterparts. Thus, what internal judicial hierarchy exists is rudimentary. However, unlike France or Germany, the prestige surrounding judicial office in the United Kingdom does not necessarily relate to rank or function. Whatever their position on the 'career ladder', the judges enjoy a comparatively high public status.

English judges are not easily removed from office; once appointed, they hold office 'during good behaviour', which invariably means until retirement age. Legal rules for removal and discipline of judges are not as abundant and detailed as rules in civil law countries or even the United States. Except for impeachment (which has fallen into disuse since the nineteenth century), the only formal sanction against High Court and Court of Appeal judges is removal by the crown on an address by both houses of Parliament. Established by the Act of Settlement in 1701,[19] this rather complex procedure has been successfully invoked on only one occasion in 1830. In practice, the professional environment, the bench and the bar control compliance with ethical rules, but on occasion the Lord Chancellor could summon a judge for a 'private meeting'. Powers granted to the Lord Chancellor over part-time judges and magistrates were more far-reaching, and he could directly remove them for incompetence or misbehaviour. The 2005 reform transferred these powers to the Lord Chief Justice.

3.2   United States

Unlike the United Kingdom, in the United States a unified legal profession exists with no separation between advocates and other practitioners, and while legal professionals

---

[19]   Article III of the Act provided that 'judges commissions be made *quamdiu se bene gesserint*, and their salaries ascertained and established; but upon the address of both Houses of Parliament it may be lawful to remove them'. Stat. 1 W. & M. Sess. 2. c. 2. s.2, available at British History Online, http://www.british-history.ac.uk/report.aspx?compid=46986.

(and therefore judges) may have different areas of specialization, they all share a common professional identity. The range of judicial recruitment methods is much broader in the United States than in the UK, as a result both of the federal structure of the US government and the legislative powers state governments possess over the administration of justice. State reforms have further diversified the methods for selecting judges, creating a complex picture. While each state has its own specific form of selection, there are three general models: (1) *appointment* (with power vested in politically representative authorities); (2) *direct election* (both partisan and non-partisan); and (3) what is generally called the *merit selection* or *Missouri plan* (whose main goal is to achieve a balance between political and professional criteria).

At the federal level, judges are recruited through a complex procedure that consists of three main stages: nomination by the president, screening of candidates by the Senate Judiciary Committee, and final approval by the whole Senate on a simple majority vote. Based on joint participation of the legislature and the executive, the process is a good example of political 'checks and balances'. The president's wide discretion in choosing candidates, especially those for the higher federal courts, does have constraints. Rejected nominations historically have occurred regularly, and over two centuries the Senate has refused to confirm 27 of the 147 Supreme Court nominees forwarded to it by the White House.[20]

The process of appointment is strongly influenced by the relationships between the two political branches: when the Senate majority and the president belong to the same political party, the process is somewhat easier. In contrast, when they are divided by party, the appointment of federal judges requires informal negotiations before and during each stage of the process. In turn, this means that the number of actors involved is much larger than formal accounts often suggest. The US Department of Justice, headed by the attorney general, plays a central role in the selection of federal judges by establishing lists of potential appointees and screening candidates. The judiciary itself participates in the preliminary phases of the nomination process, as the Justice Department and the White House usually seek the views of prominent judges at the federal and state levels. After a hiatus during the presidency of George W. Bush (2001–09), the American Bar Association (ABA) is again involved in the initial phase. The ratings of its Standing Committee on the Federal Judiciary on prospective judges' qualifications can be very influential. Senators from the state where the judicial vacancy is to be filled can also play a crucial role; provided these senators belong to the same party as the president, their opposition to a nomination usually forces the president to withdraw the name (a practice known as 'senatorial courtesy'). The executive also consults with politicians at the local level, particularly the mayors of large cities, in the same way over nominations for the lower federal courts. Interest groups actively participate in the process by expressing views on judicial candidates, and there are indications that interest group patronage is increasingly important in appointments to the federal trial and appellate courts. Thus, the federal executive (mainly the White House and the Justice Department) and the legislature are the central but not the only participants in the appointment of federal judges.

---

[20] Lee Epstein and Jeffrey A. Segal, *Advice and Consent: The Politics of Judicial Appointments* 20–21 (Oxford: Oxford University Press 2005).

In recent years, the political beliefs and party affiliation of candidates for judicial appointment in the United States appear to have increased in significance. This is often most obvious with US Supreme Court appointments: almost 90 per cent of Supreme Court justices have belonged to the same party as the president who nominated them.[21] This overtly political process of recruitment is related to the political role the judiciary plays in the American system of government. The Constitution explicitly named the judiciary as a third, co-equal branch of government, and federal judges enjoy life tenure (article III, section 1). Nevertheless, political influence tends to exert, but also to exhaust itself, at the moment of confirmation.

Even though it may appear that ideological criteria are highly significant in the appointment of federal judges in the United States, the candidates' professional qualifications and competence do play an important part in the selection process. Lee Epstein and Jeffrey Segal conclude: 'if a president is concerned with leaving a lasting legacy to the nation in the form of jurists who will continue to exert influence on the law after he leaves office, then professional merit too comes into play'.[22] The potential area of recruitment is undoubtedly larger than in Great Britain, but is still confined to professionals who usually combine legal skills and political experience in different degrees. US federal courts are mostly staffed by former practising attorneys (usually with degrees from leading law schools), law professors, former public administrators, and increasingly by judges who have previously served in high state courts. Appointees have almost invariably been active in party politics prior to their appointment to the federal bench.

At the state level, direct election of judges is widespread, even though electoral methods vary from state to state and recruitment methods vary with the type and level of state court. In all cases, provision is made for a term of office ranging from four to 15 years. The distinction between partisan and non-partisan election depends on whether it is possible for the candidate to run with the open support of a political party, although a candidate's party activity and support by local political forces can still influence non-partisan elections.[23] Not surprisingly, critics of this method stress the inherent possibility of damaging the judge's image as a neutral umpire and devaluing the professional qualifications of the bench. The Missouri non-partisan court plan, named for the state that first adopted it in 1940, is a method developed by the ABA precisely to address such problems. Variations of the ABA's original model currently operate in about 30 states, typically called 'merit plans'. The merit-plan selection process usually consists of three phases. First, a special commission of judges, lawyers and citizens nominates three to five candidates for each vacant position. Choosing from that list, the state governor then appoints a judge who will serve for the remainder of a vacated judgeship. After this probationary period, the judge must undergo public scrutiny, through a ballot, to remain in office for a specific term that varies according to state legislation and the level of court jurisdiction. Research about such ballots shows that voters usually confirm serving judges; often they run unopposed for re-election.[24]

---

[21]   Epstein and Segal (note 20) 26.
[22]   Epstein and Segal (note 20) 69.
[23]   Henry J. Abraham, *The Judicial Process* 34 (Oxford: Oxford University Press, 7th edn, 1998).
[24]   Abraham (note 23) 36–9.

The reasons behind the absence of a civil-service style career for judges in the United Kingdom also apply in the United States. However, moves from one judicial position to another are frequent, so that more than half of federal judges have served in other judicial offices.[25] For example, members of the federal judiciary are increasingly selected from among the ranks of state judges. Even though these 'advancements' follow the recruitment procedure described earlier, mobility tends to be higher in the US than in the UK. This seems to leave more room for political influence since politics provides the opportunity to move to a higher rank.

The independence of federal judges is protected by the US Constitution, guaranteeing appointment 'during good behaviour', which in practice means for life. Under a constitutional provision (article II, section 4) that applies to the president, vice-president, and all federal civil officers, federal judges can be 'removed from Office on Impeachment for, and Conviction of, Treason, Bribery, or other high Crimes and Misdemeanours'. The House of Representatives investigates such charges and can commit the individual to trial in the Senate by a simple majority vote, but conviction and removal requires a two-thirds majority of the Senate. Congress has initiated these proceedings against judges 15 times; only seven resulted in actual removal, although several judges under investigation resigned before Congress formally impeached them. For disciplinary measures against federal judges for less serious violations, the American system has much more structured legislation than the British system, and judicial councils established at the appellate court level may impose sanctions.[26] However, overall, members of the federal judiciary enjoy broad guarantees of independence, which shield them from political influence.[27]

At the state level, removal by impeachment has been widely adopted, along with other methods such as removal by address (consideration by the governor and voted by both houses of the state legislature) and recall (a public petition to remove a judge followed by a popular vote).[28] In addition, codes of judicial conduct now in force across the country provide detailed regulations for activities ranging from extra-judicial activities to campaign financing. It is up to specific institutions, usually known as judicial conduct organizations, to hear grievances against individual judges and to ensure compliance with ethical rules. While these bodies can usually only impose minor sanctions, for instance issuing a reprimand, they can always recommend to the competent authorities that more serious sanctions be imposed.

Summing up, common law judges[29] are appointed or elected only after having acquired

---

[25]   Epstein and Segal (note 20) 63.

[26]   The Judicial Councils Reform and Judicial Conduct and Disability Act (1980) does not apply to members of the US Supreme Court. The only control over them is impeachment. For the Act's implementation for the 13 federal judicial circuits, see 28 U.S.C. § 332, available at Legal Information Institute, U.S. code, http://www.law.cornell.edu/uscode (enter code section).

[27]   Although the Constitution maintains that judges' salaries 'shall not be diminished during their Continuance in Office' (art. III, § 1), recently there have been claims that they have not been adequately adjusted to inflation. Epstein and Segal (note 20) 34.

[28]   See American Judicature Society, Methods of Judicial Selection: Removal of Judges, http://www.judicialselection.us/judicial_selection/methods/removal_of_judges.cfm?state (list of removal methods for all 50 states).

[29]   The institutional setting of other common law judiciaries is largely similar (Russell and O'Brien (note 8)).

professional experience, usually, but not always, as legal advocates. There are no formal provisions for advancement. Promotions are possible but not widespread and, in general, internal controls over judges by their higher-ranking colleagues are rather weak. In any case, after appointment—a process in which politics tends to play a role—strong guarantees of both internal and external independence exist. Since judges usually have lengthy legal experience outside the judiciary, there is no particular emphasis on internal controls. As for the reference group of judges—that is, those individuals whom judges take into account when reaching a decision—it tends to lie outside the judiciary. However, while in Great Britain this is a small professional group—at least so far, especially the bar—in the United States this group seems more diversified.

4   JUDICIAL INDEPENDENCE IN CIVIL LAW COUNTRIES

In most civil law countries, the largest proportion of judges is recruited directly after university legal education (and sometimes an apprenticeship period) through public examination, and with no requirement for previous professional experience. Successful candidates are then appointed at the bottom of the career ladder, and professional training and socialization take place within the judiciary. Some form of either mandatory or optional training usually exists for both new recruits and senior members of the judiciary. Judicial training has become an increasingly important element in the administration of justice and most entry-level judges are required to complete an initial period of probationary training.

Public competition is meant to be the most effective way of ensuring both the professional qualifications and independence of the judiciary. Competitions are open to young university graduates in law, who typically have no previous professional experience. Legal education is normally multi-purpose, providing a general knowledge of all relevant branches of the law at the expense of any form of specialization. Consequently, selection incorporates little or no emphasis on the practical side of the work of the judiciary, and is made based on written and oral exams that test the candidates' theoretical knowledge of the law. Young recruits are supposed to be able to perform the entire range of tasks senior judges might assign them, from adjudicating a criminal, family or fiscal case to acting as a public prosecutor. These judges also generally supervise the recruits' legal training. Thus, judicial socialization takes place within the organization and the judiciary essentially controls it. All of these elements and, in particular, the reluctance to require professional legal experience outside the judiciary encourage both the *esprit de corps* of the judiciary and the 'balkanization' of the bench and bar. Therefore, relations between the two different sides of the legal profession are often in tension.[30]

However, in most continental European countries, recruitment by public competition has undergone some major changes. Lateral entry into the judiciary, open to experienced lawyers or civil servants, has increased in an attempt to prevent corporatist tendencies. In the same way, most of these countries have established judicial schools to provide legal

---

[30]   Giuseppe Di Federico (ed.), *Recruitment, Professional Evaluation and Career of Judges and Prosecutors in Europe* (Bologna: IRSIG-CNR 2005); Merryman and Pérez-Perdomo (note 6).

education and training for new judges to fill the vacuum that exists between university education and professional practice.[31]

Traditionally, continental European judiciaries tend to operate within a pyramid-like organizational structure.[32] Salary,[33] prestige and personal influence depend on a judge's position on the hierarchical ladder and can be improved only through promotions. These are granted on a competitive basis and according to two criteria, seniority and merit, the latter being determined through assessments by senior judges. In principle, each career step requires a specific procedure. Although the number and position of those in charge of such decisions varies from one country to another, some features are relatively constant. Hierarchical superiors play a fundamentally important role in determining judicial status in most European civil law countries. Promotions rely often on information recorded in personnel reports compiled by superiors, and this highlights the extremely delicate and critical role entrusted to the judicial elite. The process is based on the assumption that individuals in top positions can manage, and thus evaluate, the entire range of tasks performed at lower levels of the pyramid.

The decision-making process for promotions in continental European systems also involves others outside the judiciary. Traditionally, the executive (i.e., the ministry of justice) and sometimes the legislature, represented the most important institutional channels connecting the judiciary to the political system. However, in several countries the prominent role customarily played by the executive branch has been weakened substantially by the creation of new institutions—superior councils of magistrates—designed to strengthen the independence of judges.

4.1 Germany

Germany provides an influential example of the traditional education and career of civil law judges. All German jurists share a common legal education and training leading to the 'qualification for judgeship' (*Befähigung zum Richteramt*). This qualification is a necessary requirement to serve in all legal professions and the higher ranks of the civil service. Consequently, judges, public prosecutors, private attorneys, notaries and government officials are all educated through a lengthy and highly selective route and tend to identify themselves with a larger professional group, the *Juristen*. Lateral mobility among these various professions also exists. Although it is restrictive, the jurists' common educational experience appears to create a strong connection among the different legal professions that is characteristic of the German system.

Under German federal legislation,[34] a statute organizes training for future judges into

---

[31] Bell (note 13) 360–65; Cheryl A. Thomas, *Review of Judicial Training and Education in Other Jurisdictions* (London: Judicial Studies Board 2006).

[32] Carlo Guarnieri and Patrizia Pederzoli, *The Power of Judges: A Comparative Study of Courts and Democracy* (Oxford: Oxford University Press 2002).

[33] Judicial salaries are usually related to the general scales for the ordinary bureaucracy and adjust accordingly. Although the system seems capable of protecting judicial independence overall, sometimes problems arise concerning the way adjustments occur.

[34] The *Deutsches Richtergesetz*, BGBl. I S. 1665 (1961), enacted in 1961, is available at Bundesministerium der Justiz, Gesetze im Internet, http://www.gesetze-im-internet.de/Teilliste_D. html (select DRiG). Nevertheless, *Länder* also have some legislative competency in this field.

two parts: the first, devoted to theory, takes place in a university law faculty; the second, more practical, establishes training contacts with different legal environments. After completing extended university studies, candidates for the legal profession sit the 'first state examination'. If successful, they obtain the status of temporary civil servants, allowing them to carry out their practical training and receive a small salary. During this period, trainees familiarize themselves with the full range of legal roles they may have to perform in the near future: in the judiciary (both civil and criminal), bar, civil service and public prosecution. The final stage of the legal selection process is the 'second state examination', covering similar subject matter as the first stage but with a more practical orientation. The entire process lasts about ten years and has a remarkably low success rate. It is only after completion of the second state examination that new judges are selected.

Appointment to a German judgeship depends on two criteria—marks obtained in state examinations (the more important element) and information on candidates' attitudes and performance during the training period. The regional (*Land*) ministry of justice selects among candidates who apply and usually makes appointments according to a candidate's position on the examination pass-list. Judicial appointees (*Richter auf Probe*) serve a probationary period ranging from three to five years, during which their guarantees of independence are restricted. They can be moved from one position to another and required to undergo further evaluations before finally becoming life-tenure judges (*Richter auf Lebenszeit*).

Executive influence over the judiciary remains strong in Germany.[35] Within the general framework established by federal legislation, the power to appoint and promote is always vested in the *Land* minister of justice, but in eight *Länder* (out of 16), there are committees for the selection of judges (*Richterwahlauschüsse*). These committees are usually made up of representatives of the executive, legislature, bar and bench; although the proportions may vary, non-judicial members are typically in the majority. As a rule, the minister of justice presides but cannot vote, although she has veto power over the decision. However, in all cases the procedure involves the participation of the judicial council (a body established in each court and made up exclusively of judges, half of them directly elected by their peers), which is asked for an advisory opinion. Decisions concerning judges' promotions are based on evaluations drafted every four or five years by judicial superiors, who have the power of 'hierarchical supervision'. However, the jurisdiction over disciplinary matters is entrusted to specialized courts established at the *Land* level (*Dienstgerichte*): sanctions against judges can be imposed only on their ruling.

Federal judges sitting on Germany's supreme courts are appointed following the same general procedure, but with one crucial difference: the bench has no voice on the federal committee for the selection of these judges. The committee is made up exclusively of representatives of the executive and legislative branches, namely the *Länder* ministries (16) and an equal number of members elected by the federal legislative lower chamber (*Bundestag*). The federal minister of justice holds the presidency without voting rights. The committee makes appointments primarily based on the candidates' professional qualifications, but their geographic origin also carries weight to ensure that federal courts are staffed with judges drawn from the different *Länder*. This does not mean that political

---

35   Di Federico (note 30); Bell (note 13).

patronage is not a part of the appointment process; party representation on the committee plays a role and some have strongly criticized that. The federal minister (without committee involvement) decides promotions of federal judges, although an advisory opinion by the judicial council is always required.

4.2 Sweden

The traditional system has proven even more tenacious in Sweden.[36] As in Germany, the Swedish recruitment system is based on a public competition among young graduates in law who have experienced some training. In fact, at the end of the law degree a candidate can apply to become a judicial trainee. The training phase lasts for three years and involves periods in lower and upper courts as well as several formal short courses. After this initial stage, candidates are recruited to the courts as judges on probation for three years: they are not allowed to adjudicate alone, but may take part in collegial decisions. The next phase is appointment as an assessor. During this stage, an individual is not a permanent judge with a secure position in a particular court, but she has a series of fixed-term positions, which she enters as they fall vacant. The objective is to ensure broad experience. The stage as assessor lasts between six and eight years: at the end, it is possible to become a permanent judge.

The National Court Administration *Domstolsverket* (DV) is responsible for the overall management of the court and its staffing levels and equipment. The DV is separate from the ministry of justice. However, its executive board is composed of ten members appointed by the government. Besides the chief executive, there are usually four judges— among them the representative of the judicial union—two members of Parliament, one from a local government, a representative of administrative personnel and a representative of the attorneys' association.

Another independent body—the Judicial Council (*Domarnämnden*)—governs appointments to lower courts and the promotions of judges. Since 2011, it consists of five judges and two lawyers appointed by the government—after consultation with judges' and lawyers' associations—and two lay people appointed by parliament. Although in principle the government can reject the proposals put forward by the Judicial Council, it is a very rare occurrence. Traditionally, judicial positions have not gone only to career judges but also to leading practitioners, prosecutors or high-level civil servants. Once appointed on a permanent basis, Swedish judges enjoy the traditional guarantees of independence: only a judicial procedure can result in their transfer without consent or removal.

Therefore, Swedish judges are recruited according to professional, meritocratic criteria—and after a rather long period of apprenticeship. Their status is guaranteed, but higher-ranking judges influence promotions. In turn, the government appoints senior judges, although candidates must satisfy criteria of professional qualification. Therefore, the internal gradient of judicial independence does not seem particularly protected and the executive is allowed to exert some influence on the judicial elite and, indirectly, on the whole corps.

---

[36]   Bell (note 13) 240–49.

5   THE CHANGING INSTITUTIONAL SETTING OF LATIN EUROPE

Among civil law countries, remarkable changes have characterized the judiciaries of Latin Europe. These changes have involved the recruitment—with the development of forms of specialized training—and management of the judicial corps, with the creation of collegial bodies of magistrates and erosion of the traditional power of the executive branch.

5.1   France

Although reduced in scope, France still keeps the conventional influence of the executive on judicial careers. However, it has been at the forefront of reform of legal education and the training of judges and public prosecutors,[37] which it entrusts to the *École Nationale de la Magistrature* (*ENM*), an institution staffed by magistrates but under the direction of the ministry of justice. The *ENM* has provided a model for other countries, such as Spain, Portugal and recently Italy. A competition open to young law graduates (*concours étudiant*) is by far the most important recruitment channel for the *ENM*, but there are other ways to enter the school, designed to open the judiciary to candidates from different professional environments.

The *concours étudiant* is available to candidates who are not more than 31 years old and hold a university degree. The written and oral admission exams are highly competitive, and successful candidates are soon integrated into the judiciary as *auditeurs de justice* (judicial trainees). They receive a salary and enjoy certain guarantees of independence. The training period is 31 months and consists of two phases: an initial general training period in both the *ENM* and the courts and a second period, lasting six months, devoted to specialist training in the functions the *auditeur* will be assigned after the completion of training (adjudicating civil or criminal cases or acting as a public prosecutor). Recruits are continually assessed throughout the training period and their final ranking determines their ability to choose favoured assignments.

Although the ministry of justice still plays a considerable role in the management of the judicial corps, significant powers have been entrusted to the Superior Council of the Magistracy (*Conseil Supérieur de la Magistrature*). Created in 1946 to preserve the independence of judges, the Council had been the object of several changes. After a constitutional amendment in 2008, it is now a single body separated into two distinct panels, one with competence over judges and the other over public prosecutors. It consists of 15 members. These are a councillor of state elected by peers, a lawyer, six lay members appointed by the President of the Republic, the President of the Senate, and the President of the Chamber of Deputies (two each), and seven magistrates representing a variety of ranks and elected by their peers. The composition of this last segment in the Council changes according to the type of panel involved. When measures concerning judges are under consideration, it consists of the Court of Cassation's president, five judges and one public prosecutor. For decisions affecting public prosecutors, these proportions are

---

[37]   These two positions form a single professional group referred to as the *magistrature*. See section 8 on prosecutors below.

reversed and the prosecutor general at the Court of Cassation takes the place of the Court's president. Disciplinary decisions that the standing panel for the judiciary makes prevail over the wishes of the minister of justice and the range of direct appointments by the Council includes most senior positions. In all other cases, judges can be appointed only after a favourable opinion of the Council. In contrast, the reform more narrowly defined the functions of the public prosecution panel, since it can only give non-compulsory advice.

The French judicial career still resembles the civil law customary model. The judiciary's pyramid structure consists of two levels, the first and second instance. Above these two levels are the most senior judges (*hors hierarchie*) who sit in the Court of Cassation and other high courts. Advancements largely determine the position of individual judges, the functions they perform and their prestige and salary. Steps on the career path depend not only on seniority but also above all on merit. Judges undergo very detailed work evaluations every two years, and in many cases, promotion results in a transfer, although prior consent is required. The procedure for promotion is rather complicated and centres on the judicial hierarchy. Higher-ranking magistrates draft evaluations of work performance, which are recorded in personnel reports made available to everyone taking part in the decision-making process. Each year the Commission for Advancements drafts a list of magistrates qualified for promotion. Since any promotions must come from this list, the Commission holds significant power. Today, its composition includes only a few officials of the executive branch: 16 out of its 20 members are magistrates directly elected by their peers. Therefore, the proposals put forward by the executive are under the double constraints of the Commission and the Superior Council of the Magistracy.

5.2 Italy

Judicial recruitment in Italy still bears a close resemblance to the traditional continental European model. A national public competition is in effect the only way to enter the judiciary, which is a unitary organization (just as in France, both judges and public prosecutors are referred to as magistrates). Law graduates usually sit for the national examination shortly after completing their university studies. As a result, they typically have no experience in legal practice, and even if a candidate did, officials would not consider it in the recruitment process. University law faculties and various private institutions control legal education. In 2006, a law provided for a judicial school, which the state had not established by 2012. The entry test, like the current national examination, consists of written and oral questions to assess general knowledge in the main subjects included in law faculty curricula.

Selection and subsequent training of judges and public prosecutors are the responsibility of the Superior Council of the Magistracy (*Consiglio Superiore della Magistratura*), an institution controlled by a majority of magistrates. The ministry of justice is not involved in either the recruitment process or decisions concerning the status of judges and public prosecutors. Unlike France, the time devoted to training recruits (*uditori giudiziari*) in Italy is variable. In 2006, it was fixed at 18 months, but in practice varies according to the pressure to fill vacant posts. So far, in the absence of the judicial school, apprenticeship takes place in courts and prosecutor offices under the supervision of senior magistrates. Training consists of two phases. The first is devoted to familiarizing young magistrates with different legal roles, involving adjudication as well as prosecution. The second phase (lasting six months) attempts to train them in the specific functions they will have to perform once appointed (e.g., adjudication in civil or criminal courts as well as public prosecution). More importantly, no further attrition of candidates occurs during this period. The reports on individual performance that the Council drafts are almost invariably positive, which makes the initial national examination the only effective means of selection.[38]

Among European civil law countries, Italy has undergone the most radical transformation of the judiciary. It is the only country to achieve true judicial 'self-government'. Historically, the judiciary in Italy closely resembled the French, since it was established in the second half of the nineteenth century under the influence of the Napoleonic model. Since the early 1960s, a gradual process began substantially to alter the traditional set-up. The Superior Council of the Magistracy, formally established by the Constitution of 1948, finally began to operate. The Council makes all decisions related to the status of both judges and public prosecutors. It has power over recruitment, appointment, promotion, transfer, and disciplinary proceedings, which have been removed from the minister of justice.[39] The extent of judicial self-government in Italy is obvious if one considers the composition of the Council. Since reform in 2002, it consists of 16 magistrates directly elected by the whole judiciary, eight lay members elected by both chambers of Parliament from among experienced lawyers and university law professors, and three *ex officio* members (the President of the Republic and the president and prosecutor general of the Court of Cassation). In practice, the lay members are chosen to reflect the strength of the different political parties in Parliament. To understand better the internal operation of the Council, the influence of various political factions (*correnti*) in the National Magistrates Association (*Associazione Nazionale Magistrati*) is crucially important. A series of reforms has broken the traditional dominance of the judicial elite in the Council and today a proportional system of election for all magistrate members operates, assigning a significant influence to the different politically oriented magistrate groups.

The composition of the Council has had major consequences for the way promotions are managed and for the general organization of the judiciary.[40] Because of reforms carried out since the 1960s, the traditional promotion system, based on competitive examinations or senior judge assessments of judicial work, was abolished. In theory, promotions occur based on a combination of the two usual criteria—seniority and merit—the latter of which the Council assesses. In reality, advancements depend mostly on seniority, since professional evaluations are almost invariably positive. Therefore, those who meet the seniority requirements are promoted, draw their pay at the higher scale, but continue to perform their previous functions, which might be in a first instance court. In this way, almost every magistrate can attain the highest salary within 28 years of service. As a result, the Council lacks substantive information on the applicants' qualifications and generally chooses candidates based solely on seniority. Nevertheless, membership in one of the

---

[38]   Di Federico (note 30).
[39]   The minister of justice can initiate disciplinary proceedings, but in most cases, the prosecutor general of the Court of Cassation carries these out. They take place before a standing committee of the Council.
[40]   Di Federico (note 30).

magistrate groups represented on the Council plays a significant part in the process and helps explain the need for magistrates to affiliate to such groups.

Because of all these changes, the reference group of Italian judges has changed. In the past, Italian judges looked to both the decisions of the Court of Cassation and legal scholarship for their points of reference (primarily due to the role their reliance on those sources played in promotions), but today reference points are increasingly found in the political environment and the media. The Italian situation exemplifies an apparently paradoxical situation. While severing formal institutional links with the political system and dismantling all hierarchical constraints can produce high levels of judicial independence (both internal and external), it can also help judges develop a network of less visible connections that could in fact undermine the autonomy of the judiciary.[41]

5.3 Portugal and Spain

Portugal and Spain have followed the French practice of establishing a judicial school as a central element of judicial recruitment. In the Portuguese *Centro de Estudos Judiciarios*, trainees have to choose soon after admission whether to become a judge or a public prosecutor, since there are two separate professional bodies. Public competition to enter the school is similar to the French system: written and oral exams on legal subjects as well as on general social and economic issues. The separation between judges and public prosecutors is perhaps more marked in Spain. After the initial competition, open to law graduates, trainees must make their choice. The future judges are trained at the *Escuela Judicial*, managed by the General Council of the Judiciary (*Consejo General del Poder Judicial*), while prosecutors' initial training is made at the *Centro de Estudios Jurídicos* of the ministry of justice. However, both countries allow for lateral entry into the judiciary for experienced jurists 'of recognized competence', who can be appointed to a small number of positions in a variety of courts.

The Italian experience of judicial self-government has become a model for Spain and Portugal in their post-authoritarian periods. However, significant differences have emerged in these countries, especially Spain. Here, the transition to democracy and its Constitution of 1978 established principles such as the separation of powers and judicial independence, with the judiciary forming a group separate from public prosecutors. Within this framework, the Spanish General Council was created to ensure the independence of the judiciary from the executive.

Following the Italian model, the Spanish Constitution requires that the majority of the members of the General Council are judges, with the Council's functions limited to administering the status of judges. The *Ley Orgánica* of 1980 stipulated that the chief judge of the Supreme Tribunal preside over the Council, which consists of 20 members appointed for five years: 12 were judges directly elected by their peers, and the rest were appointed by both chambers of Parliament. As in Italy, the powers of the minister of justice were limited to funding the judicial system. However, in 1985, the Parliament reformed the Council's composition, since the Parliament now elects all judicial members. The reform—while fostering some collaboration between judges and political parties—

---

[41]   Guarnieri and Pederzoli (note 32).

seems to have reduced the role of judicial associations that the previous proportional system of election had helped to create. Nevertheless, since 2000, Parliament must choose among a list of candidates drafted by the more important judicial groups.

The Council is in charge of appointments and promotions according to procedures that vary with the type of judicial position to be filled. In principle, advancements depend on seniority and, to a lesser extent, on merit, but appointments to the highest judicial positions also take into account the need to ensure representation of linguistic minorities. In disciplinary proceedings, senior judges share these functions with a standing committee of the Council, which intervenes only in instances of gross violation of professional duties.

Similarly, in Portugal, after the fall of the fascist dictatorship in the mid-1970s, major reforms took place within the judicial system. The current principles regulating the Portuguese Superior Council of the Magistracy (*Conselho Superior da Magistradura*) were established in the Constitution of 1976. They entrust the Council with extensive functions, from appointments and transfers to promotions and disciplinary proceedings. Following constitutional amendments in 1982 and 1997, the 17 members of the Council now consist of seven judges directly elected by their peers through a proportional system, seven members elected by Parliament, and two other members appointed by the President of the Republic (one of whom is usually a judge). The president of the Supreme Court, a position elected by fellow judges, chairs the Council. Thus, judges typically hold the majority of the seats.

6   COMMON FEATURES OF CIVIL LAW JUDICIAL STATUS

Several common features define the judicial status in continental European countries. In all cases, recruitment occurs at a younger age than in the British and American systems. The means of educating and training new judges, whether in special schools as in France or extensive on-the-job training as in Germany, partially compensate for the recruits' lack of practical legal experience. More significantly, their professional socialization is achieved almost exclusively within the judiciary itself, which is therefore likely to become a crucial reference point for judicial attitudes. Recruitment is governed in large part by merit and no partisan considerations openly operate in the selection process. Yet, with the exception of Italy, where this process is under the full control of the judiciary itself, the ministries of justice, which might exert some influence, monitor judicial recruitment.

As for guarantees of independence, Germany and the civil law countries of central and north Europe tend to rely on the traditional approach, entrusting promotions to higher-ranking judges, whose appointment is often politically influenced. In these countries, the role of associations, representative of the judiciary, is limited. A different arrangement exists in Latin European countries such as France, Spain, Portugal and Italy, which have created superior councils of the magistracy designed to preserve the independence of the judiciary.[42] All versions of these councils share one prominent feature: members of the

---

[42]   Magistracy councils exist today in Belgium, France, Italy, Portugal and Spain and in some of the new EU countries like Poland, Romania and Bulgaria. See Daniela Piana, *Judicial Accountabilities in New Europe* (Farnham: Ashgate 2010). Other EU countries (e.g., Netherlands

judiciary are always granted representation, although in different proportions. Obviously, the level of judicial independence will tend to be higher where judges hold the majority of seats and their peers directly elected them. In the same way, guarantees of judicial independence are likely to be broader where these councils are entrusted with extensive powers.

However, in both the bureaucratic civil law and professional common law models of the judiciary, no courts are ever totally insulated from the political environment. With a professional judiciary, the influence of the political system is channelled primarily through the appointment process; in a bureaucratic judiciary, political influence is filtered through the hierarchical structure and procedures for career advancements. The way promotions are organized represents the weak point of this arrangement. While recruitment by appointment or direct election tends to align justice with politics based on shared values, hierarchical structures entail less visible but more diffused constraints. Desire for promotion is likely to produce a stronger incentive to comply with pressure or expectations from the minister of justice, judicial superiors or even a 'self-governing' body.[43]

7 THE INDEPENDENCE OF CONSTITUTIONAL AND ADMINISTRATIVE JUDGES

Constitutional review developed much later in Europe than in the United States.[44] It was only after the Second World War that European countries widely adopted judicial review of legislation through the establishment of separate constitutional courts. In 1951, Germany created the *Bundesverfassungsgericht*, followed by the Italian *Corte Costituzionale* in 1956. Two years later, the transition to the Fifth Republic in France brought about the creation of the *Conseil Constitutionnel*. Spain and Portugal joined the European trend in 1978 and 1983 respectively, with the creation of a *Tribunal Constitucional*. Finally, in the transition from communism to democracy in the 1990s, most East European countries have created constitutional courts.

Given the relevance of the task entrusted to them, it is generally argued that constitutional courts actually play a hybrid role somewhere between legal justice and politics.[45] This sort of dual nature is clear in the structure of constitutional courts. On one hand, framers intended these courts to be a check on the political branches of government to mitigate the power of the majority. On the other hand, these other branches have the power to determine the composition of the courts. Therefore, the guardians of the constitution are mainly chosen by the very institutions they have to guard. However, this arrangement reflects the principle of checks and balances and provides the courts with some political legitimacy.

---

and Denmark) have instituted councils whose main task is court administration. In 2004, several national councils created the European Network of Councils of the Judiciary (ENCJ) with the aim of cooperating especially in matters regarding judicial independence. Today, 19 countries of the EU belong to the network. See ENCJ, Home, http://www.encj.eu.

43 Guarnieri and Pederzoli (note 32).

44 Cappelletti (note 3) 117–49.

45 Alan Stone Sweet, *Governing with Judges: Constitutional Politics in Europe* (Oxford: Oxford University Press 2000).

Constitutional court judges are appointed or elected by the political branches and, in some cases, by the judiciary itself for single, non-renewable terms ranging between nine and 12 years. In Portugal, Parliament appoints ten out of 13 constitutional judges, while the other three are co-opted by the Court. Separate appointments, found in France, Germany, Italy and Spain, among others, can be understood within the separation of powers doctrine that reflects a basic reluctance in continental Europe to overlap or share power. However, political parties invariably play a role in the selection of constitutional judges, usually according to some sort of proportional criteria. In France, the President of the Republic, the President of the Senate and the President of the National Assembly each appoints three members of the Constitutional Council. No specific qualifications are required for appointment, not even a law degree. In Germany, Parliament elects the 16 constitutional judges: a committee of the *Bundestag* (reflecting the proportional weight of political parties inside the assembly) elects half of them, while the *Bundesrat* directly elects the other half by a two-thirds majority. The 12 judges of the Spanish Constitutional Court are chosen as follows: the two chambers of Parliament each elects four judges by a three-fifth majority; the executive appoints two; and the Superior Council of the Magistracy selects the remaining two. In Italy, an equal number of the 15 constitutional judges are chosen by the President of the Republic, by both chambers of Parliament sitting in joint session and with a qualified majority, and by the highest courts.

In most civil law countries (Spain being the most notable exception), administrative litigation comes under the jurisdiction of a special set of courts, staffed by a separate body of judges. Traditionally, administrative judges enjoyed a lower degree of independence, although in some countries their guarantees recently have been strengthened.

In Germany, the situation is complex since the judicial system is divided into five main groups of courts: ordinary, administrative, tax and finance, labour, and social security. Each group is divided into first instance and appeal courts at the *Land* level and a final appeal court that is a federal court. As we have already seen, the executive plays a significant role in the career of German judges. While the minister in charge of making decisions concerning the status of judges varies according to the type of court, the ministry of justice retains a prominent position over both ordinary and administrative courts.

Executive influence is even stronger in Sweden, where only in the second part of the twentieth century did the state fully develop a separate set of administrative courts. Judges are recruited and managed in the same way in Swedish administrative courts as those in ordinary courts. This allows the government some significant influence, especially on promotions.

In France, administrative courts are divided into three levels: administrative tribunals, administrative courts of appeal, and the *Conseil d'État*. Members of the *Conseil d'État* enjoy a special status and have demonstrated considerable autonomy from the executive branch. However, the position and career of lower administrative judges are managed by the *Conseil supérieur des tribunaux administratifs et cours administratives d'appel*, formed by judges (in part elected by their peers) and lay members appointed by the President of the Republic and the presidents of both legislative chambers.

In Italy, administrative cases also fall under a separate court system. However, there only two court levels exist: regional tribunals and the *Consiglio di Stato*, which hears all appeals. Administrative judges form a body separate from ordinary judges. As a result of a 1982 legislative reform, all decisions affecting the professional position of the former are made either by the *Consiglio di presidenza* (with a majority of administrative judges elected by their peers and a minority of lay members appointed by the presidents of both legislative chambers), or based on a previous advisory opinion by the *Consiglio*. Nevertheless, in both Italy and France, the executive plays a role in the recruitment and promotion of administrative judges, for example by appointing some of the state councillors.

On the other hand, Portuguese administrative judges enjoy a considerable degree of independence. A council administers their change in status, headed by the president of the highest administrative court with five other administrative judges and five lay members elected by Parliament.

8 PROSECUTORIAL INDEPENDENCE

Prosecutors, although enjoying more guarantees than ordinary civil servants, are often considered part of the executive branch and therefore under the direction of the minister of justice. However, at least in Latin Europe, the expansion of judicial guarantees of independence has also involved public prosecutors to some extent.[46] This process has been stronger in those countries in which judges and prosecutors are 'magistrates' and form a single professional group, the magistracy. In Italy, prosecutors enjoy the same guarantees as judges. Consequently, their autonomy is extremely high: the executive cannot in any way issue instructions to them. In addition, prosecutors, together with judges, elect the majority of the members of the Superior Council of the Magistracy. Also in France, where the ministry of justice has been able, at least so far, to keep most of its traditional powers, the autonomy of public prosecutors is growing. As we have seen, they enjoy some of the guarantees of judges. One can trace similar developments in Spain, where a prosecutor general, appointed by the government to head public prosecution, has to confront the growing autonomy of an increasingly unionized corps. As for Portugal, its setting most resembles Italy. Although public prosecutors are separately organized from judges, they enjoy a high degree of autonomy, since all decisions regarding their status are entrusted to a high council where prosecutors are in the majority.

As for the common law, the United States has experimented with the institution of a court-appointed Independent Special Prosecutor with the task of investigating cases involving members of the federal executive—a by-product of the Watergate scandal in the 1970s. However, the model was discontinued in 1999,[47] after dissatisfaction brought about by the investigations regarding the William Clinton presidency (1993–2001).

International organizations have promoted the trend toward prosecutorial autonomy. For instance, the 'Guidelines on the Role of Prosecutors',[48] issued by the United Nations in 1990, calls for, among other things: safeguards against appointment based on partiality or prejudice (n.2); reasonable conditions of service (n.6); and promotion based on objective factors (n.7). Prosecutorial autonomy is supported in an even stronger way in the

---

[46] Luis M. Dìez-Picazo, *El poder de acusar* (Barcelona: Ariel 2000); Di Federico (note 30).
[47] The Office of Special Counsel within the US Department of Justice replaced the United States Office of the Independent Counsel.
[48] Available at Legislationline, http://www.legislationline.org/documents/action/popup/id/7855.

'Recommendation on the role of public prosecution in criminal justice systems', issued in 2000 by the Committee of Ministers of the Council of Europe.[49] The Recommendation underlines the need that 'the recruitment, the promotion and the transfer of public prosecutors [be] carried out according to fair and impartial procedures', that prosecutor careers, promotions and mobility be 'governed by known and objective criteria, such as competence and experience', and that disciplinary proceedings be 'governed by law and should guarantee a fair and objective evaluation and decision which should be subject to independent and impartial review'.

9   CURRENT TRENDS AND PERSPECTIVES

Jurists typically consider institutional independence a necessary condition of behavioural independence, although there is no direct relationship between them. However, in the second part of the twentieth century a trend toward increasing guarantees of judicial independence and increased independence on the part of the judges developed in most democratic regimes. The growing independence of judges—and the growing political significance of their actions—has led to a general expansion of judicial power, a development often described as the judicialization of politics, that is 'the expansion of the province of the courts or the judges at the expense of politicians or administrators'.[50] The rise of judicial power has involved both the civil and the common law worlds, although it has been stronger in some countries than in others, often involving not only constitutional but also ordinary judges, who increasingly participate in the process of judicial review of legislation. However, doubts have arisen as to the extent to which judicial independence should be promoted. In fact, the enlarged visibility of judicial power has prompted the call for some form of judicial accountability: since judges are increasingly taking decisions with significant political implications, should they not be made accountable? And if so, how? How can we balance the competing needs of judicial independence and accountability? Are the existing institutional devices enough? Alternatively, is some form of political check necessary? If the answer is positive, how should this check be organized? More specifically, toward whom should judges be accountable: other judges, the legal profession, the political class, or public opinion (whatever that would mean)?

There are different ways to deal with these questions.[51] Broadly speaking, we can distinguish three general approaches. First, judicial power can be—and is—made accountable through existing devices like appeal, collegiate panels, discipline, and so on; we need only to improve them. Second, in order to make judges accountable in fact we should introduce some form of political check, that is, some institutional means by which the political system can evaluate the performance of judges—for example by intervening in the appointment or promotion process or, in extreme cases, also by provoking the removal of a judge. Last, some argue that judges can be made accountable, in a more effective

---

[49]   See *The role of public prosecution in the criminal justice system: Recommendation 19 (2000) and explanatory memorandum* (Strasbourg: Council of Europe Publishing 2001).

[50]   C. Neal Tate and Torbjörn Vallinder (eds), *The Global Expansion of Judicial Power* 13 (New York: New York University Press 1995).

[51]   Cappelletti (note 3) 57–113; Canivet, Andenas and Fairgrieve (note 9).

way and without endangering their independence, by increasing the chance that they will behave in a 'responsible' way, that is, in an efficient and competent way. This condition can be achieved by improving the selectivity of recruitment and the quality of training of judges both before and after recruitment and by a stronger emphasis on judicial discipline and ethics.

FURTHER READING

Bell, John (2006). *Judiciaries within Europe. A Comparative Review*. Cambridge: Cambridge University Press.

Canivet, Guy, Mads Andenas and Duncan Fairgrieve (eds) (2006). *Independence, Accountability, and the Judiciary*. London: British Institute of International and Comparative Law.

Cappelletti, Mauro (1989). *The Judicial Process in Comparative Perspective*. Oxford: Oxford University Press.

Di Federico, Giuseppe (ed.) (2005). *Recruitment, Professional Evaluation and Career of Judges and Prosecutors in Europe*. Bologna: IRSIG-CNR.

Feeley, Malcolm (2002). 'The Bench, the Bar, and the State: Judicial Independence in Japan and the United States', in Malcolm Feeley and Setsuo Miyazawa (eds), *The Japanese Adversary System in Context* 67–88. New York: Palgrave.

Ginsburg, Tom (2003). *Judicial Review in New Democracies*. Cambridge: Cambridge University Press.

Ginsburg, Tom and Nuno Garoupa (2009). 'Guarding the Guardians: Judicial Councils and Judicial Independence', 57 *American Journal of Comparative Law* 201–32.

Guarnieri, Carlo and Patrizia Pederzoli (2002). *The Power of Judges*. Oxford: Oxford University Press.

Merryman, John and Rogelio Perez Perdomo (2007). *The Civil Law Tradition*. Stanford: Stanford University Press.

Piana, Daniela (2010). *Judicial Accountabilities in New Europe*. Farnham: Ashgate.

Russell, Peter H. and David O'Brien (eds) (2001). *Judicial Independence in the Age of Democracy*. Charlottesville: University Press of Virginia.

Russell, Peter H. and Kate Malleson (eds) (2006). *Appointing Judges in an Age of Judicial Power*. Toronto: University of Toronto Press.

Shapiro, Martin (1981). *Courts: A Political and Comparative Analysis*. Chicago: The University of Chicago Press.

Shapiro, Martin and Alec Stone Sweet (2002). *On Law, Politics and Judicialization*. Oxford: Oxford University Press.

Shetreet, Shimon and Christopher Forsyth (eds) (2012). *The Culture of Judicial Independence*. Leiden: Martinus Nijhoff.

Stone Sweet, Alec (2002). *Governing with Judges: Constitutional Politics in Europe*. Oxford: Oxford University Press.

11 Civil court litigation and alternative dispute resolution
*Koen van Aeken**

1 INTRODUCTION

This chapter seeks to discuss civil court litigation and alternative dispute resolution from a comparative and interdisciplinary viewpoint. Comparative law and society, in section 2, lends itself perfectly to a particular empirical and interdisciplinary investigation into law, especially from the perspective of legal sociology.

In section 3, we focus on the area of litigation and alternative dispute resolution (ADR). To overcome the problem of comparing apples and oranges often raised by cross-national comparison, we consider the merits of a functional perspective. The underlying function of both litigation and ADR is dispute resolution. People attempt to solve disputes and do so by taking various paths to justice. Against the backdrop of the paths to justice, we touch upon related topics such as the advantages and weaknesses of various dispute resolution mechanisms and representations of these paths.

Drawing on statistics in section 4 from various nations including the United States, the United Kingdom, Japan, France and Australia, we see that, in actual comparative analysis, methodological pitfalls arise. This is exemplified by comparative litigation rates and comparing national paths to justice studies. We summarize the main methodological challenges, since any researcher venturing into the comparative study of judicial and extra-judicial dispute resolution will have to confront these.

In section 5, we attempt to provide a basic insight into variations in actual rates of litigation and ADR in a cross-national context. Whereas efforts to gather comprehensive comparative data often prove futile, this section strives for explanation. Several explanatory variables for national differences in levels of litigation and extra-judicial dispute resolution are examined based on direct comparisons. At this point, we look at the US, Japan, the Netherlands and Germany. The idea here is that comparative research should aim beyond description and strive for explanation. In section 6, we present a summary of the main findings.

2 THE APPROACH OF LEGAL SOCIOLOGY

Comparative law and society presents itself as a truism, that is, the comparative approach to legal systems always entails an investigation of the society in which various laws and

*   Assistant Professor of Law, Tilburg University, The Netherlands. I wish to express my gratitude to Masayuki Murayama, Dimitri Vanoverbeke and Marjolein Ledder for providing insight and advice.

legal institutions are embedded. A simple comparison of legal statutes and provisions in different nations, ignoring the societal backdrop, is generally not viable. A common illustration is the cross-national comparison of unemployment regulation.[1] Apart from the difficulties in defining unemployment—should one include arrangements for the part-time unemployed or the elderly who enjoy early retirement, for instance?—studying the legal arrangements only makes sense if their social context is taken into account. To illustrate, from the low level of legal protection for the unemployed in Italy, one might be tempted to jump to conclusions too quickly if the investigation remains limited to the codes, statutes and laws. Representing Italy as harsh for the unemployed would paint a distorted picture. Opening the scope of research to the larger social context would instantly refute such findings. In Italy, the system of invalidity benefits is extensively used in the southern part of the country as an improper yet accepted means to relieve the hardship of unemployment. Moreover, the premature conclusion that Italy lacks social support for or solidarity with the unemployed overlooks the fact that the community and the family traditionally take care of those unfortunate enough to lose their job. Social cohesion is still more significant in Italy than in other industrialized Western countries.

This general example should make us cautious about engaging in a comparative project too hastily. Mark Ramseyer expresses it as follows: 'Comparative law is . . . a bit like a good Hitchcock: Things are rarely what they are perceived to be'.[2] Does that mean that insightful comparing is never feasible? It might well lead us to the popular wisdom in the English-speaking world that you cannot compare apples and oranges.[3] Patrick Glenn refers to this as the notion of incommensurability—an idea he quickly rebuts. You can indeed compare apples and oranges, he argues, in terms of acidity, roundness, flavor, color and so on. You might also compare the trees from which the fruits spring, the markets in which the fruits are sold or the effects they have on the consumer's body. A multitude of various ways to tackle the presumed incommensurability emerges. This, in turn, provides for a new challenge: which approach do we favor when we engage in the project of comparing litigation rates, civil courts and alternative dispute resolution?

As exemplified above, one can only proceed to a meaningful comparison if one includes the societal context in which the law is embedded. With Glenn, we expect much from sociology in this respect: 'sociology and anthropology of law are open to much more information than are legal systems, and so much can be expected of them in terms of meaningful comparison of laws'.[4] This paves the way for an approach from legal sociology, which entails an interdisciplinary and empirical investigation into the relationship between law and society. Such an approach differs from legal studies in its emphasis on the use of empirical, real-life data and facts, rather than purely normative information.

---

[1]   Maurice Adams, 'Wat de rechtsvergelijking vermag: Over onderzoeksdesign', 60 *Ars Aequi* 192, 194–5 (2011).
[2]   J. Mark Ramseyer, 'The Costs of the Consensual Myth: Antitrust Enforcement and Institutional Barriers to Litigation in Japan', 94 *Yale Law Journal* 604, 645 (1984–5).
[3]   H. Patrick Glenn, *Legal Traditions of the World: Sustainable Diversity in Law* 43 (Oxford: Oxford University Press, 3rd edn, 2007).
[4]   H. Patrick Glenn, 'Com-paring' in Esin Örücü and David Nelken (eds), *Comparative Law: A Handbook* 91, 97 (Oxford: Hart 2007).

This amounts to studying 'the law in action' rather than 'the law in the books'.[5] Legal sociology is not bounded by the 'internal viewpoint' of the legal scholar. Instead, it favors an external viewpoint. This means that, whereas legal scholarship often implicitly intends to guard the coherence and consistency of the legal system, the external viewpoint allows this coherence to be challenged.[6] Such openness is key to understanding the social context in which legal systems exist.

Legal sociology thus lends itself perfectly to comparative law and society. Most prominent comparative lawyers share such a perspective: 'Comparative law is more closely related to social sciences, from where it borrowed its methods, than to "pure" normative inquiry, which seems to characterize other types of legal research'.[7] This quote not only confirms the 'truism' of comparative law and society. It also indicates that the social sciences offer the *methods* for comparative law and society. Accordingly, this chapter will discuss the methodological challenges that emerge when venturing into the comparative study of litigation and ADR.

3   A FUNCTIONAL APPROACH TO EXAMINE LITIGATION AND ALTERNATIVE DISPUTE RESOLUTION

3.1   The Functional Approach

The backdrop of dispute resolution begins our discussion here. At law faculties, the dispute resolution curriculum commonly consists solely of adjudication organized by the state. Sociologists of law, in contrast, point out that a range of functions, which jurists appear exclusively to attribute to the law, are actually shared with various social institutions. One example is the instrumental function assigned to the law. Legal instrumentalism considers a legislated rule to be a tool in the hands of a policy maker who desires some sort of social change. However, such an instrumentalist approach to law and legislation has proven sterile and untenable.[8]

So-called 'semi-autonomous social fields', able to create and enforce their own informal rules, interfere with the ambitions of the lawmaker. Whether it is a university, the New York women's garment industry or a local police corps, all these 'fields' can frustrate or stimulate the effectiveness of state legislation.[9] Likewise, the resolution of disputes is not the sole privilege of the formal legal system. Indeed, empirical research teaches us that society provides all sorts of mechanisms to deal with disputes outside the courtroom.

---

[5]   See what appears to be the first usage of this dichotomy in Roscoe Pound, 'Law in Books and Law in Action', 44 *American Law Review* 12 (1910).

[6]   See Max Weber, *Max Weber on Law in Economy and Society* (Cambridge, MA: Harvard University Press 1954, Max Rheinstein ed., orig. German 1925); Koen van Aeken, 'Law, Sociology and Anthropology: A Liaison Beginning Endlessly', in Sanne Taekema and Bart van Klink (eds), *Interdisciplinary Research into Law* 55, 60–61 (Tübingen: Mohr Siebeck 2010).

[7]   Esin Örücü, 'Developing Comparative Law', in Örücü and Nelken (note 4) 43, 48.

[8]   John Griffiths, 'The Social Working of Legal Rules', 48 *Journal of Legal Pluralism and Unofficial Law* 1, 13 (2003).

[9]   Sally F. Moore, 'Law and Social Change: The Semi-Autonomous Social Field as an Appropriate Subject of Study', 7 *Law & Society Review* 719 (1973).

The socio-legal literature is quite clear in this respect. Most problems are negotiated between the affected parties, without the interference of a third person. Once a third party is introduced to facilitate problem solving, various scenarios emerge. A third party can have a rather informal nature, as when the third party is a neighbor, a priest or a consumers' organization, or it can be increasingly formal, as in the context of arbitration and finally state-organized adjudication, where the third party is the judge in court.

This latter perspective of the judge in court has acquired a prominent role with the rise of the nation state. 'Legal statism' pushed for the creation of monopolistic legal systems.[10] The state legal system gradually absorbed a diverse array of private means of dispute resolution and manifested itself as official courts and tribunals. This explains why dispute resolution is regarded as primarily a task of the state legal system. However, research from a variety of countries has shown that relatively small proportions of most disputes eventually involve formal litigation procedures.[11] Depending on the country, field, or study, between 2 and 10 percent of all potentially legal disputes are resolved by means of state-organized adjudication.[12]

The absorption of dispute resolution by state legal systems might mask the natural kinship between litigation and ADR, but the banner of comparative law and society accommodates it well. One system of conflict resolution is nested in the legal sphere while the other predominantly resides in the social and cultural community of citizens. The alleged duality is weakened by focusing on the *function* that both the judicial and the non-judicial dispute resolution systems fulfill. Such an approach in socio-legal studies bears close proximity to the functional method that is widely applied in comparative law.[13]

The functional method requires the starting point of research to be not the law itself but rather the situation or the problem the law and its institutions seek to regulate. To start from well-defined legal concepts and institutions would not only prevent comprehensiveness, it would also create tunnel vision and hinder comparison.[14] Accordingly, we will start from the function that litigation and ADR fulfill. The departure point will be the resolution of disputes and problems that arise between citizens. The functional perspective allows not only for discussion of legal and social institutions under one standard,

---

[10]   Luigi Cominelli, 'Temi e problemi della giustizia: mediatori, giudici e avvocati', in Luigi Cominelli (ed.), *Temi e problemi della giustizia* (Milan: Giuffrè 2007); ibid., 'In search of justice between adjudication and mediation' (Treves Lecture, University of Antwerp, 9 Sept. 2010).

[11]   Herbert M. Kritzer, 'Litigation', 13 *International Encyclopedia of the Behavioral and Social Sciences* 8989, 8991–2 (Amsterdam: Elsevier, Neil J. Smelser et al. eds, 2002).

[12]   E. Delanoeije, Francis van Loon and Y. Wouters, 'Reconstructie van de pyramide van conflictafhandeling in Vlaanderen: Een empirisch onderzoek', 5 *Rechtskundig Weekblad* 144, 147–9 (1991); Marc Galanter, 'Reading the Landscape of Disputes: What We Know and Don't Know (and Think We Know) about Our Allegedly Contentious and Litigious Society', 31 *UCLA Law Review* 4 (1983); B.C.J. van Velthoven and C.M. Klein Haarhuis, *Geschilbeslechtingsdelta 2009* (Den Haag: WODC 2010).

[13]   'The functional approach, now recognized to have wide applicability, was probably comparative law's principal gift to twentieth century legal science'. Mary Ann Glendon, Michael Wallace Gordon and Paolo G. Carozza, *Comparative Legal Traditions in a Nutshell* 9 (St. Paul, MN: West Group, 2nd edn, 1999).

[14]   Adams (note 1) 195.

but it may also tackle one of the most difficult problems in comparative legal studies: the identification and definition of legal institutions and processes in a cross-national context.

Indeed, the ubiquitous variations in legal terminology from nation to nation seriously frustrate international comparisons. For instance, does the Belgian 'rechtbank van eerste aanleg' equal the Italian 'preture' or the 'general jurisdiction trial court' in the US?[15] One can distinguish two responses to this problem in the practice of comparative law: the essentialist and the nominalist traditions.[16] The essentialist definition of a court implies what a court in the Netherlands and the United States should *in essence* look like if one were to engage in a comparison. Nominalism implies that *the labels* or *names* that are attached to the institutions under scrutiny should be the same after translating them.

Both traditions have their own pitfalls. Essentialist definitions might under-include or over-include certain parts of the legal infrastructure, while nominalist definitions may suffer from 'anthropological agnosticism'. The latter problem was obvious in the early days of legal anthropology,[17] when many Western observers concluded that there was at that time no legal form of dispute resolution in so-called 'primitive' societies, simply because there were no written laws or concrete buildings in which a judge could reside as there were in their Western home countries. Dispute resolution was indeed usually informal. There appears to have been no distinct judiciary among native peoples in the Pacific islands or northern North America.[18] However, to derive from such observations that the people of the Pacific or North America knew nothing like adjudication would, of course, be false. Anthropologists only saw what they knew from back home.

3.2   Dispute Resolution as the Starting Block

The functional approach implies that a cross-national comparison of civil litigation and ADR is feasible by referring directly to the underlying function of both processes. Regardless of their formal or informal nature, both processes respond to a quest for justice, initiated by a citizen who feels that he has been wronged. In other words, this person has experienced a problem or a conflict for which he might seek either legal redress or an extra-legal solution. The dispute might concern a quarrel with a neighbor, the purchase of a malfunctioning television set or a conflict between tenant and property owner. When aggregating such experiences for the population of a country, a *landscape of disputes* stretches out.[19] The obvious question is then how citizens deal with these disputes. All these problems are *potentially* judicial. This means that, depending on the perceived seriousness of the problem, some just drop the dispute, others negotiate a solution with the other party and still others engage a third party. Third parties can take the shape of an

---

[15]   See Herbert M. Kritzer (ed.), 1–4 *Legal Systems of the World* (Santa Barbara: ABC-CLIO 2002).

[16]   David S. Clark, 'Civil Litigation Trends in Europe and Latin America since 1945: The Advantage of Intracountry Comparisons', 24 *Law and Society Review* 549, 550 (1990).

[17]   Van Aeken (note 6) 70–71.

[18]   However, the Aztecs did have a system of permanent judges and formal appeals. Glenn (note 3) 63–4.

[19]   B.C.J. van Velthoven and C.M. Klein Haarhuis, *Geschilbeslechtingsdelta 2009. Over verloop en afloop van (potentieel) juridische problemen van burgers* (Boom: BJU 2010).

acquaintance, an extra-legal institution such as a consumers' union, a lawyer, a mediator, an arbiter or, finally, a judge.

As varied as the landscape of disputes are the strategies to deal with them. Both the nature of disputes and the dispute solving strategies have inspired a voluminous body of research. We have a particular interest in the strategies that people use to seek redress for their potentially judicial problems. Indeed, these strategies coincide with the basic topic of discussion in this chapter: namely, either litigation or an alternative form of dispute resolution. Before we proceed to the comparative study of such strategies, we consider it important to explain some key concepts in the domain of dispute resolution.

3.3   From Negotiation to Adjudication in the Courts and Back

Above, we mentioned that in the modern age the state gradually pushed for the creation of monopolistic legal systems. As a result, justice became intimately linked with adjudication by state courts and tribunals. Litigation emerged as a highly structured process of dispute resolution that almost invariably invoked the power of the state to provide a means authoritatively to adjudicate a dispute between two or more parties.[20]

This evolution is less trouble-free than might appear at first glimpse. An intrinsic problem of adjudication occurs if the proceedings do not require the consent of all parties involved. Consequently, courts and tribunals may face a legitimacy crisis. Courts and tribunals responded to this crisis by substituting consent by all parties through a set of principles.[21] The first principle holds that parties should be able to participate in the procedure. Parties have an opportunity to make arguments and offer proofs on their behalf. At the same time, the court is required to respond with reasoned arguments. A second principle is the rule of law. This prohibits judges from making improvised, ad hoc decisions. They should render verdicts according to pre-existing norms or 'the rules of the game', which should be known to all parties involved. A third principle to deal with the legitimacy gap is the impartiality of the adjudicating courts. Judges should have no interest in the outcome and no reason to favor one party above the other. To this end, the judges' compensation is not dependent upon the outcome of the trial and no personal interest in the outcome of the controversy should exist. The last principle is judicial independence. This means that the judge should be free from outside influences that might cause biased decisions.

While these principles provide for legitimacy to substitute for actual consent, important developments impede these constructs. In the large majority of Western nations, increasing dissatisfaction with the length, costs and formality of legal proceedings has become apparent. Formality supersedes reality, with complicated and long lasting, expensive legal procedures. In addition, many countries face a litigation explosion. In Italy, for instance, litigation rates have increased sevenfold in the 50 years following World War II.[22] In the Netherlands, the number of cases filed in civil proceedings has increased 76 percent

---

[20]   Kritzer (note 11).

[21]   Malcolm M. Feeley and Carlo Guarnieri, 'Courts and Adjudication', *International Encyclopedia of the Behavioral and Social Sciences* 2878–82 (Amsterdam: Elsevier, Neil J. Smelser et al. eds, 2002).

[22]   Cominelli (note 10).

between 2000 and 2010 to exceed the symbolic level of two million cases (for a population of merely 16 million).[23] The pressure on many courts is soaring.

From the viewpoint of the justice-seeking citizen, the reality is that access to justice is not spread evenly.[24] Barriers to justice vary from group to group, but seem to affect those people with limited resources more strongly. In particular, the poor, the inarticulate, members of indigenous communities, the socially vulnerable and those discriminated against often cannot surmount such barriers. These barriers include the complexity of the legal and administrative system, psychological obstacles (since lawyers speak a different, specialist language, dress differently and have posh offices in the fancier parts of town), lack of knowledge of rights, high costs in terms of money, time and effort and the fear of ruining long-term relationships. The general theory of the barriers to access to justice is that the 'have-nots' overcome fewer barriers and receive less justice than the 'haves'. The haves are in an advantageous position that allows them to win a proceeding more often than the have-nots. These advantages include previous experience with adjudication, the possibility to employ top lawyers, the development of informal relationships with officials and even the ability to lobby to amend or create legislation.[25]

The longing for legitimacy and concerns about unequal access to justice, recently bolstered by endeavors to relieve the workload of the courts, have inspired a return to non-judicial dispute resolution. Grass-roots movements first revived calls for mediation on account of its promise of informal community justice. One could frame this as a wider and even worldwide judicial activism, in line with human rights movements and other demands for social change.[26] Some date the introduction or the revival of multiple forms of dispute resolution within the legal system to the 1976 US conference on the 'Causes of Popular Dissatisfaction with the Administration of Justice'. The first suggested solutions included a 'multidoor courthouse', which could meet both the immense caseload pressure on the courts and the consumer demand for 'quality of justice'.[27] From the late 1970s, ADR quickly spread from the promise that it could promote active participation of the parties in the dispute process. At the same time, it offered the prospect of increased access to justice by deprofessionalizing, decentralizing and deregulating dispute resolution.[28]

---

[23]   Koen van Aeken, 'Een rechtssociologische analyse van de juridisering van de samenleving', in *Meester over Meester?* 13, 14–15 (Leuven: ACCO 2010).

[24]   Roger Cotterrell, *The Sociology of Law. An Introduction* 245–57 (Edinburgh: Butterworths 1996).

[25]   Mark Galanter, 'Why the 'Haves' Come Out Ahead: Speculations on the Limits of Legal Change', 9 *Law & Society Review* 95–160 (1974). Some words of caution. The haves might refer to large (corporate) entities such as banks or insurance companies. In addition, the poor often enjoy some publicly funded legal aid, making it the middle class that is deprived most of access to justice. See Herbert M. Kritzer, 'To Lawyer or Not to Lawyer, Is That the Question?' 5 *Journal of Empirical Legal Studies* 875, 875 (2007).

[26]   Lia Combrink-Kuiters, AlbertKlein, Machteld Pel and S. Verberk, *Op maat beslecht: mediation naast rechtspraak 1999–2009* (The Hague: Raad voor de Rechtspraak 2009).

[27]   Carrie Menkel-Meadow, 'Mediation, Arbitration and Alternative Dispute Resolution (ADR)', 14 *International Encyclopedia of the Social & Behavioral Sciences* 9507, 9508–09 (Amsterdam: Elsevier, Neil J. Smelser et al. eds, 2002).

[28]   For instance, in the Netherlands (in 2000) the Minister of Justice distinguished four long-term goals connected to the promotion of mediation: delegalize the dispute settlement process; facilitate the settlement of disputes in a way which is qualitatively the best and optimally effective;

Table 11.1   The dispute resolution continuum

Maximum Party Control of the Process and Outcome		Minimum Party Control of the Process and Outcome	
Negotiation	Mediation	Arbitration	Court Adjudication
Two Disputants	Plus Third Person Facilitator	Plus Third Person Arbiter	Plus One or More Judges in Court
	Informal	Formal	

Table 11.2   Types of mediators

Informal		Formal	
Family Members	Volunteer or Paid Mediator	Government	State Law-Trained
Friends	Labor Union	Mediator	Professional
Neighbors	Consumer Organization		

Table 11.1 represents the various forms of conflict resolution. They are located on a continuum that stretches from negotiation to formal adjudication. The more we move to the right, the more formal the process becomes, with a corresponding reduction in participating party control of the outcome.

Negotiation is the simplest and most widely exercised process in the daily lives of citizens from America to Asia. The disputing parties try to settle the dispute without relying on a third party. A slightly more formal approach is mediation. Mediation involves a third party facilitator. The mediator can be a friend of the family, a labor union representative or a lawyer certificated in mediation (see Table 11.2). Mediation typically deals with ongoing relationships in which parties need to be reoriented to each other. The process ranges from informal to formal. The outcome is the product of deliberation between the parties themselves. The participants share payment of the mediator's fee.

Arbitration refers to the enforcement of private rules established by the parties. The arbiter acts like a judge, be it that this 'judge' is selected by the parties and not typically assigned by the state. The involved parties generally have signed a contract that states the rules of the arbitration process and proclaims the arbiter's verdict to be binding.[29] Adjudication is the most formal type of dispute resolution that, like mediation and

---

shift the responsibility for the resolution of conflicts from the state to the citizens and business; and, finally, reduce the burden on courts and tribunals. M.Guiaux, F. Zwenk and M. Tumewu, *Mediation Monitor 2005–2008*, 135 (The Hague: WODC).

[29]   Parties engaged in mediation hardly ever desire the outcome to be binding, whereas in arbitration parties sign a contract that the decision is binding (and excludes the possibility of appeal). The New York Convention also makes the outcome of arbitration legally binding in more than 140 countries, thus providing a great alternative for global business partners that were otherwise obliged to select one national jurisdiction in which to solve potential problems. See New York Arbitration Convention, Home Page, http://www.newyorkconvention.org.

arbitration, relies on an independent, third party facilitator.[30] While mediation, arbitration and state adjudication all depend on third party resolvers of disputes, the freedom of the parties to control the proceedings and the outcome of the dispute resolution process is progressively limited. Insofar as the judge is concerned in ordinary civil litigation or adjudication in the (civil) courts, this freedom is substantially reduced. The state appoints judges (but in a few places citizens elect judges), parties have little or no control over selecting the presiding judge in a panel decision and, notably, consent of the parties either to participate or to resolve the conflict is not required.

It seems clear that ADR has one obvious advantage over litigation: it adds to the legitimacy of the dispute processing since the parties control the process and outcome to a larger extent than in the courtroom. As a result, compliance rates are much higher than those for court decisions. There are additional benefits. ADR generally prevents the existing relationships from turning sour due to a legal intervention. Empirical data from the Netherlands specify that 86 percent of the parties involved in litigation have no contact with the other party after the legal procedure has ended.[31] In some jurisdictions, the shift to ADR is evident. Such is the case in Florida, where almost all lawsuits are required to be mediated before a court will allow them to be put on the trial calendar. Mediation is effective in resolving approximately 75 percent of all cases. Consequently, the trial docket of the courts is significantly relieved. From the participants' viewpoint, mediation allows parties to 'get things off their chest' and improves understanding between the involved parties, since the proceedings make clear that 'there are always two sides to a story'.[32]

Nevertheless, the ADR movement also faces criticism and raises controversy.[33] First, there are few robust empirical findings with respect to the presumed superiority over traditional adjudication in terms of speed, costs and accessibility. Some suggest that ADR is vulnerable to inequalities of bargaining power: less powerful members of society, particularly those subordinated by race, ethnicity, class or gender, will be disadvantaged disproportionately. Another cause for concern is the increasing juridification of ADR. Its early ideology has been distorted by assimilation into the conventional justice system. Indeed, as ADR gradually becomes mandated by court rules and court contracts, it risks becoming a rigid, rule- and law-based system instead of the creative, flexible and alternative process originally conceived.

Additional disadvantages derive from a functional comparison of ADR and ordinary civil litigation. One shortcoming is the privatization of jurisprudence. Since fewer cases will be available in the public arena, precedent building and its creation of rules and political values for the larger community are hindered. ADR also lacks the prospective behavior modification function or prevention, which many believe to be central to the working of the law. ADR cannot exercise such prevention whereas litigation appears to

---

[30]   Martin Shapiro, *Courts: A Comparative and Political Analysis* (Chicago: Chicago University Press 1981).

[31]   Combrink-Kuiters et al. (note 26).

[32]   See 'Mediation vs. Arbitration vs. Litigation: What's The Difference?' http://library.findlaw.com/1999/Jun/1/129206.html.

[33]   Menkel-Meadow (note 27) 9510–11; Per Henrik Lindblom, 'ADR: The Opiate of the Legal System?' 1 *European Review of Private Law* 63, 71–9; Michael Heise, 'Why ADR Programs Aren't More Appealing: An Empirical Perspective', 7 *Journal of Empirical Legal Studies* 64–96.

build morality and present deterrents to the potential law offender. Furthermore, ADR cannot exercise the control function vis-à-vis the legislative and administrative powers (judicial and administrative review). Lastly, the portion of cases addressed by ADR is overall very small. In the Netherlands, for example, a recent survey indicated that 73 percent of accredited mediators have never been engaged in mediation in their professional practice. Lawyers typically prefer adjudication because the financial gains are higher.[34]

One recurring conclusion in the discussion about whether ADR can uphold its promise of informal community justice and relief of the caseload of the courts is that more empirical investigation is required. In section 4, we will touch upon existing findings in a cross-national context.

3.4 Paths to Justice

In the preceding section, we discussed various methods of conflict resolution. An intriguing question that arises now is to what extent justice-seeking citizens call upon the various resolution mechanisms. Such is the starting point of the so-called 'paths to justice' studies. The paths to justice studies typically address two main research questions. First, to what extent are (potentially) civil law problems prevalent among the population? Second, to what extent are certain judicial or extra-judicial solution strategies used and what circumstances influence these choices?

Reconstructing such paths requires empirical research. The survey method has proven most popular here. Typically, a range of predefined problems is presented to some hundreds to thousands of citizens and the respondents are asked to select the problems they have encountered in the last three to five years. Once they identify the problems, the respondents are then asked about the way they have dealt with these. Such an approach would be most useful from a cross-national comparative perspective.

While this research strategy appears straightforward, it presupposes a theoretical model to create order out of the chaos of the huge variation in processes of dispute settlement. Two models compete. The oldest model takes the shape of a *pyramid* of conflict resolution.[35] Such a multi-layered triangle illustrates how many grievances result in legal proceedings. The total number of grievances is at the base line. Court filings are at the top, as the smallest amount, ranging between 1 and 6 percent of the initial number of grievances.[36] From bottom to top, the number of resulting disputes decreases, since parties drop or solve the original grievances after some process has occurred. The actions undertaken on each level of the pyramid are labeled, starting with the transformation of the grievance into a claim, then negotiation, followed by consulting a third party—very often predefined as a lawyer—and ending with formal adjudication (the filing of a claim in court).

---

[34]   R.J.M.Vogels and P.T.van der Zeijden, *De stand van mediation in Nederland* 31 (NMI: Stratus 2010).

[35]   See E. Delanoeije, F. Delrue and F. Van Loon, 'Reconstructie van de pyramide van conflictafhandeling in Vlaanderen', 55 *Rechtskundig Weekblad* 144–9 (no. 5, 1991); W.L.F. Felstiner, Richard L. Abel and Austin Sarat, 'The Emergence and Transformation of Disputes: Naming, Blaming, Claiming', 15 *Law and Society Review* 634–6 (1980–81); Galanter (note 12).

[36]   Van Velthoven and Haarhuis (note 19) 23.

Whereas such triangle-like representation is instructive in highlighting the wide gap between grievances and court filings, its linear approach limits its usefulness. Indeed, it imposes a strict order of actions on any potential legal dispute resolution. The pyramid does not provide for some sort of direct access to the most appropriate dispute resolution mechanism. To overcome this limitation, Dutch researchers have introduced the notion of the 'delta of dispute resolution'. The image of a delta mirrors the nautical idea of a variety of waterways, such as where the Nile River in Egypt meets the Mediterranean Sea. Paths to justice are now represented as a dynamic landscape of parallel streams that spontaneously diverge or unite. To seek a solution, the best-suited dispute solving strategy can be addressed directly. A person can negotiate a solution with a neighbor while at the same time filing a case in court for alimony in a divorce case. As with research in the tradition of the pyramid model, paths to justice studies obtain their raw data from surveying samples of the population of a country or region. With carefully designed questionnaires and sound sampling techniques, the results should be representative for the full population with a known margin of error and confidence level.

4   LIMITS TO COMPARATIVE DESIGNS

In this section, we report on traditional approaches to the comparative study of litigation and ADR and discuss whether the functional perspective might be a meaningful alternative. A striking finding is that comparative data on litigation are surprisingly scarce. Very often, scholars use and reuse the same figures, even when these data are seriously outdated. Here we look at some of the better-known overviews. Graphic representations of litigation rates across the world provide one way to consider the comparative study of formal dispute resolution. They seem to offer important insights into the rates of litigation across the globe. A well-known image is in Figure 11.1.[37]

According to this frequently cited overview, Germany appears to be the world's most litigious society with 123.2 cases filed per 1,000 inhabitants. The USA ranks substantially lower with 74.5 cases, followed by England and Wales with 64.4 cases. Denmark (very similar to the Netherlands as to litigation rates) sees 62.5 cases. Japan is definitely in the lower strata with 9.3 cases, whereas Ethiopia is at the bottom with 1.7 cases. Apart from the wide gap in litigation rates based on geography, a remarkable finding is the position of the United States. The widespread idea of the US as a notoriously litigious society is refuted by this graph.

Unfortunately, 'Litigation rates provide a notoriously difficult field for cross-national study because institutional environments vary so widely'.[38] This might be a key element in explaining the difference with the data recovered (1986) by Mark Ramseyer and Eric Rasmusen in Table 11.3.

---

[37]   Christian Wollschlager, 'Exploring Global Landscapes of Litigation Rates', in Jürgen Brand and Dieter Strempel (eds), *Soziologie des Rechts: Festschrift für Erhard Blankenburg zum 60. Geburtstag* 587–88 (Baden-Baden: Nomos 1998).

[38]   Tom Ginsburg and Glenn Hoetker, 'The Unreluctant Litigant?: An Empirical Analysis of Japan's Turn to Litigation', 35 *Journal of Legal Studies* 31, 56 (2006).

Litigation Rates

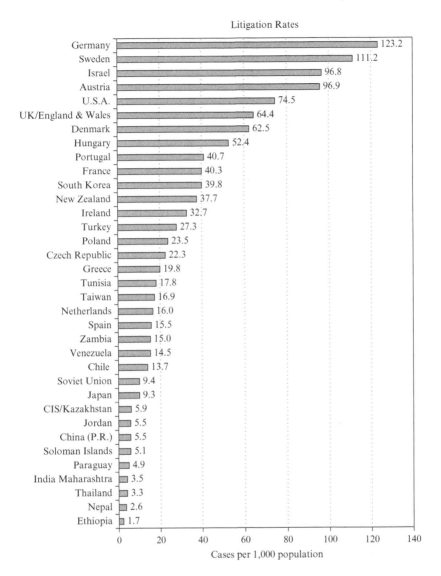

Figure 11.1 Litigation rates (cases per 1,000 population), by country

Table 11.3 is interesting in many respects. First, it displays various indicators related to civil litigation. Indeed, should we exclusively consider the number of lawsuits filed, or should we have a look at the size of the legal profession too? Second, litigation rates are in constant flux. For instance, in Figure 11.1 the US litigation rate is eight times greater than in Japan, while this ratio is reduced to 3.3 in Table 11.3. Whereas the passage of time might explain some of this dissimilarity, it appears to be very difficult to obtain steady, trustworthy and comprehensive figures. The case of Japan is illuminative: the total number of civil and administrative court cases has risen in one decade (1990 to 2000) from 1,500,000 to 3,000,000. Litigation reached a peak in 2002, amounting to almost 3,500,000 cases, to

Table 11.3   Litigation-related measures (per 100,000 population), by country[39]

	Australia	France	Japan	England	USA
Civil Cases Filed	1,542	2,416	1,768	3,681	5,806
Judges	4.00	12.47	2.83	2.22	10.81
Lawyers	357	72	23	251	391

go down again, hovering around 2,500,000 in 2005.[40] Third, international comparisons combine data from a variety of sources that most often cannot be checked for reliability and accuracy. Reliable figures are even harder to obtain when ADR comes into play, since its non-formal character cannot assure full registration of cases, leading to so-called 'dark numbers' (unregistered or undocumented cases).

In section 3 of this chapter, we argued that a functional approach might help to overcome some of the difficulties regarding identification and labeling in distinct institutional contexts. Focusing on the function that both ADR and litigation fulfill is a goal of the paths to justice studies. Does the comparative analysis of the results of paths to justice studies from different countries allow us to map dispute resolution strategies from a comparative angle?

The approach looks promising. Looking at the results from various national surveys, significant differences emerge. The percentage of respondents that has encountered potential legal problems ranges from 18.9 percent in Japan to 69.1 percent in Australia. Problem frequency differs enormously as well. The average person in the Netherland is confronted with 2.5 problems over a five-year time span, whereas this is 0.6 in three years in Great Britain and 0.7 in Northern Ireland.

Other interesting findings include the percentage of disputes that have resulted in legal proceedings. Five percent of disputes were settled in court in Australia, whereas this percentage was 3 percent in England and Wales, 4 percent in Hong Kong, 2.1 percent in Japan, 4 percent in the Netherlands, 6 percent in Northern Ireland and 1 percent in Scotland.

However tempting it is to rely on such figures as the basis for an international comparison, methodological pitfalls cast a shadow upon such comparative endeavors. In their review of various paths to justice studies, Van Velthoven and Haarhuis list the key methodological issues that hinder comparison.[41] First, representativeness of the various surveys differs. Whereas most researchers used a select sampling procedure, which enables one to generalize the results to the full population, some countries such as Australia focused on weak and vulnerable groups. This might explain why the level of judiciable problems amounts there to a sky-high 69.1. Next, various formats have been used to carry out the surveys. Australia and Canada relied upon telephone interviews, whereas face-to-

---

[39]   J. Mark Ramseyer and Eric B. Rasmusen, 'Comparative Litigation Rates', Eric Rasmusen's Homepage, http://www.rasmusen.org/papers/overheads/litigation-seminar.doc (see at 3–4: data from 1986).

[40]   See Dimitri Vanoverbeke and Jeroen Maesschalck, 'A Public Policy Perspective on Judicial Reform in Japan', 27 *Journal of Japanese Law* 11–36 (2009).

[41]   Van Velthoven and Haarhuis (note 12) 21–2.

face interviews were common elsewhere. In some instances, such as the Netherlands and Japan,[42] intricate combinations of various written questionnaires, telephone and personal interviews were used. Researchers know that the choice of a particular format for a survey imposes a bias on the outcome. Topics of a sensitive nature, such as income, money and conflict, lead to socially desirable answers when the interviewer faces the respondents. Written questionnaires provide for more anonymity and thus more trustworthy answers. Third, all questionnaires were based on predefined typologies of problems. These typologies differ from country to country. Finally, some studies ask for problems in the course of the last three years, while this period is extended to five years in other studies. Longer time spans cause memory bias but allow, on the other hand, for a much more comprehensive view of conflict-resolving strategies.

Overall, a universal and comparative listing of dispute resolution rates, both in and out of the courts, is probably a distant dream. The variety in research design and data collection appears to hinder meaningful comparison.

Where do we go from here? Some researchers recommend that they should engage in longitudinal comparisons, thus comparing dispute resolution strategies over time in one region or nation: 'Rather than enter the thicket of cross-national comparisons, which typically involve apples and oranges, we compare litigation in Japan over time to allow us to isolate which factors have the greatest impact in encouraging litigation'.[43] Others suggest that progress in understanding civil litigation trends might be feasible by means of intra-country studies that document cross-regional variations.[44] Still others approach the issue from the viewpoint that comparisons should be restricted to well-defined geographical areas with major similarities. The advantage of such perspectives is that important factors that might account for variations in the rates of civil litigation can be controlled. Such viewpoints, which are inspired by research designs in the natural sciences, underpin the well-known investigation conducted by Erhard Blankenburg of litigation behavior in the Netherlands and North Rhine-Westphalia (a German region).[45] We will discuss such side-by-side comparison of similar legal systems in the next section from the viewpoint that this might offer the best means to achieve explanation.

5 TOWARD AN EXPLANATION FOR THE DIFFERENTIAL USE OF LITIGATION AND ADR

Explanation is the key objective of most sciences. Understanding how something works or why things happen as they do, is what drives most research by scholars and scientists. This is no different for the comparative and interdisciplinary approach to legal systems: 'Generally speaking, the [comparative] analysis should seek to explain differences and

---

[42] Masayuki Murayama, 'Experiences of Problems and Disputing Behaviour in Japan', 14 *Meiji Law Journal* 1–59 (2007).

[43] Ginsburg and Hoetker (note 38) 31.

[44] Clark (note 16) 549.

[45] Erhard Blankenburg, 'Patterns of Legal Culture: The Netherlands Compared to Neighboring Germany', 46 *American Journal of Comparative Law* 1–42 (1998).

similarities as they arise from the description of the legal systems under consideration'.[46] Indeed, most scholars believe that comparing is not an end in itself but a way to foster understanding and explanation.[47]

The controversy over American litigation is illustrative of such explanatory efforts. Numerous scholars have addressed the presumed litigiousness in American society, with much of the discussion concentrating on tort lawsuits.[48] They typically present arguments based upon descriptive assessments of patterns of litigation rates, either over time or across jurisdictions. Such emphasis on description often neglects the underlying question of what factors drive litigation rates.

Much more rewarding are explanatory efforts. The central position here sees litigiousness as the result of rights consciousness and popular attitudes towards claiming.[49] This type of cultural explanation is in line with the traditional view, for instance, that the Japanese seek to avoid litigation altogether since they attribute great importance to social harmony and social relations. It is indeed tempting to explain the inclination to avoid litigation altogether in terms of the Asian Buddhist and Confucian traditions. Formal law with its formal boundaries and outspoken conflict has an unfortunate tendency to mask the underlying harmony.[50] In other words, the logic of classical adjudication necessarily juxtaposes the involved parties under the supervision of a legal arbiter who is isolated from the social relations she deals with. Litigation thus seems to deny the underlying quest for harmony and harmonious relationships that Asian culture embraces.

Asian scholars have written about the non-litigious ethos in Japan from a cultural perspective. Japan served as a prime example since it stands out as a modern, highly industrialized nation,[51] ruling out economic disparities as an explanatory variable for the difference in litigation rates between Western and non-Western nations. Only culture, then, would explain the gap.

In a landmark article, however, Blankenburg provided a viable alternative to the cultural thesis. As a German professor who migrated to the Netherlands, he was able to develop a comparative design that allowed him to isolate the key explanatory factor to explain differences in litigation rates. The design included the two countries he was familiar with: the Netherlands and a nearby region in neighboring Germany, North Rhine-Westphalia. Both geographical entities are similar in many respects. Their population and land size were almost equal: 15.5 million inhabitants and 35,500 square kilometers

---

[46]   Gerhard Dannemann, 'Comparative Law: Study of Similarities or Differences?' in Mathias Reimann and Reinhard Zimmerman (eds), *The Oxford Handbook of Comparative Law* 383, 416 (Oxford: Oxford University Press 2006).

[47]   Adams (note 1) 198–9.

[48]   Jeff Yates, Holley Tankersley and Paul Brace, 'Do Institutions Really Matter? Assessing the Impact of State Judicial Structures on Citizen Litigiousness', http://www.law.northwestern.edu/searlecenter/papers/Brace-Yates_Northwestern_conf.pdf (2005).

[49]   Erhard Blankenburg, 'The Infrastructure for Avoiding Civil Litigation: Comparing Cultures of Legal Behavior in The Netherlands and West Germany', 28 *Law & Society Review* 789, 789 (1994).

[50]   Glenn (note 3) 319–20.

[51]   See, e.g., John O. Haley, 'Why Study Japanese Law?' 58 *American Journal of Comparative Law* 1–14 (2010).

Table 11.4   *Litigation-related measures (per 100,000 population) in the Netherlands and North Rhine-Westphalia*[52]

	Netherlands	North Rhine–Westphalia
Civil Cases Filed (1992)	2,258	3,535
Civil Cases Filed (2002)[53]	3,700	13,900
Judges	12	24
Attorneys	49	102

for the Netherlands almost match the 17 million people and 34,000 square kilometers for the German region. Socio-economic indicators displayed a very similar post-war development. On the cultural level, the two communities were very much alike as well, with Protestantism being the common religious denominator. Moreover, their historic legal traditions were especially close. Both their political and legal history shared much communality, such as the introduction of the French Code Civil modified somewhat by a substantive law based on traditional values.[54]

When actual litigation behavior is compared, nonetheless, striking differences emerge. The German region ranks very high in terms of frequency of litigation, while the Netherlands ranks at the bottom with the lowest litigation rate on the European continent. This riddle becomes even more intricate when one realizes that the Netherlands have developed the most elaborate legal aid system in Europe; at that time 79 percent of the Dutch population qualified for some sort of state-sponsored legal aid.[55] Despite such easy access to justice, by all accounts 'the Dutch use less law than the surrounding countries'.[56] Table 11.4 summarizes the major litigation-related measures.

Solving this riddle is not easy. Persuasive explanation cannot flow from cultural, economic or social factors, since they are controlled in the two similar jurisdictions. Additional explanations, such as an attitudinal difference between Germans who were more righteous or 'adversarial' than the Dutch, were refuted by other findings such as European Commission surveys on values. Blankenburg's solution is that while German and Dutch inhabitants similarly prefer to avoid the mobilization of the law in their private relations, 'German legal

---

[52]   Blankenburg (note 45) 5, 19. Judges include substitute judges and trainees in the Netherlands and labor and federal judges in Germany. First instance procedures in Germany exclude summary debt procedures (1,800,000 cases). Ibid. 19.

[53]   After updating the figures for the Netherlands and Germany, the gap between both countries became wider. Albert Klein and Frank van Tulder, 'De Rechtspraak internationaal bezien: Nederland en Denemarken vergeleken', *Rechtstreeks* 44 (no. 1, 2005). The larger gap exists even with consideration of the Germany summary debt procedures.

[54]   Blankenburg (note 45) 2.

[55]   Access to the state legal aid system was based on income. The cut-off line was so high that a large majority of the population enjoyed free or very cheap legal assistance.

[56]   Fred J. Bruinsma, *Dutch Law in Action* (Nijmegen: Ars Aequi 2003). Bruinsma supplements Table 11.4 with data from neighboring Belgium: 115 attorneys and 20 judges per 100,000 population (1995).

culture offers less of an avoidance infrastructure than that of the Netherlands'.[57] The crucial word here is 'infrastructure', or the institutional context. In other words, legal behavior is determined by institutional supply rather than by popular demand.

The evidence for this finding was found in a set of institutions that exist in the most litigious areas of the law. One domain is debt collection. Whereas, in Germany, courts have a summary debt collection procedure that is widely popular, the Dutch have extra-judicial ways of collecting debt. Another field is the construction industry. In Germany, the saying goes: 'Find a lawyer before you search for a contractor'. Construction cases provide the most difficult cases in civil courtrooms, whereas in the Netherlands, the Council for Construction Firms—an arbitration service set up in The Hague—decides such cases. Contractors thus almost never see the courtroom. Similar institutions exist in several industrial sectors as well as with landlord-tenant disputes and employment protection. In addition, specific procedures (such as divorce), which have to be settled in court by law, are streamlined and simplified, thus not imposing a heavy burden upon the Dutch legal system.[58] Finally, ADR is actively promoted by the Dutch government as a way to bring justice closer to the people and as a way to relieve the caseload of the courts.

From this comparison of litigation rates of neighboring countries, we learn that institutional arrangements strongly predict the use of formal litigation to solve conflicts. Some have advocated the same theory for Japan too. In the mid 1980s, Ramseyer wrote that 'there may be indeed such a [non-litigious] ethos, but it is an ethos buttressed by an array of institutional barriers to litigation that would discourage all but the most persistent plaintiffs in any society'.[59] These findings might be framed in a larger series of attempts to attribute the Japanese litigation peculiarities to institutional factors. For instance, Joel Rosch advocates the position that the existence of the Civil Liberties Bureau in Japan might explain why the Japanese so infrequently use formal adjudication. This bureau, established after the World War II and a specialist in mediating (broadly interpreted) human rights issues by consulting the involved parties, relieved the courts of complaints that might otherwise find their way to the formal sphere of dispute resolution. While specialists now reject this thesis,[60] it exemplifies that complex societies may provide for extra-judicial institutions to resolve conflict.

Understanding international variation in the frequency of litigation thus seems to demand an in-depth scrutiny of the legal and social institutions that play a role in dispute resolution. The story does not end here, however. Recent investigation suggests that, on top of institutional factors, the economy might explain variations in litigation trends. Tom Ginsburg and Glenn Hoetker have demonstrated by means of longitudinal and cross-national Japanese data that the increase in litigation in the 1990s should not only be attributed to the expansion in institutional capacity for litigation, but also to structural

---

[57]   Erhard Blankenburg, *Patterns of Legal Culture: The Netherlands Compared to Neighboring Germany* 29–30 (Amsterdam: Duitsland Instituut 1997).

[58]   Blankenburg (note 57) 34.

[59]   J. Mark Ramseyer, 'The Costs of the Consensual Myth: Antitrust Enforcement and Institutional Barriers to Litigation in Japan', 94 *Yale Law Journal* 604 (1984–5).

[60]   Joel Rosch, 'Institutionalizing Mediation: The Evolution of the Civil Liberties Bureau in Japan', 21 *Law & Society Review* 243–66 (1987); correspondence with Dimitri Vanoverbeke.

changes in the Japanese economy.[61] Indeed, Japanese litigation rates have increased significantly after the post-bubble slowdown in economic growth in the 1990s. Understanding the role of the economy is unfortunately very difficult. While economic growth might cause invocation of the law more often through increased business transactions and thus potential conflict, the opposite seems to be true as well. Sustained economic downturn is likely to lead to the breaking of long-term relationships. To protect long-term relationships, business people typically shun formal adjudication. Indeed, empirical research has soundly documented how invocation of the law damages relationships.

The debate of culture versus institution is accordingly not over yet. Moreover, it is questionable whether one actually can distinguish culture from institutions. According to Lawrence Friedman, culture and institution are 'chicken and egg' issues,[62] inseparably intertwined to affect both perception and behavior. Indeed, from a cultural ethos, one might conclude that with few judges and lawyers, an institutional framework restrains more litigation. At the same time, the lack of an elaborated court system with many judges and lawyers may have an effect on Japanese litigation behavior and accordingly the perception of conflict handling. The relationship of structure to culture is complex and difficult to parse.

What can one now conclude with regard to explanations for the worldwide variations in litigation and ADR rates? Present day scholarship attributes a growing importance to the elemental structure of the judicial system. This structure seems to affect the degree to which citizens invoke the legal system for redress.[63] Besides, scholars have introduced several new approaches to the invocation of the law and ADR mechanisms. These study additional barriers to litigation, such as the costs of the various paths to justice, which not only include money, time and delay, but also emotional and social costs, uncertainty costs, information costs and more.[64] Others point to explanatory variables that can be given an economic interpretation, such as income, education and urbanization; they state that these can explain much of the variance among jurisdictions.[65]

Overall, it is very hard to understand the complex set of social, institutional, cultural, economic and emotional factors that predict the choice of a path to justice. We need more examples of empirical research that scholars from various countries carry out uniformly. This would provide a better understanding of the factors at stake.

6   CONCLUSION

This chapter treats civil court litigation and alternative dispute resolution from a comparative and interdisciplinary viewpoint. Legal sociology appears to fit this endeavor perfectly.

---

[61]   Ginsburg and Hoetker (note 38) 31.

[62]   Lawrence M. Friedman, 'The Place of Legal Culture in the Sociology of Law', in Michael Freeman (ed.), *Law and Sociology* 185, 199 (Oxford: Oxford University Press 2005).

[63]   Yates et al. (note 48) 5.

[64]   Martin Gramatikov, 'A Framework for Measuring the Costs of Paths to Justice', 9 *The Journal Jurisprudence* 111–47 (2009).

[65]   Richard A. Posner, 'Explaining the Variance in the Number of Tort Suits across US States and between the US and England', 26 *Journal of Legal Studies* 477–89.

However, the comparative study of litigation and ADR rates is not easy. Neither from the traditional viewpoint, nor from the functional perspective that focuses on the underlying function of dispute resolution strategies, can scholars collect reliable and comprehensive data. There is a general lack of data, they are often of questionable reliability and their volatility over time obstructs a sound and universal comparative approach.

Hence, it might be more interesting to look for explanations of variation in dispute resolution mechanisms. Various scholars have made explanatory efforts. A promising approach is side-by-side comparison of similar jurisdictions, which enables third variables to be controlled for. From such studies, including the pairwise comparing of the Netherlands and a region in Germany, and studies of the US and Japan, we learn that the institutional context in which litigation is embedded can explain a large part of the variance. This finding is in line with recent results indicating that economic and social costs can explain which dispute resolution mechanism people prefer.

FURTHER READING

Clark, David S. (1990). 'Civil Litigation Trends in Europe and Latin America since 1945: The Advantage of Intracountry Comparisons', 24 *Law & Society Review* 549–70.

Deflem, Mathieu (2008). *Sociology of Law: Visions of a Scholarly Tradition*. Cambridge: Cambridge University Press.

Fuller, Lon (1971). 'Mediation: Its Form and Functions', 44 *Southern California Law Review* 305–39.

Fuller, Lon (1978). 'The Forms and Limits of Adjudication', 92 *Harvard Law Review* 353–409.

Galanter, Marc (1974). 'Why the "Haves" Come Out Ahead: Speculations on the Limits of Legal Change', 9 *Law & Society Review* 95–160.

Genn, Hazel G. (1999). *Paths to Justice: What People Do and Think about Going to Law*. Oxford: Hart.

Glenn, H. Patrick (2007). 'Com-paring', in Esin Örücü and David Nelken (eds), *Comparative Law: A Handbook* 91–108. Oxford: Hart.

Glenn, H. Patrick (2007). *Legal Traditions of the World: Sustainable Diversity in Law*. Oxford: Oxford University Press, 3rd edn.

Friedman, Lawrence M. (2005). 'The Place of Legal Culture in the Sociology of Law', in Michael Freeman (ed.), *Law and Sociology* 185–99. Oxford: Oxford University Press.

Ginsburg, Tom and Glenn Hoetker (2006). 'The Unreluctant Litigant? An Empirical Analysis of Japan's Turn to Litigation', 35 *Journal of Legal Studies* 31–58.

Goodman, Carl F. (2001). 'The Somewhat Less Reluctant Litigant: Japan's Changing Views towards Civil Litigation', 32 *Law & Policy of International Business* 769–810.

Gramatikov, Martin (2009). 'A Framework for Measuring the Costs of Paths to Justice', 9 *The Journal Jurisprudence* 111–47.

Örücü, Esin and David Nelken (eds) (2007). *Comparative Law: A Handbook*. Oxford: Hart.

Ramseyer, J. Mark (1984). 'The Costs of the Consensual Myth: Antitrust Enforcement and Institutional Barriers to Litigation in Japan', 94 *Yale Law Journal* 604–46.

Ramseyer, J. Mark (1988). 'Reluctant Litigant Revisited: Rationality and Disputes in Japan', 14 *Journal of Japanese Studies* 111–23.

Tanaka, Kazuko (2002). 'Organization and Management of Government Legal Services of Japan'. Tokyo: Ministry of Justice, http://www.adb.org/Documents/Reports/Consultant/33069-REG/33069-01-REG-TACR.pdf.

Van Aeken, Koen (2010). 'Law, Sociology and Anthropology: A Liaison Beginning Endlessly', in Sanne Taekema and Bart van Klink (eds), *Interdisciplinary Research into Law* 55–84. Tübingen: Mohr Siebeck.

Yates, Jeff, Holley Tankersley and Paul Brace (2005). 'Do Institutions Really Matter? Assessing the Impact of State Judicial Structures on Citizen Litigiousness', http://www.law.northwestern.edu/searlecenter/papers/Brace-Yates_Northwestern_conf.pdf (2005).

12 Criminal courts and procedure
*Stephen C. Thaman**

1 HISTORICAL ROOTS OF CRIMINAL COURTS AND PROCEDURE

1.1 The Importance of Customary Procedures: An Emphasis on Victim–offender Mediation

Historically, when a criminal act was committed and someone caught the culprit in the act, he was either summarily killed or, at best, hurriedly sentenced to death by an ad hoc court, where the victim or the victim's family might act as executioner.[1] Otherwise, procedure was always accusatorial, with the victim, the victims' family or clan, accusing the suspect.[2] The community then usually pressured the victim's clan or family to negotiate with that of the suspect to resolve the case peaceably and avoid blood revenge and the prospect of a long-enduring feud.[3] Compromise was much more important than accurately assessing comparative guilt or punishment.[4] If families or clans could not regulate the matter themselves, they would call on a mediator to resolve the dispute.[5] The procedure would usually end in payment of compensation to the victim's family or clan. This payment took the form of money, livestock or other commodities. The family or clan collectively shared the guilt, which induced them to deter crimes committed by their members. The goal of the procedure was reconciliation and restoring the peace of the community, and only incidentally that of determining the truth.[6]

The mediators were respected problem solvers, such as chiefs or elders, who had no enforcement power, and thus required consensus and community involvement to make sure people respected the settlement.[7] The mediator often worked privately with each side separately to reach a compromise.[8] On the other hand, mediations would sometimes be conducted publicly in front of the entire assembled community, or a group of elders

---

* Professor of Law and Director, Summer Law Program in Madrid, Saint Louis University.

[1] Thomas Weigend, *Deliktsopfer und Strafverfahren* 36–7 (Berlin: Duncker und Humblot 1989).

[2] Accusation was a social function, falling to anyone in the aggrieved group. A. Esmein, *A History of Continental Criminal Procedure: With Special Reference to France* 3–4 (Boston: Little, Brown & Co., John Simpson trans., 1913).

[3] Weigend (note 1) 13.

[4] Karl N. Llewellyn and E. Adamson Hoebel, *The Cheyenne Way: Conflict and Case Law in Primitive Jurisprudence* 305 (New York: Legal Classics Library 1992).

[5] Uwe Wesel, *Geschichte des Rechts: Von den Frühformen bis zur Gegenwart* 53 (Munich: C.H.Beck, 3rd edn, 2006).

[6] H. Patrick Glenn, *Legal Traditions of the World* 68–9 (New York: Oxford University Press, 3rd edn, 2007).

[7] A.S. Diamond, *Primitive Law Past and Present* 185, 238–41 (London: Methuen & Co. 1971).

[8] On the similarity of mediation in European chthonic procedures and Islamic *shari'a*

who would hear the arguments of both sides and try to reach a compromise settlement. Such public decision-making processes, which were common in customary societies, were the precursors of English juries or German *Schöffen*-courts which will be discussed below.[9]

If the crime was not flagrant and immediately punished, and no 'consensual' resolution could be achieved, traditional communities often resorted to irrational forms of 'trial'. The suspect could utter a cleansing oath attesting to his innocence, and people usually accepted it, because they truly believed that someone who falsely swore would face eternal damnation.[10]

Many communities required the defendant to summon several friends or tribe members (often in a multiple of twelve), so-called oath-helpers or compurgators, to swear to his honesty or uprightness.[11] In some communities, the swearing took on an adversarial tinge when the victim was also allowed to rebut the defendant's oath-helpers with his own.[12] These groups of sworn witnesses, who had to be unanimous in their assurance of the trustworthiness of accused or accuser, represented primordial forms of early unanimous trial juries, which were expected to have knowledge of the facts of the case.[13] However, this form of trial was only open to 'honorable' or upstanding citizens, and not outsiders or the poor.

Outsiders or the poor would have to engage in painful and sometimes deadly divine ordeals, often consisting in holding or walking on hot metal, reaching one's hand into boiling water or oil or having officials throw them into a cold body of water.[14] In the ordeals, and in trial by battle, we see early forms of punishment of the suspicious through the functioning of the procedure itself, regardless of whether they were in the end found to be innocent or guilty. Thus, the thought of even having to go to 'trial' in these times might have been more of a deterrent than any punishment that might result from a guilt finding. Communities also used trial by battle to resolve unmediated disputes.[15] Here one

---

proceedings in front of the *qadi*, see Richard Vogler, *A World View of Criminal Justice* 110 (Burlington, VT: Ashgate 2005).

[9]   In Germanic lands, judicial power was exercised directly by the people, who met in regularly held great popular courts in full assembly. Over time, however, it was only the older and most experienced men of the community, the *Schöffen*, who took over the role of judges. Esmein (note 2) 32.

[10]   According to one Tibetan proverb: '[If the case is] clear, [decide it] by law; [if the case is] unclear, [decide it] by oath'; Rebecca Redwood French, *The Golden Yoke. The Legal Cosmology of Buddhist Tibet* 132 (Ithaca, NY: Cornell University Press 1995). In Europe, the oath of purgation became common with the diffusion of Roman law and the adoption of Christianity. Diamond (note 7) 300.

[11]   Thorl. Gudm. Repp, *A Historical Treatise on Trial by Jury, Wager of Law, and other Co-ordinate Forensic Institutions, Formerly in Use in Scandinavia and in Iceland* 21, 38 (London: Thomas Clark 1832).

[12]   Ian Wood, 'Disputes in Late Fifth- and Sixth-century Gaul: Some Problems', in Wendy Davies and Paul Fouracre (eds), *The Settlement of Disputes in Early Medieval Europe* 7, 10–14 (Cambridge: Cambridge University Press 1986).

[13]   Repp (note 11) 136–45.

[14]   Ordeals were used almost everywhere, 'from Iceland to Polynesia, from Japan to Africa'. Robert Bartlett, *Trial by Fire and Water* 2 (Oxford: Clarendon Press 1986).

[15]   Trial by battle was found in the early law codes of many Germanic peoples. Ibid. 103.

can see the primitive beginnings of the role of a representative or attorney in the form of 'champions' who could be hired to pitch battle on behalf of the parties.[16]

To summarize, traditional legal systems showed a clear preference for negotiation and mediation to avoid violence in the form of blood-revenge or feud. Confessions mitigated the severity of the penalty.[17]

1.2 Politicization of Criminal Law: An Emphasis on Procedural Coercion of Confessions

As kings and other potentates began to consolidate their power over kinship-based communities and as nations began to develop, the use of victim-offender mediation, oaths, duels and trial by battle gradually vanished and the procedure became politicized, a contest between offender and the state.[18] The victim gradually disappeared as a party in criminal procedure.[19] The bodies of lay judges, elders or witness-juries became co-opted and integrated into a system under the control of royal judges, as in England or under the rule of Charlemagne,[20] and eventually disappeared on the European continent, yielding to courts completely in the hands of a professional royal judiciary.[21] Two different systems replaced the customary forms: oral trial by jury in the British Isles and written inquisitorial trial by professional judges on the European continent.

A profound skepticism in relation to witness testimony, circumstantial evidence and the ability of men (that is, judges) to judge other men made its way into continental European inquisitorial procedure through the Roman Catholic canon law and made it extremely difficult to prove guilt in criminal cases in the absence of a flagrant crime.[22] Officials perceived formal rules of evidence, preventing conviction in the absence of the testimony of at least two male, Christian eyewitnesses (or other equivalents of full proof), as a check against royal judges using their discretion to convict on less than clear evidence.

Continental procedure, which lacked the inherent legitimation provided by judgment by members of the community (jurors or *Schöffen*), fell to relying almost completely on confessions to prove guilt. If someone captured the suspect in suspicious circumstances that were not sufficient under the formal rules of evidence to justify conviction, and the suspect refused to confess voluntarily, he or she would be subject to torture.[23]

---

[16] On the use of 'champions' to represent one in a duel or battle, see ibid. 306. Treating trial by battle as a precursor of modern adversarial procedure, Roscoe Pound in a speech before the American Bar Association in 1906 saw it as a 'sporting theory of justice'. Roscoe Pound, 'The Causes of Popular Dissatisfaction with the Administration of Justice', in Sheldon Glueck (ed.), *Roscoe Pound and Criminal Justice* 64 (Dobbs Ferry, NY: Oceana Publications 1965).

[17] Among the Nuer in Southern Sudan, the compensation for a confessed homicide was half of that which applied in the absence of a confession. P.P. Howell, *A Manual of Nuer Law* 59 (London: Oxford University Press 1954).

[18] On this transition, see Diamond (note 7) 339.

[19] Weigend (note 1) 94.

[20] Charlemagne found the old Germanic court of *Schöffen* already in existence when he assumed power in the eighth century and co-opted it for his own purposes. Esmein (note 2) 32.

[21] The German *Schöffen*-court disappeared in the 1400s. Ibid. 303.

[22] Ibid. 61.

[23] Ibid. 380–82.

Confessions did not mitigate. Authorities would execute the remorseful confessor anyway, the only mitigation being the possibility of receiving last rites from a priest. Torture replaced the painful ordeals as the new suspicious circumstances punishment. Officials imposed it whether or not one eventually confessed and was convicted. Many of those convicted were, of course, innocent.[24]

Inquisitorial trials were secret and based entirely on written documents in the case dossier, which the investigating magistrate pushed along to the review magistrates with little review of the credibility of the evidence.

Compared with the supposedly comprehensive investigation of the crime in continental jurisdictions, in England there was a mere cursory questioning by the justice of the peace of the suspect, witnesses and victims, theoretically to determine whether to release the suspect on bail while awaiting jury trial. Though an official did not swear-in the accused, who was not heard as a witness at trial, the justice of the peace could and often did read the accused's declaration to the jury.[25] Torture was a rarity in England, yet scholars accept that the justice of the peace used coercion, or at least took advantage of the helplessness of the suspect, to get him to talk.[26]

With the exception of torture, the pretrial situation of the suspect in England was just as horrible as on the Continent. Suspects, the great majority of whom were not bailed, waited anywhere from six months to a year for their trial in frightful dungeons where disease was rampant. When they came to trial, they were usually ill and only learned of the precise charges at that time. As on the Continent, they had no access to counsel and had spontaneously to react to the accusations of the victim or other witnesses at trial to avoid the death penalty, which awaited all convicted felons at the time. The trial still had aspects of customary procedure—that is, a victim confronting the defendant in front of members of the community—until the era when lawyers arrived.[27]

The pre-modern English procedure thus also compelled the defendant to speak. John Langbein describes the 'accused-speaks-trial' to distinguish the old arrangements from today's trials, where defendants often remain silent.[28] Though no formal rules of evidence constrained the freedom of the jury to convict on the testimony of only one eyewitness, or on solely circumstantial evidence, as on the Continent, the jury provided an instance of discretion that vanished on the other side of the English Channel with the elimination of popular judges. The jury gave popular legitimation to verdicts of guilt and innocence, which may have led to conviction of some innocent persons based on circumstantial evidence, but certainly no more than were convicted based on false tortured confessions ordered in the light of similar evidence on the Continent.

Thus, both in England and on the European continent, procedures that compelled the

---

[24]   On the conviction of the innocent, see Cesare Beccaria, *Dei Delitti e Delle Pene* 62 (Milan: Feltrinelli, 4th edn, 1995, orig. 1764).

[25]   John H. Langbein, *The Origins of Adversary Criminal Trial* 41–3 (Oxford: Oxford University Press 2003).

[26]   John H. Langbein, *Torture and the Law of Proof: Europe and England in the Ancien Régime* 9 (Chicago: University of Chicago Press 1977).

[27]   Langbein (note 25) 47–51.

[28]   Ibid. 64.

defendant to speak and admit guilt replaced those that tried to induce or coerce victim-offender mediation. Like the guilty plea, the confession has always been the quintessential vehicle for simplifying, expediting and abbreviating both the pretrial and trial phases of criminal procedure. With a confession, there was no need for law enforcement organs to gather further evidence, other than the minimal evidence needed to corroborate the confession.

In short, the monarchies on both sides of the English Channel felt they needed disproportionately gruesome punishments to consolidate their domination and deter crime. However, the more subtle approach of the Norman rulers of England to co-opt pre-existing customary institutions and not to create a massive judicial bureaucracy to over-centralize the administration of justice, led to the lion's share of decision making by non-professional justices of the peace and jurors on a local level.

1.3 Criminal Dispute Resolution in Asia (and Elsewhere): Staying out of Court

In the West, the state typically sees itself ideally as the guarantor of justice and that permitting easy access to the judicial system is required to avoid resort to self-help in resolving disputes. In the East, however, the presumption is often that one should settle his or her disputes out of court and that merely setting foot in a courtroom is shameful, an unnecessary public laundering of one's sullied linens.[29] The earliest paradigm for this way of thinking comes from ancient China. The Chinese emperors had at their disposal punishments as atrocious as those wielded by European auto-crats. Pretrial and trial procedures did not differ much from those used in inquisitorial Europe during its darkest ages, including the primacy of the confession and the use of torture.[30]

Nevertheless, the rise of Confucianism provided an interesting twist to the Asian view of the role of state criminal punishment systems. According to Chinese lore, written codified criminal laws and punishments, *fa*, came from a barbarian people who used punishments instead of spiritual cultivation to rule their peoples.[31] Any system that needed codified law was of necessity ruled by an ineffective emperor. According to Confucian and related thinking, the emperor should live an exemplary life by following the rituals and customs of proper living, *li*, a kind of 'customary, uncodified law, internalized by individuals, in which

---

[29] Reliance on out-of-court settlements, often mediated by a community elder who decides according to his cultivated ethical sense, is a Confucian legacy. Jurists consider them speedier than in-court settlements and they allow both sides to forgo the possible loss of esteem associated with a negative court decision. R.P. Peerenboom, *Law and Morality in Ancient China: The Silk Manuscripts of Huang-Lao* 269 (Albany, NY: SUNY Press 1993). The Vietnamese have tradi-tionally solved disputes locally using the informal sanctions of lineages and villages, avoiding the national courts so as not to lose face and damage existing relationships. Penelope (Pip) Nicholson, *Borrowing Court Systems: The Experience of Socialist Vietnam* 222, 227–8 (Leiden: Martinus Nijhoff 2007).

[30] The Ch'ing Code authorized torture to extract confessions from suspects, but also to extract testimony from other witnesses. Derk Bodde and Clarence Morris, *Law in Imperial China: Exemplified by 190 Ch'ing Dynasty Cases* 97–8 (Philadelphia: University of Pennsylvania Press 1973).

[31] Ibid. 13.

case no laws would ever be needed'.[32] Indeed, laws were only a bad influence over people, for when they read them, they learned how to commit crimes and avoid responsibility.[33] To the extent an unsuccessful victim-accuser in Asia would be subject to the same punishments that would have applied to the defendant had he been successfully convicted, there was an impetus for both victims and defendants to settle out of court. This avoided the potential harm that would beset the person who came out on the short end of the controversy.

The Confucian approach is the inevitable result of a justice system that is punitive in its very functioning, where even entering the courthouse doors results in punishment. Therefore, it is better to resolve the dispute out of court, using parallel institutions of victim-offender mediation, and applying a philosophy of flexible, consensual dispute resolution.[34] There is still today a reluctance to bring disputes to court in countries with a Confucian tradition, which is strengthened by a mistrust of judiciaries that people conceived of as corrupt and untrustworthy.[35]

In India, and in a similar way in the classic Tibetan legal tradition, there is a preference for resolving disputes using customary procedures despite the presence of an organized state legal system.[36] The ancient texts speak of legal procedures and severe punishments, but also of a hierarchy of procedures to which one should first turn, with the official courts being the last resort. In both India and China, the preference was for first trying to resolve the dispute through ancient methods of individual self-perfection.[37] An 'internal' settlement could also consist in an agreement among the parties or even customary methods such as singing contests, oaths, ordeals or even games of chance.[38] If this did not quell the dispute, then the parties would resort to mediation.[39] Only if these more informal methods did not bear fruit, would one resort to the court system. In Tibet, the court system consisted first in a visit to the judge and, then, if that did not end the matter, in an incredibly complex and time-consuming 44-step procedure, which ended in a trial that was humiliating in itself for the defendant, who could be whipped both before and after testifying.[40]

---

[32]   Yongping Liu, *Origins of Chinese Law: Penal and Administrative Law in its Early Development* 97 (Oxford: Oxford University Press 1998). One can find a similar anti-legal attitude in Indian history and culture. Werner Menski, *Comparative Law in a Global Context: The Legal Systems of Asia and Africa* 203 (Cambridge: Cambridge University Press, 2nd edn, 2007).

[33]   Bodde and Morris (note 30) 16–17. In the words of Confucius, 'the more laws (*fa*) and ordinances (*ling*) are promulgated, the more thieves and robbers there will be'. Ibid. 22.

[34]   Glenn (note 6) 313–14.

[35]   In Vietnam, people avoid the courts because they are arbitrary and politically controlled. In rural areas, and among the poor, anywhere from 40 to 50 percent of the people do not even know a court system exists. Nicholson (note 29) 228, 269–70. On a resurgence of Confucian values in the People's Republic of China, see Glenn (note 6) 333.

[36]   In Tibet, the goal of a legal proceeding was to calm the minds and relieve the anger of the disputants and then, through catharsis, expiation, restitution and appeasement, to achieve consensus and rebalance the natural order. French (note 10) 74.

[37]   It is still in China a commonplace that when conflicts arise, one is well advised to begin with *qing*, appeal to the other's feelings, emotions, sense of humanity or common decency. Peerenboom (note 29) 268.

[38]   French (note 10) 121.

[39]   On mediation in Tibet, see ibid. 122. On informal mediation and negotiation within the parties' socio-cultural spheres in India, see Menski (note 32) 218, 258.

[40]   French (note 10) 123–5, 322.

In India today, one reads about 'state legal systems' and 'non-state legal systems', such as local caste or regional *panchayats*, which resolve disputes in ways reminiscent of the old European popular courts.[41] The emphasis is on reconciliation, compromise and restoring the peace of the community, and less on ascertaining truth and imposing punishment.

In both Talmudic and Islamic doctrine, there is also a preference for out-of-court settlement of disputes. Talmudic law teaches that disputants should seek compromise and that it is preferable for the judge to compromise rather than to let the law 'cut through the mountain', thus creating a winner and a loser and causing the dispute to fester on.[42] In Islamic law, as well, accuser and accused should try to resolve their dispute with a *mufti* out of court before resorting to *qadi* justice, which, though based on interpretation of the Qu'ran and other Islamic texts rather than on the pure goal of restoring the legal peace, nevertheless looks a lot like mediation in customary law societies. As in customary law systems, the confession plays a mitigating role in traditional Islamic law, though, unlike in China and inquisitorial Europe, coercion of confessions was forbidden and a confession could be retracted at any time with impunity.[43]

Parallel 'non-state' systems do not, as such, exist in most Western countries, yet one can see victim-offender mediation and some types of diversion as variants of this notion of keeping criminal disputes out of the 'state legal system'. In this respect, it is interesting to see the influence of Native American law on victim-offender mediation in Canada and the United States with the use of methods derived from indigenous 'sentencing circles' and other customary law institutions.[44] Parallel systems based in customary indigenous law also exist in Latin America, for instance, in Nicaragua, Bolivia and Colombia.

Customary legal traditions also survive among certain African tribes. Some African countries provide for assessors in criminal trials who are experts in customary law. But the most interesting rebirth of such traditions has been in the *gacaca* tribunals in Rwanda, which are being used to try low-level suspects in that country's 1994 genocide, who cannot be accommodated by the International Criminal Tribunal for Rwanda and the domestic Rwandan courts.[45]

The traditional Asian approach to dispute resolution contains within it a different

---

[41] India has, according to one writer, three types of 'non-state legal systems:' caste-based, community-based and innovative-reformist. These *panchayats* are normally composed of five individuals. Upendra Baxi, 'People's Law in India—The Hindu Society', in Masaji Chiba (ed.), *Asian Indigenous Law: In Interaction with Received Law* 216, 235–6 (London: KPI 1986).

[42] Maimonides wrote that the judge 'must attempt in all his cases to have the parties compromise. If he can succeed in never deciding a case on the law, by always effecting a compromise, how praiseworthy is his accomplishment! If he is not able [to effect a compromise in a particular case], he must apply strict law'. Menachem Elon, Bernard Auerbach, Daniel D. Chazin and Melvin J. Sykes, *Jewish Law (Mishpat Ivri): Cases and Materials* 262, 267 (New York: Matthew Bender 1999).

[43] Muslim scholars claim that Islamic law was the first to recognize the presumption of innocence, the burden of proof on the accuser, and to prohibit torture and pretrial detention. Vogler (note 8) 114. They argue that the presumption of innocence burden of proof, prohibition on pretrial detention, prohibition against torture and the rights to silence and defense are all found in the Qu'ran. Ibid. 114.

[44] Glenn (note 6) 68–9.

[45] See generally Nancy Amoury Combs, *Guilty Pleas in International Criminal Law: Constructing a Restorative Justice Approach* 212–18 (Stanford, CA: Stanford University Press 2007); Mark A.

notion of 'truth' than one finds in the inquisitorial continental European tradition or in the Anglo-American view that adversarial confrontation best reveals the truth. Thus, in many of these traditions, 'truth' is equated with 'peace' and the elimination of the anger and frustration caused by confrontation in a trial situation, which might lead to further violence or disputes in the future.[46]

1.4   The European Enlightenment: Development of the Anglo-American Adversarial Trial and the European Mixed-inquisitorial System

The model for criminal procedure for both the United States and France in the late eighteenth century, and for the rest of Europe in the nineteenth century, was the new 'lawyerized' criminal trial, which had developed in England in the mid-eighteenth century. From the 1720s to the 1760s, English law turned about-face from a 'ringing endorsement' of confessions to the opinion that confessions were the 'weakest and most suspicious of evidence'.[47] With the gradual admission of lawyers in felony cases in the eighteenth century, the procedure became adversarial and the right to the defendant's silence became entrenched,[48] thus giving substance to the presumption of innocence and the prosecutorial burden of proof beyond a reasonable doubt. Defendants began letting their lawyers talk for them at trial and judges began to accept guilty pleas with a tacit promise of mitigation accompanying them.

On the European continent, the Enlightenment brought with it over the course of the nineteenth century the abolition of torture and the gradual introduction of a public trial before a jury. The early revolutionary period in France coincided with a profound distrust of professional judges and their ability justly to decide cases.[49] Despite the mistrust of judges, the preliminary investigation remained in the hands of an investigating magistrate, was secret and the defendant had little chance to influence the decision-making process. Comparatists have called this form of procedure, with an oral trial but secret inquisitorial preliminary investigation, the 'mixed' form, as it includes both adversarial and inquisitorial aspects.[50]

In the continental European version of jury trial, a special verdict, which consisted of a list of questions addressed to the jury about elements of the charged crimes and possible

---

Drumbl, 'Law and Atrocity: Settling Accounts in Rwanda', 31 *Ohio Northern University Law Review* 41 (2005).

[46]   In Tibet, people view truth as consensus on the facts. If a dispute that appeared settled flares up in the future, it has not been resolved. French (note 10) 137–8.

[47]   Langbein (note 25) 233.

[48]   Langbein believes that the privilege against self-incrimination was only officially recognized in England around 1898. Ibid. 280. Nevertheless, for a law of 1848 implementing the right to silence along with cautions, see Vogler (note 8) 147.

[49]   John Henry Merryman and Rogelio Pérez-Perdomo, *The Civil Law Tradition: An Introduction to the Legal Systems of Western Europe and Latin America* 15–16 (Stanford, CA: Stanford University Press, 3rd edn, 1985). Pound cited references to these judges as 'legal monks', utterly ignorant of human nature and the affairs of men. Pound (note 16) 57.

[50]   Esmein (note 2) 3. On the oral trial of this epoch as a mere 'repetition', or '*mis-en-scène*' of the preliminary investigation, see Luigi Ferrajoli, *Diritto e ragione: Teoria del garantismo penale* 578 (Rome: Laterza, 5th edn, 1998).

defenses, still required the judge to interpret the verdict and issue a reasoned judgment. With few exceptions, the notion of pleading guilty and moving directly to the imposition of punishment was anathema on the European continent[51] and in Latin America, where none of the liberal changes triggered by the French Revolution was introduced.

In Europe, authorities facilitated confessions by the expansive use of pretrial detention of defendants[52] and provisions in criminal codes that accorded statutory mitigation to confessing and remorseful defendants. Defendants also usually always testified in cases before a purely professional bench or a mixed court of lay and professional judges, because there was no separate sentencing stage, which would allow them to remain silent at trial and then provide evidence of mitigation relating to sentence.[53]

As guilty pleas began to be accepted in England and the US in the nineteenth century, plea bargaining was not as necessary to save time and resources, because trials were still relatively rapid. Whereas a jury in the early 'accused-speaks' trial in England sometimes heard as many as ten cases a day before retiring to deliberate on all of them simultaneously, even the later 'lawyerized' trials of the nineteenth century were quite rapid. There is, however, evidence that judges would sentence in a milder fashion upon acceptance of a guilty plea than after a jury verdict of guilt.[54]

Trials in inquisitorial systems were also speedy affairs, whether conducted in one session (as in Spain) or in installment fashion as in Germany.[55] The procedural inducement of admissions of guilt during the preliminary investigation, through aggressive interrogation or the promise of freedom from pretrial detention upon confessing, or at trial, as a means of seeking mitigation, worked in a similar manner as guilty pleas. Indeed, some writers have considered such procedural arrangements as the equivalent of plea bargaining.[56]

1.5 Jury Courts, Mixed Courts and Professional Courts

People have traditionally considered the criminal jury, with its roots in ancient England, to represent the conscience of the community. Its decisions were imbued with inherent

---

[51] The Spanish Code of Criminal Procedure of 1872 and the Russian Code of Criminal Procedure, in force from 1864 until 1917, also allowed for an admission of guilt. Stephen C. Thaman, 'A Typology of Consensual Criminal Procedures: An Historical and Comparative Perspective on the Theory and Practice of Avoiding the Full Criminal Trial', in Stephen C. Thaman (ed.), *World Plea Bargaining: Consensual Procedures and Avoidance of the Full Criminal Trial* 297, 323 (Durham, NC: Carolina Academic Press 2010).

[52] On pretrial detention as a sanction imposed due to suspicion or as 'masked torture', see Ferrajoli (note 50) 336, 562–6.

[53] Mirjan Damaška, 'Models of Criminal Procedure', 51 *Zbornik Pravnog fakulteta u Zagrebu* 477, 487 (2001).

[54] George Fisher, *Plea Bargaining's Triumph* 159 (Stanford, CA: Stanford University Press 2003).

[55] On the 'piecemeal' or 'installment' approach to criminal trials, especially in Germany, see Mirjan R. Damaška, *The Faces of Justice and State Authority* 52 (New Haven, CT: Yale University Press 1986).

[56] See David T. Johnson, 'Plea Bargaining in Japan', in Malcolm M. Feeley and Setsuo Miyazawa (eds), *The Japanese Adversary System in Context* 140, 144–5 (New York: Palgrave Macmillan 2002).

legitimacy: the jury 'spoke the truth' through its verdict,[57] which needed no other justification.[58] People accepted the verdict, as they would the results of a democratic election or parliamentary vote—even when the results appeared, on occasion, to be irrational.[59] Juries in the US and the United Kingdom return general verdicts. These merely declare the defendant (or defendants) 'guilty' or 'not guilty' of the charged crimes. Jurists can discover the logic of the verdict only by studying the record of the evidence adduced, the instructions given by the judge on the law and its application in the particular case.

In civil law Europe and Latin America, popular juries do not have the centuries-long and uninterrupted pedigree that they enjoy in the common law world. As explained above, only with the French Revolution and the Enlightenment critique of the brutality of the confession-based inquisitorial procedure did the inquisitorial system based on formal rules of evidence and torture give way to jury trial. The new French model allowed juries to decide based on its *intime conviction* (inner conviction, or conscience) and made its decision, in cases of acquittal, final.[60] Jury verdicts were by majority vote and the verdict was in the form of itemized question lists.[61]

Although the French accepted the English jury's freedom freely to evaluate evidence, the question-list form of verdict enables the bench to see the logic of how the jury decided the case. This allows judges to draft a written judgment based on the jury's factual answers. The judgment provides the legal qualification of the criminal facts that the jury found proved.[62] Yet the same Enlightenment thinkers who pushed for adopting the jury and free evaluation of the evidence were just as adamantly against professional judges doing anything but subsuming the facts to the law. As Charles-Louis de Montesquieu (1689–1755) famously said, 'the judges of the nation are nothing, as we have said, but the mouth which

---

[57]   For an opinion that the term *verdict* (truth-saying) is 'euphemistic' and was an attempt to transpose the unerring correctness of all decisions of an absolute monarch to that of a popular jury, see Reinhard Moos, 'Die Begründung der Geschworenengerichtsurteile', 132 *Juristische Blätter* 73, 76 (2010).

[58]   In the United States, verdicts, whether 'guilty' or 'not guilty', were final upon their pronouncement and not subject to appeal until 1889. *United States v. Scott*, 437 U.S. 82, 88 (1978).

[59]   Thus, Thomas Jefferson remarked once in a letter to a friend: 'Were I called upon to decide, whether the people had best be omitted in the legislative or judiciary department, I would say it is better to leave them out of the legislative. The execution of the laws is more important than the making of them.' Quoted in Jeffrey Abramson, *We, the Jury: The Jury System and the Ideal of Democracy* 30 (Cambridge, MA: Harvard University Press 2000).

[60]   Stephen C. Thaman, *Comparative Criminal Procedure: A Casebook Approach* 205 (Durham, NC: Carolina Academic Press, 2nd edn, 2008).

[61]   See section 1.2. On the French special verdict, see Bernard Schnapper, 'Le jury français aux XIX et XXème siècles', in Antonio Padoa Schioppa (ed.), *The Trial Jury in England, France, Germany: 1700–1900* at 168, 178–9 (Berlin: Duncker and Humblot 1987). On the question lists used in Russia and Spain today and in the nineteenth century, see Stephen C. Thaman, 'The Nullification of the Russian Jury: Jury-Inspired Reform in Eurasia and Beyond', 40 *Cornell International Law Journal* 357, 379–99 (2007); Stephen C. Thaman, 'Spain Returns to Trial by Jury', 21 *Hastings International and Comparative Law Review* 241, 321–53 (1998).

[62]   On the question lists and the role of the judge in drafting a judgment in the modern Russian and Spanish jury systems, see Stephen C. Thaman, 'Europe's New Jury Systems: The Cases of Spain and Russia', in Neil Vidmar (ed.), *World Jury Systems* 319, 338–47 (Oxford: Oxford University Press 2000).

pronounces the words of the law; inanimate beings who can moderate neither its force, nor its rigor'.[63]

This mechanistic approach to the role of the judge only gradually took hold in Germany, where a diametrically opposed notion of the judge had developed during the eighteenth century. According to early German Enlightenment thinkers, the judge should act as a creative savior of imperfect laws through his wise application of principles of natural law, and should nullify unwise laws and acquit suspected criminals despite the word of the law.[64]

Jury courts have never been the default jurisdiction for criminal cases on the European continent. In all non-jury courts, the judge is required to decide whether facts were proved based on his or her 'inner conviction', as would a juror. Nevertheless, in Europe there was a general reluctance to allow professional judges to decide freely, without being bound by rules of evidence of some kind. In 1846, the great German jurist, Friedrich Carl von Savigny (1779–1861) suggested a compromise when he was Prussian minister of justice. He suggested that judges would be bound in their evaluation of the facts to the 'laws of thought, experience and human knowledge'. In the same year, a Berlin ordinance instituted the requirement that the judge give reasons for his decisions. 'The judge as trier of fact must from now on decide whether the defendant is guilty or not guilty, based on a careful appraisal of all evidence for the prosecution and the defense according to his free conviction, resulting from the essence of the trial held in his presence. He is, however, obligated to give the reasons, which guided him, in the judgment'.[65] What Germans called 'free evaluation of the evidence' (*freie Beweiswürdigung*) gradually became infused with a meaning that radically diverged from the French *intime conviction*, which some now criticized as being irrational.[66] Jurists characterized the German approach as 'reasoned conviction' (*conviction raisonée*).[67]

Throughout the nineteenth and into the twentieth century, the continental jury remained the typical court for the trial of murders and other serious felonies. However, the German mixed court (*Schöffengericht*)—which is for less serious crimes and in which professional and lay judges deliberate collectively, thus allowing the professional judge to write a reasoned judgment—began to win adherents in other countries.[68] Nevertheless, it was only with the rise of Bolshevism and fascism in Europe that the anti-jury forces were able to deal a clear blow to the English transplant. The Bolsheviks

---

[63] Montesquieu, 1 *De L'Esprit des Lois* 301 (Paris: GF-Flammarion 1979, orig. 1748).

[64] Wilfried Küper, *Die Richteridee der Strafprozeßordnung und ihre geschichtlichen Grundlagen* 39–42 (Berlin: De Gruyter 1967).

[65] Regulation (Verordnung) of 17 July 1846, reprinted in Andreas Geipel, *Handuch der Beweiswürdigung* 11 (Münster: ZAP 2008).

[66] Damaška has characterized the French notion of *intime conviction* as 'romantic' and compared it with the German approach whereby the judge no longer had the 'license to disregard the extralegal canons of valid inference'. Mirjan R. Damaška, *Evidence Law Adrift* 21 (New Haven: Yale University Press 1997).

[67] Gunter Deppenkemper, *Beweiswürdigung als Mittel prozessualer Wahrheitserkenntnis: Eine dogmengeschichtliche Studie zu Freiheit, Grenzen und revisionsgerichtlicher Kontrolle tatrichterlicher Überzeugungsbildung (§ 261 StPO; § 286 ZPO)* 208 (Göttingen: V & R Unipress 2004).

[68] In France, the influential jurist Gabriel Tarde pushed for mixed courts as early as 1877. Vogler (note 8) 236–7.

eliminated the jury in 1917 and substituted a mixed court similar in form (one professional judge and two lay assessors) to the one in the 1877 German Code of Criminal Procedure.[69]

The German jury was transformed into a mixed court in 1924 by decree of the minister of justice, supposedly as a cost-saving measure during an economic depression.[70] The fascists in Italy (in 1922), Portugal (in 1927) and Spain (in 1939) also eliminated the jury, with the Italians converting it into a mixed court. In 1941, the Vichy regime in France converted its jury into a mixed court.[71] By the end of World War II, the European jury was only present in its French form in Belgium, Austria, some of the Swiss cantons, Denmark and Norway.[72]

2   MODERN CRIMINAL COURTS AND PROCEDURE

2.1   The Human Rights Revolution: From Inquisitorial to Adversarial Procedure

The defeat of German and Italian fascism in 1945, the democratization of Spain in 1978, the collapse of the Soviet Union in 1991 and the gradual removal of military dictatorships in Latin America led to a raft of new constitutions and codes of criminal procedure that have introduced a progressive array of procedural rights for defendants. The indisputable trend is away from the old inquisitorial model to an adversarial one.[73]

The centerpiece of inquisitorial procedure was always the preliminary investigation, traditionally carried out by an investigating magistrate who was usually a member of the judiciary. Even after the inquisitorial systems were reformed to include an oral trial by jury, most systems allowed reading of the reports contained in the dossier of the preliminary investigation to the jury (or the judge or mixed court where no jury was available). This constituted a pre-packaging of evidence by law enforcement organs with no opportunity for the defense to see or confront the witnesses. Some countries allowed minimal participation of defense counsel. For instance, France, since 1897, has allowed participation of counsel during judicial interrogations of the suspect, but this was of little help to the suspect, because the code allowed unfettered interrogation of the suspect by the

---

[69]   Stephen C. Thaman, 'The Resurrection of Trial by Jury in Russia', 31 *Stanford Journal of International Law* 61, 65–7 (1995).

[70]   Christoph Rennig, *Die Entscheidungsfindung durch Schöffen und Berufsrichter in rechtlicher und psychologischer Sicht* 57–59 (Marburg: N.G. Elwert 1993).

[71]   Neil Vidmar, 'The Jury Elsewhere in the World', in Vidmar (note 62) 429–32.

[72]   John D. Jackson and Nikolay P.Kovalev, 'Lay Adjudication and Human Rights in Europe', 13 *Columbia Journal of European Law* 83, 95 (2006).

[73]   On the accusatorial and adversarial reforms in the former Soviet republics, see Stephen C. Thaman, 'The Two Faces of Justice in the Post-Soviet Legal Sphere: Adversarial Procedure, Jury Trial, Plea-Bargaining and the Inquisitorial Legacy', in John Jackson, Máximo Langer and Peter Tillers (eds), *Crime, Procedure and Evidence in Comparative and International Context: Essays in Honour of Professor Mirjan Damaska* 99–118 (Oxford: Hart Publishing 2008). On Latin American reforms, see Máximo Langer, 'Revolution in Latin American Criminal Procedure: Diffusion of Legal Ideas from the Periphery', 55 *American Journal of Comparative Law* 617, 629 (2007).

police with no right to counsel before the police turned the case over to the investigating magistrate.[74]

Some jurists began to question the role of a judicial official as investigator, because the same investigating magistrate who decided the legality of arrests, orders of pretrial detention, searches and wiretaps was also conducting the investigation. They questioned whether a person could develop his/her own particular theory of guilt in a case and be independent, neutral and judicial when deciding whether the human rights of the suspect should be infringed. Since the police, in reality, did the lion's share of actual criminal investigation, and the prosecutor was responsible in most countries for preferring the charges, the typical solution was to put the prosecutor in charge of the preliminary investigation. This reduced the judicial role to that of a liberty or control judge, a neutral arbiter of invasions of human rights (authorizations of arrests, pretrial detention, seizures, searches or wiretaps) who would also preside over interrogations. Germany took this step in 1974, Italy in 1988 and Venezuela and other Latin American countries in the 1990s. In the Soviet Union and its socialist client states in Eastern Europe it was the public prosecutor who not only supervised the preliminary investigation, which was in the hands of an investigator provided by the ministry of the interior, but also authorized all invasions of protected human rights of suspects. All of the European socialist bloc countries except Belarus, however, have now ratified the European Convention of Human Rights (ECHR). The case law of the European Court of Human Rights (ECtHR) has required them to provide for judicial authorization of these measures. Similar reforms have also taken place in most of the former Soviet republics in central Asia.[75]

Increased recognition of the right to confront witnesses, guaranteed, *inter alia*, by article 6(3)(d) of the ECHR, has led formerly inquisitorial countries to require the presence of the defendant or defense counsel, where possible, while prosecution witnesses are being examined during the preliminary investigation. The ECtHR has repeatedly condemned the use of written statements when they are the sole or main evidence of guilt in criminal cases if the defendant had no pretrial chance to confront and examine the witness. The 1988 Italian Code of Criminal Procedure requires the prosecutor to initiate a hearing to preserve witness testimony in cases where it is likely that the witness may not be available for trial. At these depositions, the defendant and the victim have the right to be present and examine the witness. Otherwise, the prosecution cannot use the statement at trial. Similar provisions exist in the 1995 Spanish Jury Law and in new Latin American codes of criminal procedure.[76] Thus, procedure in formerly inquisitorial countries is now becoming closer to that which reigns in the US, where a 2004 decision of the US Supreme Court further strengthened the inadmissibility of written statements.[77]

In Italy and in cases subject to Spain's new jury law, the investigative dossier is, in principle, not to be used during the trial as a source of evidence. Officials compile a special trial dossier, including the accusatory pleading and any evidence that has been properly preserved for trial, guaranteeing defense rights of confrontation as noted above. Some

---

[74]   Stephen C. Thaman, 'Penal Court Procedures, Doctrinal Issues in', in David S. Clark (ed.), 3 *The Encyclopedia of Law and Society* 1096, 1099 (Thousand Oaks, CA: Sage Publications 2007).
[75]   Ibid.
[76]   Ibid.
[77]   *Crawford v. Washington*, 541 U.S. 36 (2004).

formerly inquisitorial countries have gone a step further, however, by allowing parallel defense investigations such as exist in the US. The 1988 Italian Code provides for defense gathering of evidence in preparation for the trial phase. Code amendments in 1999 provide for detailed procedures to regulate the gathering of this evidence and its eventual unification with the prosecution evidence in a common investigative file. The Russian Code of 2001 has also taken the step of allowing defense investigations.[78]

The trial judge in the mixed systems on the European continent traditionally acted like the quintessential investigator. After reviewing the investigative dossier, she decided which witnesses to call and she did the examination of the witnesses at trial. Since she had reviewed the investigative dossier and had it at hand, she was aware of the inculpatory premises put forward by the investigating magistrate and had usually adopted them, for she had to decide pretrial whether there was sufficient evidence to set the case for trial. It stretches the imagination to believe that such a trial judge actually entertained a presumption of the innocence of the defendant in such a procedure. Unsurprisingly, the written judgment would often closely follow the language of the written accusatory pleading.[79]

On top of that, the defendant was called to answer the charges at the beginning of the trial and asked to give a statement before any other witnesses were called or evidence presented, seemingly belying the fact that the burden was on the state to prove the charges. The judge then examined the defendant, using the materials in the dossier to guide her in the 'search for the truth'. The prosecutor and defense counsel would be able to submit questions (often only in writing to the presiding judge) to supplement the examination of the judge. If witnesses did not appear, the presiding judge would merely read the statements they had made to the investigating magistrate during the preliminary investigation.[80]

As long as European systems still had juries, the trial judge was not a judge of the facts and therefore the fact that the judge was not neutral did not necessarily directly affect the outcome of the case. But when most European systems eliminated the jury in favor of professional or mixed panels, then the same judge who 'investigated' the case at trial, using his inquisitorial skills and who had adopted the findings of the investigating magistrate, also decided the case. The adversarial model is gradually replacing this system, which still largely exists in France, Germany, the Netherlands, Belgium and other countries. In the adversarial model, the prosecution and defense are responsible for preparing and presenting the evidence and questioning the witnesses. The judge assumes the more passive role of deciding questions of admissibility of evidence and guarantying the parties have 'equality of arms' in presenting their cases.[81]

The 'search for truth' at all costs during the criminal trial has also suffered as a result of a growing recognition that evidence gathered in violation of the human rights of criminal suspects should not be used in the criminal trial even if it is otherwise relevant and credible evidence of guilt. These violations typically occur against the right to privacy, the right to human dignity or the privilege against self-incrimination. The US Supreme Court took

---

[78]   Thaman (note 74) 1100.
[79]   Ibid.
[80]   Ibid.
[81]   Ibid.

this step in 1961 with the landmark decision of *Mapp v. Ohio*.[82] The Court's famous 1966 decision in *Miranda v. Arizona*[83] greatly influenced the majority of European and Latin American countries. They now require interrogators to advise a criminal suspect of the right to silence and the right to talk to a lawyer before the state's agents question them. A failure to do so often results in a prohibition on the use of the ensuing statements.[84]

In many Western countries, such as Germany, the UK, Canada, Australia and New Zealand, the search for truth still prevails in the end because courts take a very cautious approach to exclusion of evidence, engaging in an elaborate balancing process that in the end only excludes evidence gathered in the most egregious ways. In Italy and Spain, legislatures have passed laws that require exclusion of such evidence, yet only the Spanish courts have enforced this law with any vigor. The Russian Constitution of 1993 mandates exclusion of illegally gathered evidence, as do most of the new post-Soviet constitutions and many new Latin American constitutions.[85]

In the US, the 1960s human rights revolution was spearheaded by the decisions of the Supreme Court under Chief Justice Earl Warren (served 1953–69). These finally succeeded in extending the protection of the US Bill of Rights to the entire population and in guaranteeing equal protection of the laws to African-Americans and other minorities. But the irony of this and other such 'revolutions', and the ensuing improvements in the protection of suspects and defendants in criminal proceedings, is that the states who recognize them are not willing or able to pay for the more complicated and protective procedures that the respect for these human rights necessitate.[86]

2.2 The First Counter-Revolution: Plea Bargaining and Other Consensual Processes

Plea bargaining has been expanding, in fits and starts, in the United States and now accounts for more than 95 percent of all criminal judgments.[87] Ironically, the reforms of the Warren Court in expanding the ability of the defendant to participate fully and on an equal footing with the prosecutor in the adversarial trial by jury have been substantially negated by a system of plea bargaining. Under that process, threats of Draconian punishments successfully compel nearly all defendants, whether guilty or not, to renounce their newly won rights and to plead guilty.[88] Although Spain and Russia

---

[82] 367 U.S. 643 (1961).

[83] 384 U.S. 436 (1966).

[84] On the spread of *Miranda*, see Stephen C. Thaman, 'Miranda in Comparative Law', 45 *Saint Louis University Law Journal* 581 (2001).

[85] On the use of balancing tests, see Stephen C. Thaman, 'Constitutional Rights in the Balance: Modern Exclusionary Rules and the Toleration of Police Lawlessness in the Search for Truth' 61 *University of Toronto Law Journal* 691–736 (2011).

[86] For an opinion that the activation of the right to counsel and the development of restrictive rules of evidence constituted the first steps towards making English-style jury trial unworkable without a guilty plea system, see John H. Langbein, 'Torture and Plea Bargaining', 46 *University of Chicago Law Review* 3, 11 (1978).

[87] The guilty plea rate in federal courts was around 90 percent in 1949 to 1951, fell to 79 percent around 1980, only to rise to 94 percent by the end of the twentieth century. Fisher (note 54) 222–3.

[88] On how increasingly harsh sentences over the last 20 years, coupled with steep discounts during plea bargaining, have made the US system coercive, see Jenia Iontcheva Turner, 'Judicial

have introduced new jury systems and both countries guarantee an adversarial trial with strong exclusionary rules, they are also expanding the use of forms of plea bargaining to limit the number of cases tried in the jury courts.[89] In Germany, the growing cleverness of lawyers in exploiting German procedural and evidentiary rules to draw out trials and make prosecutors and judges work longer hours has led to an increasing use of informal confession bargaining to achieve procedural economy. According to this procedure, the judge will offer a defendant a reduced sentencing range if he agrees to confess in open court.[90] In Italy, the drafters of the 1988 Code of Criminal Procedure intended it to move Italy towards an oral adversary trial with minimal use of hearsay and written testimony, similar to that in the US but without a jury. However, it also included the largest assortment of alternative procedures to avoid these expanded due process protections, including , ironically, one that allows the defendant to agree to having a written inquisitorial trial based on the material in the investigative dossier.[91]

In the literature, one reads of a growing reprivatization of criminal procedure. The paradigm of the victim and the culprit reconciling, following a show of remorse and acts of restitution or compensation, with its roots in the ancient history of criminal procedure, is very much alive today. Many new reforms of criminal procedure provide for reconciliation between victim and offender, mainly in the case of less serious crimes. The restoration of the judicial peace is the proclaimed goal of such procedures, rather than the ascertainment of the truth.[92]

The trend in Europe and Latin America towards adversarial procedure has also been coupled with the introduction of 'consensual' procedures to dispose of lesser offenses, which sometimes look similar to US plea bargaining. Penal orders, originally introduced in Prussia in the first half of the nineteenth century, allow the prosecutor to send the defendant a proposed judgment in cases involving minor crimes that normally do not include sentences to jail. The defendant is given a short time (usually from one to three weeks) to accept or decline the proposal.[93] The 1988 Italian Code of Criminal Procedure includes penal orders, but also allows the accused to make a 'request for application of punishment' if charged with a crime, the maximum term of imprisonment for which does not exceed five years, and her punishment will be reduced by one third. France (in 2004) and Russia (in 2001) introduced a similar procedure, which in Russia is now applicable to crimes punishable by up to ten years, and similar

---

Participation in Plea Negotiations: A Comparative View', 54 *American Journal of Comparative Law* 199, 202–04 (2006).

[89]   Thaman (note 51) 328.

[90]   Marcus Dirk Dubber, 'American Plea Bargains, German Lay Judges, and the Crisis of Criminal Procedure', 49 *Stanford Law Review* 547, 568–72 (1997). So-called *Absprachen* were finally codified in 2009. Karsten Altenhain, 'Absprachen in German Criminal Trials', in Thaman (ed.), *World Plea Bargaining* (note 51) 157, 179.

[91]   William T. Pizzi and Luca Marafioti, 'The New Italian Code of Criminal Procedure: The Difficulties of Building an Adversarial Trial System on a Civil Law Foundation', 17 *Yale Journal of International Law* 1 (1992).

[92]   Stephen C. Thaman, 'Consensual Penal Resolution', in Clark (ed.) (note 74) 1: 247. On victim-offender mediation, see Thaman (note 51) 335–9.

[93]   On penal orders, see Thaman (note 51) 339–42.

procedures have been adopted in other new codes in former Soviet republics and in Latin America.[94]

Wide-open US-style plea bargaining, in which the prosecutor can threaten a defendant with death, life imprisonment or decades of prison, in order to induce a guilty plea to a lesser sentence,[95] has found few adherents as of yet around the world.[96] Indeed, the coercive nature of US plea bargaining has its doctrinal roots more clearly in the inquisitorial procedures that coerced confessions than in the victim-offender mediation typical of pre-inquisitorial customary law.

Most consensual processes aim to economize on court time and unburden court dockets by simplifying procedures. The search for truth is consciously given subsidiary priority. On the other hand, some 'consensual' procedures are aimed substantively at ascertaining the truth, such as those that follow the model of American 'cooperation' agreements, which offer significant mitigation or even dismissal to an accused who agrees to cooperate in solving other more serious crimes or testify as a prosecution witness in such serious cases. Here the perceived truth of the information offered by the bargaining defendant is crucial to the acceptance of the 'bargain'. This kind of bargaining that overseas American lawyers push as an effective vehicle to fight organized crime has been adopted, *inter alia*, in Moldova, Georgia and Russia.[97] Some jurists have questioned whether use of such 'cooperation' agreements actually leads to the ascertainment of truth in the US. There have been too many innocent persons who have been cleared after being sentenced to long prison terms, or even death, based in whole or in part on testimony resulting from suspect 'crown witnesses'.[98]

The new preference for the 'uncluttered' presentation of stipulated facts, which is indicative of plea bargaining and related manifestations of 'procedural economy', over the intuitive determination of raw facts by juries or the tutored decisions of professional judges, is perhaps the best reflection of the rise of 'economic' theories of jurisprudence. These 'displace empirical interest from the ragged history of issues to the calculable consequences of their resolution'.[99]

2.3   The Future of Lay Participation

Although it was the Anglo-American jury court that gave rise to the modern model of adversarial, oral and public trial, only a few of the countries that have turned to adversarial procedures in recent reforms have introduced or returned to jury trial, even though the institution's abolition was the product of totalitarian, authoritarian and undemocratic regimes. The exceptions are the new jury systems introduced in Russia (1993), Spain (1995) and Georgia (2010).

---

94   Ibid. 348–55.
95   *Bordenkircher v. Hayes*, 434 U.S. 357, 363 (1978); *Brady v. United States*, 397 U.S. 742, 746 (1970).
96   One can find exceptions in Estonia, Latvia, Lithuania, Moldova, Georgia, Nicaragua and Venezuela. Thaman (note 51) 346.
97   Ibid. 352–5.
98   Thaman, 'Consensual Penal Resolution' (note 92) 249.
99   Clifford Geertz, *Local Knowledge. Further Essays in Interpretive Anthropology* 218 (New York: Basic Books 1983).

Despite the turn to adversary procedure, Latin America has made little use of lay judges in its criminal justice systems. Legislators have recently introduced mixed courts, in which lay and professional judges deliberate in a united panel, in Venezuela, Bolivia and the Argentine province of Córdoba. Otherwise, juries are primarily for the trial of homicide cases in Brazil, El Salvador, Nicaragua and Panama. The former Soviet republic of Kazakhstan introduced a mixed court in 2007;[100] Japan and South Korea did so in 2009. The Soviet mixed court, which replaced the Russian jury court in 1917, was adopted in nearly all countries in the socialist bloc following World War II. Most of these countries, whether or not they have become democracies, continue to use a court composed of one professional judge and two lay assessors in criminal cases (Poland, Czech Republic, Hungary, China and Vietnam, among others).[101]

The new jury systems in Russia and Spain both follow the European model based on question lists and majority verdicts, as do Belgium, Austria and Norway. Georgia, on the other hand, has introduced an American-style jury with general unanimous verdicts and non-appealable acquittals.[102] In 2010, the ECtHR decided that it could violate the right to a fair trial for a jury, in a particular case, to convict without giving reasons for its verdict.[103] Thus a conflict has arisen between the tradition of the classic jury that may decide according to its conscience or *intime conviction* and the requirement that judgments be reasoned to prevent arbitrariness and to ensure an effective right to appeal. Can a jury of twelve (as in Belgium, Russia or England and Wales) or nine (as in Spain) plausibly articulate the reasons why they determined certain facts to have been proved? The Spanish jury law, which went into effect in 1996, is revolutionary in that it requires the jurors to state the evidence upon which it relied and to give a 'succinct explanation of the reasons why they have declared, or refused to declare, certain facts as having been proved'.[104]

2.4   The Second Counter-Revolution: Victim's Rights over Defendant's Rights?

In the United States, the prosecutor still has complete discretion as to whether or not to charge a case and on what terms to propose a plea bargain for settling it. This is not true on the European continent, however, where victims can sometimes go to court to compel the prosecutor to charge a particular case where the prosecutor has refused to do so.

Victims can also sometimes file criminal charges, pursue attached civil actions for damages, and get a court-appointed attorney to represent them in court as a private prosecutor. In Spain, any member of the public may charge any crime as a 'popular

---

100   Thaman (note 73) 113.
101   Thaman (note 74) 1101.
102   The ECtHR lists the European countries that still have a 'traditional' jury system as Austria, Belgium, Georgia, Ireland, Malta, Norway (only on appeal), Russia, Spain and the United Kingdom (England, Wales, Scotland and Northern Ireland). The Swiss Canton of Geneva terminated its jury system in 2011. *Taxquet v. Belgium* (GC), no. 926/05 ECHR § 47 (16 Nov. 2010).
103   *Taxquet v. Belgium* (note 103).
104   Thaman, 'Spain Returns' (note 61) 364. On the jurisprudence in Spain relating to reasoned jury verdicts, see Stephen C. Thaman, 'Should Criminal Juries Give Reasons for their Verdicts? The Spanish Experience and the Implications of the European Court of Human Rights Decision in *Taxquet v. Belgium*', 86 *Chicago-Kent Law Journal* 613–68 (2011).

prosecutor' as well.[105] This can lead to two and sometimes three prosecutors lined up against the accused and has generated criticism for re-introducing the notion of private revenge into the criminal trial.[106]

When the victim is accorded full procedural rights parallel to those of the defendant, the public prosecutor can use the victim as its 'Trojan horse' to protect against acquittals, as has been done in Russia. There, courts and prosecutors routinely violate the constitutional procedural rights of victims to build in reversible error in case the jury acquits.[107]

FURTHER READING

Bradley, Craig M. (ed) (2007). *Criminal Procedure: A Worldwide Study*. Durham, NC: Carolina Academic Press, 2nd edn.

Damaška, Mirjan R. (1986). *The Faces of Justice and State Authority: A Comparative Approach to the Legal Process*. New Haven, CT: Yale University Press.

Damaška, Mirjan R. (1997). *Evidence Law Adrift*. New Haven, CT: Yale University Press.

Langbein, John H. (1977). *Torture and the Law of Proof: Europe and England in the Ancien Régime*. Chicago: University of Chicago Press.

Langbein, John H. (2003). *The Origins of Adversary Criminal Trial*. Oxford: Oxford University Press.

Jackson, John, Máximo Langer and Peter Tillers (eds) (2008). *Crime, Procedure and Evidence in Comparative and International Context: Essays in Honour of Professor Mirjan Damaška*. Oxford: Hart Publishing.

Thaman, Stephen C. (2008). *Comparative Criminal Procedure: A Casebook Approach*. Durham, NC: Carolina Academic Press, 2nd edn.

Thaman, Stephen C. (ed.) (2010). *World Plea Bargaining: Consensual Procedures and Avoidance of the Full Criminal Trial*. Durham, NC: Carolina Academic Press.

Vidmar, Neil (ed.) (2000). *World Jury Systems*. Oxford: Oxford University Press.

Vogler, Richard (2005). *A World View of Criminal Justice*. Burlington, VT: Ashgate.

---

[105] Many European countries allow private prosecution by victims for misdemeanor assaults or insults and similar cases, but not, as in Spain, in all cases. Thaman (note 60) 25–30.

[106] In the first year of Spanish jury trials, private prosecutors invariably asked for maximum punishments and exorbitant civil damages, whereas the public prosecutor maintained a more moderate stance. Thaman, 'Spain Returns' (note 61) 397–401.

[107] Thaman, 'Nullification' (note 61) 373–4.

13 Administrative law, agencies and redress mechanisms in the United Kingdom and Sweden
Michael Adler and Sara Stendahl*

1 INTRODUCTION

1.1 The Scope of Comparison

In this chapter, we compare administrative law, administrative agencies and redress mechanisms in the United Kingdom and Sweden from an administrative justice perspective. Before elaborating on the notion of administrative justice, we first provide a rationale for comparing the UK and Sweden.

John Bell's contribution on 'Comparative Administrative Law' in the *Oxford Handbook of Comparative Law* (2006: 1260) notes that 'much work by comparative lawyers involves the study of one other administrative law system, which is then explained in terms familiar to the author's own' and that 'comparisons of more than one system are often less successful'. It is not for us to say how successful our comparison is but, in comparing aspects of administrative law in two countries, we would appear to be avoiding the pitfalls associated with more wide-ranging comparisons. Bell points out that the grouping of public law systems into 'legal families' or legal traditions differs from the grouping of private law systems, and that variations between countries are greater in respect of public law than in respect of private law. That said, he refers to the long tradition of comparative research within and between countries in three legal traditions. First, the *common law tradition* includes the United Kingdom, much of the British Commonwealth and the United States of America. Second, the *French tradition* not only includes France but also countries that were conquered by Emperor Napoleon, in particular, Belgium, Italy, Spain, Portugal, Greece. Finally, there is the somewhat different *German tradition*.

One may note not only that this classification of legal traditions is very Eurocentric—it not only ignores the legal systems of non-European countries but also, within Europe, the *Nordic tradition*, which includes Sweden. The Nordic tradition is something of a hybrid, containing a mix of civilian and common law elements. Only a few provisions of the early civil codes are still in force, statutes are very important and the ombudsman is the trustee for the citizen vis-à-vis the state. According to a recent study, Nordic law can be characterised by its commitment to a specific set of values, which comprise an inclusive and status-oriented view of social justice and social ethics, a strong role for the citizen in law making, and its use as a tool for social engineering (Husa et al. 2007).

* Michael Adler is Emeritus Professor of Socio-Legal Studies, School of Social and Political Science, University of Edinburgh.

Sara Stendahl is Associate Professor of Public Law, Department of Law, School of Business, Economics and Law, University of Gothenburg.

Among the seemingly important differences between the legal systems of Sweden and the UK are the following:

- Sweden has a written constitution while the UK does not.
- The Swedish Constitution does not recognise the separation of powers while the separation of powers is still a hotly contested issue in the UK.
- Sweden has a separate system of administrative courts while the UK does not.
- In Sweden, the state has traditionally been trusted to promote the well-being of the people while a more critical attitude has prevailed in the UK.
- Sweden has a civil law system while the legal system of the UK is based on common law.

The main aim of this chapter is to investigate whether these differences have significant implications for administrative justice in the two countries. A secondary aim is to ascertain whether Sweden and the UK have anything to learn from each other and, if so, what that is. The chapter focuses on two areas of administrative law and procedure, namely those dealing with social security (comprising social insurance and social assistance) and immigration and asylum, which are, in both countries, not only among the most well-developed areas of administrative law but also among the most controversial ones.

1.2 Contrasting Approaches to Administrative Justice

One can identify several contrasting approaches to administrative justice. On the one hand, some see administrative justice in terms of the principles formulated by courts and other redress mechanisms that come into play when people who are unhappy with the outcome of an administrative decision, or with the process by which that decision was reached, challenge the decision and seek to achieve a determination in their favour. We can call this the *traditional administrative law approach*. Although the decisions of the superior courts are of particular importance for this approach, those of other bodies, such as administrative tribunals (which hear the large majority of appeals against administrative decisions in the UK) and ombudsmen (which play important but different roles in the two countries) are also important. Those who adopt the traditional administrative law approach assume that the principles formulated by courts and other redress mechanisms are applied and put into effect by first-instance decision makers and that administrative justice is achieved in this way.

On the other hand, others see administrative justice in terms of the justice of routine administrative decisions. This approach does not accept that the formulation of principles by the courts and other redress mechanisms is sufficient and emphasises the importance of methods designed to improve first-instance decision-making, such as recruitment procedures, training and appraisal procedures, standard setting and quality assurance systems. We can call this the *justice in administration approach*. While the administrative law approach focuses on the relatively small number of cases that come before the courts and other redress mechanisms and can be characterised as a 'top-down' approach, the justice in administration approach focuses on the huge number of first-instance decisions and can be characterised as a 'bottom-up' approach.

However, the choice is not simply between these two approaches. There is a third approach, which sees the merits in both of the above approaches and seeks to combine them. It is thus more wide-ranging than either of the first two approaches. Although it recognises the importance of courts, tribunals, ombudsmen and other external redress mechanisms for holding administrative decision makers to account, with which the traditional administrative law approach is preoccupied, it is also concerned with other (internal) means of enhancing the justice of administrative decisions, which the justice in administration approach focuses on. We can call this the *integrated approach* and it is the one adopted in this chapter. In seeking to combine the two approaches, it attaches considerable importance to feedback mechanisms that would enable first-instance decision makers to learn from the cases considered by courts, tribunals, ombudsmen and other external redress mechanisms, and to amend their decision-making procedures in light of them.

1.3   Absolute and Relativistic Approaches to Administrative Justice

The Administrative Justice and Tribunals Council (AJTC), which was established in 2007 to keep the administrative justice system in the UK under review, recently published a set of seven principles that were intended to apply 'right across the administrative justice landscape' (Administrative Justice and Tribunals Council 2010). These non-enforceable normative standards comprise:

- making users and their needs central; treating them with fairness and respect at all times (Principle 1);
- enabling people to challenge decisions and seek redress, using procedures that are independent, open and appropriate for the matter involved (Principle 2);
- keeping people fully informed and empowering them to resolve problems as quickly and comprehensively as possible (Principle 3);
- producing well-reasoned, lawful and timely outcomes (Principle 4);
- being coherent and consistent (Principle 5);
- working proportionally and efficiently (Principle 6); and
- adopting the highest standards of behaviour, seeking to learn from experience, and continuously improving (Principle 7).

These seven principles reflect an *absolute approach* to administrative justice. One can find similar principles in the Swedish Administrative Procedure Act. Unlike the AJTC's principles of administrative justice, it contains legally enforceable rules on the service duty of authorities, on their collaboration and coordination with other authorities, on rapid and simple processing of information, on the use of easily understood government language and on oral elements in the decision-making process (Regeringskansliet 1999). Although this approach certainly has its attractions, so too does a *relativistic approach*.

Jerry Mashaw is the foremost exponent of a relativistic approach. He defines administrative justice in terms of 'those qualities of a decision process that provide arguments for the acceptability of its decisions' (Mashaw 1983: 24). From this, it follows that each of the three normative models of decision-making he describes is associated with a different conception of administrative justice. According to him, each of these models is associated with a different set of *legitimating values*, different *primary goals*, a different

Table 13.1   Models of administrative justice—Mashaw's analytic framework

Model	Legitimating Values	Primary Goal	Structure or Organisation	Cognitive Technique
Bureaucratic Rationality	accuracy and efficiency	program implementation	hierarchical	information processing
Professional Treatment	service	client satisfaction	interpersonal	clinical application of knowledge
Moral Judgment	fairness	conflict resolution	independent	contextual interpretation

organisational structure and different *cognitive techniques*. Mashaw's analytic framework is set out in Table 13.1 above.

Mashaw claims that each of the models is coherent, plausible and attractive and that the three models are *competitive* rather than *mutually exclusive* (ibid.: 23). Thus, they can and do coexist with each other. However, other things being equal, the more there is of one, the less there will be of the other two. His insight enables us to see both what trade-offs are made between the three models in particular cases and what different sets of trade-offs might be more desirable. Mashaw's approach is a *pluralistic* one, which recognises a plurality of normative positions and acknowledges that situations which are attractive for some people may be unattractive for others.

We argue that the trade-offs that are made, and likewise those that could be made, reflect the concerns and the bargaining strengths of the institutional actors who have an interest in promoting each of the models. These are typically civil servants and officials in the case of the bureaucratic rationality model; professionals and 'street level bureaucrats' (Lipsky 1980) in the case of the professional treatment model; and advisers, representatives, tribunal and court personnel in the case of the moral judgment model. With the Disability Insurance (DI) scheme in the USA, for instance, Mashaw concluded not only that the bureaucratic rationality model, which he described (ibid.: 172) as 'an accuracy orientated, investigatorially-active, hierarchichally organized, and complexly engineered system of adjudication' was not only dominant in the DI scheme but, in modern parlance, 'fit for purpose'.

Although Mashaw's approach was clearly a seminal one, his claim that the three models he identified, and only these three models, are always present in welfare administration, has been disputed on the grounds that, in many countries, they have been challenged by other models of administrative justice. In particular, these are a *managerial* model associated with the rise of new public management, a *consumerist* model that focuses on the increased participation of consumers in decision-making, and a *market* model that emphasises consumer choice. In light of this criticism, Michael Adler (2003, 2006) has characterised the different models of administrative justice identified by Mashaw somewhat differently and added three more. His revised and extended analytic framework is set out in Table 13.2 below.

Mashaw's work, and the developments it has inspired, challenges the view that there are any invariant principles of administrative justice that apply in all contexts. This is because Mashaw's definition of administrative justice in terms of 'those qualities of a

Table 13.2   Models of administrative justice—Adler's revised and extended analytic framework

Model	Legitimating Goal	Mode of Accountability	Mode of Redress
Bureaucratic	accuracy	hierarchical	administrative review
Professional	public service	interpersonal	second opinion or complaint to a professional body
Legal	legality	independent	appeal to a court or tribunal (public law)
Managerial	improved performance	performance indicators and audit	none, other than adverse publicity
Consumerist	consumer satisfaction	consumer charters	'voice' or compensation through consumer charters
Market	economic efficiency	to owners or shareholders (profits)	'exit' or court action (private law)

decision process that provide arguments for the acceptability of its decisions' is a relativistic one in that different modes of decision-making provide different arguments and are therefore associated with different conceptions of administrative justice. Although the concept of administrative justice does not easily translate into Swedish discourse, Sara Stendahl has discussed Mashaw's and Adler's models in the light of theories on legal pluralism that are prevalent in Nordic legal theory (Stendahl 2010). Comparing Mashaw's and Adler's approach with Nordic ones, she has noted some strong common features as well as some marked differences in their conclusions about how best to achieve objectives such as justice, legal security and legitimacy in a pluralistic system. In a comprehensive study of the ability of Swedish administrative courts to act as providers of legitimacy, Stendahl, in a similar relativistic mode, elaborates on the notion of societal conceptions of justice (2004, 2007). However, as Paul van Aerschot (2011) has recently argued, this does not rule out the possibility that some arguments are common to all modes of decision-making and that administrative justice has some invariant features. The examples he gives of protecting clients from abuse of power and from maladministration are two cases in point.

Some political philosophers, such as John Rawls (1971) and Robert Nozick (1974), have argued that there are certain universal principles of social or substantive justice that apply 'across the board'.[1] Others, such as Michael Walzer (1985) and David Miller (1999), have

---

[1]   Thus, Rawls (1971) concluded that each person is to have an equal right to the most extensive scheme of equal basic liberties compatible with a similar scheme of liberties for others. Social and economic inequalities are to be arranged so that (1) they are to be of the greatest benefit to the least-advantaged members of society and (2) offices and positions must be open to everyone under conditions of fair equality of opportunity. Nozick (1974), on the other hand, argued that anyone who obtains what he has in a manner consistent with the principle of 'justice in acquisition' (the appropriation of natural resources that no one has ever owned before), the principle of 'justice in transfer' (which governs the manner in which someone might justly come to own something previously owned by someone else) and the principle of 'justice in rectification' (the proper means of setting right past injustices in acquisition and transfer), was entitled to it.

asserted that different principles apply to different goods in different contexts.[2] Although we favour the second of these positions, we do recognise that there is some scope for universal principles.

2   ADMINISTRATIVE LAW

2.1   The Nature of Administrative Law

According to the American political scientist Martin Shapiro,

> Administrative law as it has historically been understood presupposes that there is something called administration. The administrator and/or the administrative agency or organization exist as a bounded reality. Administrative law prescribes behavior within administrative organizations; more importantly, it delineates the relationships between those inside the administration and those outside it. Outside an administration lie both the statute maker whose laws and regulations administrators owe a legal duty to faithfully implement and the citizens to whom administrators owe legally correct procedural and substantive action.
>
> More generally, the political and organization theory that informs our administrative law has traditionally viewed public administration as a set of bounded organizations within which decisions are made collectively. On this view, these 'organs of public administration' are coordinated with one another, subordinated to political authority, and obligated to respect the outside individuals and interests whom they regulate and serve. (2001: 369)

Shapiro's characterisation of administrative law draws attention to the fact that it is a body of law with *internal* and as well as *external* reach. It both prescribes behaviour within administrative organisations and delineates the relationships between those inside the administration and those outside it. Governments and parliaments prescribe what the administrative agency should do and the rules reach citizens who are on the receiving end of administrative decision-making.

To talk of an entity such as 'administrative law' in a meaningful way, it is helpful to be able to orientate oneself on the legal map, that is, to know how administrative law relates to the rest of the legal system. From a Swedish and a UK perspective, administrative law is, alongside constitutional law, a subdivision of public law. If we consider the content of administrative law, we find that it divides into two main categories: procedural and substantive administrative law.

Under the heading of substantive administrative law are a very large number of pieces of primary and secondary legislation dealing with specific areas of interaction between the state and the citizen (for example, with social insurance, social assistance, health, education, housing, employment, planning, immigration, asylum and so on).

---

[2]   Walzer (1985) concluded that different principles, for example, need, desert or free exchange, apply to different 'goods' while Miller (1999) believes that the different principles of justice apply to different types of relationship between the people involved. Thus, in 'solidaristic communities', where people identify themselves as holding a shared culture or belief, need is the relevant consideration; in 'instrumental associations', where people are acting together with a common purpose, it is desert; while in 'citizenship', where people are related through political and legal structures, equality should prevail.

Under the heading of procedural administrative law, one can find rules that govern the way that administrative agencies are organized and how they are to perform their different activities. These include examples of 'hard law' and 'soft law' both of which receive attention. As an example of 'hard law, the Swedish Parliament passed the Administrative Procedure Act in 1986, which laid down a set of rules that, in principle, should be applied by all authorities in all fields. It has no equivalent in the UK, where procedural rules are found in separate pieces of legislation referring to specific policies. The set of seven normative principles, mentioned above, that were recently published by the UK Administrative Justice and Tribunals Council, are an example of 'soft law' since they are normative standards that are not legally binding.

2.2 Constitutional Arrangements and the Separation of Powers

A well-known textbook on administrative law in the UK opens with the claim: 'Behind every theory of administrative law lies a theory of the state' (Harlow and Rawlings 2010: 1). In this case, the theory of the state relates to the role of government in promoting or undermining the liberty and well-being of citizens.

Sweden and the UK are both constitutional monarchies but, in other respects, not least in their modes of governance, they differ markedly. Most significantly, perhaps, Sweden has a written constitution while the UK does not. Sweden has four statutes of constitutional significance, the most relevant of which, for our purposes, is the Instrument of Government (*Regeringsformen*, RF).[3] It came into force in 1974 when it succeeded the Constitution of 1809. As a document with the potential to influence the legal development of the country, the Instrument of Government has been a weak instrument (Nergelius 2006: 85). One explanation for this is that the 1809 Constitution outlived itself and that Sweden for decades had a constitution that did not reflect political realities (ibid.: 66). The 1974 Instrument of Government, although updated and modernised, has, at least so far, had little visible impact on legal reasoning and decision-making. Recently, though, there has been a renewed interest, especially in connection with the 2010 elections as the Government[4] had presented a proposal for reform in 2008.[5] Whether this is the beginning of a breakthrough for a stronger constitutional influence on Swedish politics is unclear (Nergelius 2010: 17).

A characteristic of the 1974 Instrument of Government is its neglect of the separation of powers and the fact that it sets out few restrictions on the exercise of political power. This constitutional charter is often described as one shaped by a strong commitment to popular and parliamentary sovereignty. Parliament is the main representative

---

[3] The other three fundamental laws deal with royal succession, freedom of the press, and freedom of expression. References in this chapter to the Swedish Constitution will refer to the *Regeringsformen* (RF, or Instrument of Government) unless otherwise indicated.

[4] The term 'Government' refers to the prime minister and cabinet ministers that the prime minister appoints. The broader term 'government' refers to either the executive branch in general or to all parts of state authority.

[5] See Swedish Government's Human Rights Website. The Working Committee on Constitutional Reform presented its final report (Official Reports 2008: 125), www.humanrights. gov.se (select Human rights in Sweden, then Who does what?, then final report).

of the people—it enacts laws, decides on the collection of taxes and the distribution of public funds, and has the function of holding the Government and the administration to account. Rather than specifying a division of power, the Instrument of Government sets out a division of functions, distinguishing between elected public bodies (parliament, county and municipal councils) and executive public agencies (the Government, courts and public agencies) (Warnling-Nerep et al. 2007: 27). Thus, the division of powers that characterises many constitutional systems is not present in Sweden, where many of the powers of the state rest with parliament alone.

In contrast to Sweden, the UK does not have a written constitution and the separation of powers is still a hotly contested issue. Carol Harlow and Richard Rawlings contrast so-called 'red light theories' of the relationship between government and the courts, which mistrust government and favour a strong role for the courts in scrutinising the legality of administrative decisions, with so-called 'green light theories'. These place their trust in government and emphasise the role of parliament and the use of legislation and regulation in controlling government, arguing that where the courts declare actions unlawful, they are usually substituting their own value judgments for those of the democratically elected legislature. While the green light theory is clearly dominant in Sweden, in the UK, these two competing theories generate ebbs and flows as adherents of the contrasting positions jostle for supremacy.[6]

2.3   The European Dimension

Sweden became a member of the European Union in 1995 and incorporated, somewhat hesitantly, the European Convention on Human Rights (ECHR) into Swedish law in the same year.[7] These developments have led to a more complex legal situation in which there are three tiers of regulation (national, European and international) and, arguably, to an increasing juridification of the political sphere (Brännström 2009). It has since become more common and more acceptable to put forward arguments based on the ECHR or on the Instrument of Government (RF) in Swedish courts, and the courts have also become increasingly comfortable about reaching decisions based on such arguments (Nergelius 2006: 86). The Instrument of Government includes a chapter on civil and political rights although some have argued that, after 1995, the protection of rights provided by the RF

---

[6]   Judicial review, that is, judicial scrutiny of administrative action, represents a compromise between the positions advocated by supporters of red and green light theories. Administrative decisions are subject to review by the courts but the powers of the courts are limited. The Human Rights Act 1998, which incorporated the European Convention on Human Rights into UK law, illustrates this. Section 4 of the HRA allows a superior court in the UK to issue a 'declaration of incompatibility' stating that an act of Parliament is incompatible with the ECHR but does not give it the power to strike down or otherwise invalidate legislation. When a court issues a 'declaration of incompatibility', it is then up to Parliament to decide whether to amend the law.

[7]   The Convention has the status of statutory law in Sweden, although its legal position has been strengthened by a special clause (RF 2:23) in the Instrument of Government, which states that legal acts and regulations cannot be passed if they are in conflict with the European Convention. Still, the mode of implementation has been intensively debated (Nergelius 2010: 179–80).

has been overshadowed by the international protection provided by the ECHR and the European Court of Human Rights (ECtHR).

Of interest to the discussion in the present chapter is that Sweden has had some difficulties in keeping up with its obligations with regard to article 6 of the Convention[8] (the right to a fair trial). Traditionally, conflicts between individuals and the authorities over administrative issues were not resolved in courts but through internal review procedures, sometimes with the Government as the final decision maker. This system did not provide access to court in terms of article 6. Following several critical judgments from the ECtHR in the late 1980s,[9] a new act on judicial appeal (*rättsprövning*) was passed in 1988, which made it possible to appeal to the administrative courts on administrative issues where previously the final appeal had been to the government. This reform, followed up and reinforced by a new act on judicial appeals in 2006, is an example of the ongoing process of juridification mentioned above. Thomas Bull has argued that courts in Sweden appear to have become increasingly more important as institutions for solving societal problems. One important explanation for this development, according to Bull, is the more complex and scattered legal reality that comes from having a number of parallel authoritative systems (2008: 75).

Although the UK joined the EEC (European Economic Community) in 1973, it has never been very enthusiastic about membership and is clearly a rather 'semi-detached' member of today's EU. The UK, a founding member of the ECHR, was very influential in its design and amongst the first states to ratify the treaty. However, it did not incorporate the Convention into UK law until 1997, when the Government issued a White Paper entitled 'Rights Brought Home' and introduced what became the 1998 Human Rights Act (HRA). This allows a superior court in the UK to issue a 'declaration of incompatibility', stating that an Act of Parliament is incompatible with the ECHR, although it does not allow the court to strike down or otherwise invalidate it.

Research five years after incorporation (Bondy 2003) indicates that there is little evidence to suggest that the introduction of the HRA had led to a significant increase in the number of judicial review claims. However, it also establishes that the HRA was cited in just under half of all civil claims made, although this varied considerably according to the subject matter of the application. It further found that, in the majority of cases, the inclusion of human rights arguments did not add significantly to the case or to the claimant's prospects of success. Although this might suggest that the impact of the HRA has been slight, it ignores the fact that many administrative agencies reviewed their practices and procedures to ensure that they were compatible with the ECHR. The UK Government is now committed to producing a statement of compatibility with the ECHR for all bills that are presented to Parliament and this is scrutinised by the Joint Parliamentary Committee on Human Rights.

---

[8]   Article 6(1) specifies, 'In the determination of his civil rights and obligations [or of any criminal charge against him] everyone is entitled to a fair and public hearing within a reasonable time by an independent and impartial tribunal established by law'.

[9]   The following cases were of key importance: *Sporrong and Lönnroth v. Sverige* (1982); *Pudas v. Sverige* (1987); *Fredin (I) v. Sweden* (1991).

3 ADMINISTRATIVE AGENCIES

3.1 Central Government Departments

In Sweden and the UK, ministers, who are elected politicians and represent the interests of the public, have traditionally headed central government departments. Ministers formulate policies based on their party's manifesto commitments or, in the case of coalitions, on formal agreements between the coalition parties, and on their assessment of what is in the public interest. After securing agreement to these policies from the cabinet and resources from the Ministry of Finance or Treasury, they propose legislation to Parliament, or make policy decisions that administrative agencies are responsible for implementing. Services are paid for out of general taxation, although charges may also be imposed on service users.

In both countries, central government departments are comparatively small while other administrative agencies are much larger. The senior civil service, who staff the central government departments, develop policies and, together with a relatively small number of special advisers, who are political appointments, advise ministers. Civil servants typically have long public service careers while special advisers come and go with changes in Government. Both groups are accountable to ministers who monitor their activities as they see fit. In the UK, central government as a whole is subject to a distinctive set of rules that emphasises input controls on activities, especially detailed budgetary and staffing controls (James 2003). In Sweden the organisation of government offices for a long time seemed to be unaffected by administrative reforms, although efforts were made during the 1980s and 1990s to create a more efficient and coherent organisation less marked by problems such as departmentalisation of work and stagnation due to lack of mobility of staff (Erlandsson 2007).

3.2 Regional and Local Government

In the UK, local authorities play an important, albeit secondary, role in service delivery. Their importance stems from the fact that, like central government, they also have a democratic mandate. There are 34 county-level authorities (including the Greater London Authority), 270 district-level authorities and 57 unitary authorities (which span the two tiers) in England, and smaller numbers in Wales, Scotland and Northern Ireland. Partly because local elections occur at different times from national elections and partly because the balance of political forces at the local level often differs from the balance of political forces at the national level, this often produces a different political outcome. It is important to recognise that, in the UK, which lacks a written constitution, local authorities do not have a constitutional right to exist and are the statutory creations of the UK Parliament. As such, a single Act of Parliament could abolish them. Their powers are further constrained by the legal doctrine of *ultra vires*, which means that they may only do what Parliament has empowered them to do. Thus, what local authorities do is largely determined by legislation passed by Parliament, which may, and frequently does, require them to act in ways that conflict with what they regard as being in the best interests of their local community. It follows that their democratic mandate is somewhat compromised.

The structure of government in Sweden is quite different. Some compare it with a sand-glass, which comprises a strong central government, weak regions and strong local governments (Petersson 2005: 72). At the regional level there are 21 county councils, representing conglomerates of municipalities, while, at the local level, there are 290 municipalities. County councils and municipalities have an independent and constitutionally protected position—elections to county councils and municipal assemblies are held concurrently with national elections and use roughly the same electoral system. This produces similar political outcomes. Municipalities have an open mandate to act on issues of general concern for those they represent. They also have specific obligations to carry out duties specified in statutes to secure the implementation of national policies. Taxes are paid to all three tiers of government.

In Sweden, the central government is represented at the regional level by county administrative instances (*län*) and there are branches of central government agencies working at regional and local levels, for example local social insurance and unemployment offices. While municipalities and county councils can represent the state, they are also responsible for providing the majority of public services. County councils are responsible for the provision of healthcare and hospitals and for services such as dental care, public transport, culture, tourism, environment, regional growth and development (Petersson 2005: 74). The main areas of responsibility for municipalities are primary and secondary education, social assistance and care of the elderly. Over the years, the responsibility for coordinating policies at different levels and for securing overarching political aims has become one of the most important functions of the county administrative instances.

In the UK, central government has, in recent years, imposed increasingly tight controls over local authority finances (in 2010, local authorities received, on average, 53 per cent of their income from central government grants, although this varied from around 20 per cent to around 75 per cent). They have also reduced local authorities' powers, transferred local authority services to non-elected 'quangos', discussed below, required local authorities to 'contract out' more and more services, and increased the role of markets in service delivery. Local authority powers have been cut back while local authorities have increasingly become instruments for implementing central government policies.

In Sweden, conflicts between central and local government are visible, for example, when the national interest in standard setting—to make sure that levels of service provision in different parts of the country do not differ too much—clashes with local democratic accountability. Another area of potential conflict appears when the effect of national policies puts a strain on the local economy. Municipalities have considerable freedom to make decisions about their internal organisational structure, which results in a broad spectrum of organisational arrangements.

Central and local governments in Sweden communicate informally, something that has become even more important since joining the EU. As mentioned above, the need to coordinate activities between different tiers of government has increased and thus internationalisation seems to have strengthened a development in which a seemingly clear split between central and local government has become somewhat more blurred in practice (Mattson and Petersson 2003: 154–5).

3.3   The Role of Non-governmental Organisations

In addition to using governmental agencies, governments in most liberal democracies employ non-governmental agencies to perform public functions, implement public policies and deliver public services. As central government has expanded, so too has quasi-government. In the UK, people use the colloquial term 'quango'[10] to describe quasi-public bodies that are officially at least partially independent of government but which receive public funds to carry out public functions or to deliver public services (Barker 1982). There is no equivalent of the term 'quango' in Sweden. Some quangos (known as 'executive quangos') make executive decisions, implement policy and deliver services while others (known as 'advisory quangos') provide advice to government departments. In 1980, the UK Government adopted the term 'non-departmental public bodies' (NDPBs) to refer to both types of quango. In this chapter, we are mainly interested in executive quangos.

The 1994 Democratic Audit report (Weir and Hall 1994) criticised the informality of arrangements for establishing 'executive quangos'. It was also concerned with the absence of cross-governmental rules for their governance, evidence of partisan bias and imbalance in appointments to them, the arbitrary nature of many appointment procedures, and the inadequacy of measures to secure openness and accountability. This led to growing concern in the UK about the growth of the 'quango state'.

Instead of introducing measures to 'rein in' the quango state, the widespread adoption of 'New Public Management' (NPM) has resulted in the increased use of 'executive quangos' to deliver public services. According to a report by the UK Prime Minister's Efficiency Unit entitled *Improving Management in Government: The Next Steps* (Efficiency Unit 1988), 'agencies should be established to carry out the executive functions of government within a policy and resources framework set by the [government] department'. The main features of this model of service delivery are as follows:

- The parent department, headed by a minister, determines the strategic framework, which is set out in a framework agreement. Budgetary limits and performance targets are set out in the form of a contract.
- The agency, which is semi-detached from its parent department, is a corporate unit that is free from ad-hoc, day-to-day intervention by the parent department and may be exempt from some central government-wide regulations. A chief executive, who is recruited through open competition, heads it.
- The agency as a unit is collectively accountable, and the chief executive is personally accountable, for achieving the performance targets set by the parent department. If the performance targets are unmet, the minister may reduce the resources of the agency, reorganise the agency or take it back into the department, and may terminate the employment of the chief executive.

The divide between the parent department and the executive agency (or executive quango) is a form of 'purchaser-provider' split, in which the minister and a small number

---

[10] Quango is an acronym that originates from quasi-autonomous non-governmental organisation.

of civil servants in the parent department deal with 'policy' while the bulk of civil servants work in the executive agency where they are responsible for 'operations'. Between 1988 and 2002, 173 executive agencies were created in the UK.[11]

There is at present no comparable organisational trend in Swedish public administration, although an increased interest in public-private partnerships (PPPs) has been noted as well as continued efforts to find ways of increasing cooperation between public authorities at different tiers of government and within different sectors (Petersson 2007: 96–8). Ideas derived from new public management had a distinct influence in Sweden during the 1980s, and expressed an ambition to change what some perceived as an old bureaucratic culture into a more service-oriented set of institutions. Keywords were flexibility, decentralisation, framework legislation and customer adaptation (ibid.: 27). Public institutions were exposed to competition, contracts with private partners were used as a mode of governance and centralised public authorities were decentralised (Almqvist 2004). There was thus a paradigmatic shift in approach as a system favouring detailed regulation in the 1980s and 1990s was replaced by a new mode of governance in which the overarching aims and goals were written down in legislation but responsibility for detailed implementation was decentralised (Petersson 2007: 27). What clearly remains from this period is an interest in organisational issues; the search for the 'best' form of organisation has intensified (although it is less clear what the answer to this question is). Public employees, in all sectors and at all levels, are now used to constant processes of reorganisation (Petersson 2006: 168).

Service provision in Sweden is carried out by private bodies as well as by governmental agencies, a practice that is supported by the Instrument of Government. For private actors to exercise public authority, statutory support is required. Central government, as well as county councils and municipalities, have, for quite a long time, created and owned companies that carry out public administration. There are, however, many other ways in which private bodies can become involved in public administration. For example, public grants to non-profit organisations play, and have for decades played, an important role as one means of implementing policy (Petersson 2007: 88–90). It is clear that there has been a steady increase in the role of private actors in areas previously dominated by governmental agencies. To what extent the presence of private bodies allows them to make a profit is a controversial issue, intensively debated, in relation to healthcare and hospitals as well as education and schools. Thus, the increased presence of private actors does not necessarily mean that full market forces are in play.

A strong corporatist tradition has marked Swedish public management, in which different types of organisation have been invited to participate in the political process in different ways (Rothstein 1992). Since the 1980s the traditional corporate model, in which a

---

[11]   In 2001, 367,000 civil servants, corresponding to 76 per cent of all civil servants, worked in agencies or bodies, like Customs and Excise, the Inland Revenue, the Crown Prosecution Service and the Serious Fraud Office, which operated on 'agency lines' (Cabinet Office 2002: 18). The Ministry of Defence (MOD) created the largest number of agencies, 52 executive agencies employing 26 per cent of MOD staff. The proportion of staff employed in executive agencies was highest in the Department of Work and Pensions (DWP) where, in 2001, 97 per cent of staff worked in one of its agencies and the proportion was 50 per cent or more in seven government departments (see James 2003: appendix 4).

few organisations had very privileged positions, has been challenged and there is evidence of change towards a more pluralistic organisational model in which more organisations have become involved and new forms of involvement, such as those described above, have been developed (Petersson 2007: 92–3).

In contrast to countries with an explicit system of ministerial rule, the Swedish system is based on an organisational split that prohibits ministerial intervention in decisions made by governmental agencies in specific cases. This way of regulating the relationship between government departments and governmental agencies is unique in an international perspective (Mattson and Petersson 2003: 151). In the UK, the divide between parent departments, which formulate policy, and executive agencies, which are responsible for achieving the performance targets set by the parent department, has resulted in a situation in which ministers have chosen to disclaim responsibility for administrative decisions.

The strong principle of independent governmental agencies in Sweden, which has considerable public support, has at times been questioned during the past three decades, both on legal grounds (questioning the constitutional support) and from a perspective where membership in the European Union has made it more difficult to uphold this barrier between ministries and governmental agencies (ibid.: 154). In the UK, the public has treated attempts by ministers to disclaim responsibility for administrative decisions with a fair amount of incredulity.

3.4.   Administrative Decision-making in Two Public Policy Areas

In the UK, the two areas of administrative decision-making that this chapter focuses on—social insurance and social assistance, on the one hand, and asylum and immigration, on the other—are both delivered by executive agencies. For the former, JobCentre Plus is responsible for providing benefits and services for unemployed people. It was formed when the Employment Service, which operated Jobcentres, merged with the Benefits Agency in 2002. Providing pensions and disability benefits to retired people and others who are outside the labour market is the responsibility of the Pension, Disability and Carers Service, which came into being in 2008 when the Pensions Agency merged with the Disability and Carers Service. JobCentre Plus and the Pension, Disability and Carers Service are executive agencies of the Department for Work and Pensions (DWP). The UK Border Agency, which is an executive agency of the Home Office, manages border controls for the UK, enforces immigration and customs regulations and considers applications for permission to enter or stay in the UK, and for citizenship and asylum. Although each of these agencies has so far provided services in-house, following the recommendations of a report commissioned by the previous Labour Government (Freud 2007), the Coalition Government, elected in 2010, is committed to making JobCentre Plus contract with private and voluntary sectors to provide 'individually tailored programmes for hard-to-employ adults'.

There is no standard pattern of organisation. JobCentre Plus operates through a network of local offices; the Pension, Disability and Carers Service has fewer local offices but many claims are assessed through remote processing arrangements, while the UK Border Agency has a small number of regional offices.

In Sweden, administrative decision-making in social insurance and social assistance, as well as in asylum and immigration, is the responsibility of public authorities. Provision of social insurance is a state responsibility and the two main public authorities responsible for implementation are the Swedish Social Insurance Agency (Försäkringskassan) and the Swedish Unemployment Agency (Arbetsförmedlingen), both of which have regional and local offices. Provision of social assistance is a municipal responsibility for which local authorities make the decisions. These are organised in a variety of ways.[12] To the extent that private sector organisations are involved in these areas, it is as service providers, for example, for the delivery of activation measures for the unemployed and services for the long-term sick and disabled. Decision-making in the area of asylum and migration is also a state responsibility, with the Swedish Migration Agency (Migrationsverket) the responsible public authority. Private providers exist in this area too, but only for the provision of services (for example, housing for asylum-seekers). The Swedish welfare state is comprehensive and the state has far-reaching responsibilities. Although benefits and rights are regulated by statute law, constitutional protection is weak.

3.5   Recent Developments

While the majority of administrative decisions in the UK used to be taken by officials who were employed in central government departments or local authorities, most of them are now taken by officials who work in executive agencies,[13] 'non-departmental public bodies' or 'quangos'. However, public officials still make the decisions. In Sweden, public authorities have retained their position as agencies with a core responsibility for administrative decision-making. There have been several quite dramatic changes in the organisation of public authorities as well as a number of shifts in the modes of governance—but it is still public officials, employed by public authorities, who make the decisions. In this respect, recent developments in Sweden and the UK have had very similar outcomes. In both countries, public officials make millions of decisions about a wide range of sensitive issues, including the right to enter the country and in some of those cases to obtain asylum, and about entitlement to social insurance and social assistance. These decisions have an enormous impact on people's lives and it is therefore very important that they are correct and, where those affected by the decision think they are not and are sufficiently aggrieved, they are able to challenge the decision. That brings us to the role of courts and other redress mechanisms in enabling individuals to challenge administrative decisions (section 4) and the means that are used, or could be used, to ensure that they are right in the first place (section 5).

4   COURTS, TRIBUNALS AND OTHER REDRESS MECHANISMS

4.1   Courts and Tribunals

In Sweden, there are two parallel and separate systems of courts: general courts (*allmänna domstolar*), which hear civil and criminal cases, and administrative courts (*allmänna*

---

[12]   See section 3.2.
[13]   When a new quango is set up, it is usual for staff to be transferred from the (old) government department to the (new) agency.

förvaltningsdomstolar), which hear administrative cases. Judges who are familiar with public administration and are specialists in administrative law staff the administrative courts. They, like the general courts, are organised into three tiers—with a first-instance tier, an appellate tier and a Supreme Administrative Court, whose decisions act as precedents that lower tier courts and the administration must follow. Relevant to this chapter, the administrative courts are the most important actors, although there are some possible crossovers. It is, for example, possible for an individual to claim damages from the state and such claims are handled by the general courts.

The Swedish Constitution guarantees the independence of courts and governmental agencies in chapters 11 and 12 of the Instrument of Government but there are limited possibilities for judicial review (*lagprövning*) and there is no constitutional court. There is a clause that states that courts are not allowed to apply a regulation that contradicts superior law unless it does so in a way that is manifest (Bull 2008).[14] Thus, Swedish courts, looked at from an international perspective, have a weaker position than courts in countries where the division of powers is more firmly established. At the same time, the independence of governmental agencies is comparatively strong (Nergelius 2006: 78).

Compared to the general courts, the administrative court system in Sweden is a modern innovation. Although various government committees discussed procedures for dealing with administrative matters for many years, it was not until the early 1970s that the Swedish Parliament introduced a more unitary and comprehensive administrative court system and procedure. Since then, it has steadily developed the structure and procedures of administrative courts, making them more stringent and 'court-like'. Whether general courts and administrative courts should merge, on the ground that separation is no longer needed, is debatable but there are no signs that such a reform will be enacted in the immediate future.

In Sweden, reform of the organisational structure of administrative courts is ongoing. This involves reducing the number of small local courts and centralising and increasing the size of courts. Proponents support these changes with arguments about the need to create an efficient and sustainable organisation. It is also clear that another aim of the reform is to resolve more appeals at first instance by making access to appellate courts more difficult. There also appears to be an increased interest in the award of damages; one can point to recent reforms to adjust the national system to harmonise better with the ECHR.

In the UK, on the other hand, there is a unitary court structure. There are separate courts, with separate procedures for civil and criminal cases, but administrative cases are heard in the same courts with the same judges who hear civil cases. Since the number of administrative cases in civil courts is very small compared to the number of civil and criminal cases, this has inhibited the development of administrative law in the UK.

To deal with the lack of specialist expertise in the courts, the UK established the administrative division of the High Court (known as the Administrative Court) in 2000.[15] It is,

---

[14]   Before Parliament decides on new legislation, the Legal Council (Lagrådet) scrutinizes the proposal to make sure no such conflicts should occur. Members of the Legal Council often work as judges at one of the supreme courts.

[15]   The Administrative Court is part of the Queen's Bench Division of the High Court. It comprises the list of judges authorised by the Lord Chief Justice to sit on administrative law cases.

in effect, a specialised ordinary court and appeals from it proceed to the (unitary) Court of Appeal and the Supreme Court (formerly the House of Lords).

Most of the cases heard in the Administrative Court are actions of judicial review, which is the primary means by which courts can scrutinise the actions and decisions of Parliament and of administrative agencies. In the UK, courts do not have the power to invalidate primary legislation because of the doctrine of parliamentary sovereignty, except where the legislation conflicts with EU law. It is, in any case, possible for the executive branch, because of its control over the legislature, to secure the passage of legislation, which would have the effect of reversing the impact of an adverse judgment in the courts. Thus, judicial review has a more limited scope in the UK than in some other countries, such as the United States, where any court (subject to appeal) can literally strike down legislation that violates constitutional principles. The grounds for intervention in judicial review cases are not defined in statute. However, as befits a legal system based on common law, judges have created them in cases that have come before them.

The most commonly cited classification of the grounds for judicial review, employed by Lord Diplock in the *GCHQ* case,[16] comprises 'illegality, irrationality (or unreasonableness) and procedural impropriety'. There is a very strict measure of 'irrationality', the '*Wednesbury* unreasonableness' test,[17] and a decision will be held to be irrational only if it is 'so outrageous in its defiance of logic or of accepted moral standards that no sensible person who had applied his mind to the question could have arrived at it'. Where any of these grounds are established, the court will remit the action or decision to the body that made it, and that body will then be expected to reconsider it.

The account given above ignores the existence of a large number of specialised tribunals that constitute the 'standard machinery' (Harlow and Rawlings 2010: 486) for dealing with legal disputes between the citizen and the state in the UK.[18] They hear the overwhelming majority of appeals against administrative decisions. In fiscal year 2009–10, tribunals received more than 750,000 referrals and made just under 650,000 disposals, figures that dwarf the number of applications for judicial review (6,000 to 7,000) and the number (about 750) that proceeded to a full hearing in the High Court (Bondy and Sunkin 2009: 2).

There have been two major reviews of tribunals. The *Franks Report* (1957) concluded that tribunals were properly to be regarded as machinery for adjudication rather than as part of the machinery for administration. Although this is an oversimplification of a complex position (see, for example, Thomas 2010: 5–11), it ushered in an era of juridification. The *Leggatt Report* (2001) argued that the 70 or more different tribunals had grown up in a haphazard way to meet the needs and conveniences of the departments that ran them rather than the needs of 'users', and was particularly concerned that *citizen versus state* tribunals were not sufficiently independent of the departments that sponsored them. It concluded that the separate organisation of so many separate tribunals involved considerable duplication of effort and led to an inefficient use of resources. It then recommended

---

[16]   *Council of Civil Services Unions v. Minister for the Civil Service*, [1985] AC 374.

[17]   After the decision in *Associated Provincial Picture Houses Ltd v. Wednesbury Corporation*, [1947] 1 KB 223, where it was first imposed.

[18]   Some purely private party disputes, in particular employment disputes, that is, disputes between employees and employers, are also heard by tribunals rather than courts.

that all tribunals should be brought together in a unitary Tribunals Service that would be an executive agency within the Lord Chancellor's Department (now the Ministry of Justice), and, as such, would be in an analogous position to Her Majesty's Court Service.

Most of Leggatt's recommendations were accepted by the Government and, in 2007, a two-tier Tribunals Service was established. As of early 2010, 31 former tribunal jurisdictions, including those concerned with social security and child support, and those concerned with asylum and immigration, had become part of the first tier of the Tribunals Service,[19] and the process is ongoing. In the past, the specialised nature of tribunal jurisdictions and their separate organisation did little to assist the development of administrative law as a generic body of law. It remains to be seen whether the establishment of a unitary Tribunals Service will facilitate its development.

The process of juridification appears to have been too successful for its own good. The Ministry of Justice in 2010 announced that it intended to merge the recently established Tribunals Service with Her Majesty's Courts Service into a single Courts and Tribunals Service for England and Wales. What this will mean for tribunals and for the resolution of disputes between the citizen and the state is unclear. On the one hand, there are those who think that it will make little difference because, just as tribunals have become more like courts, so courts, at least those inferior courts that deal with matters like small claims and housing disputes, have become more like tribunals. On the other hand, there are those who think that tribunals will be 'swamped' by the courts and that their distinctive characteristics are unlikely to survive. Only time will tell which of these predictions turns out to be more accurate.

4.2 Court (and Tribunal) Procedures

Some special procedural rules, which differ from the rules of the general courts, apply in the administrative courts in Sweden. A characteristic of the administrative courts is that, in general, the procedure is not oral (but handled on paper only), complainants have no right to legal aid or assistance, there are no costs involved and there is no opportunity for mediation or reconciliation. On the other hand, the courts have a responsibility actively to ensure that all the facts and circumstances that are relevant are at hand when the case is considered. In first- and second-tier courts, a legally qualified judge sits with lay people, but lay members constitute a majority. To reach the appellate courts, leave to appeal is necessary, but the Supreme Administrative Court only provides such leave on a point of law. The courts conduct a full 'merits review' of the evidence in all cases.

As noted above, Sweden, after a number of adverse decisions from the European Court of Human Rights, adopted a statute on judicial appeal with the aim of increasing access to the courts in matters that had previously been determined, in the last resort, by the Government. However, the implementation of the act on judicial appeal was followed by further adverse decisions from the ECtHR, which criticised the lack of an oral procedure in cases where an appeal to an administrative court was the first and only occasion that a

---

[19]   These include those tribunals that are outside the unified two-tier structure. See Ministry of Justice, 'HM Courts & Tribunals Service', http://www.justice.gov.uk/about/hmcts.

court had dealt with the case.[20] New cases, concerned with ordinary procedure in administrative courts and the paper hearings that were one of its characteristics, followed. In several of these cases, the ECtHR found Sweden to be in breach of article 6.[21] There is thus some pressure towards having an increased number of cases decided after an oral hearing (Bylander 2006).

In the UK, different procedural rules apply to courts and tribunals. Until recently, each of the 70 or so separate tribunals had its own set of procedural rules but the establishment of the Tribunals Service in 2007 has resulted in a degree of standardisation. To date, 31 hitherto separate tribunals have been brought into the First-tier Tribunal, which is organised into chambers dealing with cognate citizen versus state disputes.[22] There is an appeal, with leave, on a point of law from the First-tier Tribunal to the Upper Tribunal,[23] which is also organised into chambers.[24] Tribunals, in general, unlike courts in judicial review proceedings, do not merely review whether a particular decision is unlawful but can question the facts on which the original decision was based and substitute their own decision for that of the initial decision maker. Reflecting the unitary system of law in the UK, appeals from the Upper Tribunal on points of law, with leave, can be made to the Court of Appeal.

Tribunals are more informal and 'user-friendly' than courts. Thus, they often allow hearsay evidence and appellants do not present their evidence on oath. They tend to use active, interventionist and enabling procedures, and are more likely to adopt inquisitorial procedures and assist unrepresented appellants (Adler 2009). This is important because appellants are often unrepresented. Legal aid is available for pre-hearing advice and, in some cases (including asylum and immigration appeals) for representation. However, in late 2010, the UK Government published its plans to cut expenditure on civil legal aid (costing £900 million per annum) by £350 million (Ministry of Justice 2010). For instance, the state will withdraw funding from all immigration cases where the appellant is not in detention and from all routine social security cases.[25] However, it will still be available for asylum appeals, second-tier appeals involving points of law, and applications for judicial review. Those who appeal to a tribunal can choose between a paper hearing, in which the case is decided on written submissions in the absence of the parties, and an oral hearing, where the appellant and, possibly, a representative of the administrative agency are present, can address the tribunal and can be asked questions. Most appellants opt for an oral hearing—latest figures indicate that, in asylum and immigra-

---

[20]   *Fredin v. Sweden* (II) (1994); *Allan Jacobsson v. Sweden* (II) (1998); *Hellborg v. Sweden* (2006).
[21]   See, for instance, *Miller v. Sweden* (2005); *Andersson v. Sweden* (2010).
[22]   The six chambers of the First-tier Tribunal comprise a General Regulatory Chamber; a Social Entitlement Chamber (dealing with social security and other benefits); a Health, Education and Social Care Chamber; a War Pensions and Armed Forces Compensation Chamber; a Tax Chamber; and an Immigration and Asylum Chamber. Employment Tribunals constitute an additional pillar outside the chamber structure.
[23]   It follows that the Upper Tribunal does not consider the evidence on which the First-tier Tribunal based its decision.
[24]   The four chambers of the Upper Tribunal comprise an Administrative Appeals Chamber, a Tax and Chancery Chamber, a Lands Chamber, and an Asylum and Immigration Chamber.
[25]   Legal Aid will also be withdrawn from all family cases, except those where domestic violence is involved, and from all housing and employment cases.

tion cases, 65 per cent do so and, in the social security and child support cases, 72 per cent of appellants do so.

4.3 Social Security, Asylum and Immigration Appeals

While the use of the administrative court for external redress in cases concerning social security has become an established practice in Sweden, migration courts are a more recent innovation. The 2006 reform came after years of severe criticism of the body that previously heard appeals against decisions of the Swedish Migration Agency. In general, and from a longer time perspective, courts have become more important as a means for external redress against decisions made by public authorities.

Both in social security and in asylum and immigration cases, administrative courts now play an important role in Sweden. The main caseload in administrative courts consists of claims for social insurance benefits, claims under the Social Service Act (which include claims for social assistance) and migration cases (Domstolsverket 2010). In the area of social insurance, it has been possible to appeal to a court since 1962, although, until 1992, the courts were specialised social insurance courts. In the area of asylum and immigration, the availability of appeal to a court is more recent. The migration courts, which are an integrated but specialised branch of the administrative courts, were created in 2006. There are three migration courts in the country and one superior migration court (there is only one appeal in asylum and immigration cases). The superior migration court only considers cases that are important in the sense that they raise a point of law. With some exceptions, for example, where oral hearings must be held, procedure in the migration courts follows the general procedure for administrative courts. In all asylum and immigration cases, the complainant has a right to legal assistance.

In the UK, a two-tier right of appeal in social insurance cases was established in 1911, almost exactly 100 years ago, while a one-tier right of appeal in social assistance cases was introduced two decades later in 1934. Until 1983, when the two systems were aligned, appeal rights in social assistance cases were considerably weaker than in social insurance cases. The separate tribunals for social insurance and social assistance cases eventually merged in 1998. On the other hand, there was no right of appeal in asylum and immigration cases until 1969, when a two-tier system was set up. The two-tier structure was abolished in 2004 when it was replaced by a single-tier tribunal. This indicates that, in the UK, rights of redress in asylum and immigration cases, like rights of redress in social assistance cases, have been less fully elaborated than in other policy areas that deal with persons deemed to be more 'deserving'.

4.4 Other Redress Mechanisms

There are several other types of redress mechanisms in Sweden. The Swedish Parliament, according to the Instrument of Government, has responsibility for supervising the administration of the state. To that end, it is the responsible authority for two agencies: the Parliamentary Ombudsman and the Swedish National Audit Office. The Government is also responsible for supervising and controlling the administration, although this responsibility is not specified in the Instrument of Government. The Chancellor of Justice is an important agency, with a clear link to redress mechanisms, for which the Government is responsible. One could also include the media among the redress mechanisms, strengthened by a strong, constitutionally guarded, principle of access to official records and various means of protecting whistle-blowers. In Sweden, the press is referred to as the third estate, not the fourth estate as is common in countries where the principle of division of power characterises the structure of government. In the areas of social security and immigration, the media have often played an important role by highlighting individual cases and investigating injustices, thus initiating debates with political impact.

The Parliamentary Ombudsman and the Office of the Chancellor of Justice are both responsible for supervising public authorities and public officials and can deal with claims for damages. The Parliamentary Ombudsman, created in 1809, reflects the ideas of a former constitution built on the principle of division of power. The Parliamentary Ombudsman, whom the Swedish Parliament appoints, receives approximately 6,000 complaints per year but can also act in a proactive way and initiate investigations. The Office of Chancellor of Justice can negotiate reconciliation between the state and citizens in cases where there are claims for damages. This is, however, not a necessary step since it is also possible to go directly to court. The number of claims for damages handled by the Chancellor of Justice has been stable in recent years and is now about 1,200 per year. A few of these go to court anyway, since reconciliation is not always possible. Courts handle a few cases of damages each year without a prior filing through the Office of the Chancellor of Justice.

The UK Parliament is responsible for the Parliamentary and Health Services Ombudsman (PHSO), which reports to the Public Administration Select Committee of the House of Commons, and the National Audit Office (NAO), which reports to the Public Accounts Select Committee. The Parliamentary Ombudsman investigates complaints against central government departments and a range of other public bodies which have not acted properly or fairly or have provided poor service. In addition, other ombudsmen investigate complaints against local authorities and many other public and private sector organisations. The NAO holds government departments and bodies to account for the way they use public money and, in this way, seeks to improve performance and service delivery. Although the UK media do, on occasion, take up individual cases and investigate injustices, their record is a mixed one.

In a report entitled *Citizen Redress* (Dunleavy et al. 2005), published by the National Audit Office (NAO), Patrick Dunleavy and his colleagues in the London School of Economics Public Policy Group described a system of complaint procedures and ombudsmen that exists alongside the system of tribunals described above, and criticised the confusion and overlap between these parallel systems. In the UK, complaint procedures and ombudsmen investigate alleged cases of maladministration that refer to the ways in which decisions were made, rather than the decisions themselves. However, where there is no statutory appeal against the outcome of an administrative decision, citizens, for want of an alternative, may submit a complaint about the way in which the decision was made. Although both systems may enable citizens successfully to challenge administrative decision-making, the effectiveness of appeals and complaints as a means of improving first-instance decision-making would appear to be rather limited.

5 INTERNAL MEANS OF ENHANCING ADMINISTRATIVE JUSTICE

5.1 Getting Things Right the First Time

The success rate for social security appeals that are resolved at a tribunal hearing is 34 per cent and for asylum and immigration appeals it is 42 per cent.[26] Although a successful outcome clearly benefits the individual appellant, there is little evidence in the UK that successful appeals have had a significant impact on the quality of first-instance administrative decision-making. In an early study of decision-making in social security (Baldwin et al. 1992: 85), 53 per cent of the adjudication officers who were interviewed claimed that, in making decisions, they were 'not at all influenced' by a tribunal's likely response to an appeal. This compared with 25 per cent of officers who claimed that tribunals had a procedural effect in that the prospect of an appeal led them to be more thorough and document their decisions more fully. This study was carried out almost 20 years ago but there is no reason to think that, if it were repeated today, the findings would be significantly different. However, one should note that the tribunals it refers to were all first-tier tribunals and that second-tier tribunals probably have a greater impact on first-instance decision makers. Nevertheless, as a means of enhancing the quality of first-instance decision-making, these findings indicate that tribunals are not particularly effective. There are a number of reasons for this.

In an attempt to understand the impact of judicial review on first-instance decision makers, Simon Halliday (2004) has argued that it must satisfy several conditions. Decision makers must be 'knowledgeable, conscientious and competent', the administrative agency they work for must give priority to compliance with the law over other considerations, and the law itself must be clear and consistent. As Halliday (ibid.: 168) pointed out, 'the extent to which these conditions are fulfilled will vary according to context'. However, it is probably unusual for all three conditions to be met simultaneously and this inevitably limits the effectiveness of judicial review as a check on routine administrative decision-making. Moreover, if this applies to the relatively few cases that are subject to judicial review, which get a fair amount of publicity, it must apply even more to the decisions of First-tier and Upper Tribunal hearings, which get considerably less.

In Sweden, the impact of court decisions on everyday decision-making in the social security administration, or rather its lack of impact, has been described as one of the defining features of social security law and welfare law (Westerhäll 1990: 23). One should add that constant changes in legislation and regulations are a hindrance to the emergence of a strong judicial impact on initial decision-making. On the other hand, Stendahl has argued that the high level of coherence in assessments in administrative courts and public authorities (and the low proportion of cases that are overturned on appeal in Sweden) could be interpreted as a strong indication that the administrative courts act more as superior bureaucratic decision makers than as courts in the traditional sense (2004: 401). This raises questions of whether administrative justice would best be served by strengthening

---

[26] Ministry of Justice, Quarterly statistics for the Tribunals Service (2nd quarter 2010–11), tables 1.2d and 1.2e, http://www.justice.gov.uk/publications/quart-stats-tribunals.htm.

the judicial character of the administrative courts (and thus making them more 'court like') or by acknowledging their special characteristics (and making them less 'court like'). Arguably, both are possible ways of strengthening the position of administrative courts to scrutinise the administration (Stendahl 2007).

In Nordic countries, the defining character of decision-making based on welfare state regulation involves the application of law by non-lawyers using non-traditional legal sources, where traditional legal institutions have a limited impact on decision-making and where the overarching aim is often described as 'social governing' rather than the more traditional legal role of conflict resolution. This situation has given rise to a rich literature on polycentric and polyvalent law (Gustafsson 2002), which highlights the heterogeneity and plurality of legal sources that one can see, not least in the practice of law at an administrative agency level.[27]

5.2   Feedback Mechanisms

In the UK, Martin Partington and Ed Kirton-Darling (2007) recently carried out a review of the effectiveness of different forms of feedback for bringing about improvements in first-instance decision-making. They point out that simply publishing selected decisions is unlikely to be effective and identify three mechanisms for communicating feedback: official reports,[28] direct communication with the initial decision maker; and 'informal' feedback to the administrative agency.

The annual reports by the President of Appeal Tribunals—which, until 2007, were responsible for hearing social security and child support appeals in the UK—on standards of decision-making, were usually ignored by the Department for Work and Pensions (DWP). The DWP takes National Audit Office reports more seriously because it is expected to give a formal response when the report is scrutinised by the Parliamentary Public Accounts Committee. However, since these reports are one-off reports, they do not constitute a very systematic way of holding government departments to account.

The attendance of the initial decision maker, or her line manager, at a tribunal or court is perhaps the most obvious method of ensuring that front-line decision makers receive feedback but, in the case of social security, this is now the exception rather than the rule.

Finally, informal feedback to the administrative agency, by means of written recommendations filtered through senior management, bulletins sent to first-instance decision makers, regular meetings and training are more likely to be effective, but they are not activities that tribunals, courts or the NAO are equipped to carry out. The establishment of the 'unified' Tribunals Service in 2007, hearing appeals on a wide range of subjects from a large number of administrative agencies,[29] will make it even more difficult for tribunals to provide feedback than was the case in the past. Before 2007, individual tribunals had

---

[27]   An overview of the relevant literature can be found in Gustafsson (2002) along with his own contributions to the topic. Other influential contributions in this field of legal theory have been made by Jorgen Dalberg-Larsen, Hanne Petersen and Henrik Zahle.

[28]   For example, the annual reports produced by tribunals and ombudsmen and the ad hoc reports produced by the National Audit Office (NAO) and Parliamentary Committees.

[29]   See section 4.2.

narrower remits and dealt with a smaller number of administrative agencies. Ombudsmen, on the other hand, are in a better position to do so.

All the evidence from the UK suggests that external redress mechanisms, that is, tribunals (where they exist),[30] courts, ombudsmen and audit have only played, and can only play, a minor role in ensuring that first-instance decision makers 'get it right first time'. It is for this reason that Mashaw, based on an analysis of the US Disability Insurance system,[31] argued that additional safeguards, such as internal quality controls and quality assurance systems, which can be put into place by management, are needed. Recruitment procedures, induction programmes, monitoring arrangements, appropriate training and appraisal systems are also important.

In Sweden, the Administrative Procedure Act (Förvaltningslagen) regulates the substantive procedure for decision-making by governmental agencies. It provides the legal basis for internal review, while the procedure used by administrative courts is regulated separately in the Administrative Court Procedure Act (Förvaltningsprocesslagen).

If we look at these issues from a Swedish perspective, the main impression is one of the strong place held by governmental agencies, whose position as experts in the field tends to be re-enforced by the administrative courts. It is difficult for individuals to successfully appeal against the state, even when they take their case all the way to court. Figures differ depending on type of case, but for cases involving the Swedish Social Insurance Agency, claimant success rates are 20 per cent, while comparable figures for the Swedish Migration Agency are 7 per cent.[32] These figures are, at least in social insurance cases, somewhat misleading as new information might have been added when the case reached the court and thus the decision made by the court may not have been based on the same facts as the original decision. Frequently, in cases where the courts decide in favour of the complainant, there is no longer a conflict between the insured person and the governmental agency (Stendahl 2004).

Although Mashaw suggests that different rationalities steer decision-making in courts and in administrative agencies (and that this helps to explain the weak impact of courts on everyday decisions by agency officials), one could argue that the Swedish Administrative Courts to a large extent follow the logic of bureaucratic decision-making (Stendahl 2004, 2007). Still, the organisation of, and the procedure in, administrative courts have steadily been changing in a direction that has made them more like general courts.[33] To the extent that Mashaw is right in distinguishing between the underlying rationale for legal and bureaucratic decision-making, we can anticipate growing tensions in the Swedish system

---

[30] There is no general right of appeal against an administrative decision to a tribunal in the UK. Although many administrative decisions can be appealed to a tribunal, many others cannot. In these cases, where the citizen is unhappy with the decision, she can complain to the government department or public body concerned and, if this does not produce a satisfactory outcome, can then submit a complaint to the relevant ombudsman. Alternatively, where there appears to be an error of law, she can raise an action of judicial review.

[31] See section 1.2.

[32] Försäkringskassan, Årsredovisning (2010), http://www.forsakringskassan.se/omfk/styrning_och_uppfoljning/arsredovisningar; Migrationsverket, Årsredovisning (2010), http://www.migrationsverket.se/info/205.html.

[33] See section 4.2.

of administrative decision-making. One could also question whether increased juridification will necessarily achieve more administrative justice for the individual.

5.3   Decision-making in Asylum and Immigration

In the UK, the Border Agency initially considers asylum claims.[34] The principal task for decision makers in the Agency is to make findings of fact that, in the circumstances, can be extremely difficult since it involves an assessment of *both* the general social and political situation in the country from which refuge is sought and the particular circumstances of an individual's case. The burden of proof is on the applicant who must convince the decision maker that there is a 'reasonable degree of likelihood' of persecution or ill-treatment on return.

Unlike some other administrative decision-making processes, there is no system of internal review of initial decisions in asylum cases. As the discussion of administrative justice makes clear, this weakens the bureaucratic mode of decision-making to the detriment of administrative justice as a whole. Unsuccessful claimants can appeal to the First-tier Tribunal[35] and around 70 per cent do so. Appeals are determined at oral hearings that most appellants attend. Although they may be represented, publicly funded representation is restricted.[36] However, the Home Office is almost always represented (Thomas 2011: 22).

Widespread critiques of the inferior quality of the UK Border Agency initial decision-making have usually been accompanied by calls to 'get it right first-time' and thereby avoid lengthy and costly appeal proceedings. In 2004, the National Audit Office found that pressure to meet processing targets, the complexity of some applications, and a lack of clear ownership of cases once they had passed on to the next stage led to many unnecessary appeals (ibid.: 52). Before 2005, the decision-making process involved numerous officials. One official would interview the claimant, another would make a decision on the claim, while, if the claim was turned down and the claimant appealed to a tribunal, a third official, known as a 'presenting officer', would appear before the tribunal. Because of the NAO's criticisms, the Home Office introduced the 'New Asylum Model' in 2005, under which a single 'case owner' should deal with every aspect of the application from beginning to end. Since 2007, all new asylum claims have been managed in this way.

In 2009, the Public Accounts Committee concluded that, although the Home Office had made some progress, it needed to do more to enhance the quality of its decision-making. It recommended a combination of internal measures (such as adoption of targets to increase the quality as well as the speed of initial decision-making) and external measures (such as better feedback from appeal tribunals to first-instance decision makers). However, there has been persistent criticism of the quality of asylum hearings. Those who think

---

[34]   See section 3.3.

[35]   Until early 2010, the single-tier Asylum and Immigration Tribunal (AIT) heard appeals. Now appeals go to the First-tier Tribunal Asylum and Immigration Chamber that forms part of the Tribunals Service, an executive agency of the Ministry of Justice. There is a further appeal on a point of law to the Asylum and Immigration Chamber of the Upper Tribunal.

[36]   To receive legal aid for representation in England and Wales, an appellant must be assessed as having a 50 per cent or greater chance of success. This test does not apply in Scotland.

that tribunals are characterised by 'a culture of disbelief' and those who think that they are characterised by 'a culture of abuse' (ibid.: 27) appear to agree that they are of poor or indifferent quality. In our view, what is needed is a genuine effort to 'get it right first time' and the rejection of a mindset that holds that this is unimportant because any errors can be corrected when the applicant appeals. A greater emphasis on information gathering, a genuine commitment to participation in decision-making, the encouragement of representation at this stage, more feedback to applicants and their representatives, an opportunity for them to correct findings of fact and the use of internal reviews would all help to improve first-instance administrative decision-making. Unfortunately, the financial situation in the UK and the swinging cuts in public expenditure do not augur well for such developments.

The complexity of the issues involved in determining applications for asylum and immigration raises the possibility that the quality of administrative decision-making could be enhanced if the law were to be simplified. The Home Office is committed to simplifying the legal framework by rewriting the Immigration Rules and the guidance given to officials and by overhauling the administrative processes and the associated technology used in decision-making.

The Swedish Migration Agency, at least since the reform in 2006 when it became possible to appeal against decisions made by the agency to the migration court,[37] has worked intensively to ensure that its internal procedures produce correct first-instance decisions. The Government has been active in this process through instruments such as annual appropriations directives and periodic ordinances, and the agency presents its results in published annual reports available on its website.

Keywords in the annual report from the Swedish Migration Agency for 2010 are 'efficiency' and 'quality'. A new 'lean-based' mode of working[38] is planned to be operational during 2011. The main aim is to decrease the time taken to process applications, but another aim is to increase the legal quality of decision-making. Working on legal quality, the agency has proposed five different criteria: well-argued decisions; correct handling of cases; formally correct decisions; time for administration; and overall quality of processing cases (Swedish Migration Agency 2010: 10). As part of its commitment to improving legal quality, it is observing the deliberations of the migration courts. The Agency's 2010 overview of legal quality was limited in scope and resulted in only minor criticisms (ibid.: 11).

Before one can appeal a decision to court, it is reviewed internally on the initiative of the individual concerned. In 2010, the agency reviewed its initial decisions in 32,682 cases, which led to 510 revised decisions. Almost half of the revised decisions concerned residence permits for students (ibid.: 64–5). Thus, about 1.5 per cent of decisions are changed through the process of internal reviews and fewer if student cases are excluded.

---

[37] See section 4.3.

[38] There is no clear definition of 'lean-based' working methods, either in general or in the context of the Swedish National Migration Board, but an implicit aim of introducing 'lean' might be summarised as an ambition to do more with less. In industry, an explicit aim of introducing 'lean' methods of production has been to reduce or eliminate activities that do not create a surplus. The reform of working methods was initiated in 2009 and financed by EU development funding. The aim is to decrease the time required to process applications from 203 days (in 2009) to 90 days. In 2010, the average time taken to process cases at the agency was 130 days.

There were 30,983 appeals to the migration courts in 2010, out of which, as noted above, the courts decided in favour of the individual in just 7 per cent of the cases. A consequence of introducing 'lean-based' working methods has been a decision by the agency to move the handling of appeals from special appeal units (created some years ago to increase legal quality) back to the units where first-instance decisions are made. The main achievement so far has been a shortening of processing times. Another change has been a decision to minimise communications with the courts, so that specific opinions concerning cases now only occur if the courts ask for them. According to the agency, none of these changes has had a negative effect on legal quality (ibid.: 64). The Swedish Bar Association and individual advocates have criticised these developments in the media by claiming that this strong emphasis on speedy procedures puts at risk the legal position of, in particular, individuals seeking asylum (Advokaten 2009; ETC 2011).

To the extent that the 2006 reform, which made it possible to appeal to the courts, was intended to strengthen a legal rationale in the processing of asylum and immigration cases at the expense of a bureaucratic rationale, this has not happened. As the figures reveal, a high level of consistency in assessments is evident and, in most cases, the courts uphold the original decision. Reporters, advocates and citizens, and sometimes the case law of the ECtHR have condemned this failure to improve the legal position of the individual asylum-seeker.

5.4   Decision-making in Social Security

Although the UK Government was committed to publishing an annual report on standards of decision-making in social security, the most recent report appeared in 2006 and only covered the period 2002–03. In this report, the Comptroller and Auditor General was unable to confirm that a substantial part of the information in it was 'fair and balanced' and concluded that the information in it was of 'limited utility as a measure of the Department's success in improving the accuracy of decision making' (House of Commons Work and Pensions Committee 2010).[39]

In his last annual report, the President of the Appeals Service, which heard appeals in social security cases until it was incorporated into the unitary Tribunals Service in 2007, stated that 'one is left with the striking impression that there has been no significant improvement in the quality of administrative decisions coming before appeal tribunals' (President of Appeals Service 2007–08). He claimed that, since his first report was published in 2001, several themes had recurred. These included:

- decisions were frequently overturned because the tribunal elicited additional information, usually by talking with the appellant at the hearing, suggesting that initial decision makers were deficient at establishing the facts of the case;
- there was no consistent evidence to show that cases were effectively reconsidered before coming to the tribunal; and
- medical reports often underestimated the severity of disability.

---

[39]   See, e.g., DWP 2009.

Simplification has been a major concern in social security and the Department for Work and Pensions has produced a series of plans[40] that were designed to reduce the administrative burdens on decision makers. These plans have involved several factors:

- aligning permitted work rules, capital limits and disregards;
- sharing information so that people notify the government just once about a change in circumstances, such as a birth, death or change of address;
- managing customer information across programmes rather than programme by programme;
- increasing the number of services that are offered online;
- developing information technology capabilities across the department in order to support improved service delivery;
- introducing a new online enquiry service that will allow customers to track their claims and payments online; and
- giving the Citizens Advice Bureau access, with the claimant's permission, to claimant data, which will enable them to instantly address benefit queries for their clients.

In late 2010, the Secretary of State for Work and Pensions announced the new Coalition Government's intention to simplify the benefits system by introducing a new streamlined Universal Credit in place of a range of existing benefits.[41] The problem with this is that, in spite of the attractiveness of its stated aims,[42] a single benefit awarded on the basis of a simplified set of entitlement criteria will inevitably result in a measure of 'rough justice' compared to the existing range of benefits, which are designed to reflect and respond to an assortment of underlying circumstances. One should sound the same cautionary note in response to the Government's stated intention to simplify the rules relating to asylum and immigration.

One can find information on the work done to increase the quality of decision-making in Swedish social insurance offices, as with activities of the Swedish Migration Agency, in government ordinances (*regleringsbrev*) and in the annual reports of the Swedish Social Insurance Agency.[43] In these ordinances, the Government declares what aims and activities the agency should prioritise. It also gives detailed instructions on how it should report on these aims. By law, the agency is free to determine how it should organise its work to fulfil these aims.[44] Present strategies for working with increased quality in decision-making

---

[40]   See, e.g., DWP 2009.

[41]   The Universal Credit will replace the Working Tax Credit, Child Tax Credit, Housing Benefit, Income Support, income-based Jobseeker's Allowance and the income-related Employment and Support Allowance.

[42]   The aims are improving work incentives through a combination of better earnings disregards or lower benefit withdrawal rates; smoothing the transition into and out of work; reducing in-work poverty; simplifying the system, making it easier for people to understand, and easier and cheaper for staff to administer; and cut back on fraud and error.

[43]   Both agencies have informative websites, although only part of the information is available in English.

[44]   See Försäkringskassan (note 32) (select Regleringsbrev, and Instruktion för Försäkringskassan).

have been in place for several years; for example, Qben II (discussed below) was intro-- duced in 2002.

The Swedish Government implemented a large reform in 2005 when it created a new social insurance agency. Before 2005, local insurance offices were independent private insurance funds, although they had actually been acting as public agencies for a long period. The aim of the 2005 reform was to fashion a more efficient organisation and more coherent application of the law. In this process, the expectation was that the organisation would move from one characterised by a culture of investigation to one characterised by a culture of results. Government oversight was intended to become more strategic and less detailed, using traditional Swedish instruments for governing: agency instruction, yearly ordinances, specific assignments and ongoing contacts (Statskontoret 2006).

An overarching self-declared aim for work within the Swedish Social Insurance Agency is to achieve 'quality in administration', a task that builds on three core values: simplicity, speed and making correct decisions (2010). The Agency measures the goal of 'simplicity' through customer surveys in which the public rate their trust in the agency and their satisfaction with its attempts to improve its public image. It links the goal of 'speed' to efficiency that can be measured, for example, by how much time each application takes to process. To measure the extent to which the goal of making correct decisions is achieved, two indicators are used: whether there is a sufficient basis for making the decision and whether the decision was the right one to make. Overall, the three aims—simplicity, speed and making correct decisions—should lead to increased quality in administration. In its annual reports, the agency gives an account of the three aims and details its success in achieving them (ibid.).

In 2010, speedy processing was put forward as the most important accomplishment of the agency (ibid.: 6). It was less successful in improving its image and customers were less satisfied in 2010 than in the previous year. The results for making correct decisions are collected using a method called Qben II, which indicated that, in 94 per cent of the cases, there was sufficient basis for making a decision, and in 99 per cent of these cases, a correct decision was made (ibid.: 32).[45] These figures for 2010 are similar to the figures from previous years (2007, 2009). That a decision is 'correct' according to these measures does not, however, mean that the courts would reach the same conclusions. Nor does it prevent inspectors from severely criticising the agency for its standards of decision-making, claiming that the agency is obscure, inconsistent and unevenly distributed over the country (ISF 2011).

Decisions of the Swedish Social Insurance Agency, like those of the Swedish Migration Agency, can be appealed to a local administrative court, but only after the insurance office has carried out an internal review. The first step in the procedure is to ask the agency to make a reassessment of its decision. These reassessments lead to a revised decision in 19 per cent of the cases, although the figure varies from 6.6 per cent to 28.3 per cent depending on the type of application dealt with at the insurance offices. As noted above, the local administrative courts revise social insurance office decisions in 20 per cent of cases. In the

---

[45]   Qben II is an information technology support system for continuous quality control that the Social Insurance Agency has used since 2002. The aim is to measure and follow the application of law and make sure that law is applied in a coherent and correct way.

Administrative Appeal Court (dominated by lawyers), decisions are revised in favour of the applicant in 16 per cent of cases. Social insurance offices frequently appeal against decisions that are revised in favour of an insured person in the local administrative court or to the administrative appeal court.

As in Britain, there is ongoing work to strengthen and improve web-based information, self-service and telephone support. Face-to-face service centres are popular, but expensive.

6   CONCLUSIONS

In the introduction to this chapter, we identified several important differences between the legal systems of Sweden and the UK and pointed out that our main aim was to determine whether these differences have significant implications for administrative justice in the two countries. We also stated that a secondary aim was to determine whether Sweden and the UK have anything to learn from each other and, if so, what that might be.

6.1   Significance of Differences between the Swedish and UK Legal Systems

Sweden has a written constitution while the UK does not

Although Sweden does have a written constitution, the main function of the Instrument of Government is to establish fundamental principles for government. In terms of providing a basis for legal arguments in courts, it is a weak legal source. It provides limited possibilities for subjecting administrative decisions to judicial scrutiny and arguably, individual rights receive more effective protection from the ECHR and European Court of Human Rights than they do from the Instrument of Government. Sweden does, however, provide for the possibility of judicial review if a regulation contradicts superior law in a way that is manifest. However, there is no constitutional court and the work of ensuring that new legislation does not come into conflict with either the constitution or the ECHR is primarily undertaken by review procedures prior to legislation. The Instrument of Government was specifically amended (with a new paragraph) to ensure that national legislation is consistent with the ECHR.

The UK does not have a written constitution and the grounds for judicial review are not defined in statute. However, as befits a legal system based on common law, judges have created those grounds in cases that have come before them. The powers of the courts, in routine cases of judicial review, are rather limited. They can only intervene if very strict tests of 'illegality, irrationality or procedural impropriety' are met. In cases that invoke the ECHR, they are restricted to issuing a 'declaration of incompatibility' stating that an Act of Parliament is incompatible with the ECHR, leaving it to Parliament to decide whether to amend the law. However, courts can invalidate administrative decisions if they are inconsistent with the Human Rights Act 1998, which incorporated the ECHR into UK law.

The Swedish Constitution does not recognise the separation of powers while the separation of powers is still a hotly contested issue in the UK

In Sweden, the Instrument of Government provides evidence of a strong commitment to popular and parliamentary sovereignty and does not provide any support for the separation of powers. Parliament is the main representative of the people and has the function of holding the Government and the administration to account. The two different court systems (the general courts and the administrative courts) secure the implementation of laws enacted by Parliament and to that end use preparatory work as a primary source for legal interpretation.

In the UK, in contrast to Sweden, the separation of powers is still a hotly contested issue. The courts vie with Parliament in seeking to control the exercise of political power. Government departments and other public bodies are accountable to parliamentary committees and to the courts while Parliament itself can be held to account in the courts. While so-called 'green light' theories, which place their trust in government and reject a strong role for the courts in scrutinising political and administrative decisions, would appear to be dominant in Sweden, the UK position reflects an uneasy compromise between 'green light' and 'red light' theories, which mistrust government and favour a strong role for the courts.

Sweden has a separate system of administrative courts while the UK does not

In Sweden, the existence of administrative courts with their own procedural rules, which differentiate them from the civil and criminal courts, creates a less formal and more accessible means of access to justice. There is a three-tier system, which matches the general court system, and cases are considered *de novo* in all instances (if given leave to appeal). The proceedings are, in principle, inquisitorial and judges have a responsibility actively to ensure that all the relevant facts and circumstances are at hand when they consider a case. In first and second instance courts, lay persons play an essential role in decision-making. Although increasingly contested by the ECtHR, most proceedings, even in local (first instance) administrative courts, are still paper hearings in which the parties, who, in general, have no right to legal aid or legal assistance, do not appear. In practice, administrative judges, who are specialists in administrative law, tend to make the same assessments as administrative agencies and relatively few cases are overturned in favour of the individual appellant.

In the UK, there is no separate system of administrative courts although the administrative division of the High Court, with judges who specialise in administrative law, does hear judicial review cases. Regardless, the overwhelming majority of appeals against administrative decisions are heard in specialised tribunals, which have their own procedural rules, are presided over by tribunal judges who have expertise in the relevant area of administrative law, and are more informal and 'user-friendly' than courts. These administrative tribunals are very similar to administrative courts in many other countries.

In Sweden, the state has traditionally been trusted to promote the well-being of the people while a more critical attitude has prevailed in the UK

In Sweden, the state is regarded as a 'good' state—a welfare state that promotes social rights, equality, prosperity and quality of life. This perception, which is attributable to the universality of the welfare state and the fact that everyone has a stake in it (Rothstein 1998), is widespread and appears to have survived changes in Government. Together with the strong commitment to parliamentary sovereignty, it helps to explain the relatively recent introduction of judicial appeal in Sweden and the continuing reluctance of the courts to question the legality of legislation and to challenge the decisions of administrative agencies.

In the UK, there is a much more ambivalent attitude to the state. Although some people certainly do place their trust in the state and some institutions—for example, the universal National Health Service enjoys the same sort of esteem as a wide range of welfare state institutions in Sweden—other people do not and criticise the state for its inefficiency on the one hand and its parsimony on the other. This may be because of its selectivity and because many people, in particular those in the middle classes, reject public provision and opt for private provision instead.

Sweden has a civil law system while the UK has a common law system
Codification of the law started in Sweden during the eighteenth century and preceded the codifications of most other European countries. However, Sweden did not create a civil code like the Code Civil in France or the Bürgerliches Gesetzbuch (BGB) in Germany. Statute law is very important, not least in the area of administrative law. Although the Instrument of Government is undoubtedly important, setting out the powers of central government, local councils and municipalities and the relations between Government and Parliament, it does not regulate the relations between the citizen and state very effectively. As a result, the European Convention on Human Rights and the European Court of Human Rights seem to have provided greater protection for the individual citizen than the Instrument of Government. The possibility of judicial appeal against administrative decisions was introduced relatively recently as the result of a series of adverse decisions of the ECtHR, which held that the absence of a right of appeal to a court constituted a violation of Article 6 of the ECHR.

In the field of administrative law, statute law is also very important in the UK. In fact, the common law here is significant only for judicial review, which is of a relatively minor consequence overall. Administrative tribunals, as statutory creations, undoubtedly provide a greater measure of protection for individual citizens than the availability of judicial review in the higher courts, however important the latter may be in establishing the limits of the law. The impact of the ECHR and the ECtHR on judicial review in the UK appears to have been relatively slight. However, this ignores the fact that many administrative agencies reviewed their practices and procedures to ensure that they were compatible with the ECHR and that the Government is now committed to producing a statement of compatibility with the ECHR for all bills presented to Parliament.

6.2 Implications of Differences for Administrative Justice

Some of the contextual differences between administrative law in Sweden and the UK are more significant for administrative justice than others. However, considered together, they would explain why Sweden appears to place a greater emphasis on what we have called a 'bureaucratic model of administrative justice', while the UK appears to place a greater emphasis on what we have called a 'legal model of administrative justice'.

It is difficult to draw clear and unequivocal inferences from the reversal rates associated with decisions that are appealed to administrative courts or tribunals. In Sweden, reversals in 20 per cent of appeals against Swedish Social Insurance Agency decisions and 7 per cent of appeals against Swedish Migration Agency decisions could either reflect the high quality of bureaucratic decision-making in the two agencies or the weakness of a contrasting legal model of decision-making in the administrative courts. In light of the evidence reviewed in this chapter, we suspect that a combination of both factors is responsible.

In the UK, by contrast, 34 per cent of the much higher proportion of social security decisions that are appealed and 42 per cent of asylum and immigration decisions are reversed on appeal. This could indicate that the quality of bureaucratic decision-making in the two agencies is poor or that legal decision-making in the tribunals is of high quality. As in Sweden, an explanation in terms of a combination of both factors is probably better.

It would appear that there is considerable effort in Sweden to ensure that the implementation of policies harmonises with the Government's intentions while rather less effort is made to safeguard the rights of individuals. In other words, a bureaucratic model of administrative justice is emphasised at the expense of a legal one, not only in administrative agencies but also in administrative courts. This has resulted in the challenges imposed on the Swedish system by the ECtHR.

The opposite would appear to be the case in the UK. It would appear that relatively little effort is made to ensure that first-instance decision-making is of high quality on the grounds that dissatisfied individuals can appeal to a tribunal. In other words, although a bureaucratic model of administrative justice is adopted in administrative agencies, it is prone to errors that can be corrected on appeal to a tribunal where a legal model of administrative justice is more in evidence.

There are some contrasting inter-sector differences in the two countries. In Sweden, the fact that internal review, which precedes appeal to the courts, resulted in amending 19 per cent of social insurance decisions but only 1.5 per cent of migration decisions suggests that there are some significant differences in the way in which these two types of cases are handled. In the UK, the fact that there is no system of internal review of initial decisions in asylum cases and there is little evidence that social security cases are effectively reconsidered before they are heard at a tribunal implies that this problem is endemic.[46]

As we made clear in the introduction, we adopt an *integrated approach to administrative justice* that recognises the merits in both the 'traditional administrative law approach' and the 'justice in administration approach' and seeks to combine them. The achievement of administrative justice is, thus, best served by a combination of internal and external safeguards. Both the UK and Sweden do so although the balance between the two approaches differs. In the UK, bureaucratic reasoning in administrative agencies is relatively poor, but its shortcomings are frequently corrected by legal reasoning in tribunals. In Sweden, bureaucratic reasoning in administrative agencies is probably better, although it is more difficult to correct its shortcomings because administrative courts adopt a similar mode of bureaucratic reasoning. As we adhere to a relativistic and pluralistic view of administrative justice, this would be fine if it were not for some remaining concerns.

A flaw in the UK system is that to the extent that individuals who are dissatisfied with the decision of an administrative agency do not appeal to a tribunal, and common sense would suggest that many people are in this position, administrative justice is not achieved for them. The problem is all the more serious because there is so little feedback and so

---

[46]   In February 2012, the UK Government issued a consultation on its plans to introduce mandatory reviews before cases are considered by a tribunal.

few opportunities for administrative agencies to learn from their mistakes. A flaw in the Swedish system is that individuals who are dissatisfied with the decision of an administrative agency and appeal to an administrative court are unlikely to be able to present their case in person. Their appeal is decided on the papers and administrative justice is not achieved for them either. Although the resulting decisions may appear to be correct, they may not accord with the individual's circumstances.

The evidence presented in this chapter suggests that, in both countries, the systems used to achieve administrative justice could be improved. If that is to be attained, Sweden, partly in response to the criticism of its procedures by the ECtHR, needs to acknowledge the advantages of applying a legal mindset in determining appeals from first-instance decisions that were made by applying a bureaucratic mindset to the individual's claim. The priority for the UK is to develop feedback mechanisms so that administrative agencies can learn from the cases heard by administrative tribunals and improve the standard of first-instance decision-making.

One final caveat. In both countries, it is important to point out that, if the substantive outcomes of the law do not meet the requirement of providing justice—that is, if the law itself is considered unjust, no procedural safeguards can make up for that.

REFERENCES

Adler, Michael (2003). 'A Socio-Legal Approach to Administrative Justice', 25 *Law and Policy* 323–52.

Adler, Michael (2006). 'Fairness in Context', 33 *Journal of Law and Society* 615–38.

Adler, Michael (2008). 'The Justice Implications of Activation Policy in the UK', in Sara Stendahl, Thomas Erhag and Stamatia Devetzi (eds), *A European Work-First Welfare State* 95–131. Gothenburg: University of Gothenburg Centre for European Research.

Adler, Michael (2009). 'Self-Representation, Just Outcomes and Fair Procedures in Tribunal Hearings: Some Inferences from Recently Completed Research'(paper presented to Senior President's Conference for Tribunal Judges, National Exhibition Centre, Birmingham, 20 May).

Administrative Justice and Tribunals Council (2010). *Principles for Administrative Justice* (London), http://www.justice.gov.uk/ajtc/publications/418.htm.

Advokaten (2009). 'Snabbare asylprocess kan försvaga rättssäkerheten', www.advokatsamfundet.se/Advokaten/Tidningsnummer/2009/Nr-8-2009-Argang-75 (select title under Nyheter).

Almqvist Roland (2004). *Icons of Public Management: Four Studies on Competition Contracts and Control* (School of Business research report 2004:1).

Baldwin, John, Nick Wikeley and Richard Young (1992). *Judging Social Security Claims: The Adjudication of Claims for Benefit in Britain*. Oxford: Clarendon Press.

Barker, Anthony (ed.) (1982). *Quangos in Britain: Government and the Networks of Public Policy-making*. Basingstoke: Macmillan.

Bell, John (2006). 'Comparative Administrative Law', in Mathias Reimann and Reinhard Zimmermann (eds), *The Oxford Handbook of Comparative Law* 1259–86. Oxford: Oxford University Press.

Bondy, Varda (2003). *The Impact of the Human Rights Act on Judicial Review: An Empirical Research Study*. London: Public Law Project.

Bondy, Varda and Maurice Sunkin (2009). *The Dynamics of Judicial Review Litigation: The Dynamics of Public Law Challenges before Final Hearing*. London: Public Law Project.

Brännström, Leila (2009). *Förrättsligande: En studie av risker och möjligheter med fokus på patientens ställning*. Malmö: Bokbox Förlag.

Bull, Thomas (2008). 'Lagprövningens många ansikten', in Sten Heckshcer and Anders Eka (eds), *Festskrift till Johan Hirschfeldt* 75–93. Uppsala: Iustus.

Bylander, Eric (2006). *Muntlighetsprincipen: En rättsvetenskaplig studie av processuella handläggningsformer i svensk rätt*. Uppsala: Iustus.

Cabinet Office (2002). *Civil Service Statistics 2001*. London: The Stationery Office.

Department for Work and Pensions (2009). *Simplification Plan 2009–2010*. London: DWP, http://www.dwp.gov.uk/docs/simplification-plan-dwp-2009.pdf.

Domstolsverket (2010). *Court Statistics: Official Statistics of Sweden 2010*. Stockholm: Sveriges Domstolar, http://www.domstol.se/Ladda-ner--bestall/Statistik.

Dunleavy, Patrick, Helen Margetts, Simon Bastow and Françoise Boucek (2005). *Citizen Redress: What Citizens Can Do if Things Go Wrong with Public Services* (National Audit Office 'Value for Money' Report, HC-21). London: The Stationery Office.

Efficiency Unit (1988). *Improving Management in Government: The Next Steps*. London: HMSO.

ETC (2011). 'Migrationsverkets kortar ned handläggningstider', http://www.etc.se/nyhet/migrationsver ket-kortar-ned-handl%C3%A4ggningstider.

Erhag, Thomas (2010). 'Country Report on Sweden', in Ulrich Becker, Danny Pieters, Friso Ross and Paul Schoukens (eds), *Security: A General Principle of Social Security Law in Europe* 481–514. Groningen: Europa Law Publishing.

Erlandsson, Magnus (2007). *Striderna i Rosenbad: om 30 års försök att förändra Regeringskansliet* (Dissertation). Stockholm: Stockholms Universitet.

Franks, Sir Oliver (1957). *Report of the Committee on Tribunals and Inquiries* (Cmnd. 218). London: HMSO.

Freud, David (2007). *Reducing Dependency, Increasing Opportunity: Options for the Future of Welfare to Work*. London: Department for Work and Pensions.

Gustafsson, Håkan (2002). *Rättens polyvalens: En rättsvetenskaplig studie av sociala rättigheter och rättssäkerhe* (Lund Studies in Sociology of Law no. 14). Lund: Lunds Universitet.

Halliday, Simon (2004). *Judicial Review and Compliance with Administrative Law*. Oxford: Hart Publishing.

Harlow, Carol and Richard Rawlings (2010). *Law and Administration*. Cambridge: Cambridge University Press, 3rd edn.

House of Commons Work and Pensions Committee (2010). *Decision Making and Appeals in the Benefits System* (HC 313). London: The Stationery Office.

Husa, Jaako, Kimmo Nuotio and Heikki Pihlajamäki (eds) (2007). *Nordic Law: Between Tradition and Dynamism*. Antwerp: Intersentia.

Inspektionen för Socialförsäkringen (ISF) (2011). *Försäkringskassans tillämpning av den nya sjukskrivningsprocessen, Huvudrapport* (Rapport 2011:4), Stockholm, http://www.inspsf.se/publikationer/isf-rapporter.

James, Oliver (2003). *The Executive Agency Revolution in Whitehall*. Houndmills, UK: Palgrave Macmillan.

Leggatt, Sir Andrew (2001). *Tribunals for Users: One System, One Service*. London: The Stationery Office.

Lipsky, Michael (1980). *Street-level Bureaucracy: Dilemmas of the Individual in Public Services*. New York: Russell Sage Foundation.

Lundmark, Kjell et al. (2009). *Sveriges statsskic: Fakta och perspektiv*. Malmö: Liber.

Mashaw, Jerry L. (1983). *Bureaucratic Justice: Managing Social Security Disability Claims*. New Haven: Yale University Press.

Mattson, Ingvar and Olof Petersson (eds) (2003). *Svensk författningspolitik*. Stockholm: SNS-Förlag.

Miller, David (1999). *Principles of Social Justice*. Cambridge, MA: Harvard University Press.

Ministry of Justice (2010). *Proposals for the Reform of Legal Aid in England and Wales* (Consultation Paper CP 12/10), http://www.justice.gov.uk (enter title in search).

Nergelius, Joakim (2006). 'Constitutional Law', in Michael Bogdan (ed.), *Swedish Law in the New Millennium* 65–88. Stockholm: Norstedts Juridik.

Nergelius, Joakim (2010). *Svensk statsrätt*. Lund: Studentlitteratur, 2nd edn.

Nozick, Robert (1974). *Anarchy, State and Utopia*. Oxford: Blackwell.

Parliamentary and Health Services Ombudsman (2009). *Principles of Good Administration* (London), http://www.ombudsman.org.uk (enter 13/1039 in search).

Partington, Martin and Ed Kirton-Darling (2007). *Research Issues Paper (1): Feedback*, http://www.council-on-tribunals.gov.uk/adjust/item/tribunals_research.pdf.

Petersson, Olof (2005). *Statsbyggnad: Den offentliga maktens organisation*. Stockholm: SNS, 5th edn.

Petersson, Olof (2006). *Kommunalpolitik*. Stockholm: Norstedts Juridik, 5th ed.

Petersson, Olof (2007). *Den offentliga makten*. Stockholm: SNS.

President of Appeals Service (2007–08). *Report on the Standards of Decision Making by the Secretary of State*. London: The Appeals Service.

Rawls, John (1971). *A Theory of Justice*. Cambridge, MA: Harvard University Press.

Regeringskansliet (1999). *The Administrative Procedure Act* (Stockholm: Ministry of Justice), http://www.sweden.gov.se/sb/d/574/a/27808.

Rothstein, Bo (1992). *Den korporativa staten: intresseorganisationer och statsförvaltning i svensk politik*. Stockholm: Norstedts Juridik.

Rothstein, Bo (1998). *Just Institutions Matter: The Moral and Political Logic of the Universal Welfare State*. Cambridge: Cambridge University Press.

Scottish Public Services Ombudsman (2009). *Annual Report 2008–2009* (Edinburgh), http://www.spso.org.uk (enter annual report in search).

Shapiro, Martin (2001). 'Administrative Law Unbounded', 8 *Indiana Journal of Global Studies* 369–77.

Statskontoret (2006). *Den nya försäkringskassan*, Delrapport 1, 2006:1.
Stendahl, Sara (2004). *Communicating Justice, Providing Legitimacy: The Legal Practises of Swedish Administrative Courts in Cases Regarding Sickness Cash Benefit*. Uppsala: Iustus Förlag.
Stendahl, Sara (2007). 'Att bedöma arbets(o)förmåga: Rättvisa och legitimitet i förvaltningsrättsliga beslutsprocesser', in Lotta Vahlne Westerhäll (ed.), *Legitimitetsfrågor inom socialrätten*. Stockholm: Norstedts Juridik.
Stendahl, Sara (2010). 'Arbetsförmedlingen och (hoppet om) byråkratisk rättvisa', 1–2 *Nordisk Socialrättslig Tidskrift* 49–83.
Swedish Migration Agency (2010). *Migrationsverkets årsredovisning 2010*, http://www.migrationsverket.se/info/205.html.
Swedish Social Insurance Agency (2010). *Försäkringskassans årsredovisning 2010*, http://www.forsakringskassan.se/omfk/styrning_och_uppfoljning/arsredovisningar.
Thomas, Robert (2010). *Administrative Justice and Asylum Appeals: A Study of Tribunal Adjudication*. Oxford: Hart Publishing.
Thomas, Robert (2011). *Administrative Justice and Asylum Appeals*. Oxford: Hart Publishing.
Van Aerschot, Paul (2011). 'Administrative Justice and the Implementation of Activation Legislation in Denmark, Finland and Sweden', 18 *Journal of Social Security Law* 31–55.
Walzer, Michael (1985). *Spheres of Justice: A Defence of Pluralism and Equality*. Oxford: Blackwell.
Warnling-Nerep, Wiweka et al. (2007). *Statsrättens grunder*. Stockholm: Norstedts Juridik.
Weir, Stuart and Wendy Hall (eds) (1994). *EGO-TRIP: Extra-governmental Organisations in the UK and their Accountability* (Democratic Audit Paper no. 2). Essex, UK: University of Essex Human Rights Centre and Scarman Trust Enterprises.
Westerhäll, Lotta (1990). *Den svenska socialrätten*. Stockholm: Norstedts Juridik.
Westerhäll, Lotta (2002). *Den starka statens fall*. Stockholm: Norstedts Juridik.

14 Constitutional law and courts
*Tom Ginsburg**

1 INTRODUCTION

The rise of constitutional courts and the expansion of constitutional jurisdiction is surely one of the most important legal developments of the last half century. It is a major factor driving the global judicialization of politics.[1] By their nature, constitutional courts deal with inherently political issues, and are highly visible institutions with the potential to shape social understandings and expectations. It is therefore no surprise that they have attracted great attention from political actors, publics and scholars.

Traditional legal theory has problematized constitutional review from a normative perspective. Much of this work has sought to resolve the so-called 'counter-majoritarian difficulty' in which unelected constitutional courts are thought to be anti-democratic because of their power to thwart the role of the majority. Socio-legal work, on the other hand, tends to proceed from a positivist perspective and has demonstrated the increasingly important role that constitutional law and courts play in many societies, including many new democracies. In this sense, it poses an empirical challenge to traditional legal theorizing because it has demonstrated that constitutionalization and democratization tend to proceed apace.

This chapter reviews the socio-legal literature on constitutional law and courts. It begins with a historical survey of the rise of constitutional review, followed by an analysis of the various theories that scholars have offered to explain why constitutional review is adopted. The chapter then examines the various and growing number of studies of the functioning of constitutional review and its role in society. It also discusses ancillary powers of constitutional courts, beyond constitutional review, which are assuming an increasing prominence in many societies, and thrust constitutional courts into the very center of the political arena. Throughout, it elaborates on the various methods used by scholars to understand constitutional law and courts.

* Leo Spitz Professor of Law, University of Chicago and Research Professor, American Bar Foundation. The author co-directs the Comparative Constitutions Project, an effort funded by the National Science Foundation to gather and analyze the constitutions of all independent nation-states since 1789. He is also co-series editor of the Elgar Research Handbooks in Comparative Law.
1 Neal C. Tate and Thorsten Vallinder, *The Global Expansion of Judicial Power* (New York: NYU Press 1995).

2 THE RISE OF CONSTITUTIONAL COURTS AND JUDICIAL REVIEW

2.1 The First Wave

Constitutional review is typically defined as the power of courts to strike down legislation and administrative action that is incompatible with the constitution. The institution was an innovation of the early American constitutional order, originating in state constitutions and subsequently adopted at the national level. It has spread around the world in several waves: a 19th-century first wave in which it had relatively limited effect, a second interwar continental variant that became popular after World War II, and a third wave corresponding to the third wave of democracy, accelerating after 1989. As Figure 14.1 demonstrates, constitutional review has become a norm of democratic constitution-making, displacing earlier notions of parliamentary sovereignty.

The story of constitutional review originates in the founding of the United States. Legal historians and normative legal scholars have expended much energy and newsprint on this period. A central question concerns the absence of textual basis in the United States Constitution for the practice of constitutional review at the national level. While conventional analysis tends to emphasize the innovations of John Marshall in *Marbury v. Madison*, several historians and legal scholars have done important work in elucidating the antecedents of judicial review in state law.[2] From a different angle, Mark Graber has challenged the view of *Marbury* as central; he takes a more gradualist political approach to constitutional review, arguing that it was not until the election of the more moderate Madison that Marshall could truly issue the key decisions empowering the Court.[3] Graber's account emphasizes context and long-term historical interactions among various branches in establishing the practice of review, rather than a single great case, and is an illustration of the approach known as historical institutionalism.

Outside the United States, the history of judicial review was limited. Norway's Supreme Court had the power but refrained from exercising it, and other European countries only experimented with it.[4] Several early constitutions in Latin America adopted the institution, though it was exercised sparingly in the 19th century.[5] The Latin Americans initially focused on habeas corpus type issues. In the common law tradition, habeas involves a claim that one's detention is not *legally* justified; but the Latin American constitutions

---

[2] Jack N. Rakove, *Original Meanings: Politics and Ideas in the Making of the Constitution* (New York: Vintage Books 1997); Sylvia Snowiss, *Judicial Review and the Law of the Constitution* (New Haven: Yale University Press 1990); William Michael Treanor, 'Judicial Review before Marbury', 58 *Stanford Law Review* 455–562 (2005).

[3] Mark A. Graber, 'The Problematic Establishment of Judicial Review', in Howard Gillman and Cornell Clayton (eds), *The Supreme Court in American Politics* 28–42 (Norman: University of Oklahoma Press 1999).

[4] Carsten Smith, *Judicial Review of Parliamentary Legislation: Norway as a European Pioneer* (Public Law 2000); Rune Slagstad, 'The Breakthrough of Judicial Review in the Norwegian System', in Rune Slagstad and Eivind Smith (eds), *Constitutional Justice under Old Constitutions* 81–111 (The Hague: Kluwer Law International 1995).

[5] See generally Keith Rosenn, 'Judicial Review in Latin America', 31 *Ohio State Law Journal* 785 (1974).

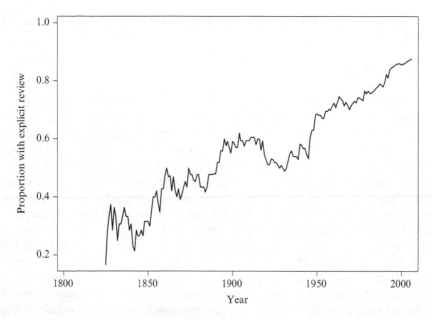

Figure 14.1   The spread of constitutional review, by year

provided a constitutional habeas right which became the basis of individual claims for constitutional protection. While initially restricted to claims of unlawful detention, Latin American jurists expanded the habeas right in creative ways. Brazilian jurists drew on a habeas right that originated in the code of criminal procedure to protect many other rights beyond physical liberty.[6] In one case, a Brazilian court used habeas corpus to annul legislative cancellation of a student's matriculation at a school.[7]

The Latin American focus tended to be on individual acts of government, and the effects of judicial review were *inter partes* rather than *ergo omnes*. The 1857 Constitution of Mexico introduced an institution called *amparo* that became an important mechanism for the protection of individual rights there, and spread to many other countries in the region.[8] Article 14 of the 1857 Mexican Constitution read: 'no one can be judged nor sentenced except by laws made prior to the facts, with the laws exactly applied to them, by the tribunal that had been previously established by law'. Litigants used the phrase 'exactly

---

[6]   Keith Rosenn, 'Procedural Protection of Constitutional Rights in Brazil', 59 *American Journal of Comparative Law* 1009–50 (2011).

[7]   Ibid. This broad use of habeas led to a significant increase in the number of suits, eventually motivating a 1926 constitutional amendment restricting the use of habeas to claims based on 'liberty of locomotion', which included traditional detention as well as some other grounds.

[8]   See Constitution of 1857, arts 101 and 102 (federal court jurisdiction); Richard D. Baker, *Judicial Review in Mexico: A Study of the Amparo Suit* (Austin: University of Texas Press 1971). On the contested origins of amparo, see Charles Hale, 'The Civil Law Tradition and Constitutionalism in Twentieth-Century Mexico: The Legacy of Emilio Rabasa', 18 *Law and History Review* 257–79 (2000). On amparo elsewhere in the region, see Alain Brewer-Carias, *The Constitutional Protection of Human Rights in Latin America: A Comparative Study of Amparo Proceedings* (New York: Cambridge University Press 2008).

applied' to allow for constitutional protection against misapplication of the law, and the amparo suit became a mechanism of appeal against decisions of lower courts.[9] To be sure, there were limitations on the exercise of amparo: courts could not strike the statute even if found unconstitutional, but could only correct its application in particular cases. It is not surprising that, until the emergence of democracy in the late 20th century, Latin American courts were hardly vigorous in using their powers of review; but the similarity in constitutional form nevertheless set the region apart from other parts of the world, as an early mover toward judicial protection of fundamental rights.[10]

2.2   The Second Wave

The second wave of judicial review began with the development of Hans Kelsen's model of constitutional review, originally embodied in the Austrian Constitution of 1920.[11] Kelsen's *Pure Theory of Law* insisted on the subservience of judges to the parliament, and thus could not tolerate any judicial role in constitutional interpretation. Instead, it featured a separate constitutional court, located outside the ordinary judiciary, whose only job was constitutional interpretation. The Austrian Constitutional Court was limited to deciding intergovernmental disputes and a handful of other polities adopted the form in the interwar period.

The model of a designated constitutional court became the basis of the post-World War II constitutional courts in Europe. These courts were initially established in Austria, Germany and Italy. Later, post-fascist Portugal and Spain adopted them as part of a general shift toward awareness of rights and natural law limitations on the power of legislatures.[12] The courts were embraced along with constitutions that had extensive rights provisions, and constitutional review became associated with protection of rights. Germany proved to be exceptionally fruitful soil for constitutional review, combining as it did a federal system with a post-fascist yearning for rights. Germany's Constitutional Court is arguably the most influential court outside the US in terms of its institutional structure and jurisprudence.[13]

Outside Europe, the wave of decolonization and constitutional reconstruction led other countries to adopt constitutional review. India's new democracy adopted a model of judicial review in which the Supreme Court had a carefully circumscribed power of review. Japan's American-drafted constitution also contained a provision for judicial review on the American example. In these and other cases, constitutional review spread to new democracies where rights traditions had been relatively underdeveloped.

---

[9]   Hale (note 8) 268.

[10]   Brewer-Carias (note 8).

[11]   Hans Kelsen, *The Pure Theory of Law* (Berkeley, CA: University of California Press 1967, Max Knight trans. from *Reine Rechtslehre*, 2nd edn, 1960).

[12]   Mauro Cappelletti, *The Judicial Process in Comparative Perspective* (Oxford: Clarendon Press 1989).

[13]   Bruce Ackerman, 'Judges as Founders', in *The Future of Liberal Revolution*, 101–04 (New Haven: Yale University Press 1992); Donald Kommers, *The Constitutional Jurisprudence of the Federal Republic of Germany* (Durham: Duke University Press, 2nd edn, 2001); Georg Vanberg, *The Politics of Constitutional Review in Germany* (New York: Cambridge University Press 2005).

France developed its own distinct form of constitutional review in the Fifth Republic.[14] President Charles De Gaulle (served 1959–1969) sought to limit the power of Parliament to constrain his scheme of executive lawmaking. Therefore, he created a new body, the *Conseil Constitutionnel,* which was empowered to conduct only pre-promulgation, abstract review of legislation. Fearing encroachment by the legislature on the executive, De Gaulle allowed the Conseil to hear challenges to 'unconstitutional' legislation only before it took effect. The orientation was less toward the protection of rights than toward the maintenance of divided and separated powers. Access to constitutional review was limited to the executive branch, leaders of the legislature, and certain other designated officials, and the institution was designed to constrain the legislature on behalf of the executive rather than on behalf of citizens directly. Gradually, however, the French Conseil was able to read the Declaration of the Rights of Man, incorporated into the preamble of the French Constitution, into a judicially enforceable set of rights, greatly expanding its bases of review. The other superior courts in the French system, the *Cour de Cassation* and the *Conseil d'Etat,* also played a role in rights protection, exercising a kind of judicial review through the backdoor but unable to strike legislation directly. With constitutional amendments in 2008 granting the *Conseil Constitutionnel* powers of prospective review for the first time, the French system has transformed itself into one with direct access to challenge legislation, and now bears closer similarity to its German counterpart.

2.3 The Third Wave

The third wave of democratization is conventionally understood to begin with the fall of the Iberian dictatorships in the 1970s, accelerating with the fall of the Berlin Wall in 1989. This wave corresponded with new constitution writing and led to the creation of a whole new set of constitutional courts. Indeed, every post-Soviet constitution has some provision for a designated constitutional court, save Estonia that adopted the American model.[15] Elsewhere, countries in Africa and Asia, from Mali to Korea, also created new courts or reinvigorated old ones. Many of these new constitutional courts took on central roles in their political systems.[16] The result is the current situation in which the vast majority of constitutions have some provision for judicial review, either by a designated constitutional court or by one or more ordinary courts. The overall shift has been in the direction of the Kelsenian model of a designated court, as demonstrated by Figure 14.2. Constitutional review also spread to countries that were less democratic and stable or had authoritarian political environments. While courts in such environments

---

[14] See generally Alec Stone, *The Birth of Judicial Politics in France: The Constitutional Council in Comparative Perspective* (New York: Oxford University Press 1992) Similar ex ante abstract review had been adopted in some Latin American countries. E.g., Constitution of Ecuador (1946) art. 67.

[15] Herman Schwartz, *The Struggle for Constitutional Justice in Post-Communist Europe* (Chicago: University of Chicago Press 2000); Shannon Ishiyama Smithey and John Ishiyama, 'Judicious Choices: Designing Courts in Post-Communist Politics', 33 *Communist and Post-Communist Studies* 166–82 (2000); Shannon Ishiyama Smithey and John Ishiyama, 'Judicial Activism in Post-Communist Politics,' 36 *Law and Society Review* 719–41 (2002).

[16] Andrew Harding and Penelope Nicholson, *New Courts in Asia* (New York: Routledge 2010).

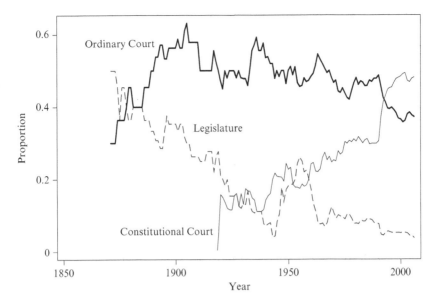

Figure 14.2   The rise of constitutional courts, by year[17]

were naturally more constrained, they were in some countries able to exercise a good deal of power.

One related development has been the spread of constitutional review in the countries of the former British Commonwealth. Britain is, of course, the motherland of parliamentary sovereignty. Nevertheless, in recent years, many previous British colonies have adopted novel forms of constitutional review.[18] One of the features that scholars have noted is that these new modes do not purport to place the courts above the legislature. For example, in Canada, the Charter of Rights and Freedoms is subject to judicial interpretation and enforcement, but provincial parliaments do have the power to pass legislation notwithstanding a judicial finding of unconstitutionality. Similarly, in New Zealand and the United Kingdom, parliament retains the last word, but a judicial finding of unconstitutionality is likely to have some political effect even if not legally dispositive.

Parliamentary sovereignty still has a formal foothold in the nominally socialist countries of China and Vietnam. However, even in these environments, there is talk of adopting constitutional courts, particularly in Vietnam. Constitutionalism, like democracy, has become so normatively desirable that even countries that do not practice it would like to pretend that they do.

---

[17]   This figure illustrates the proportion of constitutions, by year, with an explicit power of constitutional interpretation, with the actor empowered to engage in it. The study included a total of 404 constitutions.

[18]   Stephen Gardbaum, 'The New Commonwealth Model of Constitutional Review', 49 *American Journal of Comparative Law* 701–49 (2001).

3   EXPLAINING THE SPREAD OF CONSTITUTIONAL REVIEW

Some theories of the spread of constitutional review focus on cultural or ideational factors, while others emphasize institutional-functional explanations. The chief explanandum for most jurists is *rights consciousness*. The association of constitutional review with human rights was an important part of the spread of those rights to the postwar new democracies and the post-Soviet bloc countries in the third wave. A rights ideology, evident in advanced industrial economies since World War II and embodied in international human rights instruments, has spread globally. The extension of a rights culture and rights ideology, accompanied by support structures, leads to greater demand for constitutionalization.[19] The long association of courts with protecting individual rights has made judicial review the institution of choice to guard these crucial interests.

Besides the 'rights' hypothesis, Martin Shapiro discusses what he calls the 'rule of law' theory, suggesting that judicial review will flourish in countries with stronger allegiances to judicial neutrality.[20] Judicial review is more likely in cultures where judges are associated with the liberal ideal of limited government, especially former English colonies that had traditions of some judicial independence, even under non-democratic regimes. Indeed, in post-apartheid South Africa, the Constitutional Court was entrusted with authority to approve the draft Final Constitution, and its initial rejection of the draft did not provoke significant negative reaction. Nevertheless, while the rule of law hypothesis seems plausible when thinking about the founding case of the United States and its common law relatives such as Australia, it does not seem to be wholly adequate to account for the adoption of constitutional review in many other countries after World War II.

However powerful the role of rights may be in creating demands for judicial review, rights ideology alone simply cannot explain the patterns of institutional diffusion that we observe. The rights hypothesis is a demand-side theory that posits judicial review as an institutional response to social forces. There are, however, evidentiary problems with this account. It is difficult to assess the level of demand for 'rights' across countries. Furthermore, courts play an important role in generating demand for rights through their decisions. Disentangling demand from judicial supply of rights is difficult.

Demand side theories also tend to be underspecified. They account neither for variation in institutional design of constitutional review, nor for the different levels of activism that various courts engage in. They have trouble dealing with forms of constitutional review, such as the French example, in which individuals do not have access to make claims about rights-protections. In addition, they cannot explain the particular timing of the adoption of constitutional review.[21]

To examine variation in form and substance as well as the timing of the adoption of constitutional review, scholars in recent years have turned to functionalist-institutionalist

---

[19]   On support structures, see Charles Epp, *The Rights Revolution: Lawyers, Activists and Supreme Courts in Comparative Perspective* (Chicago: University of Chicago Press 1998).

[20]   Martin M. Shapiro, 'The Success of Judicial Review', in Sally J. Kenney, William M. Reisinger and John C. Reitz (eds), *Constitutional Dialogues in Comparative Perspective* 193–219 (London: Macmillan 1999).

[21]   Ran Hirschl, 'The Political Origins of Judicial Empowerment through Constitutionalization: Lessons from Four Constitutional Revolutions', 25 *Law and Social Inquiry* 91, 99–100 (2000).

approaches. A recent set of theories roots constitutional review in *domestic* political logics, which in turn suggests more theoretical payoff in terms of explanatory power to account for variation.

One set of theories originates in Mark Ramseyer's account of judicial independence.[22] Tom Ginsburg argues further that judicial review is a solution to the problem of political uncertainty at the time of constitutional design. Parties that believe they will be out of power in the future are likely to prefer constitutional review by an independent court, because the court provides an alternative forum for challenging government action. Constitutional review is a form of political *insurance* that mitigates the risk of electoral loss. On the other hand, stronger political parties will have less of a desire for independent judicial review, since they believe they will be able to advance their interests in the post-constitutional legislature. Ginsburg provides some large-sample and case study evidence for this proposition that the design and functioning of courts reflects political insurance and thus relates to features in the party system.[23]

Ran Hirschl offers a complementary political account of judicialization that he calls *hegemonic preservation*. His view is that judicialization, including establishment of constitutional review, is a strategy adopted by elites that foresee themselves losing power. In the final stages of their rule, it makes sense to set up courts to preserve the bargains embodied in legislation and constitutionalized rights. Hirschl's account has the great strength of shedding light on the *timing* of the adoption of review and also fits the classic understanding of the American experience establishing judicial review, in which the Federalists spent the months after losing the 1800 election putting their supporters into the courts. Hirschl extends the account to judicialization in other common law jurisdictions, including Canada, Israel, New Zealand and South Africa. Mexico's empowerment of its Supreme Court in the waning years of rule by the Institutional Revolutionary Party (PRI) may also make sense as a case of hegemonic preservation, and certainly fits the insurance model.[24]

Hirschl and Ginsburg's theories both rely on intertemporal electoral uncertainty as the primary theoretical driver for the adoption of constitutional review. Hirschl's hegemonic preservation seems to make strong assumptions about the information available to elites; but it has the virtue of accounting for situations where a declining power adopts the institution that then ends up hastening the party's demise. Ginsburg's insurance model is broader, as it can account for the support for the establishment of constitutional review by new, non-hegemonic, political parties (as in Eastern Europe) when they think they may not win the post-constitutional election. Both, however, are political theories that are not

---

[22]   J. Mark Ramseyer, 'The Puzzling (In)Dependence of Courts: A Comparative Approach', 23 *The Journal of Legal Studies* 721–47 (1994).

[23]   See also Rebecca Chavez, *The Rule of Law in Nascent Democracies: Judicial Politics in Argentina* (Stanford, CA: Stanford University Press 2004); Matthew Stephenson, 'When the Devil Turns . . .: The Political Foundations of Independent Judicial Review', 32 *Journal of Legal Studies* 59–81 (2003).

[24]   Jodi Finkel, *Judicial Reform as Political Insurance: Argentina, Peru and Mexico in the 1990s* (South Bend, IN: University of Notre Dame Press 2008); Beatriz Magaloni, 'Autocratic Political Order and the Role of Courts: The Case of Mexico', in Tom Ginsburg and Tamir Moustafa (eds), *Rule by Law: The Politics of Courts in Authoritarian Regimes* (New York: Cambridge University Press 2008).

purely functional in character, but consider the party system and the 'political vectors' of establishing review.[25]

These political theories also link with the literature on democratization. Declining hegemons and electoral uncertainty are crucial for the democratization dynamic. While the focus of the new political accounts of judicial review is on domestic politics, they suggest that a primary cause for the spread of the institution is the international spread of democracy. Democracy not only reinforces constitutional review, but the latter reciprocates to reinforce democracy.

In general, the dominant counter-majoritarian paradigm has been supplemented in recent years through work elucidating the majoritarian political functions of courts.[26] Keith Whittington discusses judicial activism by a court relatively friendly to the political branches and notes that courts can help overcome obstacles to direct political action. The entrenchment function emphasized by Ginsburg and Hirschl, in other words, is not the only role for courts. This suggestion has not been adequately assimilated in comparative work.[27]

Another strand of functionalist theories focused on federalism, which made sense in the American context in which the Supreme Court served as an instrument for the expansion of national power for its first several decades.[28] There are two basic complementarities between federalism and judicial review. First, whenever there are two lawmaking bodies or levels with different lawmaking jurisdictions, there is the potential for conflicts over jurisdiction, and the corresponding need for a neutral third body to resolve these disputes as they arise. Second, in a free trade system with multiple lawmakers, states face a collective action problem with regard to their own legislative powers. There is the threat that each state will put up protectionist barriers. If every state does so, then trade will not be free at all. States thus have a problem committing to a free trade system on their own. A written constitution with a neutral body in the form of a court that can evaluate state legislation can help make states' commitments to free-trade federalism more credible.[29] Indeed, the early history of the United States Supreme Court illustrates this logic, focusing as it did on consolidating national power.

The political theories do not fully explain the adoption of constitutional review functions in authoritarian regimes. Yet we do observe the use of constitutional review in dictatorships as well as democracies. For example, Iran's Council of Guardians exercises review for Islamicity and has served to constrain the democratically elected political institutions in the Islamic Republic. This draws on long religious traditions of Islamic constraint on

---

[25]   Hirschl (note 21) 91–5.

[26]   Keith Whittington, 'Interpose Your Friendly Hand: Political Supports for the Exercise of Judicial Review by the United States Supreme Court', 99 *American Political Science Review* 583–96 (2005).

[27]   But see Menachem Hofnung and Yoav Dotan, 'Legal Defeats—Politics Wins: Why Do Elected Representatives Go to Court?' 38 *Comparative Political Studies* 75–103 (2005).

[28]   Rakove (note 2); Bruce Ackerman, 'The Rise of World Constitutionalism', 83 *Virginia Law Review* 771–97 (1997); Martin Shapiro, 'Federalism, the Race to the Bottom, and the Regulation-Averse Entrepreneur', in Harry Scheiber (ed.), *North American and Comparative Federalism* 47–65 (Berkeley, CA: Institute of Governmental Studies Press 1992); Shapiro (note 20).

[29]   Yingyi Qian and Barry Weingast, 'Federalism as a Commitment to Preserving Market Incentives', 11 *Journal of Economic Perspectives* 83–92 (1997).

the state, but with the twist that it now serves to preserve a particular faction and illiberal elements of the regime used it to maintain control.[30] The basic idea of using the courts to limit a competing faction because of political uncertainty seems to fit this case, but electoral markets are not part of the story.

Another account of constitutional review in an authoritarian context is Robert Barros's work on Chile under the General Augusto Pinochet dictatorship (1973–90).[31] He argues that the junta was not a unitary actor, and faced a need for internal coordination among the different branches of the military. The new constitutional court set up under Pinochet effectively played this coordination role. This account resonates with much of the division of powers argument, illustrated by the federal cases and Fifth Republic France, but also suggests an interesting extension: even informal divisions of power in an oligarchy can generate a role for constitutional review.

In short, law and society scholars, mainly working in the political science tradition, have made significant progress in theorizing about the adoption of constitutional review. As the next section demonstrates, we also have a good number of studies that emphasize the performance of constitutional courts in various environments. These include efforts to understand judicial decision-making as well as efforts to examine success, namely why some constitutional courts fail and others succeed.

4   MEASURING PERFORMANCE

Beyond the question of *why* judges are empowered, there is a burgeoning literature on *how* constitutional courts operate in various environments. No court is more studied than the Supreme Court of the United States, but even with regard to this central case there is a very active debate concerning whether the Court is 'powerful'. Some argue that the Court's most noticeable cases did not in fact contribute to social change.[32] Others assert that courts exercise more subtle forms of power that one cannot measure simply by looking at compliance. Instead, courts shape the language and strategies of social struggles, operating at a deeper cultural level.[33] These different approaches to the Court's influence illustrate the variety of methods in law and society scholarship.

Comparative work on variations in performance is hampered by lack of a common metric of judicial power. While courts may look alike, each is embedded in a particular institutional environment. Evaluating failure is relatively easy, for there is typically evidence of a conflict between courts and other branches of government; but examining

---

[30]   Hootan Shambayati, 'A Tale of Two Mayors: Courts and Politics in Turkey and Iran', 36 *International Journal of Middle East Studies* 253 (2004).

[31]   Robert Barros, 'Dictatorship and the Rule of Law: Rules and Military Power in Pinochet's Chile', in José María Maravall and Adam Przeworski (eds), *Democracy and the Rule of Law* 188 (New York: Cambridge University Press 2003).

[32]   Michael D. Klarman, *From Jim Crow to Civil Rights: The Supreme Court and the Struggle for Racial Equality* (Princeton, NJ: Princeton University Press 2004); Gerald Rosenberg, *The Hollow Hope: Can Courts Bring About Social Change* (Chicago: University of Chicago Press 1991).

[33]   Michael McCann, *Rights at Work: Pay Equity Reform and the Politics of Legal Mobilization* (Chicago: University of Chicago Press 1994).

success is harder conceptually. Overall, the variables of number and importance of cases, and compliance with decisions, do seem to be indicia of judicial power. Nevertheless, a very powerful court may decide relatively few cases because legislators already accommodate its preferences. Furthermore, a court with very broad standing rules might have a large volume of cases, but a relatively small number of valid claims, so it may have a lower rate of striking legislation. One cannot therefore rely on simple strike rates as a metric of success or power.[34]

One approach is to rely on longitudinal variation. Alexei Trochev uses a variety of methods to trace the performance of three different Russian constitutional adjudication institutions over two decades. His analysis suggests that the tumultuous political environment in Russia has generally limited courts and led to the disbanding of the first Constitutional Court in 1994. However, the reincarnation of the court a year later suggests that it is playing some legitimating role for the regime, and indeed, it does have some impact in shaping the law. Trochev's nuanced account shows how the court did play a role in Russian politics, against somewhat long odds.[35]

Another important longitudinal study is that of Elisabeth Hilbink's account of Chile, in which she focuses on ideational factors and an institutional history that fetishized 'apoliticism'.[36] She begins historically with the introduction of positivism into Chile in the 19th century. Positivism emphasized fidelity to law along with an orientation toward elite state-building projects over democratic participation. Positivism conceptualized courts essentially as government agents whose job was to bolster a strong executive and avoid 'politics'. The problem was that politics was defined in a distinctive way. It was interpreted as anything that challenged state authority; thus, challenge was 'political' and hence anathema. Hilbink persuasively demonstrates that the nominal apoliticism of the courts was not genuinely apolitical, but rather that there was a one-way bias. The Chilean judges historically engaged in 'actively defending conservative values and interests but reverting to positivist and even formalist reasoning in cases involving defendants of the ideological Left'.[37] This gave them a certain amount of autonomy, even during Pinochet's dictatorship. While Pinochet retained rules allowing constraint of government action, including writ of amparo actions and new constitutional remedies, the courts did little with these tools and retained the same conservative approach after the return to democracy.

Hilbink rejects the role of positivism per se in producing this type of judicial ideology, and rejects other alternative explanations, including the personal policy preferences of the judges, class bias, or regime-related factors. Instead, she argues that the institutional structure and ideology of the judiciary are the crucial explanatory factors. Chile's courts were hierarchically organized in a bureaucratic structure, like other civil law judiciaries, in which the Supreme Court played a policing role. Hilbink equally emphasizes ideational

---

[34]   Cf. Erik Herron and Kirk Randazzo, 'The Relationship between Independence and Judicial Review in Post-Communist Courts,' 65 *Journal of Politics* 422–38 (2003).

[35]   Alexei Trochev, *Judging Russia: Constitutional Court in Russian Politics, 1990–2006* (Cambridge: Cambridge University Press 2008).

[36]   Elisabeth C. Hilbink, 'An Exception to Chilean Exceptionalism? The Historical Role of Chile's Judiciary' in Susan Eva Eckstein and Timothy Wickham-Crowley (eds), *The Politics of Injustice in Latin America* (Berkeley: University of California Press 2002).

[37]   Ibid. 77.

factors, including the role-conception of judges and the contextually defined notion of 'apoliticism'. This study demonstrates the power of an extended institutional analysis of a single country across time. It also demonstrates the merit of examining a case in which the proverbial dog did not bark: Chile's courts seemed to have the institutional resources and skill to play a more active role, but failed to do so.

David Law's qualitative study of the Japanese Supreme Court also reflects this approach to judicial non-activism.[38] He interviewed justices of the Japanese Supreme Court to elucidate the institutional factors that keep what is ostensibly a powerful court from intervening much in political life. He also emphasized the institutional structures that essentially limit selection to candidates who are ideologically reliable, and produce incentives to toe the line. Both Law and Hilbink do an important service in probing deeply into the self-understanding of courts. Both focus squarely on the supply side of the constitutional equation, rather than demand side variables like rights consciousness.

Beyond evaluating the exercise of judicial power, there is the question of what drives constitutional court decision-making within the court. In the American context, many scholars utilize the attitudinal model to study the Supreme Court.[39] Attitudinalism assumes that judges will vote in ways that reflect their political orientation, usually as captured by the identity of the person who appointed them. This is a somewhat problematic method for comparative work because it depends on coding separate opinions of individual judges and linking them to their appointing authorities. Because of variations in procedures for appointing judges to constitutional courts and the fact that many courts issue single 'consensus' opinions, rather than signed majority opinions and dissents, the attitudinal model has not been frequently employed as a basis for comparative research.

However, we now have several new studies that are using voting behavior to understand judicial decision-making in various comparative contexts. Nuno Garoupa, working alone and with various co-authors, has been a central figure, developing new data sets on various constitutional courts and testing the attitudinal hypotheses developed in the American context.[40] In one study, he and his co-authors find evidence of partisan voting in Portugal, with the right wing voting in favor of constitutionality more than those judges appointed by the left wing.[41] In the case of Taiwan, however, there was little evidence of partisan

---

[38] David S. Law, 'The Anatomy of a Conservative Court: Judicial Review in Japan', 87 *Texas Law Review* 1545 (2009). See Tom Ginsburg and Tokujin Matsudaira, 'The Judicialization of Japanese Politics?', in Björn Dressel (ed.), *The Judicialization of Politics in Asia* ch. 2 (New York: Routledge 2012).

[39] Lee Epstein and Jack Knight, *The Choices Justices Make* (Washington, DC: Congressional Quarterly Inc. 1998); Thomas G. Hansford and James F. Springgs II, *The Politics of Precedent on the US Supreme Court* (Princeton: Princeton University Press 2006); Jeffrey A. Segal and Harold J. Spaeth, *The Supreme Court and the Attitudinal Model Revisited* (New York: Cambridge University Press 2002); Saul Brenner and Harold J. Spaeth, 'Ideological Position as a Variable in the Authoring of Dissenting Opinions on the Warren and Burger Courts', 16 *American Politics Quarterly* 317–28 (1988); Jeffrey A. Segal and Albert D. Cover, 'Ideological Values and the Votes of U.S. Supreme Court Justices', 83 *American Political Science Review* 557–65 (1989).

[40] Nuno Garoupa, 'Empirical Legal Studies and Constitutional Courts', 4 *Indian Journal of Constitutional Law* 3 (2010).

[41] Sofia Amaral-Garcia, Nuno Garoupa and Veronica Grembi, 'Judicial Independence and Party Politics in the Kelsenian Constitutional Courts: The Case of Portugal', 6 *Journal of Empirical Legal Studies* 381 (2009).

judging.[42] Instead, Garoupa and his co-authors argue that the constitutional judges focused on institutional interests. Needing to gain credibility in a political transition from a one-party political regime to democracy, the Taiwanese Grand Justices asserted their independence from the other branches of government and, both collectively and individually, voted against the interests of the dominant party more than a simple attitudinal model would predict. Similarly, Garoupa and his collaborators find that a mix of partisan and institutional approaches best explain voting on the Spanish Constitutional Court rather than a simple confirmation of the attitudinal hypothesis.[43] Regional factors seem to play an important role in Spanish voting patterns.

Another recent study tests the correlation between the party affiliation of the pivotal judge and opposition success before the German Constitutional Court.[44] It finds that there is a positive correlation and concludes that partisan interests do play a role in constitutional court voting. In short, there is some confirmation in the comparative literature for the attitudinal hypothesis.

Even the French *Conseil Constitutionnel*, which does not publish separate opinions or reveal votes, has been subject to empirical study. Raphael Franck studied 526 decisions of the Conseil to identify the determinants of a decision for unconstitutionality.[45] The study finds that a more divided polity (in the period 1997 to 2002, while 'cohabitation' took place) increases the likelihood of an unconstitutionality finding. Nadia Fiorino and colleagues look at institutional factors and find that the share of constitutional judges elected by the magistracy and the age of the court president are significant predictors of votes of unconstitutionality on the Italian Constitutional Court.[46]

In short, a growing set of studies uses voting data to understand the behavior of courts. The weight of these studies is in line with the US literature, which has modified the attitudinal model to take into account institutional as well as partisan factors. Whether explicitly or implicitly utilized, the strategic model underpins these accounts.[47] The core insight of the strategic model is that courts can make law, but are constrained by other

---

[42]   Nuno Garoupa, Veronica Grembi and Shirley Ching-ping Lin, 'Explaining Constitutional Review in New Democracies: The Case of Taiwan', 20 *Pacific Rim Law & Policy Journal* 1 (2011).

[43]   Nuno Garoupa, Fernando Gomez-Pomar and Veronica Grembi, 'Judging under Political Pressure: An Empirical Analysis of Constitutional Review Voting in the Spanish Constitutional Court', 29 *Journal of Law, Economics and Organization* (forthcoming 2013); see Pedro C. Magalhães, 'Judicial Decision-Making in the Iberian Constitutional Courts: Policy Preferences and Institutional Constraints' (Ph.D. dissertation, Ohio State University 2002).

[44]   Christoph Hönnige, 'The Electoral Connection: How the Pivotal Judge Affects Oppositional Success at European Constitutional Courts', 32 *West European Politics* 963–84 (2009).

[45]   Raphael Franck, 'Judicial Independence under a Divided Polity: A Study of the Rulings of the French Constitutional Court', 25 *Journal of Law, Economics and Organization* 262–84 (2009).

[46]   Nadia Fiorino, Fabio Padovano and Grazia Sgarra, 'The Determinants of Judicial Independence: Evidence from the Italian Constitutional Court (1956–2002)', 163 *Journal of Institutional and Theoretical Economics* 683–705 (2007); see Fabio Padovano, 'The Time-Varying Independence of Italian Peak Judicial Institutions', 20 *Constitutional Political Economy* 230–50 (2009).

[47]   Tom Ginsburg, *Judicial Review in New Democracies: Constitutional Courts in Asian Cases* (New York: Cambridge University Press 2003); Vanberg (note 13); Lee Epstein, Jack Knight and Olga Shvetsova, 'The Role of Constitutional Courts in the Establishment and Maintenance of Democratic Systems of Government', 35 *Law & Society Review* 117–64 (2001).

actors in the political system. This work originated in the context of 'dynamic' statutory interpretation in the United States.[48]

Much recent work draws on this insight to elucidate the conditions under which courts can succeed or fail. One observation has been that judicial power expands as political fragmentation increases. As the discussion of waves of judicial review illustrated, several accounts of the emergence of judicial review are built on the fragmentation of power vertically (as in federalist polities) or horizontally (as in presidential systems like the United States and France). Political fragmentation creates the potential for conflict among different institutions and therefore the demand for a third party to resolve disputes. Fragmentation also creates the potential for political gridlock as institutional veto players make it difficult to shift policies from the status quo. In turn, this expands the space for judicial policymaking. When the political system cannot deliver policies because of gridlock, those who seek to advance particular interests will turn to the courts to obtain those policies. Constitutional review is a particularly entrenched form of judicial policymaking that one or more courts may utilize when ordinary political processes fail to deliver.

The French experience illustrates this dynamic. In 1983, when the socialists took over in France, the *Conseil Constitutionnel*, whose original role had been to buffer the executive, turned into a brake on the political program of the socialists. Fractionalization of politics opens up strategic space for the court to operate in.

The strategic perspective implies some constraints on constitutional decision-making, as the other political actors retain means of punishing courts, reducing jurisdiction, budget and powers. Consistent with this framework, Erik Herron and Kirk Randazzo find that presidential power is negatively associated with judicial review for the intuitive reason that concentrated executive power facilitates punishment of wayward courts.[49] Matías Iaryczower and colleagues show that in Argentina, antigovernment decisions rise during periods of divided government in part because leaders have less ability to sanction courts.[50]

The strategic account has mainly focused on the interaction between constitutional courts, legislatures and government. This is because the original model motivating the account emphasized over-ruling by legislative veto players. Further research is needed into the interactions between constitutional courts, interest groups and national publics, along with further theoretical refinement of effective strategies by courts. Georg Vanberg's account of Germany emphasizes the importance of public support and transparency as crucial factors in a game of executive-judicial relations.[51] Public support can insulate a constitutional court from criticism and counter-attack.

Public support for constitutional review depends not just on structural factors, such as access to the court, but on a substantive ideology of rights. A public that demands rights protection will avail itself of a constitutional court more than a public that does not care

---

[48]   William N. Eskridge, Jr., *Dynamic Statutory Interpretation* (Cambridge: Harvard University Press 1994); John A. Ferejohn and Barry R. Weingast, 'A Positive Theory of Statutory Interpretation', 12 *International Review of Law and Economics* 263–79 (1992).

[49]   Herron and Randazzo (note 34).

[50]   Matías Iaryczower, Pablo T. Spiller and Mariano Tommasi, 'Judicial Independence in Unstable Environments: Argentina 1935–1998', 46 *American Journal of Political Science* 699–716 (2002).

[51]   Vanberg (note 13).

about rights. Thus, a rights framework, while it cannot explain the adoption of constitutional review on its own, does have some power to account for the operation of particular courts and its acceptance by the public. Many a court has sought to legitimate itself through delivery of rights-enhancing decisions. For example, Pablo Rueda demonstrates that the Colombian Constitutional Court deployed changes in legal language to expand fundamental social and economic rights in the 1990s.[52]

Strategic accounts imply, though do not always directly address, the role that courts have in shaping their operating environment. Courts can use their interpretative powers to expand, or contract, their own sphere of operation, and thus contribute to their own empowerment. For example, the Indian Supreme Court transformed the original constitutional scheme greatly to expand its power.[53] The constitutional courts in Taiwan and Korea have both issued important rulings that seem to agglomerate new decision-making powers over important political questions, thus enhancing their freedom of action.

One study that addresses the self-articulation of the judicial role is Jeffrey Staton's account of Mexico, which builds on Vanberg's move to look at the role of the public.[54] Staton emphasizes a related dimension, strategic communication. Shifting the focus from judicial decision-making to the overall position of courts in the political order, Staton demonstrates that the Mexican Supreme Court pays attention to the media in its efforts to develop its own power and articulate a political role. It does so through timing and selective promotion of decisions.

Some courts have the ability to select their cases, which of course enhances this aspect of strategic consideration. Courts also seem to vary in terms of their relative focus on enforcing rights, which implies a kind of public-regarding strategy, as opposed to focusing on arbitrating inter-branch conflicts. In a recent volume, Gretchen Helmke and Julio Rios-Figueroa categorize various courts in Latin America along these dimensions.[55] They find that relatively few courts play a role in both spheres. One of the important cases in this regard is that of Costa Rica, whose Supreme Court was traditionally quiescent. A 1989 constitutional reform introduced a special constitutional chamber. Unintended by the drafters (and hence fitting problematically with theories of strategic empowerment described above), and apparently emboldened simply by their designation as a constitutional court, these judges eagerly transformed themselves into 'the central institution in the political and constitutional life of the country'.[56] This study shows how empowerment is not only a product of intentional action by constitutional drafters, in contrast with the

---

[52]   Pablo Rueda, 'Legal Language and Social Change during Colombia's Economic Crisis', in Javier Couso, Alexandra Huneeus and Rachel Sieder (eds), *Cultures of Legality: Judicialization and Political Activism in Latin America* 25–50 (New York: Cambridge University Press 2010).

[53]   Upendra Baxi, *The Indian Supreme Court and Politics* (Lucknow: Eastern Book Co. 1980).

[54]   Jeffrey Staton, *Judicial Power and Strategic Communication in Mexico* (New York: Cambridge University Press 2011); see Vanberg (note 13).

[55]   Gretchen Helmke and Julio Rios-Figueroa (eds), *Courts in Latin America* (New York: Cambridge University Press 2011).

[56]   Bruce M. Wilson, 'Enforcing Rights and Exercising an Accountability Function: Costa Rica's Constitutional Chamber of the Supreme Court', in Helmke and Rios-Figueroa (note 55) 55, 76.

electoral theories of judicial empowerment. Instead, judicial self-understanding and role designation seem to be crucial factors.

The implication of these various studies is that judges have the ability, to a certain degree, to shape their environment and to articulate a role for themselves. If courts are intentional and strategic actors, they have the ability to define their role in the political and social system. They need alliances, either with elites, other political institutions or the public, and this need may affect the type of cases they select, the way they articulate decisions and the degree to which they play an active role in society. Even the most powerful courts only exercise their power selectively. Situating the courts in the broader institutional milieu allows scholars to identify these issues of judicial strategy. For example, in tracing the history of the Turkish Constitutional Court, Ceren Belge focuses on the sociopolitical alliances of the judiciary to explain the selective nature of their activism.[57] Charles Epp provided the notion of a 'support structure' to facilitate rights revolutions, implying that constitutional courts can only be effective when there is a sufficiently rich institutional environment for litigants.[58]

Another set of relationships worthy of study is the interactions among high courts within a single legal order. In recent years, there have been conflicts among supreme and constitutional courts in several countries.[59] In traditional civil law countries, constitutional courts appear more political in nature and qualitatively different from regular courts, hardly surprising since insulation of ordinary courts from politics was one of the goals of the Kelsenian theory. However, the resulting politicization of the constitutional court may create a problem in terms of deference by the higher judicial courts. Furthermore, there may be institutional rivalries between the top courts of the ordinary jurisdiction, accustomed to their superior place in the judicial hierarchy, and the new constitutional court. This can lead to legal incoherence and gridlock.

Constitutional review also takes place in an international context. Many accounts of the European Union emphasize the alliance that developed between national courts and the supranational European Court of Justice. Others have emphasized the existence of a transnational judicial dialogue that provides content to various rights, and informs judges.[60] Cross-national citation provides a lever for judges to engage in communication across borders and to expand their collective ability to withstand encroachments of executive power.[61] Moreover, international judicial alliances can provide leverage for constitutional courts in articulating rights to constrain the government.[62] However, we do not always observe such alliance dynamics. In recent years, high courts in Venezuela, Argentina and Chile have quite explicitly ignored decisions of the Inter-American

---

[57]   Ceren Belge, 'Friends of the Court: The Republican Alliance and Selective Activism of the Constitutional Court of Turkey', 40 *Law and Society Review* 653–92 (2006).

[58]   Epp (note 19).

[59]   Lech Garlicki, 'Constitutional Courts versus Supreme Courts', 5 *International Journal of Constitutional Law* 44–68 (2007).

[60]   Anne-Marie Slaughter, *The New World Order* (Princeton: Princeton University Press 2003).

[61]   Eyal Benvenisti and George Downs, 'National Courts, Domestic Democracy, and the Evolution of International Law', 20 *European Journal of International Law* 1027–30 (2009).

[62]   Nancy Maveety and Anke Grosskopf, '"Constrained" Constitutional Courts as Conduits for Democratic Consolidation', 38 *Law and Society Review* 463–88 (2004).

Court of Human Rights.[63] We need further scholarship on the conditions that give rise to alliance dynamics among high courts: current theories of transnational judicial dialogue seem to emphasize formal citation rather than substantive impact on decision-making.

Scholars have also explored other areas, such as the performance of constitutional review in authoritarian or unstable regimes. For example, Helmke observed a pattern she called 'strategic defection' against political elites in which courts would begin to act against regime interests toward the end of the authoritarian regime.[64] Motivated by the need for institutional legitimacy, courts that challenge elites in the endgame of authoritarianism risk the imposition of short-term costs in exchange for mid-term legitimacy.[65]

Moustafa's superb study of the Egyptian Supreme Constitutional Court illustrated the effective performance but ultimate over-reaching that led to a backlash against the judiciary.[66] He traces how President Anwar Sadat (1970–81) created the Court to help make credible commitments to foreign investors and to help in a broader judicial project to discipline wayward bureaucratic agents. The Supreme Constitutional Court, however, acted with substantial independence, legalizing certain opposition parties and restraining the authoritarian regime from the use of libel laws. This eventually led to a counterattack on the Court, but many of the jurists are likely to have retained some credibility now that the authoritarian Egyptian regime has fallen.

The Egyptian story illustrates that judges are not always perfectly able to anticipate the limits of their activism. The long-term trajectory of constitutional law and courts results from strategic interaction with other actors in the political system, but information in these interactions is by no means perfect. The myriad roles that courts play in different political systems, and the factors that lead courts to articulate particular roles for themselves, are a useful area for future inquiry.

5   ANCILLARY POWERS

Besides the core task of constitutional review of legislation and administrative action, constitutional courts often have other powers, including such duties as proposing

---

[63] Alexandra Huneeus, 'Rejecting the Inter-American Court: Judicialization, National Courts, and Regional Human Rights', in Javier Couso, Alexandra Huneeus and Rachel Sieder (eds), *Cultures of Legality: Judicialization and Political Activism in Latin America* 112–38 (2010).

[64] Gretchen Helmke, *Courts under Constraints: Judges, Generals, and Presidents in Argentina* (New York: Cambridge University Press 2005).

[65] A similar dynamic has been observed in Pakistan, Indonesia and perhaps Egypt. See Paula Newberg, *Judging the State: Courts and Constitutional Politics in Pakistan* (New York: Cambridge University Press 1995); David Bourchier, 'Magic Memos, Collusion and Judges with Attitude: Notes on the Politics of Law in Contemporary Indonesia', in Kanishka Jayasuriya, *Law, Capitalism and Power in Asia* 233–52 (New York: Routledge 1999); Tamir Moustafa, *The Struggle for Constitutional Power: Law, Politics and Economic Development in Egypt* (New York: Cambridge University Press 2007).

[66] Moustafa (note 65).

legislation,[67] determining whether political parties are unconstitutional; certifying states of emergency; impeaching senior governmental officials; and adjudicating election violations.

Constitutional courts also have a wide range of other responsibilities that move even further afield from the defining role of judicial review. The Constitutional Court of Belarus, for instance, has the power to 'submit proposals to the Supreme Council on the need for amendments and addenda to the Constitution and on the adoption and amendment of laws'.[68] An Azerbaijani draft Constitution gave the Constitutional Court power to 'dissolve parliament if it repeatedly passes laws that violate the Constitution',[69] though this did not survive into the final draft. The South African Constitutional Court must certify the constitutions of provinces for conformity with the national Constitution.[70] Portugal's Constitutional Court must certify the death or incapacity of the President.[71] Lastly, the High Council of the Comoros (which serves as a constitutional court) has a role in audit and control of accounts.[72]

In some cases, Supreme Court justices even find themselves taking on direct executive roles. In Bangladesh, for example, the former Chief Justice served as interim president. After a 2000 coup in Ecuador, a member of the Ecuadorian Supreme Court served in a triumvirate running the country for a short time.

Many of these ancillary powers tend to implicate constitutional courts very deeply in politics. For example, article 21(2) of the German Basic Law, banning parties that oppose the 'free democratic basic order',[73] gave rise to two famous cases wherein the German Constitutional Court banned unconstitutional parties.[74] The first Russian Constitutional Court banned the communist party,[75] and Bulgaria's Constitutional Court issued a prominent decision to ban a Macedonian-nationalist party.[76] Thailand's Constitutional Court, which wields a broad array of ancillary powers, became embroiled in that country's deep political divisions, and may have contributed to its instability with its decisions to ban the party of the former prime minister. The Turkish Constitutional Court has also effectively used this power to constrain the rise of Islamist political parties.

Constitutional designers have quite consciously given courts this expanded set of powers, in part because the global success of judicial review has given constitutional

---

[67]   See, e.g., Constitution of Bosnia and Herzegovina art. 6 (1995); Constitution of the Chechen Republic (1992) art. 65; Constitutional Court Act of Russia art. 9.

[68]   Constitution of Belarus (1994) art. 93.

[69]   Rett Ludwikowski, 'Constitution Making in the Countries of Former Soviet Dominance: Current Developments', 23 *Georgia Journal of International and Comparative Law* 155 (1993). The Constitution was passed in 1995 without these provisions.

[70]   Constitution of South Africa (1997) art. 144.

[71]   Constitution of Portugal (2004) art. 223.

[72]   Constitution of Comoros (1996) art. 49.

[73]   Kommers (note 13).

[74]   Ibid. 217–24 describes the *Socialist Reich Party Case*, 2 BverfGE 1 (1952), concerning a neo-nazi party, and the *Communist Party Case*, 5 BverfGE 85 (1956).

[75]   Robert Ahdieh, *Russia's Constitutional Revolution: Constitutional Structure, Legal Consciousness and the Emergence of Constitutionalism from Below, 1985–1995* (University Park, PA: Penn State Press 1997).

[76]   BBC Monitoring Service, 29 Feb. 2000.

courts a reputation as effective institutions. Ginsburg and Elkins report that the average constitutional court wields three ancillary powers.[77] The most frequent are the oversight of elections, reviewing treaties, hearing charges against the executive and adjudicating the constitutionality of political parties. Constitutional review creates a kind of stock of capital that designers seek to draw on to help resolve impasses in the political system, such as those that occur in impeachment and election disputes. There is, however, a risk that courts will be drawn into explicitly political conflicts that inevitably produce angry losers. Court legitimacy may suffer in the mid-term, and there are examples of courts that were disbanded after issuing controversial decisions of this type.[78]

6 CONCLUSION: THE SOCIO-POLITICAL ROLES OF COURTS

Constitutional courts are increasingly a major locus of political decision-making, chiefly though not entirely through the vehicle of constitutional review. This has led to a 'judicialization of mega-politics', in Hirschl's pithy phrase.[79] The use of legal language, and the transformation of political disputes into constitutional ones, implies a growing juridification of society, which has been observed in many spheres. While constitutional law and courts are not the only modality for the spread of rights consciousness, they are a powerful one. The rise of constitutional courts as important fora for social and political contestation has significant implications for the quality and functioning of democracy, privileging some groups that can engage in legal mobilization and disempowering other groups.

Constitutional courts are institutions and thus are best understood using institutional analysis in its various forms. Courts have an ability to shape their operating environment, and to some degree, to articulate their own role. They interact with other political actors and the public in myriad ways, and can exercise strategic choices to enhance their own power and to provide political goods to others. Understanding how they do so requires a variety of research methods that integrate an understanding of the law with a broader social science perspective.

FURTHER READING

Brewer-Carías, Allan R. (2009). *Constitutional Protection of Human Rights in Latin America: A Comparative Study of the* Amparo *Proceedings.* Cambridge: Cambridge University Press.
Couso, Javier, Alexandra Huneeus and Rachel Sieder (eds) (2011). *Cultures of Legality: Judicialization and Political Activism in Latin America.* New York: Cambridge University Press.
Ferreres Comella, Victor (2009). *Constitutional Courts and Democratic Values: A European Perspective.* New Haven, CT: Yale University Press.

---

[77]   Tom Ginsburg and Zachary Elkins, 'Ancillary Powers of Constitutional Courts', 87 *Texas Law Review* 1432 (2009).

[78]   Ibid.

[79]   Ran Hirschl, 'The Judicialization of Mega-Politics and the Rise of Political Courts' 11 *Annual Review of Political Science* 93–118 (2008).

Garlicki, Lech (2007). 'Constitutional Courts versus Supreme Courts', 5 *International Journal of Constitutional Law* 44–68.

Frosini, Justin O. and Lucio Pegoraro (2009). 'Constitutional Courts in Latin America: A Testing Ground for New Parameters of Classification?' 3 *Journal of Comparative Law* 39–63 (no. 2).

Ginsburg, Tom (2003). *Judicial Review in New Democracies: Constitutional Courts in Asian Cases*. Cambridge: Cambridge University Press.

Guarnieri, Carlo and Patrizia Pederzoli (2002). *The Power of Judges: A Comparative Study of Courts and Democracy*. Oxford: Oxford University Press.

Helmke, Gretchen and Julio Rios-Figueroa (2011). *Courts in Latin America*. New York: Cambridge University Press.

Sadurski, Wojciech (2005). *Rights before Courts: A Study of Constitutional Courts in Postcommunist States of Central and Eastern Europe*. Dordrecht, Netherlands: Springer.

Trochev, Alexei (2008). *Judging Russia: Constitutional Court in Russian Politics, 1990–2006*. New York: Cambridge University Press.

15 Legal cultures
David Nelken*

1 INTRODUCTION

In comparative research on law and society, scholars regularly use the term 'legal culture' as a way of drawing attention to developments they seek to explain or problems that they want to change. As a recent World Bank study reported:

> Legal culture is often considered as a given feature of the local environment to which proposed legal reform projects must adapt; many argue that legal and judicial reform programs must be tailored to fit local legal culture or they will fail. Other times, the prevailing legal culture itself may be the object of reform, rather than merely a constraint. Thus, understanding the arguments related to the concept of legal culture will become increasingly important for aspiring legal reformers . . ... Does the legal system not work well because people distrust the courts, or do people distrust the courts because the legal system doesn't work well? Is the introduction of a new contract law unlikely to have an effect because the business culture prefers informal deals with family and friends, or does the preference for informal dealing exist only because no one has yet passed an efficient contract law? These sorts of problems are not easy to resolve, especially because the causality clearly runs in both directions, and the interactions between beliefs and actions are extraordinarily complex. (2005)

On the other hand, the concept is also highly contested. Academic debates about legal culture can be confusing because authors may disagree not only over what is true of a given legal culture (which should presuppose agreement about what they mean by the term), but also even about how they define legal culture and how they think it should be studied. More than this, there are even fundamental disagreements about whether the term is actually worth saving (as opposed to rival concepts). Thus, one author who previously named his book *Dutch Legal Culture* later preferred to replace it with the less question-begging *Dutch Law in Action* (Blankenberg and Bruinsma 1995; Bruinsma 2000). Even Lawrence Friedman, responsible for introducing the concept into the sociology of law, has recently described it as 'an abstraction and a slippery one', and now says that he is not sure he would want to reinvent it (2006).

An example of the first kind of disagreement is the variety of answers offered (by both inside observers and outside commentators) to the question of why the Japanese, despite living in one of the world's most advanced economies, make (or made) relatively little use of the courts. In the 1950s, it was conventional to adopt 'harmony culture' explanations, which treated Japan's legal culture as an expression of the influence of Confucian-shaped culture that emphasised harmonious and hierarchical relationships. However, by the 1970s, this approach had fallen out of favour. Since then we have had structural

---

* Professor of Law, Cardiff University, and Professor, University of Macerata Department of Social Change, Legal Institutions and Communication.

explanations that argued that limited numbers of legal professionals and courts represented institutional barriers maintained by government bureaucracies and business elites to protect their corporatist agreements from the unpredictability of court interventions. In addition, there were claims that the very predictability of Japanese courts explains the limited need to resort to them (Haley 1978). Discussion continues, with some authors suggesting that Japan sometimes actually makes more use of courts than is done in other places (Feldman 1997, 2001, 2006), and others arguing that Japan offers us an example of non-legally obsessed communitarianism that has special merits (Tanase 2009).

There are similar arguments about other countries and jurisdictions. In this chapter, however, I shall be less concerned with ongoing debates about how to explain the special features of different legal cultures or the way they may be changing—and more with the more basic questions of what we should take legal culture to mean and whether or not it can serve as a valuable term for our enquiries. Building on previous work (see, e.g., Nelken 1995, 1997a, 2004, 2006a, 2007, 2011b; Nelken and Bruinsma 2007), I shall here offer a selective overview of the literature that discusses this term. This will touch on problems of definition, objections to the concept of culture, difficulties in determining relevant units of legal culture, the use of legal culture as an explanation and the need to be reflexive about culture. My aim is to show why these issues cannot merely be side-stepped but have to be acknowledged in discussing specific legal cultures if such work is to produce valuable comparative cross-cultural insights.

2 THE MEANINGS OF LEGAL CULTURE

What is the point of calling a particular pattern of behaviour, opinions or ideas an instance of legal culture and what follows from this? If we are to develop legal culture as a 'term of art', we need to think more carefully about what exactly we are talking about and when, how and why the term is used. Taken generally, the contested ideas of 'law' and 'culture' when brought together cover a large range of possible permutations of law in culture or culture in law (Cotterrell 2004; Fitzpatrick 2005). They range from recognising that law is a cultural artefact, and not merely a form of social engineering (Kahn 1999), to seeing how law becomes present in everyday life experience, for example when filtered through the mass media (Sarat and Kearns 1993, 1998). The term legal culture is also sometimes found in common use (which itself merits study), but more often it is a concept used by lawyers or social scientists (including historians).

The concept typically plays a different role in legal science as compared to political science, or in sociology of law rather than comparative law. Given that both law and culture are words whose interpretation and definition can have illocutionary effects (such as 'this is the law' or 'that behaviour is inconsistent with our culture'), judges or others within the legal system or the culture may make reference to legal culture in claims about what is, or is not, consonant with a given body of law, practices or ideals. This use, prescriptive even as it purports to be descriptive, may help 'make' the facts it purports to describe or explain.

For jurists, legal culture is thus one way of describing legal actors' attempts to describe, ascribe, or produce normative coherence in the course of their decision-making (Rebuffa and Blankenburg 1993). As argued by Jeremy Webber:

> The concept of culture is not so much a way of identifying highly specified and tightly bounded units of analysis, then, as a heuristic device for suggesting how individual decision-making is conditioned by the language of normative discussion, the set of historical reference points, the range of solutions proposed in the past, the institutional norms taken for granted, given a particular context of repeated social interaction. The integrity of cultural explanations does not depend upon the 'units' being exclusive, fully autonomous, or strictly bounded. Rather, it depends upon there being sufficient density of interaction to generate distinctive terms of evaluation and debate. When there is that density, any examination of decision-making in that context will want to take account of those terms. (2004: 32)

Webber is thinking mainly about the role of judges. Nevertheless, the descriptive and the prescriptive may also overlap in other contexts. Politicians may advance (or reject) changes in the law or approve (or disapprove) legal decisions in the name of larger values or principles. More generally, in those jurisdictions, or parts of jurisdictions, where state rules are systematically avoided or evaded (e.g., in the former Soviet Union, Latin America or the south of Italy), there is much talk of the 'culture of legality' (or, increasingly, the 'rule of law' culture). This is intended to signal the goal of getting 'legality' into the culture of everyday social and political life, to reorient the behaviour of such populations towards (state) law.

In probably its most common use, legal culture is no more than a way of referring to a historically and geographically socio-legal field that is assumed to display some commonalities (see, e.g., Gessner, Hoeland and Varga 1996; Varga 1992). The theoretical sophistication involved in identifying the units in question varies from relatively unambitious legal or comparative law classifications of 'legal systems' to less familiar ideas of interconnections and networks taken from social theory or anthropology. All-encompassing definitions are especially recommended where the aim is to compare different units. Nelken proposes that:

> Legal culture, in its most general sense, should be seen as one way of describing relatively stable patterns of legally oriented social behaviour and attitudes. The identifying elements of legal culture range from facts about institutions such as the number and role of lawyers or the ways judges are appointed and controlled, to various forms of behaviour such as litigation or prison rates, and, at the other extreme, more nebulous aspects of ideas, values, aspirations and mentalities. Like culture itself, legal culture is about who we are, not just what we do. (2004: 1)

The tasks of the scholar who thinks of legal culture in this way (sometimes referred to as the anthropological approach) include describing these commonalities that make something into a 'culture', explaining why a given legal culture takes the form that it does, how and why it differs from others, and why it is changing or failing to change.

The other main use of the term (which follows the older notion of 'political culture') focuses on groups and individuals and their attitudes and opinions, and sometimes behaviour, towards law. For Lawrence Friedman, whose idea of legal culture has been the most influential in sociology of law, it refers to 'what people think about law, lawyers and the legal order, it means ideas, attitudes, opinions and expectations with regard to the legal system' (2006: 189). Here legal culture is itself invoked as a variable to explain how and why the legal system changes in the face of technological developments and how and when (powerful) social groups bring pressure on law to shape it to suit their ends. In particular, Friedman distinguishes 'internal' legal culture, which points to the special role judges and other legal professionals play, from 'external' legal culture, which refers to those individuals or groups who bring their expectations or pressure to bear on the law. Causal links of course do not only go in one direction. Features of life in modern industrial societies lead to increasing expectations of what he calls 'Total Justice' and such expectations increasingly mould the law (1985, 1990).

3   CULTURE IN QUESTION

For many critics culture has just too many meanings for it to be a serviceable concept to use to explain differences in socio-legal attitudes and behaviour. How are we to mark off 'the cultural' from other types of motivation or aspects of collective life? Is culture something related to and contrasted with other aspects of society, for example, legal rules, institutional resources or social structure? Alternatively, does its influence work through these elements? Should one reserve the term culture for irrational or at least value-based action, rather than purely instrumental social action? Is culture an all-embracing category or a 'residual term' to be used only where political and economic factors seem insufficient? Does it refer to unconscious sources of behaviour, or is it a 'tool kit', that one can draw on selectively? Which of these and other options one intends can make all the difference in what one claims when employing the term.

Even as culture after the so-called 'cultural turn' has become increasingly important in many disciplines, anthropologists, for whom the term was once central, have found its meanings less and less illuminating for the purpose of explanation (Kuper 1999). 'Over the last two decades', writes Sally Merry (2003: 69),

> anthropology has elaborated a conception of culture as unbounded, contested, and connected to relations of power. It does not consist only of beliefs and values but also practices, habits, and commonsensical ways of doing things. The contemporary anthropological understanding of culture envisions a far more fluid, contested, and changing set of values and practices than that provided by the idea of culture as tradition. Culture is the product of historical influences rather than evolutionary change. Its boundaries are fluid, meanings are contested, and meaning is produced by institutional arrangements and political economy. Culture is marked by hybridity and creolization rather than uniformity or consistency. Local systems are analysed in the context of national and transnational processes and are understood as the result of particular historical trajectories. This is a more dynamic, agentic, and historicized way of understanding culture.

Critics of legal culture see it as still carrying the inconsistent or misleading idea of culture as something that is homogenous, tightly bounded, unchanging and determining. Patrick Glenn reminds us that one should not treat cultures as 'super organic', or 'substantive, bounded entities', but rather as 'shreds and patches remaking themselves' (2004). Certainly, great care must be taken to avoid reifying national or other stereotypes and recognise that much that goes under the name of culture is no more than 'imagined communities' or 'invented traditions'. It is easy to fall into the opposed vices of 'Occidentalism' or 'Orientalism', making other cultures seem either necessarily similar or intrinsically 'other' (Cain 2000). If culture is, to a large extent, a matter of struggle and disagreement, the purported uniformity, coherence or stability of given national or other cultures will often be no more than a rhetorical claim projected by outside observers or manipulated by elements within the culture concerned. Any assumption that long-standing historical patterns cannot be altered can be 'dystopic' and block possible reforms (Krygier 1997). Legal culture, like all culture, is a product of the contingencies of history and is always undergoing change (Nelken 1995). For our purposes it can be salutary to recall the rapid transformations in attitudes towards 'law and order' in the short period that elapsed from Weimar to Hitler's Germany.

Given the shadow cast by the term culture, many writers see advantages in using alternative concepts: these include living law or the law in action; *épistémès*, mentalities, or formants; legal traditions, legal ideology, legal fields, legal or regulatory styles, or path dependency.[1] Patrick Glenn, an advocate of the term legal tradition, argues that it is more natural to speak of non-traditional behaviour and innovation than to make the same point when using the term culture (2004). Talking about traditions, he adds, suggests overlap rather than closure because within a given tradition there is always a range of creative possibilities. The very existence of a tradition is necessarily a result of persuasive argument and interpretation. For Glenn, because tradition is a matter of 'information' it is hard to reify it as something 'beyond us'. He also suggests that all societies have a notion of tradition, but not all use the term culture. Roger Cotterrell, who favours legal ideology, claims that such a term offers us a focus on the ideas of legal professionals and jurists and their influence over popular consciousness (1997). One of the main questions that interests him is how law succeeds in being at the same time both fragmented and abstract; how it pretends to be a gapless system while filling in the gaps. For Cotterrell, this provides us with a well-defined topic suitable for empirical investigation.

On the other hand, the political science or sociology of law approach to the term is far from using culture in the way being criticised here. Far from seeing cultures as hermetic and unchanging, Friedman argues that law is necessarily converging, and has even written about the development of 'global culture' (1994).[2] He employs the term principally as part of his effort to account for social change, not to deny it. In addition, other terms have their problems. Tradition too can be a confusing idea, one which tends too easily to distract attention from questions of power and interest (hence Merry's complaint about 'culture as tradition'). Much also depends on what we are trying to explain. As opposed to Friedman's interest in the permeability of law to wider social demands, Cotterrell's concept of ideology draws our attention to the role of legal professionals and the way rules and values of law resist modification and thrive on their inconsistencies (Cotterrell 1997). Neither tradition nor ideology may be particularly well suited to understanding why countries differ in their levels of court delay (Nelken 2004, 2008).

---

[1]   The questions at stake in speaking about legal culture are often begged even where the term is not mentioned. This is true, for example, of American discussions of US 'exceptionalism' in both civil and criminal law (Kagan 2001; Nelken 2003). Likewise, even though those who theorise about the relationship between law and society by drawing on autopoietic theory (and oppose the idea of national cultures) sometimes also mobilise inchoate notions of legal culture (Teubner 1998, Nelken 2001, 2003).

[2]   For conflicting evidence on this point, see Engel (2005, 2010).

4   THE UNIT OF LEGAL CULTURE

If we are to work with the idea of legal culture, we also need to specify what units we are referring to (and decide whether it is culture that is produced within boundaries or culture that produces boundaries). Most books and articles on legal culture still identify this with the boundaries of national jurisdictions. They write of the *Japanese Way of Justice* (Johnson 2002), *French Criminal Justice* (Hodgson 2006), or 'Dutch legal culture' (Hertogh 2011). Likewise, leading scholars seek to make sense of the specificity (see, e.g., Garapon and Papadopoulos 2003) or the 'exceptionalism' of the USA's type of legal procedure by showing its high level of 'adversarial legalism' (Kagan 2001) or the severity of its punishments (Whitman 2003; Nelken 2006b). As against the notion of 'legal families', within the classifications of comparative law, it may be important to look out for such national variation. The Netherlands and Italy are both members of the civil law world, but England and Wales and the Netherlands may have more in common in their pragmatic approach to law or in their openness to public opinion.

Nevertheless, it would certainly be misleading to limit our enquiry to the nation state. Patterns of legal culture can and must be sought both at a more micro as well as at a more macro level than the nation state. At the sub-national level, there will be considerable variation as between different areas of a nation state (and groups within it) as well as between one state and another, and this is all the more likely when we study less industrialised or less consolidated states. In many places, people live with legal pluralism or even a 'nomic din' (Harding 2001). Besides, at this level, it will often be of interest to study differences in the 'local legal culture' of the local court, the prosecutor's office or the lawyer's consulting room. Legal culture is not necessarily uniform (organisationally and meaningfully) across different branches of law (see Bell 2002). Lawyers may have less in common with other lawyers outside their field than they have with those abroad. As important, there is also increasing need to consider those processes that transcend the nation state—international courts (Nelken 2009a), *lex mercatoria* networks, non-governmental organisations and inter-governmental organisations. The history of regular transfers of legal institutions and ideas makes it misleading to argue that legal culture is embedded in its current national context (Nelken 2011c). Much domestic law in Europe in the nineteenth century, such as the law of copyright, was mainly developed as a response to its existence elsewhere (Sherman 1997). Some of the laws and legal institutions that people think of as most typically their own are the result of imitation, imposition or borrowing. Thus, there are 'Dutch' disputing mechanisms which are in fact a result of German imposition during the occupation, and which Germany has abandoned itself (Jettinghoff 2001).

The adoption of dissimilar legal models is common where third parties impose the legal transfer as part of a colonial project or insist on it as a condition of trade, aid, alliance or diplomatic recognition. Elites concerned to 'modernise' their society or otherwise bring it into the wider family of 'advanced' nations have also often sponsored it. Japan and Turkey are obvious examples. In these cases, imported or imposed law is designed to change existing contexts rather than reflect them. Thus, South Africa modelled its new constitution on the best that Western regimes had to offer rather than on constitutional arrangements found in its nearer neighbours in Africa. The hope in many cases of current transplants is that law may be a means of resolving current problems by transforming the existing society into one more like the source of such borrowed law. In what is almost a species of sympathetic magic, borrowed law is sometimes deemed capable of bringing about the same conditions of a flourishing economy or a healthy civil society that are found in the social context from which the borrowed law has been taken. In Eastern Europe legal transfers became part of the effort to become (or to be seen to be) more democratic or more economically successful. Turkey, with its eye on accession to the European Union, tried to make its laws appear more secular. Those who study these transfers, on the other hand, question their potential for producing change in the absence of the surrounding context from which they were taken. They emphasise how far such innovations are likely to be shaped by the prevailing norms and ideas in the places where they applied and were interpreted (see Nelken and Feest 2001; Gillespie 2006).

Current developments leading to the increased globalisation of markets and communications mean that the role of supranational entities, organisations and networks go well beyond cases of simple legal transfers (Heyderbrand 2001, 2007). The boundaries of the nation state as a unit are regularly traversed as transnational public and semi-public networks substitute, to an increasing extent, for national governments in building a 'real new world order' (Slaughter 1997). New challenges for those who study legal culture have to do with making sense of the forms of norm-making, dispute-channelling and regulation such as the growth of the *lex mercatoria*, the use of 'soft law' or other non-binding agreements and persuasive practices by international regulators, and the use of their power to enforce private orders by multinational companies. The use of *lex mercatoria*, for example, is said to 'break the frame' of national jurisdiction. Lawyers and accountants play an increasing role as entrepreneurs of new forms of dispute prevention and settlement (Dezalay and Garth 1996, 2002), mainly, if not entirely, to service the increasingly important international business community. In turn, the opportunities for such activity transform legal professions. The importance of private actors has also altered because of the growth of multinational and international production networks, new technology, and changes in work patterns. Rule-formulation and settlement increasingly takes place within new agencies of transnational governance, such as NAFTA, the OECD, and the WTO. Legal fields are increasingly internationalised, even if this process does not affect all fields to the same extent and varies by different areas of legal and social regulation.

All this means that it makes less and less sense to think of 'domestic' norms as forming part of distinct national jurisdictions that then interact with transnational norms. The multiple orders that grow up produce what Boaventura de Sousa Santos calls 'interlegality', a term that describes 'a highly dynamic process' where different legal spaces are 'nonsychronic' and result in 'uneven and unstable combinations of legal codes (codes in a semiotic sense)' (1995: 473). Equally important, for those seeking to mark the limits of cultural units, it becomes ever more difficult to set boundaries to our imaginations and expectations: 'we inhabit', one may argue, a 'deterritorialised world'. We can participate via the media in communities of others with whom we have no geographical proximity or common history (Appadurai 1996; Coombe 2000). Hence, 'all totalising accounts of society, tradition and culture are exclusionary and enact a social violence by suppressing contingent and continually emergent differences'. Instead, we must face the 'challenges of transnationalism and the politics of global capitalism or multiple overlapping and conflicting juridiscapes' (Coombe 2000: 31, 43). At the same time, however, even networks are themselves shaped by different contexts As Merry suggests, to keep track of these transnational flows we need to find ways to study 'placeless phenomena in a place' (Merry 2005: 44).

All this means that it would be rash to assume, in advance of empirical investigation, any necessary 'fit' between law and its environing national society or culture. However, claims about the decline of the nation state can also be taken too far (Nelken 2011a). Given the way it often sets boundaries of jurisdiction, politics and language, the nation state will often serve as a relevant starting-point for comparing legal culture. Where law is deliberately used as a unifying state-building device, practices focusing on law may have even more in common than general culture does. The state will also often be the main or only source of relevant statistics of such matters as litigation or incarceration rates. Moreover, even apparently unconnected branches of law may in fact manifest remarkable levels of cultural similarity within a given society.

5 LEGAL CULTURE AND EXPLANATION

For Friedman, legal culture is a helpful (indeed essential) concept for explanatory enquiries. To take one of his examples, legal culture provides the key to whether or not women in Italy or France turn for help to the police in cases where they have been assaulted. Another is whether Italian drivers are more or less likely than the English to comply with laws requiring the wearing of seat belts (Friedman 1997). Nevertheless, it is not always clear whether legal culture is the explanation of these differences or just the name we give to them. This is important because we need to avoid falling into the trap of 'essentialism' or 'culturalism', whereby in answer to the enquiry 'why do people use law a certain way in Japan?' we answer 'because that is their (legal) culture'! To put the point another way, when we talk about American or Japanese 'legal culture', are we already offering some sort of explanation of behaviour or only indicating that which still needs to be explained? Is legal culture the name of the question or the answer?

The problem is made worse because Friedman has applied the term legal culture to a wide variety of units in time and space—writing about individual and group attitudes, US legal culture and Latin American legal culture (Friedman and Pérez-Perdomo 2003), as well as 'modern legal culture' and 'global legal culture'. In a well-known critique, Cotterrell complained that 'this means that legal culture becomes, 'an immense, multi-textured overlay of levels and regions of culture, varying in content, scope, and influence and in their relation to the institutions, practices and knowledge of state legal systems' (1997: 17). In theory, he says, such variety in the level of supra- and sub-national units could provide a rich terrain for inquiry. Nonetheless, he rejects the idea that legal culture can be reflected in 'diversity and levels' whilst also having a 'unity'. For him, 'if legal culture refers to so many levels and regions of culture (with the scope of each of these ultimately indeterminate because of the indeterminacy of the scope of the idea of legal culture itself), the problem of specifying how to use the concept as a theoretical component in comparative sociology for law remains' (ibid.).[3]

---

[3] Friedman's reply suggested that he thought that Cotterrell's problem was with the difficulty of measuring the concept, rather than with the risks of tautology in using it as an explanation (Friedman 1997). In his later work, Cotterrell (2006a, 2006b) is less damning of the concept.

While this issue is a serious one, however, one should not exaggerate it. It is above all mainly relevant for those with an interest in prediction who hope to develop (positivist) social science explanations that connect variables and outcomes. Which types of legal systems most support economic growth? What conditions are likely to determine whether a legal transplant takes or not? However, not all scholars want to use the term for this purpose. Many comparative lawyers will be at least as interested in classification, mapping and description. These sorts of investigation of legal culture (whether or not they go on under this name) are a concern with interpretative understanding. What does this legal institution, procedure or idea mean? What, if anything, is it trying to achieve?

Whereas the positivist approach would throw light on legal culture by seeking to assign causal priority between competing hypothetical variables to explain variation in levels and types of legally related behaviour, the interpretative approach, on the other hand, is more interested in providing 'thick descriptions' (Geertz 1973) of law as 'local knowledge' (Geertz 1983). It sees its task as doing its best faithfully to translate another system's ideas of justice and fairness to make proper sense of its web of significance. It asks about the different nuances as between the terms 'rule of law', '*Rechtsstaat*' or '*Stato di diritto*', or the meanings of 'community' in different societies (Zedner 1995). It seeks to understand why litigation is seen as essentially democratic in the USA, but as anti-democratic in France (Cohen-Tanugi 1996). In this search for holistic meaning any insistence, for example, on distinguishing 'demand' for law from 'supply' of law is likely to obscure more than it reveals and could lead to mistaken practical conclusions (Nelken 1997b). Arguably, if there are differences in the significance attached to official law and legal institutions in Germany and in the Netherlands, then even if Germany had the same alternative routes to litigation that are present in the Netherlands, they could well end up producing even more work for lawyers and courts.

For the interpretative approach, concepts both reflect and constitute culture. Scholars see this in the changes undergone by the meaning of 'contract' in a society where the individual is seen as necessarily embodied in wider relationships (Winn 1994), or the way that the Japanese ideogram for the new concept of 'rights' came to settle on a sign associated with 'self interest' rather than morality (Feldman 1997). To test its hypotheses, the positivist approach is obliged to develop a socio-legal Esperanto which abstracts from the language members of different cultures use, preferring, for example, to talk of 'decision-making' rather than 'discretion'. The rival strategy, concerned precisely with grasping linguistic subtleties and 'cultural packaging', would ask whether and when the term 'discretion' is used in different legal cultures and what implications the word carries (Nelken 2002). Not least, the interpretative approach is quick to recognise the reflexivity of (legal) culture as 'an enormous interplay of interpretations in and about a culture' (J. Friedman 1994), and thus appreciate that the scholar may also be a (bit) player in the processes of legal culture that she seeks to understand.

Nonetheless, rather than treating these approaches as necessarily in competition, explanation and interpretation are often pursued as complementary strategies in the search for understanding culture (Nelken 1994, 2010a). Interesting comparative work typically starts from some puzzle about the relationship between the role of law and the rule of law within given societies (or other units). Why do the UK and Denmark complain most about the imposition of EU law but then turn out to be the countries that have the best records of obedience? Why does the Netherlands, otherwise so similar, have such a low litigation rate compared to neighbouring Germany? Why have constitutional courts managed to consolidate themselves in some post-communist societies but not in others—and why are they emerging now in East Asia? Why are the higher courts in Latin American countries such as Chile or Colombia currently seeking to guarantee minimum social security rights despite the 'formalistic legal culture' that is alleged to characterise their role? How does this connect, if at all, with the neo-liberal policies states pursue on the advice of the Chicago-educated technocrats in government? Why in the United States and the UK does it often take a sex scandal to create official interest in doing something about corruption, whereas in Latin countries it takes a major corruption scandal to excite interest in marital unfaithfulness![4] Such contrasts can lead us to reconsider broader theoretical issues in the study of law and society. How does the importance of 'enforcement' as an aspect of law vary in different societies? What can one learn, and what will one likely obscure, by defining 'law' in terms of litigation rates? Under what conditions can courts condition political actors? How do shame and guilt cultures condition the boundaries of law and in what ways does law help shape those same boundaries?

6   LEGAL CULTURE AND LEGAL CONSCIOUSNESS

In a recent attempt to sum up the field, Merry argues that legal culture is a valuable concept but that it is important to distinguish the various issues that one examines under this rubric. She distinguishes between studying the practices and ideologies of those with legal roles, the public's attitudes towards law, how readily people turn to law or 'legal mobilization', and legal consciousness—how people see themselves in relation to the law (Merry 2011). However, others, such as Franz and Keebet von Benda-Beckmann (2011) object that if we can identify its constituent parts there is no reason to continue to use the more general term. For them, legal culture refers 'to the knowledge, meanings and values inscribed into social phenomena at different layers of social organisation'—and each of these phenomena can and should be studied as such. It thus remains very much an open question whether or when it is better to study the elements that go to make up legal culture in their own right and when it can be useful to try to put them together.

It may often be appropriate to separate the study of culture as a 'variable' from what Glenn (2004) has called culture as 'holistic signifier'. Insofar as this coincides with the difference between what I have described as 'the political-science approach' to legal culture and the anthropological sense of the term applied to cultures as wholes, this could help deal with the confusion that Cotterrell points to. He describes the use Friedman makes of the term both for the variable of 'legal dynamics' as well as for a variety of large aggregates

---

[4]   Any given culture, and hence legal culture, is of course, always undergoing change. Since I first used this example, Italy has witnessed (unsuccessful) attempts to weaken the Silvio Berlusconi government by focusing on the sex liaisons of the Premier, whilst the UK has seen outrage over the abuse of parliamentary expenses (over which a few individuals had to resign). The relation between the synchronic and dynamic aspects of legal culture over time requires further study. Surprising continuity may often point to the influence of legal culture. For instance, consider the similarities in using prosecution for political purposes in countries such as Russia and Poland (Polak and Nelken 2010) even after the end of communism.

Table 15.1   Legal culture as a variable and an aggregate

	Legal Consciousness	Legal Culture
As Explanation	1. How attitudes and feelings about law influence the choice to use it	3. How interrelated attitudes, uses and discourses produce 'effects'
As Needing Explanation	2. Why people and groups have the attitudes they do	4. What makes patterns of attitudes and behaviours different

such as 'American culture' (Cotterrell 1997). Nevertheless, as we will see, the difference between legal culture as a variable and as an aggregate is not a firm one. We tend to think of aggregates as large, often national, units of legal culture. However, one could see all variables for some purposes as aggregates. For example, attitudes to law, which Friedman treats mainly as a variable, could be disaggregated where appropriate into the different elements that make them up. This is even true at the level of the individual, where one could take a person's 'attitude' to represent the sum of opinions tested in a survey instrument. Conversely, even large aggregates, such as American legal culture, can serve as explanations if one can configure them as variables that produce effects on attitudes or behaviour.

Table 15.1 distinguishes between legal consciousness and legal culture more generally. It shows that one can examine Friedman's interest in the reason why people turn to law as a topic that serves both as an explanation and as something that needs to be explained (cells 1 and 2). Micro-social qualitative studies into this in the USA and elsewhere over the past 20 years have been especially concerned to probe the role of legality for different social actors as it emerges from their life experience narratives. They have tried not to assume that law is or should be a priority in everyday life and have sought to tease out its often-contradictory role in people's lives (Silbey and Ewick 1998; Silbey 2001, 2005; Pélisse 2005; García-Villegas 2006). Quantitative survey research has also shown that people distinguish between confidence in the technical efficiency of legal remedies and their views about its social legitimacy (Toharia 2003).

The other two cells (3 and 4) concern legal culture more holistically as both a tool of explanation and as something to be explained. It is important to notice with respect to cell 3 that claiming that legal culture can also exert influence on attitudes and behaviour does not have to take the form of a tautological argument. For example, behaviour within one 'legal culture' may be influenced by imitation or perceptions of what is going on elsewhere. In a multitude of transnational economic, health, criminal, human rights and other initiatives, governmental and non-governmental agencies, networks of regulators and others exert pressure intended to change behaviour through processes of signalling and monitoring conformity (Nelken 2006c). When 'league tables' of legally relevant behaviour—such as incarceration rates or levels of corruption—are published, countries may try to come into line so as not to be too distant from the norm or average of other countries. Likewise, one of the most pressing tasks of the comparative sociologist of law is to try and capture how far current practices connected with what is described as globalisation in fact represent the attempted imposition or imitation of one particular legal culture, in particular the Anglo-American model (Ferrarese 2001).

Where legal culture is that which needs to be explained, rather than that which does the explaining (cell 4), a host of economic, political, social and wider cultural factors may be found relevant. The threat of circular argument is much less evident here, but this sort of enquiry risks becoming unwieldy and inconclusive. Almost everything about a society (or other unit) can turn out to be relevant to explaining why its legal culture, or even just one aspect of it, differs from another's. Why does Italy, for example, have such long court delays? The answer involves looking at the relevant laws, especially those to do with civil and criminal procedure, as well as the management and organisation of the courts and legal profession. In addition, one should give attention to economic interests and political priorities amongst other factors (Nelken 2004). It can prove surprisingly difficult to decide which of these factors is crucial (especially as the relevant facts can be elusive). Interpretations of these facts can be even more controversial. Do economic interests, such as those represented by small businesses, gain from the current situation, or are they its chief victims? If the latter, why do they not put more pressure on the politicians to do something?

7   THE COHERENCE OF LEGAL CULTURE

The most ambitious enquiries concerning legal culture have to do with making (and testing) claims about the coherence between its various elements. Cotterrell is certainly right to remind us that such unity may be question begging: often all that we have are social processes in which coherence is being asserted (1997). This certainly applies even to the supposed coherence of law itself (Balkin 1993; Dewar 1998), never mind its 'fit' to the larger society (Nelken 2009b). On the other hand, just as variables that explain will sometimes also need explaining, so too we can sometimes treat as coherent that which one can further disaggregate. Therefore, we should not rule out the possibility that, for some purposes, various elements add up to more than the sum of their parts. As James Whitman has claimed recently, in replying to criticisms of his culturalist approach to penal law,

> the pattern that we see in comparative punishment is also the pattern we see in many other areas of the law. Indeed, I would claim it as a virtue of my book that it shows that punishment law cannot be understood in isolation from the rest of the legal culture. For example, American workplace harassment law differs from German and French workplace harassment law in very much the same way. The same is true of comparative privacy law . . . just as it is true of the law of hate speech and everyday civility . . .. I think these studies carry cumulative weight. (2005: 392)

In speaking about the coherence of legal culture, we may be making one or more of the following claims:

(1)   There is some intrinsic causal link between the elements that make up a given unit (for example, some influential Italian observers attribute their court delays to the increasing number of lawyers; one might analyse the US case to cast doubt on this); or

(2)   the supposed coherence is one *imposed* on units by the observer and commentator, for example, through processes of classification such as the construction of 'ideal types', or on other theoretical grounds; or

(3)   the connection exists (only) insofar as participants talk about it 'as if' it exists, for example, when legal actors are obliged to assume or attempt to create such internal consistency. In this case, as Glenn puts it, 'culture may be an effect of our descriptions, not its precondition' (2004).

Table 15.2   Types of coherence

Internal Coherence	External Coherence
1. That which holds together given elements of legal culture	3. The relationship between legal culture and general culture
2. Legal culture as an aspect of political, economic, or social culture in the same unit	4. Given units of legal cultures compared to other legal cultures

All students of culture know how important it is to take seriously what participants think they are trying to do—since this is what gives meaning and purpose to their actions. However, we have to balance this against the need for analytic distance where our claims about legal culture rely on factors or findings which may be unknown to the participants themselves. This is especially true of ideas about comparative similarities and differences. Even well-informed people living in India wrongly think that the courts are slow because the country has such a relatively high rate of litigation (Galanter and Krishnan 2003). Likewise, Americans, as well as many others, are convinced that the US tort system regularly produces excessive and undeserved awards. Nevertheless, it turns out that in large part the media manufactures this impression (Haltom and McCann 2004). More generally, those societies where legal professionals express the least concern for what Anglo-American writers since Roscoe Pound have called the 'gap' or gulf between the 'law in books' and 'law in action' may not be those where the gap is least problematic, but those where the gap is overwhelming.

As Table 15.2 makes clear, we can also distinguish between types of coherence in what we are describing as legal culture by thinking about patterned relationships between legal culture and its elements, or its relationship to other external phenomena.

The first type of coherence (cell 1) concerns elements that the researcher hypothesised to hold together units of internal or external legal culture. Mirjan Damaška's well-known attempt to show the 'affinities' between the rules of criminal procedure in common law as compared to civil law countries is a good example (1986). Another is Cotterrell's suggestion to think about 'ideal types' of community that have different propensities to structure their relationships in terms of law (2001). The second kind of internal coherence (cell 2), on the other hand, invites attention to variability in the connections between legal culture and other interrelated aspects of the same culture (Brants and Field 2000). Returning to Damaška's argument, many commentators have suggested that in civil law, 'strong state' systems, law tends to be more linked to politics, whilst in common law systems it is more linked to the market. For this reason, the privatisation encouraged by neo-liberalism and the de-coupling of law from politics associated with globalisation has been more of a 'shock' for the civilian world.

The third type of coherence (cell 3) concerns the relationship between legal ideas and other practices and ideas in the wider society. For example, it can be instructive to examine what there is in common between what are considered appropriate methods of truth finding within and 'outside' of legal institutions (Chase 2005). Does one find the same methods of persuasion in law and other forms of enquiry? 'Legal' and 'scientific' forms of truth telling may be symbiotic because they use somewhat different approaches to truth finding. Scholars often assume that the direction of influence is mainly from culture in general to legal culture in particular. However, those who argue for 'constitutive' theories of 'law in society' would see things also working the other way round. It is law, or at least different forms of ordering practices, which help shape common behaviours and ideas (Calavita 2001). Societies may also differ in the extent to which they actually encourage similarities in legal and wider cultural practices. An insistence on 'formalism' in legal matters may often go together with the presupposition that there is (or should be) less formalism in the 'life world' of ordinary social interaction.

The last type of coherence (cell 4) refers to the traditional type of legal or socio-legal attempt to compare larger legal cultures as relatively independent units (often national ones). Freek Bruinsma, for example, argues that the specificities of legal culture lie in social valuations. One can best understand Dutch legal culture, compared to other legal cultures, if we consider the typically pragmatic way the Dutch handle issues such as drugs, prostitution and euthanasia (1998). Whether or not such differences are intrinsic to the object being described, such 'imagined' differences help to reproduce the boundaries of culture.

8   LEGAL CULTURE AND REFLEXIVITY

Despite the problems with the idea of culture, there is still much to be said for seeking to make sense of cultural variation in the ways law is thought about and lived in different societies and contexts (Chiba 1989). Not least, it can remind us of the need to examine our own cultural common sense. Can there be a culturally transcendent idea of legal culture? The 'culture of legality' has different implications in societies with weak state administrations. Amidst all the effort to reform the efficiency of legal institutions in developing countries, few have stopped to consider that in many such societies (and in all societies in at least some contexts) official law may often be experienced as a source of unpredictability that threatens to disrupt other normative patterns and agreements. Likewise, it is unlikely to be happenstance that Friedman thinks that external legal culture—the demand side—gives law its shape, whereas continental European scholars tend to assume that its dynamics must be located more in internal legal culture, or what Erhard Blankenburg called 'the supply side of infrastructural institutional arrangements (1997).[5] This disagreement is likely to be at least in part a reflection of differences in notions of the state and consequent different expectations about legal culture in the common law and civil law world. More recently, David Engel has suggested that Friedman's ideas about internal and

---

[5]   Blankenburg defines legal culture to include four components: law in the books, law in action as channelled by the institutional infrastructure, patterns of legally relevant behaviour, and legal consciousness, which he sees as a distinctive attitude towards the law among legal professionals (Blankenburg and Bruinsma 1994).

external legal culture may reflect the cultural aspiration of modernity to keep law separate from other spheres—an aspiration that is quite foreign to many past societies or current sacred legal systems (2011). He warns us that one would need a different starting-point when dealing with such diverse types of legal cultures. Even though Friedman's lifework has been to try to persuade lawyers that their idea of autonomy from social pressures is in fact an illusion, it turns out that the framework he uses to make this point itself reflects his own legal culture.

REFERENCES

Appadurai, Arjun (1996). *Modernity at Large: Cultural Dimensions of Globalization*. Minneapolis: University of Minnesota Press.

Balkin, Jack M. (1993). 'Understanding Legal Understanding: The Legal Subject and the Problem of Legal Coherence', 103 *Yale Law Journal* 105.

Bell, John (2002). *French Legal Cultures*. Cambridge: Cambridge University Press.

Benda-Beckmann, Franz von and Keebet von Benda-Beckmann (2011). 'Why Not Use Legal Culture?', in David Nelken (ed.), *The Uses of Legal Culture* (special issue of the *Journal of Comparative Law*).

Blankenburg, Erhard (1997). 'Civil Litigation Rates as Indicators for Legal Culture', in David Nelken (ed.), *Comparing Legal Cultures* 41–68. Brookfield, VT: Dartmouth.

Blankenburg, Erhard and Freek Bruinsma (1994). *Dutch Legal Culture*. Deventer: Kluwer Law and Taxation Publishers, 2nd edn.

Brants, Chrisje and Stewart Field (2000). 'Legal Culture, Political Cultures and Procedural Traditions: Towards a Comparative Interpretation of Covert and Proactive Policing in England and Wales and the Netherlands', in David Nelken (ed.), *Contrasting Criminal Justice* 77–116. Aldershot: Ashgate.

Bruinsma, Freek (1998). 'Dutch Internal Legal Culture', in Jürgen Brand and Dieter Strempel (eds), *Soziologie des Rechts. Festschrift für Erhard Blankenburg* 369–80. Baden-Baden: Nomos Verlagsgesellschaft.

Bruinsma, Freek (2000). *Dutch Law in Action*. Nijmegen: Ars Aequi.

Cain, Maureen (2000). 'Orientalism, Occidentalism and the Sociology of Crime', 40 *British Journal of Criminology* 239–60.

Calavita, Kitty (2001). 'Blue Jeans, Rape, and the "De-Constitutive" Power of Law', 35 *Law & Society Review* 89–116.

Chase, Oscar (2005). *Law, Culture, and Ritual: Disputing Systems in Cultural Context*. New York: New York University Press.

Chiba, Masaji (1989). *Legal Pluralism: Toward a General Theory of Law through Japanese Legal Culture*. Tokyo: Tokai University Press.

Cohen-Tanugi, Laurents (1996). 'The Law without the State', in Volkmar Gessner, Armand Hoeland and Casba Varga (eds), *European Legal Cultures* 269–73. Dartmouth: Aldershot.

Coombe, Rosemary J. (2000). 'Contingent Articulations: A Critical Cultural Studies of Law', in Austin Sarat and Thomas R. Kearns (eds), *Law in the Domains of Culture* 21–64. Ann Arbor: University of Michigan Press.

Cotterrell, Roger (1997). 'The Concept of Legal Culture,' in David Nelken (ed.), *Comparing Legal Cultures* 13–32. Brookfield, VT: Dartmouth.

Cotterrell, Roger (2001). 'Is There a Logic of Legal Transplants?', in David Nelken and Johannes Feest (eds), *Adapting Legal Cultures* 71–92. Oxford: Hart Publishing.

Cotterrell, Roger (2004). 'Law in Culture', 17 *Ratio Juris* 1–14.

Cotterrell, Roger (2006a). *Law, Culture and Society: Legal Ideas in the Mirror of Social Theory*. Ashgate: Aldershot.

Cotterrell, Roger (2006b). 'Comparison, Community, Culture', 2 *International Journal of Law in Context* 1–10.

Damaška, Mirjan R. (1986). *The Faces of Justice and State Authority*. New Haven: Yale University Press.

Dewar, John (1998). 'The Normal Chaos of Family Law', 61 *Modern Law Review* 467–85.

Dezalay, Yves and Bryant Garth (1996). *Dealing in Virtue*. Chicago: University of Chicago Press.

Dezalay, Yves and Bryant Garth (eds) (2002). *Global Prescriptions: The Production, Exportation and Importation of a New Legal Orthodoxy*. Ann Arbor: University of Michigan Press.

Engel, David M. (2005). 'Injury Narratives: Globalization, Ghosts, Religion, and Tort Law in Thailand', 30 *Law & Social Inquiry* 469–514.

Engel, David M. (2010). *Tort, Custom, and Karma: Globalization and Legal Consciousness in Thailand*. Stanford: Stanford University Press.

Engel, David M. (2011). 'The Uses of Legal Culture in Contemporary Socio-Legal Studies: A Response to Sally Engle Merry', in David Nelken (ed.), *The Uses of Legal Culture* (special issue of the *Journal of Comparative Law*).

Feldman, Eric (1997). 'Patients' Rights, Citizen Movements and Japanese Legal Culture', in David Nelken (ed.), *Comparing Legal Cultures* 215–36. Brookfield, VT: Dartmouth.

Feldman, Eric (2001). 'Blood Justice, Courts, Conflict and Compensation in Japan, France and the United States', 34 *Law & Society Review* 651–702.

Feldman, Eric (2006). 'The Tuna Court: Law and Norms in the World's Premier Fish Market', 94 *California Law Review* 313.

Ferrarese, Maria Rosaria (2001). *Le Istituzioni della Globalizzazione*. Bologna: Il Mulino.

Fitzpatrick Peter (2005). 'The Damned Word: Culture and its (In)compatibility with Law', 1 *Law, Culture and the Humanities* 2–13.

Friedman, Jonathan (1994). *Cultural Identity and Global Process*. London: Sage.

Friedman, Lawrence M. (1985). *Total Justice*. New York: Russell Sage Foundation.

Friedman, Lawrence M. (1990). *The Republic of Choice*. Cambridge, MA: University of Harvard Press.

Friedman, Lawrence M. (1994). 'Is There a Modern Legal Culture?' *Ratio Juris* 117.

Friedman, Lawrence M. (1997). 'The Concept of Legal Culture: A Reply', in David Nelken (ed.), *Comparing Legal Cultures* 33–40 Brookfield, VT: Dartmouth.

Friedman, Lawrence M. (2006). 'The Place of Legal Culture in the Sociology of Law', in Michael Freeman (ed.), *Law and Sociology* 185–99. Oxford: Oxford University Press.

Friedman, Lawrence M. and Rogelio Pérez-Perdomo (eds) (2003). *Legal Culture in the Age of Globalization: Latin America and Latin Europe*. Stanford: Stanford University Press.

Galanter, Marc and Jayanth K. Krishnan (2003). 'Debased Informalism: *Lok Adalats* and Legal Rights in Modern India', in Eric G. Jensen and Thomas C. Heller (eds), *Beyond Common Knowledge: Empirical Approaches to the Rule of Law* 96–141. Stanford: Stanford University Press.

Garapon, Anton and Joannis Papadopoulos (2003). *Juger en Amérique et en France*. Paris: Odile Jacob.

García-Villegas, Mauricio (2006). 'Comparative Sociology of Law: Legal Fields, Legal Scholarships, and Social Sciences in Europe and the United States', 31 *Law & Social Inquiry* 343–82.

Geertz, Clifford (1973). 'Thick Description: Towards an Interpretive Theory of Culture,' in Clifford Geertz, *The Interpretation of Cultures: Selected Essays*. New York: Basic Books.

Geertz, Clifford (1983). *Local Knowledge: Further Essays in Interpretive Anthropology*. New York, Basic Books.

Gessner, Volkmar, Armand Hoeland and Casba Varga (eds) (1996). *European Legal Cultures* 269–73. Dartmouth: Aldershot.

Gillespie, John Stanley (2006). *Transplanting Commercial Law Reform: Developing a 'Rule of Law' in Vietnam*. Ashgate: Aldershot.

Glenn, H. Patrick (2004). 'Legal Cultures and Legal Traditions', in Mark van Hoeck (ed.), *Epistemology and Methodology of Comparative Law* 7–20. Oxford: Hart.

Haley, John Owen (1978). 'The Myth of the Reluctant Litigant', 4 *Journal of Japanese Studies* 359–90.

Haltom, William and Michael McCann (2004). *Distorting the Law*. Chicago: Chicago University Press.

Hamilton, Valerie and Joseph Sanders (1992). *Everyday Justice: Responsibility and the Individual in Japan and the United States*. New Haven: Yale University Press.

Harding, Andrew (2001). 'Comparative Law and Legal Transplantation in South East Asia', in David Nelken and Johannes Feest (eds), *Adapting Legal Cultures* 199–222. Oxford: Hart Publishing.

Hertogh, Marc (2011). 'The Curious Case of Dutch Legal Culture: A Reassessment of Survey Evidence', in David Nelken (ed.), *The Uses of Legal Culture* (special issue of the *Journal of Comparative Law*).

Heyderbrand, Wolf (2001). 'From Globalization of Law to Law under Globalization', in David Nelken and Johannes Feest (eds), *Adapting Legal Cultures* 117–37. Oxford: Hart Publishing.

Heyderbrand, Wolf (2007). 'Globalization and the Rise of Procedural Informalism in Europe and America', in Volkmar Gessner and David Nelken (eds), *European Ways of Law: Towards a European Sociology of Law* 93–140. Oxford: Hart Publishers.

Hodgson, Jacqueline (2006). *French Criminal Justice*. Oxford: Hart Publishers.

Hofstede, Geert (1980). *Culture's Consequences: International Differences in Work Related Values*. Beverly Hills, CA: Sage.

Jettinghoff, Alex (2001). 'State Formation and Legal Change: On the Impact of International Politics', in David Nelken and Johannes Feest (eds), *Adapting Legal Cultures* 99–116. Oxford: Hart Publishing.

Johnson, David (2002). *The Japanese Way of Justice*. Oxford: Oxford University Press.

Kagan, Robert (2001). *Adversarial Legalism: The American Way of Law*. Cambridge, MA: Harvard University Press.

Kahn, Paul (1999). *The Cultural Study of Law: Reconstructing Legal Scholarship*. Chicago: Chicago University Press.

Krygier, Martin (1997). 'Is There Constitutionalism after Communism? Institutional Optimism, Cultural Pessimism, and the Rule of Law', 26(4) *International Journal of Sociology* 17–47.

Kuper, Adam (1999). *Culture: The Anthropologists' Account*. Cambridge, MA: Harvard University Press.

Merry, Sally Engle (2003). 'Human Rights Law and the Demonization of Culture (and Anthropology Along the Way)', 26 *PoLAR: Political and Legal Anthropology Review* 55–77.

Merry, Sally Engle (2005). *Human Rights and Gender Violence: Translating International Law into Local Justice*. Chicago: Chicago University Press.

Merry, Sally Engle (2011). 'What is Legal Culture? An Anthropological Perspective', in David Nelken (ed.), *The Uses of Legal Culture* (special issue of the *Journal of Comparative Law*).

Nelken, David (1994). 'Whom Can You Trust?' in David Nelken (ed.), *The Futures of Criminology* 220–42. London: Sage.

Nelken, David (1995). 'Understanding/Invoking Legal Culture', 4 *Social and Legal Studies* 435–52 (David Nelken (ed.), special issue on Legal Culture, Diversity and Globalization).

Nelken, David (ed.) (1997a). *Comparing Legal Cultures*. Brookfield, VT: Dartmouth.

Nelken, David (1997b). 'Puzzling out Legal Culture', in David Nelken (ed.), *Comparing Legal Cultures* 55–88. Brookfield, VT: Dartmouth.

Nelken, David (2001). 'Beyond the Metaphor of Legal Transplants? Consequences of Autopoietic Theory for the Study of Cross-Cultural Legal Adaptation', in Jiří Přibáň and David Nelken (eds), *Law's New Boundaries: The Consequences of Legal Autopoiesis* 265–302. Aldershot: Ashgate.

Nelken, David (2002). 'Comparing Criminal Justice', in Michael Maguire, Rod Morgan and Robert Reiner (eds), *The Oxford Handbook of Criminology* 175–202. Oxford: Oxford University Press, 3rd edn.

Nelken, David (2003). 'Comparativists and Transferability', in Pierre Legrand and Roderick Munday (eds), *Comparative Legal Studies: Traditions and Transition* 329–44. Cambridge: Cambridge University Press.

Nelken, David (2004). 'Using the Concept of Legal Culture', 26 *Australian Journal of Legal Philosophy* 1–28.

Nelken, David (2006a). 'Rethinking Legal Culture', in Michael Freeman (ed.), *Law and Sociology* 200–24. Oxford: Oxford University Press.

Nelken, David (2006b). 'Patterns of Punishment', 69 *Modern Law Review* 262–77.

Nelken, David (2006c). 'Signalling Conformity: Legal Change in China and Japan', 27 *Michigan Journal of International Law* 933.

Nelken, David (2007). 'Defining and Using the Concept of Legal Culture', in Esin Örücü and David Nelken (eds), *Comparative Law: A Handbook* 109–32. Oxford: Hart.

Nelken, David (2008). 'Normalising Time: European Integration and Court Delays in Italy', in Hanne Petersen et al. (eds), *Paradoxes of European Integration* 299–323. Aldershot: Ashgate.

Nelken, David (2009a). 'The Temple of Rights', 15 *European Journal of Public Law* 447 (review essay of Nina-Louisa Arold, *The Legal Culture of the European Court of Human Rights*, 2007).

Nelken, David (2009b). *Beyond Law in Context*. Aldershot: Ashgate.

Nelken, David (2010a). *Comparative Criminal Justice: Making Sense of Difference*. London: Sage.

Nelken, David (2010b). 'Human Trafficking and Legal Culture', 44 *Israel Law Review* 479–513.

Nelken, David (ed.) (2011a). *Comparative Criminal Justice and Globalisation*. Aldershot: Ashgate.

Nelken, David (ed.) (2011b). 'Using Legal Culture', in David Nelken (ed.), *The Uses of Legal Culture* (special issue of the *Journal of Comparative Law*).

Nelken, David (2011c). 'Theorising the Embeddedness of Punishment', in Dario Melossi, Maximo Sozzo and Richard Sparks (eds), *Travels of the Criminal Question: Cultural Embeddedness and Diffusion* 65–92. Oxford: Hart.

Nelken, David and Freek Bruinsma (2007). *Exploring Legal Cultures*. Amsterdam: Elsevier.

Nelken, David and Johannes Feest (eds) (2001). *Adapting Legal Cultures*. Oxford: Hart Publishing.

Pélisse, Jérôme (2005). 'A-t-on conscience du droit? Autour des *Legal Consciousness Studies*', 59 *Genèses* 114–30.

Polak, Paulina and David Nelken (2010). 'Polish Prosecutors, Political Corruption and Legal Culture', in Alberto Febbrajo and Wojciech Sadurski (eds), *East-Central Europe after Transition: Towards a New Socio-Legal Semantics* 219–54. Aldershot: Ashgate.

Rebuffa, Giorgio and Erhard Blankenburg (1993). 'Culture juridique', in André-Jean Arnaud (ed.), *Dictionnaire encyclopédique de théorie et de sociologie du droit* 139–42. Paris: LGDJ, 2nd edn.

Santos, Boaventura de Sousa (1995). *Towards a New Common Sense*. London: Routledge.

Sarat, Austin and Tom R. Kearns (eds) (1993). *Law in Everyday Life*. Ann Arbor: University of Michigan Press.

Sarat, Austin and Tom R. Kearns (eds) (1998). *Law in the Domains of Culture*. Ann Arbor: University of Michigan Press.

Sherman, Brad (1997). 'Remembering and Forgetting: The Birth of Modern Copyright Law', in David Nelken (ed.), *Comparative Legal Cultures* 237–66. Aldershot: Dartmouth.

Silbey, Susan (2001). 'Legal Culture and Consciousness', in *International Encyclopedia of the Social and Behavioral Sciences* 8623–29. Amsterdam: Elsevier Science.

Silbey, Susan (2005). 'After Legal Consciousness', 1 *Annual Review of Law and Social Science* 323–68.

Silbey, Susan and Patricia Ewick (1998). *The Common Place of the Law: Stories from Everyday Life*. Chicago: Chicago University Press.

Slaughter, Anne-Marie (1997). 'The Real New World Order', *Foreign Affairs* 183–97 (Sept.).

Tanase, Takao (2009). *Community and the Law*. Cheltenham, UK and Northampton, MA, USA: Elgar.

Teubner, Gunther (1998). 'Legal Irritants: Good Faith in British Law or How Unifying Law Ends Up in New Divergences', 61 *Modern Law Review* 11–32.

Toharia, José Juan (2003). 'Evaluating Systems of Justice through Public Opinion: Why? What? Who? How? and What for?', in Eric G. Jensen and Thomas C. Heller (eds), *Beyond Common Knowledge: Empirical Approaches to the Rule of Law* 21–62. Stanford: Stanford University Press.

Varga, Casba (ed.) (1992). *Comparative Legal Cultures*. New York: New York University Press.

Webber, Jeremy (2004). 'Culture, Legal Culture, and Legal Reasoning: A Comment on Nelken', 26 *Australian Journal of Legal Philosophy* 25–36.

Whitman, James Q. (2003). *Harsh Justice*. Oxford: Oxford University Press.

Whitman, James Q. (2005). 'Response to Garland', 7 *Punishment and Society* 389–96.

Winn, Jane Kaufman (1994). 'Relational Practices and the Marginalization of Law: Informal Financial Practices of Small Businesses in Taiwan', 28 *Law & Society Review* 193–232.

World Bank (2005). *Legal Culture and Judicial Reform* 1–2, available at World Bank Search, http://search.worldbank.org.

Zedner, Lucia (1995). 'In Pursuit of the Vernacular: Comparing Law and Order Discourse in Britain and Germany', 4 *Social and Legal Studies* 517–34.

16 Legal education
*David S. Clark**

1 INTRODUCTION

1.1 European Origins

The first large-scale use of systematic education to train legal professionals occurred in Europe during the twelfth and thirteenth centuries. Two universities distinguished themselves in developing and transmitting knowledge to such an extent that they attracted students from throughout Europe. The University of Bologna became famous for its instruction in Roman law and canon law while the University of Paris, renowned for its faculties of theology and liberal arts, influenced legal education through the structure of its organization. By 1400, 46 universities existed in Europe, most of which had a faculty of Roman law and canon law.[1]

England, which participated in this European development, offered Roman and canon law in its two universities at Oxford and Cambridge. This served the lawyers and judges who worked in church courts and in certain special royal courts, but it was only near the end of the twentieth century that law school education replaced apprenticeship (in London) as the dominant avenue to legal careers.[2] The English historical variation from university legal education in continental Europe helps to explain in part the divergence between the civil law and the common law traditions.

1.2 The Dominating Role of Church, State and Market

Figure 16.1 sets out a simplified macro-social model for illustrating the relationships in society between university legal education and dominating spheres of influence such as church, state and market. It is a premise of this model that at different times in the history of cultures a particular organizing influence comes to prevail in these relationships, although one or both of the other spheres may also be significant in promoting its

* Maynard and Bertha Wilson Professor of Law and Director, Certificate Program in International and Comparative Law, Willamette University. I thank Galin Brown, access services manager at the Willamette University College of Law library, for interlibrary loan assistance, especially for difficult to find statistical data.

1 David S. Clark, 'The Medieval Origins of Modern Legal Education: Between Church and State', 35 *American Journal of Comparative Law* 653–54, 717 (1987). Most universities had the traditional three higher faculties—law, medicine and theology—as well as the general faculty of (the seven) liberal arts. Ibid. 700–01.

2 Ibid. 654; John H. Langbein, Renée Lettow Lerner and Bruce P. Smith, *History of the Common Law: The Development of Anglo-American Legal Institutions* 169, 190–98 (New York: Aspen Publishers 2009). After Henry VIII broke with Rome, he closed the canon law faculty in 1535 and the Church of England used lawyers trained in Roman law. Ibid. 191.

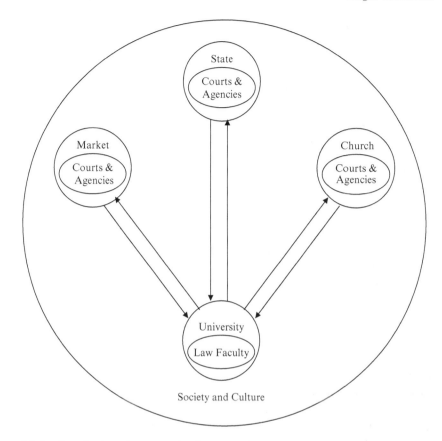

Figure 16.1   Legal education in societal context

own political or economic interests. An imperative of each type of order—whether it is church, state or market—aims to control and thereby to benefit from universities and legal education. Since control is often indirect, and even when direct may be benign, scholars usually ignore this high-level control when thinking about legal education. This distorts our understanding of the subject, especially in a comparative context. Other macro influences, such as technology, are instrumental and do not exist independently of the three major orders. Similarly, abstract ideals, such as justice, economic equality or dharma, serve the larger forces.

The medieval mind saw *sacerdotium, imperium* and *studium* as three mysterious powers that together sustained the life and health of Christendom. Beginning in the twelfth century, spontaneously developing medieval universities felt the need to combat external encroachments of a potentially stifling nature. These struggles against the rising power of church and state helped to formulate evolving views of corporate and individual academic freedom, which were crucial to the growth of universities as a separate estate in the medieval European community. Despite their semi-autonomous status, law faculties reacted to political, religious and economic pressures by providing church and state with the type of officials or jurists needed to promote their respective interests. This included the need to maintain order and to further other values. Law faculties also developed and transmitted new ideologies about law and government as well as methods of argument that filtered into and molded the larger culture.[3]

1.3   The Cognitive and Practical Dimensions

By focusing on the cognitive aspect of law training—knowing rather than doing—in particular on the role university law faculties have played in educating jurists, one discovers an unbroken history during which modern legal professions emerged. As mentioned, the study of law in continental Europe (only Roman and canon law until the eighteenth century) has been associated for centuries with instruction at the university. To a significant extent, this defines the salient characteristic of the civil law tradition, which followed European colonization and influence in Latin America, Asia and Africa with university legal education.[4]

In England, already by the late thirteenth century, before the Inns of Court in London, lawyers had tended to specialize in two distinct types of professional activity. Serjeants, who in 1300 numbered about 30, exercised the more prestigious, skillful and remunerated role when they spoke and argued for their clients in royal courts, especially the Court of Common Pleas at Westminster. Attorneys, a larger group of about 210, handled the preliminaries to civil litigation such as hiring and briefing the serjeant for the client and making sure the opponent appeared in court. Both professionals were trained through apprenticeship as in other guilds. They learned by watching, reading and doing (such as recording colloquies), working with the English common law.

Those men aspiring to become serjeants learned at court. The Common Bench apprentices had a special place in the courtroom (the crib), where a justice would sometimes instruct them on interesting legal points in a case. Some apprentices could also meet a county quota and serve as an attorney with the desire to qualify later as a serjeant. A 1292 royal ordinance ordered Common Bench justices to limit the number of professional attorneys by county. However, the evidence is that this cap was ineffective and that the difference between professional attorneys and would-be attorneys was that the former could attract clients, be recognized by a court, and earn a livelihood. The larger portion of professional attorneys learned their craft with occasional lectures, reading, attending court, practice exercises and helping other attorneys.[5]

In the fifteenth century, the Inns of Court took on the teaching mission for serjeants,

---

[3]   Clark, Medieval (note 1) 654–6.

[4]   See Edward Shils and John Roberts, 'The Diffusion of European Models outside Europe', in Walter Rüegg (ed.), 3 *A History of the University in Europe: Universities in the Nineteenth and Early Twentieth Centuries* (1800–1945) 163–231 (Cambridge: Cambridge University Press 2004). The University of Paris was one of the earliest to add a version of French law, a *jus proprium*, in 1679, to the two universal *jus commune*. David A. Bell, *Lawyers and Citizens: The Making of a Political Elite in Old Regime France* 33 (New York: Oxford University Press 1994).

[5]   Paul Brand, 'Legal Education in England before the Inns of Court', in Jonathan A. Bush and Alain Wijffels (eds), *Learning the Law: Teaching and the Transmission of Law in England, 1150–1900*, at 51, 61–84 (London: Hambledon Press 1999); see J.H. Baker, 'The English Legal Profession, 1450–1550', in Wilfrid Prest (ed.), *Lawyers in Early Modern Europe and America* 16–41 (London: Croom Helm 1981).

mixing lectures with problem-case mooting and practical pleading exercises. When the Inns gained a monopoly over admission to the bar, the term barrister became more common for some exercising the advocate's role. The Inns lost their teaching function in the seventeenth century, so aspiring barristers apprenticed with a solicitor or barrister, read the law and kept a commonplace book before petitioning an Inn for admission to the bar. Attorneys and solicitors joined in 1729 to form the Society of Gentlemen Practisers (incorporated as the Law Society in 1826). Apprenticeship was the route to admission to the Society. This apprenticeship system for a legal career followed the British to its colonies and, until recently, constituted the core element in learning the law in those places comparatists classify as common law countries.[6] Paul Brand concludes his excellent study of early English legal education:

> It was in large part the separation of the teaching of the common law from university legal education that made the common law so resistant to the influence of Roman law which elsewhere in Western Europe exercised a powerful influence over the development of national legal systems. One consequence of this was to make English judges and lawyers resistant to abstract thought and theoretical speculation: they had not been trained to think about law in that kind of way and saw no need to do so. The common law tradition of legal education produced tough and sharp thinkers, but not generally speculative ones. The consequences are perhaps still with us.[7]

2   FINDING A BALANCE BETWEEN THEORY AND PRACTICE IN LEARNING THE LAW

2.1   Tenacity of the University Education Tradition

As section 1 suggests, dozens of universities in Europe from the fifteenth century taught Roman and canon law.[8] The characteristic methods of instruction from the thirteenth century on were *lectura*, *disputatio* and *repetitio*. Professors (masters) conducted these in Latin, both to facilitate discussion of the sources and to accommodate the students who came from various parts of Europe speaking their peculiar languages and dialects. The lecture covered the source material, introducing and summarizing it, and reading it aloud,

---

[6]   J.H. Baker, *An Introduction to English Legal History* 160–64 (London: Butterworths-LexisNexis, 4th edn, 2002); see C.W. Brooks, 'The Common Lawyers in England, c. 1558–1642', in Wilfrid Prest (ed.), *Lawyers in Early Modern Europe and America* 42–64 (London: Croom Helm 1981).

[7]   Brand (note 5) 83–4.

[8]   See notes 1–2 and accompanying text. Farther away from the Mediterranean, in the north and east of Europe, the creation of universities with law faculties occurred in the late fifteenth century or even later. For instance, a papal bull founded Uppsala University, the oldest in Scandinavia, in 1477. Paolo Nardi, 'Relations with Authority', in Hilde de Ridder-Symoens (ed.), 1 *A History of the University in Europe: Universities in the Middle Ages* 84 (Cambridge: Cambridge University Press 1992). Empress Elizabeth decreed the founding of Moscow University in 1755, the first in Russia with law, continuing Peter the Great's opening to the West. Lomonosov Moscow State University, 'History of Moscow University', http://www.msu.ru/en/info/history.html.

together with glosses and comments (*lectio textus et apparatus*).[9] Professors mentioned similar and contrary legal provisions, solving apparent contradictions by revealing how a distinction might lead one text to apply in a certain situation and another text in a different situation. They might also continue to clarify the text with *argumenta* and pairs of opposing arguments (*brocardica*). A later school of scholarship offered more complex lectures with categorization of the textual sources, use of hypotheticals (*casus*), examination of contrary interpretations (*oppositiones*) and exploration of actual cases with question and answer (*quaestiones de facto*).

Masters and sometimes students (scholars) presented disputations in a dialectical style of argument (*quaesita et opposita*), defending a thesis against all comers. These stimulated student interest in points of law and helped to develop student ability to argue *pro et contra*. Professors also prepared *repetitiones*, which were elaborate discussions of some particularly difficult question reserved from a recent lecture or of an important timely topic.[10]

Law students in most of the world today would recognize elements of this scholastic approach to learning the law. Since World War II, university law teaching has become near universal. Even in England, where the Inns of Court organized instruction for barristers from about 1500 until 1640, they took on something of the form of a 'third university'. The difference between the Inns and the two English universities (and those of continental Europe) was that barristers and judges rather than professors conducted lectures and exercises at the Inns. In Europe, many professors wrote scholarly works about what they taught. They spent time organizing and conceptualizing the law and were less interested in legal practice with clients than were barristers. In addition, the core Roman and canon law source material was textual in nature, perhaps more amenable to sophisticated classification and conceptualization. With English common law, by contrast, cases constituted the primary source material. Compilers classified cases according to illogical writs and then organized them within yearbooks, nominate reports and abridgments. In the seventeenth century, a few English barristers undertook a more analytical categorization of the law, which led to encyclopedias and treatises, but by this time, apprenticeship had replaced the teaching function at the Inns.[11]

2.2   Creation of Guilds for Lawyers

Historically there were, and today in most countries there are, more than one legal career, with varied educational requirements of a learned or practical nature.[12] Castile in the sixteenth century provides an interesting example. There were three principal types of private lawyers: *abogados*, *procuradores* and *solicitadores*. The first two categories reflected Roman influence on the structure of legal representation. *Abogados* (advocates) had the most prestige since they had earned a law degree at a university;

---

9   Clark, Medieval (note 1) 681, 696–7. The university typically regulated the book trade, since generally students could not afford books. Some students rented a small part of a book at a fixed price per quire (*pecia*), four sheets with writing on both sides in a portfolio. Ibid. 698.
10   Ibid. 697–8.
11   Langbein et al. (note 2) 179–90, 933–6.
12   See Chapter 17 this volume on the variety of legal professions.

they could plead for a client in court and file appeals. In 1495, there was no bar organization to limit the number of advocates and apprenticeship was unnecessary. Rather, universities certified that a person had studied both Roman and canon law for five years and thus qualified for a doctoral law degree. He could use the title *letrado* or *licenciado* and apply to the crown's judges in an *audiencia*, which was the general jurisdiction court for a region. They examined him, verified his credentials and admitted him to plead in court.[13]

However, as the sixteenth century progressed, the number of advocates increased to such an extent that leading members of the profession decided to organize in a guild-like structure to control the supply of authorized practice. Between 1592 and 1595, they formed two *colegios de abogados* (bar associations), one each in Madrid and Valladolid. Nevertheless, the *colegios* did not effectively curb access, so the advocates petitioned the crown, which decreed in 1605 that its judges reduce the number of advocates by half. The purported rationale was to protect litigants from the corruption and greed of desperate advocates. This pattern of private independent bar and state cooperation was repeated throughout Europe.[14]

Procuradores (procurators) and *solicitadores* (solicitors) had no university requirement and learned the law through clerkship or apprenticeship. *Abogados* depended upon *procuradores* to bring them cases, and sometimes the former would have an agreement with the latter to promote business. Procurators were primarily responsible for litigation strategy, finding witnesses and securing admissible documents. If they could help a client resolve a dispute without litigation, they would keep all the fees. Most cities enacted laws limiting the number of procurators, often to about 30 or 40. They had to purchase their office and royal courts only permitted those licensed to practice. In the 1570s, procurators began organizing into *colegios* to protect their livelihood from the emerging practitioner branch known as *solicitadores*.[15]

As litigation increased in the sixteenth century, procurators were unable to accommodate all who wished to sue. Solicitors learned law by having worked for another private practitioner or in a court and were unregulated by the state. In general, they assisted procurators in preparing cases, acted as agents in the disbursement of funds, and greased

---

[13]   Richard L. Kagan, 'Lawyers and Litigation in Castile, 1500–1750', in Wilfrid Prest (ed.), *Lawyers in Early Modern Europe and America* 181, 184–6, 189, 193 (London: Croom Helm 1981). Charles I, king of Spain from 1516 to 1556, and later Habsburgs preferred that law professors rather than advocates serve on royal courts or councils. Ibid. 186, 198. The scholarly bias carried over to German imperial courts, since Charles was also emperor of the Holy Roman Empire from 1519 (as Charles V).

[14]   Ibid. 189; Richard L. Abel, *The Legal Profession in England and Wales* 37–46 (Oxford: Basil Blackwell 1988). One could sometimes see the same collaboration between the Roman church and those lawyers admitted to practice in ecclesiastical courts. In eleventh century Castile, clerics expert in canon law had a right of audience in ecclesiastical courts. Kagan (note 13) 185. In England, the archbishops of Canterbury and York provided a right of audience in ecclesiastical courts to Cambridge and Oxford law graduates in Roman and canon law, who were known as advocates. They formed Doctors' Commons in the late fifteenth century to further their interests, including practice in admiralty courts. Baker (note 6) 169–70; see Brian P. Levack, 'The English Civilians, 1500–1750', in Wilfrid Prest (ed.), *Lawyers in Early Modern Europe and America* 108–28 (London: Croom Helm 1981).

[15]   Kagan (note 13) 184–6.

litigation with bribes and gifts. When litigation declined in the seventeenth century, procurators saw the investment in their position decline in value and petitioned the crown to intervene. In 1632, Philip IV prohibited solicitors from practice in royal courts and, to procure revenue, sold a new office called *agente de negocio*, limited in number, that granted the buyer exclusive right to serve as legal agent in a royal court.[16]

As a result, by the seventeenth century, Castile had the two Roman professions associated with litigation, advocate and procurator, found throughout Europe (including England as barrister and attorney or solicitor). Through their respective associations, first with the advocates' *collegios*, they began to create an independent identity separate from the state, with a right to set their own admission standards, ethical rules and fee schedules. In addition, advocates aspired to associate their status with that of the landed aristocracy to elevate the rather low prestige of lawyers in general.[17]

France provides another example similar to that of Castile. In the seventeenth century, there were *avocats* and *procureurs*, who divided litigation activities as in Spain. The advocates who desired to practice law requested admission to a regional *ordre des avocats*, the guild for advocates. Unlike Castile, which required a doctorate in law, the Paris bar found the three-year degree (*licence*) sufficient, but students could obtain it under low standards or even purchase it at some French universities. If accepted, the *ordre* entered their names on a list (*rôle*), printed annually and available to judges and procurators as the *tableau*. Another difference was that many men who took the title *avocat* did not intend to practice law, but some accepted positions in government or joined princely councils to manage real estate holdings or provide legal and political advice. By the end of the century, the bar had succeeded in establishing standards of conduct for its members and effective discipline, in effect, creating its own culture and character.[18]

Procurators, as in Castile, did not need to attend a university, but about two-thirds of the 400 Paris *procureurs* had a diploma. The French crown raised money by selling the office, which made the procurators royal officers subject to direct royal discipline. However, procurators first needed to complete a long apprenticeship as a clerk, usually for ten years. Once obtaining office, procurators paid a share of their regulated fees to the crown, which manipulated the arrangement to the procurators' disadvantage. Consequently, they used an organization, the *communauté des procureurs*, to serve their interests, including negotiating with the crown and facilitating loans to help members.[19]

2.3 Development of an Apprenticeship Requirement

Apprenticeship for a career in law developed spontaneously in continental Europe (as in England) and requirements grew incrementally. As the two civil law examples of Spain and France suggest, it was associated with the guilds that private lawyers created to further their welfare. One of the guilds' primary concerns was to improve the prestige of their members. For advocates, this aspiration was to achieve the status of the landed

---

[16] Ibid. 189–92.
[17] Ibid. 196–9.
[18] Bell (note 4) 27–33, 35–6, 38–9, 50–56, 58, 125. The University of Reims, for example, was notorious for selling the *licence* after minimal attendance. Ibid. 34.
[19] Ibid. 30, 39–40, 61–2, 124, 172.

aristocracy or perhaps educated nobility.[20] For procurators, whose image was worse, particularly in France where the monarchy was often devising new charges (for further procurator privileges) that they passed on to clients, the goal was to gain acceptance as a profession closer to that of advocacy. Both professions believed that improving the training of their members would help in these endeavors. The guilds' emphasis was on the practical and technical aspects of their members' work. This meant learning by supervised doing.

The practical side of training had always been the focus of procurator guilds. For advocates, however, apprenticeship became supplemental to the learned core that served as the primary basis for their prestige. For instance, in France after 1693, the Paris *Ordre*, reacting to the poor quality of many French university law faculties, instituted a two-year internship (*stage*) for *avocats écoutants* prior to formal acceptance. Interns had to attend court hearings and have six senior *avocats* attest to their accomplished ability. In 1710, the bar began a series of seminars on selected legal topics of a vocational nature with senior advocates and magistrates as lecturers. Finally, about a third of advocates served as clerks to procurators, either before or during their *stage*.[21]

An important dimension of bar associations was their origin and development independent of the state as a liberal profession. The office of advocate was never a royal office or sold for income by the state.[22] However, as nation states in Europe gained power vis-à-vis intermediate entities in society, including trade and professional guilds, this independence became problematic. Bar associations lost some of their prerogatives over training, admission, conduct, fees and discipline. Nevertheless, in most countries, the importance of apprenticeship for private legal practice, and in fact for most modern legal careers including judges, remained.

3   THE DOMINANCE OF UNIVERSITY LAW FACULTIES OR LAW SCHOOLS

3.1   Recent Common Law Acceptance of University Legal Education

In England, Australia and Canada it was not until the second half of the twentieth century that university legal education replaced apprenticeship as the dominant avenue to legal careers. For instance, of the solicitors admitted to practice in 1985 in England and Wales, only 75 percent had graduated from a university law school.[23] In Canada, a law degree became mandatory in every province for admission to the law society in 1960. In addition, most Canadian law students completed more than two years in a university

---

[20]   Michael P. Fitzsimmons, *The Parisian Order of Barristers and the French Revolution* 10 (Cambridge, MA: Harvard University Press) (treatises referred to *avocats* as *demi-noblesse*).

[21]   Ibid. 15, 28, 31, 34–7, 39–40, 56, 58–9. Provincial bars sometimes required a three-year *stage*. Lenard R. Berlanstein, 'Lawyers in Pre-Revolutionary France', in Wilfrid Prest (ed.), *Lawyers in Early Modern Europe and America* 164, 167–8 (London: Croom Helm 1981).

[22]   E.g., Fitzsimmons (note 20) 8.

[23]   For the English history, see Andrew Boon and Julian Webb, 'Legal Education and Training in England and Wales: Back to the Future', 58 *Journal of Legal Education* 79, 85–100 (2008).

liberal arts program only in the 1980s, following the US model of law as a graduate university curriculum. By 2000, most common law Canadian law schools required an undergraduate degree to enroll in the law program of three years' study for the bachelor of laws degree (LL.B) and by 2011 the degree was renamed at most universities the juris doctor (JD) to coincide with US practice, augment prestige and emphasize its graduate-level status.[24]

In the United States, however, university law schools at the end of the nineteenth century had already adopted important elements related to the goals, method, structure and ceremony of European—and especially German—legal education. By the 1920s, accredited law schools had largely replaced apprenticeship as the avenue to the profession. Modern legal education in other parts of the common law world also followed the European example and therefore one can better understand it as part of a long and rich university tradition now nine centuries old.[25]

3.2   Some Comparative Illustrations in Civil Law and Common Law Countries

Current examples from civil law and common law countries will illustrate the function that university legal education serves as the initial gatekeeper to the legal professions.[26] University legal education became virtually universal in the last three decades for the exclusive (or at least dominant) path of entry to the legal profession. This was so for solicitors and barristers in the 1980s in Canada and the United Kingdom, *notarios* in Uruguay, and *conseils juridiques* up to 1991 when they became *avocats* in France. At the same time as the university requirement brought greater status to certain law professions, a push to democratize opportunities in law to the middle and lower social classes led to the creation of many new law faculties and much larger law student enrollments. In the late 1960s and 1970s, law studies also opened up to women, who progressively have made up a larger proportion of the student body. By 2009, women had reached parity or beyond with men in law enrollment in Europe, North America and many other places.[27]

Table 16.1 demonstrates some of these generalities since World War II for both civil law and common law systems.

---

[24]   David S. Clark, 'Comparing the Work and Organization of Lawyers Worldwide: The Persistence of Legal Traditions', in John J. Barceló III and Roger C. Cramton (eds), *Lawyers' Practice and Ideals: A Comparative View* 9, 25–6 (Hague: Kluwer Law International 1999); see, e.g., UBC Faculty of Law, UBC Board of Governors Approves Request for LL.B (Bachelor of Laws) degree to be renamed JD (Juris Doctor), http://www.law.ubc.ca/news (select 18 Mar. 2008).

[25]   Richard L. Abel, *American Lawyers* 71–3 (New York: Oxford University Press 1989); Robert Stevens, *Law School: Legal Education in America from the 1850s to the 1980s*, at 172–80, 205 (Chapel Hill: University of North Carolina Press 1983); David S. Clark, 'Tracing the Roots of American Legal Education—A Nineteenth-Century German Connection', 51 *Rabels Zeitschrift für ausländisches und internationales Privatrecht* 313–33 (1987).

[26]   A good example of the state dominating control of legal education occurred in former East Germany. The communist government permitted only one law school, at Humboldt University in Berlin, to train its judges and lawyers. In an attempt to guarantee the political reliability of future jurists, the ministry of justice controlled the admission process. Most lawyers were party members and one-third of their law training at the university was in Marxism-Leninism. Clark, Comparing (note 24) 28–9.

[27]   Ibid. 26, 105.

Table 16.1   Total number of law students, by country and year[28]

	1950	1970	1990	2009
Europe				
France[29]	39,000	127,000	158,000	170,000
Germany[30]	12,000	32,000	83,000	101,000
Italy	37,000	59,000	142,000	216,000
Spain	17,000	21,000	160,000	112,000
United Kingdom[31]	4,500	9,000	17,000	92,000
United States[32]	42,000	78,000	127,000	145,000
Japan[33]	29,000	145,000	190,000	168,000

Perhaps surprisingly, population size has not been a major determinant of national enrollment in law study when one investigates the question comparatively. In Europe, for instance, France, Italy and the United Kingdom have approximately the same number of inhabitants (between 60 and 63 million in 2009). Nevertheless, while France, Italy and Spain—three civil law countries—had similar increases in law students from 1950 to 1990, the UK in 1950 had very few students studying law at the university. It did not really shift to university legal education in a major way until 1990, after which its student number approached that for Germany in 2009 (which had a population of 82 million).

What might explain some of these European variations? In England and Wales during the 1950s, about three-fourths of barristers admitted to the bar were university

[28]   Sources: Abel (note 14) 465 (for England and Wales 1970); John Henry Merryman, David S. Clark and John Owen Haley, *The Civil Law Tradition: Europe, Latin America, and East Asia* 870–71 (Charlottesville, VA: Michie Co. 1994) (for Germany, Italy and Spain 1950–90); American Bar Association, 'Legal Education Statistics from ABA-Approved Law Schools', http://www.americanbar.org/groups/legal_education/resources/statistics.html (for 2009); David S. Clark, 'American Legal Education: Yesterday and Today', 10 *International Journal of the Legal Profession* 93, 97 (2003) (for 1950–90); Eurostat, Home Page, http://epp.eurostat.ec.europa.eu (select Statistics, then Education and Training, then Tertiary Students (ISCED 5–6) by Field of Education and Sex) (for France, Germany, Spain and UK 2009); C.J. Hamson, 'The Teaching of Law: Reflections Prompted by the UNESCO Enquiry, 1950–52', 2 *Journal of the Society of Public Teachers of Law* 19, 21–2 (new series, 1952–4) (for UK 1950); Institut National de la Statistique et des Études Économiques, 58 *Annuaire Statistique 1951*, at 61 (1952) (for France 1950); ibid., 76 *Annuaire Statistique de la France 1970/71*, at 104 (1971) (for 1969); 96 ibid. *1991–92*, at 308 (1992) (for 1990); Istituto Nazionale di Statistica, Annuario Statistico Italiano 2010, at 185–8 (2011) (for 2009); Statistics Bureau, 1 *Japan Statistical Yearbook* table 214 (1951) (for 1950); 21 ibid. 1971 at table 373 (for 1970); 41 ibid. 1991 at 661 (for 1990); 61 ibid. 2011 at table 22-16 (for 2009); John Wilson, 'A Third Survey of University Legal Education in the United Kingdom', 13 *Legal Studies* 143, 146, 155 (1993) (for Scotland 1950–90, England and Wales 1990).

[29]   The 1970 number is from 1969.
[30]   For unified Germany in 1990 and 2009.
[31]   Excluding Northern Ireland 1950–90.
[32]   Enrolled in JD degree programs at ABA-approved schools.
[33]   Including 5,000 and 19,000 students in 1950 and 1970 who combined law studies with economics or literature. For 1990 and 2009, an undifferentiated number of law students also studied politics.

graduates, although most had degrees in liberal arts and not law. This changed by the 1980s, when four-fifths of new barristers had law degrees. For the much larger group of solicitors, it was not until after 1970 that a majority of new solicitors had even graduated from a university. By 1985, however, three-fourths of new admissions were law graduates, with another 15 percent graduates in other disciplines.[34] While, before 1990, most law students went on to a law career, today only about half of UK law students do so.[35]

This latter phenomenon of attending university law studies with no serious intention of pursuing a traditional legal career has been common in many places, especially civil law countries. After World War II, law was a popular course of study at the university (see Table 16.1). In continental Europe and Japan, law faculties often also included tracks emphasizing economics or political science. The creation of the first European-style law faculty in Japan in 1877 had the objective of educating government officials in Western statecraft based on European legal systems. In addition, about one-third of French students in law faculties were primarily studying economics from 1950 through the 1970s.[36] Many students did not graduate, but went on to work in a non-law career. Some who graduated did not qualify for a law job or chose government or business employment. In some nations, such as France and Japan, there were many types of law or quasi-law occupations which law graduates could pursue.[37] Furthermore, France from 1970 had several university credentials for law—*certificat, diplôme, licence,* and *maîtrise*—that involved progressively more course work which permitted employers to differentiate among candidates.[38]

The enrollment in law faculties doubled (or more) between 1950 and 1970 in many European countries and the United States. However, in Italy and Spain it took until 1990 to catch up with the general postwar European expansion. Francisco Franco's fascist regime delayed Spain's growth until after his death in 1975. Italy was slower to reform university education than France.[39] In Japan, law enrollment increased by a factor of five between 1950 and 1970. This increase in the number of law students occurred as central governments eased university entrance requirements to accommodate more applicants from the middle class, students viewed law as a useful preparation for many careers and women determined that law would provide a practical profession to earlier alternatives and a chance to extend the equality agenda. By 1990, this trend peaked (in Spain and Japan) and the growth rate slowed elsewhere up to 2009 apart from the UK.

In the first two decades after World War II, civil law nations had substantial enrollments in law faculties compared to other university disciplines. This was due to the traditional importance of law studies in civil law Europe and Latin America as an avenue to many

---

[34]   Abel (note 14) 47–8, 143, 319, 391.

[35]   'Qualifying as a Lawyer', http://www.legaleducation.org.uk.

[36]   76 *Annuaire Statistique de la France 1970/71* (note 28) 105; Emmanuelle Pautler, 'The Links between Secondary and Higher Education in France', 16 *European Journal of Education* 185, 187 (1981); Kahei Rokumoto, 'Legal Education', in Daniel H. Foote (ed.), *Law in Japan: A Turning Point* 190, 192–5 (Seattle: University of Washington Press 2007).

[37]   See Chapter 17 this volume for detail on types of law or quasi-law occupations.

[38]   See 76 *Annuaire Statistique de la France 1970/71* (note 28) 103, 105; 96 ibid. 288, 312.

[39]   Higher education reform began in France in 1966. Between 1964 and 1969, the number of law students (some in new programs) increased from 65,000 to 127,000. Ibid. 103.

Table 16.2   Percentage university students in law, by country and year[40]

	1950	1970	1990	2009
Europe				
France[41]	23	22	13	8
Germany	10	9	6	4
Italy	16	9	15	11
Spain	31	10	22	6
United Kingdom[42]		4	2	4
United States[43]	2	1	1	1
Japan	13	11	10	7

types of careers, including business. The percentage of law students in universities in the UK and the US, however, was in the low single digits (see Table 16.2).[44] For the US (and Germany at 10 percent), some university disciplines had already evolved as options for a professional career prior to 1950. However, after 1950, even with rapidly expanding law student numbers, universities and other new institutions of higher education opened, added new departments, and in general grew faster than law faculties. Consequently, by 2009, only Italy in Table 16.2 had law faculty enrollment greater than 10 percent of that for the entire university. The mass university law faculties of the 1990s had a large ratio of students to teachers, ranging from about 40 to one in Germany to more than 50 to one in Italy and Spain. Approximately a third of these teachers were full professors. This ratio had not improved by 2009, when it was 56 to one in Italy with the same fraction of full professors.[45]

Another feature of law study beyond the *relative* decline in the percentage of law students at the university was its *feminization*. This trend, noticeable almost everywhere after 1970, was part of a larger movement of women training to enter the professional marketplace generally and the expansion of universities in many countries facilitated it. In Europe, for example, 6 percent of the law students in Germany in 1950 were women, whose percentage

---

[40]   Sources: Table 16.1 provides the numerator. I derived the number of university students from the same sources listed in Table 16.1, except as further noted in Table 16.2. There are variations in the definition of universities and newer forms of higher education in some countries.

[41]   See Jean-Claude Eicher, 'The Recent Evolution of Higher Education in France: Growth and Dilemmas', 32 *European Journal of Education* 185–6 (1997).

[42]   Eurostat, *Yearbook 2002*, at 89 (2002) (for 1990); Isabelle Musnik, 'Student Flows in Higher Education 1970–1977', 13 *Paedagogica Europaea* 37, 42 (1978) (for 1970).

[43]   Enrolled in four-year institutions. US Census Bureau, *Statistical Abstract of the United States 2011* table 275 (2010) (for 1990–2009); ibid., *Historical Statistics of the United States: Colonial Times to 1970*, at 383 (1975) (for 1950–70).

[44]   In Canada, the percentage in law study was 2 percent in 1962 and 3 percent in 1983. Harry W. Arthurs, Richard Weisman and Frederick H. Zemans, 'Canadian Lawyers: A Peculiar Professionalism', in Richard L. Abel and Philip S.C. Lewis, 1 *Lawyers in Society: The Common Law World* 123, 127 (Berkeley: University of California Press 1988).

[45]   Merryman et al. (note 28) 870–72; Istituto Nazionale di Statistica (note 28) 189. Seventeen percent of the Italian full professors in 2009 were women. Ibid. 189.

Table 16.3   *Total number of law students and as a percentage of university students in Latin America, by country and year*[46]

	1950		1965		1985		2000	
Argentina[47]			29,000	13%			164,000	15%
Brazil[48]			33,000	22%	135,000	9%	370,000	14%
Chile	2,000	25%	3,000	8%			24,000	5%
Colombia[49]	2,000	21%	5,000	12%	27,000	8%	67,000	7%
Mexico[50]			17,000	13%	84,000	9%	188,000	12%
Peru	1,000	9%	5000	6%			37,000	9%
Venezuela	1,000	14%	7000	13%			44,000	7%

increased to 12 by 1970, 42 by 1991 and 53 in 2009.[51] Women were 17 percent of the entering law students in the UK in 1967, but increased to 59 percent of all law students in 2009.[52] In the US, women represented 3 percent of total law students in 1960, 9 percent in 1970, 43 percent by 1990, and 47 percent in 2009.[53] Today, women are the majority of students studying law in Italy and Spain and reached 66 percent in France in 2009.[54] Japan tells a somewhat different story, which may be typical for developed Asian nations. In 1950, 1 percent of law students were women, whose percentage increased to 5 by 1970, but only 16 by 1991 and 29 in 2009.[55]

As Table 16.3 illustrates, some similar patterns exist in Latin America, where the number of law students increased dramatically after 1965. All of the countries listed are

---

[46]   Merryman et al. (note 28) 873, 878, 882–3; Rogelio Pérez-Perdomo, *Latin American Lawyers: A Historical Introduction* 105 (Stanford, CA: Stanford University Press 2006); Sergio López-Ayllón and Héctor Fix-Fierro, '"Faraway, So Close!" The Rule of Law and Legal Change in Mexico, 1970–2000', in Lawrence M. Friedman and Rogelio Pérez-Perdomo (eds), *Legal Culture in the Age of Globalization: Latin America and Latin Europe* 285, 319–20 (Stanford, CA: Stanford University Press 2003); Rogelio Pérez-Perdomo and Lawrence Friedman, 'Latin Legal Culture in the Age of Globalization', in ibid. 1, 8.

[47]   The 1965 number is from 1970 and the 2000 number is from 1998.

[48]   The 1985 number is from 1980. For 2000, Instituto Nacional de Estudos e Pesquisas, *Censo da Ecucação Superior 2003: Resumo Técnico* 21 (2003) (university students); Roberto Fragale Filho, 'Brazilian Legal Education: Curricular Reform that Goes Further without Going Beyond', 10 *German Law Journal* 751, 753–4 (2009) (law students).

In 2009, there were 652,000 Brazilian law students, who constituted 13 percent of total university enrollment excluding distance learning (which was not available for law). Instituto Nacional de Estudos e Pesquisas (ibid.) *Censo 2009* at 14 (2010), http://portal.inep.gov.br/web/censo-da-educacao-superior/resumos-tecnicos.

[49]   The 1985 number is from 1983 and the 2000 number is from 2001.

[50]   The 1985 number is the average between 1979 and 1991. See Héctor Fix-Fierro, 'The Role of Lawyers in the Mexican Justice System', in Wayne A. Cornelius and David A. Shirk, *Reforming the Administration of Justice in Mexico* 251, 253–4 (Notre Dame, IN: University of Notre Dame Press 2007).

[51]   Merryman et al. (note 28) 871–2; Eurostat (note 28).

[52]   Abel (note 14) 276; Eurostat (note 28).

[53]   Clark, American (note 28) 99; American Bar Association (note 28).

[54]   Eurostat (note 28); Istituto Nazionale di Statistica (note 28) 185–8. Women were already a majority of law students in France in 1990. 96 *Annuaire Statistique de la France 1979–91* (note 28) 308.

[55]   Statistics Bureau (note 28) (same volumes and pages).

typical civil law nations with a long history of university legal education that traditionally served as general training for the non-medical professions. That means that many
law students did not intend to enter the legal professions.[56] Alternatives to law study at
the university in general developed more slowly than in Europe, which the percentage
of university students in law suggests. By the mid-1980s, nevertheless, new departments
had opened and law represented about 10 percent or less of the university population.
Surprisingly, by comparison with Europe, the continued strong growth in Latin American
law enrollment in the 1990s was perhaps responsive to the liberalization in market economies following the collapse of Soviet socialism and to continued democratization within
the political system.[57] This might explain the substantial creation of new and expansion
of existing private university law schools in Mexico by a factor of almost six compared to
public university law enrollment from 1991 to 2000.[58]

Brazil provides an interesting example of the growth cycle. The fraction of university
students studying law in 1961 was 24 percent, a large percentage that nevertheless represented only 24,000 law students. With the ruling military regime substantially expanding
university enrollment after 1977, the law percentage declined to 9 percent in 1980. After
that, increased interest in law promoted by economic and political liberalization led to the
huge law enrollment of 370,000 in 2000, 14 percent of the university total. That percentage remained steady through 2009 with a continued law expansion to 652,000 students.[59]
As for women studying law, in Brazil in 1950 they represented 3 percent of law students,
which increased to 25 percent in 1983, when women were already 45 percent of Colombian
law students. The ratio of female law students in Mexico rose from 28 percent in 1979 to 49
percent in 2002 and in Argentina was 56 percent in 1997. There were also more students
from lower-income social strata gaining admission to law faculties after 1990.[60]

Law enrollment grew almost as much in Mexico as in Brazil and it continued into the
new century to reach 240,000 in 2007. Much of that increase was in private university
law schools, some of which have gained in national prestige. Thus, private law schools
enrolled 16 percent of the total students in 1991, but 45 percent in 2001.[61] Nevertheless,

---

[56]   Merryman et al. (note 28) 881; López-Ayllón and Fix-Fierro (note 51) 319.

[57]   E.g., Filho (note 53) 756; Eliane Botelho Junqueira, 'Brazil: The Road of Conflict Bound
for Total Justice', in Lawrence M. Friedman and Rogelio Pérez-Perdomo (eds), *Legal Culture in the
Age of Globalization: Latin America and Latin Europe* 64, 85–6 (Stanford, CA: Stanford University
Press 2003). The 1990s expansion in law enrollment in some countries increased its percentage
importance at the university. Ibid. 85–7.

[58]   López-Ayllón and Fix-Fierro (note 51) 320, 323–4. The phenomenon of mass public universities and their decline in quality also contributed to the growth of private options. Ibid. 323. The same
pattern of expansion for private university law schools occurred in Chile between 1990 and 1998.
National law student enrollment increased during that period from 9,000 to 25,000, mostly at private
law schools. Edmundo Fuenzalida Faivovich, 'Law and Legal Culture in Chile, 1974–1999', in
Lawrence M. Friedman and Rogelio Pérez-Perdomo (eds), *Legal Culture in the Age of Globalization:
Latin America and Latin Europe* 108, 119 (Stanford, CA: Stanford University Press 2003).

[59]   Merryman et al. (note 28) 878, 883; Filho (note 53) 752–4.

[60]   Merryman et al. (note 28) 873, 882–3; Pérez-Perdomo (note 51) 106–07; Fix-Fierro (note 55)
253–4.

[61]   Fix-Fierro (note 55) 254, 256: Luis Fernando Perez Hurtado, 'Transnationalizing Mexican
Legal Education: But, What About Students' Expectations?' 10 *German Law Journal* 767, 770
(2009).

the huge public university law faculty—Universidad Nacional Autónoma de México (UNAM)—dominated in its influence on other law school curricula and teaching and had 16,000 students in 2001. UNAM and other law schools typically have about 10 percent of their faculty working full time with the remainder practicing lawyers who teach one course a year. Sixty percent of law graduates become licensed to practice law (*licenciado* or *titulado*), while the remaining 40 percent simply graduate (*egresado*) by taking the required courses, but fail to fulfill the social service requirement, write a thesis, or pass an oral professional exam. These *egresados* may work in government or with corporations and in some states represent clients although they cannot register with the bar. Surveys and commentators in general have considered the quality of education poor. In other respects, Mexican legal education shares characteristics with civil law legal education.[62]

Law schools in the United States in the late 1960s faced many of the same social changes that precipitated student revolutions in Europe and elsewhere, which opened up universities more broadly to the middle class. The agents of change in America were the civil rights movement and student hostility to the Vietnam War. As in other countries, student demand for greater economic and political democracy fueled change. Feminism, consumer rights and environmentalism added to the interest in law in the 1970s.[63]

The enormous jump in enrollment in US law schools occurred during the 15 years after 1960, when the number of students grew 194 percent from 38,000 to 111,000 in 1975, then to reach 127,000 by 1990.[64] The 1990s were a stable decade in terms of law enrollment, as in much of Europe, but the numbers gradually increased to 145,000 law students in 2009. In 1990, the American Bar Association (ABA) had approved 176 law schools. The average-size school enrolled 736 students taught by 30 full-time professors (for a ratio of 25 students per professor), plus 20 part-time teachers, and spent $9.1 million (or $12,350 per student). This was and continues today to be the most expensive system of legal education in the world. In 2009, the ABA approved 200 law schools. They collectively enrolled 155,000 students, of whom 10,000 were studying in an advanced degree or special program. About 5 percent of the total students enrolled dropped out of law school, most during the first year. The average annual law school tuition for students domiciled in the state in which they attended a public institution was about $18,000, but averaged $36,000 at private law schools. There were almost 8,100 tenured or tenure-track law teachers, yielding a student–faculty ratio of 15 to one. About 38 percent of these teachers were female, 17 percent were ethnic minorities and 1 percent foreign citizens.[65]

---

[62]   Stephen Zamora et al., *Mexican Law* 44–6, 52–4, 59 (Oxford: Oxford University Press 2004); Fix-Fierro (note 55) 255–6, 259–61.

[63]   Clark, American (note 28) 96.

[64]   Ibid. 97. Law student enrollment also expanded at a high rate in Australia, doubling from 1,500 in 1950 to 3,000 in 1965, and then almost quadrupling to 11,300 in 1984. In Canada, the number of law students almost tripled from 2,500 in 1960 to 7,200 in 1970, leveling off in the late 1980s at about 10,500. Clark, Comparing (note 24) 28.

[65]   Clark, Comparing (note 24) 28; American Bar Association (note 28). In 2009, the law schools included 11 that were provisionally accredited and the US Army Judge Advocate General's School. The tuition for non-resident students at a public state law school averaged $30,000.

4 CONTEMPORARY APPRENTICESHIP TRAINING[66]

Law study at the university is not the only requirement that students must meet to become a lawyer. In most developed countries, one must also serve an apprenticeship period, typically as a trainee lawyer, and pass an examination.

4.1 Civil Law Countries

German law faculties have traditionally aimed at training standardized jurists (*Einheitsjuristen*) who can meet the qualifications to become a judge.[67] In fact, one must pass two state examinations. Most students traditionally take the first test after about five to six years in the university.[68] Once a candidate passes the first state examination, with its written and oral components, she may proceed to the stage of training known as preparatory service (*Vorbereitungsdienst*), which lasts two years. The trainee, a *Referendar*, receives an allowance from the state as a temporary civil servant. She typically spends several months in each of the four obligatory stations—a civil court, a criminal court or public prosecutor's office, an administrative agency, and an attorney's office—leaving four to six months for one elective experience. The *Referendar* must also attend courses taught by judges and civil servants aimed at the analysis of complex practical cases. At the end of the preparatory period, a *Referendar* who passes the second state examination becomes a *Volljurist* and is eligible to apply for a judgeship.[69]

The state also requires these same judicial service qualifications in Germany by statute or regulation to become a prosecutor, government lawyer, attorney or notary. In addition, by custom this standardized education, although sometimes without the apprenticeship service, also applies to lawyers whom business firms, banks and insurance companies employ. Austria, Greece, Sweden, Switzerland, Turkey and Japan follow this model. Austria and Sweden have the longest apprenticeship period in the world at five years.

Other countries in the civil law tradition use a separate apprenticeship or training program for different legal careers. For instance, in France a law student after four years

---

[66] Much of this section is derived and updated from Clark, Comparing (note 24) 29–33.

[67] This ideal arose in eighteenth-century Prussia, which wanted to educate a qualified, loyal corps of judicial and administrative officers to run its heterogeneous territories. For peculiarities of the German legal training system and attempts to reform it, see Nigel Foster and Satish Sule, *German Legal System and Laws* 94–103 (Oxford: Oxford University Press, 4th edn, 2010); Ulrike Schultz, 'Legal Education in Germany—An Ever (Never?) Ending Story of Resistance to Change', in Vittorio Olgiati (ed.), *Higher Legal Culture and Postgraduate Legal Education in Europe* 125–49 (Naples: Edizioni Scientifiche Italiane 2008); Reinhard Zimmermann, 'Characteristic Aspects of German Legal Culture', in Mathias Reimann and Joachim Zekoll (eds), *Introduction to German Law* 1, 34–43 (The Hague: Kluwer Law International, 2nd edn, 2005).

[68] The state assumed responsibility for the administration of this examination. It considered the university, although it tested and might grant an academic degree, inadequate to license lawyers. This illustrates the dominant role for the state in controlling legal education in Europe, which has few private university law schools. See section 1.2 above. Today the state court of appeals supervises these exams. Since the end of the nineteenth century, professors have participated along with practitioners in examining and grading students. About a quarter of the candidates fail the exam.

[69] In most German states only judges, senior civil servants and attorneys serve as examiners. About 15 percent of the candidates fail this exam.

at the university (today more commonly five years) earns the master's degree. After 12 more months of study in an *institut d'études judiciaires*, the person desiring to become an advocate takes a state examination to enter a *centre régional de formation professionnelle des avocats* (CRFPA), attached to a court of appeal. The pass rate is about 40 percent.[70] The successful candidate has 18 months of practical study and training at the *centre*, takes another exam and if she passes, receives a *certificat d'aptitude à la profession d'avocat* (CAPA). The program consists of courses on professional conduct, drafting documents, oral argument, law office management and foreign languages together with short periods of training with advocates. Since 2005, one of the 182 local bars will record a lawyer who has obtained the CAPA on its *grand tableau* as an inscribed *avocat* without the formerly required internship *stage*.[71]

The Dutch have a three-year apprenticeship program for the aspiring advocate, who works under the supervision of an attorney. The Italians have a similar system, but lasting two years, for *practicanti*. The Dutch applicant must then complete a postgraduate training program and pass a state examination to be qualified for enrollment as an *advocaat*. The Italian applicant must pass a written and then an oral exam. In 2006, Spain introduced an apprenticeship system of one to two years through *escuelas de práctica jurídica* run by bar associations, universities and other entities. Apprenticeship training and courses in Mexico and Uruguay are under the supervision of the university. In Turkey, the one-year apprenticeship divides between work at courts and in a law office.[72]

4.2   Common Law Countries

Legal education nowadays in common law countries approximates in functional terms the civil law system. Law study is thus an undergraduate curriculum at the university and is generally followed by apprenticeship training—called variously pupilage, articling, or clerking—or enrollment in a special training program, or both. An examination may precede or follow apprenticeship, which serves to reduce the number of lawyers. In England, prospective barristers spend one year in a vocational course followed by one year as pupils in a barrister's chambers; trainee solicitors enroll in a one-year legal practice course and then clerk with senior solicitors for two years.[73] Lawyers article in Canada for one year and attend a bar admission course for two weeks to six months, depending on the province.

In Israel, law graduates clerk for 18 months for a judge, a private practitioner with at least five years standing or government legal services offices such as those of a state

---

[70]   The examiners consist of two law teachers, two judges from the ordinary and administrative courts and three *avocats*. They also test candidates for the CAPA at the end of their training. The *institut* can also prepare one to enter the competition for the École Nationale de la Magistrature, the training program for judges and prosecutors.

[71]   *Experts' Report on the Legal Education and Training System in Turkey* 111–16 (2009), http://ssrn.com/abstract=1677818.

[72]   Ibid. 8, 10, 18, 23–33, 37–8, 179–80.

[73]   Boon and Webb (note 23) 81–2; see Michael Zander, *Cases and Material on the English Legal System* 615–17, 632–3 (London: Butterworths, 8th edn, 1999).

attorney or district attorney. The written and oral examination follows, administered by the Chamber of Advocates, which candidates must pass before the Chamber will register them as lawyers.

In Ghana, Kenya and Nigeria, law graduates enter training schools where they work with advocates and judges. Law students in Tanzania must complete a six-month internship to obtain the LL.B degree. To enroll as an advocate, the candidate takes an oral examination before the Council of Legal Education, which passes about 20 percent on the first attempt.

The United States stands as a singular exception to these generalizations on three points. First, law students must complete a four-year undergraduate college or university curriculum before they are eligible to apply to law school. (Canada now also follows this procedure.) University legal education is then a three-year graduate curriculum (four years for evening part-time students), isolated in a separate college or school, sometimes independent of any university. Second, the majority of the 200 approved law schools in the US are private institutions, independent from the state or bar associations, with competitive entrance requirements that force public law schools to compete for the best law students. Finally, no apprenticeship or special training is required to enter any legal career, including that of law professor, after a law student receives a university law degree (JD) and passes a state bar (attorney) examination.

5   AMERICAN LEGAL EDUCATION AND GLOBALIZATION[74]

As section 1.2 described, historically the dominating power on the form and substance of legal education came from the church, state or market. After the intellectual revolution in Europe and North America in the eighteenth century, the role for religion continued to wane, but still exists today in varying degrees depending on the nation. The unremitting proliferation or consolidation of nation states since the nineteenth century accentuates the power of statism and the role of government in all parts of society, including university education. It is the diverse balance between plan and market among countries that today generates the variety of approaches to legal education. In that spectrum, the United States represents the market prototype, while many civil law nations illustrate the preference for plan and uniformity. We begin with the US approach and its influence, particularly through processes of globalization.[75]

---

[74]   Much of sections 5, 6 and 7 are derived from David S. Clark, 'American Law Schools in the Age of Globalization: A Comparative Perspective', 61 *Rutgers Law Review* 1037, 1044–75 (2009).

[75]   Even before globalization became the dominant theme that one sees today, some legal educators in the United States were involved with the exportation of the US law school model. This occurred under the strategy of 'law and development'. See M.C. Mirow, *Latin American Law: A History of Private Law and Institutions in Spanish America* 187–91 (Austin: University of Texas Press 2004); Jayanth K. Krishnan, 'Academic SAILERS: The Ford Foundation and the Efforts to Shape Legal Education in Africa, 1957–1977', 52 *American Journal of Legal History* (forthcoming 2012).

5.1   From Nativism to Globalism

International and comparative law research and teaching have been present in American law schools for over 100 years. This cannot hide the fact that the dominant view of law worldwide, certainly since the nineteenth century, has focused on the law promulgated by the state and in particular the national state. By the nineteenth century, the civil law countries of Europe had replaced the university study of Roman-canonic *jus commune* (in Latin) with the study of national law in the vernacular. In common law countries, such as the United States, law study through apprenticeship and law office training began to diverge from the English common law as Americanized versions of William Blackstone's *Commentaries on the Laws of England* (1765–9) became available and American jurists wrote their own commentaries on law. In the second half of the nineteenth century, more legal scholars abandoned natural law philosophy and embraced the genius revealed in their local positive law.

After World War II, some legal educators realized that this nativist perspective had been harmful and began to make efforts to find wisdom in universal law, foreign examples, or increased transnational contact. The victorious countries founded the United Nations in 1945. In Europe, the European Economic Community, formed in 1958, showed another approach. By 1990, the collapse of the former Soviet Union opened up the possibility for even greater transnational legal relations than had existed in the bipolar world of communism and capitalism, totalitarianism and democracy. What effects have these and similar events had on the practice of law and legal education?

5.2   The 1990s

To say that the impact of economic and cultural globalization has been transformative almost seems an understatement. Already in the 1990s, there were calls to organize global American law schools.[76] The Europeans in 1995 built on the successful Erasmus support program to encourage student study (including law students) in another European Union (EU) member state by extending it to include professors also. Besides this initiative (called Socrates), the EU in the 1990s broadened its support to include non-member East European universities and to foster foreign language fluency (Lingua).[77]

At the 1995 ABA annual meeting, the Section of Legal Education and the Section of International Law and Practice co-sponsored a program entitled 'The Globalization of the American Law School'. Panel members noted that globalization was opening up new legal markets. Lawyers trained in foreign, comparative, and international law would come to dominate these markets. Already American law firms were in the vanguard of participating in these developments, but new methods for training lawyers and practicing law would be necessary. The ABA president suggested that lawyers should become fluent in second languages effectively to practice law internationally. Others recommended that more professors teach the international aspects of their subjects, or that law schools

---

[76]   David S. Clark, 'Transnational Legal Practice: The Need for Global Law Schools', 46 *American Journal of Comparative Law* 261–74 (Supp. 1998).

[77]   One also can find the idea of foreign language study in law schools outside Europe. For example, since 2005, Mexico's UNAM has required a mandatory foreign language course to obtain the basic law degree (plans 1138 or 1342).

undertake to educate the judiciary and the bar about these new global legal developments. The Association of American Law Schools (AALS) continued this emphasis by making globalism the topic of its 1998 annual meeting: 'Thinking and Teaching about Law in a Global Context as an Exercise in Common Enterprise'.

In 1994, the private New York University (NYU) announced the creation of the world's first global law school program. Supported by a large endowment, the initiative intended to invite foreign law professors (most to teach for a full or half semester), foreign scholars (professors, judges, and government officials for one to six months) and foreign graduate students to NYU to interact and collaborate with resident professors and students. Some of the funds would generate innovations in the curriculum and finance conferences that reflect the impact of an emerging global economy. In 1997, NYU School of Law had almost 225 foreign citizens—representing over 50 countries—enrolled out of 1,500 students. At this level of commitment, as foreign and American faculty and students spend time together, they will both learn about the international legal order in a more denationalized manner as well as gain new perspectives on American law.

5.3   The Current Situation

The challenge of the 1990s was to develop various alternatives in response to economic and cultural globalization and then to assess which approaches work best. American law schools can be more or less global depending on their resources, setting and commitment to competing missions. However, there are certain facts worth keeping in mind. First, international law firms and increasingly any law firm will want graduates conversant in comparative and international law. Second, foreign law students are more and more interested in studying in the US. In 1995, about 3,500 attended American law schools, primarily in LL.M programs. Third, between 2004 and 2008, there was a drop of 17,000 in domestic law applicants to ABA law schools, so it was a matter of good business sense to look abroad.

In 2000, the AALS sponsored the Conference of International Legal Educators, held in Florence. NYU provided the forum. Participants attended from 27 countries. Panelists discussed topics such as cooperation among different systems of law and legal education, faculty and student exchange, enrichment of curricula through international cooperation and development of a global curriculum and educational outcomes. This led to a second AALS event in 2004 held in Hawaii, the Conference on Educating Lawyers for Transnational Challenges. Legal educators from 47 countries attended. Sessions covered issues relevant to lawyers in business transactions, governmental organizations, and non-governmental organizations (NGOs), identifying a curricular core for the transnational lawyer, and special methods for educating that lawyer using clinics, exchanges or technology. The participants agreed to form a new organization, the International Association of Law Schools, created in 2005. Its mission serves to strengthen the role of law in the development of societies through the improvement of legal education and to better prepare lawyers as they increasingly engage in transnational or global legal practice, including governmental, non-governmental, academic or corporate careers.[78]

---

[78]   The International Association of Law Schools has been meeting annually in different countries since 2007. See IALS, Meetings, http://www.ialsnet.org/meetings/index.html.

In addition, both the Law School Admission Council (LSAC) and the ABA Section of Legal Education and Admissions to the Bar have responded to the effects of globalization. In 2008, the LSAC amended its bylaws to permit membership by law schools outside the US and Canada to include those in Australia. The first of these members was Melbourne Law School, which transformed its undergraduate LL.B degree program into a graduate curriculum with a JD degree. Enrolling students since 2008, the Law School offers this justification: 'The shift to graduate law at Melbourne is part of a worldwide trend responding to the challenge of providing the best legal education to support the increasingly international profession of law.'

In 2011, 113 US law schools had one or more ABA-inspected summer programs abroad, with some institutions making this an important offering that would permit most of their students to find something to meet their interests. Notable examples are Santa Clara (14 locations), American (13), Pennsylvania State (8), San Diego (8), and Tulane (7). Ten schools have semester abroad programs that they administer, typically including mainly American students. Thirty-three schools have ABA-inspected cooperative programs abroad with a foreign law school, usually for a semester. These programs are part of a pre-existing foreign course of law study, in which a few American students participate with local law students. Some US schools emphasize this approach, such as North Carolina, with five locations, and Columbia, Connecticut, Cornell, and New Mexico, each with three partner schools.

Based on information from the ABA and the Institute of International Education, about 4,600 foreign law school graduates and lawyers in 2008 enrolled in LL.M degree programs in the United States. Fifty US law schools have a special LL.M program for foreign lawyers. In addition, there are many LL.M programs in some aspect of international or comparative law, which would have many American JD students enrolled along with some foreign students. For instance, there are 33 programs classified under international law (and/or comparative law), 18 in comparative law, 11 in international business, trade, or tax law and three in human rights law. In 2007, the average tuition required from a foreign student at a public law school was $27,000; that charge was $32,000 at a private law school. Making a rough calculation for the approximately 4,600 foreign students in non-JD programs, the total law school revenue from that source would be about $136 million.[79]

Although the number of American law school LL.M programs specifically for foreign lawyers has more than doubled since 1997, another important development is the increase in foreign students and lawyers who enroll in the JD degree program. In 2008, US law schools enrolled 2,017 foreign nationals in that program, awarding 582 JD degrees. Some law schools have a foreign lawyer program that permits someone who has earned her law degree abroad to complete the JD degree in two years.

---

[79]   For a study of the American LL.M market, see Carole Silver, 'The Variable Value of U.S. Legal Education in the Global Legal Services Market', 24 *Georgetown Journal of Legal Ethics* 1 (2011).

5.4 Illustrative US Law School Programs in International and Comparative Law

There are many excellent international and comparative law centers and programs at American law schools.[80] Two law school examples will have to suffice as illustration. How has NYU, which declared itself in the mid-1990s the world's first global law school program, developed?[81] In 1997, its School of Law enrolled 225 foreigners from 50 countries out of 1,500 students. Today's operations are coordinated through the Hauser Global Law School Program. 'The goal has been to transform legal education and make NYU Law a "global" rather than merely a national law school.' The program supports up to 20 foreign professors and judges each year who teach at the law school and it enrolls more than 300 foreign students from 50 countries, including those with special Hauser global fellowships, out of about 1,700 students. This major commitment represents about 18 percent of the student body, up from 15 percent foreign students in 1997. The program has also introduced global material into first-year courses and 'with the largest international student body among American law schools, lively, informed global discussions are a staple in both academic and social spheres'.

Traveling uptown in Manhattan, there is Columbia University School of Law. Its commitment to international and comparative law is older than that at NYU, but the two schools have strongly competed since the mid-1990s to distinguish themselves among American law schools as to that commitment. Columbia Law School states that it has been 'internationalizing' US legal education since its founding before the American Civil War in the 1860s. 'Long before global markets and instant worldwide communications forced US practicing lawyers to become aware of laws outside the territory of the United States, Columbia faculty and its students were developing the precepts and principles of public international law, international economic law, and comparative law.' Especially over the past ten years, the law school's programs in international and comparative law have grown, for instance with double-degree offerings, semester study abroad, international internships, and video conferencing that provides international contact for courses and symposia. Columbia enrolls about 200 foreign lawyers and students from 50 countries in its LL.M program, which together with the JD foreign participation gives the law school over 300 foreigners. With a student body of around 1,450, this constitutes about 21 percent of the total. There are also many opportunities for visiting foreign scholars in the school's seven centers and institutes that specialize by country, region or topic in dealing with global legal issues.

6 THE SINGULARITY OF US LEGAL EDUCATION

American legal education is unusual in several respects. First, the basic program to train lawyers is a graduate degree course, which requires prior study, usually for four years, at

---

[80] A few US law schools have recently established a satellite campus in a foreign country. John Flood, 'Legal Education in the Global Context: Challenges from Globalization', *Technology and Changes in Government Regulation* 9 (London: Report for the Legal Services Board 2011).

[81] Flood suggests that perhaps SOAS in London was the first global law school. He provides examples of global initiatives in other countries. Ibid. 9–10.

a university or college to obtain a bachelor's degree. Second, there is no national ministry of justice that oversees the major elements in legal education: admission of students, hiring instructors, setting tuition and fees, designing a curriculum and mandating certain courses, or even forming a new law school. Third, among more economically developed nations, the United States is virtually alone in not requiring a significant apprenticeship period before a person becomes a fully authorized lawyer. Elsewhere, apprenticeship is not normally the task of a university, although it may be in some nations. Fourth, American law schools lead the world in the use of electronic technology both in teaching and accessing legal materials. Finally, in the aggregate, and especially for the leading law schools, American legal education has a reputation, largely deserved, as the best in the world. It is also the most costly calculated on a per student basis.

6.1   A Graduate Degree Program

American legal education in the nineteenth century grew out of an apprenticeship and law office training system (analogous to the English approach, but without Inns of Court for social activities) into a university program more like that in civil law countries, especially Germany. Harvard in the 1870s first developed the idea of making law more scientific and thus more prestigious as a discipline. Charles Eliot, president at Harvard University from 1869 to 1909, favored a classroom laboratory method, with its inductive reasoning process, to replace the lecture and recitation methods used in law-office type law schools. He hired Christopher Langdell as law dean in 1870. Over the next 15 years, the two men worked together to institutionalize several measures that made the study of law more rigorous: an entrance examination, a progressive curriculum ending with a bachelor of laws degree (LL.B), annual examinations and a research function. Langdell's most significant innovation was the introduction of an instructional method utilizing Socratic dialogue to discuss appellate cases and to encourage the compilation of the materials into casebooks.

Harvard's success stimulated the spread of this approach to other universities. Prior to the end of World War I, only Harvard and Pennsylvania had decided to make an undergraduate degree a serious requirement for admission to their law schools. However, with the help of the ABA and its accreditation process, this idea prospered. There were over 100 ABA-approved law schools just prior to World War II and the large majority of states then required at least two years of college education before law school to be able to take the state bar examination. By the 1960s, most law schools recognized the shift toward law as a graduate curriculum and began to offer the doctor juris degree in place of the LL.B. Until recently, the only country to transplant this American innovation of law as a graduate program had been Canada.

6.2   Flexible Regulation by a Non-Governmental Organization

Most countries regulate university legal education through a central ministry of education. In other countries, regulation comes in whole or in part from the ministry of justice, given the subject matter of law. This regulation typically occurs within a nationwide system of public universities, although it might also apply in some respects to private institutions. In the public sector, decisions about budgets, professor salaries, student admissions, buildings, mandatory curricula, and so on are centralized. Complaints about underfunding, overcrowding, stale lecturing, out-of-date curricula, inadequate technology and libraries, and general inefficiencies are common.

The United States Secretary of Education, however, does not take a direct interest in American legal education, nor do state departments of education, either as to admission standards, curricula, or degrees offered. Alternatively, a private NGO, the ABA's Section of Legal Education, has developed standards for these matters (and others, such as finances and administration, faculty, library, and building facilities) that it uses to decide periodically whether first to accredit and then to reaccredit an American law school. Although some law school administrators complain about the ABA's regulation of their operations, or the undue influence of state bar examinations on their curricula, by comparison, the diversity and high quality of American law school programs is remarkable.

It is fully imaginable that the US government, or perhaps individual states, might consider it in the national or local interest more directly to regulate legal education. Because of the periodic and widespread nativist political sentiment expressed, not unlike that in other nations, the consequence would probably be harmful for further globalization of legal education. One should see current efforts to globalize American legal education, consequently, primarily as a decentralized reaction to market forces.

6.3   Clinics and Professional Skills Training, but No Apprenticeship

In the 1950s and 1960s, disenchantment with the predominant emphasis on the Socratic case method of instruction in US legal education, as useful as it might be to teach analytical skills, led to curricular reform that began to consider other skills that lawyers use. In addition to document drafting, seminar research, moot court and interdisciplinary courses, some advocated teaching professional and practical skills with courses, clinics, externships or simulations on counseling, negotiation, mediation, advocacy and later values and ethics. By the 1990s, when the *MacCrate Report* embraced professional skills with the active assistance of practicing lawyers and judges who sometimes felt academic lawyers had left the law, clinics and professional skills had found a home in most law schools.[82]

However, tension between the place of theory and the place of practice in legal education was not resolved.[83] Prior to 1870, of course, there was no tension since American legal education was entirely practical, as it was in all common law countries. It was only with the introduction of the civil law scientific university education at Harvard Law School, motivated to bring prestige to the discipline of law, which introduced the dualism.

Since a foreign transplant created the problem, perhaps the comparative law method of examining how other countries deal with the issue of practical training for young lawyers

---

[82]   Joan S. Howland and William H. Linberg (eds), *The MacCrate Report: Building the Educational Continuum* (St. Paul, MN: West Publishing Co. 1994). Over a decade later, this found support in the Carnegie Foundation's two-year study of legal education, with results and recommendations reported in William M. Sullivan et al., *Educating Lawyers: Preparation for the Profession of Law* (San Francisco: Jossey-Bass 2007) and Roy Stuckey et al., *Best Practices for Legal Education* (New York: Clinical Legal Education Association 2007).

[83]   See section 1.3.

could guide an alternative response to the US use of in-house practical training.[84] The approach in most economically developed civil law countries (and common law nations as well) is apprenticeship independent of the university. Leading examples are France, Germany, Italy, Japan and Korea for the civil law and Australia, Canada and the United Kingdom for the common law. Their programs range from six months to three years in length and may include a single area of practice or a rotation among several law jobs. In all of these countries, established lawyers consider it irresponsible to permit an unsupervised university law graduate to practice law on an unsuspecting public. Furthermore, their experience is that academic jurists, as scholars, are simply incapable of providing sufficient practical instruction. Bifurcation benefits everyone.

6.4   Teaching and Information Technology

The use of electronic technology for teaching and research is pervasive in American law schools today, with schools generally extending wireless computer and smartphone connections to students in law buildings and their environs. A leading example as it relates to international and comparative law is the Cornell Law School Legal Information Institute (LII), founded in 1992. In addition to instruction in how to find and use electronic information, LII organizes law materials by topic and source. The LII collection of world legal materials gathers, country by country, continent by continent, the Internet-accessible sources of constitutions, statutes, judicial opinions and related legal material from around the globe as well as international law resources and document collections.

6.5   Prestige Ranking Worldwide

American legal education, especially among the top tier of 50 schools, has the highest prestige of any legal education in the world. It certainly is the most expensive. The evidence that supports this assertion includes the decision of a large number of foreign lawyers who enroll for further education in the United States, more than study in any other foreign country. However, these foreign nationals are as likely to enroll at schools outside the top 50 as with elite schools, which should broaden the prestige among more American schools. In addition, several countries, reacting to the forces of globalization, are transplanting some features of American legal education. These include graduate law schools for the primary law degree in Australia, Japan and Korea. Finally, international academic ranking systems recognize the quality of American university education. An example is the ranking conducted annually by Shanghai Jiao Tong University's Center for World-Class Universities. Of the top 50 universities worldwide in 2008, 36 are in the

---

[84]   The US has also been an active exporter of its legal institutions, such as the law school clinic. Prior to 2000, the Ford Foundation promoted this model in the People's Republic of China, which the ministry of education authorized for seven law schools in 2000. Ford funded the Chinese Clinical Legal Education Network and by 2007, 64 law schools had clinics to provide students with practical training. The social justice mission, however, was more controversial. Sarah Biddulph, 'Legal Education in the People's Republic of China: The Ongoing Story of Politics and Law', in Stacey Steele and Kathryn Taylor (eds), *Legal Education in Asia: Globalization, Change and Contexts* 260, 271 (London: Routledge 2010).

United States (of which 26 have a law school). Of the global top 100 universities, 54 percent are in the United States, followed by 11 percent in the United Kingdom and 6 percent in Germany.

Foreign nationals enroll in American law schools for many reasons. Some may want to reside long term in the United States and hope they may take advantage of their foreign background in the practice of law. Others may already be lawyers in another country, wish to add prestige to their credentials with an American law degree, and return home to practice law with an LL.M on their letterhead. The next step would be to pass an American state bar examination, with that offered in New York the most popular with foreign LL.M students, since that credential is sufficient to qualify to take the exam. Increasing numbers of foreign lawyers pass the New York test each year. For the July 2008 administration, for instance, 2,872 foreign-educated lawyers took the examination and 1,290 or 45 percent were successful. This further augments their prestige, since it allows the foreign lawyer to practice American law and makes the individual more attractive to a transnational law firm either in the US or abroad. Of course, a JD degree would make the graduate eligible to take the bar exam of any American state.

7   GLOBALIZATION AND THE INFLUENCE OF US LEGAL EDUCATION ABROAD

Legal education is experiencing significant reform in Europe and East Asia, as well as in some other regions. These reforms are primarily a response to economic and cultural globalization as it has affected the practice of law. Some pejoratively call this process Americanization, perhaps to rally support in cultural defense, and it is clear that in some cases an American model is the starting point for national discussion.[85] A UK commentator states that from 'an empirical point of view there is an inexorable move in the world towards the Americanization of legal education'.[86]

7.1   The Europeanization of Legal Education and the Bologna Process[87]

Pressures for the Europeanization of legal education have come from both the EU and national governments, and within the latter, from both universities and the legal profession.[88] First, the EU Erasmus and Socrates programs for student and teacher mobility have had a limited impact on legal education. The idea was that law schools would coop-

---

[85]   See, e.g., Norbert Reich, 'Recent Trends in European Legal Education: The Place of the European Law Faculties Association', 21 *Penn State International Law Review* 21, 24–6 (2002); Veronica L. Taylor, 'Legal Education as Development', in Stacey Steele and Kathryn Taylor (eds), *Legal Education in Asia: Globalization, Change and Contexts* 215, 218–28 (London: Routledge 2010).

[86]   Flood (note 80) 1.

[87]   In addition to Clark, Globalization (note 74) 1063–8, see Laurel S. Terry, 'The Bologna Process and Its Impact in Europe: It's So Much More than Degree Changes', 41 *Vanderbilt Journal of Transnational Law* 107 (2008).

[88]   Illustrative studies include Jan M. Smits, 'European Legal Education, or How to Prepare Students for Global Citizenship?' Maastricht Faculty of Law Working Paper No. 2011/02 (2011).

erate across borders among the now 27 EU member states to facilitate student exchange and mutual recognition of credits through the ECTS (European Credit Transfer System). The EU provided financial incentives to students, teachers and law faculties to promote this process but did not intervene in the curricula or accreditation processes. Perhaps 5 percent of European law students participated in these programs. The effects on curricula were more indirect than direct. For a law school to be more attractive, it had to develop European and comparative courses, frequently in English. This weakened the traditional nationalistic approach to law.

Second, since the EU was committed to liberalize trade in services, which meant foreign access to the legal profession, it adopted (after protracted negotiations) diploma recognition directives. These allow lawyers established in one EU country to practice law in another EU country under their home titles, and after either an additional exam or three years of actual and continuous legal practice, under the host country title. This stimulated multi-jurisdiction practice, especially with neighboring countries that already had close historic, academic and linguistic ties in legal education.

The Bologna Process to reform all of higher education, a 1998 initiative of European university rectors, complemented these legal education concerns. After an initial meeting in Paris, the European ministers of higher education in 1999 assembled in Bologna. Their *Bologna Declaration* recommended the restructuring of tertiary education with a uniform three-five-eight-year sequence of degrees, modeled on the typical American university that begins with a bachelor's degree. Since European students are better educated than Americans are after secondary education, that first degree would take only three years of studies. For motivated students, a master's program averaging two years might follow. Finally, for those desiring an academic career, a doctoral degree would be available for three more years of study and research. The goals are to increase the quality, transparency and competitiveness of the European Higher Education Area (EHEA) and to shorten the length of studies that might reduce high dropout rates. In 2011, 47 countries were participating in the Bologna Process and the EHEA.

There are five goals relevant for legal education in the Bologna Process, as it has evolved through a series of biennial meetings. These include developing:

(1) 'outcomes' or competences that European students should have;
(2) recognition processes for students (and lawyers) who have studied outside their home country;
(3) transnational quality-assurance standards;
(4) more responsive higher education for the needs of business and industry to help Europe become the most competitive knowledge-based economy in the world; and
(5) common curricular standards.[89]

This latter point is particularly important for American legal education. If 47 European countries decide that European law students should master certain legal concepts, then the size of Europe and the global nature of the US economy would require transnational lawyers to be familiar with those concepts as well.

---

[89] Terry (note 87) 112.

In 1989, the EU introduced the ECTS as part of the Erasmus program. Initially a credit transfer system, it was based on the principle that 60 credits measure a full-time student's course load during one academic year. This would provide an institution with a uniform basis for evaluating each course as it applied to foreign study. More recently, the ECTS has evolved to encompass an accumulation system that officials should implement at institutional, regional, national and European levels. They now use ECTS to measure what is required for a student to receive a particular degree, regardless of whether the student has studied abroad.

The implementation of the Bologna Process for higher education within Europe as it relates to legal training is supposed to make it easier for those who have commenced law study to move from one country to another to further their studies, earn a degree or other credential, or successfully seek employment. Bologna proponents, moreover, argue that it will also make European higher education more attractive to non-Europeans who might come to study or work in Europe.

For example, France implemented from 2003 to 2006 the LMD Reform (for *Licence-Master-Doctorat*) called for in the Bologna Process. By 2007, most university law departments used these three diplomas awarded after three years (*licence*), then one or two years (master 1 or 2, needed to enter legal apprenticeship training, replacing the former *maîtrise en droit*) and finally three years of study for the advanced *doctorat* degree. The law departments also now use the ECTS credit system, for instance, requiring 180 ECTS for the *licence*. France's oldest law faculty (from the twelfth century), today called the Université Paris 1, Panthéon-Sorbonne, has five departments in which law is taught: Administrative and Public Sector Law; Business Law; International and European Studies; Economics, Labor, and Social Law; and General Legal Studies. The General Legal Studies Department works with the other four law departments and with the political science department. All law students enrolled for their first degree (*licence*), and first and second-year politics students, enroll in General Legal Studies. Other university law faculties also usually combine with the political science or economics discipline and develop special curricula in addition to their core courses.

Implementation of the Bologna Process in Germany has been more difficult for two major reasons. First, after years of debate, the federal government adopted changes to legal education in 2002 that were its response to the most pressing issues. To reconsider those reforms so soon after their enactment would require substantial political pressure. Second, the Bologna Process itself is an initiative of ministers of education and is a university-wide reform. The federal German Judges Law, however, controls legal education and state-level ministers of justice administer the two state examinations required to become a judge or a lawyer. Nevertheless, some German law faculties and state ministers of education have tried to reach a compromise position, which the programs and curriculum at the University of Hamburg Law Faculty illustrate.

In 2003, the Hamburg Law Faculty instituted two new programs to satisfy the obligations of the Bologna Process: the *Baccalaureus Juris* (six semesters) and *Magister Juris* (eight semesters) degrees. A student can now get a university degree in law without taking the First State Exam, which the Judges Law requires to enter the apprenticeship program to become a judge or lawyer. Time will tell whether the *Baccalaureus Juris* degree is useful for a law-related or other job in government or commerce. The degree does not prohibit students from continuing their studies and then taking the state examination. A student must enroll at Hamburg for a full year before making application for either degree. A person who receives the *Magister Juris* degree will also satisfy the admission requirements for the First State Exam.

7.2   Japan: 'Training Doctors for the People's Social Life'[90]

In 1999, the Japanese government established the Justice System Reform Council (JSRC) to study and recommend to the prime minister reforms to improve the justice system. The JSRC's report recommended less trial delay, lay judges in serious criminal cases, legal aid to persons immediately after arrest instead of only after indictment, a national network of full-time staff lawyers to provide civil and criminal legal aid, a system to accredit alternative dispute resolution programs, and the deregulation of practicing attorneys (*bengoshi*).

The JSRC found that a larger number of lawyers, particularly *bengoshi*, would be required to implement these reforms and set a goal to triple the number of new lawyers by 2010. To accomplish this, it recommended establishing postgraduate law schools by 2004. The traditional Japanese system of legal education and lawyer training consisted of (1) earning a degree at an undergraduate four-year law faculty, (2) passing the justice ministry's national bar examination, and (3) completing the Supreme Court's apprenticeship program run by the Legal Training and Research Institute (LTRI).[91]

Since the late nineteenth century, when Japan transplanted the European civil law system, it included the typical European undergraduate law faculties. However, it established these to educate not primarily future lawyers, but rather government bureaucrats and judges. Even after World War II, law faculties primarily functioned as general education programs to produce a workforce for business and government. Although a law faculty is the only place to receive a comprehensive legal education, an undergraduate law degree (*hō-gakushi*) is not required for one to take the national bar examination. In 2009, over 100 undergraduate law faculties, with most of the 168,000 students, trained more law students than studied in the United States.[92]

A large number of university graduates take the national bar examination. Nevertheless, until 1990, only about 500 per year passed since the LTRI had set a pass rate of about 2 percent. Due to pressure from outside the legal profession, that number increased steadily during the 1990s to reach 1,000 in 1999, a pass rate of 3 percent. Those who passed the exam then spent two years in apprenticeship (reduced to 18 months in 1999 and now to one year) as trainees with stipends paid by the government. The LTRI faculty provided practical instruction at the beginning and end of this period. For the remainder of the time, trainees received field experience at courts, prosecutor's offices and *bengoshi* law offices in designated regions all over the country. Upon completion of the apprenticeship, trainees could choose one of the three branches of the legal profession (judiciary, prosecution or the bar) for their career.

The old system resulted in an extremely small number of *bengoshi*, only 15,000 attorneys

---

[90]   In addition to Clark, Globalization (note 74) 1068–73, see Setsuo Miyazawa, Kay-Wah Chan and Ilhyung Lee, 'The Reform of Legal Education in East Asia', 4 *Annual Review of Law and Social Science* 334, 339–49 (2008).

[91]   The traditional system is admirably described in Rokumoto (note 36) 191–205.

[92]   See Table 16.1 above.

in the 1990s for Japan's 120 million people. In addition, the distribution of attorneys was also highly skewed, with 60 percent in Tokyo and Osaka. Many jurisdictions—referred to as zero-one districts—had either no attorney or one attorney.

Hideo Tanaka, an Anglo-American law professor at the University of Tokyo, who also taught at Harvard Law School, was an early critic of this system. He argued for the transformation of university legal education to professional legal education. Since the LTRI was the major impediment, preventing an increase of lawyers and maintaining a conservative judiciary, Setsuo Miyazawa, who taught law at Harvard and other North American universities, proposed establishing law schools that would provide professional legal education at postgraduate level and replace the LTRI with clinical programs at these new law schools.

The political dynamic in Japan changed when the business community began to exhibit a strong interest in justice system reform. It had sought deregulation of business activities and independence from government regulations to revitalize the Japanese economy, and the government responded by introducing a series of deregulation measures and administrative reforms. Political slogans supported transparency of administrative processes and citizen responsibility to protect their own interests without depending on the government. By the late 1990s, the focus turned to the judicial system and legal profession as alternatives to government bureaucracy to protect the business community's interests.

The JSRC was able to build on this support with an argument that the rule of law needed improvement through a more accessible justice system with a stronger popular base. It was remarkable for a government committee to announce so clearly the need to change a system deeply entrenched in Japanese legal culture. The agenda called for the establishment of professional law schools as a measure designed to produce a larger number of better-educated lawyers as 'doctors for the people's social life'.

The JSRC's final recommendations in 2001 set in motion efforts to create graduate law schools. These, in the beginning, would supplement undergraduate legal education, but would come to replace it for the careers of judge, prosecutor and attorney. The JSRC wanted to:

(1) increase the number of successful bar examination takers from 1,000 in 1999 to 1,500 by 2004;
(2) create a new system for training lawyers through a process that organically connected legal education, the national bar exam, and apprenticeship with graduate law schools (*hōka daigakuin*) as its core;
(3) introduce these graduate law schools in 2004; and
(4) introduce a new bar examination for these law school graduates that would produce 3,000 new lawyers per year by 2010.

The JSRC expected that the total number of practicing attorneys would reach 50,000 by 2018, a huge increase from the 20,000 in 1997.

One can see the parallel between the new Japanese graduate law schools and the American system of legal education. The JSRC rejected the idea of converting undergraduate law faculties into professional schools for two main reasons: (1) they had never provided the new kind of teaching envisioned and changing their culture would be too difficult; and (2) it would be impractical to transform all undergraduate law faculties with their enormous number of students into professional schools. The JSRC wanted to turn out a larger number of practicing attorneys with an education more relevant to its social goals and to the globalized business world that preferred the transnational talent found in large law firms. It also desired to educate attorneys with diverse academic and social backgrounds and reduce applicant numbers for the new bar examination. The latter would lead to a higher pass rate closer to that in the United States, so that students would devote themselves to law school study rather than going to exam cram schools.

By 2005, Japan had 74 new law schools with about 5,800 new entrants. The admission process required an aptitude test similar to the one used in the US. About 60 percent of the new students were law faculty graduates, with the remainder from other undergraduate fields and a significant group that had 'life experience'. Tuition is substantially higher than at undergraduate law faculties, ranging from $7,000 at public law schools to between $10,000 and $18,000 at private law schools. These schools, which have now formed the Japan Law School Association, will award the JD degree (*homu hakushi*). The education ministry has delegated the accreditation and reaccreditation process (at five-year intervals). At least 30 percent of the full-time faculty should have practical experience, often as judges or prosecutors. The maximum student-faculty ratio should be 15 to one. Besides basic doctrinal courses, schools have introduced new subjects, such as international human rights, and added practical skills classes, clinics and simulations. Interested professors formed the Japan Clinical Legal Education Association in 2008.

Speed bumps appeared almost from the beginning.[93] The justice ministry, which controls the LTRI examination, refused to accelerate the pass rate to 70 percent, as the JSRC had recommended. For the new exam's first round in 2006, which emphasized the reform curriculum, the pass rate was 48 percent, which then declined to 40 percent in 2007, 33 percent in 2008 and 25 percent in 2010.[94] This led to a substantial reduction in law school applicants, with only 30 percent applying without an undergraduate law degree. The cram schools have increased their enrollment again with new products aimed at the reformed bar exam. Commentators expect that several of the new law schools will soon close. Over 25 of the new schools have failed to obtain certification—often for failure to broaden their curricula—from the accreditation bodies approved by the education ministry.[95] Some predict that soon there will be only 20 to 25 graduate law schools remaining.[96]

---

[93]   The tension between the justice ministry and the education ministry is described in Kent Anderson and Trevor Ryan, 'Gatekeepers: A Comparative Critique of Admission to the Legal Profession and Japan's New Law Schools', in Stacey Steele and Kathryn Taylor (eds), *Legal Education in Asia: Globalization, Change and Contexts* 45, 54–61 (London: Routledge 2010).

[94]   Gerald Paul McAlinn, 'Japanese Law Schools: "A Glass Half Full"', 15 *Zeitschift für Japanishes Recht/Journal of Japanese Law* 225, 229 (no. 30, 2010).

[95]   Ibid. 58–9. Taiwan's ministry of education, influenced by the US and new Japanese graduate legal education models, proposed in 2006 the creation of graduate legal professional institutes that would be operational in 2008. At that time, undergraduate law programs would end and their law graduates would have ten years to pass the legal professionals exam. The reaction from existing law faculties was swift and the president in 2007 suspended this reform. Tay-sheng Wang, 'The Development of Legal Education in Taiwan', in Stacey Steele and Kathryn Taylor (eds), *Legal Education in Asia: Globalization, Change and Contexts* 137, 146–9 (London: Routledge 2010).

[96]   McAlinn (note 94) 230.

7.3   New Graduate Law Schools in Korea[97]

Japanese influence on Korea's modern legal institutions, beginning at the end of the nineteenth century and increasing during Japan's colonial occupation from 1905 to 1945, continues in the twenty-first century. When Japan undertook reforms in legal education in 2004, Korean jurists and business people monitored the situation. Since 1995, Korean jurists have considered changes in their own legal education system in the face of criticism that it was failing to meet the needs of contemporary society and especially an economy dependent on international trade.[98]

In 2007, Korea's National Assembly enacted legislation to implement American-style professional law schools. This resulted from a thorough study of the US system and Japanese proposed reforms.[99] The Establishment and Management of Law Schools Act was the last formal hurdle after much contentious debate. Korea's current legal education system (ending in 2013) is remarkably similar to that in Japan prior to 2004, with undergraduate study at a law faculty leading those who desire to be judges, prosecutors or practicing attorneys to take the national judicial service examination. The reality is that students enroll in cram schools, typically for two or three years, to prepare for the exam (available until 2017) and only 1,000 (or 5 percent) are successful each year. They then attend the Judicial Research and Training Institute (JRTI), under the Korean Supreme Court's supervision, for a two-year apprenticeship program.

In 2008, the education ministry issued regulations under the 2007 Act and selected 25 universities to house the new graduate law schools leading to a JD degree. Fifteen are in Seoul and the largest school, at Seoul National University, will admit 150 students for each class in a three-year curriculum. The nationwide law school enrollment is set at 3,000 per class and operations began in 2009. The annual tuition at these schools is $24,000.[100] The major bottleneck to becoming a lawyer or judge now occurs with the stringent admission criteria to law school, which includes an English competency test. The new emphasis is on a more practical curriculum, with students preparing at undergraduate school in political science or international relations. There will be clinics and clerkships and the students' English competency will allow comparative and international law courses taught by foreign lawyers. Unlike Japan, where a substantial gap between the number of law school graduates and those permitted to pass the national bar exam already endangers many law schools, the enrollment size in Korean graduate law schools should be kept close to the expected number that the JRTI will allow to pass the examination. It anticipates a rise to 2,400 per year for an 80 percent pass rate.[101]

Although one might contend that this illustrates a Japanese legal transplant in Korea,

---

[97]   In addition to Clark, Globalization (note 74) 1073–5, see Miyazawa et al. (note 90) 351–5.

[98]   Simon Spencer Reyner Lee, 'Legal Education in Korea: New Law School Reforms', in Stacey Steele and Kathryn Taylor (eds), *Legal Education in Asia: Globalization, Change and Contexts* 169, 172, 176 (London: Routledge 2010).

[99]   Ibid. 169, 174–5.

[100]   Ibid. 173–4, 177–8. The new system will run in parallel with the undergraduate programs until 2013, when the last of those undergraduates will take the test to enter the JRTI training program. Ibid. 170, 173, 177.

[101]   Ibid. 174–7.

another perspective is that the Korean solution is a reaction to the same economic and cultural globalization that has affected the practice of law in developed countries world-wide.[102] Its reality is represented by the huge transnational law firms, already in Tokyo and soon to be in Seoul, and the pervasive presence of global NGOs. The large number of Korean government officials, judges, prosecutors, academics and practitioners obtaining advanced degrees or occupying visiting scholar positions in US law schools could also serve as agents for cultural transmission. Since 2000, Korean law faculties have increasingly adopted certain American law school elements, such as clinics and legal ethics and other specialized courses on subjects such as international business transactions. English language proficiency is a requirement for entrance to graduate law schools and became a required subject on the Korean bar examination. In addition, the JRTI added international contracts and other international subjects to its curriculum.

8   CONCLUSION

What can one learn about the status and improvement of legal education in light of this brief survey? First, law study is still an important discipline at the university, but not as significant as it was 60 years ago. In many countries, it still serves as more than the initial preparation for a legal career. It may also provide training for positions with government or in politics, corporations, insurance companies and banks.

Second, those who enter law study today more broadly represent the demographic makeup of their societies. Thus, women have reached parity with men in most countries. However, ethnic minorities—although they have made some progress—still are underrepresented in most places. In addition, social class continues to plays a part in admission to law faculties, even with the dramatic expansion of mass public universities for those from the middle class in Europe, Latin America, and Asia since the 1970s.

Third, apprenticeship is an important part of professional training to enter a legal career almost everywhere. The US model, of using clinics and skills training within a law school, has influenced some curricula elsewhere, but it has not generally replaced apprenticeship outside the university.

Fourth, the current development of law study is dynamic in response to worldwide pressures of economic and cultural globalization. Legal education systems in Europe, the Americas and Asia—public and private—are striving to catch up with the United States, and perhaps even to surpass it. European regional associations, including the European Union, in particular are engaged in a full-scale effort to produce transnational and global lawyers. The EU primarily promotes these activities as an economic issue, that is, as competition for legal service fees. This also seems to be motivating changes in Japan and Korea.

Fifth, most countries recognize the importance of lawyers learning a foreign language as the principal method to better understand another culture and to become less parochial. Sometimes an entire national legal educational and training system mandates that

---

[102]   The Korean Supreme Court's Judicial Reformation Committee held a conference in 1995 to discuss reforming legal education. Ibid. 169.

language, often English, as in Korea, but more frequently a choice of several languages, as in Germany. Other times, a particular educational institution mandates the foreign language, such as English at the Bucerius Law School in Germany, or the option of English as part of the foreign language requirement at the National Autonomous University of Mexico Faculty of Law.

FURTHER READING

Abel, Richard L. (1988). *The Legal Profession in England and Wales* 37–64, 142–68, 261–82, 463–80. Oxford: Basil Blackwell.

Boon, Andrew and Julian Webb (2008). 'Legal Education and Training in England and Wales: Back to the Future', 58 *Journal of Legal Education* 79–121.

Bush, Jonathan A. and Alain Wijffels (eds) (1999). *Learning the Law: Teaching and the Transmission of Law in England, 1150–1900*. London: Hambledon Press.

Clark, David S. (1987). 'The Medieval Origins of Modern Legal Education: Between Church and State', 35 *American Journal of Comparative Law* 653–719.

Clark, David S. (1987). 'Tracing the Roots of American Legal Education—A Nineteenth Century German Connection', 51 *Rabels Zeitschrift für ausländisches und internationales Privatrecht* 313–33.

Clark, David S. (1999). 'Comparing the Work and Organization of Lawyers Worldwide: The Persistence of Legal Traditions', in John J. Barceló III and Roger C. Cramton (eds), *Lawyers' Practice and Ideals: A Comparative View* 9–155. The Hague: Kluwer Law International.

Clark, David S. (2003). 'American Legal Education: Yesterday and Today', 10 *International Journal of the Legal Profession* 93–108.

Clark, David S. (2009). 'American Law Schools in the Age of Globalization: A Comparative Perspective', 61 *Rutgers Law Review* 1037–78.

Miyazawa, Setsuo, Kay-Wah Chan and Ilhyung Lee (2008). 'The Reform of Legal Education in East Asia', 4 *Annual Review of Law and Social Science* 334–60.

Rokumoto, Kahei (2007). 'Legal Education', in Daniel H. Foote (ed.), *Law in Japan: A Turning Point* 190–232. Seattle: University of Washington Press.

Steele, Stacey and Kathryn Taylor (eds) (2010). *Legal Education in Asia: Globalization, Change and Contexts*. London: Routledge.

17 Legal professions and law firms
David S. Clark*

1   INTRODUCTION

Comparative lawyers have often used the legal profession as a window to observe important features of different legal systems. This chapter examines the legal professions—especially the private independent professions—in several nations to determine if there remain significant variations in the world.[1] This examination reveals that the standard comparative law division between the civil law tradition and the common law tradition still provides important explanatory power. Geographic location and the level of economic development are also important variables. Even in the face of the process of economic and cultural globalization, it remains true that national history and local culture matter.

1.1   One or Many Professions?

In Canada and the United States, lawyers tend to view the legal profession as a single entity, a unified bar. In common law countries in general, people believe it is normal for a lawyer to switch positions without special training, perhaps from government work to a corporate counsel's office, to a law firm, or maybe to the judiciary. However, in civil law jurisdictions young law graduates tend to think of several legal professions, calcified by their own career images. A civil law lawyer, especially in Europe, must be ready at an early age to select her career either in the private sector as an advocate, notary or with a corporation, or in the public sector as a judge, prosecutor or government official or attorney. Subsequent lateral mobility is minimal.

If we broaden our inquiry into legal professions to encompass East Asia, we find that the practicing bar is quite small. In Japan, the legal profession (*hōsō*) of judges, prosecutors and attorneys defines itself by its common apprenticeship training, leaving outside the formal profession a large number of quasi-lawyers. Finally, one can characterize the nature of legal professions in the developing countries of Africa, Asia and Latin America by the influence of a wide variety of cultural elements peculiar to each country and by the low degree of integration of a formal legal system into the larger society.

---

*   Maynard and Bertha Wilson Professor of Law and Director, Certificate Program in International and Comparative Law, Willamette University. An earlier version of some material in this chapter appeared in David S. Clark, 'Comparing the Work and Organization of Lawyers Worldwide: The Persistence of Legal Traditions', in John J. Barceló III and Roger C. Cramton (eds), *Lawyers' Practice and Ideals: A Comparative View* 9–155 (Hague: Kluwer Law International 1999).
    [1]   Chapter 10 in this volume examines variability in the position of judges and their careers within national legal cultures.

1.2   Legal Traditions

Scholars have used several models and approaches to examine legal professions, ranging from a focus on lawyers' public service and professional independence, their collective ability to control the market for their services, functionalism, contingencies of history and tradition, dominance of state structures, and socialism. In this chapter, I rely on insights from most of these models, viewing them as complementary rather than mutually exclusive approaches. Consequently, I adopt a pragmatic approach toward examining recent developments in the work and organization of lawyers in illustrative nations worldwide, drawing on the comparative law idea of legal traditions, while briefly discussing certain supranational developments. In attempting to avoid distancing myself too far from reality, I have used as much empirical data as I could find.

An influential definition of legal tradition is

> a set of deeply rooted, historically conditioned attitudes about the nature of law, about the role of law in the society and the polity, about the proper organization and operation of a legal system, and about the way law is or should be made, applied, studied, perfected, and taught. The legal tradition relates the legal system to the culture of which it is a partial expression. It puts the legal system into cultural perspective.[2]

By adopting the idea of legal traditions and grouping national legal professions into the two dominant examples of civil law and common law, I have been able to test certain propositions stemming from models as diverse as market control and state structures. I supplement the major traditions with occasional information from Asian, Islamic, and developing nations. On many issues I attempt to let national lawyers explain their own reality, whether as ideology or as sociological insight. I often refer to more than one legal system within a tradition to illustrate the substantial variability that exists, giving credence to the historical model that emphasizes the contingencies existing in all societies.

If one adopts a broad definition of lawyers, we discover that the traditional comparative law categories still offer substantial insight into the work and organization of law-trained professionals. This broad view helps us understand why there has been a distinction between advocates and procurators, why there is a special role for notaries and legal scholars in the civil law tradition, and how the relationship between judges and lawyers varies greatly among legal traditions. These elements grow out of and are a staple of European legal history. They spread worldwide via the conduit of European colonization. The expectation was that legal systems in general and legal professions in particular on the continents beyond Europe would eventually conform, at least at the formal level, to either the common law or civil law tradition.

Today there is serious debate about whether these separate legal traditions continue to reflect reality. Since the collapse of the Soviet Union the existence of a socialist legal tradition has been validly questioned, although the Chinese maintain their own form of socialist law. Furthermore, several comparatists have argued that scholars should collapse

---

[2]   John Henry Merryman and Rogelio Pérez-Perdomo, *The Civil Law Tradition: An Introduction to the Legal Systems of Europe and Latin America* 2 (Stanford, CA: Stanford University Press, 3rd edn, 2007).

the civil law and common law into one category.[3] I hope to show that the historical and cultural underpinnings of these legal traditions will not disappear so easily, at least in relation to the legal professions and specifically the work and organization of private lawyers.

It is true that the locus of influence for the development of the world's legal professions has shifted from the individual nations of Europe. One now finds the engine for change in the United States and to a lesser extent England, where it takes the form of the large law firm, and in the European Union (EU), which has successfully broken the parochial restraints of national bar organizations to promote transborder and multidisciplinary practice. This is not entirely accidental, since the United States has the world's largest number of lawyers and a long tradition of legalism and the EU is the most successful example of supranational cooperation after the end of colonialism.

Since the late 1960s, the number of students studying law in most parts of the world has increased noticeably, which directly led to much larger national legal professions.[4] The response in the United States to this new interest in legal rights and the role of law in society was to absorb more and more lawyers in ever-larger law firms and further to develop specialized practice. Other countries, such as France, undertook to eliminate historic divisions in the legal professions and to liberalize law practice. Since the 1990s, economic and cultural globalization have accelerated interest in transnational transactions and dispute resolution that in the twenty-first century developing nations participate in along with the post-World War II economic powers of Europe, North America and Japan. Have these developments overwhelmed the entrenched differences that have marked legal professions in the civil law and common law world? It is still too soon to tell, but the past two decades have witnessed tremendous change in national legal professions worldwide.

2   CURRENT TRENDS AND ISSUES

The legal profession is changing dramatically because of several trends that transcend any one country or even any one legal tradition. These changes will affect the future of the profession. First, since 1950, the number of students studying law has increased by a multiple of four to eight in Europe, North America and Japan, yielding substantial increases in the number of lawyers and judges.

Second, the opening of the legal profession to women, who have entered all careers in significant numbers, even in most non-Western nations such as Japan and Singapore, explains much of this increase. When one turns to ethnic minorities in the law, however, reflecting society's interest in democratization or pluralization of cultural viewpoints among the powerful, progress everywhere has been minimal.

Third, how many private lawyers does a society use to carry out the tasks of law and justice? That number appears to be highest in common law countries, followed by European and Latin American civil law nations, with Asian and African nations at the bottom. Japan deserves special attention because its private legal professions are as small

---

[3]   E.g., Harold J. Berman, *Law and Revolution: The Formation of the Western Legal Tradition* (Cambridge, MA: Harvard University Press 1983).

[4]   See Chapter 16 this volume.

as in other Asian societies, even though its economy is among the most developed. The United States is distinct within the common law tradition because its legal culture supports an extreme adversarial legalism. Lawyers have substantial influence on the cost of maintaining a legal system, although that cost is difficult to measure. The ratio of law-trained professionals working in the private sector (with some directly hired by corporations) to those employed as judges or government attorneys tells us something about a culture's view of the desirability of public versus private order in social life. The relative number of lawyers that an economy supports gives us a sense of the demand for law (compared to other constructs) as a mechanism for social ordering and for resolving disputes.

Fourth, by the 1990s, with expanded business in international trade and investment, many countries—especially in Europe—had liberalized their rules permitting lawyers to organize in firms (sometimes with other professionals such as accountants), practice in more than one city or country, advertise and in general compete for a lucrative worldwide market for lawyers' services. In the United States and Europe, governments have gradually opened local legal practice to foreign lawyers who provide advice on international and foreign law. As a reaction to economic and cultural globalization, some analysts argue that in fact this is an Americanization of legal culture.

Fifth, related to this liberalization in the transnational and multidisciplinary practice of law is the growth of specialization among lawyers and the sea change in the size and competitiveness of law firms. This is centered in the United States and England but now also prominent in the Netherlands and elsewhere. The form of large law firms has spread to European civil law countries and some Asian nations under the pressure of Europeanization on a regional level and globalization in trade and investment. The growth in transnational lawyering signals the creation of a vastly more complex international legal system with its own distinct values of order and justice that transcend the interests of national sovereignty.

Sixth, perhaps because of these trends, the image of lawyers competing aggressively among themselves has led to complaints in many countries that law has become simply a business, sometimes referred to as the legal services industry. The importance of rapidly changing technology affects most lawyers and further separates them from personal interaction with their clients. The focus on efficiency in the twenty-first century has led to some use of offshore (especially in India) legal process outsourcing (LPO) for document review and memorandum writing for law firms and corporate legal departments. CPA Global and Integreon are two of the worldwide enterprises pursuing this business.[5] Many large firms now use e-discovery software to sort through email and documents. One hears more discontent, especially among advocates, about the demise of professionalism. Further, women complain about the hierarchy in firms and the glass ceiling that precludes them from exercising their full potential. Senior practitioners are retiring earlier, sometimes with a majority of partners forcing them out of their firms.

Seventh, professional associations historically were important in defining private legal professions, especially in common law nations. England was the archetypical example, since its associations controlled apprenticeship and access to the bar and the law society.

---

[5]   See Anthony Lin, 'Inside the Revolution', 32 *American Lawyer* 140–45 (Oct. 2010). In 2009, the top ten Indian LPOs each had more than 300 employees. Ibid. 144.

In continental Europe, legal education was at the university. Most lawyers were until recently judges, prosecutors and civil servants who did not need to associate together to promote their status, guarantee security and regulate conduct; the state assumed this task.

Professional associations today have lost part of their monopolistic power over lawyers. In some countries, they no longer have exclusive power to discipline members, and, in many nations, they cannot prohibit lawyers from advertising or set mandatory minimum fee schedules. Many associations, often together with a supervising high court or legislature, are discussing and responding to requests to permit incorporation of law firms, limited liability, multidisciplinary practice and branch offices. In the United States, the proliferation of specialized groups of lawyers and controversial social issues fragment the politics of local, state and national bar associations such that they are often unable to formulate a unified stand even on issues of practical concern to the legal profession.

Finally, the financial status and social prestige of lawyers seem more closely tied to a nation's wealth or to political factors than to a legal system's alignment with the civil law or the common law. It is true that lawyers are concentrated in urban practices, often in the capital city, a trend seemingly more pronounced in developing nations than in the developed world.[6] Successful urban practice normally determines income and prestige. There are complaints in many countries, however, about reduced income, maybe even a trend, for significant segments of the private bar associated with the overproduction of lawyers. During the 2009–10 recession, for example, the largest 250 US law firms fired 9,500 lawyers.[7]

3   TYPES OF LAWYERS

3.1   Broad View

A broad functional definition of the legal profession would encompass persons who have devoted several years to formal legal education and who then enter a career using law and legal argument. This would include advocates, procurators, notaries, corporate lawyers, judges, some bailiffs and judicial clerks, prosecutors, legislators, other government lawyers and law professors.

All countries have one or more types of lawyers beyond the traditional advocates, procurators and in the civil law, notaries, who work for a particular client: normally either for the state or in the private sector for a corporation. The state employs judges and prosecutors, bailiffs and clerks, as well as other government lawyers who legislate, resolve disputes or advise a ministry, department or public entity. In some jurisdictions, the bar excludes lawyers who work for private concerns because of their perceived lack of independence. These lawyers work for banks, insurance companies, trade unions, business corporations,

---

⁶   For instance, in Korea in 2009, 82 percent of attorneys practiced in Seoul or adjacent communities. This geographic concentration makes it difficult for rural people to obtain assistance for litigation. Youngjoon Kwon, 'Bridging the Gap between Korean Substance and Western Form', in E. Ann Black and Gary F. Bell (eds), *Law and Legal Institutions of Asia: Traditions, Adaptations and Innovations* 151, 172 (Cambridge: Cambridge University Press 2011).

⁷   'How To Curb Your Legal Bills', *Economist* 14 (7 May 2011).

nonprofit organizations and other entities. Law professors are yet another type of lawyer in all nations. They either work for the state in public universities as civil servants or as part-time employees or they work for nonprofit or for-profit private universities with varying degrees of job security.

3.2   National Conceptions of Lawyers

In most countries, the usual conceptualization is an outgrowth of its history and culture. Lawyers in the United States, for instance, tend to view the legal profession as a single entity, a unified bar. An attorney may after a few years in practice stand for election (or be appointed) to a state judgeship, from which she may later resign to join a law firm that values her special knowledge of the judiciary. In the Netherlands, alternatively, the traditional idea of lawyers consists of *advocaten* and *procureurs*. This traditional view of the profession is historically rooted in the idea of a liberal profession (that is, one free from outside political, religious or economic control). In England, the term 'bench and bar' refers to judges and barristers as a continuation of one profession, historically excluding solicitors.

Thus, there are many different views of the concept 'lawyers'. For the purpose of comparison, one needs a broad viable definition to remain open-minded about the experience of young graduates from law faculties and the evolution of the legal profession in the twenty-first century. The Netherlands illustrates this situation. Since there is no monopoly for attorneys providing legal advice, some legal services are provided by law graduates and half-trained persons not admitted to the bar. Social advocacy attorneys, for instance, compete with legal aid bureaus and trade unions that hire law graduates as labor lawyers. General practice attorneys compete with insurance companies for legal costs and automobile clubs that hire law graduates for tort advice. Business clients often turn to tax advisers and accountants rather than to attorneys. Old age pensioners might take their legal problems to social workers.

3.3   Notaries

Some types of lawyers commonly exist beyond advocates and procurators in many nations. A category of practicing lawyer who serves to separate the civil law from the common law tradition is the notary. In common law nations, the law-trained notary is unknown; the position of notary requires no special education or expertise. In civil law nations, however, the notary is a lawyer who holds a public or ministerial office (or has the credential of public faith) to verify particular facts (such as decisions in general meetings of public companies), maintain certain registries, and draft such legal documents as wills, incorporations or land contracts that are regarded as authentic and enforceable.

In most civil law countries, the notariat is a liberal profession whose prestige parallels or exceeds that of attorneys. In several European countries, a statute determines the number of notaries and the government fills positions with a public competition. Virtually all of the notaries in Japan come from the ranks of retired judges, prosecutors and ministry of justice officials, who must leave their posts at age 65. In a few places, notaries work for the state as civil servants, for instance in the German state of Baden-Württemberg and in the Swiss canton of Zurich. Notaries in many countries are at the same time attorneys. In other places, however, such as Quebec, which has 3,500 notaries, the profession is inconsistent with that of advocate and one must choose one or the other. Finally, a mixed system continues in 2011 in Germany, where some states have attorney-notaries (6,356 *Anwaltsnotare*) and others have a separate notarial profession with a total of 1,561 notaries.[8]

3.4   In-house Corporate Counsel

When a corporation employs lawyers full time there is concern in some countries that they will become progressively associated more closely with the corporate goals of their employers. Such a lawyer's livelihood and potential for promotion are dependent on the discretion of a single client. This concern increases if an in-house counsel joins the corporation's management team.

In most common law countries, in-house counsel are also members of a bar association or law society. They have the same ethical duties and must observe the same rules of professional conduct as self-employed lawyers. Civil law countries often take an alternative approach and segregate in-house corporate lawyers from advocates. These corporate lawyers practice a separate profession and in some nations may not represent their employer in court or in arbitration. In other jurisdictions, they may not practice law privately. Germany has a hybrid system. Some law students who pass the first exam decide not to enter apprenticeship training but instead go to work for a corporation or take another job. Many of these corporate lawyers use their legal training on a regular basis but they are not qualified as 'full jurists'.

3.5   Government Lawyers

Besides the professions of judges and prosecutors, which have special responsibilities in the administration of justice, many lawyers are also employed by governments to advise a ministry, department or public agency or otherwise to use their legal skills in tasks such as resolving disputes or rule making.[9]

In most civil law nations, government lawyers may not join the bar association because they are perceived to lack independence from the state. Sweden, however, permits advocates who work in one of its public law firms to remain members of the bar, but other civil servants must resign their bar membership. In Spain, civil servants may register with the local bar but may not participate in cases in which their agency is a party. In Italy and Spain, a single agency, such as the Avvocatura dello Stato or Cuerpo de Letrados del Estado, provides legal advice to the state and its entities, including government corporations. In France and Germany, agencies employ their own lawyers as in-house counsel to provide advice, although they may hire private attorneys to represent the state in civil or administrative litigation.

---

[8]   Statistisches Bundesamt, *Statistisches Jahrbuch 2011 für die Bundesrepublik Deutschland* table 10.3 (Stuttgart: 2011).

[9]   In most countries, lawyers are not elected to the legislature as frquently as the public might expect, based on their educational training to work with laws. Where legislatures have significant permanent staffs, however, many of those senior employees are law-trained.

In many common law nations, government lawyers are also members of a bar association or law society and are expected to follow the same rules of professional conduct as ordinary attorneys. Nevertheless, government lawyers generally are required to regard the ministry or agency that they represent as their client and should follow the lawful instructions received from responsible authorities. Sometimes the understanding is that government lawyers represent the 'public interest', which is fulfilled by following adopted policies and superiors' directions. However, as with corporate lawyers, professional conduct rules only allow government lawyers to use confidential information for whistle blowing if they have reasonable grounds to believe that a crime is likely to be committed.

The government lawyer who prosecutes criminal cases stands between two poles of lawyering. The magisterial pole represents the ideal of a judge, that is, one who sees that the process of justice is fair and efficient. The adversarial pole invokes a system in which the prosecutor represents the state as the client and, in worrisome cases, the prosecutor's overriding duty de facto is to convict an accused.

Modern legal systems seek to come closer to the magisterial pole. A prosecutor's duty is to serve the public interest, which jurists in the civil law tradition argue is the search for justice in a role similar to that of the judge. In some civil law nations, the government procurator or advocate participates ex officio in supreme court decisions or intervenes on behalf of the public interest in certain civil actions. In Japan, for instance, the Public Prosecutor's Office is separate from the judiciary and organized in a centralized, hierarchical form under the ministry of justice. A prosecutor's main function is to investigate crimes and to prosecute the offender, but he may also represent the public interest in a civil case. A prosecutor has discretionary power not to proceed and there are some citizen controls on this discretion. This must be a strong filter, since the conviction rate exceeds 99 percent. Some civil law nations, such as Germany, Italy and Japan, have constructed educational programs or apprenticeship and career paths to merge the two professions of judge and prosecutor. France refers to both judges and prosecutors as magistrates in a *corps unique*, the former sitting on a bench and the latter standing on the floor (*parquet*).

In common law countries, the adversarial pole pulls more strongly. Prosecutors often interpret the duty to serve the public interest to make them more like an ordinary government lawyer. The adversarial emphasis makes winning very important. Being part of a hierarchical organization puts assistant prosecutors in the position of treating their superior as the client with established policies or specific orders. In the United States, the president appoints a chief prosecutor in each federal judicial district in a partisan political process while in most states the voters elect chief prosecutors in each county. These political pressures erode independence as the prosecutor desires to please a local citizenry outraged by excessive crime.

Increasing interest in the principle of equality as applied to the administration of justice has led to sustained efforts at national and supranational levels (particularly in Europe) to make accessibility to justice a reality for poor persons, ethnic minorities and politically repressed individuals. Part of the solution toward achieving equal justice in some countries has included subsidization of court costs, waiving security bonds, expanding small claims jurisdiction and reducing delay before final judgment. Another approach is to provide attorneys to persons who previously were unrepresented or underrepresented. Where the state takes direct responsibility for providing legal assistance to poor persons in criminal or civil matters, it hires full-time lawyers to perform this task. In many countries, however, the government only indirectly supports legal aid lawyers by paying their fees for specific tasks.[10]

4   ADVOCATES AND PROCURATORS

A comparative study of legal professions shows that the Roman distinction between advocate and procurator is not useful for dividing the civil law world from the common law world. Rather, prominent examples from both traditions maintain the distinction, although there is a clear tendency toward merger of these two liberal professions everywhere.

4.1   Common Law Countries

England, the progenitor of the common law tradition, borrowed the Roman distinction and carried it over as barrister and solicitor, with some lateral mobility between the two professions after 1990. Solicitors deal with about 95 percent of the financially significant legal matters in England and Wales, today more often as specialties (such as criminal defense advocacy in magistrates' courts and out-of-court preparation in the Crown Court) or in large law firms representing corporations, leaving the job of pleading and advocacy in higher courts and certain other specialized work to barristers. Barristers deal with clients only when so instructed by a solicitor, although this rule was relaxed in 2004 for some matters. In general, England exported this division to its colonies, where today in independent nations it is eroding. Ireland has the same separation, but since 1971 it has permitted solicitors the right of audience (although normally only exercised in lower courts) that barristers enjoy. Scotland maintains the distinction as one between advocates and solicitors. South Africa preserves a divided profession, prohibiting dual practice as both an advocate and an attorney.[11]

Barristers in England and Wales often are specialized, practicing in limited fields such as chancery, common law, criminal law, commercial law or admiralty. Some of these specialties, such as tax, labor or regulatory (planning) law, involve little courtroom work.[12] Barristers (or advocates in Scotland) begin as junior counsel. After a minimum of 15 years experience, one may apply (since 2006) to a panel, which recommends to the monarch that candidates 'take silk' and become queen's counsel.[13] Only about 11 percent of the self-employed bar is queen's counsel, and it is from their ranks that most judges are selected.

---

[10]   For the increase in the number of law professors, often employees of the state, along with the expanded importance of university legal education worldwide, see Chapter 16 in this volume.

[11]   General Council of the Bar of South Africa, 'South African Legal System', http://www.sabar.co.za/legal-system.html.

[12]   The increasing specialization of solicitors in firms is functionally reducing the separation with barristers as solicitors increasingly offer the type of expert advice formerly provided by barristers.

[13]   Prior to 2004, the lord chancellor made the recommendation. Complaints by women and ethnic minorities about bias and the lack of transparency led to the use of a panel. QC Appointments, 'About Us', http://www.qcappointments.org.

Barristers involved with criminal law have unusual flexibility not found in the civil law or in much of the common law world. This need for flexibility stems from their prosecution of a major case on behalf of the Crown Prosecution Service one day and their representation of defendants directly or on behalf of the Legal Services Commission the next day.[14] Supporters of this system argue that this develops a degree of objectivity and independence in advocates important for the cause of justice. Detractors find that too many barristers take 'late briefs' that allow them to see their client only on the day of the hearing.

One of the most important developments for private legal professions in the United Kingdom in the 1980s and 1990s was the elimination of certain monopolies that these professions historically enjoyed. The government premised these reforms on the notion that market forces would require a more efficient delivery of legal services to consumers. First, barristers (and advocates in Scotland) lost their exclusive right of audience in the higher courts in 1990.[15] Second, solicitors lost their monopoly over property conveyancing in 1985 and Parliament created the new non-legal career of licensed conveyancer.[16] Third, in 1990, solicitors lost their monopoly over the preparation of litigation and probate cases. Banks, building societies, insurance companies and regulated legal executives may now provide probate services.[17]

In 2007, the UK Parliament further sought to liberalize the legal services market. The Legal Services Act created the Legal Services Board that began its regulatory function in 2010 and included a consumer panel.[18] The Act defined legal activity as either 'reserved' or merely the ordinary provision of legal advice (generally excluding probate, notarial or property law) or assistance with non-litigation dispute resolution or the application of law. Only authorized persons who are subject to approved regulators such as the Law Society, Bar Council, Institute of Legal Executives or Council for Licensed Conveyancers may provide reserved services. In addition to expanding who could provide legal services, the Act included the possibility of multidisciplinary practice with non-lawyer 'alternative business structures' in management or ownership roles.

Australia illustrates the haphazard erosion of the division between the two professions. The distinction between barristers and solicitors continues in New South Wales and Queensland. Most barristers are sole practitioners, tend to specialize, and generally have no direct contact with clients other than through instructing solicitors. Barristers engage

---

[14]   The Crown Prosecution Service has been reducing its reliance on private barristers and now has the largest UK law firm of employed barristers and solicitor advocates. Crown Prosecution Service, 'Careers at the CPS', http://www.cps.gov.uk/careers.

[15]   The Courts and Legal Services Act 1990 eliminated the barristers' exclusive right of audience in higher courts. However, solicitors must qualify by experience and examination to appear in the Crown Court or the High Court. In 2002, there were 1,400 solicitor advocates. See Solicitors Association of Higher Court Advocates, Home Page, http://www.sahca.org.uk.

[16]   Administration of Justice Act 1985. This type of 'lawyer' also handles other type of property transactions and exists in Australia, New Zealand and South Africa.

[17]   Legal executives have law training and generally specialize in an area of the law. They also exist in Australia, New Zealand and Singapore. The UK Legal Services Act 2007, ss 182–7, describes licensed conveyancers, trade mark or patent attorneys, immigration advisers or service providers and claims management services as 'other lawyers'.

[18]   The new Office for Legal Complaints reflects the consumer focus. It established a legal ombudsman who began receiving complaints in 2010.

in advocacy before the courts and prepare legal opinions. Senior (or queen's) counsel in 2008 represented 17 percent of the bar, from whom the government selects almost all of the superior court judges. The government also employs barristers, typically as prosecutors.[19] Solicitors are the general practitioners who may and do work in partnerships. They give general advice to clients, deal with non-litigious matters such as contracts and testaments and typically make court appearances only in minor matters. South Australia, Tasmania, Victoria, Western Australia and the two territories have fused the professions; nevertheless, an independent bar still exists in those places.[20] However, most lawyers practice as both barrister and solicitor, although interest in specialization has kept some practicing only one profession. As in England, some states have recently reduced restrictive practices. For instance, solicitors in New South Wales lost their monopoly over conveyancing in 1992.

In Canada and New Zealand, there has been de facto merger. All Canadian lawyers are automatically both barristers and solicitors (except in Quebec, which borrowed the French *avocat* and *notaire*). Ontario was the last province (in 1857) to fuse the two professions. Canada is similar to the United States in that the term 'lawyer' is universal and the public sees it as embracing all qualified members of the legal profession. In New Zealand, almost all lawyers practice as both barristers and solicitors.

In the United States and elsewhere, there has always been a fused profession of lawyer (or attorney or counselor). A member of a state bar association in the US can practice any law job from prosecutor to corporate lawyer to judge and many lawyers undertake more than one position during their careers. The dominance of the sole practitioner has eroded dramatically since the end of World War II, however, when individual lawyers were still in the majority of all legal professionals. From a sociological perspective, of course, there can be many professions. One study found that the great division in the United States is between lawyers who serve corporations and those whose clients are individuals and small businesses. The former are prestigious law firm lawyers who are bar leaders. The latter graduated from lesser law schools, have different social origins, practice in more varied office environments, and are more likely to litigate in state rather than federal courts.[21]

Singapore by necessity developed a single practicing bar during its nineteenth-century colonial relationship with the British East India Company. Trained lawyers were scarce. Since the Supreme Court had to license law agents for them to be able to represent litigants, qualifications were relaxed. The Court admitted the first fully qualified person in 1859 and only in 1873 were law agents required to possess qualifications as British barristers or solicitors, although they could exercise either or both professions. Today, the Supreme Court admits every practicing lawyer as an 'advocate and solicitor'. The National University of Singapore trains most of these lawyers.

---

[19]   Law Council of Australia, 'How Many Lawyers Are There in Australia?', http://www.law-council.asn.au (select Resources/About the Profession). Senior counsel earned 36 percent of barrister income. Ibid.

[20]   See Australian Bar Association, Home Page, http://www.austbar.asn.au (select Barristers in Australia, then Practising Requirements).

[21]   John P. Heinz and Edward O. Laumann, *Chicago Lawyers: The Social Structure of the Bar* (Evanston, IL: Northwestern University Press, rev. edn, 1994).

Since its creation in 1948, Israel has had a unitary bar. Once admitted to the Israeli Bar Association (formerly the Chamber of Advocates), an advocate may engage in any legal activity anywhere in the country. To be appointed to the bench (or as a court registrar) or to a government legal services office, one must be a bar member.[22] Tanzania, likewise, has fused the professions of barrister and solicitor since its independence. There were too few law-trained persons, known as advocates, to maintain the division. Today the unified profession is justified based on reduced costs to litigants.

4.2 Civil Law Countries

In the civil law world, one should distinguish between the French (Romanist) model and German patterns. Traditionally, France took on the Roman division of the liberal professions of *avocat* and *avoué*, which it almost completely merged into *avocat* in 1971.[23] The former category of legal advisers, *conseils juridiques*, became more closely regulated in 1971, including the requirement that they have law degrees. In 1990, the government also merged them into *avocats*. Advocates have a nationwide right to provide legal advice and to plead in any courts (except the high courts),[24] but their right of audience in representing a client is generally restricted territorially to the *tribunal de grande instance* of their local bar and other courts in its district. This rule has come under increasing attack in both French and European courts.

Nations in the Romanist tradition in Europe and Latin America have followed the late twentieth-century French trend toward merger of the two liberal professions. For instance, the two professions exist in the Netherlands, as *advocaat* and *procureur*, but today the same person normally practices both. In Italy, experience differentiated an *avvocato* and *procuratore* by years in practice, but the distinction is now gone. Today a law graduate practices for two years as a *praticante*; if then successful with the state exam, he becomes an *avvocato*. In Belgium, only *avocats* may appear in court, but unregulated *conseillers juridiques* may handle administrative cases.

In Costa Rica and Venezuela, the category of *procurador* has disappeared and it is nearly gone in Uruguay. *Abogados* now practice the full liberal profession. Egypt has a merged liberal profession of advocates. Some countries that abandoned the socialist law tradition in the 1990s, such as Romania, have adopted the model of the unitary French *avocat*.

The German pattern has been different. By the nineteenth century, in German-speaking lands such as Switzerland, authorities fused the liberal profession into *Rechtsanwälte*. *Advokater* in Sweden and lawyers in Greece are also part of a unitary profession. They provide clients with the full range of legal advice but in many countries may represent

---

[22] See Israeli Bar Association, Home Page, http://www.israelbar.org.il (select English).

[23] At the same time, *agréés près les tribunaux de commerce* also became *avocats*. In 2008, the French government announced the merger of the 440 remaining *avoués* with *avocats* to promote free competition, which the Constitutional Council approved for 2012.

[24] There are 102 *avocats aux conseils*, who handle appeals to the highest French courts. The ministry of justice grants these lawyers a *charge*, which is a monopoly for their *office ministériel* that they can sell or devise with ministry permission. This type of special bar also exists in Belgium and Germany.

them, at least for private law matters, only in courts that are subject to the territorial jurisdiction of the district court where their law office is located (*Lokalisationsprinzip*).

German law requires that a litigant use a *Rechtsanwalt* in certain courts (*Anwaltszwang*), namely for civil and criminal matters (other than for misdemeanors or in limited jurisdiction local courts). However, litigants may appear unrepresented in all social courts or local administrative, labor or tax courts, although the majority retains the services of a lawyer. Upon qualification, a lawyer joins a local bar and registers with the local court (*Amtsgericht*). The rationale for this requirement was to foster a sense of community among local attorneys, allow those judges to know them and to protect practice in towns and villages as an issue of access to justice. Since the early 1990s, however, the Federal Lawyers Act (BRAO) has permitted attorneys to open a second office elsewhere in Germany or abroad and has broadened access to appellate courts. Nevertheless, the Federal Supreme Court in 2011 only permitted 41 attorneys to practice before it.[25]

Restraint of trade challenges brought in the European Court of Justice during the 1970s and 1980s stimulated these developments. The increased competition among a growing number of lawyers similarly convinced the German legislature to enact a Specialist Lawyers Act (FAO). This permits a local bar association to authorize a lawyer with at least three years' experience to hold herself out as a specialist in one of several designated fields. BRAO also now authorizes advertising, which it previously had banned. In 2004, the legislature approved a liberalized statute on lawyers' compensation (RVG), which provides for contractual deviation from the civil claim-value scale or criminal fee guidelines. Even so, BRAO still prohibits pure contingent fee agreements; to pass muster, an agreement may call for a successful outcome bonus. As in most civil law nations, the prevailing party can recover FAO fees from the loser.[26]

Export of the German *Rechtsanwalt* to non-European nations has resulted in interesting mixtures of modern and traditional. For instance, Turkey has the equivalent of German lawyers (*avukatlar*) who practice a liberal profession. In addition, two types of traditional licensed legal counselors still exist, especially in rural areas. First, a dispute agent (*dava vekili*) with five years of judicial experience can represent litigants in localities that have no bar association and fewer than five attorneys. Second, a dispute pursuer (*dava takipçisi*) may represent litigants in areas with fewer than three attorneys or dispute agents. Both of these traditional types of lawyers are in decline as more attorneys graduate from universities in Turkey.

4.3   Islamic Law Countries

Islamic law countries inherited the profession of advocates from their European colonial relationship, but they also had a parallel profession that practiced primarily before *shari'a* courts. In Morocco, for example, *oukils* represented clients in personal status and succession matters before *châa* (*qadi*). They also appeared for parties in ordinary courts with a

---

25   Nigel Foster and Satish Sule, *German Legal System and Laws* 108–10, 125–6 (Oxford: Oxford University Press, 4th edn, 2010).

26   Ibid. 111–12, 127–8. For transaction work, the attorney may negotiate a price with her client.

written mandate or even before the Supreme Court with permission of the chief justice. The profession of *oukils* gradually disappeared in Morocco as well as in Tunisia.

4.4 Japan

Another example of mixing Western and traditional ideas about lawyers occurred in Japan. To accommodate the West, the Japanese ministry of justice opened the University of Tokyo Law Faculty in 1877 and adopted the German legal education model with a *Referendar* apprenticeship.[27] This focused on the production of lawyers to serve the state, principally judges and prosecutors. To keep the number of attorneys (*bengoshi*) small, until the mid-1990s, the state bar examination (for the apprenticeship to enter these three positions) passed only about 2 percent of test takers. These three careers constitute the legal profession (*hōsō*). Most notaries (*kōshōnin*), whom the ministry of justice selects, are retired judges and prosecutors.

Until globalization accelerated transnational lawyering in the 1990s, the best students tended first to select a judgeship, then the positions for prosecutor, but now often choose to work as an attorney, typically in a firm with an international clientele. Nevertheless, most *bengoshi* practice alone and are concerned with litigation. In 1990, for instance, there were only 179 lawyers working in the four largest firms, while 57 of these were partners. By 2002, their number had increased to 451 lawyers and 135 partners.[28] Law graduates also work in corporate legal departments (*homubu*), whose size has been increasing significantly since 1990. Finally, some highly qualified law graduates take the first-tier civil service exam. The pass rate is low, about 3 percent, but success provides one with a good chance of a position in one of 28 ministries and agencies. Those not hired and other law graduates, of course, may apply for other government positions.[29]

Meanwhile, traditional types of quasi-lawyers remain in Japan. Many if not most of these people are university law-trained and they perform tasks similar to those that lawyers undertake in Western nations. This is a matter of continued misunderstanding by journalists and even some legal scholars. They insist on comparing the total number of lawyers in the United States with *bengoshi* in Japan, two countries of similar economic development, typically then decrying the excessive number of US lawyers.[30]

Among the variety of quasi-lawyers are judicial scriveners (*shihō shoshi*), administrative scriveners (*gyōsei shoshi*), patent agents (*benrishi*), tax agents (*zeirishi*) and certified public accountants (*kōnin kaikeishi*). Judicial scriveners take a government test, with a pass rate of about 4 percent, for a license to practice in real estate and corporate registration, but also to provide documents to courts. They often offer general legal advice in rural

---

[27] See Chapter 16, section 4.1, this volume.

[28] Yasuharu Nagashima and E. Anthony Zaloom, 'The Rise of the Large Japanese Business Law Firm and its Prospects for the Future', in Daniel H. Foote (ed.), *Japanese Law: A Turning Point* 136, 142–5 (Seattle: University of Washington Press 2006). In Korea in 2009, 59 percent of attorneys were in sole practice. Kwon (note 6) 172.

[29] Curtis J. Milhaupt and Mark D. West, 'Law's Dominion and the Market for Legal Elites in Japan', 34 *Law and Policy in International Business* 451, 459–62, 464–8, 476–7 (2003).

[30] See Richard S. Miller, 'Apples vs. Persimmons: The Legal Profession in Japan and the United States', 39 *Journal of Legal Education* 27–31 (1989).

regions or towns with few attorneys and play a silent role in summary court or district court proceedings in which neither party has an attorney. Since 2004, some of them may represent clients in summary courts. Administrative scriveners primarily represent small businesses in license applications and compliance with government regulations. Patent and tax agents work in their respective fields, advising clients and preparing and filing documents. Lastly, certified public accountants handle much of the securities work for large corporations.[31]

In 2010, there were 20,000 judicial scriveners (12,000 of whom had the right to appear in summary courts), 40,000 administrative scriveners, 8,100 patent agents, 72,000 tax agents and 20,000 certified public accountants.[32]

4.5   China

A liberal, independent legal profession and socialist law were mutually inconsistent. In former communist nations, law—guided by the communist party—was a tool in the class struggle of workers and peasants against entrenched capitalist interests. The state must clearly marginalize if not eliminate free-acting lawyers, representing traditional private interests and values. The bar as a group (*advokatura*) took the view that an advocate, more than the representative of a client, was a collaborator with the judge and prosecutor in furthering socialist legality. Thus in a criminal proceeding, if a lawyer were convinced of the client's guilt, the lawyer was relieved of the duty to maintain professional secrecy. A lawyer, as a result, was independent, not from the state but from the client.

That was the standard analysis for attorneys in socialist law countries through the 1980s. What requires further consideration is the interesting case of China, which started as a classical Asian culture, added communism, and then injected in the 1980s a desire for a market economy based on law. How do attorneys fit into the political framework of China in the twenty-first century?[33]

China never really had a distinct profession of advocates or procurators until its contacts with the West in the nineteenth century. There were a few self-trained litigation agents, often translated as shysters (*song shi*) or tricksters (*song gun*), who advised their fellow subjects about criminal matters and drafted complaints or other legal documents for litigants, but the advisers could not argue in court. Most shysters were former government clerks, without systematic legal education, who had a low reputation in the community. Chinese law, interwoven with Confucianism and feudal ethical rules, aimed toward protecting governmental powers, community social interests and patriarchy while minimizing individual rights. Law had an educational function useful in maintaining social harmony.

---

31   Dan Fenno Henderson, 'The Role of Lawyers in Japan', in Harald Baum (ed.), *Japan: Economic Success and Legal System* 27, 28–35, 55–6, 58–59 (Berlin: Walter de Gruyter 1997); Milhaupt and West (note 29) 476.

32   Japanese Federation of Bar Associations, *White Paper on Attorneys: 2010*, at 22, http://www.nichibenren.or.jp/library/en/about/data/WhitePaper2010.pdf.

33   See Elizabeth M. Lynch, 'China's Rule of Law Mirage: The Regression of the Legal Profession since the Adoption of the 2007 Lawyers Law', 42 *George Washington International Law Review* 535 (2010).

Westernization in Chinese law began with the Opium War (1840), when the minister in charge of legal reform invited Japanese legal scholars to translate and prepare draft laws for the Qing Dynasty. After 1912, the republican government continued the program of Western (largely German) inspired legal reform, which was inconsistent with traditional law and culture. The People's Republic (PRC) from 1949 to 1956 then undertook to transform these layers of law into a socialist legal system appropriate for an economy based on public ownership and centralized planning, a polity guided by the supremacy of the party for a people's democratic dictatorship and a culture dominated by Marxist ideology.

In 1954, the government promulgated a constitution and established judicial and public procurator structures along with a system of lawyers. The PRC saw law as manipulable to serve the more important policies of the party and the state, an idea still present in China. From 1956 until 1966, the legal system was in decline and the feeble legal profession disbanded. During the Cultural Revolution from 1966 to 1976, the PRC praised lawlessness.[34] What rules there were came from Chairman Mao Zedong's writings and the party's policies.

The disastrous political and economic consequences of these developments led to a reconsideration in the late 1970s of the role of law in a socialist society. From that time, and especially under the leadership of Deng Xiaoping, economic growth replaced the class struggle as the country's basic task. The PRC rejected a rigid planned economy in favor of a 'socialist market economy' with private ownership, foreign investment and trade. Government was decentralized, and there has been some liberalization of individual rights. To facilitate these changes the government dramatically altered the legal system and gave law a new importance under the 1978 and 1982 constitutions. Legal scholars debated the desirability of the rule of law, the necessity of private law and its separation from public law and the importance of legal rights. By 1994, in addition to the Supreme People's Court, there were 30 high courts, 391 intermediate courts and 3,074 basic courts. All of this has required the restoration of the legal profession, which in 1995 worked out of 7,263 law firms and 3,148 notarial offices, totaling 76,000 lawyers and notaries.[35] By 2004, there were 145,000 lawyers compared to 191,000 judges, an extremely low lawyer/judge ratio even for a civil law country.[36]

The Provisional Regulations on Lawyers took effect in 1982 and article 1 proclaimed that 'lawyers are the state's legal workers'. The profession's role, since lawyers were salaried civil servants, was to safeguard socialism and the public interest. By 1985, however, the ministry of justice permitted some attorneys to practice privately outside state law firms. The 1996 Lawyers Law validated this decision, which termed lawyers 'legal service workers'. Some firms became economically independent from the state. The Provisional

---

[34]   During the period 1956 to 1980, there were about 3,000 lawyers. William P. Alford, 'Tasselled Loafers for Barefoot Lawyers: Transformation and Tension in the World of Chinese Legal Workers', in Stanley Lubman (ed.), *China's Legal Reforms* (Oxford: Oxford University Press 1996).

[35]   Bin Liang, *The Changing Chinese Legal System: 1978–Present* 45–54 (New York: Routledge 2008). In 1981, there were 1,465 law offices and 5,500 lawyers. Daniel C.K. Chow, *The Legal System of the People's Republic of China in a Nutshell* 232 (St. Paul, MN: Thomson Reuters, 2nd edn, 2009).

[36]   Jianfu Chen, *Chinese Law: Context and Transformation* 169 (Leiden: Martinus Nijhoff 2008); Chow (note 35) 54.

Regulations did permit local law societies, which acted to protect the legitimate rights and interests of lawyers. In 1986, the ministry of justice required all lawyers and law societies to join the All China Lawyers Federation. It promulgates rules for attorney qualification, practice, fees and discipline.

In 2000, there were 9,500 law firms and 117,000 lawyers (for a population of 1.3 billion), which grew to 13,000 firms and 154,000 lawyers in 2005. The need for updating rules regulating lawyers was apparent. The PRC adopted the 2007 Lawyers Law, which set higher qualification standards, continued the movement toward private legal services and established ethical rules with a disciplinary body to enforce them.[37]

As with Turkey,[38] China also had its own indigenous version of legal service worker outside the Roman law tradition followed in Europe. In the 1980s, the PRC decided to supplement the effort to educate lawyers with already existing quasi-lawyers known as 'basic-level legal workers' (*falü fuwuzhe*). By 1987, there were about 60,000 legal workers working from 23,000 legal service centers. In 1990, their number reached 100,000 (compared to 50,000 lawyers). In 2000, these legal workers still outnumbered lawyers (122,000 to 117,000) and handled more civil cases, provided more legal advice and drafted more documents. About that time, the growing number of lawyers lobbied the ministry of justice to end efforts to regularize legal workers with a qualifying exam, since these were a relic of the past. Lawyers argued that a de-emphasis on legal workers was necessary to demonstrate progress toward a rule of law and to professionalize legal services so that foreign lawyers would respect the Chinese legal system.

Many legal workers were former government employees, sometimes judges, who often used unscrupulous practices, including corruption, fraud and influence peddling. They frequently were the only agents available in rural areas, but by the end of the twentieth century, more were moving to cities along with millions of peasants looking for work. Under measures from the justice ministry, the number of legal workers declined to 80,000 by 2006. The 2007 Lawyers Law prohibited non-lawyers from representing clients in court, but so far enforcement at the local level has been uneven. Some predict that an inadequate supply of lawyers or their unwillingness to practice in rural areas will provide work for legal workers for many years.[39]

Another type of agent also provides legal advice in civil cases and other non-litigation services in China, primarily in rural areas. These are the so-called 'barefoot lawyers' (*tu lüshi*), who are likely to have no formal legal qualifications. In some regions, they may handle more cases than either lawyers or legal workers. Although most cases involve

---

[37] Chow (note 35) 232–4, 250–58; Liang (note 35) 54. In 2007, 22 percent of the bar exam takers (who need not have a law degree) passed. Chow (note 35) 234–7. Official statistics list 165,000 lawyers in 2006, which declined to 144,000 lawyers in 2007. *Law Yearbook of China* 607, 630 (Beijing: Press of Law Yearbook of China 2009).

[38] See text following note 26.

[39] William P. Alford, 'Second Lawyers, First Principles: Lawyers, Rice-Roots Legal Workers, and the Battle over Legal Professionalism in China', in William P. Alford, Kenneth Winston and William C. Kirby (eds), *Prospects for the Professions in China* 48–63 (Routledge: New York 2011); Randall Peerenboom, 'Economic Development and the Development of the Legal Profession in China', in Margaret Y.K. Woo and Mary E. Gallagher (eds), *Chinese Justice: Civil Dispute Resolution in Contemporary China* 114, 123–4 (Cambridge: Cambridge University Press 2011). The ministry of justice stopped publishing statistics on legal works after 2003. Alford (note 39) 63.

family matters or minor property disputes, they sometimes are willing to take on controversial cases involving land acquisition, environmental issues and local corruption.[40]

5   COMPARING THE SIZE AND DISTRIBUTION OF LEGAL PROFESSIONS

The number of lawyers in a society provides a rough indicator of the importance of law and its complexity within a country.[41] Most would agree that modern society, over the course of the nineteenth century to the present, has become more rational. Rationalism, as a state of mind, has been central to Western societies since the Enlightenment. As gradually implemented, it includes a variety of notions—frequently contradictory—associated with the expansion of market exchange and the rise of bureaucracy. Max Weber, in particular, in explaining the emergence of industrial capitalism in Europe emphasized the importance of rational law and legal institutions in the modernization process.[42]

As nations modernize and become more rational, their social structures divide and grow more complex in response to an economic division of labor. The differences between citizens increase. Informal means of social control are ineffective. Law, however, can substitute an effective network of solidarity by providing a common set of symbolic representations to foster social integration. The two dominant legal models in this regard for the past century have been decentralized market exchange and central bureaucratic administration.

The movement toward market or plan should have a direct impact on the composition of a country's legal profession. In nations where political leaders prefer an indirect regulative role for government, private attorneys seem to predominate. This role includes differentiation of routine administration (especially judicial) from the political process. If, in addition, large-scale organizations such as business corporations emerge in society, this type of change in the social structure should be reflected in the evolution of a distinct class of attorneys to service corporate interests. On the other side, a shift toward plan— public bureaucratization—absorbs lawyers into bureaucratic roles. Nevertheless, just as corporations are subject to law, a country where government decision making is subject to legal restraint may stimulate in response a group within the legal profession to control both private and public bureaucracies 'in the public interest'.

Although the structure of a nation's polity and economy are important in determining the size and breakdown of its legal profession, factors internal to the legal system may also be significant. For instance, the percentages of private attorneys, corporate counsel and government lawyers may reflect the political and economic structure, while the percentage of judges may more closely relate to the judicial role vis-à-vis attorneys within a particular

---

[40]   Peerenboom (note 39) 123–4; see Xing Ying, 'Barefoot Lawyers and Rural Conflicts', in You-tien Hsing and Ching Kwan Lee, *Reclaiming Chinese Society: The New Social Activism* 64–82 (New York: Routledge 2010).

[41]   See David S. Clark, 'The Legal Profession in Comparative Perspective: Growth and Specialization', 30 *American Journal of Comparative Law* 163–75 (Supp. 1982).

[42]   David M. Trubek, 'Max Weber on Law and the Rise of Capitalism', 1972 *Wisconsin Law Review* 720–25 (1972).

Table 17.1   Number of common law lawyers by country and year[43]

Year	England and Wales[44]	Canada[45]	United States[46]
1850	13,000		24,000
1880	17,000		64,000
1900	21,000		114,000
1930	18,000	8,000	139,000
1950	20,000	9,000	222,000
1960	21,000	12,000	286,000
1970	27,000	16,000	327,000
1980	42,000	34,000	575,000
1990	61,000		756,000
2000	93,000	64,000	1,022,000
2011	166,000	85,000	1,225,000

legal tradition. Finally, one can best explain certain aspects of a society's legal profession with variables unique to that country's particular history.

For the three common law nations in Table 17.1, the decade of dramatic expansion in lawyer populations was the 1970s, a trend that has continued through 2011. In England and Canada, the relative size of the legal profession prior to 1970 grew slightly more than the general population. Even in the United States, where absolute figures increased faster, population also grew more. The number of lawyers per 100,000 US inhabitants in 1850 was 103, a figure that increased moderately to 160 in 1970. By contrast, in 2011, there were 392 lawyers for 100,000 people, the second highest ratio in the world. In England and Wales, the ratio was 301 lawyers and in Canada, it was 246 lawyers.[47]

---

[43]   Excludes retired or non-practicing lawyers as well as lawyers employed in government or the private sector who do not maintain their practicing license or bar membership.

[44]   Richard L. Abel, 'England and Wales: A Comparison of the Professional Projects of Barristers and Solicitors', in Richard L. Abel and Philip S.C. Lewis (eds), 1 *Lawyers in Society: The Common Law* 23, 67–72 (Berkeley: University of California Press 1988) (for 1851, 1880–1980); Bar Council, 'Statistics', http://www.barcouncil.org.uk/about/statistics (select Annual Statistics: 2010); David Dixon, *Entry to the Solicitors' Profession: 1980–2010*, at 3, 5 (London: Law Society 2011) (for solicitors 1990–2010); Michael Zander, *Cases and Materials on the English Legal System* 618 (London: Butterworths, 8th edn, 1999) (for barristers 1990–2000).

[45]   Harry W. Arthurs, Richard Weisman and Frederick H. Zemans, 'Canadian Lawyers: A Peculiar Professionalism', in Richard L. Abel and Philip S.C. Lewis (eds), 1 *Lawyers in Society: The Common Law* 123, 169 (Berkeley: University of California Press 1988) (for 1931, 1951, 1961, 1971, 1981); Federation of Law Societies of Canada, 'Publications and Resources', http://www.flsc.ca/en/resources (select Statistical Report for 2000, 2009).

[46]   Richard L. Abel, 'United States: The Contradictions of Professionalism', in Richard L. Abel and Philip S.C. Lewis (eds), 1 *Lawyers in Society: The Common Law* 186, 239 (Berkeley: University of California Press 1988) (for 1850); American Bar Association, 'Public Resources', http://www.americanbar.org/portals/public_resources.html (select Statistics, then Lawyers) (for 1880–2011).

[47]   From 1996 to 2011, the number of lawyers in Israel increased from 17,000 to 46,000, for a rate of 589 lawyers per 100,000 population. Israeli Bar Association (note 22) (select Israel Bar Association, then General Information).

Table 17.2   Number of civil law advocates, by country and year

Year	Germany[48]	Italy[49]	Netherlands[50]	Japan[51]
1880	4,100	13,000	(3000) 700	500
1900	6,700	20,000	(3000) 700	1,600
1930	16,000	25,000	(5700) 1,100	6,600
1950	13,000	29,000	(8600) 1,600	5,900
1960	18,000	37,000	(11,000) 1,900	6,300
1970	23,000	40,000	(16,000) 2,100	8,500
1980	36,000	45,000	3,700	11,000
1990	57,000	69,000	7,000	14,000
2000	104,000	108,000	11,000	17,000
2011	156,000	198,000	16,000	29,000

When considering civil law countries in Table 17.2, one must note that governments generally only collect regular statistics about advocates, notaries, judges and sometimes prosecutors. The total number in law-trained professions would be substantially larger than the figures for advocates alone, as the comparative Netherlands data illustrate. As in the common law nations considered, the rapid growth in the size of the advocate group began in Germany and the Netherlands in the 1970s. Italy was a decade behind in reforms to its legal profession that would permit the growth of the 1980s. Japan did not implement serious reform to facilitate law firms until the twenty-first century. In 2011, the number of advocates per 100,000 inhabitants was 326 in Italy, 190 in Germany, 96 in the Netherlands and a diminutive 23 in Japan.[52] It would appear that Italy has had a severe overproduction

---

[48]   Erhard Blankenburg and Ulrike Schultz, 'German Advocates: A Highly Regulated Profession', in Richard L. Abel and Philip S.C. Lewis (eds), 2 *Lawyers in Society: The Civil Law World* 124, 150 (Berkeley: University of California Press 1988); Bundesrechtsanwaltskammer, 'Rund um den Anwaltsberuf: Statistiken der BRAK', http://www.brak.de/fuer-journalisten/zahlen-zur-anwaltschaft (select Lawyers since 1915).

[49]   Includes procurators until 1998, when the government merged that class with advocates. Vittorio Olgiati and Valerio Pocar, 'The Italian Legal Profession: An Institutional Dilemma', in Richard L. Abel and Philip S.C. Lewis (eds), 2 *Lawyers in Society: The Civil Law World* 336, 346, 358 (Berkeley: University of California Press 1988); John Henry Merryman, David S. Clark and Lawrence M. Friedman, *Law and Social Change in Mediterranean Europe and Latin America* 470 (Stanford, CA: Stanford Law School 1979); European Commission for the Efficiency of Justice, *European Judicial Systems: 2010*, at 237 (Strasbourg: Council of Europe Publishing 2010); Sabino Cassese, 'The Italian Legal System, 1945–1999', in Lawrence M. Friedman and Rogelio Pérez-Perdomo (eds), *Legal Culture in the Age of Globalization: Latin America and Latin Europe* 220, 233–4 (Stanford, CA: Stanford University Press 2003); Istituto Nazionale di Statistica, *Censimento Generale della Popolazione e delle Abitazioni* (Roma: 1991, 1981, 1971).

[50]   The total for all lawyers is in parentheses. Kees Schuyt, 'The Rise of Lawyers in the Dutch Welfare State', in Richard L. Abel and Philip S.C. Lewis (eds), 2 *Lawyers in Society: The Civil Law World* 200, 214 (Berkeley: University of California Press 1988); Centraal Bureau voor de Statistiek, *Rechtspraak in Nederland 2007*, at 94–6 (The Hague: CBS 2008).

[51]   John Owen Haley, *Authority without Power: Law and the Japanese Paradox* 96–104 (New York: Oxford University Press 1991); Japanese Federation of Bar Associations (note 32) 1.

[52]   In 2009, there were only 11,000 attorneys in Korea or 23 per 100,000 inhabitants. Kwon (note 6) 172.

of lawyers in the past decade that will lead to some being unable to make a living in the private sector.[53]

Women began to enter the legal professions in substantial numbers in the 1970s. This was part of a larger movement of women entering the professional marketplace generally, which the expansion of universities in Europe and elsewhere facilitated. Prior to 1970, women represented 5 percent or less of the profession in the three common law countries examined here.[54] In European civil law countries, likewise, women in 1970 were 5 percent of the profession in Germany and Italy, only 2 percent of *bengoshi* in Japan, but 10 percent of advocates in the Netherlands.[55] By 2011, the percentage of female lawyers in Canada was 38, in England and Wales it was 36 percent for barristers and 46 percent for solicitors and in the US 31 percent.[56] Civil law countries had a similar pattern, with 40 percent of advocates female in the Netherlands, 32 percent in Germany but only 16 percent in Japan.[57]

Some sectors of the legal profession are more attractive to or receptive of women than others. In general, women have more often settled on positions with governments (including civil law judiciaries), corporations and small firms or solo practice and less often as equity partners in firms or chaired positions in law teaching.[58] For instance, in England in 2010, 54 percent of employed barristers were female, while only 32 percent of self-employed barristers were female. In the US in 2011, women represented 15 percent of equity partners, 26 percent of state and federal judges and 53 percent of assistant law professors.[59]

The situation for ethnic minorities, in terms of democratization or pluralization of cultural viewpoints within the legal profession, for most countries is much bleaker than the relative success of women. There has been some progress, however, especially in the UK and the US.

Germany and the United States illustrate the wide variation in distribution among a nation's legal professions. Table 17.3 has three data points: 1975, before the age of huge national law firms and when there were only a few transnational law firms; 1995, as globalization pressures increased; and 2011, when the competition for transnational legal services was fierce. In 1975, the entire legal profession in the US was much more highly

---

[53]   See James Faulconbridge et al., 'Training and Education in the International Context: The Case of Italy', at 5 (2009), http://www.lancs.ac.uk (enter title in search bar).

[54]   Richard L. Abel, *The Legal Profession in England and Wales* 342, 415 (Oxford: Basil Blackwell 1988; Abel, United States (note 46) 199, 202; Arthurs et al. (note 45) 169.

[55]   Bundesrechtsanwaltskammer (note 48) (select Proportion Women since 1970); Schuyt (note 50) 218; Japanese Federation of Bar Associations (note 32) 1.

[56]   Dixon (note 44) i, 5; Bar Council, 'Statistics' (note 44); ABA Commission on Women in the Profession, 'Statistics', http://www.americanbar.org/groups/women/resources/statistics.html (select A Current Glance at Women in the Law 2011).

[57]   Bundesrechtsanwaltskammer (note 48) (select Proportion Women since 1970); Centraal Bureau voor de Statistiek (note 50) 96; Japanese Federation of Bar Associations (note 32) 1. All of the Japanese quasi-lawyer professions had a smaller percentage of women than the bar had. Ibid. 22; see text accompanying notes 29–32.

[58]   See Ulrike Schultz and Gisela Shaw (eds), *Women in the World's Legal Professions* (Oxford: Hart Publishing 2003).

[59]   Bar Council (note 44); ABA Commission on Women in the Profession (note 56); Association of American Law Schools, 'AALS Statistical Report on Law Faculty', http://www.aals.org/resources_statistical.php.

Table 17.3   Percent distribution of lawyers in Germany and the United States, by year[60]

Type of Lawyers	Germany[61]			United States[62]		
	1975	1995	2011	1975	1995	2011
Judges	17	12	8	3	3	3
Government Lawyers	37	30	17	11	10	9
Attorneys (and Notaries)	33	41	65	74	76	78
Corporate Lawyers	12	16	8	11	10	9
Law Teachers	1	1	2	1	1	1
Total Number	85,000	185,500	241,900	404,800	896,100	1,225,500

privatized than in Germany. This pattern existed between common law and civil law nations almost everywhere outside Asia and Africa.[63] Only 14 percent of the profession in the US served as judges (and judicial support personnel) or worked as government lawyers (including legal aid and public criminal defenders). This public sector was 54 percent in West Germany in 1975, declining to 42 percent in 1995. The ratio of judges to private attorneys in the two countries also reveals the much greater role in Germany that judges took to make the procedural system function properly: one judge for 1.9 attorneys in 1975, still high (with the larger population of unified Germany) in 1995 at one judge for 3.4 attorneys and one to 8.1 in 2011. This compares to the stable US ratio of one judge for 25 attorneys (or 26 attorneys in 2011).[64]

Prior to the twenty-first century, most German lawyers worked in salaried positions. In the private sector, this included business—usually large corporations—and trade unions, which employed 12 percent of the total in 1975, increasing to 16 percent in 1995. Employed registered lawyers (*Syndikusanwälte*) could not represent their employer in court, which has continued to be a task for attorneys. The significant number of lawyers

[60]   Clark, Comparing (note *) 101 (for all 1995 percentages and German lawyer total); Clark, Legal Profession (note 41) 167, 171 (for all 1975 percentages and West German lawyer total).
[61]   Foster and Sule (note 25) 115–16 (for government and corporate lawyers in 2011); Statistisches Bundesamt (note 8) tables 6.6.10, 10.2, 10.3 (for other 2011 data).
[62]   Clara N. Carson, *The Lawyer Statistical Report: The U.S. Legal Profession in 2000*, at 28 (Chicago: American Bar Foundation 2004) (for percentages in 2000, with retired omitted); American Bar Association (note 46) (for all lawyer totals, including 2011). The US percentages for 1975, 1995 and 2011 are from 1970, 1991 and 2000 respectively.
[63]   To illustrate, in England and Wales in 1975, 80 percent of barristers and solicitors were in sole practice or firms, corporations paid salaries to 10 percent, leaving 7 percent for government employment, 2 percent as judges and 1 percent as law teachers. Abel, Legal Profession (note 54) 111–12; Zander (note 44) 13; Abel, England and Wales (note 44) 67. In the Netherlands in 1971, by contrast, only 26 percent of all lawyers were advocates and notaries, but 32 percent were salaried at corporations. The remainder worked for government, 28 percent in various departments, 4 percent as judges and 10 percent at public universities. Freek Bruinsma, *Dutch Law in Action* 27–39 (Nijmegen: Ars Aequi Libri 2000); Schuyt (note 50) 214–16.
[64]   In Japan in 2009, the ratio was one judge for 8.2 attorneys (*bengoshi*). Kent Anderson and Trevor Ryan, 'Japan: The Importance and Evolution of Legal Institutions at the Turn of the Century', in E. Ann Black and Gary F. Bell (eds), *Law and Legal Institutions of Asia: Traditions, Adaptations and Innovations* 120, 141 (Cambridge: Cambridge University Press 2011).

in private organizations not registered as attorneys signals a certain management style that was comfortable with integrating lawyers into the everyday administration of an organization. By comparison, from 1975 to 2011 in the US, 11 percent of the legal profession (declining to 9 percent) worked in corporations and other organizations. These are licensed attorneys, who commonly work in a company's legal department, with full power to represent their company in court.

By 2011, although the number of US lawyers more than tripled from 1995, there was little change in the distribution of these lawyers among the major types. The basic paradigm of a highly privatized profession, increasingly employed in large law firms (as we will see below), with a huge ratio of attorneys to judges, held steady. However, in Germany, a somewhat smaller growth in the legal profession, under the forces of globalization, drew most of the new lawyers into private practice as attorneys and typically into law firms.

6   LAW FIRMS AND SPECIALIZATION

The increased complexity of modern society, accelerated by the globalization process of the past two decades, has led to functional specialization in the delivery of private legal services, primarily through the vehicle of the law firm. Firms have great diversity, ranging from simple office-sharing arrangements to legally recognized partnerships and even corporations with or without limited liability. Although most specialization occurs in the context of division of labor in larger law firms, some of it is stimulated by market forces that convince lawyers to specialize in a particular field individually or in small firms. Such is the case for barristers in England and Wales.

A few countries authorize recognized specialties for lawyers beyond separation into system-specific types of legal professionals rooted in historical experience. In the Netherlands, for instance, three types of specialized law practice occupy approximately one-third of the bar. About 15 percent specialize in commercial advocacy or business consulting. Ten percent serve legal aid clients in developing or protecting welfare rights, tenant rights and immigration rights. Finally, 9 percent specialize in family law practice.

In Germany, the legislature expanded the certified fields of expertise to four in 1989: administrative law, labor law, social welfare law and tax law. It added family law and criminal law in 1998. By 2010, there were 20 recognized specialties, including law and medicine and computer law. About 27 percent of the 156,000 lawyers were qualified as *Fachanwälte* in 2011, with the largest numbers in labor and family law (9,000 and 8,000 respectively).[65] France authorized certification for specialization if an advocate had worked in a field for two years and passed a test on that subject.

6.1   United States

The United States, the world's leader among larger nations in the absolute and relative size of its legal profession and in the number of private practitioners, also leads in taking the

---

[65]   BRAO § 43c, 59b II (2)(a); Bundesrechtsanwaltskammer (note 48) (select 2011). The number of specialty lawyers increased from 11,000 in 1990 to 42,000 in 2011. Ibid.

law firm to its logical extreme. In 1991, 55 percent of lawyers in private practice worked in firms: 213,000 as partners and 112,000 as associates. This is an increase from 36 percent in 1960 and 51 percent in 1980, when for the first time a majority of attorneys no longer worked as sole practitioners. Law firm associates are in effect salaried employees of the firm and normally do not participate in sharing profits or deciding on firm policies. This development has led to the bureaucratization of most law practices, adding firms to the functional ranks of in-house corporate counsel and government lawyers. The ideal of independence becomes harder to achieve as more and more lawyers are simply employees. Besides affecting the new middle ranks of lawyers who are not on a track to partnership, bureaucratization takes the time of senior partners who must attend meetings to develop policy and write memoranda to communicate with a large number of colleagues.

As recently as 1980, there were only 287 US firms with more than 50 lawyers. In 1991, that number increased to 751 firms, while 324 of those had more than 100 lawyers. In 1960 American law firms were clearly identified with a particular city. By 1980, however, the largest firms had branches. In the twenty-first century, large law firms operate on a national and increasingly an international basis with branch firms.

In 1996, the 100 largest law firms generated fees in the United States of $18 billion, about 10 percent of which came from foreign clients. This amount for large firms represented about one-sixth of total American law firm domestic revenues. These top revenue-producing firms totaled 40,000 lawyers. The largest three—Baker & McKenzie, Jones Day, and Skadden Arps—each had over 1,000 attorneys. Senior partners structured huge firms to generate large profits for themselves. On average, each partner oversaw three associate lawyers to whom the firm paid a salary. The average partner in the top 100 firms in 1996 drew a profit of $492,000.

Forty thousand attorneys in 100 firms represent a significant concentration of power over the delivery of legal services. These firms' role in making and administering law and in resolving disputes is opaque, but to the degree that it replaces the transparent functioning of the legal system in a democratic society it poses a risk to that society. Huge global law firms with national governments as clients may also be supporting a surrogate international legal system whose outline is only dimly perceptible. In any case, concentration of law firms is continuing. Between 1986 and 1996, the top ten revenue-producing firms increased their share of the largest 100 firms' revenue from 21 to 23 percent.

By 2010, the top 17 American law firms each had revenue in excess of $1 billion. Two of the firms exceeded $2 billion. Of the five top earners, Baker & McKenzie, DLA Piper and Hogan Lovells now structure themselves under the protection of Swiss law as an association (*Verein*). This permits unified management, but without integrating the predecessor law firm partnerships financially. It also allows limited liability for each constituent element vis-à-vis the others. This has proven particularly useful for UK-US firm mergers.[66] Two firms in 2010 had more than 3,000 lawyers worldwide in their offices. There were 19 firms with more than 1,000 lawyers.[67]

---

[66]   Seventeen Firms (note 56) 121; see note 95 and accompanying text. The *Verein* structure is responsible for the separate UK financial reporting for DLA Piper and Hogan Lovells in Table 17.5. See notes 80–81.

[67]   Seventeen Firms (note 56) 121.

Table 17.4   Highest American lawyer revenue earners (2010), by law firm[68]

Name of Firm	Revenue (million $)	Total Number of Lawyers	Partners (Equity Partners)	Profit per Equity Partner (thousand $)
Baker & McKenzie	2,104	3,738	0 (717)	1,125
Skadden Arps	2,100	1,859	0 (430)	2,320
DLA Piper	1,961	3,348	802 (416)	1,135
Latham & Watkins	1,929	1,931	145 (451)	1,995
Hogan Lovells	1,664	2,363	297 (512)	1,120
Kirkland & Ellis	1,625	1,379	337 (280)	3,075
Jones Day	1,616	2,502	0 (828)	820
Sidley Austin	1,341	1,538	319 (297)	1,465
White & Case	1,278	1,814	128 (269)	1,555
Greenberg Traurig	1,236	1,721	594 (317)	1,320

Twenty firms distributed profits averaging more than $2 million per equity partner, with Wachtell, Lipton, Rosen & Katz leading for its 84 equity partners at $4.3 million. The average for equity partners in the top 100 firms was $1.4 million. A strategy used to maximize partner profits is to eliminate the non-equity partner category and to leverage the firm hierarchy so that there are as many worker-bee associate lawyers and contract lawyers as possible employed for each equity partner. Almost all of the 20 high payout firms used the non-equity approach, as did three in Table 17.4, but not Kirkland & Ellis, the most profitable for equity partners among high-revenue firms. Many lawyers hope that 2010 marks the end of the recession years of easing senior partners into retirement, de-equitizing underperformers and outright firings.[69]

Firm profit margins and equity-partner leverage over all firm lawyers varied substantially among the 100 American highest revenue-earning firms in 2010. Leverage figures varied from 7.5 to 1.4, reflecting a variety of law firm environments. Profit margins (profits over revenues), related to efficiency, ranged from 63 to 19 percent. Kirkland & Ellis, for example, had leverage of 3.9 lawyers for each equity partner and a profit margin of 53 percent.[70]

Baker & McKenzie was the largest law firm in Table 17.4, both in the number of lawyers and in revenue. It began with two partners in Chicago in 1949, but today has offices in 42 countries. No single nationality dominates the firm since its lawyers come from 60 countries and four-fifths practice outside the United States. The lingua franca within the firm is English. It adopted the Swiss *Verein* structure in 2004.[71]

American law firms come in all sizes; attorneys in private practice are a very heterogeneous group. In urban centers, one likely will find large firms representing major

---

[68]   'The Am Law 100 at a Glance', 33 *American Lawyer* 108–20 (May 2011); 'Seventeen Firms Gross More than $1 Billion', ibid. 121–6.

[69]   Robin Sparkman, 'Back in Black', 33 *American Lawyer* 79, 82–3 (May 2011); 'Profits Show a Healthy Increase', ibid. 139–40; 'A Little More Pay for Partners', ibid. 145–6.

[70]   'The Efficiency Analysis', ibid. 152–4.

[71]   Baker & McKenzie, 'Firm Facts', http://www.bakermckenzie.com/firmfacts.

corporations, banks and governments. In addition, there are specialty firms (handling matters such as patent applications, labor relations and white-collar criminal defense) and small firms with a general practice (based on probate, real estate, small business matters and debt collection). Solo practitioners may wait for the personal injury client or divorce case to walk into the office or more aggressively seek business at the criminal court. In rural areas, private practice is one of small firms and solo practitioners carrying on a general practice of whatever the community demands.

By the 1960s, most American states had authorized the creation of professional corporations to permit persons such as attorneys to take advantage of favorable tax rules. Another benefit stemming from this form of organization was that an attorney might be able to limit her personal liability. No state permits a lawyer to limit liability for professional malpractice, but almost all states do limit liability for the firm's ordinary business debts up to the value of the corporation's assets. More controversial is the question of personal liability for the malpractice of other attorneys or employees in the corporate firm. Some states do not limit this liability but treat the relationship as similar to a partnership. Other states put an annual monetary maximum on individual vicarious liability. Another variation limits liability unless an attorney participated in collective conduct or had direct control or supervision over the attorneys or employees who committed the malpractice.

A new type of law firm made possible by advertising appeared in the United States in the 1970s: the private legal clinic. Today, there are thousands of clinics, some are nonprofit, run by law schools or community groups, as well as some run for profit in storefront offices. Their services are cheap, with fixed fees at about half to three-fourths of the normal charge; they specialize in routine wills, uncontested divorce and other matters for lower- and middle-income customers. Turnover among lawyers is high. The best known operate as chains, spending millions of dollars on advertising.

In the 1990s, increased competition from large numbers of young lawyers cut into the profitability of these chain legal clinics. For instance, Hyatt Legal Services was the largest in the late 1980s; it had 192 offices in 22 states with over 675 lawyers and spent $5 million on television advertising. In 1990, under competitive pressure, Hyatt spun off Hyatt Legal Plans (HLP), which MetLife (the biggest life insurer in the US) acquired in 1997. In 2011, HLP was the leading provider of group legal plans with two million members and 12,000 plan attorneys.[72]

Even before the US Supreme Court permitted lawyer advertising, an effort to reach lower-income persons with group and prepaid legal service plans began to expand in the 1960s. Besides the general lawyer advertising ban, the Court also held unconstitutional most bar association restraints on group and prepaid legal service plans, refusing to accept the argument that they were an unauthorized practice of law. Today, as with Hyatt's transformation, many businesses include prepaid plans as part of employee benefits packages.

---

[72] Hyatt Legal Plans, Home Page, http://www.legalplans.com (select About Us, then Brief History & Timeline). Another legal clinic, Jacoby & Meyers, shrunk from 300 to 150 lawyers in the 1980s. Today, it has 100 offices in five states and employs 150 attorneys. Jacoby & Meyers, Home Page, http://www.jacobymeyers.com (select About Jacoby & Meyers). Australia also saw the development of this type of clinic in the 1980s.

In addition, some unions, fraternal groups and credit card companies include them as a perquisite of membership. About 122 million persons enroll in a legal service plan.[73]

6.2   England and Wales

In England and Wales, law firms of solicitors in recent decades have grown to the size where specialization allows them to compete directly with the expert advice previously available only from specialist barristers. In 1990, 39 percent of solicitors worked for firms with 11 or more partners.[74] In the 1980s and 1990s, several huge firms appeared in the part of London known as the City through mergers to provide corporate clients the services they desired and to compete in the emerging global legal services market. The largest firm in 1995 was Clifford Chance (with 894 solicitors), but there were 50 other firms with more than 100 solicitors. (By comparison, the Netherlands had nine firms of the 100-plus size, France six and Germany five. No other country in Europe had more than two firms larger than 100 lawyers). Clifford Chance emerged from the successful merger of two London firms in 1987. In 2000, it created the first non-franchise global law firm by its merger with a leading firm in Germany and the US and today provides legal services to clients throughout Europe, Asia, the Middle East and Brazil.[75]

By 2010, 54 percent of solicitors worked in firms with more than 11 partners, which represented 5 percent of all private solicitor firms. Nevertheless, the concentration of lawyers in the largest category of firms (with more than 25 partners) was notable, at 41 percent of solicitors. This latter group of firms comprised only 2 percent of the total number. At the other end of the profession, the percentage of solicitors in one-partner law firms was only 8 percent, but it had already dropped to the low rate of 9 percent in 1990.[76] The economic realities of transnational activities convinced English and Scottish law societies in the 1990s to allow solicitors to set up multidisciplinary partnerships and to practice together with accountants, stockbrokers, chartered surveyors and certain other professionals. Solicitors may also form multinational partnerships.[77] In 2000, the British government permitted law firms to form limited liability partnerships, although most have not embraced this form.[78]

---

[73]   American Prepaid Legal Services Institute, 'History', http://www.aplsi.org/about/history.cfm.

[74]   Stephen Harwood-Richardson, *Annual Statistical Report 1991*, at 16–18 (London: Law Society 1991). These large firms represented 0.5 percent of all the private solicitor firms. Ibid.

[75]   Clifford Chance, 'Our Story', http://www.cliffordchance.com/about_us/our_story.html.

[76]   Nina Fletcher and Yulia Muratova, *Trends in the Solicitors' Profession: Annual Statistical Report 2010*, at i, 6 (London: Law Society 2010); Harwood-Richardson (note 74) 18.The Law Society organizes its categories by the number of equity partners in the firm. Thus, a single principal in a law firm may pay a salary to another solicitor and still be classified as a sole proprietorship. In 1990, for instance, 3,018 principals worked in the same number of 'firms of one', employing 1,038 assistant solicitors. Ibid. 18, 52–53.

[77]   Courts and Legal Services Act 1990 ss. 66, 89; see Solicitors Regulation Authority rule 14. Solicitors in Scotland have been able to incorporate their law firms since 1985, even with limited liability.

[78]   Limited Liability Partnerships Act 2000.

Table 17.5   Highest English solicitor revenue earners (2010), by law firm[79]

Name of Firm	Revenue (million £)	Total Number of Lawyers	Partners (Equity Partners)	Profit per Equity Partner (thousand £)
Clifford Chance	1,219	2,466	552 (379)	1,005
Linklaters	1,200	2,126	473 (442)	1,225
Freshfields Bruckhaus Deringer	1140	2,032	445 (416)	1,308
Allen & Overy	1,120	2,112	487 (398)	1,100
DLA Piper[80]	605	2,181	647 (201)	564
Hogan Lovells[81]	582	1,380	380 (250)	740
Norton Rose	488	1,512	420 (277)	445
Herbert Smith	465	1,061	265 (131)	900
Slaughter and May	448	561	125 (122)	1,930
Eversheds	354	1,228	328 (132)	555

Table 17.5 illustrates the sizeable revenues earned by English solicitors who belong to the largest firms. Four London firms generated revenue over a billion pounds in 2010 (about 1.6 billion US dollars). They are among the leading global fee-generating law firms, with six US-based firms filling out the top ten. The expenses subtracted from revenue to yield profit distributed to equity partners included office and staff expenses and other operating costs, which incorporated the salaries and bonuses of non-equity partners and other lawyers. Although the total revenue of English firms dropped off sharply after the top four, equity partner profits in other principal firms can be comparable to the leaders and depend on factors such as lawyer productivity, cost management and leverage (the ratio of total lawyers to equity partners). Profit margins varied significantly among the firms from a low of 19 percent (at DLA Piper) to a high of 51 percent (at Slaughter and May). Among the ten firms, the leverage ratio varied from 3.6 to 9.9, which identifies the degree of lawyer hierarchy within an organization. Besides levels among associate solicitors, some firms differentiated more between equity and non-equity partners than others did. Partners design these organizational elements to motivate the capture and execution of law work in a highly competitive global environment. Clifford Chance's 2010 revenue

---

[79]   The Lawyer, 'UK200 2011', http://www.thelawyer.com/1009501.article. Firms paid most of the revenue in 2010, but many firms use a fiscal year that included part of 2011. E.g., Clifford Chance's figures came from the period May 2010 through April 2011.

[80]   The revenues listed here excluded the firm's US operations that were financially separate as DLA Piper US. Ibid. (select DLA Piper).

[81]   Hogan Lovells is an international law firm, co-headquartered in London and Washington DC, which formed from the May 2010 merger of Washington-based Hogan & Hartson and London-based Lovells. Hogan Lovells, 'History', http://www.hoganlovells.com/aboutus/history. The revenues listed here came from operations in Europe (including England), the Middle East and Asia. The global revenues were £1.1 billion, which included the legacy Hogan & Hartson operations. The Lawyer (note 79) (select Hogan Lovells).

Table 17.6　Highest English barrister revenue earners (2010), by set of chambers[82]

Name of Set	Revenue (million £)	Total Number of Barristers	Queen's Counsel	Revenue per Barrister (thousand £)
Brick Court Chambers	47.0	73	36	644
One Essex Court	46.5	73	26	637
Essex Court Chambers	43.6	71	35	614
Fountain Court Chambers	43.0	57	27	754
Blackstone Chambers	42.4	84	34	504
Wilberforce Chambers	40.0	50	23	800
No5 Chambers	36.5	204	23	179
39 Essex Street	36.3	84	30	432
3 Verulam Buildings	35.8	63	19	568
7KBW	34.9	48	21	727

(in million £), by region of its offices, was continental Europe (467), UK (430), Asia (145), Americas (140) and Middle East (37).[83]

The English bar council traditionally required barristers to work as self-employed individuals if they were to have the right to appear in most courts. Often they joined with other barristers in a set of chambers, administered by a senior barristers' clerk, but they could not form partnerships. Nevertheless, they can have 'purse sharing' agreements with pooled fees distributed according to a formula.[84] After 2000, the growing number of employed barristers—working in-house for a company or for local or the central government—gained the same right of audience that self-employed barristers and solicitor advocates had.[85]

Since 2010, barristers may join legal disciplinary practices (LDPs), which so far have included solicitor law firms, while issues of share ownership are under discussion.[86] The highest earning barristers work in sets of chambers, as shown in Table 17.6. Each independent barrister is a tenant in the set under an agreement to pay a fixed monthly amount, or a percentage of her income, or a mixture of the two. The set provides offices, clerical support and the allocation of clients.

In 2010, the top ten barrister sets had revenue of £406 million, while the next 20 barrister sets had revenue of £440 million. This reveals the significant drop-off in size among

---

[82]　Katy Dowell, 'The Bar', http://www.thelawyer.com/the-bar/1009265.article.

[83]　Clifford Chance, 'How We Performed', http://www.cliffordchance.com/about_us.html (select Annual Reviews).

[84]　Bar Council, 'Fee Sharing and CFA's', http://www.barcouncil.org.uk/guidance/feesharingan-dcfas. Barristers working in a set of chambers functionally permit a similar type of specialization found in solicitor law firms, but coordinated by the barristers' clerk.

[85]　Bar Council, 'Guidance for Employed Barristers', http://www.barcouncil.org.uk/guidance/guidanceforemployedbarristers; see notes 15–17 and accompanying text; Abel, Legal Profession (note 54) 111–13, 124–5.

[86]　Bar Council, 'Legal Services Act 2007', http://www.barstandardsboard.org.uk/standards andguidance/LegalServicesAct; see Legal Services Act 2007.

London bar sets. The revenue of all the top 30 was £846 million, a 6 percent gain over 2009.[87]

In 2010, the major ten solicitor law firms had revenues of £7.6 billion, 19 times more than the principal barrister sets. The cost of running the sets, however, was significantly lower than law firms, with the expense ratio ranging between 10 and 22 percent. This reflects the much smaller size of bar sets and the reduced need for staff and office space. Nevertheless, the largest barrister set (No5) had 204 tenants, a number unimaginable even as late as the 1990s. The top ten barrister sets comprised 6 percent of all self-employed barristers in England and Wales in 2011.

6.3   Other Common Law Countries

Since the 1980s, other common law countries have been participating in the expansive role that lawyers have undertaken in their own societies in addition to their role in the process of economic globalization. Much of this increased presence has occurred through specialization, particularly as it occurs in the law firm. Nevertheless, from a relative perspective, the US and UK in 2010 dominated among huge law firms, both in terms of total revenue and in the number of lawyers. The two countries had 90 of the top 100 global firms by revenue and 85 by size.[88]

Canada has tended to follow the pattern of the United States, including the growth of large law firms and the development of branch offices. In Ontario, for example, in 1961 the largest six law firms had between 22 and 39 lawyers. By 1989, these same firms ranged in size from 154 to 225 lawyers. In some ways, law practice in Canada still exists in traditional forms, although there has been a trend since the 1960s toward fewer lawyers practicing alone. In 2009, only about 16 percent of lawyers were solo, a ratio one-third of that in the United States. Partnership is an important form for groups of lawyers not in solo practice. Partners share in the profits and losses of the firm and assume personal liability for debts. Today, the Federation of Law Societies' Model Code of Professional Conduct permits law firms to form limited partnerships or to incorporate, which provides certain tax advantages and limited liability (but not for the general partner or lawyer). In 2011, there were 104 firms with more than 50 lawyers. The 30 largest firms totaled almost 10,200 lawyers, with the average at 340 lawyers.[89]

In 2010, Canada had three law firms among the world's largest 100 by number of lawyers and one firm measured by total revenue. These were primarily huge national firms centered in Toronto with Canadian branch offices, although Borden Ladner Gervais (with 775 lawyers) and Fasken Martineau (with 677 lawyers) also had overseas offices in

---

[87]   Ibid.

[88]   'Most Revenue', 33 *American Lawyer* 157 (Oct. 2011); 'Most Lawyers', ibid. 160. By revenue, the UK had 12 firms and by size, it had 16 firms. Ibid.

[89]   Federation of Law Societies of Canada (note 45) (for 2009); ibid., Model Code of Professional Conduct 12 (2011), http://www.flsc.ca/en/conduct-of-the-profession (definition of law firm); Lexpert, 'Canada's Largest Law Firms', http://www.lexpert.ca/directory/canadas-largest-law-firms (for 2011).

London. McCarthy Tétrault had US$444 million in revenue and ranked number 77 (while its 571 lawyers ranked number 100 in size).[90]

Australia is a good example of a country that has taken advantage of its location in the southern hemisphere and proximity to Asia. In 1985, only 24 firms had more than 20 lawyers and half of those were in New South Wales. Nevertheless, these figures hid the mergers that occurred during the 1980s as corporate clients let firms know that their interest in the efficient delivery of increasingly complex services meant that they preferred to deal with the same firm nationwide and even internationally. Thus, by 1990, four Australian firms or federations had more than 375 solicitors and two more firms had more than 200 solicitors.

In 2010, six Australian firms were on the 'Global 100' list based on gross revenues as well as on total number of lawyers. These firms, largely headquartered in Sydney but with other national offices, had a stronger international presence than the largest Canadian firms did. Minter Ellison, the leading firm, earned revenues of US$484 million, and ranked 67. Its 1,061 lawyers (ranked 25 in size) worked in Australia and overseas offices (London and China). Other top firms had offices in South and East Asia.[91]

No other common law country has a firm among the world's largest 100. In Singapore, the profession grew from 809 advocates in 1980 to 2,650 in 1995. At that time, the largest firms had more than 80 advocates and medium firms were in the 20- to 30-lawyer range. There were 110 firms with five or more advocates. Bigger firms divided into departments (for instance, litigation, intellectual property or shipping). Some had already joined with English or American firms to follow business opportunities in China and East Asia. This has led some smaller firms to turn away from the traditional areas of criminal law, traffic accidents, debt collection and conveyancing to develop lucrative specialties in construction law or family law.

A few common law countries have been more conservative and resisted moving away from the traditional ideal of law practice as a homogeneous, individual and liberal profession. India is an important example. The Indian Partnership Act 1932 capped law firms at 20 partners, a limit that firms sometimes evaded using multi-tier structures that allowed a few firms of about 100 lawyers. In 2008, the Limited Liability Partnership Act introduced that type of partnership to India with no upper limit on firm size. However, the Bar Council of India does not permit foreign lawyers to practice in India, so most arrangements with US and UK firms are alliances with local firms.[92]

6.4   Agents for Legal Globalization

Law firms are important vehicles for the spread of Western law. American and English firms have taken the lead in this development, indirectly stimulating the acceptance of

---

[90]   Most Revenue (note 88) 159; Most Lawyers (note 88) 165. Fasken Martineau also had offices in Paris and Johannesburg.

[91]   Most Revenue (note 88) 158–9; Most Lawyers (note 88) 161–5.

[92]   Ben Lewis, 'A Breakthrough in India: Or Another False Spring?' *Asian Lawyer* (3 Oct. 2011), http://www.law.com/jsp/tal (enter title in search bar); Shikhil Suri, 'Comparing Law Firms in the United States and India: An Indian Lawyer's Perspective', http://www.mansfieldtanick.com/CM/Articles/Comparing-LaFirms.asp.

common law ideas in the field of international commercial law, especially for business, trade and investment contracts. Some of these ideas then filter down to affect domestic legal concepts. There also is some influence in the area of procedure, particularly for pre-trial discovery, which comes from law firm attorneys who serve as international arbitrators.

As an illustration of this phenomenon, consider the arrival of American and English law firms in Islamic Arab countries. Egypt and Middle Eastern nations accepted many legal concepts and institutions from the civil law world, especially from France, modified by the resurgence in Islamic law. Nevertheless, in the past 30 years, common law legal concepts, particularly in the commercial law field, have arrived principally through the action of lawyers working in international commerce. Research from the early 1990s examined the 17 largest multinational law firms involved in Egypt and the oil-rich Middle Eastern nations from the Red Sea to the Persian Gulf.[93]

Ten of these firms originated in the United States, six in England, and only one in France. Most began in the twentieth century and first established branch offices after World War II. They have grown most dramatically in the last 40 years. In the early 1990s, all but two of these firms had offices in London and 11 had offices in Paris, partly because international arbitration was available in those cities. Seven had offices in Brussels, the administrative headquarters of the European Union. About 40 percent of these 17 firms had established more than one branch in the Arab Middle East. Fox & Gibbons was the first to locate there in 1969 with an office in Dubai, United Arab Emirates. It has since created a specialization in this region, with 45 lawyers and five of its seven worldwide offices located in Egypt and the Persian Gulf area.

For the last 15 years, Fox & Gibbons has been typical of many transnational law firms engaged in the globalization process, illustrating the fierce competition for clients, weak loyalty of partners, and shifting economic and political realities. In 1998, a much older London firm, Denton Hall, acquired Fox & Gibbons, but only accepted one of its 11 partners as a new equity partner. Two years previously, four Fox & Gibbons equity partners had left the firm for greener pastures.[94] In 2000, Denton Hall merged with another London firm, Wilde Sapte, to create Denton Wilde Sapte, which grew to 600 lawyers by 2010. At that time, it merged with the US law firm, Sonnenschein Nath & Rosenthal, forming SNR Denton. This new firm structured itself as a Swiss *Verein* under unified management, but without integrating the predecessor partnerships financially. SNR Denton today is one of the world's largest 25 law firms with 1,400 lawyers in 43 countries. It has five offices (and another five associate firms) in the Middle East and an extensive network of associate firms in Africa.[95]

Arab law firms are of recent vintage, including those with an international affiliation, and were not large in the 1990s. Using ten lawyers as a standard, Egypt had seven firms

[93]   Jean-Claude Delaunay, *Services Cultures Mondialisation: Les Services Juridiques dans les Relations Économiques Euro-Arabes* 226–326 (Bruxelles: De Boeck Université 1994).

[94]   Richard Tyler, 'Dentons Swallows Fox & Gibbons', http://www.thelawyer.com/dentons-swallows-fox-and-gibbons/88723.article (13 Oct. 1998).

[95]   Luke McLeod-Roberts, 'A New Transatlantic Firm Born as SNR Denton Goes Live', http://www.thelawyer.com/a-new-transatlantic-firm-born-as-snr-denton-goes-live/1005630.article (30 Sept. 2010); SNR Denton, 'About Us', http://www.snrdenton.com/about-us.aspx. The Swiss *Verein* will permit the two constituent member firms to operate separately in the UK and US.

at least this size, Saudi Arabia had three (including two with international liaisons) and the United Arab Emirates and Tunisia each had one. Before 1974, only six firms existed in Egypt, although a French *avocat* and an English solicitor founded the oldest one in 1872. Elsewhere in the Arab world, there were only a few firms before 1975.

6.5   France and the Netherlands

A few civil law countries have been relatively hospitable to the development of law firms, which then tended to capture the best corporate clients. For expansion to occur, a necessary rule was that a firm could establish secondary offices in locales apart from the principal office. This was the situation in France, where law firms (*cabinets d'avocats*) were typically either SCP (*sociétés civiles professionnelles*) or, since 1992, SEL (*sociétés pour l'exercice d'une profession libérale*). The legislature created the latter form to allow French firms to compete better with American and English firms. Professionals in the company must hold more than half the capital and votes of an SEL. The remaining shares can belong to lawyers in other firms or to those in other legal professions (such as notaries) or quasilegal professions (such as accountants or *experts comptables*). The firm, depending on its type, might raise a maximum of 25 to 49 percent of its capital from external sources. *Avocats* may now practice as salaried employees (previously permitted only for legal consultants), but if so, they cannot have their own clients. Young attorneys often begin their careers associating with firms, most of which have two or three members, but 38 of which in 1995 had more than 25 lawyers. Six of these were larger than 100 lawyers and the biggest, Fidal, had over a thousand lawyers. In 2010, Fidal was one of three French firms on the 'Global 100', ranked 22 in size (with 1,176 lawyers) and number 84 in revenue (US$398 million).[96]

The Netherlands was the civil law country that most aggressively copied the American and English approach to law firms in the 1980s. It reflected the common law pattern for the national distribution of attorneys by firm size. Thus in 1992, there were 2,114 law units: 45 percent were sole practitioners, 42 percent consisted of firms of two to five attorneys, and 13 percent were firms of six or more attorneys. Thirteen percent of the attorneys, however, worked in one of the five largest firms. In 1995, the biggest firm, Nauta Dutilh, had 300 lawyers. Eight more had at least 100 lawyers, while 19 others exceeded 25 lawyers. Dutch firms could be a partnership (*maatschap*), a limited liability company (*besloten vennootschap*) or a nonprofit enterprise (*stichting*). The latter usually consisted of attorneys providing state-funded legal aid. In 2010, Loyens & Loeff was the largest Dutch law firm, ranked 57 on the 'Global 100' in size with 781 lawyers (in 11 foreign countries) and number 86 in revenue (US$391 million).[97]

6.6   Other Civil Law Countries

Most civil law nations were slow to follow the American and English model of huge law firms and branch offices. In 2010, Spain was the only other civil law country besides

---

[96]   Most Revenue (note 88) 159; Most Lawyers (note 88) 161.
[97]   Most Revenue (note 88) 159; Most Lawyers (note 88) 162.

France and the Netherlands with 'Global 100' law firms. Garrigues had offices in seven foreign countries and throughout Spain. It was number eight on the 'Global 100' in size with 2,037 lawyers and ranked 71 in revenue (US$468 million). Cuatrecasas, Gonçalves Pereira had offices in eight foreign countries with 885 lawyers, ranked 41 in size.[98]

Traditional norms often stood in the way. The usual form of cooperation included office-sharing arrangements in which attorneys had a common infrastructure to reduce expenses, but independent control over their income and expenses. Spain in the early 1990s permitted up to 20 lawyers from the same local bar to establish a partnership (*despacho colectivo*) with shared liability. Nevertheless, by 1995, the largest Spanish firm with offices and affiliates throughout the country had 180 lawyers and there were ten other firms with more than 25 lawyers.

In Germany, until 1989 an attorney could maintain only one office, which was located in the jurisdiction of the court that admitted her. In that year, the German Constitutional Court permitted lawyers and law firms to establish branch offices in other cities. By 1995, there were five multi-city firms with more than 100 lawyers registered in their respective courts.

In 1980, only 14 firms had as many as ten partners, which by 1985 had increased to 42 firms. The largest, in Cologne (in 1990), had 40 members. By 1991, with the one-office rule gone, there were 91 firms with ten or more attorneys and by 1995, 34 firms larger than 25 lawyers. This proliferation of firms (*Kanzleien*) was a response to market pressures and the mandate of the European Union to liberalize the delivery of legal services. Many large firms used an association agreement among smaller firms to accomplish their merger. Since 1995, the Federal Lawyers Act permitted attorneys to cooperate among themselves or with certain other professionals such as tax advisers (*Steuerberater*) or certified accountants (*Wirtschaftsprüfer*) to establish nationally or internationally something similar to a general commercial partnership with unlimited liability.

Germany also now allows foreign lawyers to offer advice on the law of their home country if registered with a local bar association under the Federal Lawyers Act. In 2010, there were 213 such lawyers, with the largest number in Frankfurt. The US provided the most at 97 lawyers, with Turkey next at 43, followed by Russia at 12. EU nationals have special practice rights within all member states and there were 351 such EU lawyers, 96 from the UK and 51 and 50 from Italy and Spain respectively.[99] This development permits the largest UK and US law firms to have a presence in Germany, which in 2010 they largely staffed with German lawyers. The largest 68 firms (each with more than 40 and an average of 126 lawyers) employed together 8,600 attorneys.[100]

In Switzerland, law firms typically organized as partnerships, with only a few employed attorneys. In 1995, there were, however, eight firms with more than 25 attorneys. In the 1990s, some firms organized as trust companies and the largest firm in 1995 had 59 attorneys. Firms in Zurich and Geneva had merged to form a nationwide presence. Attorneys could practice in cantons other than that of their residence by qualifying for a

---

[98]   Most Revenue (note 88) 159; Most Lawyers (note 88) 160–61.
[99]   Bundesrechtsanwaltskammer (note 48) (select § 206 Bar Members and EU Bar Members); see BRAO § 206.
[100]   Christoph Luschin, 'Large Law Firms in Germany', 14 *Touro International Law Review* 26, 36–42 (2010).

license based on reciprocity. Some Swiss cantons maintain specialty lists of attorneys, but everywhere specialization—particularly in family law, social law and real estate law—was growing.

In other places, resistance to market forces was stronger. Greece first permitted law firm partnerships in 1986, but according to a 1989 decree, they must be personal and not commercial in nature. The partners must belong to the same local bar. Some countries, for instance Italy, prohibited attorneys from forming corporate firms. Other countries, such as Austria, permit corporations but prohibit them from having limited liability. In the mid-1990s, the larger Italian firms (*studi associati*)—12 with more than 25 lawyers countrywide—had to remain professional associations with individual responsibility.

Japan and Turkey had similar restrictive rules. The largest firm in Turkey in 1995 had 21 lawyers. Firms in Japan tended to be loose arrangements in which the income did not flow to a partnership. Often the arrangements only covered sharing office space and other overheads. Ninety percent of *bengoshi* in the 1990s worked in this manner or individually. Loose partnerships also were characteristic in Italy and Turkey. The larger firms in Japan, stimulated by international business, had about 12 attorneys. Combining attorneys and quasi-lawyers (such as patent and tax agents), the largest three firms had 40 or so members, primarily located in Tokyo and Osaka. In 1993, 53 firms had five or more lawyers.

Latin America has been slow to encourage large law firms. In 2000, there were only seven with more than 100 lawyers, although Brazil had four of those.[101] In 2011, the São Paulo chapter of the Brazilian national bar association, reflecting the protective interests of most national lawyers, ruled that formal alliances between foreign and local attorneys were unethical. The national bar association is now considering its position on this issue and whether such law firm alliances should be dissolved. Currently, foreign-qualified lawyers cannot work in firms that employ local attorneys or offer any advice on Brazilian law (even if based on that of a local attorney).[102]

6.7   China

Under the 2007 Lawyers Law, a law firm needed approval from the judicial administration department at the provincial level before it would receive a practice certificate. This is then subject to annual renewal. Firms can be sole practices or general or limited partnerships (with at least three partners). Firms with more than 20 attorneys may establish branch offices and a small number have foreign branches.

Two other types of law firms include those that are state funded and cooperatives. In the former, lawyers charge low fees, forward them to the state and earn a salary. In 2004, there were 1,742 state-funded firms, 1,746 cooperatives, 8,024 partnerships and 179 solo firms: a total of 11,691 firms. Lawyers in state firms, judges and most law professors earn between

---

[101]   Rogelio Pérez-Perdomo and Lawrence Friedman, 'Latin Legal Cultures in the Age of Globalization', in Lawrence M. Friedman and Rogelio Pérez-Perdomo (eds), *Legal Culture in the Age of Globalization: Latin America and Latin Europe* 1, 11–12 (Stanford, CA: Stanford University Press 2003).

[102]   Ross Todd, 'The Future is Now', 32 *American Lawyer* 146–56 (Oct. 2010); 'Keep Out', *The Economist* 77–8 (25 June 2011).

US$3,500 and $6,000. This explains why some have left for private firms, where they will earn significantly more. An associate in a top Beijing firm will earn almost $30,000 and many partners earn $200,000 or even more.[103]

By 2009, there were 15,000 law firms in China, with 40 firms each employing more than 100 lawyers. These 40 firms had about 5 percent (or 8,100) of all Chinese lawyers. In 2011, King & Wood (established 1993) had 990 lawyers and other legal professionals in 11 Chinese cities plus Hong Kong, Tokyo and New York.[104]

Foreign law firms have set up Chinese branches since 1993 under rather strict guidelines. They cannot practice Chinese law; if they hire a Chinese lawyer, she must surrender her practice license and work as a consultant. These restrictions, which should ease due to China's admission to the World Trade Organization, have led some foreign law firms to establish branches in Hong Kong. Chinese lawyers who have a US JD degree and US permanent resident status can receive a salary of $160,000 as an associate in an American firm's Beijing branch. Even with the substantial formal impediments, 150 foreign firms from 20 countries, plus another 50 Hong Kong firms, have a branch in China. Most of these branches have fewer than ten lawyers and associates.[105]

7 TOWARD A EUROPEAN AND GLOBAL LAWYER

7.1 European Developments

Since the end of the jus commune period in Europe, when nationalism and statism in the nineteenth century led jurists to look inward rather than outward toward a universal law, the focus of legal systems has been national and local. The excesses of nationalism and the deleterious consequences of colonialism, however, have stimulated jurists to reconsider the appropriate balance in law, economy and politics between the local and the universal.[106]

This reconsideration was especially strong in Europe, where from the ashes of war in the 1940s, visionaries in the 1950s created new institutional frameworks. The Rome Treaty (1958), the first comprehensive convention for European economic integration, set out articles that encompassed the freedom of professional practice as part of the trade in services. Vigorous European Court of Justice decisions as well as Council directives have progressively implemented these articles. In 1998, the Parliament and Council approved a directive on the permanent establishment of law offices for self-employed or salaried lawyers in another member state of the European Union.

Under the Council's series of directives, a state could not substantially impede lawyers from carrying out the tasks of procurator or solicitor from their home office or from a host-state office in providing legal advice. The 1998 directive made it clear that lawyers

---

[103] Chow (note 35) 137–42, see notes 37–9 and accompanying text.
[104] Peerenboom (note 39) 127–30; see Harvard Law School, 'Program on the Legal Profession: Comparative Analyses' 3, http://www.law.harvard.edu/programs/plp/pages/comparative_analyses. php (select China); King & Wood, Home Page, http://www.kingandwood.com (select Firm).
[105] Chen (note 36) 165; Chow (note 35) 246–8; Peerenboom (note 39) 130–31.
[106] See generally David B. Goldman, *Globalisation and the Western Legal Tradition: Recurring Patterns of Law and Authority* (Cambridge: Cambridge University Press 2007).

from another member state may give advice on EU law, international law or the domestic law of their home or host country. By contrast, the host country might require the services of a local advocate or barrister as co-counsel to assist a foreign EU lawyer in representing a client in court according to accepted national rules for registration with that court.

These new European lawyers are subject to the professional conduct and indemnity insurance rules of both their home and host states, including enforcement by disciplinary proceedings. They practice, however, under their home professional title. To encourage further integration of foreign lawyers into the local bar, EU lawyers who have practiced 'effectively and regularly' under their home title for three years may petition the competent local authority for admission to the bar without examination, which normally it should grant.

In addition to branch firms (which the 1998 directive permits), sometimes created by merger, multinational practice within Europe has accelerated with the creation of law firm networks and alliances. Networks involve agreements to cross-refer clients and may range from informal arrangements to legally binding exclusive links. Alliances are similar but may involve the joint opening of a foreign office to reduce overhead expenses.[107]

For attorneys who are non-EU citizens, the task of establishing a presence in one of the 27 EU member states is more difficult. France was the first European Community country hospitable to foreign lawyers; many of the firms established in the 1960s still practice there. However, provincial barriers to supranational practice with non-European lawyers have only slowly eroded. Two countries that earlier took a different approach were the UK and the Netherlands. In England, foreign lawyers since 1992 have registered with the Law Society; they practice foreign and international law individually under their national professional title or with solicitors in multinational firms. In 1995, approximately 2,000 foreign lawyers practiced under their home title in London and 130 foreign law firms (half of them American) were listed. Registered foreign lawyers are subject to the Law Society's major client protection rules, indemnity insurance and discipline.

7.2   US and UK Support for Global Lawyers[108]

The relentless march of market capitalism in many parts of the world after the collapse of the Soviet Union stimulated an economic globalization that finds its counterpart in the need for world lawyers. US lawyers have been particularly aggressive in opening law offices in foreign countries where opportunities exist. Conversely, important commercial centers in the United States have been hospitable to foreign lawyers. Already in 1971, the New York City bar association had initiated the formation of a statewide committee to look into the advisability of creating a liberal regime for the licensing and regulation of foreign lawyers in New York. Between 1972 and 1974, the legislature and the court of appeals adopted rules detailing the conditions under which foreign-educated lawyers

---

[107]   See Julian Lonbay, 'Assessing the European Market for Legal Services: Developments in the Free Movement of Lawyers in the European Union', 33 *Fordham International Law Journal* 1632–69 (2010).

[108]   See generally Carole Silver, Nicole De Bruin Phelan and Mikaela Rabinowitz, 'Between Diffusion and Distinctiveness in Globalization: U.S. Law Firms Go Glocal', 22 *Georgetown Journal of Legal Ethics* 1431–71 (2009).

could take the New York bar examination, gain membership in the bar without examination or practice as legal consultants in New York.

By 1996, 21 states and the District of Columbia had adopted a foreign legal consultant rule, which increased to 31 in 2011.[109] These rules create a new category of licensed law-trained person, the legal consultant (LC). Applicants are foreign country lawyers (subject to discipline by their home professional bodies) who are interested in maintaining a law office in an American state. They must satisfy the local attorney standards of good moral character and general fitness to practice law. There are significant limitations on the scope of practice. First, LCs cannot represent clients in court; they also may not hold themselves out as attorneys but may use the title 'legal consultant'. Second, they provide legal advice in the areas of foreign and international law. In most states, they may only comment on US law to the extent that they base their advice on that received from an attorney. Third, LCs are explicitly precluded from practicing law related to American real property transactions, wills and estates, or families.

By 1995, 31 states permitted foreign law graduates admission to their bar examination on liberal terms. In a typical state, the foreign applicant from a common law nation must show that she has successfully completed a government-approved course of study of at least three years duration. The civil law applicant must also complete a one-year program (usually an LL.M) at a law school approved by the ABA.

In the late 1970s, the ABA lobbied the US government to present the issue of liberalizing transborder practice to Japan. After about ten years, the result in Japan was the 1987 Special Measures Law Concerning the Handling of Legal Business by Foreign Lawyers (Foreign Lawyers Act). Still quite restrictive, the ministry of justice received only 175 applications from foreigners to register as legal consultants. About two-thirds came from the United States and 20 percent from Europe. Foreign lawyers (*gaiben*) still could not enter into partnerships with *bengoshi* or practice under their firm name.

In the 1990s, the US contested these restrictions as trade issues and the Japanese government promised to reform the law as a compromise to conclude the GATT round. In 1994, it amended the Foreign Lawyers Act to eliminate a reciprocity requirement and to allow firms to use their own name. However, the provisions on joint enterprises between *bengoshi* and *gaiben* were still restrictive and many US law firms left Tokyo by the late 1990s. In 2003, there were 27 of these joint enterprises and about 200 *gaiben* in Japan. Continued pressure by the governments and legal communities in the US, UK and now the EU convinced Japan to further liberalize the Foreign Lawyers Act, which since 2005 eased practice rules and allowed *gaiben* to employ *bengoshi* or to share offices and fees. This opened up the possibility of real partnerships, including through merger, so that firms of Japanese and foreign lawyers could provide integrated services to global corporations. Both UK and US firms took advantage of this change through merger or acquisition.

In other parts of the world, UK and American lawyers have had an easier path, both in establishing law firms or alliances abroad as well as in obtaining foreign clients for domestic offices. In the United States, this latter activity generated $1.6 billion in 1994, about 10 percent of the total revenue of the largest 100 firms. This was an increase from

---

[109] American Bar Association, 'Foreign Legal Consultant Rules', www.americanbar.org (enter title in search bar).

$451 million in 1990.[110] By the economic recession of 2008–09, US law firm export earnings leveled at $7.3 billion through 2010.[111]

As the amount of fees that American lawyers earned annually from foreign clients passed the $1 billion mark in the early 1990s, the ABA and the US government increased its role in encouraging this trend. The ABA's interest, through the Section of International Law and Practice, was to open foreign markets to American lawyers who had already shown their competitive advantage vis-à-vis the relatively staid legal professions in most countries. The ABA Section believed that a liberal model rule for the licensing of legal consultants, based on the New York rule, would buttress the bargaining position of the United States in negotiating for lower barriers for US lawyers desiring to practice in European Union countries and Japan. The ABA House of Delegates adopted such a rule in 1993.

US and UK law firms have reaped huge benefits stemming from the internationalization of business, the dominance of American investment banks and the crucial role that New York and London capital markets play in the world economy. In the twenty-first century, civil law countries—especially in Europe—are striving to export their lawyers abroad as part of law firms owned and centered in their own nations.

7.3   GATS and Trade Liberalization

The United States Trade Representative (USTR), combating years of American trade deficits in goods, agreed to support the introduction of legal services into the Uruguay Round of multilateral GATT negotiations for trade liberalization that resulted in GATS (General Agreement on Trade in Services). The US Congress approved GATS in 1994 and it, along with membership in the new World Trade Organization (WTO), went into effect. There were 153 WTO members in 2011.

GATS opened a new era of visibility for international trade in legal services. Most important, GATS adopted the previous GATT (now WTO) principle of most-favored-nation (MFN) treatment. Governments should now refrain from conditioning market access for the supply of legal services from other member-state lawyers on a requirement of reciprocity. In addition, signatories should adopt measures for the recognition of the education or experience obtained, requirements met or licenses or certifications granted in a particular country. Finally, GATS aims for a progressive liberalization of worldwide trade in services through successive rounds of negotiations. Progress has been slow in these matters.[112]

As part of the negotiation strategy during the Uruguay Round, the ABA/USTR team

---

[110]   Other common law countries also saw the advantage of promoting the export of their legal services. For instance, Australian law firms earned Aus$194 million in 2000 for services abroad. Law Council of Australia, 'What is the Export Value of the Legal Services Industry?' http://www.lawcouncil.asn.au (select Resources/About the Profession).

[111]   Jennifer Koncz-Bruner and Anne Flatness, 'U.S. International Services: Cross-Border Trade in 2010', at 20, http://www.bea.gov (enter either author's name in search bar). From 2008 to 2010, the US import of legal services declined from $1.9 to $1.5 billion. Ibid. 21.

[112]   See Laurel S. Terry, Carole Silver and Ellyn S. Rosen, 'Transnational Legal Practice 2009', 44 *International Lawyer* 563, 572–6 (2010).

promised (particularly to the European Union representatives) improved conditions for foreign lawyers who desired to establish US offices. The ABA had adopted the Model Rule for the Licensing of Legal Consultants. The USTR encouraged American states to adopt this Model Rule as well as rules facilitating the recognition of foreign legal education as partial or full qualification to sit for the local bar examination. This process has borne fruit. For example, South Korea adopted the Foreign Legal Consultant Act in 2009 providing access to lawyers from countries with which it has a free trade agreement. The US Congress approved the US-Korea Free Trade Agreement in 2011.[113]

GATS recognizes the existence of preferential trading areas such as the European Union or the North American Free Trade Area (NAFTA). It permits these under certain conditions to deviate from the MFN principle by maintaining trade barriers that otherwise would be precluded. During negotiations for NAFTA, the ABA pushed for the inclusion of legal services and especially for the adoption of the category of foreign legal consultants. In particular, it saw this as an opportunity to open the Mexican market to US lawyers. NAFTA entered into force for Canada, Mexico and the United States in 1994. NAFTA's chapter 12 (Cross-Border Trade in Services) requires each of the three member nations to give service providers of another state-party the better of national or MFN treatment. Furthermore, foreign lawyers have a right of 'non-establishment' in providing cross-border services because a party may not require residence or establishment in the jurisdiction as a condition to practice. The three NAFTA parties have designated national professional bodies to consult with each other to develop joint recommendations for licensing FLCs.

FURTHER READING

Abel, Richard L. (1988). *The Legal Profession in England and Wales*. Oxford: Basil Blackwell.

Abel, Richard L. (1989). *American Lawyers*. New York: Oxford University Press.

Abel, Richard L. and Philip S.C. Lewis (eds) (1988–9). 1–3 *Lawyers in Society* (The Common Law World; The Civil Law World; Comparative Theories). Berkeley: University of California Press.

Clark, David S. (1999). 'Comparing the Work and Organization of Lawyers Worldwide: The Persistence of Legal Traditions', in John J. Barceló III and Roger C. Cramton (eds), *Lawyers' Practice and Ideals: A Comparative View* 9–155. Hague: Kluwer Law International.

Clark, David S. (2002a). *The Organization of Lawyers and Judges* (16 *International Encyclopedia of Comparative Law* (Civil Procedure, ch. 3). Tübingen: Mohr Siebeck and Martinus Nijhoff.

Clark, David S. (2002b). 'Legal Education and the Legal Profession', in David S. Clark and Tuğrul Ansay (eds), *Introduction to the Law of the United States* 13–33. The Hague: Kluwer Law International, 2nd edn.

Cummings, Scott L. (ed.) (2011). *The Paradox of Professionalism: Lawyers and the Possibility of Justice*. Cambridge: Cambridge University Press.

Drolshammer, Jens and Michael Pfeifer (eds) (2001). *The Internationalization of the Practice of Law*. The Hague: Kluwer Law International.

Friedman, Lawrence M. and Rogelio Pérez-Perdomo (eds) (2003). *Legal Culture in the Age of Globalization: Latin America and Latin Europe*. Stanford, CA: Stanford University Press.

Harvard Law School. 'Program on the Legal Profession'. http://www.law.harvard.edu/programs (select Program).

---

[113] Korea will implement the legal services rules in stages during the 2010s. Sheppard Mullin, 'Korea Passes Foreign Legal Consultant Act', http://www.antitrustlawblog.com (enter title in search bar).

Indiana University Maurer School of Law, 'Center on the Global Legal Profession'. http://globalprofession.
    law.indiana.edu.
Pérez-Perdomo, Rogelio (2006). *Latin American Lawyers: A Historical Introduction*. Stanford, CA: Stanford
    University Press.
Sarat, Austin (ed.) (2010). *Law Firms, Legal Culture, and Legal Practice*. Bingley, UK: Emerald Group.
Schultz, Ulrike and Gisela Shaw (eds) (2003). *Women in the World's Legal Professions*. Oxford: Hart Publishing.

18 Legal protection of the environment
Stephen C. McCaffrey and Rachael E. Salcido*

1 INTRODUCTION

The natural environment sustains all life on Earth. It is our life-support system. The field of environmental law has grown substantially over time as citizens and policy makers have recognized the need to safeguard the health of the environment. This legal field relies on multiple scientific fields, such as biology, geology, hydrology, toxicology, as well as social science fields such as public health, to achieve its aims—a healthy, functioning and resilient natural environment.

Environmental law is closely related to the fields of both natural resources law and land use law. These fields all focus on human interactions with the natural world. Traditionally the field of environmental law was primarily concerned with the effects of pollution on components of the environment, such as air, water and soil. Natural resources law regulates extraction of raw materials including minerals development, oil and gas, water and forestry, focusing on effects upon the environment—flora and fauna. Land use law focuses on the development of real property for housing and commercial purposes, transportation, energy development and transmission, among other things. Over time, the basic field of environmental law has broadened into several subfields such as toxics regulation, wildlife and biodiversity preservation, ocean and coastal law, and climate change to name only a few.

2 NATIONAL AND INTERNATIONAL ENVIRONMENTAL LAW

In the United States, the environmental movement of the 1960s and 1970s created a legacy of statutory protections. The National Environmental Policy Act (NEPA)—the first instrument requiring environmental impact assessment—was adopted in 1969.[1] Congress created the Environmental Protection Agency in 1970. It was during this era that Americans became more concerned about human health and recognized the importance of clean air, water and soil to thriving, healthy human populations. The Clean Air Act (1963),[2] Clean Water Act (1972),[3] the Coastal Zone Management Act (1972),[4] the

---

* Stephen C. McCaffrey is Distinguished Professor of Law and Scholar, University of the Pacific, McGeorge School of Law as well as Counselor of its Institute for Sustainable Development.
Rachael E. Salcido is Professor of Law, University of the Pacific, McGeorge School of Law.

[1] Codified at 42 U.S.C. § 4321 (2006) and following sections.
[2] Codified at 42 U.S.C. § 7401 (2006) and following sections.
[3] Codified at 33 U.S.C. § 1251 (2006) and following sections.
[4] Codified at 16 U.S.C. § 1451 (2006) and following sections.

Comprehensive Environmental Response, Compensation and Liability Act (CERCLA, 1980),[5] and the Resource Conservation and Recovery Act (1976)[6] were initially adopted during this period. There have been major amendments to all these statutes up to the present.

Beyond the statutory environmental protections adopted by national legislatures, many nations around the world have adopted a right to a healthy environment in their constitutions. For instance, nations such as Costa Rica,[7] India[8] and Kenya[9] have recognized this right in the supreme legal document of the land. Whether a constitutional right results in strong environmental protection in practice differs from place to place. The United States Constitution does not contain a right to a healthy environment, but some state constitutions, such as that of Montana, do.[10]

Given the global aspects of the environment we share, the necessity of cooperation among nations to address particular environmental issues such as ocean pollution, ozone depletion and climate change is well recognized. A robust body of international environmental laws complements domestic environmental law. Nations may often need to adopt specific legislation to meet their international treaty obligations. For example, the United States adopted the Migratory Bird Treaty Act of 1918[11] to carry out its treaty obligations with Great Britain (for Canada) entered into in 1916 for migrating birds. Treaty obligations expanded with additional agreements related to migrating birds, such as those between the US and Mexico (1936), Japan (1972), and the then Union of Soviet Socialists Republics (1976) with amendments to domestic law implementing such treaty obligations. There are now many international agreements relating to the environment and protection of wildlife. Some examples include the United Nations Convention on Long-Range Transboundary Air Pollution (LRTAP)[12] adopted in 1979 as well as the 1973 Convention on International Trade in Endangered Species of Wild Fauna and Flora (CITES),[13] the 1992 Convention on Biological Diversity (CBD)[14] and the 1992 UN Framework Convention on Climate Change (UNFCCC).[15]

Nations have created major international institutions to focus on the challenges of environmental degradation. The United Nations Environment Programme (UNEP), established by the General Assembly following the 1972 Stockholm Conference on the

---

[5]   Codified at 42 U.S.C. § 9601 (2006) and following sections.

[6]   Codified at 42 U.S.C. § 6901 (2006) and following sections.

[7]   Political Constitution of the Republic of Costa Rica art. 50 ('Every individual has a right to a healthy and ecologically balanced environment').

[8]   Constitution of India, sec. 48A ('The State shall endeavor to protect and improve the environment and to safeguard the forests and wild life of the country').

[9]   Constitution of the Republic of Kenya art. 42 ('Every person has the right to a clean and healthy environment, which includes the right (a) to have the environment protected for the benefit of present and future generations through legislative and other measures').

[10]   Mont. Const. art. II, § 3 and art. IX. § 1. Other state constitutions, such as those of Hawaii and Illinois, also announce the policy of the state to protect the environment.

[11]   16 U.S.C. § 703–12 (1918).

[12]   T.I.A.S. no. 10,541 (13 Nov. 1979), 18 *International Legal Materials* 1442 (1979).

[13]   T.I.A.S. no. 8,249, 27 U.S.T. 1087 (3 March 1973, Washington Convention).

[14]   31 *International Legal Materials* 818 (1992), available at http://www.cbd.int/convention/text.

[15]   See United Nations Framework Convention on Climate Change, Home Page, http://unfccc.int/2860.php.

Human Environment, strives to improve capacity for ecosystem management as well as environmental protection and restoration in many parts of the world. Virtually all of the major multilateral treaties in the field of the environment—for instance, the 1985 Vienna Convention on the Protection of the Ozone Layer and its 1987 Montreal Protocol, the 1992 UNFCCC and its 1997 Kyoto Protocol, and the 1992 CBD—provide for a conference of the parties (COP) and are serviced by a secretariat. Other international organizations active in the field of the environment include the Food and Agricultural Organization of the UN (FAO), the World Meteorological Organization (WMO) and the UN Educational, Scientific and Cultural Organization (UNESCO).

Another important development is the creation of special courts and other tribunals to hear grievances based on harm to the environment. New Zealand has a specialized environment court with expert judges dealing specifically with environmental cases.[16] Its Resource Management Act of 1991 installed sustainable development as the law of the land, and created this specialized court. The University of Denver Environmental Courts and Tribunals Study identified over 80 such forums in 35 different countries.[17]

Finally, the right to a healthy environment as a human right has also gained recognition in some forums, such as the European Court of Human Rights. The United Nations General Assembly voted to recognize a fundamental human right to water in 2010.[18]

3   CHALLENGES INHERENT IN ENVIRONMENTAL REGULATION

3.1   Temporal Dimension of Environmental Harms

There are recurring difficulties in regulating pollution and its effect on the environment. One constant challenge is the time lag between the onset of an activity and a possible harmful outcome manifested in people, wildlife or other aspects of the environment. This compounds the difficulty of identifying the causes of environmental degradation and the actors causing harm. Some types of harm occur from an accumulation of inputs or extractions from the environment rather than from one isolated activity. Pollution respects no boundaries, thus some environmental effects are transboundary, where the activity causing harm is in one location but the harm is experienced in a different location.[19] As discussed later, environmental justice focuses on the unequal distribution of harm to people.

---

[16]   32 Reprinted Statutes of New Zealand 131(1) (1994). For an analysis of the innovative expert court model see Bret Birdsong, 'Adjudicating Sustainable Development: New Zealand's Environment Court', 29 *Ecology Law Quarterly* 3 (2002).

[17]   George (Rock) Pring and Katherine (Kitty) Pring, 'Specialized Environmental Courts and Tribunals at the Confluence of Human Rights and the Environment', 11 *Oregon Review of International Law* 301–30 (2009).

[18]   GA Resolution 64/292, The Right to Water and Sanitation (28 July 2010), U.N. Doc. A/Res/64/292. Art. 1 states: [The General Assembly] '*Recognizes* the right to safe and clean drinking water and sanitation as a human right that is essential for the full enjoyment of life and all human rights'.

[19]   A famous example is the *Trail Smelter* arbitration between the United States and Canada arising from smelting activities in Trail, British Columbia approximately seven miles from the

Climate change is a particular challenge since it involves the accumulation of green-house gases over time that gradually affects the environment. Climate is not a linear system, making it even more difficult to predict the effect of large concentrations of green-house gases in the atmosphere. Although scientists have voiced concerns about harm to the environment caused by the accumulation of greenhouse gases in the atmosphere for several decades, it is only recently that significant visible harms have been appearing, such as the melting of the ice caps, rising sea levels, retreating glaciers and ocean acidification.

3.2   Inter-generational and Intra-generational Equity

Two related concepts, inter- and intra-generational equity, play an important role in the development of just laws related to the environment. As Earth's natural amenities are finite, one challenge is the equitable distribution of environmental goods among those living today, known as intra-generational equity. Governments also struggle with balancing the needs of the current generation with those of future generations. Inter-generational equity requires that those living on Earth today leave the environment in a condition that supports options for future generations to thrive.

3.3   Environmental Law is Inherently Interdisciplinary

A further challenge is the complex and interdisciplinary nature of environmental regulation. The environment is complex and we still do not fully understand the inter-working of particular spaces on Earth. For example, the deep oceans have become new frontiers of exploration, and the lack of knowledge and understanding of this environment stunted our ability to respond to the Deepwater Horizon offshore well blowout in the Gulf of Mexico on 20 April 2010.[20] Collaboration among experts in different disciplines is required to address environmental challenges.

4   PHILOSOPHICAL BASES OF REGULATION

The following are the most frequently discussed philosophical bases of environmental law.

4.1   Anthropocentrism

Under this view of the world, humans are at the center of the universe, and nature is separate from humans and exists to serve humanity. Traditionally, environmental law and policy decisions flowed from this perspective. Most environmental laws are designed from an anthropocentric view. For example, the US Clean Water Act standards call for water that is 'fishable and swimmable', which is clearly linked to human activities. Further, the

---

US border that caused harm downwind in the American state of Washington. 3 *U.N. Reports of International Arbitral Awards* 1911, 1938 (1941); reprinted in 35 *American Journal of International Law* 684 (1941).

   [20]   See, e.g., 'Oil Spills', *New York Times* (6 Aug. 2010), http://topics.nytimes.com/topics/reference/timestopics/subjects/index.html (select O, then Oil Spills).

US Clean Air Act provisions use a standard tethered to human health. On the global level, Principle 1 of the 1992 Rio Declaration on Environment and Development provides that: 'Human beings are at the centre of concerns for sustainable development. They are entitled to a healthy and productive life in harmony with nature.'[21]

4.2   Biocentrism, Ecocentrism and Deep Ecology

Contrasted with anthropocentrism, from a biocentric or ecocentric viewpoint humans beings are a part of the larger universe of equals and should strive to live in harmony with the living and non-living world. Limiting the amount of environmental degradation caused in the pursuit of human civilization is an obligation owed to non-humans. Norwegian philosopher Arne Naess developed the philosophy of deep ecology, first introduced in 1973.[22] This philosophy goes beyond the worry of pollution and resource depletion and is concerned with diversity, egalitarianism, and the ethic of respect for nature and other creatures. His work created the deep ecology movement, which he founded on a set of principles. The first of these principles is that all life on Earth, including human life, is to be respected.

4.3   Conservation and Preservation Ethics

There has long been a conservation ethic in the United States. The natural beauty of the continent led to nature preserves and the establishment of the first national park, Yellowstone, on 1 March 1872.[23] Gifford Pinchot led the National Forest Service and popularized the concept of 'wise use'.[24] Under this view, he promoted conservation of natural resources for the future prosperity of the nation.

A distinction between the terms conservation and preservation became more pronounced as environmental law evolved in the United States. Conservation or wise use of resources will literally conflict with preserving the environment in its existing state. For example, re-seeding a small area following a timber harvest may be consistent with sustainable forestry, however, the area will literally not be preserved in its pre-harvested state. For this reason, government authorities no longer allow activities such as mining and logging in US federal public lands designated as statutory wilderness under the Wilderness Act of 1964.[25] The Wilderness Act is a land management statute seeking to set aside large tracts of land for preservation as reference landscapes and opportunities for rustic recreation. In general, no commercial activities are allowed in statutory wilderness.

The federal government also manages the National Park System under a model of preservation, seeking to keep the natural environment as close as possible to its unimpaired state for future generations. However, its use for recreational and educational purposes

---

[21]   'Report of the United Nations Conference on Environment and Development', U.N. Doc. A/CONF. 151/26 (12 Aug. 1992), 31 *International Legal Materials* 849 (1992) (Rio Declaration).

[22]   Arne Naess, 'The Shallow and the Deep, Long-Range Ecology Movements: A Summary', 16 *Inquiry: An Interdisciplinary Journal of Philosophy* 95–100 (1973).

[23]   Yellowstone National Park Act of 1872, 30 U.S.C. §§ 21–2, 17 Stat. 32 (1 Mar. 1872).

[24]   Gifford Pinchot, *The Fight for Conservation* (New York: Doubleday, Page & Co. 1910).

[25]   16 U.S.C. §§ 1131–6; 1133(d) (2006) (mining).

necessarily degrades it. This is a consistent challenge with a preservation mandate. In general, even where land is set aside for preservation, some active management is involved. Other preservation-oriented statutes in the US include the Antiquities Act of 1906,[26] the National Historic Preservation Act of 1966[27] and the Endangered Species Act of 1973.[28]

Another way to frame this debate is to focus on the distinction between a utilitarian approach to environmental protection and a moral imperative to act as a steward of Earth and its living inhabitants. As previously explained, most environmental laws are anthropocentric.

4.4 Religious Bases and Theocentrism

Biocentrists rely to some extent on a moral argument for environmental protection. The moral imperative is further supported by some religions, which value the entire living world and support environmental protection as a responsibility to recognize all life on Earth as sacred. Theocentrism reconciles human relationship to nature in a way that recognizes an order created by a higher being. Thus, degradation of the environment and nature is a moral wrong as it interferes with the creation of God.[29]

5 NATURE OF ENVIRONMENTAL LAWS

There are various approaches to the protection of the environment, including prescriptive controls, market-based methods, information-based laws and voluntary or incentive-based laws.

5.1 Prescriptive Controls

Most frequently environmental laws prohibit certain actions, such as the release of pollutants from discrete sources, for instance, industrial facilities. In the US, the predominant tool for environmental protection is this type of command and control mandate. For example, the Clean Water Act prohibits the discharge of a pollutant to the navigable waters of the United States except in permitted instances. In this way, the government seeks to achieve a standard of clean water by taking into account how much pollution it permits actors to introduce into the environment. In setting these standards, the government might consider human health or wildlife health, and the technological feasibility of pollution control equipment.

There are also outright bans on the introduction of particular materials into the environment, such as chemicals prohibited under the Toxic Substance Control Act (TSCA)[30]

---

[26]   16 U.S.C. §§ 431–3 (2006).
[27]   16 U.S.C. §§ 470–470w-6 (2006).
[28]   16 U.S.C. §§ 1531–43 (2006).
[29]   For an example of contrasting philosophical bases, see Andrew J. Hoffman and Lloyd E. Sandelands, 'Getting Right with Nature: Anthropocentrism, Ecocentrism and Theocentrism', 18 *Organization & Environment* 141–62 (no. 2, June 2005).
[30]   15 U.S.C. §§ 2601–92 (2006).

or bans on the introduction of a particular waste to land or other open medium, as with regulation under the Resource Conservation and Recovery Act (RCRA).[31] There may also be restrictions on various modes of operation, one example being the flaring of gas during oil refining operations under the Clean Air Act.

Here, the practices of nations may vary. For example, the use of DDT was banned in the United States after the popular book *Silent Spring* (1962) by Rachel Carson brought the scrutiny of the regulating agency on this potent pesticide.[32] However, it is not banned in all nations. In fact, in 2006, the World Health Organization backed the use of DDT to combat malaria.[33] Gas flaring is a contentious issue under the Clean Air Act in the United States, and in other gas-producing states such as Nigeria.

We use the term 'command and control' to describe the prescriptive mode of regulation. Yet, there is still disagreement over the exact meaning of the term 'command and control'. Practically speaking, in the US, Congress or a government agency determines what actions are unacceptable and bans that activity, or the governing body sets a limit or amount on the pollution that is acceptable and leaves it up to private actors to determine how to stay within the limits during their operations.

5.2 Market-based Approaches

Market-based approaches seek to harness the power of markets instead of allowing a central government to make decisions about the release of pollution from particular private actors. Economists argue that it is more efficient to rely on the markets to allocate environmental 'goods' such as clean air, water, soil and biodiversity. As the argument goes, interference by the government causes the cost of environmental regulation to be higher than necessary to achieve the same environmental benefits using free market principles.

Some instances of market-based approaches have been successful. Market-based regulation has been used to control acid rain air pollution in the United States. The European Union's creation of a market for permits to emit greenhouse gases is another example of the use of market mechanisms, in this case to combat climate change. Related market tools include effluent discharge fees, taxes and subsidies to consumers of energy-efficient products.

Market principles may also be combined with command and control approaches. For example, 'cap-and-trade' and similar programs are being used to protect the environment and spur innovation. Under the cap-and-trade approach, the government imposes a 'cap', or limit, on the total emission level of a pollutant. Then, emission allowances are divided among industry sources and these sources may trade emission allowances among themselves. For example, a more efficient producer with excess allowances may trade (sell) those allowances to a less efficient producer in need of additional allowances.

---

[31]   See note 6 and regulations at 40 C.F.R. pts. 239–82 (2011).
[32]   Rachel Carson, *Silent Spring* (Boston: Houghton Mifflin 2002, orig. 1962).
[33]   Joanne Silberner, 'WHO Backs Use of DDT Against Malaria', at NPR (15 Sep. 2006), http://www.npr.org/templates/story/story.php?storyId=6083944.

5.3   Information-based Laws

Requiring robust dissemination of information to the public is another means of environmental regulation that may complement the approaches just discussed. The federal Emergency Planning and Community Right-to-Know Act (EPCRA) is an example of an information-based law.[34] The EPCRA created the Toxic Release Inventory (TRI), a publicly available database reporting the amount of toxic chemicals used and released by certain industries. This approach also can achieve environmental protection if pollution behavior is influenced by public pressure. The requirement to disclose this information may be sufficient to create an incentive to minimize pollution to reduce public scrutiny.

5.4   Voluntary or Incentive-based Laws

In a complete shift from the focus on command and control laws, multiple voluntary associations and labels have emerged that capitalize on the public's increasing demand for sustainable practices. For example, voluntary initiatives related to greenhouse gas pollution were created in response to the lack of regulation on the subject. One illustration is the California Climate Action Registry launched by the State of California. Firms voluntarily report their greenhouse gas emissions and seek to make voluntary reductions. These reductions may be credited in future implementation of California's Global Warming Solutions Act of 2006.[35] This incentive program spurred early action prior to the law's being fully implemented. The US Environmental Protection Agency also has a voluntary environmental project program.

Scholars analyzing these efforts criticize the effectiveness of voluntary programs to achieve improved environmental results, and posit that such programs may change the perception of entitlements to clean air, water and land. An analysis of voluntary efforts in Denmark, Germany, Japan, the United Kingdom and the United States concluded that mandatory programs are necessary for environmental protection, but voluntary programs could play an important role particularly when mandatory programs are challenging to administer or environmental gains are small in comparison to the investment in regulation.[36]

6   IMPLEMENTING ENVIRONMENTAL LAWS

6.1   Federalism and Preemption

In the United States, there are multiple levels of environmental decision-making—federal, state, and local. Many environmental effects are both generated and experienced in the same location. In such situations, local regulation might be preferred as responsive to the

---

[34]   42 U.S.C. §§ 11004–49 (2006).
[35]   Cal. Health & Safety Code § 38500 (2010) and following sections.
[36]   Richard D. Morgenstern and William A. Pizer (eds), *Reality Check: The Nature and Performance of Voluntary Environmental Programs in the United States, Europe and Japan* (Washington, DC: Resources for the Future 2007).

problem. Yet some effects are generated in one location and experienced in many locations, which may support regulation at a broader regional or national scale. Examples include interstate air pollution and the production and broad distribution of toxic chemicals. There is a large body of scholarship on the doctrine of federalism, focused on the division of authority between the federal and the state and local governments. Federal law is supreme under this system. Any laws that conflict with federal law are preempted, and local laws that conflict with state law are also preempted.

A related concern is the need to establish a baseline of protection across the country. If states competed for business and jobs without environmental standard setting by a central government, there is a concern that a 'race to the bottom' would occur, whereby states would compete for polluting but economically productive industries by lowering their environmental standards. Some environmental laws balance these concerns by facilitating federal and state cooperation to achieve environmental goals. This approach is called 'cooperative federalism', whereby the federal government sets minimum standards and otherwise incentivizes states to engage in environmental protection. One case in point is the Coastal Zone Management Act (1972).[37] States must prepare Coastal Management Plans (CMPs) which include elements required by the federal law. The federal government approves the CMP and thereafter, federal activities must be consistent with the enforceable provisions of the CMP. States that participate in the federal program receive federal funding for coastal management.

6.2   Standing to Sue

To seek to prevent environmental harm or have a continuing harm stopped, an individual must have the right to seek redress in court. Only those with legal standing to sue—generally, persons who have suffered some form of harm or legally recognizable 'injury'—can challenge agency action. The standing requirement is derived from article III of the US Constitution. Standing requirements have denied some persons and entities access to the judiciary to vindicate various environmental harms. This has led environmental advocates to agitate for relaxed standing requirements in cases involving the public interest.

There are constitutional standing requirements as well as prudential doctrines that the US Supreme Court uses to limit federal judicial involvement in particular disputes. The constitutional standing requirements generally look to whether a particular plaintiff has a personal stake in the outcome of the case. Because of the 'case or controversy' requirement of the federal Constitution's article III, there is no general right to sue to protect the environment in the United States. Nevertheless, US standing requirements are more liberal that those in some other countries, allowing, for example, members of an environmental organization to sue to protect an area in which they hike or otherwise enjoy.[38]

A cognizable injury may be not only an economic interest, but also an aesthetic, environmental or recreational interest.[39] The Court established three prongs that must be met:

---

[37]   See note 4.

[38]   *Sierra Club v. Morton* required that individuals must have a 'direct stake in the outcome' to meet the first prong of standing, injury in fact. 405 U.S. 727, 740 (1972).

[39]   Ibid. at 734–5.

(1) injury in fact, (2) causation and (3) redressability. The Court's jurisprudence on standing in environmental cases has changed over time. In a 2009 Supreme Court case, *Summers v. Earth Island Institute*, an organizational plaintiff was held not to have the 'imminent injury' required to establish standing to sue.[40] The Court rejected organizational standing based on a statistical probability that some of the organization's members would be injured in the near future by the defendant's alleged illegal conduct, since application of regulations allowed exemption for salvage timber sales of fewer than 250 acres in fire-damaged areas of the Sequoia National Forest without the notice, comment and appeals process. The case emphasizes the importance of a plaintiff identifying injury in fact with specificity.

In another high profile decision, many were surprised by the Supreme Court's standing approach in *Massachusetts v. EPA*, in which twelve states and several cities were held to have standing to sue the US Environmental Protection Agency to compel it to regulate carbon dioxide and other greenhouse gases as pollutants. A divided Court determined that Massachusetts was suffering imminent injury in the form of a sea level rise, causation was widely recognized, and finally a judgment could redress the harm alleged (effects of climate change) even if action by the federal government alone would not completely eliminate climate change.[41] This standing analysis might be specific to state government plaintiffs.

6.3   Environmental Justice

Social class and racial disparities in the distribution of environmental conditions are prevalent in many places. The siting of hazardous waste facilities is one illustration. For example, chemical plants and refineries are situated along the lower Mississippi River, in areas where the descendants of former slaves still live. An executive order issued in 1994 by President William J. Clinton requires that federal agencies pursue efforts to address these disparities.[42]

6.4   Cost-benefit Analysis

In evaluating whether a particular regulation should be imposed on human activities, the cost of the regulation can be weighed against the benefit of the regulation. Scholars and jurists have criticized this approach as a crude method of evaluating whether or not to impose a particular regulation, as costs can easily be inflated while benefits may be more diffuse and difficult to assess, particularly in the case of environmental regulations. The benefits of such regulations frequently take the form of improved human and environmental health, reduced mortality and morbidity rates, which may become manifest only

---

[40]   555 U.S. 488 (2009). After a settlement was reached in the case, the plaintiff sought to challenge the regulation in the abstract, without identifying a national forest where application of the regulation would result in injury to any particular individual.

[41]   Bradford C. Mank, 'Standing and Future Generations: Does *Massachusetts v. EPA* Open Standing for Generations to Come?' 34 *Columbia Journal of Environmental Law* 1 (2009).

[42]   Executive Order 12898, Federal Actions to Address Environmental Justice in Minority Populations and Low-Income Populations, 59 *Federal Register* no. 32 (11 Feb. 1994).

over time. Thus, critics also point out the difficulty of monetizing the benefits of improved environmental and human health and reduced deaths.[43]

Chemical regulation is one instance where the benefits of regulation were perceived to outweigh the costs in the European Union, which adopted the REACH legislation as discussed below in section 7.5. However, in the US, cost-benefit analysis has generally prevented regulation of chemicals that is more stringent.[44]

6.5   Risk-benefit Analysis

Risk-benefit analysis compares the economic benefit of an activity with the risk and severity of the potential environmental harm it may cause. If risk outweighs the potential benefits, a government agency may not allow the activity to proceed. The acceptable level of risk in a society appears to be evolving as knowledge of the nature of environmental harm develops. The US Environmental Protection Agency now endorses a risk-based corrective action approach to hazardous waste clean-ups under CERCLA.

Natural disasters, such as the 2011 tsunami in Japan that resulted in a nuclear meltdown at the Fukushima Dai-ichi plant, have influenced risk perception. Following this incident, plans in some countries for nuclear power plants were cancelled.[45]

6.6   Ecosystem Management

Originally, governments enacted environmental laws to address specific sectors, such as air, water and chemicals. Ecosystem management is an approach to environmental regulation that takes a broader inventory of activities and resources with an eye to holistic regulation. All parts of the environment work together synergistically, and ecosystem management is a way to look at the larger picture. The United Nations Environment Programme (UNEP) has an Ecosystem Management Sub-programme to promote this approach to natural resource management in member countries.[46]

6.7   Ecosystem Services

The United Nations refined the term 'ecosystem services' to facilitate valuation of the benefits, or services, provided by a healthy, resilient environment in economic terms.[47] For

---

[43]   Frank Akerman and Lisa Heinzerling, *Priceless: On Knowing the Price of Everything and the Value of Nothing* (New York: The New Press 2004).

[44]   Richard Revez and Michael Livermore, *Retaking Rationality: How Cost-Benefit Analysis Can Better Protect the Environment and Our Health* (New York: Oxford University Press 2008). See Dan Farber, 'Rethinking the Role of Cost-Benefit Analysis', 76 *University of Chicago Law Review* 1355 (2009).

[45]   See, e.g., public concerns in Italy that led to a change in policy. 'Italy Moves a Step Closer to Shelving New Nuclear Plants', *Guardian News* (24 May 2011), http://www.guardian.co.uk/world/2011/may/24/italy-shelving-new-nuclear-plants.

[46]   See UN, UNEP Home Page, http://www.unep.org.

[47]   The United Nations Millennium Ecosystem Assessment (2004) was a four-year study that involved more than 1,300 scientists worldwide. See Millennium Ecosystem Assessment, Guide to the Millennium Assessment Reports, http://www.maweb.org/en/index.aspx.

instance, it is relatively easy to calculate the value of a grove of trees in terms of its board feet when cut, and the number of jobs potentially created or supported by the work of logging. However, it is much more difficult to convey the value of the standing grove in terms of providing habitat to wildlife, shade to river ecosystems, aesthetic and recreational pleasure, water purification and carbon sequestration. Valuation of ecosystem services developed as a method better to compare the amount of money it would take for human activity to replace the human-valued services provided by the environment. Ecosystem services include things like air and water purification, breakdown of waste, stabilization of the climate and protection of the integrity of soils. UNEP also focuses on the value of ecosystem services to humans.

7   CURRENT ISSUES IN ENVIRONMENTAL LAW

7.1   Climate Change and Greenhouse Gas Regulation

Global climate change is the most challenging environmental issue of this era. Greenhouse gases—carbon dioxide and methane, among others—trap heat in the atmosphere, which has already begun to change the climate on Earth. Nations have collaborated to study the impact of greenhouse gas accumulation. The Intergovernmental Panel on Climate Change (IPCC), a panel of the world's leading climate scientists formed by UNEP and the World Meteorological Organization (WMO) in 1988, has produced multiple reports detailing the causes and effects of climate change and warning of the dangers of unchecked emissions.[48]

The United Nations Framework Convention on Climate Change (UNFCCC), a treaty to which nearly all countries are parties, entered into force in 1994.[49] In turn, many countries first pledged legally to reduce emissions of greenhouse gases during a UN Convention in Kyoto, Japan in an agreement known as the Kyoto Protocol to the UNFCCC. Thereafter, progress on actually reducing emissions has been limited, with the most recent targets from Kyoto left unmet and a new agreement containing specific emission-reduction targets and timetables far from being completed.

The European Union has made progress in combating unchecked emission increases by the creation of a greenhouse gas emissions trading regime. The EU Emissions Trading System (or Scheme, EU ETS) was launched in January 2005. It covers installations in all 27 of the EU member states, as well as in Iceland, Liechtenstein and Norway. It is the first and largest multi-nation greenhouse gas-trading regime. Analysis produced by the PEW Center on Global Climate Change indicates the EU ETS is poised to deliver actual, though modest, reductions in greenhouse gas emissions.[50] The EU ETS works on the 'cap-and-trade' principle previously explained. The goal is to reduce emission allowances over time so that by 2020 emissions will have been reduced 21 percent from 2005 levels.

The United States has not adopted a national program of greenhouse gas emission

---

[48]   See IPCC, Home Page, http://www.ipcc.ch.
[49]   See note 15.
[50]   PEW Center on Global Climate Change, *The European Union Emissions Trading Scheme (EU-ETS): Insights and Opportunities*, www.pewclimate.org (enter title in Search).

reduction to address climate change. However, the US Environmental Protection Agency has begun to use its authority pursuant to the Clean Air Act to undertake regulatory initiatives related to climate change. States such as California are nevertheless forging ahead in the void of national leadership. California's ambitious program grows out of The Global Warming Solutions Act of 2006.[51] The state is creating a carbon emission trading program in which participants will have a right to emit or trade a set amount of greenhouse gases, and the amount of emissions will be reduced over time.

7.2   Deforestation

Contributing to the challenge of combating the greenhouse effect, forests around the world are being cut down at an alarming rate. Some forests are being cleared to make way for urban development, while other deforestation is occurring to accommodate growing agricultural and mining practices. Forests act as carbon sinks (that is, they remove carbon dioxide from the atmosphere) and can influence the climate, by providing shading. Of course, forests also provide an important habitat for wildlife.

7.3   Overfishing and Ocean Degradation

The collapse of many commercially important fisheries followed the industrialization of fishing fleets. Destructive fishing methods, such as trawling, have played a significant role in damaging the marine environment by turning the ocean floor into a marine desert. The technology has so progressed that in some areas there is literally nowhere for fish to hide. Although the United Nations Convention on the Law of the Sea[52] makes coastal nations responsible for stewardship of fishery resources (since the high seas beyond the 200-mile exclusive economic zone (EEZ) are beyond the limits of national jurisdiction), the problems of harmful fishing methods and overfishing have continued. The loss of certain species of fish—or the reduction of the numbers to the point that fishing for them is no longer commercially viable—leads to 'fishing down the food chain' where new fish are targeted then ultimately overfished as well. Fish are an important part of the marine environment, and the loss of abundance has led to a degradation of habitat.

The problem is acute around the world. Fish have become an important source of protein for the world, and the people of many nations depend on fish for their diet. Without this source of food, for example, some African nations have seen increased consumption of bush meat, leading to the jeopardizing of monkey and ape populations, among others. The situation has also caused severe economic displacement for fishermen and associated industries and port towns. Communities dependent on a robust fishing industry suffer due to unsustainable overfishing.

Governments and the fishing industry have pursued few solutions, in part because the principle of the freedom of the seas makes oceans a perfect venue for the operation of

---

[51]   See note 35.

[52]   See UN Division for Ocean Affairs and the Law of the Sea, Oceans and Law of the Sea, http://www.un.org/Depts/los/index.htm (links for text of Convention, ratifications, and other information).

the tragedy-of-the-commons phenomenon.[53] A regime of individual tradable quotas in some commercial fisheries replaced the 'first come first served' traditional approach in US waters. The US is also now experimenting with marine protected areas, a small percentage of which allow recovery in no-take zones.

7.4 The Polluter Pays Principle

This principle requires that if there is injury from pollution, the actor causing the pollution must bear the cost. The principle takes account of the fact that often the polluter gains financially from its activity, and thus fairness requires the polluter to internalize pollution costs or to compensate others who suffer from the negative impact of the activity.

There are various formulations of the polluter pays principle (PPP). Originally, an economic principle of cost internalization put forward by the Organisation for Economic Co-operation and Development (OECD) in 1972,[54] jurists have more recently seen the PPP as a liability principle.[55]

7.5 Precautionary Principle

Yet another way to deal with risk is through the application of the precautionary principle. The precautionary principle requires that when there is uncertainty about the impact of a course of action, and that activity carries a risk of serious or irreversible harm, it should not be undertaken.[56] Scholarship identifies the origin of the principle as either Swedish or German (*Vorsorgeprinzip*). There are many articulations of the principle. In one form or another, the principle has been adopted in international agreements on environment and health. For example, the Rio Declaration approach is that the absence of rigorous proof of danger does not justify inaction. Many nations have incorporated the precautionary principle into their environmental laws as a method of preserving a healthy environment. For example, in India, the Supreme Court in *M. C. Mehta v. Union of India* embraced the precautionary principle as a part of the 'law of the land'.[57]

The use of genetically modified organisms (GMOs) provides a good illustration of cases in which a precautionary principle has given rise to differential national policies. European nations rejected the use of GMOs, identifying the unknown risks and potential catastrophic impacts to the agricultural sector. On the other hand, GMOs have been widely introduced into agriculture in the United States, from which many farming products are exported to other nations. This conflict led to a dispute settlement panel final decision in the World Trade Organization (WTO) known as the

---

[53] See Garrett Hardin, 'The Tragedy of the Commons', 162 *Science* 1243 (1968).

[54] 14 *International Legal Materials* 236 (1972); see Principle 16 of the 1992 Rio Declaration (note 21 and text).

[55] See, e.g., Sanford E. Gaines, 'The Polluter-Pays Principle: From Economic Equity to Environmental Ethos', 26 *Texas International Law Journal* 463, 471–87 (1991).

[56] The Precautionary Principle, UNESCO World Commission on the Ethics of Scientific Knowledge and Technology (COMEST) (Paris, France: 2005).

[57] *M.C. Mehta (Badkhal and Surajkund Lakes Matter) v. Union of India and Others*, Supreme Court of India (10 Nov. 1996), (1997), 3 S.C.C. 715.

EC-Biotech decision. This case, brought by the US, Canada and Argentina against the European Communities (EC), alleged that the EC imposed a de facto moratorium on the approval or marketing of GMO foods in the period of June 1999 to August 2003.[58]

Some researchers criticize the precautionary principle as being unscientific.[59] These critics also charge that it slows economic progress and development. Regulated industrial businesses in the United States have lobbied strenuously against the application of a precautionary principle. Similar to burden shifting, the precautionary principle puts the onus on proponents of activities that might cause harm to the environment to demonstrate its likely impact and safety.

An example of the different approaches to chemical safety helps to illustrate the precautionary principle in action. Often, scientists know very little about existing and new chemicals. The lack of information available to assess the impact on human health and the environment led to the adoption of the EU Registration, Evaluation, Authorisation and Restriction of Chemicals (REACH) legislation, which entered into force in 2007.[60] REACH puts the burden on chemical producers to prove that their products are safe before they can be placed on the market. The REACH legislation addresses all new substances, defined as those on the market after 1981. It created the European Chemicals Agency that has implemented testing of existing chemicals phased over the period of 11 years. As explained by the Environment Directorate General of the European Commission, REACH is based on the principle that 'industry itself is best placed to ensure that the chemicals it manufactures and puts on the market in the EU do not adversely affect human health or the environment'.[61] In contrast, the Toxic Substances Control Act (TSCA)[62] in the US puts the burden on the government to acquire information about chemicals, and then prove that a chemical substance poses an 'unreasonable risk' to health or the environment and, finally, justify any regulation as the 'least burdensome'.[63]

Given the great uncertainty that often accompanies new activities, chemicals and modes of operation, the United States has nevertheless frequently allowed activities to move forward with disastrous consequences. Perhaps in part for this reason, the precautionary principle has made its way into policy discussions in the US. For example, President Barack Obama's 2010 action plan for restoring degraded ocean ecosystems (as well as the coastlines and the Great Lakes) proposes that management agencies use the

---

[58] European Communities: Measures Affecting the Approval and Marketing of Biotech Products, DS 291, 292, 293. The panel determined that the EC was not acting in accordance with their obligations in the Agreement on the Application of Sanitary and Phytosanitary Measures (SPS Agreement). The panel also struck down national GMO bans imposed by individual EC member states.

[59] David B. Resnick, 'Is the Precautionary Principle Unscientific?', 34 *Studies in History and Philosophy of Science* 329–44 (June 2003).

[60] See EC Regulation no. 1907/2006, 2006 O.J. (L 396) 1 (30 Dec. 2006).

[61] European Commission Environment Directorate General, REACH, http://ec.europa.eu/environment/chemicals/reach/reach_intro.htm (select 'REACH in Brief').

[62] See note 30.

[63] *Corrosion Proof Fittings v. EPA*, 947 F.2d 1201 (5th Cir. 1991).

precautionary principle as a component of decision-making.[64] Policy makers perceive the precautionary principle as particularly useful in this field given the lack of baseline information regarding the ocean environment and the significant amount of research now undertaken better to understand the marine environment.

7.6   Sustainable Development

Development can lift people out of poverty and provide an improved quality of life. However, development can also lead to a degraded natural environment, leading to reduced opportunities for humans to thrive. The concept of sustainable development seeks to reconcile and achieve the benefits of development while avoiding detrimental by-products. For instance, while oil and gas drilling may in theory fund new schools and economic prospects, if done without due regard to all the aspects of human well-being— social, economic and environmental—the promise of development may be squandered. Sustainable development emphasizes that all these aspects of development must be considered. These aspects may be in tension and conflict with one another in the short term despite working toward a long-term balance among all three components.

There are various interpretations of the concept of sustainable development. Some consider that any type of development must be done under a set of best-practice principles. Another view is that there is a limit to how much development can disturb the natural world, beyond which more development is unsustainable.

In 1987, the World Commission on Environment and Development, known as the Brundtland Commission (after its chair, Gro Harlem Brundtland), produced a report entitled *Our Common Future*.[65] According to the report, sustainable development is 'development that meets the needs of the present without compromising the ability of future generations to meet their own needs'.[66] This will often be a difficult balance to strike, given pressing needs for the improvement of living conditions, particularly in developing countries. The Brundtland Commission's report counsels factoring into the balance considerations of future harm and benefits in addition to those relating to the present.

New Zealand has been most aggressive in implementing sustainable land use development. Its Resource Management Act of 1991 installed sustainable development as the law of the land, and created a specialized environment court to facilitate improved decision-making.[67]

7.7   Ecological Restoration and Rewilding

Biological diversity, or biodiversity, is dwindling at an alarming rate. Some extinction of species occurs naturally as part of evolution. Yet unlike other periods of major extinctions,

---

[64]   See White House, Executive Order: Stewardship of the Ocean, Our Coasts, and the Great Lakes (19 July 2010), http://www.whitehouse.gov/the-press-office/executive-order-stewardship-ocean-our-coasts-and-great-lakes.

[65]   World Commission on Environment and Development, *Our Common Future* (Oxford: Oxford University Press 1987).

[66]   Ibid. 43.

[67]   Resource Management Act 1991, Public Act no. 69, as amended to 2011, http://www.legislation.govt.nz/act/public/1991/0069/latest/DLM230265.html.

there has not been a catastrophic geologic event associated with the current extinctions. Humans have caused the rapid rate of extinction today. By developing land, we fragment habitat, which either directly or indirectly can lead to the extinction of interdependent species. This threatens the survival of the human species itself; humans affect other species that provide key functions such as air and water purification. The Intergovernmental Panel on Climate Change has predicted that climate change will also bring about mass extinctions, and some of this may already be occurring.[68]

International organizations such as UNESCO and treaties such as the 1992 Convention on Biological Diversity recognize the need to reverse this dangerous trend.[69] Likewise, scholars have played an important role. The eminent biologist E.O. Wilson's work on extinction galvanized a movement—conservation biology (a discipline with a deadline)— that includes biologists and other scientists.[70]

Ecological restoration and rewilding focus on healing the environment by reintroducing and cultivating native flora and fauna. The practice first began on a small scale, but there are now very large rewilding projects that are primarily focused on creating cores of healthy habitat and corridors for wildlife to use to connect the cores and reintroducing to the land top predators that have been nearly exterminated by humans. The recognition that predators have an important relation to the land and interconnection with the entire ecosystem has led to projects such as reintroducing wolves in US national parks and supporting elephant protection in African nations. The work of Michael Soule illustrated the critical role of predators, and led to the understanding that by creating conditions for predators or 'keystone species' to thrive, we would be creating an 'umbrella' under which countless interdependent other species will also thrive.[71]

The importance of this interconnection evaded our understanding for many years. Thus, policy makers omitted measures from land management practices even in those places dedicated to environmental conservation or preservation. While it has taken longer to move this discipline offshore to marine ecosystems, it has become clear that living species have a relationship to their environment and one another that extirpation of any particular part can easily disrupt negatively. One difference between land and offshore restoration is that in the ocean removing negative impacts, such as pollution and overfishing, will lead to significant environmental improvement. Nonetheless, overfishing has so devastated fisheries and fish stocks and legal tools have yet to reverse the trends appreciably.

7.8   The Use of Property Rights in Conservation

The 'tragedy of the commons', alluded to above, refers to the possibility that a system of common property tends to lead to overexploitation because for each individual there is little incentive to conserve the resources.[72] In contrast, some scholars argue that a system

---

[68]   See note 48 and text.

[69]   See note 14.

[70]   Edward O. Wilson, 'On the Future of Conservation Biology', 14 *Conservation Biology* 1 (Feb. 2000).

[71]   See Caroline Fraser, *Rewilding the World: Dispatches from the Conservation Revolution* 18 (2009).

[72]   See Hardin (note 53).

of private property supports conservation, as there is an incentive for longer-term stewardship of the resource in question. There is much disagreement about this proposition generally, with examples of common property regimes also effectively used to conserve resources when appropriate cooperation is involved.[73] Nonetheless, there have been devastating effects related to a 'tragedy of the commons' in open access regimes, such as fisheries. Thus, the use of private property has emerged as one potential tool to promote sustainability. As mentioned in section 7.3 above, individual tradable (or transferable) quotas (ITQs) have been adopted in some US fisheries as a management tool limiting the commercial harvest of marine species. Other nations, such as Iceland and New Zealand, have followed this path.

In the law and economics literature, the Coase Theorem, developed by Nobel Laureate Ronald Coase, proposes that in the absence of transaction costs bargaining will lead to an efficient allocation of goods and services regardless of the initial allocation of property rights. Published in 1960, 'The Problem of Social Cost' clarifies that transaction costs cannot be ignored, and thus the initial allocation of property rights must be scrutinized because it may ultimately be the final allocation due to transaction costs.[74] The ideal option for achieving efficiency is that the initial allocation should be to those actors who can obtain the most utility from those rights. These concerns animate the debate over the allocation of ITQs.

8   CONCLUSION

Pressing environmental challenges await resolution and decisive action. As humans rely on Earth to support their ever-growing population, the challenges outlined here will become more acute. Interdisciplinary collaboration and international cooperation is increasingly necessary since all of human society will be required to respond to these challenges. Some believe that proactively approaching stewardship of Earth is essential for future generations. Environmental law will undoubtedly play a role. It is a dynamic field, constantly growing and changing just like our knowledge of planet Earth.

FURTHER READING

Carson, Rachel (2002). *Silent Spring*. Boston: Houghton Mifflin (orig. 1962).
Jordan III, William R. (2003). *The Sunflower Forest: Ecological Restoration and the New Communion with Nature*. Berkeley: University of California Press.
Leopold, Aldo (1966). *A Sand County Almanac*. Oxford: Oxford University Press.
McCaffrey, Stephen and Rachael Salcido (2008). Global Issues in Environmental Law. St. Paul, MN: West Group.
McKibben, Bill (2006). *The End of Nature*. New York: Random House (orig. 1989).
Safina, Carl (1997). *Song for the Blue Ocean: Encounters Along the World's Coasts and Beneath the Seas*. New York: Henry Holt & Co.

---

[73]   See Elinor Ostrom et al., 'Revisiting the Commons: Local Lessons: Global Challenges', 284 *Science* 278–82 (1999).

[74]   Ronald Coase, 'The Problem of Social Cost', 3 *Journal of Law and Economics* 1 (1960).

Sax, Joseph L. (1973). 'Standing to Sue: A Critical Review of the *Mineral King Decision*', 13 *Natural Resources Journal* 76.
Sax, Joseph L. (1980). *Mountains without Handrails*. Ann Arbor: University of Michigan Press.
United Nations Department of Economic and Social Affairs (2006). *Agenda 21: The United Nations Programme of Action from Rio*, http://www.un.org/esa/dsd/agenda21 (orig. 1992 from the UN Conference on Environment and Development).
Wilson, Edward O. (1996). *In Search of Nature*. Washington, DC: Island Press.
Wilson, Edward O. (1999). *The Diversity of Life*. New York: W.W. Norton & Co.
World Commission on Environment and Development (1987). *Our Common Future*. Oxford: Oxford University Press.

19 Preventive health at work
Julie C. Suk*

1 INTRODUCTION

The delivery of preventive healthcare is a central challenge for overall healthcare reform in the United States. Much more is spent on healthcare providers and delivery in the US than in most other countries, but US health outcomes are much worse, in significant part due to the cost of treating chronic disease. European countries have done much better than the United States on this score. The American healthcare crisis has invited comparative perspectives, as many US reformers seek to learn from, and perhaps import, successful European models.

This chapter exposes one important but often ignored aspect of preventive healthcare in European countries: the integration of preventive medicine into employment law. In France, for instance, the law requires every employer to provide a workplace doctor, who performs regular checkups on each employee, identifies workplace health risks and makes policy recommendations to the employer to protect employees' health. As American employers begin to experiment with onsite preventive health clinics, what might they learn from the French experience? Rather than proposing a transplant of French or European workplace health services on American soil, this chapter explores the reasons why such a transplant would flounder, not only politically, but also legally. The purpose is to develop a critical perspective on the wide range of social and legal factors that impede preventive health services in the United States.

2 THE FRENCH LAW OF OCCUPATIONAL MEDICINE

2.1 Origins

French law has required every employer to have a *médecin du travail*, a workplace doctor, since 1946. The purpose of the 1946 statute was to avoid 'any impairment of workers' health due to the fact of their work'.[1] Prior to World War II, there were 'factory doctors' in the manufacturing sector who performed regular checkups on employees to monitor

---

* Professor of Law, Yeshiva University, Benjamin N. Cardozo School of Law. A fuller version of this chapter is at Julie C. Suk, 'Preventive Health at Work: A Comparative Approach', 59 *American Journal of Comparative Law* 1089–134 (2011). All translations, unless otherwise noted, are my own. The use of the singular pronoun he or she also includes the other unless referring to a specific person.

1   Loi 46-2195 du 11 octobre 1946, Organisation des services médicaux au travail [Organization of workplace medical services], *Journal Officiel de la République Française* [hereinafter J.O.] [Official Gazette of France], 12 Oct. 1946, p. 8638.

their health and ability to work. Although workers and their unions initially viewed these factory doctors as allies of the employer, they eventually advocated the expansion of workplace health services.[2] The unions favored the idea of regular compulsory medical examinations for all employees, whereas employers resisted it.[3] These practices evolved to shape the current system, whose purpose is to protect and promote employee health and safety. The 1946 law envisioned the doctors' role as 'exclusively preventive, consisting of avoiding all impairments of the health of workers due to the fact of their work, notably in monitoring the conditions of hygiene at work, the risks of contagion, and the workers' state of health'.[4]

2.2   Compulsory Checkups by Law

Today, the French Labor Code requires every employer to organize a 'Workplace Health Service'.[5] The law requires every employee to be examined by the workplace doctor before beginning a new job, or at the very latest, at the end of the trial period.[6] The checkups have three main purposes: first, to ensure that the employee is 'medically apt' for the job for which he has been hired; second, to propose adaptations to the job or a transfer to other jobs if any health conditions require it; and third, to determine whether the employee poses a danger to any other workers.[7]

Although the occupational medical examination is not intended to replace primary preventive healthcare, it does include many essential elements of a routine preventive checkup with a primary care physician. Consequently, in practice, it makes all employees learn new facts about their own health that they might not otherwise investigate through primary healthcare. The occupational checkup typically consists of an interview to learn of the employee's professional and personal medical history,[8] urinalysis[9] and a clinical exam.[10] The employee's height, weight, heart rate, blood pressure and body mass index are recorded. The urine test checks for protein, blood and glucose, as they can be indicators for a variety of health conditions including kidney failure, kidney stones, diabetes and many others.

In addition, the workplace doctor checks the individual's state of health in relation to the full range of health concerns that would arise in the particular workplace, with attention to the professional calendar and the tasks assigned to each employee. During these medical examinations, the workplace doctor consults with each employee, providing advice regarding best health and safety practices on the job, as well as on personal health, such as

---

[2]   Stéphane Buzzi, Paul-André Rosental and Jean-Claude Devinck, *La santé au travail: 1880–2006* 34–7 (Paris: La Découverte 2006).

[3]   Ibid. 36.

[4]   Ibid. Codified at Code du travail [hereinafter C. trav.] [Labor Code] art. L. 4622-3.

[5]   C. trav. art. D. 4622-1.

[6]   C. trav. art. R. 4624-10.

[7]   C. trav. art. R. 4624-11.

[8]   See Pol Dyèvre and Damien Léger, *Médecine du travail: Approches de la santé au travail* 47 (Paris: Editions Masson, 3rd edn, 2003).

[9]   Ibid. 44.

[10]   Ibid. 49.

tobacco use, alcohol use, exercise and nutrition.[11] The confidential consultation between the workplace doctor and the employee is the central component of these checkups.[12] The doctor asks the employee if he is satisfied with his work, and asks a variety of follow-up questions designed to identify any sources of emotional or physical discomfort on the job.[13] The clinical exam should seek to 'put in debate the problems not yet expressed, made banal or problems that are passing through the body but not yet thought of'.[14]

If the hiring checkup reveals a health condition that the employee did not disclose to the employer, the employer is not entitled to withdraw the employment contract based on a failure of consent.[15] If there are any individual health problems that require medical treatment, the doctor advises the employee to seek treatment from a 'treating physician'.[16] Based on the particular risks associated with the job, the doctor orders a variety of complementary tests, including x-rays, blood and urine tests to check for the presence of various toxic substances, hearing, vision or respiratory function tests.[17] During this checkup, the workplace doctor creates an 'aptitude file', which remains with the workplace health service throughout the employee's career.[18]

In addition to the hiring checkup, the Labor Code requires each employee to undergo checkups every 24 months.[19] The checkups are similar to those performed when the employee is hired.[20] Their purpose is to ensure the continuing aptitude of the employee for her job.[21] In some sectors and situations, employees undergo 'reinforced medical surveillance', meaning that the periodic checkups are more frequent than every 24 months.[22] Annual exams are required if a regulation has classified a job as higher-risk. More frequent exams are also given to employees who have recently changed their type of work, those who have recently arrived in France, disabled workers, pregnant and nursing women and workers under the age of 18.[23] During these regular preventive checkups, the doctor discusses the changing work environment in relation to the employee's health, including stress management. One workplace doctor reports that she tends to the full range of stress issues, including the management of work-family conflict, especially for female employees. The workplace doctor might offer non-medical prescriptions during the consultation, such as urging the employee to hire a housekeeper to reduce the employee's stress.[24]

---

[11]   Interview with Dr. Lina Barouhiel, Médecin du travail, Nouvelle Messagerie de la Presse Parisienne (NMPP), Paris, France (25 Jun. 2009).

[12]   See Dominique Huez and Odile Riquet, 'Savoir-faire: Clinique et action en médecine du travail', 23 *Les Cahiers Santé Médecine du Travail* 30 (2009).

[13]   See ibid. 30–31.

[14]   Ibid. 31.

[15]   See Evelyn Bledniak, *Santé, hygiène, et sécurité au travail* 213 (Paris: Delmas 2008).

[16]   See, e.g., Odile Riquet, 'Contrées et Horizons', 23 *Les Cahiers Santé Médecine du Travail* 36, 40 (2009).

[17]   See Dyèvre and Léger (note 8) 43–9.

[18]   Interview with Dr. Phillippe Ginel, Association Inter-professionnelle des centres médicaux et sociaux de la region Ile-de-France, Suresnes, France (15 Jun. 2009).

[19]   C. trav. art. R. 4624-16.

[20]   Dyèvre and Léger (note 8) 43.

[21]   Ibid.

[22]   C. trav. art. R. 4624-19.

[23]   C. trav. art. R. 4624-18.

[24]   Barouhiel (note 11).

Finally, checkups with the workplace doctor are required when an employee returns to work from certain types of absences authorized by the Labor Code. These include maternity leave, absence due to occupational diseases, absence of at least eight days resulting from a workplace accident, absence of at least 21 days resulting from a sickness or accident unrelated to work, and repeated absences for health reasons.[25] The employer can refuse to allow the employee to return to work until she undergoes an examination with the workplace doctor.

In what sense are all of these checkups obligatory? The Code provides that the employee 'benefits from' a medical exam, which suggests that the employee may accept or refuse the 'benefit'. However, the French *Cour de cassation* or Supreme Court has held that an employee's refusal to submit to an obligatory medical examination can result in termination for 'real and serious' cause, even when the employee's refusal was based on religious convictions.[26] In another case that did not involve any religious reasons, the *Cour de cassation* held that such refusal constituted 'misconduct',[27] which enabled the employer to terminate without a severance. The costs of the regular preventive checkup are borne entirely by the employer.

2.3 Individual Accommodations

Through these clinical checkups designed to certify employee fitness to work, the French workplace doctor plays a central role in shaping workplace accommodations for all workers whose working conditions may undermine their health. An inaptitude determination by the workplace doctor cannot serve as the basis for the employee's summary dismissal. Such a dismissal would violate the prohibition of discrimination based on the employee's state of health.[28] Instead, the law requires the employer to accommodate the employee.

When the workplace doctor determines that an employee is unfit for his current job, the employer must propose an alternative position. The proposal must take into account the opinions of the workplace doctor regarding the existing tasks within the company that the employee might be capable of performing. The Code requires that the job proposed should be 'as comparable as possible' to the job previously occupied, even if this means that modifications and accommodation to the job or a reduction in working hours are needed.[29] Furthermore, the *Cour de cassation* has interpreted this provision as requiring the employer to consider these accommodations for the employee even when the workplace doctor has declared her inapt for every job in the company.[30] In such circumstances,

---

[25]   C. trav. art. R. 4624-21.

[26]   Cour de cassation, Chambre sociale [hereinafter Cass. soc.] no. 83-45409, 29 May 1986, Bull. civ. V, no. 262, p. 201.

[27]   Cass. soc. no. 97-45286, 17 Oct. 2000 (unpublished).

[28]   The Labor Code prohibits discrimination in hiring, firing and all terms and conditions of employment based on origin, sex, morals, sexual orientation, age, family situation or pregnancy, genetic characteristics, membership or non-membership, real or supposed, in an ethnicity, nation, or race, political opinions, union activities, religious convictions, physical appearance, family name, state of health or disability. See C. trav. art. L. 1132-1.

[29]   C. trav. art. L. 1226-2.

[30]   See Cass. soc. no. 98-41351, 18 Jul. 2000 (unpublished); Cass. soc. no. 98-43970, 10 Jan. 2001 (unpublished).

the employer must consider all the possible modifications and accommodations to every job so that the employee may remain employed.

If an employee's aptitude is in question, the doctor cannot simply declare partial or limited inaptitude without researching and proposing solutions that would resolve the difficulties of the employee's inaptitude.[31] Indeed, in such situations, the employee is not declared 'inapt,' but rather the employee is declared 'apt with restrictions' or 'apt with an accommodation of the job'.[32] In such cases, the doctor highlights the aspects of the job that the employee is medically capable of performing, with recommended limitations. The doctor might indicate a limitation to the hours the employee can tolerate in a particular position or a limit on the weight the employee can lift. She might also identify any tasks that the employee cannot perform.[33]

Nevertheless, due to medical confidentiality rules, which unambiguously apply to the workplace doctor's relationship with the employee, the doctor may not provide a justification for these recommendations by reference to the particular medical circumstances of the employee.[34] If the employer cannot pursue the limitations or accommodations recommended by the workplace doctor, the procedures for inaptitude are then followed. The workplace doctor may not declare an employee inapt without first doing a study of the job, a study of the working conditions in the company as a whole, and two medical examinations of the employee spaced two weeks apart.[35]

In this legal regime, accommodations are not limited to those who fit the statutory definition of the 'disabled'. Disability is defined by the Labor Code as 'any person for whom the possibilities of obtaining or keeping a job are effectively reduced due to the impairment of one or many physical, sensory, mental, or psychic functions'[36] and disabled employees have rights to special accommodations.[37] In France, however, *all* employees can get some accommodations based on the relationship between their state of health and their jobs through the framework that requires each employee to be declared apt or else to be reclassified.

The purpose of the mandatory regular checkups is not to fire those who are no longer medically fit for their jobs, but to adapt work conditions to the employee's state of health.[38] If the doctor determines that the employee is not medically fit for her assigned job, the employer has a duty to adapt the job to make it compatible with the worker's state of health or to reclassify the employee into a different job for which she is apt, taking into account the recommendations of the workplace doctor.[39]

If these attempts at adapting work conditions or reassigning the employee fail because

---

[31]   See Sylvie Bourgeot and Michel Blatman, *L'Etat de santé du salarié* 399–400 (Rueil-Malmaison: Editions Liaisons, 2nd edn, 2009).

[32]   Ibid.

[33]   Ibid.

[34]   Conseil d'État [highest administrative court], no. 25400, 3 Dec. 2003, Rec. Lebon.

[35]   C. trav. art. R. 4624-32.

[36]   C. trav. art. L. 5213-1.

[37]   See C. trav. art. L. 3122-26.

[38]   See Gabriel Fernandez, 'Quelle clinique en médecine du travail?', in Yves Clot and Dominique Lhuilier (eds), *Travail et santé: Ouvertures cliniques* 145, 149 (Toulouse: Editions Érès 2010).

[39]   C. trav. art. L. 1226-2.

the employee's health is incompatible with every job in the company, the employer can terminate the employee. Still, such a firing is considered a termination with a 'real and serious
cause' under the Labor Code, and such terminations are strictly regulated. Employers
must pay a severance that is calculated based on various factors including the employee's
seniority when terminating a worker under these circumstances.[40] It is only when the termination is for misconduct by the employee that the employer would be exempt from the
severance obligations.[41] As is the case with all other disputes surrounding an employee's
termination, the employer bears the burden of proving that the termination is justified.
Thus, the employer must show that the employee is unfit for every job in the company, and
that reclassification is impossible. The cases applying this provision suggest that, even if
the workplace doctor determines that the employee is inapt for every job in the company,
the employer must still search for ways of reclassifying the employee by modifying some
existing position.[42] When the quest for reclassification is exhausted because the employee
is truly unfit for every available job in the company, only then can the employer legitimately terminate the employee for 'real and serious' cause.[43]

Since it is illegal or costly to fire a worker who has become medically unfit for his job,[44]
most French workers do not have reason to fear that they will lose their jobs because of
the regular visits to the workplace doctor. Such a visit can even lead to an improvement
in the employee's job situation. Furthermore, the regular checkups are an opportunity
for employees to discuss and request health-based accommodations and modifications
to their working conditions, because the workplace doctor has significant power to bring
about individual changes in the workplace.[45] Although the doctor cannot require the
employer to make changes, the law forces transparency by requiring the employer to give
reasons for rejecting the doctor's recommendations.[46] It also catalyzes processes of change
that can take effect if the employee appeals to the relevant state authorities.

2.4   Policymaking

In addition to performing individual clinical assessments of the employees, the workplace
doctor also functions as a workplace regulator. The French Labor Code provides that
the employer must 'take steps necessary to ensure safety and to protect the physical and
mental health of workers'.[47] The workplace doctors are assigned a central role in assisting
the employer in fulfilling this statutory duty. They function as internal health and safety
officers within the workplace.

---

[40]   C. trav. art. L. 1226-12.

[41]   See C. trav. art. L. 1234-1 (providing for terminated employees' right to severance, except
when the termination is justified by the employee's serious misconduct).

[42]   Cass. soc. no. 03-42744, 10 Mar. 2004, Bull. civ. V, no. 84, p. 75.

[43]   Cass. soc. no. 87-43243, 29 Nov. 1990, Bull. civ. V, no. 600, p. 361.

[44]   See C. trav. art. L. 1132-1; Cass. soc. no. 95-41,491, 28 Jan. 1998, Bull. civ. V, no. 43, p. 32;
Cass. soc. no. 96-45394, 16 Feb. 1999, Bull. civ. V, no. 76, p. 56.

[45]   A Code provision authorizes the doctor to propose changes to work stations based on the
health circumstances of the workers. The employer is required to consider these proposals and give
reasons if rejecting the doctor's proposals. See C. trav. art. L. 4624-1.

[46]   Ibid.

[47]   C. trav. art. L. 4121-1.

The employer's positive duty includes steps to prevent professional risks, information and training measures and the implementation of adapted methods.[48] Workplace doctors participate in shaping company policies to protect workers' health and safety. The workplace doctor is a central figure in facilitating the employer's fulfillment of these duties. The Labor Code regulations assign the workplace doctor the role of adviser to the employer on many matters, including improvement of life and work conditions in the company, protection of workers against the totality of nuisances, general hygiene of the establishment and prevention and health education within the workplace in relation to professional activity.[49]

The 'third-time rule' requires workplace doctors to devote a third of their time to learning about the work environment.[50] Thus, the doctors have free access to the workplace, and can visit at their own initiative or at the request of employers or employee committees.[51] These visits can aid the doctor in fulfilling her statutory duties to study new methods of production and to receive safety training,[52] and to learn about the composition of products and materials used in work, as well as any measures or analyses done on new methods of production or safety training.[53]

In practice, the doctor's 'third-time' activities are focused towards the production of an annual report, which the doctor is legally required to submit to the employer and to the company's health and safety committee.[54] In this work, the doctor brings together his study of the workplace and his knowledge of the workers' health. Medical facts about the workers are anonymous for the purpose of studying and reporting them statistically.[55] Thus, the doctor is able to evaluate and bring to the employer's attention the effects on workers of exposure to various risks—chemical, biological, organizational and psychosocial.

The head of the company must inform the doctor any time an employee declares an occupational disease or accident. If the doctor deems it necessary, she prepares a report on measures to avoid the repetition of such incidents in the future. The report goes to the employee health and safety committee, as well as the head of the company, who then must submit it to the labor inspector and the medical labor inspector.[56]

The regulatory function of the workplace doctor is largely one of gathering information that becomes available, to both employees and public authorities, rather than ordering change. As Cynthia Estlund has recently noted, information disclosure can play a central role in making workplace regulation more efficient.[57] In France, the workplace doctor is required to author two important documents: the 'company file' on professional risks, and the annual activity report. The 'company file' identifies all of the risks faced by

---

[48]   Ibid.
[49]   C. trav. art. R. 4623-1.
[50]   See C. trav. art. R. 4624-1 to R. 4624-9.
[51]   C. trav. art. R. 4624-1.
[52]   C. trav. art. R. 4624-3.
[53]   C. trav. art. R. 4624-4.
[54]   See Dyèvre and Léger (note 8) 64.
[55]   See ibid.
[56]   C. trav. art. R. 4626-19.
[57]   See Cynthia Estlund, 'Just the Facts: The Case for Workplace Transparency', 63 *Stanford Law Review* 351, 354 (2011).

its employees[58]—physical, chemical, infectious, those related to particular work situations and accident risks. It also identifies the measures taken by the employer to address these risks. Typically, the file includes statistics concerning workplace injuries and illnesses, as well as any measures that the company has taken over the past year to prevent or reduce risks. The workplace doctor evaluates the effectiveness of any such measures and notes any relevant training programs.[59] She submits the company file to the employer, who must send a copy to the labor inspector and the medical labor inspector.[60]

In addition to the roles and duties assigned to the workplace doctor by the Labor Code, there is a duty stemming from the Social Security Code with regard to the prevention of workplace diseases. The workplace doctor is obligated to declare and report toxic exposures and diseases to the relevant public authorities.[61] This regime treats workplace doctors as internal regulators. Even when these doctors are employees of private enterprises, the law imposes public health duties on them. In fact, the law makes clear that workplace doctors' purpose is to protect employee's health. By contrast, these doctors have no duty to protect or advance private employers' needs, preferences or profits.

2.5   The Medicalization of Workplace Regulation: Psychosocial Risks

Thus, the French *médecin du travail* plays a regulatory role in the French workplace on a wide variety of social issues that one can characterize as public health issues, including workplace harassment. The Labor Code prohibits 'moral harassment', behaviors 'which have for their purpose or effect the degradation of an employee's work conditions that may undermine his rights and dignity, or alter his physical or mental health or compromise his professional future'.[62] The concept of 'moral harassment' includes, but is not limited to, sexual harassment.[63] Coined by the psychiatrist Marie-France Hirigoyen in a 1998 book,[64] moral harassment is a term that can refer to a variety of abusive, humiliating behaviors that Americans might call 'bullying'.[65]

Most interestingly, 'moral harassment' includes conduct that violates other employment-law norms, when they have the purpose or effect of psychologically harming the employee. For instance, one court has upheld the liability of an employer who made an employee work during his holidays and Friday afternoons without pay, and without breaks except at the supervisor's discretion. This constituted moral harassment because of the 'real moral

---

[58]   C. trav. art. D. 4624-37.
[59]   Dyèvre and Léger (note 8) 71.
[60]   C. trav. art. D. 4624-40.
[61]   See Code de la sécurité sociale [Social Security Code] art. L. 461-6.
[62]   C. trav. art. L. 1152-1.
[63]   See Gabrielle Friedman and James Q. Whitman, 'The European Transformation of Harassment Law: Discrimination versus Dignity', 9 *Columbia Journal of European Law* 241, 242 (2003).
[64]   Marie-France Hirigoyen, *Le harcèlement moral: La violence perverse au quotidien* (Paris: La Découverte 1998).
[65]   See David C. Yamada, 'The Phenomenon of "Workplace Bullying" and the Need for Status-Blind Hostile Work Environment Protection', 88 *Georgetown Law Journal* 475, 480–84 (2000) (defining bullying).

prejudice' sustained by the employee, who cried, was unable to sleep and just could not contain himself.[66]

In authorizing the workplace doctor to propose environmental changes in the interests of workers' physical and mental health, the 2002 statute explicitly envisioned a role for these doctors in addressing the problem of workplace harassment. Given the range of workplace behaviors and norms violations that can constitute 'moral harassment' and cause harm to the mental health of employees, the workplace doctor's power to intervene on physical and mental health matters is considerable.

Harassment is one area in which the workplace doctor's power to recommend individual accommodations by way of clinical aptitude determinations intersects with the larger regulatory role. If an employee's supervisor or co-workers are harassing her, such that the employee bears risks or sustains harm to her mental health, the workplace doctor can propose changes such as the reassignment of the employee or the alleged harassers to minimize the occurrence of harassment.[67] In extreme cases, the workplace doctor can declare the harassed employee partially or totally inapt for his job, or for any job in the company.[68] In instances of severe harassment, the employee might welcome a declaration of inaptitude, since the employer may, and ordinarily does, terminate any employee that the workplace doctor declares totally inapt for any job in the company. Although being fired is not ideal, a termination for inaptitude is more attractive to most employees than voluntarily resigning one's job, since a justified termination entitles the employee to a severance payment,[69] whereas resignation does not.[70]

The doctor's role in regulating workplace harassment—both through policy recommendations and through remedies for individual disputes—demonstrates the extent to which social problems in the French workplace are reframed as health problems. Another example is workplace stress, which is a major preoccupation of workplace doctors.[71]

---

[66]   Cours d'appel Riom, soc. no. 1293/01, 1 Oct. 2002 [excerpted in Bourgeot and Blatman (note 31) 183].

[67]   See Bourgeot and Blatman (note 31) 194–5.

[68]   Ibid. 195.

[69]   C. trav. art. L. 1234-9.

[70]   See art. C. trav. art. L. 1237-1. In the case of resignation, the employee is required to give notice. The notice periods are set by collective agreements. If the employee does not observe the notice period, the employee may have to pay damages for resignation to the employer. See Cass. soc. no. 83-44747, 18 Dec. 1986, Bull. civ. V, no. 625, p. 473. Note, however, that as of 2008, the law now makes it possible for employers and employees to negotiate a termination agreement, thereby multiplying the possibilities for the terms under which a harassed employee might depart. See Loi 2008-596 du 25 juin 2008 portant modernisation du marché du travail [Law on modernization of the labor market] art. 5, J.O., 26 Jun. 2008, p. 10224.

[71]   See Michel Niezborala and Anne Lamy, *Travailler sans dérouiller: Le bien-être au travail est-il encore possible?* (Toulouse: Editions Milan 2007); Bernard Salengro, *Le Stress des cadres* (Paris: Editions L'Harmattan 2005); Dominique Steiler, *Prévenir le stress au travail: De l'évaluation à l'intervention* (Paris: Editions Retz 2010); Philippe Nasse and Patrick Légéron, *Rapport sur la détermination, la mesure, et le suivi des risques pychosociaux au travail* 5 (Paris: La Documentation Française, 12 Mar. 2008), at http://lesrapports.ladocumentationfrancaise. fr/BRP/084000156/0000.pdf (report submitted to the Ministry of Labor, Social Relations and Solidarity).

France has a strong tradition of psychiatric literature on 'suffering at work'.[72] The highly publicized suicides of 34 France Telecom workers during 2008 and 2009 are widely thought to have resulted from workplace stress.[73] Discussions of workplace stress tend to focus on other big policy issues in employment regulation, such as working time,[74] the impact of globalization and technology on work and work-family balance.[75] The France Telecom suicides involved workers who suffered from a particular source of workplace stress: anxiety about the future of their jobs in a company that was in the midst of restructuring to respond to new technologies and globalization.[76] The 35-hour workweek is debated as a workplace stress issue, because the shortening of the workweek has allegedly led to the intensification of work.[77] In addition, another major social issue, the conflict between work and family, is framed as a question of workplace stress.[78] Americans typically view these problems primarily through other employment-law frameworks, such as job security[79] and gender equality.[80] The French law of occupational medicine enables the internal regulation of these issues through the concept of 'psychosocial risks'.

---

[72] See, e.g., Christophe Dejours, *Travail, usure mentale: Essai de psychopathologie du travail* (Paris: Bayard Editions, 3rd edn, 2008) (existing modes of organizing work, and the resulting working conditions, have caused workers' mental suffering in France); Bernard Cassou, *Les risques du travail: Pour ne pas perdre sa vie à la gagner* (Paris: La Découverte 1985) (evolution of work organization had detrimental effects on workers' mental and physical health); Michel Gollac and Serge Volkoff, *Les conditions de travail* (Paris: La Découverte, 2nd edn, 2007) (impact of the organization of work on health, with particular attention to mental health effects).

[73] See generally Ivan du Roy, *Orange stressé: le management par le stress à France Télécom* 172–9 (Paris: La Découverte 2009) (workplace doctors' documentation of the stress and depression of France Télécom workers). See also Yves Clot, *Le travail à coeur: pour en finir avec les risques psychosociaux* 6–7 (Paris: La Découverte 2010); Annie Thébaud-Mony and Nathalie Robatel, *Stress et risques psychosociaux au travail* 5 (Paris: La Documentation Française 2010); Richard Tomlinson and Gregory Viscusi, 'Suicides Inside France Telecom Prompting Sarkozy Stress Testing,' *Bloomberg*, 25 Jan. 2010, http://www.bloomberg.com/apps/news?pid=newsarchive&sid=a3Esvz92Fko4.

[74] See, e.g., Patrick Légéron, *Le stress au travail* 23–5 (Paris: Odile Jacob 2003).

[75] See ibid. 113–21.

[76] Max Colchester, 'France Telecom Addresses Suicides', *Wall Street Journal*, 15 Sep. 2009, http://online.wsj.com/article/SB125291498468308169.html.

[77] See Gollac and Volkoff (note 72) 73–80; Rodolphe Cole, 'L'amélioration du bien-être des salariés par les temps de travail à la carte', in Emmanuel Abord de Chatillon and Olivier Bachelard (eds), *Management de la santé et de la sécurité au travail: Un champ de recherche à défricher* 203 (Paris: L'Harmattan 2011).

[78] See Ministre du travail, de l'emploi, et de la santé, 'Les risques psychosociaux, Les RPS: De quoi parle-t-on?', http://www.travailler-mieux.gouv.fr/Les-RPS-c-est-quoi.html.

[79] See, e.g., Katherine V.W. Stone, *From Widgets to Digits: Employment Regulation for the Changing Workplace* 67–86 (Cambridge: Cambridge University Press 2004); Steven Greenhouse, *The Big Squeeze: Tough Times for the American Worker* 117–35 (New York: Anchor Books 2009).

[80] See Vicki Schultz and Allison Hoffman, 'The Need for a Reduced Workweek in the United States', in Judy Fudge and Rosemary Owens (eds), *Precarious Work, Women, and the New Economy: The Challenge to Legal Norms* 131, 133 (Oxford: Hart Publishing 2006); Rachel Arnow-Richman, 'Incenting Flexibility: The Relationship between Public Law and Voluntary Action in Enhancing Work/Life Balance', 42 *Connecticut Law Review* 1081 (2010).

2.6   A Preventive Health Infrastructure

In combining individual preventive care checkups with policymaking to reduce occupational health risks, the French system of occupational medicine constitutes a robust system for the delivery of preventive care and the improvement of public health. Every employed person in France is required to undergo regular checkups as a condition of remaining employed. Forty percent of Parisian workers get regular checkups only from their workplace doctors;[81] for whatever reason, they do not attend regular checkups with any other physician.

Although the purpose of these checkups is to ensure that the employee's health is compatible with her job, the examinations, in effect, deliver preventive healthcare to a significant portion of the French population. Due to the nature of the tests performed at these exams, many health conditions that could worsen if left untreated are detected early. Diabetes, thyroid conditions, kidney conditions, skin lesions and digestive issues become apparent through urinalysis, blood tests, mouth, throat and full-body exams.[82] Recent data suggest that French workplace doctors have detected 35 percent of cancer cases, and of those, 73 percent of the diagnoses are made at a very early stage. By contrast, of the cancer cases diagnosed by ordinary physicians, only 42 percent are detected at an early stage.[83]

The regular checkups also operate as a comprehensive workplace wellness program. Through individual consultations, employees obtain regular advice about how to maintain good health. Many *médecins du travail* also conduct group workshops within the workplace on these health issues.

2.7   Challenges

The French system of occupational medicine faces numerous challenges. There is an ongoing debate about the effectiveness of workplace doctors in preventing workplace health risks. Recently, employers have been exercising more control over the governance of workplace health services.[84] A 2011 law appoints employers' representatives as the presidents of the committees governing workplace health services, reserving to employees' representatives the subordinate role of treasurer.[85] Thus, in situations of conflict over the direction of any particular company's workplace health service, the management voice will play a tiebreaking role. This recent reform suggests that the strong pro-employee model of preventive health in the workplace is under attack.

---

[81]   Alain Bérard, Christian Courtonne and Ange Mezzadri, *La santé au travail 2009: Enfin une vraie réforme* (Feb. 2009), at Fondation Concorde, http://www.fondationconcorde.com/publications.php.

[82]   Ibid.

[83]   Ibid. at 16.

[84]   See Loi 2011-867 du 20 juillet 2011, art. 3; J.O., July 24, 2011 (Fr.) (codified at C. trav. art. 4622-11).

[85]   Ibid. The statute explicitly provides that, in cases of disagreement on the governing committee, the president's voice shall prevail.

3　UNITED STATES ANALOGUES

3.1　Onsite Clinics

Even in its weakened form, the French system of legally mandated, employer-provided, onsite preventive health, including a broad occupational health law, is robust in comparison with what is plausible in the American workplace. At the same time, it is worth noting a recent development in the US workplace that bears a family resemblance. In the last few years, employers have been voluntarily establishing onsite company clinics that provide primary care, focusing on preventive health services, to their employees.[86]

In 2007, about 10 percent of the largest employers in the US had onsite medical services; in 2009, a third of these large employers did. Forecasts predict that company clinics will grow from 2,200 in 2009 to about 7,000 in 2015. By the latter date, these clinics are likely to serve between 10 and 15 percent of the American population under the age of 65.[87] Large self-insured companies have been creating onsite medical clinics to provide primary care to employees, and in some instances, their dependents.[88]

The new American onsite clinics, like the French clinics, focus on preventive care. These clinics help employees manage chronic diseases by regularly monitoring conditions like diabetes and asthma, and addressing occupational health issues.[89] Unlike the French workplace medical services, US onsite clinics offer medical treatment (such as prescriptions for medications) in addition to preventive screenings.[90]

Thus far, the snapshot of the American company clinic looks remarkably similar to the French workplace health service. Nevertheless, the French model is a creature of law, whereas the American clinics are products of the market. Company clinics have become popular with employers, not only to save lives, but more importantly for employers, to save money.[91] Many employers see the provision of primary care services to employees at an onsite clinic as a way of reducing the costs of healthcare and lost productivity.[92] Company clinics save employers as much as 25 percent in employee healthcare fees,[93] even as the majority of employers providing this benefit do so with no cost sharing by

---

[86]　See Ha T. Tu, Ellyn R. Boukus and Genna R. Cohen, 'Workplace Clinics: A Sign of Growing Employer Interest in Wellness', *Research Brief* 1 (Dec. 2010, no. 17, Center for Studying Health System Change), at http://www.rwjf.org/files/research/71564.pdf.

[87]　See Fuld and Company, *White Paper: The Growth of On-Site Health Clinics* 2 (Feb. 2009).

[88]　A. Michael La Penna, 'Workplace Medical Clinics: The Employer-Redesigned "Company Doctor"', 54 *Journal of Healthcare Management* 87 (2009).

[89]　See Paula S. Katz, 'Big Employers Bring Health Care In-House', *American College of Physicians Observer* (Jan.–Feb. 2007), at http://www.acpinternist.org/archives/2007/01/clinics.htm.

[90]　See Susan J. Wells, 'The Doctor Is In-House: The Company Doctor is Back, Helping Workers Remain Healthy and Employers Reduce Health Care Costs', *HR Magazine* 26 (Apr. 2006).

[91]　See Watson Wyatt, *Realizing the Potential of Onsite Health Centers* 4 (New York: Towers Watson 2008).

[92]　See Tu et al. (note 86) 2; Lydell G. Bridgeford, 'Employers Adjust Workplace-Clinic Models to Achieve Goals', *Employee Benefit News* 1 (Apr. 2011), at http://ebn.benefitnews.com/news/employers-adjust-workplace-clinic-models-goals-2710650-1.html.

[93]　See Maureen Glabman, 'Employers Move into Primary Care', *Managed Care Magazine* (Jun. 2009), at http://www.managedcaremag.com/archives/0906/0906.companydoc.html.

employees.[94] Employers tend to outsource the management of the onsite clinic to companies who are in the business of running medical clinics.

Furthermore, employers generally take an interest in preventive care and chronic disease management, regardless of whether or not they operate a company clinic. Many firms offer some sort of chronic care program, in an effort to cut their healthcare costs.[95] The most extensive of these includes treatment in onsite company clinics, but there are also pared-down programs in which employees receive calls from health professionals employed or otherwise engaged by the firm to remind them to get their regular checkups and keep track of prescriptions.[96]

The recent proliferation of company clinics, locating preventive health services in the workplace, raises the question of whether these clinics can function as a preventive health infrastructure in the United States. Can they reduce healthcare costs in ways that promote and protect employee health in the long run? Should employees be suspicious of the health services they receive when provided by employers to cut their own costs? This question is particularly salient in light of the history of company doctors in the US.

3.2   Company Doctors

The United States, like France, has a history of industrial medicine dating back to the nineteenth century, involving company doctors performing checkups on employees. The company doctors preceded both the new company clinics and the modern-day employer-based health insurance schemes. They conducted periodic and pre-employment health examinations, and were concerned with the health supervision of workers. Companies provided a broad range of welfare services, such as healthcare, schools, housing and social and religious programs,[97] to instill long-term loyalty in workers.

In the US, employees have historically perceived the company doctors as siding with management. Many thought the company doctor was pro-management in determinations regarding workers' compensation claims.[98] For instance, doctors would perform physical examinations to find grounds to discharge miners who were active in the union.[99] The doctors also had incentives to reduce healthcare costs in ways that were detrimental to workers' health. For instance, they were required to pay for medical supplies out of their salaries.[100] These company clinics rapidly declined during the Great Depression in the 1930s, in part because they were too costly for employers to maintain, but also because workers and unions advocated the removal of healthcare from the workplace.[101]

---

[94]   See Watson Wyatt (note 91) 8.
[95]   See Walecia Konrad, 'For Chronic Care, Try Turning to Your Employer', *N. Y. Times* (23 Jul. 2010), at http://www.nytimes.com/2010/07/24/business/24patient.html.
[96]   Ibid.
[97]   See Paul Starr, *The Social Transformation of American Medicine: The Rise of a Sovereign Profession and the Making of a Vast Industry* 200 (New York: Basic Books 1982).
[98]   Ivana Krajcinovic, *From Company Doctors to Managed Care: The United Mine Workers' Noble Experiment* 21 (Ithaca, NY: Cornell University Press 1997).
[99]   Ibid. See Elaine Draper, *The Company Doctor: Risk, Responsibility, and Corporate Professionalism* 82–3 (New York: Russell Sage Foundation 2003).
[100]   Krajcinovic (note 98) 22.
[101]   See Starr (note 97) 202–03.

Although company doctors went into decline after that time, many large corporations in the United States have continued to employ them. Like their French counterparts, company doctors still perform pre-employment physicals on some newly hired employees. The purpose of these physicals is to evaluate employee suitability for certain jobs, in light of health conditions that might increase their risk of injury or illness. American company doctors also provide some preventive health services: they supervise fitness centers, health education and wellness programs.[102] In some industries, they provide regular checkups to employees to monitor their exposure to toxic substances[103] or to determine whether they are disabled and entitled to accommodations under the Americans with Disabilities Act.[104] Company doctors advise the employer on these accommodations. These activities make modern American company doctors look similar to the French *médecins du travail*.

4 DIFFERENCES AND COMPARATIVE LESSONS

These similarities, however, are largely cosmetic. They mask deep differences between the two systems' abilities to deliver preventive healthcare effectively to employees. First, a significant difference between the French and American onsite clinics is that the French system requires all workers to get regular preventive checkups. In the United States, the law does not (and perhaps cannot) require employers to do so. Employers are also constrained in their ability to require their employees to undergo regular checkups by the Americans with Disabilities Act (ADA). When preventive health checkups are offered to employees on a voluntary basis, the take-up rate is likely to be disappointing, especially in the United States.

This highlights a second and related difference between the legal landscapes in which French and American workplace clinics operate. The stark differences between French and American employment law on unjust dismissals account for the significant disincentives for the American employee to visit a company doctor or clinic.

Third, American company doctors were and continue to be constrained by their lack of independence from management. If a US company doctor attempts to protect employees, when doing so is at odds with the employer's interests, there is no job security protection for the doctor. By contrast, French law has long protected the independence of workplace doctors, both through the Labor Code and through the Code of Medical Ethics. As a result, French workplace doctors tend to align themselves with workers and unions rather than with management.

Finally, the differences between French and American approaches to occupational safety and health are remarkable. French law imposes positive duties on the employer to prevent risks, and the expansion of this field of law into mental health risks has enabled reconceptualization of the full range of workplace problems as health matters. By contrast, occupational safety and health law in the United States tends to be narrowly limited

---

[102]   Draper (note 99) 13.
[103]   Ibid. 16.
[104]   Ibid. 13; see Americans with Disabilities Act, 42 U.S.C. § 12101 and following (2006).

to regulating recognized hazards to physical health. As a result, the complex health consequences of a broad range of workplace problems remain unrecognized.

4.1   Mandatory Checkups

The mandatory nature of French occupational medicine is what ensures that preventive medicine is delivered to a large swath of the population. Every employed person in France must attend regular checkups as a condition of remaining employed. Employees simply cannot avoid the regular visits to the doctor based on laziness, fear or cost. Thus, it is unlikely that a chronic disease or health condition will go undetected and unmanaged.

The new company clinics in the United States only provide preventive health screenings to employees who want them, when they want them. In fact, the Americans with Disabilities Act makes it difficult for an employer to require all its employees to submit to regular physical examinations as a condition of remaining employed. The ADA prohibits employers from subjecting job applicants to pre-employment physical examinations.[105] Employers may require a physical examination after extending a job offer to the candidate and condition hiring on a satisfactory medical examination, but only if 'all entering employees are subjected to such an examination regardless of disability'.[106] Furthermore, the employer cannot require physical examinations of any employees 'unless such examination or inquiry is shown to be job-related and consistent with business necessity'.[107]

In the US, the federal Third Circuit Court of Appeals has held, for instance, that 'an examination that is "job related" and "consistent with business necessity" must, at minimum, be limited to an evaluation of the employee's condition only to the extent necessary under the circumstances to establish the employee's fitness for the work at issue'.[108] The US Equal Employment Opportunity Commission (EEOC) has read this standard to exclude periodic or regular physical examinations, except in a limited class of jobs affecting public safety (for instance, police officers and firefighters). 'In most instances', the EEOC guidance reads, 'an employer's need to make disability-related inquiries or require medical examinations will be triggered by evidence of current performance problems or observable evidence suggesting that a particular employee will pose a direct threat'.[109] As a result, it would be extremely difficult for a US employer to adopt a mandatory system of regular preventive health checkups for all its employees. Because of the 'job-related and consistent with business necessity' standard, the types of physical examinations that employers can require tend to be narrow as compared to the broad checkups performed by the French workplace doctors.

In France, there is no 'business necessity' standard to justify the occupational medicine framework, but even if there were, it would be easy to demonstrate that comprehensive preventive health screenings are job-related and consistent with business necessity in a

---

[105]   42 U.S.C. § 12112(d)(2) (2006).

[106]   Ibid. § 12112(d)(3)(A).

[107]   Ibid. § 12112(d)(4)(A).

[108]   *Tice v. Centre Area Transp. Auth.*, 247 F. 3d 506, 515 (3d Cir. 2001).

[109]   EEOC, Enforcement Guidance: Disability-Related Inquiries and Medical Examinations of Employees under the Americans with Disabilities Act (ADA) (27 Jul. 2000), at http://www.eeoc.gov/policy/docs/guidance-inquiries.html.

legal regime that imposes positive duties on employers to protect employees' physical and mental health.[110] In sum, a wide range of medical tests, including chronic disease screenings, are job-related in France, because the employer's duty to protect the employees' health is further elaborated by another provision that requires the workplace doctors to 'avoid all impairments of the health of the workers by the fact of their work'.[111] This requires periodic clinical assessments to determine whether there is actually an alteration in workers' health.

4.2 Voluntary Checkups

Furthermore, the voluntariness of preventive health services in the new American company clinics is unlikely to reach the employees who need them the most, because those employees can reasonably fear adverse employment consequences as a result of visiting a company clinic or a company doctor. A medical examination could enable management to find out about costly ailments, which could lead to the employee's termination. In the past, employers screened employees through company doctors as a way of avoiding hiring or retaining workers who would threaten the company's financial health.[112] Employees may hesitate to use these clinics out of skepticism about the employer's motives for launching them.

These fears are reasonable. As is well known, the default rule in the United States, setting it apart from most European countries, is that an employer can terminate the employee at will, for any reason or no reason, without notice and without a severance package.[113] In France, by contrast, an employer can only terminate the employee for cause, and even when the termination is justified, the employer must give the employee notice or a severance.[114] Without job security protection, the American employee has every reason to be fearful of adverse consequences stemming from the employer's knowledge of the employee's health conditions, especially if the employee might have conditions that could cause drops in productivity or additional healthcare costs. Given that the openly acknowledged *raison d'être* of the American company clinic is to save money for the employer, the employees who are most likely to need preventive care, that is, the most likely to develop costly conditions, are also most likely to fear termination based on information revealed to the employer's physicians.

---

[110] See C. trav. art. L. 4121-1.

[111] See C. trav. art. L. 4622-3.

[112] See Mark Rothstein, *Medical Screening and the Employee Health Cost Crisis* 4–6 (1989); Draper (note 101) 157.

[113] The classic articulation is found in *Payne v. Western and Atl. R.R.*, 81 Tenn. 507 (1884). For a discussion of the American rule, its origins, and its contrast with European approaches, see Clyde W. Summers, 'Employment at Will in the United States: The Divine Right of Employers', 3 *University of Pennsylvania Journal of Labor and Employment Law* 65 (2000). For a comparison of American employment at will and the French regime of just-cause termination, see Julie C. Suk, 'Discrimination at Will: Job Security Protections and Equal Employment Opportunity in Conflict', 60 *Stanford Law Review* 73, 78–9, 87–91 (2007).

[114] See C. trav. art. L. 1231-1 to L. 1232-6 (governing terminations for reasons pertaining to the individual employee).

4.3   Confidentiality and the Doctors' Independence

In addition, US law does not prohibit the company doctor from revealing employees' confidential medical information to management. Although American professional ethics rules generally bind doctors to respect patient confidentiality, this duty is not legally recognized as applying to company doctors. For example, in *New York Times v. Horn* (2003), Dr. Horn, a company doctor for the *New York Times*, brought a wrongful discharge action against the newspaper, challenging the termination for her refusal to disclose employees' medical records to the Labor Relations, Legal, and Human Resources departments without the patient-employees' consent.[115] She also claimed that the *Times*'s Human Resources Department instructed her to misinform employees about whether their injuries were work-related in order to limit the workers' compensation liability at the *Times*.[116] The New York Court of Appeals held that the physician-patient privilege was not central to the company doctor's conduct of her practice on the employer's behalf.[117] The Court noted that the doctor had 'responsibilities as a part of corporate management', and thus she could not work simply 'for the benefit of the employee'.[118]

Another difference between French and US law concerns the protection of occupational physicians' job security. The Court in *New York Times* noted that, since Dr. Horn was an at-will employee, the company could legitimately discharge her for refusing to violate her patients' confidentiality.[119] In the United States, the company doctors' lack of independence from the employer stems in part from the enduring doctrine of employment at will in most American jurisdictions.

In France, by contrast, workplace doctors are protected from termination. In addition to ordinary French employment law, which protects all employees from unjust dismissals, there are special provisions that shield workplace doctors from unjust dismissal. Employers cannot fire the workplace doctor without first consulting the works council, an employee representative body that large companies must have as a matter of law.[120] Furthermore, the termination of a workplace doctor is not valid until the labor inspector authorizes it.[121]

Under the regulations, the employer must petition the labor inspector to terminate a workplace doctor in writing, with the reasons articulated. A hearing is held with the employee representative body or the inter-enterprise governing committees.[122] The labor

---

[115]   *Horn v. New York Times*, 790 N.E. 2d 753, 754 (N.Y. 2003).

[116]   Ibid.

[117]   Ibid. 758–9.

[118]   Ibid. 758.

[119]   Ibid. Horn had argued that her case fit within an exception to employment at will, by which professional employees have an implied contract under which the professional is obligated to follow its professional code of ethics. The court held that this exception did not apply to Horn because there was no common professional enterprise between Horn and the *New York Times*.

[120]   C. trav. art. L. 2322-1 and following. A works council is required in companies with 50 or more employees. Smaller companies need not establish a works council, but those with 11 or more employees must allow them to elect representatives who represent the employees' interests and concerns in meetings with management. See C. trav. art. L. 2312-1 and following.

[121]   C. trav. art. L. 4623-5.

[122]   C. trav. art. R. 4623-22.

inspector then conducts an adversarial investigation, in which any person of the work-place doctor's choice belonging to the employer's health service can accompany her.[123] Even when the labor inspector authorizes termination of a workplace doctor, the Ministry of Labor or an administrative court can review the decision.[124] If either invalidates the termination, the doctor has a right to return to her job or an equivalent job, and the employer is liable for damages.[125] Due to these extensive protections, French workplace doctors do not fear termination because of exercising independent medical judgment that may be contrary to the preferences and productivity goals of the employer.

French medical ethics rules also protect the confidentiality of the employees' medical information obtained by the workplace doctor in the course of her duties. In France, medical ethics rules have the force of law. Drafted by the National Council of the Order of Doctors, the medical profession's organization, the Code of Medical Ethics became law by decree in 1995.[126] Special provisions of this Code apply to 'salaried' physicians such as workplace doctors. However, the Code makes clear that they must observe the same professional duties of medical confidentiality and independence as ordinary doctors. 'The fact of a doctor tied in his professional practice by a contract or status to an administration, a collectivity, or any other public or private organism has no effect on his professional duties and in particular on his obligations concerning medical confidentiality and independence in his decisions'.[127]

Furthermore, article 4 of the Medical Ethics Code provides, that '[m]edical confidentiality, instituted in the interest of patients, is necessary for every doctor according to conditions established by the law'.[128] Criminal sanctions are imposed for breaches of medical confidentiality under the French Penal Code: 'The disclosure of confidential information by a person who is its agent, whether for the state or for a profession, even if it is by function of a temporary mission, is punished by one year of imprisonment and a fine of 15,000 euros'.[129]

French medical ethics law also prevents the conflicts of interest that have significantly limited American company doctors' ability to promote employee health. A good example of this problem surfaces in the facts of *Millison v. E.I. DuPont de Nemours & Company*. Former employees of DuPont sued the company and company doctors. They argued that, 'although the physical examinations performed by the company doctor and the x-rays indicated asbestos-related injuries, the doctors did not inform plaintiffs of their sicknesses, but instead told them that their health was fine and sent them back to work under the same hazardous conditions that had caused the initial injuries'.[130] The *DuPont*

---

[123]   C. trav. art. R. 4623-23.

[124]   C. trav. art. L. 4623-6.

[125]   C. trav. art. L. 4623-7.

[126]   By contrast, in the United States, the American Medical Association's Code of Medical Ethics does not have the force of law. Indeed, some of its rules coincide with provisions of state and federal law. However, for the most part, American medical ethics are distinct from law.

[127]   Décret 95-1000 du 6 septembre 1995 portant code de déontologie médicale [Code of Medical Ethics], art. 95, J.O., 8 Sep. 1995, p. 13305, 13310.

[128]   Ibid. art. 4.

[129]   Code pénal [Penal Code] art. 226-13.

[130]   *Millison v. E.I. du Pont de Nemours and Co.*, 501 A.2d 505, 516 (N.J. 1986). The legal issue was whether the plaintiffs' claims could move forward in light of the New Jersey workers'

case demonstrates the conflict faced by company doctors between employers' production and profit interests and employee health.

In France, the law clearly and explicitly directs the workplace doctor to protect employee health, even when there is a conflict:

> In no circumstance may the doctor accept limitations on his independence in his medical practice on the part of the enterprise or the organism that employs him. He must always act, as a priority, in the interests of the public health and in the interests of the persons in the companies or organisms and their safety.[131]

Another broadly-worded provision prohibits doctors from operating under any monetary incentives based on the norms of productivity: 'A salaried doctor may not, in any case, accept any compensation founded on norms of productivity, scheduled output, or any other arrangement which would have as its consequence a limitation or abandonment of his independence or an effect on the quality of care'.[132]

This comparison illustrates why American employees have historically feared, and perhaps should continue to fear, visits to the company doctor. At the same time, the new company clinics may be more independent because the doctors who staff these new onsite clinics are not employees of the company. As mentioned, the current trend among employers is to outsource the clinic to a third-party vendor. Under these arrangements, the doctors would not have responsibilities as part of corporate management, and one could argue they would be covered by the privacy rule in the Health Insurance Portability and Accountability Act (HIPAA).[133] HIPAA restricts the disclosure of a patient's protected health information without the patient's written consent.[134] Doctors would thus be bound to respect the privacy of patients' medical information to the extent required by the statute. Many of the third-party healthcare vendors that run the company clinics guarantee the confidentiality of employee-patient health records, precisely to overcome employees' well-known fears of the past practices of company doctors.[135] Thus,

---

compensation law's provision of exclusive remedies for injuries on the job, with an exception for intentional wrongs. The New Jersey Supreme Court held that the doctors' alleged concealment of the plaintiffs' illnesses came within the intentional wrongs exception. Nonetheless, the case illustrates the mixed incentives faced by company doctors in a legal order that allows them to protect the employer's interests above those of the employee.

[131]   Décret 95-1000 (note 127) art. 95.

[132]   Ibid. art. 97.

[133]   Health Insurance Portability and Accountability Act, Pub. L. 104-191, §§ 261-264 (authorizing the Secretary of Health and Human Services to issue privacy regulations governing health information); 45 C.F.R. pt.160, 164. Authorities would likely consider an onsite clinic providing primary care services that go beyond urgent care a 'health care provider', to which the statute and the regulations would apply.

[134]   45 C.F.R. pt. 160, 164.

[135]   For example, QuadMed, one of the leading operators of employer-based onsite clinics, has a policy of promising not to share patients' medical records with the company's human resources department. The doctors wear a different uniform from plant employees to emphasize that they are not 'company doctors' but patient advocates. See Douglas McCarthy and Sarah Klein, 'QuadMed: Transforming Employer-Sponsored Health Care through Workplace Primary Care and Wellness Programs', *Case Study: Organized Health Care Delivery System* 4 (51 The Commonwealth Fund pub. 1424 (July 2010).

employees' disincentives to take advantage of the preventive health services offered by the onsite clinics may decrease.

The potential of employer-based onsite clinics in the United States to become a preventive healthcare infrastructure will depend on their ability to earn the trust of a critical mass of employees, especially those most likely to develop costly chronic conditions. Yet, those employees are most inclined to fear adverse employment consequences based on medical information revealed to the employer. Thus, significant attention will need to be paid to the problems of doctor independence from employers if the public preventive health potential of American onsite clinics is to be realized.

4.4 Occupational Safety and Health Law

Another significant difference between the French and American integration of health services into the workplace is the scope of occupational safety and health law. French employment law imposes on employers the positive duty to prevent risks to employee health. This duty is the foundation of the institution of *la médecine du travail* in France.

There is no parallel duty under the Occupational Safety and Health Act (OSH Act) in the United States. Under the OSH Act, the employer's only duties are to 'furnish to each of his employees employment and a place of employment which are free from recognized hazards that are causing or are likely to cause death or serious physical harm to his employees' and to comply with the specific standards promulgated by the Secretary of Labor under the statute.[136] The first clause, known as the 'general duty clause', only requires employers to address 'recognized' hazards. The French workplace doctors, by contrast, are charged with the task of identifying new risks by spending a third of their time surveying the workplace. Furthermore, the American statute imposes a duty to remove hazards that are 'causing or likely to cause death or serious physical harm'. The general duty clause is thus only concerned with the most egregious risks of substantial harm, whereas the French workplace doctors are required to 'avoid all impairments of the health of the workers by the fact of their work'.[137]

These differences are not merely textual. In the United States, many of the factors that cause or exacerbate chronic conditions relate to work. Occupational deaths are the eighth leading cause of death in the US.[138] Although occupational deaths include those from accidents, one can attribute a significant proportion to chronic diseases. For example, various workplace factors, including exposure to toxins, noise, sedentary work and stress, can cause or exacerbate cardiovascular disease, which is the number one cause of death in the United States.[139] OSH Act's general duty clause, however, does not regulate these problems.

---

[136] Occupational Safety and Health Act, 29 U.S.C. § 654 (2006).

[137] See C. trav. art. L. 4622-3.

[138] See Kyle Steenland, Carol Burnett, Nina Lalich, Elizabeth Ward and Joseph Hurrell, 'Dying for Work: The Magnitude of U.S. Mortality from Selected Causes of Death Associated with Occupation', 43 *American Journal of Industrial Medicine* 461 (2003).

[139] See Jiaquan Xu, Kenneth D. Kochanek, Sherry L. Murphy and Betzaida Tejada-Vera, Centers for Disease Control National Vital Statistics Reports, Deaths: Final Data for 2007, at 1 (20 May 2010).

Another distinguishing feature of French employment law that makes it possible for workplace medical services to protect workers' health is employee participation in workplace governance. French workers have more power and voice in the workplace than their American counterparts, and this is formalized in the various provisions of the Labor Code.[140] Since 1945, the French Labor Code requires all large employers to form a *comité d'entreprise*, or works council, comprised of representatives of management and workers.[141] The workers' representatives are elected and, in companies with 300 or more employees, a union representative must be included.[142] The law requires the employer to consult the works council on a variety of matters, including the general management of the company, policies on the research and development of new technologies,[143] changes in the company's economic organization,[144] and most relevantly, working conditions.[145]

The Labor Code also provides for employers with 50 or more employees to form workplace health and safety committees, comprised of management and workers.[146] The workplace doctors attend the committees' meetings.[147] The purpose of the health and safety committee is: (1) to protect the physical and mental health of the workers; (2) to improve working conditions; and (3) to ensure compliance with relevant legal norms.[148]

In the United States, by contrast, workers have few opportunities to participate formally in workplace policies affecting health and safety conditions. There is significant scholarly interest in developing new modes of employee participation in the self-regulation of the American workplace, since scholars believe such participation is essential to meeting workers' needs, particularly with regard to health and safety.[149]

4.5   Conclusion

Employer-provided onsite preventive health services operate in radically different employment law regimes in the two countries. These regimes shape each country's potential to pursue the public health goal of broad-based prevention of costly chronic conditions. American employers are instituting company clinics to cut their own healthcare costs, not to promote the public health goal of reducing societal healthcare costs. In the past, employers' concern with their own bottom line has created conflicts of interest for company

---

[140]   For an extensive history of the evolution of French employees' status with a voice in the workplace, see Jacques Le Goff, *Du silence à la parole: Une histoire du droit du travail des années 1830 à nos jours* (Rennes: Presses Universitaires de Rennes 2004).
[141]   See C. trav. art. L. 2322-1; L. 2324-1.
[142]   C. trav. art. L. 2324-2.
[143]   C. trav. art. L. 2323-13.
[144]   C. trav. art. L. 2323-19.
[145]   C. trav. art. L. 2323-27.
[146]   C. trav. art. L. 4611-1; L. 4613-1; L. 4613-2.
[147]   C. trav. art. L. 4613-2.
[148]   C. trav. art. L. 4612-1.
[149]   See, e.g., Cynthia Estlund, *Regoverning the Workplace* (New Haven, CT: Yale University Press 2010); Orly Lobel, 'Interlocking Regulatory and Industrial Relations: The Governance of Workplace Safety', 57 *Administrative Law Review* 1071, 1128–40 (2005); David Weil, 'Are Mandated Health and Safety Committees Substitutes for or a Supplement to Labor Unions?', 52 *Industrial and Labor Relations Review* 339 (1998–9).

doctors, which in turn have stymied the potential of onsite clinics since employees could not trust and effectively use them. State regulation of company doctors and clinics *à la française* may offer some solutions. Nevertheless, the French system demonstrates the legal complexity—and ongoing political conflict—involved in such an endeavor.

FURTHER READING

Bérard, Alain, Christian Courtonne and Ange Mezzadri (2009). *La santé au travail 2009: Enfin une vraie réforme.* Paris: Fondation Concorde, at http://www.fondationconcorde.com/publications.php.

Bledniak, Evelyn (2008). *Santé, hygiène, et sécurité au travail.* Paris: Delmas.

Bourgeot, Sylvie and Michel Blatman (2009). *L'État de santé du salarié.* Rueil-Malmaison: Editions Liaisons, 2nd edn.

Buzzi, Stéphane, Paul-André Rosental and Jean-Claude Devinck (2006). *La santé au travail: 1880–2006.* Paris: La Découverte.

Dejours, Christophe (2008). *Travail, usure mentale: Essai de psychopathologie du travail.* Paris: Bayard Editions, 3rd edn.

Draper, Elaine (2003). *The Company Doctor: Risk, Responsibility, and Corporate Professionalism.* New York: Russell Sage Foundation.

Dyèvre, Pol and Damien Léger (2003). *Médecine du travail: Approches de la santé au travail.* Paris: Editions Masson, 3rd edn.

Estlund, Cynthia (2010). Regoverning the Workplace. New Haven, CT: Yale University Press.

Friedman, Gabrielle and James Q. Whitman (2003). 'The European Transformation of Harassment Law: Discrimination versus Dignity,' 9 *Columbia Journal of European Law* 241.

Hirigoyen, Marie-France (1998). *Le harcèlement moral: La violence perverse au quotidian.* Paris: La Découverte.

Krajcinovic, Ivana (1997). *From Company Doctors to Managed Care: The United Mine Workers' Noble Experiment.* Ithaca, NY: Cornell University Press.

Nasse, Philippe and Patrick Légéron (2008). *Rapport sur la détermination, la mesure, et le suivi des risques pychosociaux au travail.* Paris: La Documentation Française, at http://lesrapports.ladocumentationfrancaise.fr/BRP/084000156/0000.pdf (report submitted to the Ministry of Labor, Social Relations and Solidarity).

Starr, Paul (1982). *The Social Transformation of American Medicine: The Rise of a Sovereign Profession and the Making of a Vast Industry.* New York: Basic Books.

Suk, Julie C. (2011). 'Preventive Health at Work: A Comparative Approach', 59 *American Journal of Comparative Law* 1089–134.

Tu, Ha T., Ellyn R. Boukus and Genna R. Cohen (2010). 'Workplace Clinics: A Sign of Growing Employer Interest in Wellness', *Research Brief* no. 17 (Center for Studying Health System Change), at http://www.rwjf.org/files/research/71564.pdf.

Index